# ROUGH JUSTICE:

## *Perspectives on Lower Criminal Courts*

**John A. Robertson**

*Professor of Law*
*University of Wisconsin—Madison*

**Little, Brown and Company**
**Boston    1974    Toronto**

*Published simultaneously in Canada*
*by Little, Brown & Company (Canada) Limited*

PRINTED IN THE UNITED STATES OF AMERICA

TO THE TUESDAY MORNING GROUP

*"Allow None to Labor in the Gardens of the*
*Temple Save Those Who Despise Weeds" — Confucius*

# *PREFACE*

No formal legal institution, except the police, has as much direct contact with people as the lower courts. For millions of people these courts embody the law and judicial process. For most people the words "judge," "trial," and "court" have no experiential referent other than their encounters with the municipal, misdemeanor, traffic, and magistrate's courts of their community. As the following essays show, that encounter seldom is a happy one.

If these courts represent the law, and determine in some significant way its influence in our lives, then it is a national shame that the lower court conditions described in this book have been tolerated for so long. Not that reform efforts have been wanting. They spring up repeatedly, like cyclical purification ceremonies in a primitive tribe. Philadelphia, for example, has investigated its magistrate system at least six times in a 40-year period, and once went so far as to indict 24 of 25 magistrates. In Massachusetts, at least one legislative or executive commission every decade since the 1870s has addressed problems in the lower courts. Yet the problems resist change. Reforms seldom occur, and when they do, the problems crop up again, like hardy insects that defy every chemical. The occasional exposé, the official inquiry that garners headlines, satisfies legislators, leaders of the bench and bar, and apparently the public.

Meanwhile the lower court system continues to churn up people and cases, providing further evidence for Chief Justice Hughes' often quoted statement on the importance of lower courts — a statement impossible not to quote in a book such as this:

> A petty tyrant in a police court, refusals of a fair hearing in minor civil courts, the impatient disregard of an immigrant's ignorance of our ways and language, will daily breed bolshevists who are beyond the reach of your appeals. Here is work for lawyers. The Supreme Court of the United States and the court of appeals will take care of themselves. Look after the courts of the poor, who stand most in

need of justice. The security of the Republic will be found in the treatment of the poor and the ignorant; in indifference to their misery and helplessness lies disaster.*

The purpose of this book is to illuminate the problems of the lower criminal courts and the forces maintaining them. It proceeds somewhat in the manner of a cubist painter depicting simultaneously the multiple angles from which his subject can be perceived. The several perspectives that follow approach the subject with varying vision, complaint or emphasis. None alone is sufficient. As with the painting, each perspective is necessary to grasp the full reality of the lower courts. .

It is hoped that this collection of basic documents on lower courts will inspire researchers and students to reconsider the social and moral implications of this neglected institution. Although the judicial process has recently gained subspeciality status in some academic departments, the focus has been on appellate courts, particularly the United States Supreme Court. Too little research has been directed to trial courts, and even less to lower level criminal courts. These materials should provide a sufficient nucleus for law, sociology, political science, or criminal justice courses concerned with trial courts, and will serve any teaching context where the subject is the gap between rules and reality.

The essays have been chosen for their relevance to and exposition of lower court problems. While a few of the essays are well known and have been previously anthologized, an effort has been made to bring together materials not generally available, at least in this context. Most deal directly with lower courts, though one or two discuss lower court issues in a general trial court setting. Several excellent essays and empirical studies were excluded because of their focus on higher trial courts. Nearly every essay has been edited to some extent, hopefully without distortion of meaning, to save space without sacrificing meaning and clarity. Retained footnotes carry their original numbering.

Finally, even as modest a scholarly effort as this has incurred debts. Perhaps the greatest debt is owed that group of Massachusetts lawyers to whom this book is dedicated. They took on a lower court system and actually changed it, and in doing so not only excited my interest in lower courts, but taught me many things that I needed to know. One member of that group, Melvyn Zarr, provided materials, support and, most important, well-founded criti-

* 42 Rep. N.Y. State Bar Assn. 240, 241 (1919).

cism at a crucial point in this project, for which I am very grateful. My wife Mary gave love and understanding when a lesser person would have given less. Joseph Zekas gave invaluable help with proofreading and indexing. Finally, I am grateful to the Russell Sage Foundation's Residency Program in Law and Social Science, which provided me with a year of study at Harvard University, and exposed me to Gary Bellow who, unbeknown to him, is the intellectual mentor of this work.

John A. Robertson
University of Wisconsin Law School
Madison
September 1973

"THE CONVEYOR BELT WAS A GREAT IDEA."

# TABLE OF CONTENTS

# PART V: ALTERNATIVE MODELS: THE PARENTAL FUNCTION AND DISPUTE RESOLUTION, 345

# PART VI: REFORMING THE LOWER COURTS, 433

# INTRODUCTION:
# THE LOWER COURT PROBLEM

If courts, like prisons, are a measure of a society's commitment to justice, then the lower criminal courts raise serious questions about the American system of justice. In its ideal form, the criminal process has much to recommend it. Guilt or innocence is determined through an open adjudicative process in which witnesses confront the accused and the state has the burden of proof. The accused may present evidence, although he need not testify; with the assistance of counsel he participates in shaping the outcome. The judge impartially applies rules of law and protects the rights of the defendant. Appellate review corrects errors and assures that the rules of law have been followed. Underlying this ideal model is a moral commitment to the dignity of man, the efficacy of rules, and the need for procedural limits on the exercise of state power.

In actual operation, however, the criminal process presents an altogether different face. A semblance of the ideal exists in serious felony cases, but becomes more elusive as the possible penalties grow less severe; in the lower criminal courts — known variously as municipal, district, police, county, magistrate, or justice of the peace courts — one finds a justice system that bears little resemblance to the ideal.

One manifestation of the disjunction between the ideal and reality found in the lower criminal courts is the unequal distribution of power between judge and defendant. Despite a legal structure that carefully confines and limits official power through procedural rules, through the countervailing power of the defendant acting through counsel, and through substantive limits on the court's intervention in a person's life, lower court judges nonetheless exercise enormous discretion that is largely unsupervised and unreviewable, having major impact on defendants and local communities. Thus, the limited jurisdiction of the courts — often cited as a reason for a less punctilious concern with procedure — is limited only in a relative sense.

In addition to ordinance violations and petty offenses, jurisdiction of the lower courts usually encompasses serious misdemeanors, lesser felonies, and, in some jurisdictions, felonies punishable by five years imprisonment or more. Even if final jurisdiction is limited, nearly all lower courts also play an important role in major felony cases by setting bail and determining whether probable cause exists to try a person at all. With these powers, the decisions made· by lower court officials quite clearly impinge on individuals in significant ways. In deciding whether criminal complaints and arrest warrants are issued, the lower courts decide who is charged with crime and arrested. Bail decisions involve possible loss of freedom, financial loss, and often the disposition of a case. Typically, a judge sitting alone will decide guilt or innocence, or some alternative disposition if he feels it to be warranted. Finally, decisions about disposition — dismissal, continuance, fine, probation, prison, social services, or restitution — will affect a defendant's future and his relationships with others. In addition to the effect on the individual, the courts' decisions indirectly determine the quality of life in the community — integrating or alienating individuals from the social order, reinforcing or undermining legal norms, alleviating or intensifying the urban crises.[1]

In exercising these extensive powers, the lower court judge is relatively unaccountable to legal authority. Lifetime appointment or party politics provide job security. Defendants usually have no organization to protect their interests, and until recently have seldom been represented by counsel in the lower courts. (But, given the complex web of relations in lower court criminal practice, even the presence of counsel hardly guarantees against the arbitrary assertion of power by the judge.) The absence of easily available procedural remedies for the abuses that do occur contributes to the stewardlike role of the lawyer in lower court proceedings. For example, the trial de novo system found in many jurisdictions provides a dissatisfied defendant with a new trial in an upper court rather than appellate review of the propriety of a judicial ruling, effectively shielding judges from appellate scrutiny. Although extraordinary remedies may exist, and appellate courts — if pushed — occasionally do intervene, on the whole the lower courts remain untouched. Similarly, the Supreme Court has seldom dealt directly with lower criminal courts and, if recent decisions are an indication,

---

1. The National Advisory Commission on Civil Disorders reports at 337: "Too often the courts have operated to aggravate rather than relieve the tensions that ignite and fire disorders" (1973).

has little impact when it does.[2] While many lower court systems have a chief judge or an administrative committee, their powers often are only nominal. Neither administrative structure nor intra-court organization encourages effective supervision.

For these reasons, lower courts are visible institutions that, for purposes of supervision and evaluation, function invisibly. Only when corruption is uncovered or the periodic study commission enters the scene do judicial actions receive public attention. Even then the scrutiny is likely to be short-lived and easily deflected to other issues before permanent reform occurs.

In such a setting judicial style tends to emphasize outcome over process, leaving the judge free to draw on extralegal criteria in his determinations. Thus, we find the actual decision-making process of the lower court to be a mere shadow of the formally prescribed adversary procedure of reasoned adjudication. Most cases are handled by well-developed routines. Guilty pleas predominate. Trials occur swiftly, often with the presumption of innocence and the burden of proof inverted. Right to counsel may be slighted, or presented as a liability, as when an indigent defendant is told on first appearance that if he pleads guilty his case will be "taken care of" that day. Defendants may also be persuaded or coerced into waiving rights to trial, appeal, discovery, or confrontation of witnesses. Fact-finding and sentencing turn on rough rules of thumb, rather than on an orderly exploration of the individual case. Contributing to the atmosphere of rough justice is a pervasive sense that the defendant, once he has entered this legal machine, has lost his claim to be treated as a unique being with an intrinsic moral worth. All too often he is verbally abused, addressed disrespectfully by the judge and court officials, not informed of the meaning of rapid-fire procedures, not listened to if allowed to speak, and, in general, treated like an unsavory object on an assembly line that is running behind schedule.

The catalogue of vices is long, and it is well-documented in the pages that follow. In addition to judicial arbitrariness, other pervasive problems include noncompliance with procedural rules, racial or economic discrimination, corruption, and nonfeasance. While in a few cases it might be argued that such behavior and attitudes

2. See Colten v. Kentucky, 407 U.S. 25 (1972); Ward v. City of Monroeville, 409 U.S. 57 (1972); Shadwick v. City of Tampa, 407 U.S. 345 (1972). An exception may be Argersinger v. Hamlin, 407 U.S. 25 (1972), found herein at 464.

have no substantial effect on the final outcome — for example, both the defendant and the court might actually benefit from a guilty plea, without counsel, to a minor offense at first appearance — in most instances derogation of process leads to abuse, and cannot be tolerated in a system based on authority regulated by rules.

Other legal institutions share the lower courts' inability to conform actuality to the ideal, but few other parts of the justice system touch so many people so directly. For the millions of people who pass annually through the lower courts as witnesses, complainants, observers, or defendants, these courts *are* the justice system, and in a real sense represent the power and majesty of the law. Thus the performance of the lower courts can have a powerful socializing or alienating effect, influencing the quality and extent of order found in society.

The lower courts also merit special attention because they reflect social and institutional barriers to achieving justice through rules — a problem confronting most legal institutions in a liberal, democratic society. In the lower court setting of few resources, voluminous caseloads, and conflicting roles, the problem is starkly presented. Examination of the dilemma in the lower courts will both clarify immediate needs and identify the obstacles to achieving justice throughout the system.

### DEVELOPMENT AND CAUSES OF THE LOWER COURT PROBLEM

An important facet of the lower court problem is the amazing intransigence with which these courts have faced scandal, chronic public dissatisfaction, and the reform movements that periodically have arisen to challenge abuses of the system. The pervasiveness of the lower court problem is matched only by its longevity, which merits separate discussion.

Today's lower court is a modernized replica of the police and criminal courts which, due to industrialization and population growth in the nineteenth century, gradually replaced the justices of the peace and magistrates who, since colonial times, had been the machinery of justice at the lower level. Although an innovation, police and municipal courts retained the decentralized organization of the old system, and were unequipped to deal with the burgeoning problems of an urbanized society. The law reform movements of the late nineteenth century did little to improve the situation. At the turn of the century, the excesses of machine politics led progressive reformers to look more closely at the corruption and abuses of urban lower courts. Official commissions in many cities uncovered widespread venality and political influence, and sought a solution in the concept of a centrally administered municipal court organized on "modern business methods," statistical reporting, and a judicial executive with broad powers. First established in Chicago in 1905, the centrally administered municipal court was hailed as the answer to court problems, and was rapidly emulated in other jurisdictions. That era's belief that structural change could dissolve problems involving politics and the court's social role set the tone for all later reform efforts.

The progressive reforms, if they succeeded at all, were short-lived. From 1920 to 1930 lower court abuses again confronted the public in Chicago, New York, and Cleveland — the very cities that had been in the vanguard of reform. Roscoe Pound and Felix Frankfurter, for example, in their landmark study of the justice system in Cleveland, found the same problems flourishing in the municipal court that had led to its creation only eight years previously. The public response led to another wave of commission studies. The best known — the Seabury Investigation in New York, the Illinois Crime Survey, and the Wickersham Commission — further documented the shortcomings that had become synonymous with lower courts, and attempted to exorcise the problems with procedural and structural changes that seldom succeeded. Public dissatisfaction was not overcome, although its fever lessened considerably from the scandal-ridden days of 1925 through 1935.

In the 1960s, with the Warren Court and the civil rights and poverty movements highlighting social injustices, the lower courts once again became a source of concern. Legal service and public interest lawyers, citizens' groups, and federally funded projects have in recent years brought increased visibility to the lower courts and have attempted, within their means, to reform them. Interestingly, contemporary solutions hardly differ from those of earlier eras. The 1967 President's Commission on Law Enforcement and Administration of Criminal Justice describes the same problems that had been exhaustively described by studies in the 1920s, and proffers an institutional solution[3] — abolishing the lower courts by integrating them into a higher trial court — that reiterates Roscoe Pound's earlier recommendations. The most recent proposals, those of the National Advisory Commission on Criminal Justice Standards,[4] also focus on structure, and ignore the institutional barriers to due process. Again, the preferred solution is a unification of upper and lower trial courts. Detroit, however, has had a unified system since

3. See 54-58, infra.
4. A National Strategy to Reduce Crime, 157-159 (1973).

1920 — without notable success in resolving the problems of lower court justice.[5]

The orthodox explanation for the tenacity of the lower court problem stresses high caseload, inadequate resources and staffing, low prestige, and archaic structure. The lower courts fail, the argument runs, because of insufficient funds to hire the judges, probation officers, and defense and prosecution lawyers, which the ideal of due process requires. Moreover, structural elements such as trial de novo, decentralized or nonexistent administration, and politicized selection procedures impose further limitations. If the courts were unified, if judges were selected strictly on merit, if officials were better trained, if salaries were raised, and if petty offenses such as drunkenness were removed from the criminal courts, *then* the lower courts would become bastions of legality and monuments to a just society.

This view, while certainly accurate as far as it goes, combats the symptoms without diagnosing the problem itself. More resources and structural improvements will help, but if history is any guide they will help only marginally. Since 1890 structure has been tinkered with, altered, and reformed continually. Court budgets have increased. An unprecedented number of defense attorneys, judges, prosecutors, and probation officers now staff these courts. Despite growing caseloads, many judges still manage to hurry through their dockets in two or three hours a day. To be sure, increased funds are a necessary condition for reform, but money alone will not solve the problem.

The general public and the leaders of the bench and bar frequently exhibit a particular attitude toward the lower courts (and toward those who appear before them) that leads to either an evasion or a denial of the very real problems of such courts. Relative to other social problems, the need for increased salaries for municipal court officials or for a unified court system appears trivial and is easily ignored. The lower criminal court is viewed like any other state agency — a welfare department or a registry of motor vehicles — where impersonal, exasperating procedures are to be expected and tolerated, because the cases are of no great moment and affect only a small portion of the population. If traffic offenders, drunks, petty thieves, assaulters, and society's other misfits receive

5. One of the few commentators pessimistic about the success of the standard approach is Arnold Enker. See his essay. The Lower Courts, in C. Whitebread, Mass Production Justice and the Constitutional Ideal, pp. 191-194 (1970).

less than ideal treatment, what does it matter? More important problems demand solution; more deserving people need society's protection. Although the individuals and groups that have sparked reform movements hold a different view, they have always been a minority that has been difficult to mobilize and hold together over the long course of judicial reform.

The majority's lack of concern over the problems of the lower courts, however, is difficult to justify. That the lower courts are sometimes referred to as "inferior courts" should not be taken to imply that the *function* of these courts is inferior, somehow unworthy of attention or concern. To the contrary — in terms of quantity of cases, contact with the citizenry, and impact on individual lives, the lower courts are a major social institution. And while they often service the poor, the disputes and indiscretions of the middle class also surface in these courtrooms. Most importantly, the lower courts symbolize lawful order, and inevitably influence the power of law to regulate behavior. To justify complacency on the grounds that these courts are "inferior" or trivial, then, is to confess a cynical parochialism. If law means anything, the lower courts matter.

A more fruitful approach to the lower court problem, and one to which the articles in this book repeatedly advert, would examine the conflicting principles and purposes inherent in the social fabric of the lower court. Like any social organization, the lower court serves a number of purposes, both formal and informal, many of which conflict with each other. Paralleling the system's formal goals and norms are sets of organizational, political, and personal norms which often clash with the formal goals and which lead to trade-offs that give priority to administrative and personal convenience over the constitutional ideal of due process.

We can identify several functions of the lower criminal court. The most obvious set of functions is related to the court's manifest goals of maintaining order and social control. Through decisions on bail, probable cause, guilt, and sentence, the court acts directly to protect the community's security — preventing crime and punishing offenders. Closely related is a social service or rehabilitative function. The lower criminal court process operates in part to identify persons in need of nonpunitive social services. In cases of alcoholism, drug abuse, mental illness, and certain first offenses, the court links services with those who would appear to need them. Unlike other agencies, the court cannot easily avoid this role, and often is the only agency available, or able, to act. The recent emphasis among professionals on pretrial diversion programs reflects this concern, and if the proper services are made available, such programs could greatly enhance the court's rehabilitative role. Finally, a significant portion of the court's criminal caseload involves the resolution of disputes within families, among individuals, and between individuals and organizations. The court's job here may often be to restore parties to amicable relations rather than to adjudicate guilt or innocence. Arguably, such controversies should not appear before the criminal courts at all, and often judges lack the skills or the inclination to mediate effectively. Yet the courts cannot easily ignore the task when it confronts them. While the style and techniques of fulfilling the social control functions vary, satisfactory performance of this role pays off in publicity, approval, and funding; generally, it receives high priority from court officials.

Another set of functions concerns the equilibrium of the entire court system. If the lower court can filter most cases out of the system, the caseloads of the felony courts will be more manageable. Thus, many judges explicitly recognize a need to keep cases from "going upstairs" and adding to the heavy backlogs of superior courts. For his part, the defendant has an incentive to have his case concluded in a court where sentencing power is limited and may use the system accordingly, sometimes to the detriment of the community in need of protection from crime. The need to limit the caseload of the superior courts also leads to pressure on innocent defendants to plead guilty. Often serious charges will be reduced, plea bargains struck, or defendants persuaded to waive the right to appeal. In addition, the higher court judges who administer the court system implicitly expect lower courts to dispose of their business without engendering adverse publicity that will disturb the equilibrium of the system by causing the higher courts to take corrective action. Judicial advancement or prestige may rest on such a low profile, and of course it is in the interest of lower court judges to avoid actions that will induce appellate supervision of their activities.

The lower court also has functions involving internal organization. Most prominent is the expeditious handling of cases — the court's effectiveness measured in terms of its "production." Cases must be handled quickly to clear the way for more cases and also to free court officials for other tasks (or simply for leisure). Increasing caseloads add to pressures for haste and contribute to a characteristically cavalier attitude toward the rights of the defendant and the considered adjudication of factual issues. The bureaucratic ingenuity with which some courts meet these demands is remarkable. Oath-taking and the apprisal of rights are done en masse. Unstated rules of thumb are used to decide bail, guilt, and sentence. Legal arguments which prolong proceedings are discouraged; written motions and briefs become the exception rather than the rule. Defendants asserting rights may be perceived as threats, and deviations from the court routine are quickly sanctioned.

Included in this set of functions are the needs of court personnel for power, security, and advancement, requiring larger court budgets, new facilities, salary increases, and additional staff. Protection of one's present position and promotion to the next level of clerk, prosecutor, or judge are also important concerns. For the private defense counsel, dependent on a high-volume business for a livelihood, the chief concern may be a rapid turnover of cases. The career goals of public defenders may entail deference to judges and court procedures, at times conflicting with vigorous assertion of defendant rights. Personal and career considerations inevitably influence role performance in the lower courts.

A fourth set of lower court functions is political. Courts at any level are an integral part of the political system, but in the lower courts the political concerns are often manifest, unobstructed by case citations and elaborate opinions. Politics influences the selection of personnel, the matters which the police bring to the courts, the amount of time spent on cases, and even the decisions reached in particular cases. At one extreme, local political machines or politicians may use the lower court's services to enhance their own power, and staff the courts through patronage. Even the lower court free from overt political influence mirrors in its handling of cases the dominant assumptions, attitudes, and political choices of the community. To remain a viable institution, the court needs community acceptance and its officials need personal security; the court can hardly be independent of its milieu. Thus society's out-groups find the law, as refracted through the political culture of the lower court, less than neutral.

Finally, the lower courts owe a duty to the law itself. The values of legality — of legal constraints on state power — have little substance if they do not inform the procedures and decisions of lower courts. Between most citizens and official lawlessness stands only the lower court judge. On him falls the burden of transforming the abstract rules articulated by higher courts into living law. In the rules he applies to the police, to the prosecution, and to his own actions, the judge identifies the boundaries of state power, educates officials and the public, and reaffirms the societal commitment to due process. Thus a key function of the lower courts is maintenance of the rule of law.

This brief account of manifest and latent functions shows the conflicting currents buffeting the lower court. Achieving due process of law is but one function of many and, given the social and political relationships affecting the court, one seldom exerting a dominant influence. Functions of defending society clash not only with due process but also with intra- and intercourt needs, and sometimes with political demands. Conflicts among the other functions are easily visualized: the influence of politics on the lower courts, for instance, jars with the concept of an ideal, unbiased legal system. The balance among these functions, though varying with time, locality, judge, and other factors, often deprecates the due process ideal. Due process may obstruct factual determinations, and frequently will not help the judge deal with the cases of pain, misery, and human deterioration which daily face him. A Boston judge noted for his antipathy to the Supreme Court reveals a common attitude of the lower courts:

> "Take those two bitches screaming at each other! What's the Supreme Court got to do with them? Or those drunks! It's a farce that I have to ask every one of them if he wants a lawyer.... The trouble with the Court is that it ignores the reality of what day-to-day criminal courts are like.... The Court just doesn't know what goes on in a place like this. And the reformers are even worse. They have a priori concepts about poor people and black people and believe that they can be changed in their attitudes and habits. That's just unrealistic." [6]

If informal adjudication keeps most cases out of higher courts, there will be little pressure from above to formalize procedures, and hierarchical supervision, when it occurs, will be ad hoc, individualized, and unlikely to have systemwide impact. A commitment to rehabilitative functions, like a commitment to due process, may entail more work for clerks, court officers, lawyers, and judges, or may threaten the entrenched position of probation officers. In addition, both goals imply a respect for the individual, which the crime prevention perspective of the lower court frequently dilutes. The mix of functions deemphasizes the ideal of due process in favor of personal, political, and administrative needs — and the lower court problem persists.

The balance struck among these conflicting functions becomes apparent in the techniques of case resolution employed by individual judges. A few judges adhere closely to the due processs ideal of adjudication, with a formal approach to evidence, procedure, and

6. R. Harris, In Criminal Court, The New Yorker, p. 72 (April 14, 1973).

fact-finding. Other judges, while following this model in particular cases, rely on an administrative–bureaucratic approach: factual issues are resolved by routine acceptance of the accounts of certain witnesses, such as the police, and cases are fitted into a limited number of categories tied to specific dispositions. Still other judges prefer to avoid decision-making and encourage the prosecutor and defense counsel to reach a settlement which the judge then ratifies. If informal resolution is not possible, the judge will then adopt the adjudicative or administrative technique, or a combination of the two. With the exception of the adjudicative approach, these varying techniques enable the judge to meet the exigencies of caseload and role without undue concern for formal procedure.

### ACTUALIZING DUE PROCESS IN THE LOWER COURTS

The main obstacles to realizing due process in the lower courts are three: (1) the lack of judges with a strong commitment to due process values; (2) competing norms and interests; and (3) the lack of organizational support for procedural due process. Despite the rhetoric of the investiture ceremony, few judges reach the bench because of fidelity to legal principles. Further, the complicated role demands of the lower court force other interests to the fore and diminish the attraction of legality per se. No matter how committed an individual judge may be to the rule of law and to the dignity of the individual — and many such judges grace the lower court bench — preserving that commitment against political, systemic, organizational, and caseload pressures is an exhausting and difficult task.

While it is true, as one observer has remarked, that "there is no particular reason to expect an individual's behavior to coincide with the behavior prescribed by the formal goals of the system,"[7] the dilemma faced by the lower courts is the creation of such congruence. But how to proceed? Structural, political, and judicial reform, more resources, and selective decriminalization would, no doubt, partially right the balance. Beyond workload and resources, however, remains the task of blunting the force of competing incentives and norms, and inspiring allegiance to due process itself. Yet few routes to this end are available. Enforcement mechanisms — litigation, appellate review, or grass-roots citizen activity — are too expensive, time-consuming, and highly specific for permanent impact. Reform

---

7. J. Feeley, Two Models of the Criminal Justice System: An Organizational Perspective, 7 Law & Soc. Rev. 421 (1973).

movements generally aim at clarifying or formulating rules, but success in obtaining a set of rules does not guarantee their implementation: Reformers who lack the resources to assure compliance soon learn that they have won a symbolic victory that has had no true effect on the lower courts. Rules, of course, even if primarily symbolic, serve useful functions and may rectify the worst abuses. However, they are an incomplete solution to the problem. Absent large-scale social change and an infusion of moral values into political and governmental institutions, the chances of reordering value priorities in the lower courts are slim.

There remains, then, the possibility of recruiting judges so dedicated to the moral values of due process that other factors, however strong, will lose their force. Recently, reformers in a few jurisdictions have partially succeeded in bringing to the bench judges committed to community accountability and a respect for defendant rights, but the permanence of this success is unclear. In any case, without major changes in selecting and disciplining judges — an unrealistic possibility — such reform is unlikely to occur. Moreover, in an age of moral skepticism and regard for technical efficiency, it is perhaps understandable that the moral and ethical dimensions of the judicial role give way to the pragmatic operational requirements of running a court. And in many instances an overly formalistic concern with procedure may even frustrate substantive justice.

In the end, the lower courts face the difficult task of reconciling goals that may at times appear mutually exclusive: they must lose sight neither of the ideal nor of the "real" problems that confront them; they must match formal and substantive justice; they must reduce the conflict between the courts' social role and the social context in which the courts operate. Ready solutions, it should be clear, are lacking. Rather than justifying inaction, however, the absence of solutions is cause for confronting the situation openly and achieving what is possible within prevailing limits. The present state of the lower courts is far from the limits of the possible. If those limits were first reached, a final solution might well prove to be less of a problem.

The selections that follow explore the problems of the lower courts and are grouped under six headings. In Part I the historical development of lower court problems is discussed, and an overview of issues currently facing the courts is provided. Part II includes several essays on the social organization of the lower courts, in which the authors take a functional system or exchange approach to show the influence of nonlegal factors in the application of formal rules. Part III presents a political perspective that indicates the intensity and the strength of ties between lower court systems and politics. Part IV focuses on the actual performance of lower criminal courts — their atmosphere, their decisions, and their impact on minority groups. Part V turns to nonadversarial modes of judicial decision-making as a potential alternative to the formal demands of due process. Finally, Part VI deals with the problems and processes of reform. Several alternatives to the present system are discussed, and the factors determining the potential for change in the lower criminal courts are analyzed.

# PART I.
# THE EVOLUTION OF
# LOWER CRIMINAL COURTS

This section presents materials documenting and describing the evolution of lower criminal courts discussed in the Introduction. Like all history, the purpose here is to reveal the present through an understanding of the past. The current state of the courts derives in an important sense from the tradition here described.

The selections attempt this task with varying degrees of generality. Perhaps the most general is the short selection from Max Weber. Weber, who among other achievements was an imaginative legal historian, finds in the West a progression from informal and irrational to more formal and rational modes of adjudication — from the khadi, who decides according to his own view of the just result, to the judge applying formal rules and precedent. On a micro-level, lower courts illustrate a parallel development. The khadi-like justice of the peace or rural magistrate with unfettered discretion has gradually been replaced by centralized municipal courts, appellate review in theory, and the obligation to apply law. In practice khadi elements still exist in the lower court judicial role. The history of the lower court has been an attempt to minimize those elements.

The excerpt from the Wickersham Commission recounts the same development in more specific terms. It describes the English and early colonial roots of the magistrate system and its gradual absorption into systems of formal courts. Its description of inferior courts in 1931 is a useful benchmark for consideration of contemporary problems.

With justices of the peace the precursor of, if not the actual, lower court in many parts of the country, some consideration of their decline is essential, and this Kenneth Vanlandingham provides. His essay shows both the functions which make them almost irradicable, and the problems that make eradication essential. The waxing and waning of the justice of the peace shows how difficult it is to achieve true reform. The problems are merely displaced to another level or they reappear in a different form, a theme explored by Warren Lehman in Section VI.

Given the importance of the municipal court movement in the development of contemporary lower courts, two aspects of that optimistic endeavor are here presented. One describes the original reform movement in Chicago, the paradigm and inspiration for municipal courts elsewhere. The second is a description of the Cleveland Municipal Court in 1922, eight years after the municipal court replaced the police court in that city.

The latter selection provides an interesting comparison to the contemporary state of the lower courts described in the last selection in this section. The President's Commission on Law Enforcement and Administration of Justice found similar problems and recommended similar solutions. Like the remainder of this book, it shows that the history of the lower criminal court is not yet complete. It has yet to achieve the goals for which it aims.

# Petty Offenses and Inferior Courts*

## Wickersham Commission

### 1. IMPORTANCE OF PETTY PROSECUTIONS

There has been little appreciation of the importance of magistrates' courts and police and municipal courts in the system of criminal justice. It is only in the present century that there has been a beginning of adequate provision for petty prosecutions. Even where modern municipal courts have been set up, there has been a tendency to take advantage of their better organization and simpler procedure to impose upon them an increasing burden of civil litigation, more appropriate to the superior courts, to be carried at the expense of the work for which magistrates' courts primarily exist. But it is in the latter that the administration of criminal justice touches immediately the largest number of people. Apart from all other considerations, arbitrary methods, incompetent magistrates, tribunals governed by petty politics, and slovenly proceedings, at the point at which the great mass of the population come in contact with law enforcement, give a bad impression of the administration of justice as a whole and most seriously affect respect for and observance of law generally.

In addition to the preliminary examination as a stage in the prosecution of major offenses, and the relatively unimportant petty prosecutions which were in the jurisdiction of magistrates in the formative era of our institutions, in the large city of to-day they have to deal with traffic offenses, involving the public safety to a degree far beyond anything which formerly came before magistrates, and a multitude of police regulations, required by the conditions of urban life. These new types of offense have given a new and much greater significance to the inferior courts. The bulk of prosecutions for felony involve preliminary examination before a magistrate, and in our report on prosecution we pointed out the need of thorough sifting at the beginning of such prosecutions, and the ill results at later stages where there is perfunctory or incompetent investigation at this point. Moreover citizens come before these tribunals as complainants and witnesses at preliminary hear-

* From: National Commission on Law Observance and Enforcement (Wickersham Commission), Report on Criminal Procedure, 6-15 (1931).

ings much more frequently than before the superior courts. Great numbers of citizens who have no other contacts with the courts come before these tribunals in traffic cases. Probably the chief point of contact of the ordinary law-abiding citizen with the criminal law is in connection with police regulations. To do their work properly and to command the respect which will give to the average man a right attitude toward criminal justice, these tribunals should be manned by strong judges, equipped as befits agencies of the justice of the state, and conducted with dignity.

Unhappily the old-time police court has too often furnished the model even for municipal courts organized in the present century. In too many cities little or no provision is made for men of the caliber demanded for the work to be done. Too often the judges are chosen at elections for short terms, are compelled to campaign for nomination and election, and thus are subjected to politics. The surveys of criminal justice everywhere have shown the ill effects of this system at the very root of criminal justice. The legal profession has very little interest in petty prosecutions which to-day are chiefly the concern of the lowest stratum of the profession. Also the public has assumed that a petty judge is good enough for petty cases. But what is of little profit to the lawyer may none the less be of much profit to the law. The importance of petty prosecutions for the sum total of criminal justice can not be measured by the amount of the fine or duration of imprisonment in the average of such cases. They must be looked at with reference to their place in the scheme of criminal justice as a whole and the part played by them and by the offenses to which they relate in the whole process of urban life. . . .

### 3. PETTY OFFENSES IN THE STATE COURTS

There are no reasonably complete or reliable statistics as to the relative volume of petty prosecutions in the States. But in such urban localities as publish full and well-compiled statistics, the average proportion of such prosecutions to prosecutions within the jurisdiction of the superior courts is about 7 to 3. It should be noted, however, that the number of causes which go to the superior courts is swollen by appeals from convictions before magistrates, often resorted to because the crowded criminal dockets of those courts make possible or even require bargains with the prosecutors whereby the accused escapes with a lesser penalty than that imposed in the lower courts, or, even, through delay and loss of

evidence or dispersion of witnesses, compel dismissal. If allowance is made for these cases, in which the system of double appeals from magistrates' convictions, with its resulting advantages
to the accused, tends to a congestion of appealed petty cases in
the superior courts, an analysis of such statistics as are at hand
indicates a proportion of 9 to 2.1. Moreover, in our large cities the
work of these tribunals in connection with domestic relations may
have an intimate bearing on the causes of crime. It may be a large
factor in the preventive justice which we must increasingly develop. When it is added that all but a minute fraction of prosecutions for felony involve preliminary examination before a magistrate, the importance of courts of summary jurisdiction in the
State polity is manifest.

Magistrates' courts were the first to be organized in America and
the first American law books were books of practice before justices
of the peace. At the end of the sixteenth century, on the eve of
colonization, the English system of justices of the peace had taken
on the form which it kept substantially till the present century.
In origin the justices of the peace were administrative rather than
judicial officers. Their function in the beginning was to keep the
peace. They kept their administrative functions, but developed
also as a part of the judicial organization. As their work came to
be organized it included, in addition to much of local administration, preliminary examination of accused persons, a considerable
superior criminal jurisdiction, and an exclusive petty jurisdiction.
Keeping the peace involved, what to-day we should call criminal
investigation. In time the function of criminal investigation was
set off from their judicial tasks. In the end it was turned over to
a specialized administrative agency. But at the end of the sixteenth
century, the Lord Chief Justice of England, as the highest conservator of the peace, was expected on occasion to do something
very like what we now in the United States expect of a prosecuting
attorney. At the time of colonization a differentiation was still far
distant. Preliminary examination of accused persons had its begin-
nings in statutes of the sixteenth century. From a present-day
standpoint it was partly a police and partly a judicial examination,
and in England it did not become definitely judicial till the nineteenth century. Hence as it came to us, it had its original twofold
character. But our American insistence on the separation of powers
led us to make it judicial. Unfortunately it became judicial before
the development of the modern police system. As the magistrates'
examinations were judicial, all examinations of accused persons

were subjected to the guaranties attaching to judicial proceedings, and so in a measure the system compelled an extra-legal practice of examinations by prosecuting attorneys and police.

By the time of colonization, the principal judicial work of the justices of the peace in England had become organized in courts of general sessions or quarter sessions held for the whole county, with jurisdiction of all crimes but treason, although in practice difficult cases were sent to the assizes to be tried by the superior justices. Later petty sessions were set off. In these a certain number of justices had power to impose penalties under the provisions of statutes. Also there were borough courts exercising criminal jurisdiction under charters. It was usual to make the mayor and some of the aldermen justices of the peace, and often the charter gave authority to hold courts of quarter sessions. In important boroughs there was usually a recorder who was a lawyer and in practice became the real judge.

In the United States we took over the idea of laymen conducting preliminary examinations and administering justice as magistrates in petty causes. In some States we took over the idea of municipal criminal courts in which the mayor or aldermen sat as judges, sometimes with a recorder as judge also. In many States we took over the system of concurrent jurisdiction in county and municipal tribunals, which, indeed, only disappeared in New York in the present century and still obtains in some parts of the land. In some States also we took over the administrative features of the English system, so that the justices of the peace, or their analogues, have general administrative functions hardly compatible with efficient handling of judicial work under the conditions of to-day. With respect to organization of courts, the chief legacy of the colonial period is the system of numerous local petty tribunals manned by laymen which still obtains, except as superseded by modern municipal courts in some of our largest cities.

Organization of inferior courts has come to vary greatly in the different States. Generally, but not everywhere, there are justices of the peace, commonly one for each of the ultimate local political subdivisions. There are still in some places courts of mayors or aldermen or equivalent officials. Police courts for municipalities, with a magistrate's jurisdiction and jurisdiction over petty police offenses, were formerly general but are coming to be superseded by municipal courts with a better organization. In some parts of the country there are local criminal courts with magistrates' jurisdiction. In many States, concurrent with the local justices of the peace and the municipal petty courts, there are county courts, with a concurrent magistrate's jurisdiction extending over the whole county. A few States have a higher type of inferior courts, organized in districts. In the present century there have come to be municipal courts in many large cities, some of them exceptionally well organized. But taking the country as a whole, our inferior courts are conspicuously the least satisfactory part of our judicial system.

Except in a few jurisdictions in which the inferior courts have been completely reorganized, dignity long since ceased to attach to the position of magistrate. The old-time country squire, a leader in his community, exercising a sort of patriarchal jurisdiction, is as much in the past as the conditions in which he administered justice. Election in a self-sufficient neighborhood, in which everyone knew the squire, was a very different thing from election in the city of to-day. The short tenure, the mode of choice, the want of dignity in the position, and the manner of compensation very generally by fees, lent themselves to a low personnel which for the most part made these tribunals petty in fact as well as inferior in name. Nowhere is a proper organization more called for. With modern conditions of transportation there is no need of a magistrate at every man's back door. About all that is left of the fee system of compensation is in inferior courts in different parts of the country. Wherever it remains, it ought to be abolished and magistrates with salary and a modern organization into a unified court should be substituted.

Even in the modern municipal courts in some of our large cities, the physical conditions and decorum are often those of the old-time police court of a small town when the police magistrate knew the town drunkard, as did all his neighbors, and could dispose of his case offhand with the assurance of one who knew. The methods of the rural magistrate are out of place without the personal knowledge on the part of the court and the community which they presuppose. Without this check, there are opportunities for questionable influences in the case of real offenders, and there is danger of irreparable injury to the occasional offender who is not able to command such influences. The bad physical surroundings, the confusion, the want of decorum, the undignified offhand disposition of causes at high speed, the frequent suggestion of something working behind the scenes, involved in the casual conferences of magistrate and politician lawyers, not audible to the public in attendance — in short the atmosphere of the inferior criminal courts — create in the minds of observers a suspicion of the whole process of law enforcement which, no matter how unfounded,

greatly prejudices respect for and observance of law. Even in jurisdictions in which the judges of these courts are appointed and are
distinctly above the average for the country generally, they are
sometimes permitted to practice in other courts and their professional connections are sometimes such, or appear to be such, as
to give rise to unfortunate suspicions. Taking the country as a
whole there has been and continues to be scandal in connection
with these inferior tribunals in noteworthy contrast with the almost uniformly clean record of the superior courts during a century of immersion in politics. After starting out well, few of the
more recently organized municipal courts have been able to maintain the requisite high type of personnel, nor are they likely to be
able to do so until the bar and the public become thoroughly alive
to the importance of these tribunals for an efficient administration
of justice.

As to procedure in the inferior criminal courts of the States,
there is relatively little to be done. Chiefly, improvement must be
sought in the personnel, tenure, and mode of choice of the magistrates. Neighborhood quarrels, petty depredations, small-scale pred-
atory activities, very serious to the participants or victims, and
often most irritating in a crowded urban community, are not to
be dealt with effectively by the contentious procedure which has
developed for and is appropriate to the superior courts. It has been
a universal experience that such cases are best disposed of summarily by a strong magistrate with a large measure of discretion
applying to them his common sense, but within the limits of the
law. This involves conferring large powers, as between man and
man, on magistrates who to-day are seldom of the requisite caliber.
The power of passing upon conduct and appraising its moral aspects untrammeled by many rules, is a royal one. It requires a
magistrate equal to exercise of royal powers, if it is to be employed
wisely and well. In tribunals or causes where there is not a defined,
contentious procedure, with both sides represented by competent
counsel, the fundamental guaranties may be made effective only
by putting on the bench magistrates who understand these guaranties and how and when to give effect to them on their own
motion. It is important not only that justice be done but that
those who come before the tribunals or take part in or watch the
proceedings, feel it is done. The casual arbitrariness characteristic
of proceedings in the inferior courts, to a greater or less extent
everywhere, contributes to suspicion of and disrespect for law.

Next to organization of the courts and better personnel, the matters most deserving of attention are the overburdening of our inferior courts with matters which in the rest of the world are confided to administration, the excessive resort to arrest as a mode of beginning minor prosecutions, and the system of double appeals.

In nineteenth-century America we sought to make the courts do the bulk of what to-day we have been learning to do through administration. In particular we cast upon courts a heavy burden of what is more appropriately administrative work. Particularly prosecutions were relied on to do what would have been done better by administrative inspection and supervision and adjustment. It is worth while considering whether much of traffic regulation in the city streets could not be achieved more effectively, and with less annoyance to the parties and expenditure of public time and money, by administrative agencies rather than by magistrates' courts. Certainly such things as violations of parking rules need come before criminal tribunals only in exceptional cases.

In some jurisdictions civil suits for penalties in which arrest is not involved are used ordinarily for breaches of municipal ordinances. In England summons, rather than arrest, is used regularly for minor prosecutions, and this practice obtains in some States, although even in those States arrest is employed too indiscriminately. At common law all prosecutions began with arrest and this is the staple method of beginning petty prosecutions in the United States. The practice of summons in such cases should be introduced wherever it is not provided for, and its use should be extended everywhere. Indiscriminate exercise of the power of arrest is one of the most reprehensible features of American criminal justice.

One of the most significant improvements in connection with the municipal courts set up in many of our cities in the present century is the provision for doing away with two trials on the merits in minor prosecutions through reviewing proceedings in those courts, in cases within their summary jurisdiction, only for errors of law. In some of these courts an appellate division has given them a specially effective organization. The inferior courts should be so organized and so manned that they may be trusted to do the work in their sphere as we trust the superior courts to do the work in theirs. Instead of retrial of all cases where the accused has the means to appeal, a modern organization of courts would provide for general visitatorial powers over the inferior tribunal, exercised by responsible superior judges. The system of double appeals from magistrates' courts and retrial of the facts in a superior court as a matter of course, gives a great and unjust advantage to delinquents of means or delinquents with an organization behind them.

The absolute right of having any conviction before a magistrate retried before a jury in a superior court, which obtains in so many jurisdictions, clogs the dockets of the higher courts with long lists of minor cases awaiting jury trial and has much to do with compelling wholesale dismissals and bargain penalties. It adds to the overburdening of jury trial which makes citizens generally seek to avoid jury service. It deprives the convictions in magistrates' courts of efficacy as to those who can appeal. It interferes with the proper disposition of the primary business of the superior courts. It has had much to do with the growth of a system of disposition of prosecutions out of court. In some jurisdictions it has almost paralyzed administration of the laws as to serious traffic violations. It should be done away with everywhere. But provision of courts equal to their tasks must go along with this change.

Another significant improvement, introduced in some of the municipal courts set up in the present century, deserves to be adopted in all inferior urban courts and to be developed further. More and more we must put the emphasis upon preventive justice; and preventive criminal justice is emphatically the field of the inferior criminal tribunals. It was a great step forward when the municipal court of Chicago set up a bureau of information where the citizen could ascertain something of his rights and duties instead of being compelled to guess, subject to prosecution if he guessed wrong. The conception of such a tribunal not as a mill for grinding through prosecutions but as a bureau of justice has great possibilities for law and order in the city of to-day. But it calls for an adequate personnel both as to the magistrates and as to the administrative officials. Without this, no improved organization or machinery will effect much.

## *The Chicago Experiment**

## Journal of the American Judicature Society

Inasmuch as the exceedingly loose structure of courts and organization of judges is a heritage of simpler conditions of life, it is easily seen why complaints concerning the failure of justice are more pointed and emphatic in large cities than elsewhere, because the larger the city, the greater the departure from the primitive conditions which shaped our judicial institutions.

First, let us have a look at Chicago's judicial system, if it can be called a system, at the time when agitation was approaching its legislative goal. The constitutional amendment which permitted of creating the Municipal Court of Chicago, was adopted by the voters in November, 1904. At that time Chicago had a population of about 1,800,000. There was a County Court with one judge and an anomalous jurisdiction comprising chiefly insanity proceedings and those involving taxation and elections. There was the Cook County Probate Court with one judge and three assistants. The courts of general trial jurisdiction were the Circuit and Superior Courts with twenty-six judges in the two. These were, and still are, distinct courts, but with identical jurisdiction, the only difference being that in the Superior Court yellow paper is used for process. They had civil jurisdiction from $100 up and from them were drawn the justices of the intermediate Appellate Court for the First District. They also delegated certain of their members to sit in the Criminal Court and try causes involving offenses of the grade of felony. The inferior civil and criminal jurisdiction was vested in fifty-four justices of the peace.

The damnable condition of certain of the justices' courts furnished much of the incentive to remedy affairs in the judicial field. But it deserves to be said that some of the justices were capable lawyers who did the best they could under the impossible conditions which were imposed upon them. But for others the environment was too hard; they became mere judicial buccaneers. And in one respect the situation was not as bad as in certain other cities,

* From: The Success of Organized Courts, 1 J. Am. Jud. Socy. 134-151 (1917). Reprinted by permission of Judicature, Journal of the American Judicature Society.

because Chicago justices were not elected. They were appointed
by the judges of the Circuit and Superior Courts, just as masters
are now appointed, which accounts for the fact that some of them
were faithful and efficient within their limits. But on the criminal
side there was one especially untoward feature, for the justices who
sat as police judges were designated for this work by the mayor *at
the suggestion of aldermen*. Politics, graft, and the judiciary were
thus linked together.

The Municipal Court was created to meet two very definite
needs. One of these needs grew out of the fact that the dockets of
the Circuit and Superior Courts were seriously overloaded. The
commercial interests of the city especially suffered from the fact
that it took two or three years to adjudicate ordinary commercial
causes. The other need rested on the scandalous condition of the
justices' courts which had exclusive jurisdiction in civil causes involving less than $100 and criminal causes less than the grade of
felony.

The first need was met by giving the new court unlimited jurisdiction in contract causes. The second by abolishing the office of
justice of the peace and conferring justices' jurisdiction on the
Municipal Court. In respect to jurisdiction in contract causes involving more than $100 the new court was designed to compete
with the Circuit and Superior Courts within the city's boundaries.
In respect to criminal jurisdiction it was intended to divide the
field with the Criminal Court. Further, in order to relieve the
County courts of the less important tort actions, the Municipal
Court was given jurisdiction in this field over causes involving not
more than $1,000. No chancery jurisdiction was conferred.

Thus far there was no real innovation. Chicago was merely doing
on a large scale what had been done previously in many cities
where it became necessary to get rid of the primitive justices'
courts. In respect to jurisdiction the new court presented no striking features. It was just about what would be expected of lawyer-
legislators. But business men had a large part in shaping the new
court. They, naturally, viewed the problem from the business
standpoint. Here were twenty-seven new judges to take over the
work of fifty-four justices, to relieve as far as possible the glutted
calendars of the courts of general trial jurisdiction and to meet
the demands, if possible, of a rapidly growing city. In this last
respect they gave the new court a harder problem than they conceived, as figures to be presented will show.

To simply create so many new judges and permit them to go
as they pleased would obviously result in failure. At least the busi-

ness men appeared to think so. To provide a fixed salary instead of fees would go far to remove the evils of the justices' courts, but for twenty-seven judges to do business all "on their own" without direction and management, without co-ordination and united responsibility, would inevitably result in every kind of judicial shirking. In a short time litigants would be as bad off as before, at least as far as delays were concerned.

## STAFF IS ORGANIZED

So the citizens' committee which assumed the drafting of the municipal court act, decided to organize these new judges just as any business man would organize a staff of workers. They decided to create a head for the court with such powers that he could be held responsible for the administrative acts of its judges. So the office of Chief Justice was created and in this official was centered the administrative control of the entire court. It was done very simply by providing that the Chief Justice should assign judges to sit in the various branches of the court and that he should superintend the making of calendars and classify business upon various calendars. . . .

1. The court was given power to create and regulate procedure subject to the details enumerated in the act. This fact alone would have made the experiment one notable in American legislation for it was the first conspicuous acknowledgment of a principle which has become indispensable to the success of courts in all other English speaking countries.

2. The power to classify causes upon separate calendars, conferred upon the Chief Justice, enabled him to group causes of an allied nature, or concerning like persons or arising from like causes, along natural administrative lines, rather than upon the traditional and often meaningless lines observable in other courts. The full employment of this power, in a strikingly successful way, came about in the creation of the Domestic Relations Court, to which reference will be had later. A new tribunal may be created for any special purpose which appears to justify it by a mere executive order of the Chief Justice. There is nothing comparable to this outside the organized court. If in St. Louis or San Francisco a special tribunal is needed it is to be obtained only by legislative action, and when established it is an awkward piece of furniture. Its judge may or may not be adapted to its peculiar and limited jurisdiction. The fact that it is created for a special purpose limits its usefulness in many causes which do not classify wholly within

the scope of the specialized court, so that what is really but one controversy has to be adjudicated in two or more tribunals, and is almost certain to be a "judicial botch."

3. The power of the Chief Justice to direct the activities of the associate judges is one essential to the success of the specialized branch court. In order that judicial business may be done expertly and economically it must be classified and come before specially designated branches and these branches must be manned by *specialist judges*. Some guiding mind must determine the judge best qualified for particular classes of causes. No lawyer can succeed in every field of law, nor can any judge. It would be a good thing, at least, if every judge were as well versed in the law as the lawyers practicing in his court. He can become such an expert, or specialist judge, if the branch is one suited to his native powers and training and if he is kept there long enough to master the substantive law involved.

The assignment of judges is, of course, essential to any plan for promoting judicial efficiency. Judicial efficiency without this power is as little to be expected as would be commercial efficiency if all employes in any enterprise performed indiscriminately the functions of buyer, salesman, stockkeeper, accountant, credit manager, and so forth. Most of our existing inefficiency is to be ascribed to its absence and wherever we have a measure of efficiency among any considerable number of judges of equal jurisdiction, it will be found that some approach to the principle of assignment has been worked out.

4. The requirement that associate judges report the number of hours which they devote to their work is one doubtless quite essential to the success of this court. In this connection it must be remembered that conditions were not, and are not now, what they should be in Chicago courts. Such a provision may be considered by some persons a reflection upon the judges of this court, but the people are entitled to know how much their judges do, and the judges are favored in being permitted to keep their own time. When one realizes the slackness and irresponsibility of certain of the judges of the other courts in Chicago, he appreciates the need for the requirement. A judge of one of those courts absented himself in California for a year or more before being exposed by a newspaper. He was drawing $10,000 a year salary and paying a country judge $10 a day to substitute for him. There are plenty of other cases, not so extreme — and when no substitute is hired. Even as it is it is hard to keep a few of the Municipal Court judges at their work until half past four. Without this requirement

the Municipal Court probably could not have made its wonderful record and this fact is sufficient justification.

5. One of the wonderful features of the act is the one which requires judges to attend monthly meetings to receive and investigate all complaints brought before them and to consider opportunities to improve the service generally. At every such meeting every judge is enabled to obtain guidance with respect to knotty problems, to unload responsibility upon his colleagues, to point out the omissions of another judge and to share generally in the dignity of managing a great institution.

### RESULT IS RESPONSIBILITY

All these factors together make for the one essential of success, responsibility. The judges are responsible, just like all other judges, to the appellate courts for their decisions with respect to particular causes. But as members of this organized court they are also responsible for the due administration of justice within the jurisdiction conferred by the act. The ablest among them, who ordinarily tries only important civil causes, finds himself shouldered with responsibility for the conduct of the police branches in the slum wards, because he has power to influence judicial conduct in these branches, indirectly at least, and because the public will charge all blunders and scandals, more or less, to the entire body of judges. Every judge is made his brother's keeper and the protector of the reputation of the entire court. This is self-government and self-discipline, the only real government and the only real discipline. It is the only remedy for the complaints which have found expression in the demand for the recall of judges which promises any measure of success. Organized responsibility is prophylactic. The judicial recall is surgery.

This act gave the people of Chicago a new court utterly different from any court ever created in this country. The people were hopeful but there was no undue assurance that the problem had been solved. It yet remained to get the right judges, and particularly the right chief justice as administrative head, or business manager, for this unique business court, and then much would depend upon the way in which the powers conferred by the act would be developed.

There was one big element making for success which was not taken into account at that time. It lay in the importance of the role of chief justice, as head of a powerful, wieldy organization committed to the task of redeeming the enforcement of law in a great city, which importance made it possible to negotiate the candidacy of a man full-statured, broad-gauged, ambitious, experienced, and strong-willed. Such a man was Harry Olson, then and for ten years previously assistant state's attorney. Olson was the super-dreadnought of the state's attorney's office. He intended to enter private practice where his powers as trial lawyer would insure gratifying returns.

But the opportunity for distinguished public service drew him more powerfully than the chance to acquire wealth; he accepted the nomination. At that time the convention system of nominations was still in vogue in Illinois. It was in order to select candidates for the twenty-seven associate judgeships. The selections were made in advance of the convention, in accord with custom, by a committee consisting of Harry Olson, John J. Healey, then state's attorney for Cook county and John F. Smulski, then state treasurer. The committee was given such a free hand in selecting, that the resulting candidates were practically "hand picked." This ticket prevailed at the polls so that the new court was instituted December 1, 1906, with a willing and ambitious force of judges. They were young men, it is true, and mostly without judicial experience, but this may have been in their favor.

Within a few months the court and its friends had 44 of the 67 sections of the act amended. Provision was made for economical record writing by adopting a set of abbreviated forms corresponding by serial-numbers to regular amplified forms which were used only in cases in which transcripts were required. This put the records of the court on what might well be called a card catalogue system.

Taking over the business of the justices of the peace and assuming the vast amount of commercial litigation which was offered, gave the court an arduous regime during its first year or two, and prejudice on the part of the bar and the judges of other courts had to be overcome. But the court had a genuine leader, tireless in his work at judges' meetings, in the city council, in the press, in the upper courts, in the legislature, with political committees, and before the people in campaigns. The court had to be defended on numerous constitutional questions, the act had to be amended several times, and every amendment had to be ratified at a popular election.

In the first year 30,877 civil causes were disposed of and 6,227 were left on the docket. Fifty-eight thousand two hundred and twenty-seven criminal and quasi criminal causes were disposed of.

Before two years had elapsed the court was a going concern, keeping abreast of its work in spite of continual increases; it had won the confidence of the public and commercial lawyers were enthusiastic about it. The time had arrived for tackling the problem of simplifying procedure in first class civil causes, a problem quite generally considered insuperable among the common law practitioners of Illinois.

Judge Stephen Foster was sent to London to study the modern English practice, and upon his return a few simple rules, thirty-four in number, were drafted. Over a period of nine years these rules were not altered at all but in 1917 some improvement was made by incorporating a few lines concerning statement of the cause of action taken from the model rules drafted by the American Judicature Society. . . .

The act required monthly reports from the judges and at the end of the first year the Chief Justice made up a public report on his own initiative. Subsequently the act was amended to cover this important feature. The reports of this court comprise a larger body of judicial facts than are to be found elsewhere in this country. Outside of the reports of similar organized courts one will look in vain for judicial statistics. Our demand for published opinions has resulted in thousands of volumes of reports, a considerable part of which could never survive editing, but concerning the business end of administering justice there was never a page until the Chicago Municipal Court issued its first annual report.

One of the features which has proved indispensable is the efficiency audit month by month by a firm of accountants employed just as any business concern might employ them. This not only relieves the Chief Justice of worry concerning the balancing of the court's books, but it works like a charm in checking up everybody in the entire establishment of nearly 400 persons so that nobody can be ten cents in arrears at the end of the month. Harry Olson, as prosecutor of a crooked Circuit Court clerk, $50,000 in arrears, had learned how the books for a court should be kept.

One of the significant stories concerning the early career of this court, turns on the relationship of court to police. The new court act made the police ex officio deputy bailiffs for the service of all process. Now the police, under the former regime, had held warrants instead of serving them, had let news concerning warrants leak, and had generally enforced the law or not in accordance with instructions emanating no doubt from politicians high up in administration circles. There was a standing order that no patrolman should serve a warrant until it had been countersigned by his superior officer.

Municipal Court warrants for the arrest of gambling devices were issued and, of course, foozled. A big, powerful, self-respecting court could tolerate no trifling with its process. The Chief Justice was in the arena in a minute. He instituted at once a warrant docket in which was entered the name of every officer receiving a warrant. The police force scented danger and tried to bluff. The Chief Justice threatened to jail for contempt the chief of police for disobeying the mandates of the court. Nobody had dreamt of such an outcome from the wording of the act; it was because they had not foreseen what a courageous and efficient administrator could do to translate words into action.

The police knuckled under. They became in truth and fact officers of the court from the moment an arrest was made, or an offender booked, or a warrant received for service.

The victory for the court had a profound influence upon police administration. The patrolmen were to a considerable extent relieved from political pressure and soon came to like this situation. . . .

### SPECIALIZATION

The next experiment with specialization in the judicial field segregated all the causes involving violation of the state and city automobile laws in the Speeders' Court. To this new branch was assigned a judge who did not own an automobile and who was not owned by the owner of any automobile. Fines went up immediately from ten and twenty-five dollars to fifty and one hundred dollars, but better than this was the adoption of a uniform and systematic increase regardless of social eminence. At that time Chicago's streets were speedways. In sixty days the automobile drivers had learned their lesson fairly well. They had contributed $10,000 in fines. Highways were safer. The breath of life had been breathed into laws which formerly had been valueless. The customary way would have been to go on enacting more laws with heavier penalties which juries would have refused to inflict, while the evil persisted. In the typical American jurisdiction we have no knowledge as to the sufficiency of penal legislation for the reason that we have no adequate means for enforcement. We try to conjure our evil spirits by voluminous statutory incantations when a bright axe would do more good.

The next class of causes which defied uniform and consistent treatment when scattered throughout the police court branches was found to comprise those arising from vice conditions, and this led to the creation of the Morals Court. The Chicago vice district had been officially closed. Of course, this was a policy, not a solution. Nobody had discovered legal measures for repression of vice which would be other than sources of corruption for the police. The Chicago Morals Court is a step nearer than any other measure yet devised. At least the Morals Court does not despoil the prostitute so that she will be more dependent after discharge than before arrest. A woman physician is on the staff and opportunity is afforded for examination and free hospital treatment. Most of the offenders accept the offer.

A few years ago Chief Justice Olson met a tremendous need by the creation of the Boys' Court. Male offenders between the ages of seventeen and twenty-one had always been treated the same as adult offenders. Statistics showed that a majority of all first offense felonies were committed by boys under twenty-one. Olson's ten years in the prosecutor's office had given him a world of experience with these types. He had begun also a serious study of mental defectiveness, and he had suspicions as to the mental fitness of much of the human flotsam drifting through the criminal branches. It was obvious too, that from this class of boys must be recruited the ranks of professional criminals.

So the Boys' Court was established by a simple order directing the officers to present all male offenders under the age of twenty-one at a certain branch court, designated by number, and another order assigning a certain specially chosen judge to sit in this branch. The public had been prepared for this development through the press. On the day for instituting the new branch the judge's desk was banked with the most costly roses. Heads of the leading social organizations, judges from other courts, newspaper men and prominent citizens generally were present and an impressive ceremony marked the first day's session. The new court was instituted with a moral momentum sufficient to keep it in the grooves of efficiency for at least a year. This specialization on youthful offenders did not reform Chicago in a day or a year but it has made scientific conclusions possible and slowly a wise policy is developing, which will permit of saving as large a proportion of these boys as lies within human possibility. . . .

### PRESENT SHORTCOMINGS

The reader must not get the opinion that the Municipal Court of Chicago is a perfect institution. It is an amazing and illuminating instance of pioneering, but far from a complete and perfect court. Nearly as much is to be learned of the ideal court of the future from the shortcomings of this first great experiment as from its obvious successes.

Notwithstanding the efficient management of the Court Chicago has a dark record for crime. The explanation is not difficult.

The Municipal Court has no criminal jurisdiction beyond that formerly exercised by justices of the peace. In cases of felony, after finding that probable guilt exists, the court can do no more than hold the accused to the grand jury. From that stage the powers of irresponsibility rule. The State's attorney has almost undisputed power to nolle pros at any stage. He can ignore the Municipal Court entirely by beginning before the grand jury. If he should be disposed to let an offender slip after probable guilt has been established in the preliminary examination, he has only to fail to subpoena all of the people's witnesses before the grand jury.

The grand jury is the grand humbug. Beyond it lies the Criminal Court, presided over by judges of the Circuit and Superior courts. The people's witnesses are exhausted by former appearances and months of waiting before they arrive in the Criminal Court. Dangerous criminals give bail and succeed in prolonging the time before trial. Some undoubtedly commit new offenses to earn their lawyers' fees. The procedure in the Criminal Court is cumbersome, and beyond it lies the Court of Appeal and the Supreme Court. Of course, there are unfortunates, and friendless persons and some whose offenses are too sensational to permit of escape, and these make up the ten per cent of those held to the grand jury who are eventually convicted. If the Municipal Court were given felony jurisdiction the percentage of convictions would be nearer ninety than ten, and Chicago would speedily become a different city.

The Municipal Court has other limitations. The political price of passing the act originally was making the offices of chief clerk and chief bailiff political. The judges of the court ought to have the power to fill these positions and this would undoubtedly permit of running the court with a smaller staff than at present. . . .

There is another and most serious political limitation. Illinois has many elections and Cook County, with 144 elective offices, has one of the longest ballots in the country. The new court started with men selected for nomination by the assistance of the man who was to be responsible as chief executive for the success of the court. These nominees chanced to be elected. But every two years thereafter nine new judges were put on the bench. The direct primary, a very good thing in small cities and rural districts, is a cursed thing in a metropolis. Supposed to curb the political bosses and restore power to the people, it does exactly the opposite. Unfortunately for the court, under the direct primary, men with little legal experience are likely to be selected for a judgeship, thus lowering the average of the court.

A very serious problem is presented. The court pays its judges $3,000 a year less than the judges of the Cook County courts. Their term is but six years. Lucky is the candidate for judicial office who can fight through a primary and election with an expenditure not exceeding $4,000, to say nothing of months of time devoted to his canvass. The men at the bar who might bring the greatest support to the distinguished leadership in this court, who might by their reputations command confidence in the profession, are hardly to be induced to accept a nomination.

### BLIND CHANCE A FACTOR

The direct nomination principle has not killed the political boss but has added to the necessity for his existence as a useful middleman in politics. But it has sufficiently interfered with his former clear prerogative of selecting candidates so that now there is no responsibility in any quarter. It is impossible to restore such a function to an electorate of three-fourths of a million, and to wrench it from party leaders — who formerly exercised the power of nominating with considerable discretion — simply means that blind chance is now invoked as an important agency. Being a scholarly and esteemed lawyer does not recommend a man for the primary ballot so much as being a representative of some faction, political or racial, so that we have candidates running for the nomination because their names indicate Irish, German, Scandinavian, Polish or Jewish descent. Of course, in the final election the result is likely to turn on national politics. In the fall of 1914, one of the ablest of the Municipal Court judges was defeated for re-election by about 4,000 votes; but in the spring of 1915 he was elected by 139,000! But this was not all of his burden, for he had only been elected to fill a vacancy and was obliged to submit a third time in two years to the expense and worry of the primary and election.

Under such cataclysmic conditions the outlook for real juristic material is indeed foreboding, not only for this court, but for the Circuit and Superior Courts as well.

If means are discovered for introducing some measure of responsibility with respect to nominations, as by recommendations by the bar, or by some special body similar to the Municipal Voters' League, it will not be restoring political power to the mass of voters. It will be merely vesting, in a measure, and extra-legally, the nominating power in an imperfectly defined body only *slightly* responsible for the administration of justice, and possessed of no very high degree of expertness.

There has been some slight improvement in the political situation by a recent increase of judge's salaries from $6,000 to $9,000. (In the Circuit and Superior Courts salaries have been raised from $10,000 to $12,000.) The hook is more liberally baited than before and some improvement in the quality of candidates is believed to be observable. But the gamble from the standpoint of the voters, who cannot possibly know the respective merits of candidates, remains much the same.

In this same city there are always a number of eminent lawyers ready to accept appointment to the Federal District bench and receive a salary of $6,000.

Come to Chicago and you will hear pessimistic estimates of the Municipal Court. You will hear certain Municipal Court judges ridiculed and mocked. Of course there are enough able lawyers willing to become judges who would earn the large salaries now provided if any sane means existed for their selection. But to enter the lists with three or four score others for the primary race is something that only a few of them have the courage, or the foolhardiness, to do. Ordinarily real legal ability is unable to play the courtier to nearly a million voters. The terms of the game almost exclude the type of lawyer who is needed. There are always exceptions and some capable judges are gifted in keeping themselves before the public. But the efforts of some of the others are enough to make the angels weep.

Perhaps the most miraculous feature of the Municipal Court after all is that it is able to maintain a pretty good standard in spite of the weak material it has to operate through. The Circuit and Superior Courts have the advantage of higher salaries, but they too have individual judges who are no credit to the bench either as lawyers or as citizens. They have been saved in some measure from worse consequences through the developing practice of re-electing sitting judges as the only safe policy under the primary system. This has kept for them some pretty good judges who were originally the product of the convention system of nominating. Of course the principle of re-electing sitting judges is simply the choice of what is esteemed the lesser evil of the election dilemma.

But critics of the Municipal Court dare not compare existing conditions with what would be the conditions if the court possessed as little organization as the Circuit and Superior Courts. Nor dare they compare the present situation with that existing before the creation of the Municipal Court. They can go no farther than to say that some of the old justices were better than some of the present judges. The situation on the whole is inestimably better than it once was and inestimably better than it would be if the court lacked its closely knit organization and responsible direction.

### CONSUMES ITS OWN REFUSE

This Municipal Court has been aptly described as an "internal combustion" court. Its judges exercise unusual powers. They are made clearly responsible for results within the range of their jurisdiction. They are obliged to work together and to act together and to share in a considerable measure each other's shortcomings. The monthly and annual reports and the meetings all tend to center responsibility.

Their work is open to the public and the public always has it in its power to criticize effectually. Any litigant who has a grievance of the sort which cannot be remedied by appeal — and this is the kind by no means infrequent for which no remedy exists in the traditional judicial system — can complain to the head of the Municipal Court and get action. Such complaints are common. If found to be unjustified, as many of them are, the judge who is complained of is protected from unfair criticism. If not satisfactorily explained the complaints become the subject of discussion at judges' meetings held "for the consideration of such matters pertaining to the administration of justice in said Court as may be brought before them."

Where the statute says "At such meetings they shall receive and investigate, or cause to be investigated, all complaints presented to them pertaining to the said Court, and to the officers thereof, and shall take such steps as they may deem necessary or proper with respect thereto," it lays down a vital and practical procedure which is ever active to prevent or remedy abuses. In many a stormy session this "internal combustion," self-disciplining body determines a policy which it is willing to stand upon publicly.

The Court was comparatively new when a precedent was set in discipline. A judge assigned to a criminal branch instituted an original system of jurisprudence. He played the "cat and mouse game" with offenders. He would sometimes suspend sentence and order the defendant to keep out of mischief and to attend church or do something else calculated to effect his moral regeneration. If, after some months, he lapsed from the appearance of virtue and obedience, he was brought again before this judge and sentenced under the earlier conviction.

The judge had the faculty of winning popular applause for his policy. When criticized by his colleagues he became the newspaper sensation of the day. Soon the question was presented whether he was greater than the court. He thought that he was.

But meanwhile orderly steps for discipline were being taken. A committee of judges was appointed to review his work. They examined several hundreds of cases and found that he was violating the constitution. The committee recommended that he be removed from the trial of criminal cases.

When the Chief Justice acted upon the recommendation the judge became defiant. At that time the Court was temporarily housed in a building on Michigan avenue. Judge Olson pointed out of a window and said: "You see that tool shed there in Grant Park? Under the powers conferred upon me by statute I will create a special district one hundred feet square and you shall hold court in that tool shed!" The judge saw the point. He accepted assignment to a class of civil causes which left him no opportunity for mischief or newspaper notoriety.

### OTHER CITIES SEIZE BENEFITS

At the time the Municipal Court of Chicago was instituted the administration of justice was disgracefully bad in a number of other cities. The worst feature, in most instances, was the persistence of the political magistrate for a long time after he should have been abolished. Chicago's drastic action interested other cities and the first organized court had only made a good start when steps were taken to copy its general plan elsewhere. In Cleveland the justices were ousted after a hard struggle and the Municipal Court was established with organization and powers very similar to that of the pioneer court. But instead of unlimited contract jurisdiction the Cleveland court was restricted to $1,000. In Milwaukee the Civil Court was created with rule-making powers and a Chief Justice as business manager. In Pittsburgh the Allegheny County Court was established with similar organization.

The New York legislature created a commission headed by Mr. Justice Page which made a thorough study of the subject and rendered a voluminous report. The result appeared in the Municipal Courts of Buffalo and of New York City. The next in chronological order was the Municipal Court of Atlanta. A constitutional amendment was put through to permit of freeing this progressive city from inefficient magistrates and a very successful court was created with the necessary powers and structure.

The newest experiment is that made in Philadelphia, which now has a Municipal Court similar to those already mentioned. In all of these courts the judges are subject to assignment by a responsible chief executive or business manager, sometimes called President Judge and sometimes Chief Judge or Chief Justice. In all of them a special branch can be created by an executive order on short notice. All have comparatively wide rule-making powers. In all of them the associate judges participate in the management of the court and in all the requirement of meetings and reports is imposed. . . .

Every one of these new municipal courts has been successful in marking a great advance over previous conditions. All of them are able to point to very creditable performances. In no instance has there been any trouble arising from the peculiar characteristics of the system. In every one of them judicial procedure has ceased to be the acute problem which it still generally is in the traditional courts of the same localities.

## SUCCESS UNDER ADVERSE CONDITIONS

But they all fall short of the greatest possible efficiency by reason of the limitation upon jurisdiction. They are all in a sense inferior courts; they work side by side with courts of higher trial jurisdiction and higher judicial salaries. In respect to limits of jurisdiction the Chicago court is most fortunate but it has some limitations more embarrassing than the others. The independence of its chief bailiff and chief clerk, already referred to, is a serious burden. Its manner of selection is doubtless worst of all owing to the vast size of the electorate. In New York the Municipal Court judges are elected by districts, and while this plan has some faults, because some districts are controlled by spoilsmen, it probably yields a higher average than the Chicago plan.

There is reason to believe also that the extremely simple organization of the Municipal Court of Chicago could be improved upon. The administration of so many branches by a single executive calls for almost superhuman energy and vigilance. The court appears to need departmentalizing. If it had three departments, civil jury, civil non-jury and criminal, each with a presiding justice, the Chief Justice would have three capable adjutants who would relieve him of considerable work, who would feel a special responsibility for their respective departments and who would be able to devote more time to the small details of daily administration than a single head can possibly do. The court's head would also be afforded dependable supporters for administration plans when submitted to the entire body of judges.

There can be little doubt as to the ultimate working out of the basic principles now so well tried in this court. For several years the progressives of the Chicago bar and bench have been looking forward to the unification of all the courts of the city or county. It is coming to be realized very generally that it is an absurdity to have more than one court in any given locality. By departments and divisions within the departments it is possible to have an orderly and efficient organic court comprising all trial jurisdiction, of whatever sort, and there are many sorts.

It is only a question of time when the Municipal Court of Chicago will be merged into a unified metropolitan court. The great plan for giving Chicago efficient local government embodies the unified metropolitan court idea. The striking success of Illinois in the past year in organizing its executive department along efficiency lines gives promise for the ultimate success of the plans now urged for the city government and the city's courts. . . .

## *The Municipal Court of Cleveland**

## Reginald Heber Smith and Herbert B. Ehrmann

The present Municipal Court was launched in 1912 with fine civic enthusiasm, in the belief that Cleveland had finally attained a modern city court. It is not within the scope of this report to consider whether or not the high hopes of those days have been realized so far as its civil jurisdiction is concerned, but nine years of

* From: Criminal Justice in Cleveland: Reports of the Cleveland Foundation Survey of the Administration of Justice in Cleveland, Ohio 254-275 (R. Pound & F. Frankfurter eds. 1922). Reprinted by permission of the Cleveland Foundation.

experience do not justify any satisfaction with the handling of criminal causes. Lawyers and public officials appraise the criminal division of the Municipal Court when they persist in calling it, as they called its predecessor, a "police court."

## PHYSICAL CONDITIONS

Civil causes, however small, are heard in the imposing new City Hall on the lake front, in court-rooms of dignity and charm; criminal causes, outside of the few jury trials held in the City Hall, are tried in the old police court-rooms at the corner of West Sixth Street and Champlain Avenue, N.W. This small building is used for police headquarters, bureau of criminal identification, office of city prosecutor, probation office, clerk's office, city jail, as well as court-house, and is inadequate for all these purposes. Several years ago the city voted $1,250,000 for a new jail and criminal court. The commission began work on the lake front and then asked for additional bonds for the building. The voters of Cleveland refused the request, and the city has, therefore, gained nothing but an excavation. It is not necessary to build edifices like the City Hall or County Court-house, but a community which could erect those buildings should not accept the present stalemate with respect to an institution even more vital to its citizenship. A simple, modern criminal court-house and jail is an immediate necessity. One way of securing it speedily would be to compel the leading citizens of Cleveland to attend one of the daily sessions of the "police court." A former municipal judge has recommended that "the place should have a hose turned on it." After this is done, a carpenter, a painter, an electrician, and an expert on ventilation should be called. Their services would make the place tolerable until new quarters are available. Little can be done, however, to relieve the extreme congestion of the auxiliary departments. It is greatly to the credit of the clerks' and probation officer's staffs that they have been able to work with any degree of success amid such an environment.

## DECORUM

Accepting the court-rooms as they are, little can be said for the conduct of cases therein. From 150 to 300 cases a day are assigned to the two court-rooms, and the visitor is immediately struck with the lack of orderliness in handling the list. The lawyer who has only an occasional case, perhaps an ordinance violation, may wait with his clients and witnesses from nine o'clock until two, not knowing when his case will be reached. This apparent chaos is, of course, to the advantage of the regular "police court lawyer," who has a number of cases each morning.

The decorum in Room 1 is somewhat better than in Room 2, but the first room has higher ceilings and is better adapted for hearings. On a day during the period covered by the survey Judge Howells was sitting in Room 1 and Judge F. L. Stevens in Room 2. In neither room did the proceedings reveal the necessary dignity of a court. The rooms were crowded with lawyers, defendants, witnesses, police, hangers-on, and sightseers, many chewing gum or tobacco, even when addressing the court. In Room 2 an attorney was waving a cigar in the judge's face by way of emphasizing his argument. Crowded around the bench were lawyers, witnesses, and officials, almost screening from view the testifying witness. Others in the court-room were standing about talking and were occasionally asked by the judge to be quiet in order that he might hear the testimony — this, although the witness chair was placed directly against the judge's bench. The only person who seemed to be able to follow the testimony was a young woman reporter from one of the newspapers who took up a position behind the witness-chair.

In order to make themselves heard in this court-room, lawyers and others have to lean over the bench to address the judge.[1] This produces an impression of a confidential communication, which, although false, lends color to the belief that certain lawyers have "pull with the judge."

The question of decorum lies with the judges. A space should be cleared before the bench and on both sides, marked off with a railing, and no one should be allowed within the inclosure except attorneys in good standing. Everyone should be compelled to sit while the court is in session, and if every seat is taken, no additional persons should be admitted. Any talking during a hearing should be immediately suppressed. Several years ago Judge Selzer had the witness-chair moved away from the bench so that its occupant could not give the appearance of talking for the judge's ears only. On account of the poor acoustics and confusion in the court-

1. Formerly the end of the bench was open so that attorneys, politicians, etc., could go in back of the bench to whisper. When Judge Levine was in the Municipal Court he had long arms put on the ends of the bench, so that all conversation had to be held across it. These arms are now a permanent part of the equipment.

room the chair is again next to the bench. It should be moved away, and if order is maintained, a witness can make himself heard clearly enough.

### SEPARATE SESSIONS RECOMMENDED

Separate sessions dealing with different groups of cases should be established, as, for example, one for misdemeanors and ordinance violations criminal in nature; one for felony examinations; one for women offenders; and one for violations of ordinances only quasi-criminal in their nature. Possibly the last mentioned might be held in the City Hall in order that otherwise law-abiding citizens may await their turn and have their cases heard in an atmosphere less suggestive of crime and degradation. During the trial of a sexual offense the court-room should be cleared of everyone not concerned in the particular case. It may also be possible to hold different sessions in the morning than in the afternoon. . . .

### SHIFTING CASES FROM ONE JUDGE TO ANOTHER

One of the assistant clerks has discretion to decide whether the list in one room is congested so that cases should be transferred from one session to the other. Since a lawyer may get along better with a certain judge than another, or the disposition of a judge may be known to be strict or lax in certain classes of cases, this discretion often exposes the clerks in charge to great pressure to transfer cases from Room 2 to Room 1, and vice versa. It is impossible to ascertain how many cases are shifted upon solicitation, but the atmosphere is charged occasionally with rumors that certain cases are "thrown" before a particular judge. . . .

### SCANT ATTENTION TO INDIVIDUAL CASES

With the cases organized into different lists for different sessions, it may be possible to avoid some of the waste time now involved in waiting for cases to be reached. The principal advantage, however, would be to enable the judges to give more attention to individual cases. Unless a case is of public importance, has news value, or has interested influential people, it is apt to be disposed of before one can say the proverbial "Jack Robinson." This results practically in depriving of his day in court the poor or ignorant petty offender, and plays directly into the hands of the defendant with "wire-pulling" friends. Table 12* gives the number of dispositions in the criminal branch compared with the number in the civil branch of the Municipal Court, showing the amazing discrepancy between the time devoted to deciding questions involving, on the whole, petty property rights, compared with those involving individual liberty. . . .

In the hurly-burly of the day's work the judge cannot examine closely into statements and excuses of lawyers, police prosecutors, and police officers, and this affords opportunities either to escape the law by "putting it over" the judge or hastily to punish the innocent.

### BAD EFFECTS OF MANY CONTINUANCES

Most serious of all is the practice of continuing or passing cases. Rule 3, of the Municipal Court,[1] criminal branch, relating to continuances, has become atrophied. It is the object of every police court lawyer to get his case continued as many times as is necessary to disgust the witnesses for the State, — who have been wasting their time in a most disagreeable place, — and to cause the prosecuting police officer to lose interest in the case in the face of more pressing matters.

Table 13,† based upon a study of every tenth case in the criminal branch for a period of two years, gives the average time between arrest and disposition. It is to be noticed that it takes the least time to find a defendant guilty, a longer time to discharge him, and the longest time to "noll" or dismiss his case. . . .

Cases in which continuances are of most advantage to the defendant are those in which the witnesses are disinterested bystanders, as in automobile accident cases resulting in charges of manslaughter or driving while intoxicated. "Continuances kill accident cases," says a police officer posted in the court-room. "The witnesses won't come down and swelter, or else they move in the meantime. The regular lawyer's game is to tire out the witnesses."

Such continuances not only enable the guilty to escape, but play into the hands of unscrupulous lawyers who desire to use the criminal court to exact payment of a civil claim for damages, whether well founded or not. If the case were tried immediately

---

* Omitted.

1. "Motions for a second continuance must be in writing, setting forth the facts and reasons therefor (unless dispensed with by the court). . . ."

† Omitted.

upon its merits, such lawyers would be unable to use the machinery of criminal law as instruments for extortion.

## THE "MOTION IN MITIGATION"

The tendency cannot be effectively curbed, however, unless the "motion in mitigation" is eliminated from the practice of the court. This motion, apparently peculiar to the police court, makes a farce of judicial business, more than any other single factor. After a defendant has been adjudged or has pleaded guilty, the court imposes sentence. To the uninitiated the case is over, but this is not so. A "motion in mitigation" is then made, which is sometimes granted the same day, after trial, and sometimes ruled upon weeks and even months later, after many continuances.[2] Thus the court satisfies the complaining witness in open court, and has the opportunity later to placate the defendant's lawyer. Lawyers report instances where their clients were found guilty, although clearly innocent (in the belief of the defendant's lawyer), and upon protesting against the "outrage" of a conviction, were advised to make a "motion in mitigation." This they did, and the motion was later granted.

The "motion in mitigation" affords the setting for the performing judge, enabling him to do "stunts" which get into the front page of the newspapers, and then to undo the damage quietly at a later date. Mention has already been made of Judge Stevens' campaign against liquor law violators during January, 1921, and the notoriety which resulted from it. Considering the fines for this offense during 1919 and 1920 (taking every tenth case), 61 per cent. were less than $200 and 99 per cent., less than $400. About 26 per cent. of these sentences were suspended. The average original fine imposed by Judge Howells for January, 1921, was $299.12, and the average fine imposed by Judge Stevens (exclusive of five appealed cases) for the same period was $468.72. Excluding cases sentenced to the workhouse for failure to pay fines, Judge Stevens' average fine was $376.62. The average amount actually paid in Judge Howells' cases was $180.17 and in Judge Stevens' cases (ex-

2. On November 23, 1920, Louis Ettkin was fined $200 and costs for violating the liquor law, and the same day the fine was changed to $100 and costs. Notice of motion in mitigation was given, and the case continued eight times until February 21, 1921, when the execution docket shows the entry, "motion in mitigation overruled." The original file, however, shows that at some stage $75 was suspended, so that Ettkin paid $25 and costs on February 21. Meanwhile bond had been forfeited twice and the forfeitures set aside.

clusive of workhouse commitments), $176.61. The "motion in mitigation" is thus seen to be a leveler of fines in this particular group of cases.

It is said that the "motion in mitigation" serves the purpose of allowing a defendant time to pay his fine, and after the fine is paid, the motion is overruled as a matter of form. Undoubtedly the motion is used for this purpose and also to allow the court time to investigate the defendant to ascertain whether the fine imposed is a just one. The vice of the motion is that the court apparently disposes of the case, and at a later date, when no witnesses are present, makes a change. This vice is intensified by a system of record keeping, discussed later, which makes it difficult to find out what actually happened in a particular case. The court should make its investigation *before* sentence, not afterward, and the sentence once imposed, should stand. This could be accomplished by continuing a case for sentence to a certain day after the issue of guilt is determined, in case the court wishes further advice as to the condition of the defendant. This method would be more apt to impress the defendant with the seriousness of the court than the game of thimble played with motions in mitigation. . . .

### THE "POLICE COURT RING"

Owing to the fact that no record is kept of attorneys in cases before the criminal branch of the Municipal Court, no statistical data can be submitted of the attorneys practising in this court. It is common knowledge, however, that certain attorneys monopolize most of the business, and in a rough fashion divide the practice among themselves. Thus one group represents prostitutes, another pickpockets, another suspicious persons, etc. Any one connected with the court knows the names of these attorneys.

Theoretically, there is no objection to a limited group practising in a particular court. Indeed, under wholly different conditions a limited group of advocates would serve to facilitate the administration of justice by focusing responsibility for the ethical conduct of cases on a definite group. In the "police court" of Cleveland exactly the opposite has resulted. Men of ability as lawyers, or of fine sensibilities, shun this court, so that there is a tendency for men of less refinement to drift into the practice. The activities of these men are nowhere spread upon the record; they involve people who dare not or do not know how to complain. Some of these lawyers were formerly police prosecutors, in which capacity they made the acquaintance of habitual offenders and professional crooks; some are city councilmen with a voice as to the salaries of certain court attendants and a control over votes, which a weak judge cannot entirely overlook; others are connected in various ways with people of political importance.

In the trail of the police court lawyer come the "runner" and the "professional" bondsman, not even subject to the slight check of belonging to the legal profession. Some of the bondsmen are notorious characters, others operate gambling places in the guise of "political clubs." The presence of these men in the corridors of the court-rooms gives rise to rumors of "underground" connections with certain prosecutors, which, even if false, greatly damage respect for the courts in the minds of the unfortunate and their friends.

In some cases these lawyers and "runners" have been compelled to pay back to clients money which they extorted under the claim of "influence." ... Judge Howells became for a time so disgusted with lawyers defending prostitutes that he arbitrarily refused to permit any lawyer to represent a prostitute before him. He had just fined a prostitute $10 when the police prosecutor whispered to him to suspend the sentence. The lawyer also urged suspension on the grounds that his client could not pay the fine. On inquiry the judge learned that the girl had paid the lawyer a fee of $75. It is said that formerly a custom obtained of raiding prostitutes when the city needed money, and although this custom has been stopped if it ever existed, there is some opinion to the effect that they have been occasionally arrested when their lawyers needed money. Except in an unusual case, the prostitute fares as well or better in court *without any police court lawyer.* ...

It is no longer necessary for police court runners to look over the contents of the "bull pen" for old and new clients.[2] Some look over the police blotter, and, it is charged, sometimes secure the release of prisoners on personal bond (without surety) in order to make them retain the lawyers in question. For some of the

---

2. "One visit to the central court is usually sufficient for a stranger — one day's visit to the place being as complete as a month's sojourn within its desolate walls. ... Yet there are a few lawyers in this city who make a practice of habituating the place, picking up such crumbs as these, managing somehow to exist on them. They can be seen every day, a half-dozen or so of them, waiting in eager expectation for the herd to be driven in from the pen; and if one of them looks as though he might have $5 about him, he is besieged by anxious solicitors, ready and willing to take his case." — Kennedy and Day, Bench and Bar of Cleveland, 1889. The spirit of the place has not altered greatly in over thirty years.

lawyers this is unnecessary because their clientele and reputation are established. . . .

It cannot be said that the judges are individually responsible for the record shown by these cases. In the great majority of the felony charges the defendants were bound over for the grand jury. In the other cases the story is told in the number of cases "nolled" and "no-papered" by the police prosecutor. The former is done by motion before the court; but the absence of centralized judicial administration through a watchful and directing administrative head, the great confusion of the court, and lack of a courageous, highly skilled, and completely disinterested prosecutor, or failing that some "amicus curiae" upon whom the court can rely for disinterested advice, are largely responsible for the court's part in cases "nolled" and sentences suspended. The police court lawyer is most adept in taking advantage of those conditions which inevitably make for abuse of law and the defeat of its purposes.

## BAIL BONDS

Because of the reaction occasioned by the "crime wave" and obvious breakdown of the courts, the bail bond situation in the Municipal Court has received a wrong emphasis. In the matter of assuring the attendance of the defendant in court, bail is not a serious problem. During the nine years of the Municipal Court to January, 1921, there have been approximately 2,200 forfeitures of bail bonds which had not been set aside either by producing the defendant or through purging him of contempt. Compared with 170,137 cases disposed of during this period, this is a relatively small number. Of 562 cases of liquor law violation before the court in January, 1921, only six bond forfeitures were still outstanding on April 19, 1921.

The real evil in the situation is not the matter of easy bail, but the disreputable professional bondsmen who make a business of exploiting the misfortunes of the poor, and whose connection with "runners" and "shysters" tends to prostitute the administration of justice in the inferior courts. To eliminate the professional bondsman requires not a stiffening in the matter of bail, but a removal of the necessity of bail wherever possible, and a relaxation where such a removal cannot be accomplished.

A step forward was made in the provision for cash bail in G.C., Section 1579-20. The tendency of cash bail to drive out the professional bondsmen to some extent is apparent. Another excellent provision is Rule 10, of the criminal branch of the Municipal

Court, providing for the release of a defendant upon a personal bond without surety, where the offense charged is a misdemeanor punishable by fine only or a violation of a city ordinance. This rule should be extended to cover other minor infractions of the law which may be punishable by short terms of imprisonment. From what can be learned, however, the administration of this rule has not been wholly successful. The clerks in charge have established a practice of requiring someone to "vouch" for the defendant before releasing him on personal recognizance. This has apparently revived the opportunity for the professional bondsman and the runner, who are active on the trail of arrested persons in order to get them out on a bond without sureties. . . .

A most beneficial step would be the establishment in petty offenses of beginning process by means of a summons instead of a warrant. It is absurd that known residents of Cleveland should be arrested for violation of traffic and other ordinances and for misdemeanors not serious in their nature. This not only provides opportunity for the professional bondsman and imposes unnecessary hardship upon the accused, but also involves an enormous waste of time by members of the police force, the clerk's office, and the jail attendants. In such cases it should be sufficient, if the policeman handed the accused a summons to appear in court upon a certain day. The summons has replaced the warrant in many other cities. In Detroit it has an extensive use and has proved to be a most successful labor-saving device. In that city a warrant is not issued unless the accused fails to respond not only to the original summons, but to an alias summons issued on the day of his non-appearance in court. In Cleveland an informal summons has already been established in the police prosecutor's office. In certain classes of cases, notably neighborhood quarrels and the like, the police prosecutor summons the party into his office in an endeavor to straighten out the difficulty without the intervention of the court. In theory, at least, this informal procedure is a considerable step forward, but it is obviously vulnerable to abuse and does not go far enough. The summons should not be a discretionary matter with the prosecutor, but should be made the normal mode of beginning of judicial process in certain classes of cases.

There will always remain, however, a residue of cases in which a bail bond with sureties is necessary. The number of such cases may be considerably reduced by the prompt compulsory trial of cases and by the erection of a jail with decent and adequate facilities.

These steps should reduce to a minimum the number of cases

in which a professional bondsman may hope to make a profit. By eliminating the opportunity for such business, those who are now engaged in it will seek a living elsewhere. So far as it may be impossible to eliminate the professional bondsman, his business should be regulated like that of the "loan sharks" in many jurisdictions.

### THE CLERK'S OFFICE

In this section is discussed only that part of the clerk's office which handles the records for the criminal division. This office is in the Police Court Building, and is altogether inadequate for records, files, or human beings working therein.

The Chief Clerk, Peter J. Henry, devotes most of his time and attention to this office rather than the civil branch. He is well intentioned, quick in human sympathy, and his popularity with his employees does much for the esprit de corps of the staff. The first assistant, James Cantillon, is an earnest, hard-working man, who was unfailing in his patient cooperation with the survey. Like all those who have known only one way of doing things for a long time, both are inclined to be somewhat hostile to suggested innovations. To one acquainted with the lack of physical facilities and the antiquated method of record keeping which prevails, it is a constant source of wonder that the system works at all, however badly.

The method has apparently been inherited from the old Police Court, and is not in any sense adequate for the present needs.[2] A record system should accomplish three things: first, enable the clerks and the judges to prepare and follow each day's business; second, leave an accurate, easily accessible record of what has happened in each case to date; third, automatically build up statistics which the Chief Justice and the public ought to know as an authoritative basis for appraisal of the courts' work and the basis of its continuous improvement.

Under the system in use the clerks can make up a day's docket fairly well, but there is no adequate way of following the day's business and there is complete failure to secure the second and third objects. . . .

The only approach to a history of the case is found on the file

2. In 1912, when the Municipal Court succeeded the Police Court, the total number of cases was 7,788. In 1920 the number was 26,088, an increase of 235 per cent.

papers themselves, where the plea is entered, with the continuance date, the final disposition, and the name of the judge making final disposition. Nowhere is there a record of the attorney who appeared, or the prosecutor in charge, or the judge in any preliminary stage. As the notes are in pencil, it is not unusual to find an entry cancelled or erased and a new disposition written above the old.

To locate the case of John Stewart it would be necessary to perform the following acts, which might be profitably contrasted with the process of finding the history of a sales order in any modern mercantile business. A beginning is made by consulting an index book where the names are entered alphabetically according to the first letter only, so that one must go through a long list of names beginning with the letter "S". If the name is finally found (and the index has some omissions), the reference is to a folio page of "Execution Docket." If there are several cases of the same name, it is necessary to know the approximate date or else employ a process of elimination. With the folio page one finds an entry relating to John Stewart. It is then necessary to follow the entry forward through all the continuances, trying to pick the name out of many others on the dates given. Finally an entry is reached which disposes of the case, and unless a motion in mitigation is made, with further continuances, the case receives a number, usually in combination with other cases.[1] At the end of each day's cases in the "Docket" the names of both judges are stamped, so that it is not possible from this record to ascertain the judge who disposed of the case.

With the number of the case one goes to the files, which are kept numerically.[2] The penciled notations in the file will then tell the dates of the warrant and plea, continuances and disposition, and the name of the judge disposing of the case is stamped on the margin. If one wishes to know before whom John Stewart was originally arraigned, or before whom a new trial was held, or if one has so many cases that it is impractical to hunt through the original files, then one consults the "Judge's Docket," which is a journal of each day's work kept in two series of books, one for Room 1 and the other for Room 2. The names of judges regularly sitting in these rooms do not ordinarily appear in the "Judge's

1. If bail was forfeited, the case is not given a number and is not filed with the other cases. When the forfeiture is set aside, the clerk usually remembers to go back to the forfeiture entry and note the new folio page.

2. On account of lack of room, files more than three years old are stored in the loft under a thick layer of dust.

Docket," so that it is necessary to know the handwriting of each judge to be certain as to identity. This procedure for studying cases in this court is naturally complicated further by occasional errors inevitable in a system of this kind, and by some cases with unusual features, which do not fit comfortably into it.[3] Moreover, the information when obtained is incomplete. The only record books which are at all adequate are the bail forfeiture book, showing the history of such forfeitures, — exclusive of the question whether they have been collected, which is the work of the prosecuting attorney, — and a little volume giving the dates when cases are bound over for the grand jury, and the dates when transcripts are made out in such cases. . . .

We regard the question of record keeping as one of first importance. The activities of police court hangers-on are to a large extent dependent upon the assurance that they will leave no tracks behind them, and the watchful interest of the press and the public is baffled into inaction by obstacles which make vigilance too difficult. Moreover, the failure of the system to meet modern needs makes for informal action on the part of some of the judges, and informality in the court breeds suspicion and disrespect.

### RECOMMENDATIONS

. . . If the Municipal Court is retained as an institution,[1] the following recommendations are made at this time:

1. Adequate court-house and jail, pending the securing of which the present building should have all alterations necessary to make conditions tolerable, and to remove the sordid aspect of the surroundings.

2. A few physical devices for keeping the crowds in the court-room away from the judge's bench.

3. Increased formality in the court-room and strict maintenance of decorum.

4. A division of the cases into sessions according to their nature and the requirements of decency.

5. Orderly handling of the list, together with an established policy as to transferring cases from one session to another.

---

3. To obtain a reliable history of cases of liquor violation appearing in the "Execution Docket" for January, 1921, only, required many days, when a ledger system of keeping records would have yielded the information in as many hours.

1. Its amalgamation with the Common Pleas Court has already been recommended. . . .

6. A stricter rule as to continuances, enforced absolutely.

7. Abolition of the "motion in mitigation."

8. The registering, before being heard, of every attorney who appears for a defendant.

9. Extension of the judge's term on the criminal division from three months to six months or a year, discretion remaining in the Chief Justice to alter such terms.

10. Conferences before each swinging of terms between the judges going out, the judges going in, and the Chief Justice, to determine policies in handling cases so as to avoid injustice resulting from the whims or political exigencies of judges, and to promulgate, alter, and secure enforcement of court rules.

11. Close coöperation between the Chief Justice, the clerk, and the police in ridding the court-room and corridors of "runners" and their kind.

12. Formation of a permanent committee of the Bar Association to assist the Chief Justice in cleaning out and keeping out the "shysters" and their followers, this committee to designate as associate members certain probation officers and representatives of social agencies actually working in the police court.

13. Legislation giving the judges summary power to award damages to any defendant in the court, equal to twice the amount paid by such defendant to any runner or lawyer, upon solicitation or upon any representation as to influence with any judge or other public official.

14. A statute or ordinance fixing the charges of professional bondsmen, scaled according to the security given such bondsmen, and clothing the judges with summary power to award damages equal to twice the amount paid in violation of such statute or ordinance. The bondsman should be required to file his affidavit with the bond as to the fee and securities received.

15. Blanket permission to any defendant pro se, or any private attorney representing such defendant, to conduct prosecution for any alleged violations of any statutes or ordinances intended to regulate the business and practice of the court. It would help the situation greatly if the Legal Aid Society undertook to enforce penalties for these violations.

16. Extension and closer supervision of the rule allowing for personal recognizances.

17. The formal beginning of process in minor offenses by means of a court summons.

18. The establishment of an entirely new filing system in the criminal branch of the Municipal Court.

# The Decline of the Justice of the Peace*

## Kenneth E. Vanlandingham

### PRESENT STATUS OF THE JUSTICE OF THE PEACE

One of the most significant developments in American local government during comparatively recent years has been the attempt, frequently successful, to modify or abolish the traditional justice of the peace system. The justice of the peace conducts both misdemeanor and civil cases, but for most justices civil cases are few compared with misdemeanor cases; and since most abuses occur in connection with misdemeanor cases, this article in pointing up defects in the system emphasizes the justice's role in them. Abuses do exist, however, in civil cases conducted by the justice. Sometimes he solicits business by acting as a collection agency for small debts. In 1959, Illinois, which has since abolished his office, enacted legislation forbidding him to engage in this practice. Courts replacing the justice usually have a small claims division in which civil cases are heard.

Ordinarily, the traditional justice of the peace system may be defined as the administration of petty justice by lay officials paid by fees. As late as 1928, no state had eliminated the office of justice of the peace throughout its borders; yet, today, it does not exist in eight states, and is in the process of being terminated in three others. Although the justice is a constitutional officer in 35 states, statutory action in some of them has reduced his judicial status to the point where he has little or no significance. In most states where he exists, he is inactive as a judicial official. In 1955, only 167 of Kentucky's 678 justices were active, and probably not more than half of them tried many cases. In Kansas, it is reported that, of a net minimum possible number of 3320 justices authorized by the state constitution, only 233 were elected and qualified following the 1958 election. A 1956 Wisconsin survey found also that 51 per cent of the state's justices who had qualified to hold office did no judicial business.

* From: 12 Kan. L. Rev. 389-403 (1964). Reprinted by permission of the Kansas Law Review.

Throughout New England, the justice does not hold court save in Vermont where in the occasional absence of the municipal court judge he accepts pleas in traffic cases. In the United States, he tries misdemeanor cases in some 32 states, but his importance as a judicial officer varies considerably among them. He appears most active in the mountain and western states of Arizona, New Mexico, Wyoming, South Dakota, Idaho, Montana, Oregon, and Washington, and in the southern states of Mississippi and Alabama. Justices have no jurisdiction to try misdemeanor cases in Louisiana and Georgia, throughout much of Kansas, and in most metropolitan areas of Kentucky. Wisconsin by greatly reducing his jurisdiction has rendered him largely inactive; and his court has been superseded by municipal courts throughout much of Arkansas and in the metropolitan areas of Nebraska and Minnesota. It appears also with the passage of time his judicial role will further decline. In 1962, Montana voters rejected by a narrow margin an amendment which would have removed him from its constitution; and in 1964, a similar amendment will be submitted to Wyoming voters. In 1963, a bill to replace the justice with general sessions courts passed one house of the Oklahoma legislature but failed of final enactment. In the same year, the Kansas legislature directed the state legislative council to study state constitutional provisions respecting the justice, and to make recommendations concerning creation of new minor courts to replace his court. In several states, state bar associations and judicial councils, agencies most usually responsible for judicial reform, have made studies of the justice, and have recommended that he be replaced by courts better equipped to administer justice. For instance, the state bar of Utah has recommended county justice courts, the Florida Judicial Council has recommended magistrate courts, and the Iowa state bar has recommended district courts.

REASONS FOR THE DECLINE OF THE TRADITIONAL JUSTICE

## Outmoded in Present-Day Society

The traditional justice of the peace is now outmoded as a judicial officer primarily because conditions of life formerly prevailing have greatly changed. Brought from England to early colonial America, the justice was intended to be a keeper or conservator of the peace in his local community. He was to provide readily available and inexpensive justice. Hence, his selection from a small unit, usually the magisterial district or the township. Generally, he was a person of high moral character and possessed considerable wealth and dignity and thereby enjoyed the confidence and respect of his community. Since lawyers were few, the lay justice he administered was considered to suffice. Evidently, he served very well the judicial needs of his day. Indeed, during the early centuries of America, he was the principal guardian of county government. In today's urban and highly mobile society, there remains, however, little justification for his existence. Because of various abusive practices usually associated with his court, his name almost everywhere has become an object of ridicule and scorn. Occasionally, he is called an in-justice of the peace. In many places, he is paid by fees, collectible sometimes only when he convicts; and hence, J.P. has come to denote "justice for the plaintiff." One county attorney in Kentucky recently observed that "it is a judicial disgrace to retain the justice as judge."

Undoubtedly, the justice's political responsibility to a small area affects in no small measure his judicial behavior. In many states, his court has become almost solely a traffic court; and the quality of justice he administers seriously impedes uniform traffic-law enforcement, and thereby imperils traffic safety. Usually, he administers unequal justice without regard to law. The out-of-state motorist frequently receives no mercy before his court, but the local offender may have his case fixed in advance and receive only a slight or no penalty.

### Lack of Legal Training

The one universal criticism of the justice is his ignorance of proper judicial procedure. The justice, and particularly the fee-paid justice, is prone to regard his office as a business operation rather than a vehicle for the administration of justice. Most states do not require him to possess legal training. In 1963, Kentucky, the author discovered, had only one county, Jefferson (Louisville), with lawyers as justices, and Nevada had only one lawyer serving as justice in the entire state. A 1956 Wisconsin survey found only nine per cent of that state's 1059 justices were lawyers. On the other hand, New York State requires any justice, not a lawyer, whose term begins after 1962 to complete a course of training and education approved by a committee of the state judicial council. A few other states also try to improve the qualifications of justices. Washington State requires the justice in its most populous counties to be lawyers, and many of Maryland's trial justices designated by the governor are attorneys. Texas holds frequent conferences, institutes, and seminars to furnish the justices some legal training.

As a result of his judicial ignorance, the justice is probably taken advantage of occasionally by lawyers practicing before his court, but more often it seems his lack of judicial knowledge causes harm to defendants. Some ten years ago, a case involving title to an automobile was brought before an Alabama justice of the peace. The defendant in this instance was accompanied by an attorney. Since the value of the automobile caused the case to exceed the justice's jurisdiction, he could not conduct it. Later, however, he confessed to an interviewer, a graduate student of the author, that, if the defendant had not been accompanied by an attorney, he would have, despite his lack of jurisdiction, tried the case anyway.

## Absence of Judicial Decorum

In many states, the justice represents the most frequent contact of the public with the state court system; and it is commonly believed that the usually bad impression which his court creates lessens public esteem and respect for the entire state judicial process. One county attorney in a Kentucky mountain county recently observed that "the haphazard system of justice administered by justice courts cause more disrespect for law than any other factor." Lack of judicial decorum by the justice is also illustrated by a recent Montana study of the justice of the peace. One justice in that state, an auto mechanic, was reported to have tried a case without ever emerging from under an automobile which he was repairing, and another justice there, a farmer, was alleged to have tried a case while sitting on his tractor during a pause while plowing a field. These are, to be sure, extreme examples, but usually the physical surroundings of the justice's courtroom leave much to be desired.

## The Fee System

The worst feature of the justice of the peace system is compensation of the justice by fees. Wherever this method of compensation prevails, there is strong likelihood that official bias is present in the administration of justice. That this method of paying the justice is bad is evidenced by the fact that no state has adopted a new minor court system without abolishing it. Presently, only nine states pay the traditional justice by salary. He is paid fees throughout all or in some portions of twenty-four states (twenty-one after Colorado, Michigan, and North Carolina abolish his office). In some states, for instance, Indiana, Montana, Texas, Iowa, and Washington, he is a salaried officer in the larger units, and is paid fees only in the less populous places. In a few states, notably North Carolina, Alabama, Tennessee (six counties), and Utah, he receives payment only when he convicts and collects from the defendant. In still other states, including Delaware, Kansas, Nebraska, Mississippi, New Mexico, South Dakota, and Washington the defendant pays costs when he is convicted, and the county or state pays costs when he is acquitted.

Compensation of the justice by fees, whatever the arrangement for payment, usually raises serious questions concerning the fairness of trials he conducts. As stated in a recent dissenting opinion of a justice of the Washington Supreme Court, "The income of the fee justice of the peace depends directly upon the volume of cases filed. If no cases are filed, he receives nothing. Vice inheres in the system. That under this system there is a very real likelihood of bias is demonstrated by the published studies of the law's scholars both here and in England." In the celebrated case of Tumey v. Ohio,[26] decided in 1927 by the United States Supreme Court, the rule was laid down that a judge in a misdemeanor case is disqualified when his compensation for conducting it depends upon his verdict. Although, since the Tumey case several states have replaced the justice with new minor courts presided over by salaried judges, some other state supreme courts, distinguishing judicial circumstances prevailing in Ohio at the time of the Tumey case from those in their own states, still have not accepted the Tumey ruling. The Kentucky Court of Appeals accepted it only in 1956, twenty-nine years following its pronouncement, and North Carolina and Michigan as a result of constitutional change accepted it only in 1962 and 1963 respectively. Michigan will abolish it within five and North Carolina within ten years.

The United States Supreme Court has not passed directly on the constitutionality of that compensation system wherein the justice derives fees from defendants upon conviction and from the state or county upon acquittal. This method of payment is sometimes defended on the ground that it does not require a justice to convict in order to obtain compensation. Moreover, assuming good faith and honesty on the part of law-enforcement officers, a high percentage of persons brought before the justice's court are usually guilty; and, thus, most expenses for conducting trials fall on them.

26. 273 U.S. 510 (1927).

Officials in some states, notably Delaware, South Dakota, Washington and Kansas report that payment of the justice in this manner works satisfactorily; that is, it does not encourage unjust convictions. A recent survey by the Kansas Legislative Council of traffic court cases handled by Kansas justices during the fiscal years 1958 and 1959 revealed that, although the great bulk of persons accused pleaded guilty, justices were not unduly disposed to convict those who pleaded innocent. In 1958, out of 391 persons who pleaded innocent, 197 or slightly above 50 per cent were found guilty; and in 1959, out of 393 such persons, only 166 or slightly above 42 per cent were convicted. In Kansas, like in some other states, the county does not assume liability for court costs for acquittal in cases not instituted with the advice and instruction of the county attorney. Kansas and other states paying the justice in this manner require him to keep dockets of all cases, and they are subjected to periodic audits.

Despite the apparent success of these states, certain objections seem to inhere in this manner of compensation, particularly when justices are extremely active or when the county places a limit on its financial support to them. In Mississippi, the county pays the justice an annual lump sum of 200 dollars for conducting cases wherein he acquits, and reports from there indicate that he has a normal disposition to convict in order to obtain costs. New Mexico also found that the county's slowness to pay costs in the event of acquittal tended to make the justice more zealous in returning convictions. It has now amended its law to provide that, when the justice acquits or when he convicts and can not collect from a defendant, costs are to be paid by the state court administrator.

Evidently, this method of payment can sometimes result not only in denial of justice, but also it presents some difficulties in administration. Where many justices are very active, it seems that the county attorney can not give proper attention to cases they conduct. Nebraska law, for instance, provides that a justice can not collect costs from his county for conducting a trial when he acquits unless the county attorney approves the trial's institution. In a 1958 case, the Nebraska Supreme Court in the public interest granted a writ of prohibition to prevent trial by a justice, a woman, not observing the statutory requirement of obtaining the county attorney's approval. In 1954, this justice, the record showed, had tried 833 misdemeanor cases in which she rendered 798 convictions. She did not bill the county for costs, because she knew she had not obtained the county attorney's permission to conduct the trials. It thus appears that, in this instance, the rule of Tumey v. Ohio was violated. In these states and in other states using similar methods of compensation seemingly circumstances are not such as to encourage a justice to observe the suggestion of the United States Supreme Court in the Tumey case "to hold the balance nice, clear and true between the state and the defendant."

The states of Minnesota and Washington permit a defendant before a fee-paid justice as a matter of right to remove his case to a salaried judge, and almost all states allow a person convicted before a justice to appeal to a higher court. This, however, places an undue burden on the defendant in obtaining justice. The justice's court, because it is believed to administer justice on an inexpensive basis is sometimes referred to as the "poor man's court"; however, an appeal from it to a higher court is sometimes time consuming and expensive. The expense involved in an appeal by an out-of-state motorist is usually prohibitive. The Kentucky Court of Appeals and the West Virginia Supreme Court assert that a defendant is entitled to a fair trial in the first instance. It seems very difficult to refute this point of view. It is doubtful, moreover, whether some justice courts, as they now function, offer fair trials. Perhaps the only solution is establishment of new minor courts not possessing the characteristics of traditional justice courts.

### PRINCIPLES AND OBJECTIVES OF REFORM

Although the United States Supreme Court's decision in Tumey v. Ohio is not fully observed in some states, it has focused attention upon the poor quality of justice administered by justice and other minor courts; and its long-run effect has been to induce reform. On the local level, along with justice courts there usually exist other minor courts exercising conflicting and duplicating jurisdiction. These latter courts are scarcely better than justice courts; and judicial reform should include them as well as justice courts. One primary aim of judicial reform should be that of simplifying the local court structure. Judicial reform must also take into account the position occupied by the lower courts in the state court structure, for contrary to popular public fallacy, the administration of justice by lower courts is not a matter of only local concern. Recognizing this fact, the Model Judicial Article approved by the House of Delegates of the American Bar Association in 1962 vests the state judicial power in one court of justice consisting of four divisions, including one trial court of limited jurisdiction, known as the magistrate's court. Magistrates are appointed by the Chief Justice of the Supreme Court for three-year terms and may be retired for incapacity or removed for cause by the Supreme Court after appropriate hearing. To provide prompt disposition of cases, the Chief Justice of the Supreme Court is empowered to assign any magistrate or judge to any court in the state. During recent years, several states, including New York, New Jersey, Alaska, North Carolina, Hawaii, Illinois, and Idaho when adopting constitutional judicial change have attempted to establish unified and integrated court systems, or at least have tried to vest higher courts with supervisory authority over local courts. Such state supervision should increase public respect for lower courts.

The traditional justice of the peace system with its part-time lay justices paid by fees may have been satisfactory for frontier days when travel was slow, but it no longer suffices to serve the judicial needs of modern society. In most states now using this system, the vast majority of justices are inactive, but there remain still too many unqualified and low-paid justices. Even if a state could economically afford to pay them salaries and furnish them proper court-room facilities, they would remain unqualified as judicial officers. They exist in excessive numbers in some states because the state constitution authorizes their election from small units, such as the township or the magisterial district. The Kansas Constitution, for instance, authorizes election of two justices from each township. Reform of the justice of the peace — if the justice is to be at all retained — must therefore begin with a marked reduction in the number of justice courts. New Mexico, for instance, began its reform of the justice in this manner. In most instances, a single court consisting of several divisions, including a small claims division, and exercising county-wide jurisdiction is sufficient to handle all petty cases. Such a court, staffed with salaried judges who are lawyers, should be created to replace justice and all other minor courts.

Beginning with Virginia in 1934, several states have inaugurated reforms in their minor courts, including justice courts. These reforms have been adopted by different methods and have taken various forms. Some states, including Alaska, Colorado (by 1965), Michigan (by 1969), North Carolina (by 1971), Illinois, Missouri, New Jersey, and California have eliminated the justice either through adoption of new constitutions or through amendments to existing ones, while other states, including Virginia, Kansas, Tennessee, and Wisconsin have, by reducing his jurisdiction, rendered him mostly inactive and unimportant. Still other states, such as Ohio and North Dakota, have eliminated him by statutory enactments. The fact that the justice may be a constitutional officer does not necessarily preclude reform or elimination of his office. Constitutional change is necessary *only* when the existing constitution vests the justice with jurisdiction, or when it, like the Kentucky Constitution, prohibits creation of new courts. Unlike the justice in most other states, the New England justice, who is, for instance, a constitutional officer in all states except Maine and Rhode Island, has not for a long period of time had a very significant judicial role. Misdemeanor cases are now usually conducted in that region by district or equivalent courts presided over by salaried judges who are lawyers. The district court system in Rhode Island, for instance, dates from the 1880's. Even in those New England states where the justice of the peace has never constituted a "serious problem," it has been considered desirable to eliminate him entirely as a judicial officer. In 1957, New Hampshire, where the justice was in practice inactive, repealed all jurisdiction of justice courts to conduct cases; and in 1960, Connecticut replaced all minor courts with state-operated circuit courts. Since 1961, Maine has been in the process of replacing its trial justices, who were lawyers, with a district court system. Judges of the district court are appointed for a seven-year term by the governor with the advice and consent of the governor's council. . . .

## *Khadi Justice\**

## Max Weber

Finally, the administration of justice by honoratiores† presents two aspects depending on what legal interests there are involved,

---

\* Reprinted by permission of the publishers from pp. 230-1, 317, 350-2, and 354-6 of Max Weber on Law in Economy and Society, Max Rheinstein, ed., tr. by Edward Shils and Max Rheinstein. Cambridge, Mass.: Harvard University Press, Copyright, 1954, by the President and Fellows of Harvard College. A khadi is the judge of the Mohammedan *sharia* court. Khadi justice is used by Weber as a term of art to describe the administration of justice which is oriented not to fixed rules of a formally rational law, but to the ethical, religious, political or otherwise practical value judgments of a substantively rational law. It has become a synonym for substantive justice meted out by a judge with discretion to ignore formal rules in order to achieve the just result.

† Honoratiores (Latin, "those of higher honor"). Weber uses the term to designate those classes of persons who (1) in some way made the occupation

those of the honoratiores' own class or those of the class dominated by them. In England, for instance, all cases coming before the central courts were adjudicated in a strictly formalistic way. But the courts of justices of the peace, which dealt with the daily troubles and misdemeanors of the masses, were informal and representative of khadi-justice to an extent completely unknown on the Continent. Furthermore, the high cost of litigation and legal services amounted for those who could not afford to purchase them to a denial of justice, which was rather similar to that which existed, for other reasons, in the judicial system of the Roman Republic. This denial of justice was in close conformity with the interests of the propertied, especially the capitalistic, classes. But such a dual judicial policy of formal adjudication of disputes within the upper class, combined with arbitrariness or de facto denegation of justice for the economically weak, is not always possible. If it cannot be had, capitalistic interests will fare best under a rigorously formal system of adjudication, which applies in all cases and operates under the adversary system of procedure. In any case adjudication by honoratiores inclines to be essentially empirical, and its procedure is complicated and expensive. It may thus well stand in the way of the interests of the bourgeois classes and it may indeed be said that England achieved capitalistic supremacy among the nations not because but rather in spite of its judicial system. For these very reasons the bourgeois strata have generally tended to be intensely interested in a rational procedural system and therefore in a systematized and unambiguously formal and purposefully constructed substantive law which eliminates both obsolete traditions and arbitrariness and in which rights can have their source exclusively in general objective norms. . . .

Safety valves are also provided against legal formalism. As a matter of fact, in the sphere of private law, both common law and equity are "formalistic" to a considerable extent in their practical treatment. It would hardly be otherwise under a system of stare decisis and the traditionalist spirit of the legal profession. But the institution of the civil jury imposes on rationality limits which are not merely accepted as inevitable but are actually prized because of the binding force of precedent and the fear that a

---

with legal problems a kind of specialized expert knowledge, and (2) enjoy among their group such a prestige that they are able to impress some peculiar characteristics upon the legal system of their respective societies. The context makes it clear, however, that persons of this kind can be honoratiores even though they receive a more than nominal remuneration for their activities.

precedent might thus create "bad law" in a sphere which one wishes to keep open for a concrete balancing of interests. We must forego the analysis of the way in which this division of the two spheres of stare decisis and concrete balancing of interests is actually functioning in practice. It does in any case represent a softening of rationality in the administration of justice. Alongside all this we find the still quite patriarchal, summary and highly irrational jurisdiction of the justices of the peace. They deal with the petty causes of everyday life and, as can be readily seen in Mendelssohn's description, they represent a kind of khadi justice which is quite unknown in Germany. All in all, the Common Law thus presents a picture of an administration of justice which in the most fundamental formal features of both substantive law and procedure differs from the structure of continental law as much as is possible within a secular system of justice, that is, a system that is free from theocratic and patrimonial powers. Quite definitely, English law-finding is not, like that of the Continent, "application" of "legal propositions" logically derived from statutory texts. . . .

Above all, bureaucratization offers the optimal possibility for the realization of the principle of division of labor in administration according to purely technical considerations, allocating individual tasks to functionaries who are trained as specialists and who continuously add to their experience by constant practice. "Professional" execution in this case means primarily execution "without regard to person" in accordance with calculable rules. The consistent carrying through of bureaucratic authority produces a leveling of differences in social "honor" or status, and, consequently, unless the principle of freedom in the market is simultaneously restricted, the universal sway of economic "class position." The fact that this result of bureaucratic authority has not always appeared concurrently with bureaucratization is based on the diversity of the possible principles by which political communities have fulfilled their tasks. But for modern bureaucracy, the element of "calculability of its rules" has really been of decisive significance. The nature of modern civilization, especially its technical-economic substructure, requires this "calculability" of consequences. Fully developed bureaucracy operates in a special sense "sine ira ac studio." Its peculiar character and with it its appropriateness for capitalism is the more fully actualized the more bureaucracy "depersonalizes" itself, i.e., the more completely it succeeds in achieving that condition which is acclaimed as its peculiar virtue, viz., the exclusion of love, hatred, and every purely personal, especially irrational and incalculable feeling from the execution of official tasks. In the place of the old-type ruler who is moved by sympathy, favor, grace, and gratitude, modern culture requires for its sustaining external apparatus the emotionally detached, and hence rigorously "professional," expert; and the more complicated and the more specialized it is, the more it needs him. All these elements are provided by the bureaucratic structure. Bureaucracy provides the administration of justice with a foundation for the realization of a conceptually systematized rational body of law on the basis of "laws," as it was achieved for the first time to a high degree of technical perfection in the late Roman Empire. In the Middle Ages the reception of this law proceeded hand in hand with the bureaucratization of the administration of justice. Adjudication by rationally trained specialists had to take the place of the older type of adjudication on the basis of tradition or irrational presuppositions.

Rational adjudication on the basis of rigorously formal legal concepts is to be contrasted with a type of adjudication which is guided primarily by sacred traditions without finding therein a clear basis for the decision of concrete cases. It thus decides cases either as charismatic justice, i.e., by the concrete "revelations" of an oracle, a prophet's doom, or an ordeal; or as khadi justice non-formalistically and in accordance with concrete ethical or other practical value-judgments; or as empirical justice, formalistically, but not by subsumption of the case under rational concepts but by the use of "analogies" and the reference to and interpretation of "precedents." The last two cases are particularly interesting for us here. In khadi justice, there are no "rational" bases of "judgment" at all, and in the pure form of empirical justice we do not find such rational bases, at least in that sense in which we are using the term. The concrete value-judgment aspect of khadi justice can be intensified until it leads to a prophetic break with all tradition, while empirical justice can be sublimated and rationalized into a veritable technique. Since the non-bureaucratic forms of authority exhibit a peculiar juxtaposition of a sphere of rigorous subordination to tradition on the one hand and a sphere of free discretion and grace of the ruler on the other, combinations and marginal manifestations of both principles are frequent. In contemporary England, for instance, we still find a broad substratum of the legal system which is in substance khadi justice to an extent which cannot be easily visualized on the Continent. Our own jury system, in which the reasons of the verdict are not pronounced, frequently operates in practice in the same way. One should thus be careful not to assume that "democratic" principles of adjudication are identical with rational, i.e., formalistic, adjudication. The very opposite is the truth, as we have shown in another place. . . .

A typical instance of nonrational and yet "rationalistic" and highly traditional empirical justice is to be found in the responses of the rabbis of the Talmud. Purely untraditional khadi justice is represented in every prophetic dictum of the pattern: "It is written — but I say unto you." The more the religious character of the khadi or of a similarly situated judge is emphasized, the freer he is in his treatment of individual cases within the sphere which is not bound by sacred tradition. The fact that the Tunisian ecclesiastical court (*Chara*) could decide in real property matters in accordance with its "free discretion," as a European would say, remained a hindrance to the development of capitalism for a generation after the French occupation. . . .

Now it is perfectly clear that "objectivity" and "professionalism" are not necessarily identical with the supremacy of general abstract rules, not even in modern adjudication. The idea of a gapless system of law is, as we know, under heavy attack and there have been violent objections against the conception of the modern judge as a vending machine into which the pleadings are inserted together with the fee and which then disgorges the judgment together with its reasons mechanically derived from the Code. This attack has, perhaps, been motivated by the very reason that a certain approximation to that type of adjudication might actually result from the bureaucratization of the law. Even in the sphere of adjudication there are areas in which the bureaucratic judge is instructed by the legislators to arrive at his decision by "individualizing" the case in its peculiar circumstances. But in the domain of administration proper, i.e., of governmental activity other than legislation and adjudication, the claim of freedom and of the decisiveness of the circumstances of the individual situation has been put forth, in the face of which general norms should play but a negative role as mere limits on the positive, unregulatable, and creative activity of the official. The full implications of this proposition will not be discussed here. The important point is that this "freely" creative administration is not, as in prebureaucratic forms, a sphere of *free* discretion and grace, or of *personally* motivated favor and evaluation, but that it implies the supremacy of impersonal ends, their rational consideration, and their recognition as obligatory. Indeed, in the sphere of governmental administration in particular, that very proposition which does most to glorify the creative will of the official has put forward as his ultimate and highest guide the furtherance of the specifically modern and thoroughly impersonal idea of the *raison d'état*. To be sure, with this canonization of the abstractly impersonal there are fused the sure instincts of the bureaucracy for what is necessary to maintain their power in their own state, and, therewith, also as against other states. Finally, these power interests confer on the by no means unambiguous ideal of *raison d'état* a concretely applicable content and, in doubtful cases, the very decisive element. This point cannot be elaborated here. What is decisive for us is only that, in principle, behind every act of purely bureaucratic administration there stands a system of rationally discussable "grounds," i.e., either subsumption under norms or calculation of means and ends.

Here, too, the attitude of every democratic movement, i.e., in this instance, one aiming at the minimization of "authority" must necessarily be ambiguous. The demands for "legal equality" and of guaranties against arbitrariness require formal rational objectivity in administration in contrast to personal free choice on the basis of grace, as characterized the older type of patrimonial authority. The democratic ethos, where it pervades the masses in connection with a concrete question, based as it is on the postulate of substantive justice in concrete cases for concrete individuals, inevitably comes into conflict with the formalism and the rulebound, detached objectivity of bureaucratic administration. For this reason it must emotionally reject what is rationally demanded. The propertyless classes in particular are not served, in the way in which bourgeois are, by formal "legal equality" and "calculable" adjudication and administration. The propertyless demand that law and administration serve the equalization of economic and social opportunities vis-à-vis the propertied classes, and judges or administrators cannot perform this function unless they assume the substantively ethical and hence nonformalistic character of the khadi. The rational course of justice and administration is interfered with not only by every form of "popular justice," which is little concerned with rational norms and reasons, but also by every type of intensive influencing of the course of administration by "public opinion," that is, in a mass democracy, that communal activity which is born of irrational "feelings" and which is normally instigated or guided by party leaders or the press. As a matter of fact, these interferences can be as disturbing as, or, under circumstances, even more disturbing than, those of the star chamber practices of an "absolute" monarch.

## *The Lower Courts* *

## The President's Commission on Law Enforcement and Administration of Criminal Justice

In many big cities the congestion that produces both undue delay and unseemly haste is vividly exemplified in the lower courts — the courts that dispose of cases that are typically called "misdemeanors" or "petty offenses," and that process the first stages of felony cases. The importance of these courts in the prevention or deterrence of crime is incalculably great, for these are the courts that process the overwhelming majority of offenders. Although the offenses that are the business of these lower courts may be "petty" in respect to the amount of damage they do and the fear they inspire, their implication can be great. Hardened habitual criminals do not suddenly and unaccountably materialize. Most of them committed, and were brought to book for, small offenses before they began to commit big ones. This does not suggest, of course, that everyone who commits a small offense is likely to commit a big one.

The criminal justice system has a heavy responsibility, particularly in cities where so many men are so nearly anonymous and where the density of population and the aggravation of social problems produce so much crime of all kinds, to seek to distinguish between those offenders who are dangerous or potentially dangerous and those who are not. It has an additional responsibility to prevent minor offenders from developing into dangerous criminals. It is a responsibility that the system is in some ways badly equipped to fulfill.

The Commission has been shocked by what it has seen in some lower courts. It has seen cramped and noisy courtrooms, undignified and perfunctory procedures, and badly trained personnel. It has seen dedicated people who are frustrated by huge caseloads,

* From: The Challenge of Crime in a Free Society 128-130 (1967).

by the lack of opportunity to examine cases carefully, and by the impossibility of devising constructive solutions to the problems of offenders. It has seen assembly line justice.

A central problem of many lower courts is the gross disparity between the number of cases and the personnel and facilities available to deal with them. For example, until legislation last year increased the number of judges, the District of Columbia Court of General Sessions had four judges to process the preliminary stages of more than 1,500 felony cases, 7,500 serious misdemeanor cases, and 38,000 petty offenses and an equal number of traffic offenses per year. An inevitable consequence of volume that large is the almost total preoccupation in such a court with the movement of cases. The calendar is long, speed often is substituted for care, and casually arranged out-of-court compromise too often is substituted for adjudication. Inadequate attention tends to be given to the individual defendant, whether in protecting his rights, sifting the facts at trial, deciding the social risk he presents, or determining how to deal with him after conviction. The frequent result is futility and failure. As Dean Edward Barrett recently observed:

> Wherever the visitor looks at the system, he finds great numbers of defendants being processed by harassed and overworked officials. Police have more cases than they can investigate. Prosecutors walk into courtrooms to try simple cases as they take their initial looks at the files. Defense lawyers appear having had no more than time for hasty conversations with their clients. Judges face long calendars with the certain knowledge that their calendars tomorrow and the next day will be, if anything, longer, and so there is no choice but to dispose of the cases.
>
> Suddenly it becomes clear that for most defendants in the criminal process, there is scant regard for them as individuals. They are numbers on dockets, faceless ones to be processed and sent on their way. The gap between the theory and the reality is enormous.
>
> Very little such observation of the administration of criminal justice in operation is required to reach the conclusion that it suffers from basic ills.

There are judges, prosecutors, defense attorneys, and other officers in the lower courts who are as capable in every respect as their counterparts in the more prestigious courts. The lower courts do not attract such persons with regularity, however. Judging in the lower courts is often an arduous, frustrating, and poorly paid job that wears down the judge. It is no wonder that in most localities judges in courts of general jurisdiction are more prominent members of the community and better qualified than their lower court counterparts. In some cities lower court judges are not even required to be lawyers.

In a number of jurisdictions the State is represented in the lower court not by the district attorney but by a special prosecutor or by a police officer. Part-time attorneys are sometimes used as prosecutors to supplement police officers. In jurisdictions where assistant district attorneys work in the lower courts, they usually are younger and less experienced men than the staff of the felony court. The shift of a prosecutor from a lower court to a felony trial court is generally regarded as a promotion. Movement back to the lower courts by experienced men is rare. As a result there often is inadequate early screening of cases that are inappropriate for prosecution, lack of preparation for trials or negotiated pleas, and little prosecutor control over the proceedings. These inadequacies add to the judge's burdens and increase the likelihood of inadequate attention by the judge to the processes of adjudication and the goals of disposition.

In many lower courts defense counsel do not regularly appear, and counsel is either not provided to a defendant who has no funds, or, if counsel is appointed, he is not compensated. The Commission has seen, in the "bullpens" where lower court defendants often await trial, defense attorneys demanding from a potential client the loose change in his pockets or the watch on his wrist as a condition of representing him. Attorneys of this kind operate on a mass production basis, relying on pleas of guilty to dispose of their caseload. They tend to be unprepared and to make little effort to protect their clients' interests. For all these shortcomings, however, these attorneys do fill a need; defendants probably are better off with this counsel than they would be if they were wholly unrepresented.

In most jurisdictions there is no probation service in the lower courts. Presentence investigations are rare, although the lower courts can and do impose sentences as long as several years' imprisonment. While jail sentences of 1, 2, or 3 months are very common, probation appears to be used less frequently than it is for presumably more serious offenses in the same jurisdictions.

Every day in large cities hundreds of persons, arrested for being drunk or disorderly, for vagrancy or petty gambling, for minor assaults or prostitution, are brought before the petty offense part of the lower courts. In some cities these defendants are stood in single file and paraded before the judge. In others, 40 or 50 or more people are brought before the bench as a group. Almost all plead guilty, and sentence is imposed in such terms as "30 days or $30." A large part of the jail population in many cities is made up of persons jailed in default of the payment of a fine. The offender subjected to this process emerges from it punished but unchanged. He returns to the streets, and it is likely that soon the cycle will be repeated in all its futility.

Those few cases in which the defendant demands a trial may be inordinately delayed by the unavailability of judges to try cases. One result of this can be that witnesses, who are grossly under-compensated at rates as low as 75 cents a day, become weary and disappear. The courthouse in which the lower court sits is likely to be old, dirty, and extremely overcrowded. Witnesses, policemen, lawyers, and defendants mill around halls and courtrooms. Office facilities for clerks and prosecutors are commonly inadequate.

Study commissions have pointed out the scandal of the lower criminal courts for over a century. More than 30 years ago the Wickersham Commission concluded that the best solution to the problem would be the abolition of these courts. The Commission agrees. While the grading of offenses as felonies, misdemeanors, and petty offenses is an appropriate way of setting punishments, is dictated by history and constitutional provisions, and is necessary for such procedural purposes as grand jury indictment and jury trial, the Commission doubts that separate judicial systems are needed to maintain these distinctions. A system that treats defendants who are charged with minor offenses with less dignity and consideration than it treats those who are charged with serious crimes is hard to justify. The unification of these courts and services may provide a sound way to bring about long overdue improvement in the standards of the lower courts. Existing differences in punishment, right to grand jury indictment and jury trial, and the like should be retained unchanged, but all criminal cases should be tried by judges of equal status under generally comparable procedures.

*The Commission recommends*:

Felony and misdemeanor courts and their ancillary agencies — prosecutors, defenders, and probation services — should be unified.

As an immediate step to meet the needs of the lower courts, the judicial manpower of these courts should be increased and their physical facilities should be improved so that these courts will be able to cope with the volume of cases coming before them in a dignified and deliberate way.

Prosecutors, probation officers, and defense counsel should be provided in courts where these officers are not found, or their numbers are insufficient.

# PART II.
# THE SOCIAL ORGANIZATION
# OF THE LOWER
# CRIMINAL COURTS

Courts are first of all groups of people organized in particular ways to achieve certain ends. Like any organization, a court creates distinctive patterns of recruitment and socialization of its personnel. It develops norms related to its goals and punishes deviations from those norms. Often organizational survival counts more than success in achieving formal goals.

The sociological perspective is essential to understanding lower court performance, for it reveals the social and organizational pressures that animate the court's actions and push it away from formal due process considerations. Every essay in this section shows some aspect of that phenomenon. Maureen Mileski's study of courtroom encounters in a Connecticut city shows how the bureaucratization of adjudication determines the quality and length of exchanges between judge, court personnel, and defendants; affects case disposition; and influences on-the-bench behavior of the judge.

Her emphasis on work-production norms is echoed in the selections by Jerome Skolnick and Alexander Smith–Abraham Blumberg. Skolnick analyzes control devices utilized by court actors to keep caseloads moving, and shows how these devices deviate from the ostensible adversary nature of the criminal trial. His account of prosecutor–public defender relations challenges the easy assumption that the defender and prosecutor come to share the same work norms and thus sacrifice defendants. The Smith–Blumberg piece approaches the question of efficiency from the perspective of judicial background, recruitment patterns, and role perception. Their study shows the importance of background and career paths to an understanding of role performance, and by implication suggests that reform must deal with those factors.

George Cole's research on the Seattle prosecutor's office is included because it neatly summarizes the series of exchanges that occur in the court environment, only a few of them directly in the courtroom. Again, the theme is the irrelevancy of formal rules to the actual purposes and decisions of court actors. While the rules set limits or serve as benchmarks, a variety of adaptations — in Cole's view, based on a market system — occurs to achieve or frustrate the system's formal goals.

Herbert Packer's famous essay "Two Models of the Criminal Process" posits an ideological or value genesis for the cult of courtroom efficiency. Taking the justice system's formal goal of crime control as key, it is this concern which produces the administrative processing of cases and the blithe disregard of defendant rights. He recognizes and describes the countervailing due process values, and shows how their conflict with crime control values leads to the central tension in contemporary criminal procedure.

For reform-minded readers, this section is bound to be ambiguous. One possible lesson to be drawn is that reform is possible if the proper intervention occurs. In this case, a rule alone may not be the answer. Rather, one must work directly on the organizational and social setting that influences rule application, injecting new or countervailing incentives to overcome bureaucratic reluctance. Yet even assuming that social engineering is feasible, changes here will not totally eliminate the influence of role and setting. The sociological perspective, while helpful in focusing efforts, only reveals in depth the complexity of the legal enterprise in a lower court setting.

# Courtroom Encounters: An Observation of a Lower Criminal Court*

## Maureen Mileski

This is a study of the criminal trial court as a formal organization. The processing of defendants through court can be seen simply as a task for the courtroom personnel — the cases presenting not only occasions for moral outrage or legal acumen but also presenting problems for the legal bureaucracy as such. From one perspective, defendants are as deviant if they do not conform to the routines of the court as they are if they do not conform to the rules of the state. Like the wider society it supports, the court has a social integrity which can be disrupted. The court processes persons alleged to have been deviant in the larger society. The defendants are then subject to the moral exigencies of the court itself. The discussion treats the court as a business as well as a prime sanctioning center for the outer society. But the control of crime is more than a business; it is an industry. The immediate suppliers of the court — the police — act upon and in turn are conditioned by courtroom configurations. Several features of this police-court interrelation also form a part of this study.

This paper divides into two basic parts. In the first, compositional features of courtroom encounters are discussed. This section concerns the types of offenses lower courts process, the rapidity of courtroom encounters, the processing of defendants in groups, the apprising of rights, the presence of legal counsel in encounters, and the pleas of defendants. The second section investigates the dispositions of cases. The overall task of this paper is to detail some prominent patterns in the lower court's day-to-day operations.

### Method and Setting

Attention directed toward criminal courts displays an emphasis on matters apart from courtroom encounters themselves. Thus, for instance, it is widely believed that in order to understand many courtroom outcomes it is essential to understand the place of the negotiated plea. Nevertheless, the courtroom encounter can be approached in its own right. Although some stages may be set and

* From: 5 Law & Socy. Rev. 473-533 (1971). Reprinted by permission of The Law and Society Association and the author.

some denouements may be neatly written in prosecutors' offices, the ways in which these sketchy plots are acted out in the courtroom remain largely unexplained. . . .

Data for this study were gathered over a three-month period by direct observation on Mondays and Fridays in a criminal court of the first instance of a middle-sized eastern city. Two judges presided over the court. The prosecutor and five of his assistants rotated during the observation period. A total of 417 cases comprise the final sample. These are arraignments and final dispositions. Many more than 417 defendants passed before the judge during the 11 full days of observation, but encounters that fall within the broad category of continuances (under half of the cases observed) are not analyzed. . . .

The city where observation was done, like many, has two levels of trial courts, the court of the first instance and a higher-order court. The court of the first instance has final jurisdiction over all municipal ordinances and all offenses punishable by a fine of no more than $1,000, one year's incarceration, or both. The lower court may also take final jurisdiction over crimes punishable by a $1,000 fine, five years' incarceration, or both, if the prosecutor deems that a penalty of no more than $1,000 and/or one year is necessary in a given case. The court thus has final jurisdiction over misdemeanor cases and minor felony cases. If a defendant has been charged with a crime carrying more than a five-year maximum or if the prosecutor decides that a suspect might receive more than one year's incarceration, the suspect must be bound over to the higher court for final disposition. However, the lower court does handle serious cases at preliminary stages — arraignments and probable cause hearings — before they reach the higher court.

The city parcels the business of the lower court system into two physically separate rooms. The proportional volume of serious cases is smaller in one of these rooms. This courtroom disposes of most of the city's minor cases — matters of public drunkenness, breach of the peace, and so on. This was the room selected for observation. The observational method suits it both because the volume of cases is high and because plea bargaining has little or no relevance in the handling of lesser offenses. Two attorneys and a language interpreter employed by the court reported that plea bargaining is simply nonexistent in routine cases of intoxication and disturbances of the peace. Since most defendants are charged with minor offenses of this sort, a field observer frequently witnesses the total post-police processing. . . .

## A Sketch of the Lower Court

The great bulk of criminal cases start and end at the lower court level. Our understanding of courts does not reflect court volume since accumulated knowledge disproportionately pertains to the higher courts. Offenses break down into the legal categories of felony and misdemeanor. Within each of these categories, offenses divide into three finer classes for purposes of analysis: offenses against the public order, against property, and against the person. Examples of misdemeanors against the public are intoxication, breach of the peace, and underage possession of alcohol. Typical misdemeanors against property are petty larceny and minor but malicious destruction of property. Simple assault and resisting arrest are misdemeanors against the person. In the felony category, a narcotics offense is an offense against the public, breaking and entering an offense against property, and robbery or aggravated assault an offense against the person.

Charges in this lower courtroom overwhelmingly (81%) accumulate in the misdemeanor categories:

| Offense Charged | Percentage | |
|---|---|---|
| Misdemeanor against Public | 66 | |
| Misdemeanor against Property | 6 | |
| Misdemeanor against Person | 7 | 81 |
| Misdemeanor, Unspecified | 2 | |
| Felony against Public | 2 | |
| Felony against Property | 4 | |
| Felony against Person | 5 | 14 |
| Felony, Unspecified | 3 | |
| Other Offenses, e.g., Traffic or Unspecified | 6 | |
| Total Percentage | 101 | |
| Total Number | 417 | |

From the standpoint of legal seriousness, the operations of this court are of minor importance. The court rises in importance, on the other hand, from the standpoint of volume.

Court sessions are called to order in the morning at approximately ten and run until one or two o'clock in the afternoon, depending on the caseload. On many days there is one recess of roughly a quarter-hour. Unlike some more informal courts, the prosecutor is always present in the courtroom along with the judge. Other personnel routinely present include a clerk, a reporter, a bailiff, a policeman, a probation officer, a secretary for the public defender, and a family court and juvenile court liaison man. In addition a female probation officer and a female police officer are present when a female defendant is scheduled for appearance, as is a Spanish interpreter when a defendant who would need his services is scheduled for appearance. Bail bondsmen and attorneys frequently work their way up to the front of the courtroom to pass the time with others while awaiting cases. Thus at least twelve officials or their assistants may literally surround a defendant as he goes before the bench. All but the most obvious three or four of them may have functions ambiguous to the average defendant.

The public area of the courtroom seats about sixty persons; it is more than full at the opening of the day's session. Adjacent to the courtroom is the "lock-up," as it almost always is called by the participants. Its door bears three locks and a sign reading "No admittance. Attorneys only. No food, candy or cigarettes." The door's trappings symbolize a great deal, but those behind it are not treated like outsiders to the extent that it might first appear. It is not uncommon for a wife, sister, or friend to have a hamburger passed to a prisoner through the guard at the door. Relations between the policeman-guard and the prisoners are rather cordial. Slightly over one-half of the defendants enter the courtroom through the lock-up, the others approaching the bench from the public seating area. The remaining public, of course, is witness to the courtroom encounters.

### COMPOSITIONAL FEATURES OF ENCOUNTERS

*Mass Justice*

Many American courts have a workload problem. Court systems have what their participants, spokesmen, and critics consider too much to do. Heavy workloads do not pressure all bureaucracies; in fact, some bureaucracies are faced with the opposite problem, that of having work insufficient even to justify their maintenance.... Such is not the plight of the court.

One obvious way the court can allay pressures from heavy case-loads is to handle the accused rapidly. In this court 72% of the cases are handled in one minute or less.... It is noteworthy that routine police encounters with citizens in the field last on the average far longer than court encounters. The climax of many an alleged offender's contact with the criminal justice machinery is dwarfed by his police contact on the one side and the time he is incarcerated on the other. The sluggishness that often characterizes governmental organizations does not carry over to the courts. The notion of delay in the courts refers to the number of weeks, months, or even years necessary to bring various cases to a close. Furthermore, it is usually used with reference to courts that handle civil or private law cases. Once a criminal case surfaces in the courtroom, the encounter often has an extremely short life. In this city, it usually takes one or two hours to obtain auto license plates, but it takes a matter of minutes to dispose of accused auto thieves in court. Typically, justice in court is quick.

An additional device to allay caseload pressures is to process two or more defendants simultaneously. Not infrequently in a lower court the prosecutor strings defendants out in a line before the judge and processes them partly as a group. When the prosecutor mass-processes defendants, he calls out a list of names from his records. Those called step up to the bench from the public area of the courtroom or from the lock-up adjacent to the courtroom. This allows the judge to accomplish part of his task more efficiently than he could if defendants were sent to him one by one. For example, if it takes a given judge one-half minute to apprise one defendant of rights, four-and-one-half minutes would be saved if he were to apprise an assembly of ten defendants. If this is done twice or thrice per session, an extra full trial can be worked into a day of the same length. After the judge handles the defendants as a group — this usually consists only of rights apprisings — he considers each case separately. Yet the line in front of the bench remains.

Only half (51%) the defendants see the judge individually. Thus only half the defendants in the lower court engage in what fits the popular and even academic image of the judge-defendant confrontation. The remainder of the defendants see the judge only in conjunction with others. Sometimes the group is large; 15% of the total defendants face the judge with ten or more others alongside them. Most criminal defendants presumably commit their offenses alone and go on to receive their sanctions in the midst of strangers. Decisions as to dispositions may historically have become more individualized, but numerous encounters in contemporary lower courts are not.

The shape of courtroom encounters surely conditions the legal outputs thereof. One characteristic of many preliterate control systems is that they are relatively informal and nonbureaucratic, whereas contemporary societies maintain bureaucratized systems of control. A corresponding distinction is found in the study of legal control within the two types of societies. Anthropologists almost consistently use the conflict resolution model; sociologists more frequently use the rule enforcement model in investigations of control systems. This analytical difference is no doubt to some extent a result of empirical differences. The extent to which the outputs of the two polar types of control systems differ — whether primarily rule enforcement or conflict resolution — may in part be due to differences in the structures into which legal problems are poured and from which solutions emerge. Conflict resolution or order maintenance literally takes time and requires attention to individuals on a case-by-case basis. Highly bureaucratized courts with caseload problems lend themselves more easily to rule enforcement than to conflict resolution. Legal decision-making with a goal of conflict resolution almost necessarily entails particularism; with a rule enforcement end, it entails a greater degree of universalism. Thus where encounters are rapid and where defendants are processed in groups, more universalistic rule enforcement would be expected. A consequence may be that the recent trend toward individualized treatment of offenders is stunted by the bureaucratization of the processing organizations. Similarly, when citizens complain about the movement away from the foot patrolman on the neighborhood beat, a movement to a highly bureaucratic police force, the real touchstone of their complaints may be an increase in rule enforcement over conflict resolution. The form of any social activity affects its substance and, consequently, its impact.

### Apprising of Rights

... Apprisings of rights in the lower court generally are like so many clerical details performed and reperformed. From one perspective they simply are part of the job of the judge. There are a number of forms by which the judge informs suspects of their rights, if he informs them at all. He may inform a group in the audience, a smaller group assembled before the bench, a group before the bench with an individual follow-up, or an individual before the bench. These four forms are elaborated below.

First, to launch the day's session of the lower court, the prosecutor requests the judge to apprise all defendants seated in the public area of the courtroom of their rights. Such announcements roughly run as follows:

> All of you who have charges against you, listen. You have a right to remain silent if you wish. If you speak, what you say can and

probably will be held against you. You have a right to an attorney and to have time to get one. You also may have a right, in some cases — if you have no money — to apply for a court-appointed attorney, and under certain conditions one will be assigned to you. And if your offense is bondable you have a right to bond.

If a defendant happens to be talking to his neighbor, if he is for some other reason inattentive, or if he arrives in court later than the scheduled ten o'clock, he is not formally informed of his rights unless the judge later informs him in a face-to-face encounter, as he sometimes does. Inattention or tardiness, then, may carry with it whatever are the consequences of ignorance of constitutional rights. Moreover, there is the matter of the defendant's inability to comprehend various rights — something that is inaccessible to an observer. The degree of comprehension may vary according to the form of apprising.

A second form is the apprising of rights to a group of defendants who are lined immediately before the judge's bench. The groups range from a pair to a dozen. While the content of the apprising usually is the same as that for the courtroom audience, the form is doubtlessly more effective for a more thorough transmission of rights. Because these defendants are arrayed before the judge, they undoubtedly are more aware that he is speaking to them than are those when apprising takes the first form. Those before the judge are on stage, the center of attention; the members of the audience obviously are not. In short, the spatial arrangement of rights apprisings may have a bearing on the extent to which defendants are informed. What is more, defendants immediately before the judge have a license to speak, a license that audience members lack; a defendant on stage before the judge may say that he does not understand, may ask for elaboration, and so on. For at least these two reasons, defendants warned of their rights in groups before the judge probably understand these rights better than those warned through general announcements to the larger courtroom.

In the third setting, the judge apprises some defendants in a group before him, after which there is an individual follow-up. Here the judge warns the defendants as a group and then asks each if he "heard" and/or "understood" his rights. This embellishment surely adds to the probability that the defendant is made aware of his legal options. In the fourth form, the judge informs defendants of their rights individually, in a one-to-one interchange.

It may be that only those defendants who fall into the fourth category are apprised of their rights in a way that an appellate judge would deem adequate. In any case, it is not clear that any of the first three forms of apprising is deviant from a sociological standpoint. That is, even though these apprisings may not stand high against the spirit of procedural law, judges are rarely if ever sanctioned through reversal or through orders for retrial for using these forms. Perhaps judges risk sanctioning only when they do not warn defendants of rights at all.

There is reason to believe that the four forms in their respective order — group in audience, group before bench, group before bench with individual follow-up, and individual before bench — are progressively more effective ways to transmit rights to defendants. In *reverse* order they contribute progressively to an efficient judicial bureaucracy. It is work and time for the court to apprise individual defendants of their rights. If there are to be apprisings at all, it is most expedient, from a bureaucratic point of view, to apprise as many defendants as quickly as possible in a situation where questions are not likely to be asked. Moreover, if a defendant understands and asserts his rights, it can be to the detriment of court efficiency. For instance, if a defendant decides that he will seek an attorney, his case must be delayed. Where bail is involved, another officer of the court — the bailiff — is interjected into the process. If the defendant successfully obtains an attorney, it often happens that the attorney will request a delay. The prosecutor again has to reschedule the case for a later date. Complicating the situation is the fact that the involvement of an attorney increases the likelihood of a "not guilty plea." While the not guilty plea is a basic right on which the system rests, from another standpoint it gives rise to the expenditure of a relative wealth of court resources. Not guilty pleas in turn introduce the potential of acquittals — blemishes on the prosecutor's record. On the other hand, when the judge apprises groups of defendants simultaneously, the defendants are less likely to be fully informed, and the court bureaucracy is less likely to be heavily overloaded. Thus, a norm of justice and a need of the formal organization run counter to one another.

In a quarter (26%) of the lower court cases, the judge does not apprise the defendant of his constitutional rights at all (see Table 1). Moreover, defendants are warned in groups of one type or another in half (52%) of the cases. The judge warns a defendant of his rights as he stands alone before the bench in only 22% of the cases. Thus, of those who are apprised, most are apprised in groups. Not infrequently, the judge transforms his manner after the apprisings. That is, after a routine apprising he then pauses and directs his full attention to the defendant for the first time. It is as

## TABLE 1
### Percentage of Courtroom Encounters According to the Offense Charged, by Apprising of Rights

| | Offense Charged | | | |
| | Misdemeanor | | | |
| Apprising of Rights[a] | Minor[b] | Serious[c] | Felony | All Cases |
|---|---|---|---|---|
| None | 35 | 06 | — | 26 |
| In courtroom audience | 22 | 11 | 05 | 18 |
| Groups before bench | 20 | 23 | 38 | 23 |
| Groups before bench with individual follow-up | 06 | 28 | 25 | 11 |
| Individual before bench | 18 | 31 | 32 | 22 |
| Total | 101 | 99 | 100 | 100 |
| (n) | (220) | (35) | (37) | (292) |

(Brace grouping "In courtroom audience" through "Groups before bench with individual follow-up" = 52)

a. Highest possible code category was used; e.g., if defendant was present for general announcement but also was apprised alone, apprising was coded in the latter category. Defendants who had previous encounters were not tabulated if they were not apprised since they may have been apprised on a previous occasion.

b. Misdemeanors against public and against property.

c. Misdemeanors against persons.

if the case only then begins. The judge or prosecutor inquires: "Well, do you want to wait or do you want to get this over with now?" "Getting it over with" perhaps sounds desirable to many defendants, and they agree, proceeding without attorneys.

The seriousness of the offense charged has an effect on whether and how defendants are apprised. When the offense is serious, the judge more often apprises defendants of their rights; when the case is more serious, the chances are greater that the judge apprises defendants individually. In minor misdemeanor cases, the judge fails to apprise 35% of the time. There is a failure to apprise in only 6% of the serious misdemeanor cases and in none of the felony cases where an apprising was clearly required. Individual apprisings are likewise more common in felony and serious misdemeanor than in minor misdemeanor cases (32, 31, and 18%, respectively).

If individual warnings were required for each case, the judge would have to alter his work style in two-thirds of the cases. One consequence of this sort of constraint might be an even further routinization of apprisings. If the judge were to repeat the catalog of rights roughly forty or fifty times each day, it is likely that the intonation and clarity with which the words are spoken would decline. The present permissible variability in forms of apprisings allows for certain more emphatic apprisings from time to time. These more emphatic apprisings attach to the more serious cases, where full recognition of rights may be more crucial for the defendant's future.

There is more control operating over the judge and prosecutor when they handle serious cases than when they handle minor cases. Because appeals — even though very improbable — are more likely in serious cases, there is a higher probability in these cases that any judicial errors will be caught. It is therefore not surprising that the court processes these cases with relative care. In serious cases, a good deal of each defendant's liberty is at stake; the judge often takes precautions against unduly intruding on that liberty by giving individual rights apprisings. However, these precautions guard against an upset of the lower court's integrity at the same time as they guard against the violation of individual rights. The court does not so often guard against a violation of individual rights when the likelihood of appeal is extremely low. Lower court judges, like policemen . . . , may relate to procedural rules largely as obstacles, dodging them when their behavior is unlikely to be monitored at a later time. A very serious case for a defendant, then, is a very serious case for a judge.

### Legal Counsel

Legal counsel attends only 16% of the defendants. Very typically, it is a defendant rather than a lawyer who contends with the judge and prosecutor. The judge and prosecutor, correlatively, do not usually go through the screen of an attorney in their relation to the typical defendant. The lower court is by and large a court without attorneys; both the legal and bureaucratic intricacies of the defendant-court relationship are minimal.

Counsel is far more likely to be present, as would be expected, in encounters involving relatively serious charges: Felony suspects are not only more likely to be apprised of their rights; they are also more likely to have an attorney's aid in taking advantage of their rights. Excluding arraignments, only 12% of the misdemeanor suspects were professionally represented, whereas over five times as many (64%) of the felony suspects were represented. Nonetheless, one out of three defendants charged with a felony provides his own defense. . . .

The court presents the defendant or his lawyer not only legal battles to be dexterously fought and won, but also a configuration of bureaucratic relationships to be manipulated more or less adeptly. When a defendant obtains a lawyer to fight his case, he not only obtains a legal buffer between himself and the judge, he also — even if unwittingly — wedges his fate into a series of organizational battles irrelevant to the legal status of his case. The prosecutor balances his need to prosecute cases against his need to maintain good relations with the judge, public defender, and many other attorneys who frequently take cases to court; all are members of the "team" that maintains orderly operations of the court. They share a worksite. Together they can make their worksite a fractious, turbulent one or an orderly and predictable one. Though the interests of some of the parties are formally at odds, in operation they share common interests. A certain level of cooperation between them obtains. Where relationships between parties are enduring, cooperation or bargaining may often be found beneath a formal façade of conflict or coercion, as they are, for example, in the relations between prisoners and prison guards. . . . Adversarial behavior is often disruptive in the court, a formally adversarial organization. . . . There may be more conflict between the police and the court than between the average attorney and the prosecutor. . . .

The question arises as to whether the assignment of the public defender is to the benefit of the court, the defendant, or both. On one hand, the defendant is assured of at least some legal assistance free of charge. On the other hand, it is to the benefit of the court that the public defender be at least as adept at working well within the court bureaucracy as he is at legal matters as such. Because the public defender is in that class of attorneys generally cooperative within the bureaucracy, his attachment to serious cases deflates an underlying potential for disruption. There is a felicitous meshing between the formal requirements of law and those of the courtroom bureaucracy. Sixty-three percent (27 cases) of the public defender's load concerned a client charged with a felony, even though felony cases comprise only 19% of the cases observed. Furthermore, in a few of the most serious of felony cases, the judge assigned the public defender without even requiring the defendant to apply formally for his services. Court-funded counsel not only protects the defendant from the state, it also protects the state from the potential disruption of defendants in serious cases.

Lawyers no doubt receive positive or negative reinforcement for their own behavior in the judicial bureaucracy. One attorney, to give a minor example, noted that whenever he obtained an "unreasonable" acquittal, the prosecutor penalized him by not calling his cases until the end of the day's session. This "penalty" would last about a week after the disapproved disposition. Not only the lawyer but also his client, then, must sometimes sit all day in court for reasons irrelevant to the substance of the cases at hand. Ordinarily, clients with attorneys have their cases scheduled for very early or very late in the day's session. The court thus allows the attorneys to salvage most of each day for out-of-court matters. Defendants without attorneys are told the day, but not the time, of their court appearances. This favor may add to the court's leverage in coaxing attorneys toward routine cooperation. . . .

To be sure, the attorney also serves important functions in the courtroom. Nevertheless, in a typical case the facts are not problematic because the plea is guilty. Indeed, because the guilty plea is so common, it is somewhat misleading to call trial courts fact-finding courts. Much of the attorney's function in court in the cases observed is to enter particularistic appeals — and sometimes words of contrition — on behalf of his client. Particularistic appeals have to do with the offender rather than with the offense. An unrepresented defendant may not be cognizant of the relevance of such information. He may feel that it is inappropriate or unwise to report on potentially mitigating circumstances. By contrast, attorneys observed almost invariably inject such information in seeking low or no bond or low or no punishment. Their clients are hard workers, new fathers, long residents of the city, ordinarily upstanding, good students, unfamiliar with English, respectable businessmen, or even caring for sick mothers. . . .

Thus it is not that the attorney in the courtroom plays no adversarial role whatever, even when he enters a guilty plea for his client. His strategy very commonly is adversarial at the sentencing stage. Instead of arguing that his client is innocent, he argues that his client does not deserve a severe penalty. The lower court is largely a sentencing court, rarely a trial court — more a sanctioning than a truth-seeking system. The lawyer may step into either context as an advocate. It is not insignificant that one attorney, when asked to evaluate the court in this city, remarked that the court is "pretty good, pretty fair." By this, he said he meant "pretty lenient." He evaluated his success and the court's quality by the severity of sentences rather than by the rate of acquittals. In the lower court, the attorney *is* an advocate, but an advocate for freedom rather than for innocence. . . .

While lower courts are called fact-finding courts, most fact-finding goes on before the court-appearance stage. Operationally, the police and the prosecutor play more of a fact-finding role than does the judge. The highly bureaucratic form of contemporary courts and the heavy caseloads almost force much of the judicial function to be relegated to the police and prosecutor. In many instances, the judge simply ratifies the judicial decisions of the processing agents who work at earlier stages of the process. It should therefore be no surprise that a main function of the attorney in court is to enter particularistic appeals for his client. It is about all there remains to be done.

### The Plea

. . . Various factors are associated with the likelihood of a guilty plea. The more serious the offense charged, the less likely is the guilty plea (see Table 3). In felony cases, there is a guilty plea 44% of the time; in serious misdemeanor cases, 68%; and in minor misdemeanor cases, 89%. Further breaking down the category of minor misdemeanors, in public drunkenness cases the guilty plea rate jumps to 98%. Those who have made very minor trouble for the larger society by their offenses also make extremely little trouble for the court organization.

Black defendants plead not guilty more often than do white defendants. Twenty-one percent of the black defendants but only 8% of the white defendants enter not guilty pleas. . . . Spanish-American defendants, too, have a rate of not guilty pleas that is almost double (14%) that of other white defendants. Even when the nature of the offense charged is held constant, black defendants pro-

TABLE 3

Percentage of Courtroom Encounters According
to Offense Charged, by Plea

| | Offense Charged | | | | |
|---|---|---|---|---|---|
| | Misdemeanor | | | | |
| Plea | Minor | Serious and Other | All | Felony | All Cases |
| Guilty | 89 | 68 | 86 | 44 | 84 |
| Not guilty | 11 | 32 | 14 | 55 | 16 |
| Total | 100 | 100 | 100 | 99 | 100 |
| (n) | (246) | (37) | (283) | (18) | (301) |

test their innocence more often than do whites. In minor misdemeanor cases, white defendants plead guilty 95% of the time; black
defendants, 83% of the time. In all other misdemeanors, the respective percentages are 88 and 69. It is unclear whether the race difference in pleas stems from more numerous instances of innocence
among black defendants, fewer opportunities for them to engage
in plea bargaining, greater willingness to undertake the risks of
"going for broke," an unwillingness to submit to "white man's justice," a higher level of combativeness, or even ignorance of the
fact that in the long run they might be better off pleading guilty.
Whatever the source of the race difference in guilty pleas, it remains that blacks make a disproportionate amount of work for
the court in their pursuit of justice....

THE DISPOSITION

... Along with situational correlates of dispositions there is an
underlying concern in this section with some implications of court
dispositions for deterrence and for police practice. Both deterrence
and police practice feed back upon the court. To the extent that
the court deters both those it finds guilty and other potential offenders, it lessens its own workload. Complicating the courts' deterrent role, however, is the relation between the court and the
police. It is the police relation to appellate courts that is emphasized in discussions of the criminal justice system. Surprisingly,
students of the criminal process have slighted the routine, day-to-
day relations of trial courts and the police.... The practices of
trial courts surely are highly associated with police behavior. Faced
with a lenient court, police officers sometimes take the law into
their own hands, becoming self-appointed judges and applying informal sanctions from time to time.... Or, police themselves may
not sanction suspects at all when they have reason to believe that
the judge will not uphold their sanction with one of his own. A
consistently harsh court might give rise to more professional police
behavior. Trial court practice feeds back on police practice; together both have implications for deterrence. The manner and
degree to which the specific deterrence function is served by the
court can only stem from the cases that the court obtains for
processing, which depend primarily upon police arrest practices.
But the court's handling of these cases in turn affects police arrest
practice to some degree. The impact of any control system is always limited by the nature of the cases it comes to process....
Aside from the statutory maxima and minima, the court or-

ganization is such that the judge's decisions can be swayed by the prosecutor on one occasion, an attorney, the defendant, the public, probation and prison authorities, or personal predilections on other occasions. It is not that the judge deliberates amid some cloak of informal pressures each time he sentences a defendant. His modus operandi becomes routinized so that he handles typical cases in typical ways, deviating primarily in the face of an extraordinary offense or offender or under sporadic pressures from the public or the prison. Still, on paper he has legitimate use of a wide range of discretion.

The set of final dispositions that immediately precedes a case sometimes exerts an influence on a given disposition. What could be called situational precedents and standards are set and then destroyed again and again as the court grinds out its cases. It appears that the judge gauges the desirable severity of a given punishment partly in relation to the punishment or punishments he has just meted out. Thus, for example, while there is relatively little variability between the sanctions for all defendants who have the same charge and who are brought before the judge in one group, there is variability between the groups themselves. When the judge requires five days in jail for the first defendant in a group of defendants with intoxication charges, he is quite likely to require the same for all or most of the remaining defendants in the group. Later, when another group is before him, however, the judge may begin and follow through with a sanction of ten days in jail, suspended sentences, or whatever. This procedure might be called a pattern of situational justice; it is neither individualized justice nor justice with absolute standards. The pattern might be understood in terms of the larger legal and organizational context; it flows from the great range of legal discretion and the general lack of external supervision over consistency on the part of the judge. Neither purely legal nor purely social factors operate in such a way as to compel the judge to follow any clear principles of disposition. Within this seeming void, the judge allows his dispositions to be carried along by the rhythms of clusters of cases as they come before him.

### Offense and Disposition

... The offense charged in each encounter observed (except one case of trespass) is punishable by incarceration. Still, a mere 17% of all persons convicted of any offense in this court are incarcerated.... Hence it is first of all evident that rarely does the court punish defendants to the extent that it is able. In fact, the propor-

tion of incarceration is lower than that for police arrest in the field
when they have evidence of a criminal violation. When a suspect
is available in the field situation, the police make arrests of adults
in felony incidents roughly 60% of the time and in misdemeanor
incidents roughly 50% of the time. . . .

Overall, the outstanding pattern is that of legal leniency in the
treatment of persons convicted by the court. It is difficult to say
whether the court is more or less lenient than are the police, since
the court has a variety of sanctions and the police formally have
only the arrest. Considering incarceration alone, the court is far
less harsh than the police. In general, the police are legally required
to make an arrest whenever possible when a criminal offense is
made known to them. They plainly do not. . . . The judge is under
no such formal obligation to penalize all convicted offenders. Likewise he does not. The formal law is different for the police and for
the judge, but the rates of sanctioning are quite similar. Unless
social control agents themselves are regularly penalized for failing
to sanction, there is no reason to expect that any control system,
formal or informal, would penalize all the offenders it could. Instead they select from among the available deviants those that are
to be sanctioned formally. Overlapping this group are those each
social control system selects to sanction informally. The criteria of
selection could be many: those singled out can be the ones who
most flagrantly violated the rules, the ones who are disrespectful
toward the social control agents, the ones who have a particular
ascriptive characteristic such as a certain ethnicity or a certain age,
or whatever.

The deterrence value of any social control system, it seems likely,
is ordinarily, though not always, undermined by under-enforcement
of rule violations. And, among the instances of deviance that are
in fact controlled, the deterrence function surely is served for the
better or worse depending upon the criteria of selection. From all
available evidence, neither the court nor the police appear to select
for sanctioning purely on the basis of race. . . . Both the police and
the court in part select to sanction on the basis of the seriousness
of rule violations; the more serious the violation, the more likely
some sort of sanction. Furthermore, the police and, it seems im-
pressionistically, the court select to sanction on the basis of suspects' disrespect toward control agents. What deterrence there is,
then, might reach into two pockets: prevention of relatively serious
victimization of the general public and prevention of victimization
of the control system itself. . . .

A factor that increases the probability of incarceration is the

offender's criminal record. We can safely assume that persons convicted of intoxication have disproportionate records. In fact, the
police-court-drunken suspect relation has been characterized as a
"revolving door." ... No defendants in intoxication cases who had
clean records were incarcerated. Nearly all (92%) were released on
suspended sentences.... Incarceration increases quite strikingly
as the length and recency of records increase. The judge incarcerates
7% of those with light records, 20% of those with intermediate records, and 41% of those with heavy records. Thus the court tends
to sanction through incarceration not so much for public intoxication per se but rather for repeated instances of court appearances
for intoxication, to say nothing of actual repeated instances of
public intoxication. It is of some interest that when the judge
inquires into the criminal history of a petty misdemeanant he
usually asks whether the defendant has ever been *in court* before,
whereas when he inquires into the past of a more serious offender,
it is more common for him to ask whether the individual has ever
*committed such an act before.* Never does the judge ask whether
a defendant in an intoxication case has previously been intoxicated
in public. To the extent that the comparison can be made, routine
drunks seem more of an administrative problem for the court than
their deviance is a problem of disruption for society. Individuals
who commit crimes without victims, who are repeatedly arrested
and processed through court, in some sense victimize the court
itself, or at least they are responded to as though they do....

*Situational Excuses*

There is a sufficient number of intoxication cases, finally, to investigate the relation between situational excuses by defendants,
and dispositions. It is rare for a defendant in the courtroom to give
an "account" ... for his violative behavior or to try to excuse himself from punishment on the grounds that his future behavior
will be inoffensive. In only 14% of the intoxication cases did the
offender present an excuse. Yet, virtually all of them had earlier
pleaded guilty to their charges. The data show that penalties of
self-excusers are considerably more severe than those of other defendants. While over half the latter receive suspended sentences,
merely 18% of the former are freed on suspended sentences (see
Table 8). Furthermore, 54% of the self-excusers are incarcerated,
whereas only 15% of the other defendants are incarcerated.

Numerous explanations of this pattern could be suggested. Perhaps defendants who somehow realize that their chances for suspended sentences are slight tend to excuse themselves from punish-

TABLE 8
Percentage of Intoxication Cases Encounters
According to Situational Excuse, by Disposition

| Disposition | Did Defendant Attempt to Excuse Himself? | | All Cases |
| | Yes | No | |
| --- | --- | --- | --- |
| Suspended sentence | 18 | 56 | 51 |
| Fine  $1-10 | 18 ⎫ | 20 ⎫ | 20 ⎫ |
|      $11-20 | 05 ⎬ 28 | 10 ⎬ 30 | 08 ⎬ 29 |
|      $21 or more | 05 ⎭ | — ⎭ | 01 ⎭ |
| Jail  5 days | — ⎫ | 02 ⎫ | 02 ⎫ |
| Term 10 days | 27 ⎬ | 03 ⎬ | 06 ⎬ |
|      15 days | 18 ⎬ 54 | 07 ⎬ 15 | 08 ⎬ 20 |
|      20 days or more | 9 ⎭ | 03 ⎭ | 04 ⎭ |
| Total | 100 | 101 | 100 |
| (n) | (22) | (136) | (158) |

ment. On the other hand, an underlying factor may again relate to considerations of bureaucratic efficiency. The court is a system whose currency of operation is information. Citizen witnesses, police reports and testimony, prosecutorial investigations, the defendants, and sometimes attorneys together provide information through which the judge sifts to determine guilt or to set penalties. Information allows the court to work, but *extra* information drives the court toward *extra* work. If the court disproportionately uses the sanction of jail as a defense against the injection of extra information during the courtroom encounter, then defendants might come to offer it less often. Were the court to bend immediately to the excuses of the defendants, defendants might in a short time learn always to excuse themselves. Alternatively, were the court to probe further into the defendants' excuses to find whether they could be considered justified, much time would be lost. To respond more often with jail sentences to defendants who excuse themselves is at least a relatively rational way to respond not necessarily from an ideological standpoint but from the standpoint of the court as a bureaucracy. Even if such does not *account* for the pattern, it speaks to part of the consequences of the pattern.

## Mass Justice and Disposition

. . . Thus the court seemingly orients itself more to the varieties of its workload than to race, a legally irrelevant characteristic of the individuals it processes. In serious cases, defendants are more likely to protest their innocence; trials are therefore more common. Further, in serious cases, lawyers more often are present; witnesses may be heard; the judge may set penalties more carefully; and procedural restrictions and requirements are more stringent. Minor cases are simple. The court handles so many minor cases that it can and does establish routines for processing them. Each legally serious case is a relative novelty for the court. Consequently, the court cannot feed it as quickly through its machinery. The court can handle rapidly what it handles most often. It should not be assumed that minor cases are quickly disposed of only because they are legally petty. While they are minor in the formal legal system, they likewise are common and routine in the legal bureaucracy. There is a convergence between the formal and organizational networks of the law.

Pressures toward rapid processing derive not only from an overloaded court but also from the defendants themselves. In other words, at times there is an identity of interests between the parties at conflict — the state and the defendant; they contribute for different reasons to a rapid system of justice. For example, when the judge asks, as he frequently does, if the defendant has "anything to say" the usual reply is a brief "no." Also, defendants often say such things as, "I'd like to get this over with." One defendant, assuming he would be fined rather than incarcerated, said he would plead guilty so that he could salvage more of the remaining day for his job. In brief, while the court cannot allow lengthy moments in court for all defendants, most defendants do not appear to want them anyway. After all, any given defendant or his representative need only speak longer if he cares to stretch his encounter.

There could be a point beyond which this option remains open only with certain negative consequences for the defendant. It seems that the judge and the prosecutor have a notion of a defendant who "talks too much." For example, the three most loquacious defendants in the study met with treatment uncharacteristic of the court. The first of the three, a middle-class, white young man, inquired with some detail into his rights. He then embarked on a relatively lengthy account (roughly two minutes) of his alleged offense (vagrancy). He concluded with a statement as to why he should be fined rather than incarcerated. He was more than reasonably polite, but he apparently also was too verbose. The judge interrupted him, dismissed him with, "That will be all, Mr. Jones," and asked that the police officer on duty place him in the courtroom lock-up. The second loquacious defendant — a black in his thirties charged with breach of the peace — behaved similarly, although with antagonism toward the judge and prosecutor. He, too, was interrupted and placed in the lock-up. Moreover, when he knocked on the lock-up door to ask the police officer if he could see the judge, the prosecutor announced that he would be found in contempt of court upon the next rap at the door. The third, a white lower-class female, was more subtly stopped from taking up court time. However, she received a penalty more severe than most in her offense category. Defiance of authority may be what more basically is at issue; but devouring time may in and of itself defy the court. Even though the number of cases is minute, and though other factors could be at work, these cases do suggest that behavior which uses extra time may not be advisable for the defendant. . . .

A number of dimensions along which felony and misdemeanor cases are handled differently have been discussed. Overall, felony cases take longer to process; the court more often processes felony suspects alone instead of in groups; the judge more often apprises them of their rights; he more often apprises them individually; and they more often receive the services of the public defender. The misdemeanant does not nearly so frequently meet this kind of treatment by the court. At the same time, he also does not receive the kind of punishment that the felon receives; nor does he receive the informal approbation from peers and relatives, nor does his criminal record follow so closely and consequentially on his heels when he finally emerges from the criminal justice system. He is handled with less caution, but his trip through the system has relatively few ramifications for him. So little does his penalty affect his future that it is not worth his while to appeal. The lack of control from the minor defendants on one side and from the higher courts on the other allows the lower court to send misdemeanants routinely and smoothly through the system. . . .

A higher proportion of those incarcerated than of those fined are recidivists. Moreover, a disproportionate number of those both incarcerated and mass-processed are recidivists. Repeaters are thus the most apt to be handled impersonally and in turn incarcerated. The court takes relatively little care with its failures, more care with its newcomers. It would appear that, in so doing, the court may in part abdicate its deterrence role with those it has not been able to deter. It is as if the court gives up.

A slightly different but fundamentally similar pattern obtains in the relation between the duration of encounters and dispositions. Exactly half of all offenders who are jailed are disposed of very quickly, that is, in less than one minute. . . . Offenders whom the judge fines are not quite so often processed with this rapidity (41%). This mirrors the relation between mass processing and dispositions, although the percentage difference is not nearly so great. At the other end of the time scale, 13% of those who are incarcerated have encounters of four or more minutes; this is true of only 5% of those fined. Thus, even though it is common for an offender to be sentenced to jail in very short order, the judge does spend more time with slightly over one out of ten offenders he sends to jail. Again, however, what is of far greater interest is that decisions to incarcerate are very quick decisions more often than are decisions to fine.

Augmenting this contrast between the fine and incarceration are the contrasts within the two categories. As the fine increases, it is *less* likely that the encounter lasts *less* than one minute. By contrast as the jail term increases it is *less* likely that the encounter lasts *more* than one minute. Hence, not only is the briefest of meetings characteristic of encounters that result in incarceration; in addition, extremely short encounters are still more likely as the length of time in jail increases.

These dual patterns — between and within the categories of incarceration and the fine — may seem surprising, since a jail term is obviously a greater deprivation of an offender's liberty than is a fine. The court does not allocate its time and resources according to the severity of the punishment imposed. A possible factor underlying this finding is that the rapidly processed incarcerated defendants are very likely to be the "regulars," well-known in intoxication cases. While these defendants repeatedly "cause trouble" on the street, they uncommonly "cause trouble" in the court. The court is familiar with them, and they are familiar with the workings of the court. They neither question their charges nor do they say that they do not understand their rights. In brief, they present no trouble to the court during the encounter itself, and the court need not anticipate a protest about court treatment once they are released. The court can afford to process these defendants quickly, even though in doing so it often sends them to jail. They are routine failures; the court routinizes its failures.

*Situational Sanctions*

Defendants face the teeth of material sanctions, if they face
them at all, only after they depart from the courtroom. They must
work off days in jail or months in prison, muster funds to pay
fines, or arrange their lives to accommodate periodic rendezvous
with probation officers. On occasion, defendants also receive what
could be called situational sanctions during their courtroom encounters with the judge. The judge's manner toward them may be
harsh or severe rather than good-natured or distant and bureaucratic. Besides the relative subtlety of a harsh manner, the judge
at times openly reprimands defendants in the courtroom. The
judge traditionally has been a moral agent not only in his actions
but also in his style.

Only a small portion of defendants are singled out to be situationally sanctioned during courtroom encounters, and the selection does not directly follow the seriousness of the charge. The
courtroom is removed from the immediacy of the criminal event.
Thus it is removed from the tension, disgust, outrage, or defensive-
ness that might attach to the witnessing of violative behavior and
its consequences in the field. The courtroom is usually the stage
for the comparatively dull aftermath of the passion, disruption,
fun, or danger of deviance.

It appears that a minor disruption in the courtroom or a show
of disrespect for its personnel is more likely to give rise to situational sanctioning than is the allegation of a serious criminal
offense. Details from some of the more dramatic instances of such
informal deviance and response are presented in the preceding
discussion. Unfortunately, there are not enough cases to control
for offense and to show quantitative findings on the matter of
court disruption and situational sanctioning. Instead, we examine
situational sanctions, first in relation to the offense charged and
then in relation to the disposition.

The judge's manner toward the defendant may be classified into
four categories: good-natured, bureaucratic, firm, and harsh. First,
the judge may be very courteous, affable, or even subservient
toward the defendant. For example, in one case three brothers,
middle-class and neat in appearance, were brought in on breach
charges. One was still in uniform, having just been discharged
from the service. When the judge learned that their behavior consisted of some raucous but seemingly harmless antics on a public
street, he smiled knowingly and said, "Well, I guess you just got a
little overly excited to see your brother back. Okay. Sentences suspended."

Secondly, the judge might behave in a routine, bureaucratic, businesslike way toward the defendants, a manner that at least borders on the impersonal. Many times these cases run as follows: The judge frequently apprises the defendant of his rights at the outset. The prosecutor then says, "Mr. Jones, you're charged with intoxication; what is your plea?" "Guilty." The judge, speaking for the second time, says, "Twenty dollars," or "Five days," or whatever. The case is over. Sometimes the judge does not even make the disposition decision. For example, the prosecutor says, "I recommend twenty-five dollars," and the judge echoes, "Twenty-five dollars." Some cases are more lengthy, but the personal involvement of the judge remains minimal. He is routine and affectively neutral in his outward behavior.

In other encounters, the judge is firm and displays his legal authority over defendants. While this third manner does not imply that the judge orally reprimands defendants, the tone, force, and sometimes the content of his words and his demeanor convey moral authority. Instances of firmness are: "I hope you understand that you are in serious trouble"; "Now I'm going to fine you twenty-five dollars for this. But I want you to pay it out of your own pocket so you can appreciate the consequences of what you have done. You can pay me on a weekly basis, but I don't want your father to pay for you."

Last, and to be clearly separated from the third type of judicial demeanor, is a harsh, nasty, abrasive style of behavior. The judge's demeanor is so categorized only when it goes beyond firmness to personal vindictiveness. For example, a white defendant charged with abusing an officer and breach of the peace protested: "I have never been arrested before. This is ridiculous. The record says I abused a police officer. I never touched him. This was a traffic violation." The judge responded, "Don't give me that disgusting look. Your case is bondable. Your bond is one hundred and fifty dollars."

The judge is formal or firm in 14% of the encounters. To the extent that a formal demeanor is the stereotype of judicial behavior, the stereotype is far from accurate. Secondly, it is extremely rare for the judge's demeanor to take on either extreme: he is harsh in a mere 5% of the cases, good-natured in only 3% of the cases. By far the most common demeanor of the judge in the courtroom encounter is routine and bureaucratic. In over three-quarters (78%) of the cases, he behaves in this fashion.

Perhaps the high proportion of cases in which the judge is routine and affectively neutral should not be surprising since the lower court, after all, is a bureaucracy — one in which criminal legal work happens to be done. The patterns of judicial demeanor may be very close to those for bureaucratic workers in other legal or even nonlegal settings. Crime, however, is a topic which periodically generates a great deal of moral outrage on the part of the citizenry. Yet the judge in the courtroom usually does not behaviorally uphold these moral sentiments. Most often he remains personally detached while he sanctions offenders or allows them to go free. Judicial affective neutrality may be compared to that of police officers, the control agents who are closer in social space to the deviant act. In a contrastingly low 60% of their contacts with suspects, police officers behave bureaucratically. . . . Thus the police officer is less often distant or detached even though, formally, he is not empowered to perform a judicial function.

On the average, a businesslike manner is slightly more frequent in felony than in misdemeanor cases (see Table 13). One might have expected the opposite. This pattern surely is the opposite from that of the larger community's response to violations. A firm demeanor is in general more frequent in misdemeanor cases: the judge is more often firm in either level of misdemeanor cases (13% in minor misdemeanor cases and 27% in serious misdemeanor cases) than in minor felony cases (5%), and is more often firm in serious misdemeanor cases than in serious felony cases (21%). Thus the judge's demeanor does not *parallel* the gradations in the law; instead it seemingly *complements* these gradations. Perhaps the judge can afford to be routine and impersonal in a greater majority of felony cases: the charges alone extend a good deal of moral authority and official condemnation. Accordingly, the judge can be impersonal, allowing the rules themselves to impart official morality. When the charge is not serious in the legal hierarchy of offenses, the judge more often attempts to impress upon the defendant the seriousness of the matter. Formal and informal authority mesh in such a way as to homogenize condemnation across the categories of offense.

Rarely is the judge affable and good-natured, and even then it is only in misdemeanor cases, never in felony cases. Although a felony charge might appear sufficiently serious so as not to call for judicial firmness, at the same time a felony charge might be rather dissonant with judicial affability. Whether or not this is the motive for the judge's avoidance of affability with felony suspects, it is the pattern. The case of the three drunken brothers is an example of good nature and friendliness, implying that even the judge does not seriously relate to petty matters. In one case the judge was kind toward a man who could barely hear. At other times the

TABLE 13

Percentage of Courtroom Encounters According
to Offense Charged, by Judge's Situational Demeanor

| | Offense Charged | | | | |
| | Misdemeanor | | Felony | | |
| Judge's Demeanor | Minor | Serious | Minor | Serious | All Cases[a] |
|---|---|---|---|---|---|
| Good-natured | 03 | 04 | — | — | 03 |
| Bureaucratic | 79 | 65 | 85 | 79 | 78 |
| Firm | 13 | 27 | 05 | 21 | 14 |
| Harsh | 05 | 04 | 10 | — | 05 |
| Total | 100 | 100 | 100 | 100 | 100 |
| (n) | (278) | (26) | (20) | (19) | (343) |

a. Arraignments had to be included in the tabulation to supply a number of cases sufficient for analysis. However, this presents problems for interpretation since proportionately more felony cases were arraignments, cases in which the defendants are still legally innocent. Nevertheless, on a number of occasions judicial harshness did not appear to be inhibited by the presumption of innocence. Furthermore, judicial firmness is not unexpected in an arraignment. Were the judge merely to say, for example, "Now you're charged with a felony; this is a serious matter," his demeanor was categorized as firm or formal.

judge's demeanor simply takes on the cast of a concerned, helpful social worker rather than that of a stern or impersonal authority figure. Overall, though, judicial good nature is extremely uncommon.

At the other extreme, in only 5% of all cases does the judge behave harshly toward the defendant. In serious felony cases the judge is never harsh. While harsh treatment is more characteristic of minor felony cases (10% of the total) than of misdemeanor cases (an average of 5%), there were only two cases of the former. One of them seemingly can be rather easily explained. The defendant in this case was a boy home on leave from the service. He had been arrested for possession of drugs. The judge, feeling that he should not detain the defendant from his military duty, let him off with no penalty whatsoever. He was not, however, let off without situational sanctioning. The judge behaved quite harshly toward him. The harshness, in short, seemed to be a substitute for formal punishment. In the remaining cases, the judge's harshness may have been a response to some situational violation on the part of the defendants; they were disrespectful, unrepentant, argumentative. Again, it is very uncommon for the judge to vent any hostility during the courtroom encounter. . . .

When the court expends its time and facilities to process a case, and when it requires a defendant to go to the trouble of submitting to its processing but ultimately gives that defendant only a minor penalty, a situational lecture or judicial firmness perhaps goes part of the way toward upholding the legitimacy of the court. A minor material penalty alone might seem pointless to the defendant, given the effort both he and the court had to go through to reach it. By situationally sanctioning the defendant whom he only penalizes lightly, however, the judge in effect says that the defendant is indeed a "bad man," even if his behavior does not merit a harsh material punishment. Not only might situational sanctioning somehow compensate for the legitimacy lost, it might in some small part compensate for the deterrence value lost by a lenient court.

In sum, the judge typically does not bother to condemn or chastise defendants with his tone or with his words. The fact that the persons processed by the court are official deviants slips beneath the surface of courtroom interaction. The style of in-court work belies its content; the routines hide the substance. There are no formal or informal requirements that the judge be the personal moral spokesman for the state, and he usually is not. While the fundamental elements of a "status degradation" . . . are present in the courtroom encounter, the degradation usually is not dramatized; it is unceremonial. The judge's work becomes routinized, as do all work roles. Surely some deterrence value of the encounter is lost to the extent that routinization sets in.

The situational sanctioning that the judge does engage in is woven in unexpected patterns. First, it is suggested that persons who violate the informal rules of the court, regardless of their violations of legal rules, are particularly susceptible to situational condemnation. Indeed, when the disruption is sufficiently severe, the court can invoke the legal rule against contempt of court. The court protects itself as it protects the larger society, responding to its own victimization at the same time as it responds to the victimization of others.

Second, situational sanctioning relates to the seriousness of the charge and to the seriousness of the material penalty. It seems, overall, to be more common with minor than with serious charges. Thus it is possible that situational sanctioning works in such a way as to compensate for the lesser degree of condemnation that a minor charge itself carries. Furthermore, situational sanctioning is more common, in all but petty misdemeanor cases, when the penalty is slight. Indeed, when a defendant is not punished severely, his encounter with the judge more often outwardly appears as a degradation ceremony. With opprobrious words the judge might buoy the legitimacy of processing minor offenders and offenders he does not severely punish. In a greater majority of felony cases and in a greater majority of cases where the penalty is relatively stiff, by contrast, the judge can remain uninvolved without jeopardizing the manifest condemnation of the offender.

### CONCLUSION

This paper reports findings from an observational study of a criminal court which handles primarily minor cases. Because the empirical patterns examined here are somewhat diverse and numerous, the discussion closes with a list of generalizations, some of which are clearly more tentative than others.

(1) The lower court processes defendants with striking rapidity.

(2) The lower court frequently processes defendants in groups rather than individually.

(3) The judge typically but not always apprises defendants of their legal rights. However, most apprisings are to groups rather than to individual defendants.

(4) The judge is less likely to apprise accused persons individually or at all in legally nonserious cases, cases where the defendants are least likely to protest their dispositions.

(5) Attorneys represent only an extremely small portion of the defendants.

(6) Attorneys handle more serious than minor cases.

(7) The attorney's involvement in informal relational networks of the court generally has beneficial consequences for the fate of his client; but the court sometimes sanctions uncooperative attorneys by sanctioning their clients.

(8) The attorney's role as an advocate for leniency supersedes his role as an advocate for freedom.

(9) Since the vast majority of defendants, particularly those in minor cases, plead guilty, the court is much more a sentencing than a fact-finding enterprise.

(10) Black defendants plead not guilty more often than do white defendants.

(11) The court is legally lenient in its dispositions, releasing many offenders on suspended sentences, incarcerating very few.

(12) In drunkenness cases, a criminal record and a situational excuse increase the likelihood of incarceration.

(13) There is no clear evidence of racial discrimination in dispositions.

(14) A reduced charge nets the defendant roughly the same type of punishment as that typical for a higher charge; in these cases, many a defendant is punished for what he seems to have done rather than for what he was convicted of having done.

(15) The court allocates its time and official energy according to the nature of cases rather than according to race.

(16) In minor cases the more severe the punishments, the less time and official energy the court spends.

(17) The judge very rarely moralizes to or lectures defendants in the courtroom.

(18) In all but drunkenness cases, the probability of judicial moralizing and lecturing increases as the charge is relatively minor and as the disposition is milder.

One theme in this analysis concerns the court in relation to segments of its larger environment — the prosecutor's office and the police. Ideally, a broad approach to the court would include other external organizations and actors that play a part in molding court operations, such as trial courts with jurisdiction over more serious cases, appellate courts, some municipal officials, the general public, and correctional personnel and facilities. These organizations and actors exert a constant, largely indirect set of pressures over time. In short, part of what occurs inside the court is conditioned by and conditions factors outside of it.

Besides this broader approach to the court, this analysis directly confronts courtroom encounters as units of study in their own right. It is shown that various characteristics of face-to-face encounters cohere with others. Encounters are in turn analyzed in the context of their immediate environment, the court itself. The court can be seen as a formal organization with a legal content; its workers are bureaucrats with legal roles. Thus encounters come into being and are played out in a bureaucratic setting. The control of crime is as much a bureaucratic as it is a moral enterprise.

# Social Control in the Adversary System*

# Jerome H. Skolnick

To understand the social control problem of the adversary system, we begin with what is admittedly a conceptual oversimplification — that social organizations are based upon norms of either conflict or cooperation. The family, the university, the industrial enterprise are institutions predicated upon the idea of cooperation. It is believed that the more smoothly the actors within it work together, the more likely will the institution achieve its aims. For such institutions, the key problem of social control is to find means for countering forces that precipitate conflict.

There are, however, institutions experiencing just the opposite problem. The most striking example of an institution based upon conflict is the *sporting event*. Not only are most sporting events zero-sum games in which one player must lose and the other win; even more fundamental is the condition that each player try to win. Should a fight be "fixed," it might be that the outcome would be the same as if the fight had not been fixed. Underlying the sporting event, however, is the principle of conflict. Within the ethic of the institution it is understood that each fighter will attempt to throw his best punches, that each will strain to achieve victory. Otherwise, the fight is not considered genuine. *Procedure* is as important as *outcome*.

As a procedural matter, the adversary system may similarly be viewed as resting upon an assumption of genuine conflict. As the Allen report . . . states:

> The adversary system is the institution devised by our legal order for the proper reconciliation of public and private interests in the crucial areas of penal regulation. As such, it makes essential and invaluable contributions to the maintenance of the free society. The essence of the adversary system is *challenge*. The survival of our system of criminal justice and the value which it advances depends upon a constant, searching, and creative questioning of official de-

* This excerpt from Social Control in the Adversary System, by Jerome H. Skolnick, is reprinted from the *Journal of Conflict Resolution*, Vol. XI, No. 1 (March 1967) pp. 52-70 by permission of the publisher, Sage Publications, Inc., and the author.

cisions and assertions of authority at all stages of the process. The proper performance of the defense function is thus as vital to the health of the system as the performance of the prosecuting and adjudicatory functions [... italics added].†

The introduction of this quotation should not be taken to mean that the adversary system is the only, or even the best, system possible "for reconciling public and private interests in the crucial areas of penal regulation." All it is intended to suggest is that, as a procedural matter, there seems to be a fundamental norm of challenge underlying the system. It is therefore like the sporting event in that it presupposes an underlying ethic of genuine conflict. Furthermore, as in all institutions based on conflict, there is a perception of "deviance" when actors who are supposed to be genuinely antagonistic begin to cooperate. Adam Smith expresses a social control problem of the free enterprise economy as follows:

> People of the same trade seldom meet together even for merriment and diversion, but the conversation ends in a conspiracy against the public, or on some contrivance to raise prices. It is impossible indeed to prevent such meetings by any law which either could be executed, or would be consistent with liberty and justice. But though the law cannot hinder people of the same trade from sometimes assembling together, it ought to do nothing to facilitate such assemblies, much less to render them necessary....*

Just as it is sometimes argued that monopolies are more economic than free enterprise, the aims of truth and justice may be considered better achieved through the institution of the interrogating magistrate. From the point of view of the sociological analyst of the system, however, the argument is relevant mainly insofar as it provides a resource for actors in the system who deviate from the norm of adversariness, that is, it gives them a justification for "deviant behavior." It may even be that all conflict systems are unnecessary, but that is not the point. The point is that all conflict systems share a similar problem of social control; that problem is conflict maintenance, or the control of tendencies toward cooperation....

† Report of the Attorney General's Committee, Poverty and the Administration of Federal Criminal Justice at 10-11 (1963).
* A. Smith, An Inquiry into the Nature and Causes of the Wealth of Nations at 116 (McCullock ed. 1776).

*Source of Data and Method*

Data are based upon a study of one California county, which shall be called La Loma. La Loma County has a population of approximately one million, and is dominated by one city, which shall be called Westville. Westville's population is nearly 400,000, approximately 20 percent of whom are nonwhite.

Two criminal trial courts operate at the felony level. There are seven municipal courts and a traffic court in Westville, two municipal courts in Elmwood, and another municipal court serving the western part of the county. Municipal courts hold preliminary hearings and misdemeanor trials. Both levels of court were studied, but most of the data in this paper derive from observations relating to the felony courts. In the fiscal year 1961-62 there were 1,893 felony cases in the county, with Westville accounting for more than 60 percent. Of all felony cases, 61 percent were handled by the public defender's office.

The research method . . . was participant observation in a face-to-face professional community of about 100 attorneys and judges. The principal investigator spent three months in the office of the public defender (who had a staff of fifteen), four months in the office of the prosecutor (who had a staff of forty), and six months in the police department (about 700 men) over an eighteen-month period commencing in the summer of 1962. Attorneys and police usually were aware of the investigator's true identity, while defendants were not. In studying public defenders, for example, the investigator would select one who was not scheduled for trial and follow him on his daily round of interview and negotiation, since the main subject of interest was the system of justice without trial. . . .

*The Prosecutorial Role and Prosecutor Discretion*

In law and in practice, the prosecutor enjoys wide discretion, especially in the details of charging the defendant. A simple view of the prosecutor's role would principally emphasize the prosecutor's responsibility to argue the case for the state. In fact, however, the responsibilities of the prosecutor were observed to be more extensive and complex, taking into account administrative concerns as well as the task of prosecution.

Most organizations within a bureaucracy seek to expand their authority; the prosecutor is also interested in expansive authority, but he already has it; thus his greatest concern is with maintaining his present latitude, that is, with avoiding action that might limit his future enjoyment of present discretionary power. He is, therefore, interested in making a favorable impression on a diffuse public — including courts, political authorities, and the man in the street. His specific task is to strike a balance between those cases which, for a variety of reasons — usually related to public interest — he cannot deal out; and those which, in deference to his administrative responsibilities, he needs to settle before trial. In brief, he is required to keep the calendar moving, at the same time not appearing to be "giving anything away" to the defense.

If criminal procedure were to be analyzed through statutes and cases alone, the pervading importance of administrative concerns would hardly be apparent. Viewing the system in action, however, it becomes clear that system norms can be inferred from sanctions within the system itself, with the values of the system expressed through its penalties. In the system studied there were strong informal controls to enhance the smooth *functioning* of the system itself. Thus an assertion regarding the pertinence of administrative concerns is evidenced by the weight of the sanctions favoring administration.

Judges, for example, typically exhibit a strong interest in calendar movement. The criminal court judge who allows his calendar to lag will in turn be cautioned by his presiding judge. Judges observed and interviewed made clear their potent interest in maintaining the administrative security of the courts. . . .

Finally, and also connected to public relations, is the prosecutor's interest in nondefeat. In the county studied, the prosecutor's office cared less about winning than about *not losing*. This norm is so intrinsic to the rationale of the prosecutor's office that one does not often hear it articulated. Nevertheless it is very powerful. It cannot be attributed to such a simple and obvious fact as the periodic requirement of reelection. Indeed, reelection seemed to be taken for granted, and an observer would be hard put to relate prosecutorial decisions directly to electoral requirements. Not only does the prosecutor desire to maintain a respectable record, but more than that, he seeks to maintain, insofar as possible, a reputation for utter credibility, inevitable truth, almost of invincibility.

Why this should be so is initially puzzling. The phenomenon may be best explained, however, in terms of the stratification of statuses within the criminal justice system. The defendant occupies a position at the bottom of this hierarchy, the judge a position at the top. In this perspective, each actor may be regarded as attempting to maximize his status. The defendant strives to be a citizen unencumbered by the stigma of conviction; the defense attorney represents the defendant, but at the same time faces the problem of disaffiliating himself from the stigma associated with the status of defendant. The prosecutor seeks to rise above the adversarial role to that of judge. The trial judge seeks to maximize his esteem through the acceptability of his decisions, not only to appellate courts, but also to the community of practitioners. Even in an elective system, judges are not motivated principally by the requirement of reelection, largely because there is a tradition of reelection.

The role of the prosecutor in an adversary system is accusatorial. He brings a charge, and the merit of the accusation is weighed by judge and jury. He is expected, however, before bringing the charge, to weigh its merits, including statements of fact. Thus, when a prosecutor brings a charge, he has himself made an investigation. It is as if the prosecutor were addressing the community as follows: "I have investigated, I have charged, I have found the man guilty; so should you." That the defendant is represented by counsel, that counsel has usually discussed the case with the prosecutor, tends to reinforce the prosecutor's confidence in the merits of his accusations. The adversary system is not, as it is frequently presented, a model of charge by complainant and defense by accused. Rather, the complainant's charge is considered by the prosecutor, the defense attorney usually discusses its merits, and the prosecutor comes to a decision to present the accusation, to act as attorney for the complainant. When the prosecutor makes such a decision to accuse, he does not care to be "reversed" in his judgment. His conception of esteem is recognition as a quasi-magisterial functionary. Such a status implies credibility, not only as to the prosecutor's belief in his own assertions, but also as to his capacity to assess the assertions of others before making his own.

The advantages of preserving such a magisterial posture are obvious for the routine functioning of the office, if the image can be maintained. If there is a presumption of innocence aiding the accused, when the prosecutor achieves a quasi-magisterial acceptance, he enjoys the countervailing advantage of a presumption of administrative regularity. Nothing can be more destructive to this posture, however, than a series of defeats in the courtroom. Credibility leads to victory, victory to the quasi-magisterial status, and quasi-magisterial status to enhanced credibility, all of which eases the task of the prosecutor.

In this context, prosecutor discretion itself puts certain pressures on the prosecutor. He is not only allotted the task of repre-

senting the interests of the state in the particular case but, given
his discretion, he is also expected to play an administrative and
public relations role. If prosecutors were selected from a community of lawyers, to represent the state in the individual case, the
office itself would not have the administrative concerns or the
public-relational concerns that presently characterize it. Most important, perhaps, there would be little need to enhance the status
of the *office* itself. Thus the very structure of the prosecutor's office,
and the tasks that are allotted to it, tend to create a social control
problem for the adversary system. The prosecutor must attempt
to "work with" defense attorneys to achieve goals wider than those
ordinarily contemplated by a "squaring off" between two individual contestants, the state and the accused.

## The Calendar Man and the Defense Community

If, as suggested, the calendar man not only is responsible for
the conviction of the accused but also bears a heavy administrative
responsibility for court functioning, he must elicit the cooperation
of defense attorneys. From the point of view of the prosecutor,
however, the idea of "prosecutor–defense attorney relations" is an
oversimplified conception. He does not view a defense attorney
solely in terms of his formal role as legal representative of an accused, but rather in light of the attorney's history of relations with
the prosecutor's office and his position in the defense attorney
community. Or, from the vantage point of the defendant, the
strength of his defense depends in part upon the actual "facts" of
his case, in part on how the defense is presented to the prosecution,
and in part on who his defense attorney is. Principally, the prosecutor views the defense attorney in terms of the latter's "reasonableness," that is, the attorney's ability to discern a generous offer of
settlement, and to be willing to encourage his client to accept
such an offer. Prosecutorial discretion thus creates the fundamental
conditions for the reduction of conflict.

From the vantage point of the prosecutor's office studied, there
were at least four categories of defense attorney. One category
comprised defense attorneys who tried relatively few criminal
cases. These attorneys had variable relations with the prosecutor.
One might think that, because of the inexperience of such attorneys, the prosecutor's office would prefer to deal with them. On the
contrary, the more inexperienced the defense attorney, the more
likely he was to pose an *administrative* problem for the prosecutor's
office. Since the prosecutor is concerned not merely with convictions but with administrative efficiency, he tends to prefer to deal

with attorneys who "know their business." To be sure, the prosecutor has an advantage over the inexperienced attorney in court trial, but that is relatively unimportant. Court trials waste time and money. Furthermore, in dealing with an inexperienced defense attorney the prosecutor is often faced with a man who, because of his own lack of knowledge, will be unnecessarily mistrustful of collaboration, even though in such cases the prosecutor may lean over backward to give the neophyte a fair shake. Experienced attorneys who maintain a general practice frequently forward criminal cases to experienced defense attorneys, believing that they serve their clients more advantageously.

There was also a group of defense attorneys who maintained both a small but active criminal practice and rather hostile relations with the prosecutor's office. Most defense attorneys and members of the prosecutor's office regarded them as "gamblers." They might occasionally gain an acquittal for their clients in cases where a "cooperative" defense attorney would have advised a plea of guilty. At the same time, the practices of such attorneys exemplified the dangers of adversariness for the rest of the criminal law community. In order to make it in the interest of the clients of other defense attorneys to plead their clients guilty, the district attorney had to demonstrate the negative consequences of adversariness through his victories over adversarially-oriented defense attorneys. Thus such attorneys tended to "win big" or "lose big," and the more successful defense attorneys preferred to avoid such tactics. Had the entire defense community united to frustrate the operations of the district attorney's office, they might have succeeded in changing the power structure of the system. As it was, however, the highly adversarial attorneys succeeded mainly in demonstrating the negative consequences of an adversarial posture, thereby unintentionally contributing to the power position of the prosecutor.

From the point of view of the prosecutor's office, greatest concern is with defense attorneys who represent the most numerous defendants, and also those who represent defendants in the most important cases. From this viewpoint the most important defense attorney is the public defender, whose office represented more than 60 percent of the accused felons in the county studied. The prosecutor also perceived a "group" of five or six "successful" criminal lawyers, with whom he had close and continuing relations. Still, because of the volume of cases that he handled, the public defender (PD) was the most important defense "agency" in the community.

The remainder of this paper will concentrate upon prosecutor–PD relations. We will attempt to show, first, that differences in demeanor and attitude between PD and "regular" or "successful" private defense attorneys have been exaggerated by critics of the PD; and second, to offer reasons, based upon the character of the PD's clientele, for the criticisms to have arisen. Particular consideration will be given to examining PD–private defense attorney differences regarding "client control," an issue that is fundamental to social control in the adversary system. The main argument of the remaining portion of the paper will be that, given the prevailing system of prosecutorial discretion, the public defender operates on much the same principles as the private defense attorney, and that perceived differences can be largely explained by the character of the public defender's clientele.

*Similarities Between the PD and the Private Defense Attorney*

To analyze similarities between the public defender and the private defense attorney, it is instructive to consider the statements of two critics of the PD. The noted defense attorney, Edward Bennett Williams, has said that:

> ... the public defender and the prosecutor are trying cases against each other every day. They begin to look at their work like two wrestlers who wrestle with each other in a different city every night and in time get to be good friends. The biggest concern of the wrestlers is to be sure they do not hurt each other too much. They don't want to get hurt. They just want to make a living. Apply that to the public defender and prosecutor situation and it is not a good thing in a system of justice that is based upon the adversary system. . . .*

Similarly, David Sudnow, a sociologist who studied a PD's office, writes:

> He [the Public Defender] will not cause any serious trouble for the routine motion of the court conviction process. Laws will not be challenged, cases will not be tried to test the constitutionality of procedures and statutes, judges will not be personally degraded, police will be free from scrutiny to decide the legitimacy of their operations, and the community will not be condemned for its segregative practices against Negroes. The PD's defense is completely

* D. McDonald, The Law: Interviews with Edward Bennett Williams and Bethuel M. Webster at 10 (Santa Barbara, Cal., Center for the Study of Democratic Institutions 1962).

proper, in accord with correct legal procedure, and specifically amoral in its import, manner of delivery, and perceived implications for the propriety of the prosecution enterprise.

In "return" for all this, the district attorney treats the defendant's guilt in a matter of fact fashion, doesn't get hostile in the course of the proceedings, doesn't insist that the jury or judge "throw the book" but rather "puts on a trial" (in their way of referring to their daily tasks) in order to, with a minimum of strain, properly place the defendant behind bars. Both prosecutor and public defender thus protect the moral character of the other's charges from exposure. . . .†

There is a degree of truth in the observations of Williams and Sudnow, especially regarding the "teamwork" conception of DA-PD relations. Each, however, tends to draw conclusions that are partly false or misleading, because of a fundamental flaw in the assumptions underlying their analysis. This consists in taking given institutional categories — such as "public defender" — at face value. A better understanding of the system is achieved, however, by considering the PD to represent a more general phenomenon, that of the "cooperative" defense attorney. Indeed, one of the pitfalls of studying the administration of criminal law from the point of view of only one of the institutional participants is that the analyst may fail to see the possibilities of reconceptualization. To the prosecutor, it matters not so much whether a defendant is being represented by a PD as whether the defense attorney, regardless of his institutional base, can be counted upon as a "cooperative" defense attorney, a category that usually includes leading private defense attorneys and only some of the members of the PD's office.

In the county studied, for example, of the six leading private defense attorneys, five report that they settle a greater percentage of their cases by plea of guilty than does the public defender. The one exception settles approximately half his cases in this manner, as compared with upwards of 90 percent for the remainder of the private defense attorney community. There are, however, characteristics distinguishing him from the other leading private defense attorneys. As the leading Negro defense attorney in the area, he represents a predominantly Negro clientele. Some of his clients are small-time "professional" criminals for whom it is difficult to make attractive deals because of prior records. In addition, he is an exceptional courtroom advocate, likely the most articulate in

† D. Sudnow, Normal Crimes: Sociological Features of the Penal Code in a Public Defender Office, 12 Social Problems at 273 (1965).

the community, and therefore fares well in the courtroom. Furthermore, his clients generally expect a posture of challenge and defiance, and would mistrust an attorney who appeared to cooperate too closely with the prosecutor and the police. Finally, he tends himself to share the disestablishmentarian view of his clientele, and argues with other defense attorneys over the wisdom of their cooperative tactics. Since he is reinforced in his beliefs by client opinion, he maintains a more challenging posture than the leading white defense attorneys.

A similar report of cooperation, however, was made to the writer by a leading criminal defense firm in an eastern city (employing Negro as well as white lawyers). Each of the other private defense attorneys interviewed made statements *vis-à-vis* relations with the prosecutor which were similar to each other's and also to statements made by the members of the public defender's office. One such statement will suffice to illustrate:

> You have to know the law to practice criminal law, but you also have to know the ropes. Our office is on very good terms with the prosecutor's office, because they trust us. We never misrepresent to them, and we don't degrade them, or the police or their witnesses. But don't get the idea that we don't represent our clients well. If we didn't do that we wouldn't get all the criminal business that we now have — and we could treble our criminal practice if we were to charge smaller fees. When we settle cases, we get a reduction of the original charge in virtually every case. Not only that, but our clients are treated better by the police, and as a result, the prosecutor often has a weaker case against them than he might have. Whenever we can, we have our client bailed out as soon as possible, and instruct the police that we don't want them talking to the client. We're on very good terms with the police. — Of course [one of his partners chimed in], we've handled civil matters for a lot of detectives, and we give them a break on the fee.

Every leading white defense attorney interviewed insisted that the layman's notion of adversariness was not in the interests of their clients, and that their clients did better as a result of a "cooperative" posture. It should also be noted, of course, that "cooperation" is in the interests of the defense attorney as well as the prosecutor. Usually, defense attorneys charge a set fee for a defense regardless of whether a trial takes place, although in civil cases it is customary to charge by the hour. Thus it may be to the economic advantage of the private defense attorney to plead his client guilty. Indeed, in this respect, the PD enjoys greater flexibility to maintain an adversarial posture than the private defense attorney. One judge interviewed, critical of the practices of some private attorneys, suggested that the fee sometimes deters private defense attorneys from pleading their client guilty. "They often find it hard to collect a fee after their client has been convicted. While a defendant is out on bail, he tries to raise his legal fees, sometimes in illegal activities."

As for the question of testing the constitutionality of procedures and statutes, defense attorneys generally regard this as a naive view of the practice of criminal law in the routine criminal case. There is a great deal of publicity given to constitutional decisions, but appellate courts overturn relatively few decisions of trial courts, although the publicity given to such cases tends to create an appearance of review and instability. It is rare, however, for the average local defense attorney to base his strategy of defense on procedural error in the routine case, whether he is a private attorney or a PD.

Most private defense attorneys usually operate on a theory of defense similar to that of the public defender, and "bargain" as willingly as he. This theory presupposes the guilt of the client, as a general matter, and the fact that pleas of guilty are so common tends to reinforce the presumption of guilt throughout the system. It is a theory that stresses administrative regularity over challenge, and emphasizes decisions most likely to maximize gain and minimize loss in the negatively valued commodity of penal "time." As a leading private defense attorney writes:

> The public image of a criminal lawyer, as well as that of a general practitioner, is of a trial gladiator eloquently arguing for the acquittal of his client. But it has long been clear to the criminal law specialist, and should be to the general practitioner, that at some points the criminal process is moving away from a strictly adversary proceeding, and the district attorney as well as the criminal defense lawyer is interested in arriving at a settlement or compromising the matter in a way that will bring substantial justice to the defendant and to society. . . .*

By law, judges are usually responsible for calculating the sentence. It sometimes happens that the defense attorney will ask the judge for an indication of sentence prior to a plea of guilty. Some defense attorneys are on close enough personal terms with some

---

* S. P. Golde, Interviewing Clients: Initial Steps, California Criminal Law Practice, California Continuing Education of the Bar, at 118 (1964).

judges that they may speak to them "off the cuff." In most cases, however, when the defense attorney approaches the judge he seeks to implement an agreement already worked out with the prosecutor. Since the judge is also under administrative pressure, he rarely rejects a plea of guilty, and also rarely fails to cooperate with the defense attorney and prosecutor who have worked out a "deal." Thus a typical plea bargain encompasses a reduction of charges, a limitation of the potential sentence, and an agreement from the prosecutor to urge the judge to sentence in accord with an agreement between defense attorney and prosecutor.

In such negotiations, a norm of "rationality" or "reasonableness" prevails; the defense attorney is expected to accept a sentence that would be in the "interests" of the community as well as his client. While the adversary system contemplates an aggressive defense, the "cooperative" system alters the nature of the services that the defense attorney is capable of performing for his client. He may often act less as an advocate than as a "coach," preparing his client to meet the behavioral and attitudinal standards acceptable to criminal law officialdom. For example, one case was observed in which a young man had been convicted of stealing a purse from an eighty-five year old woman. When his attorney asked what he would say to the parole officer, the youth replied with an answer that was exculpatory and defensive, "Well, I needed the money. Anyhow, all we did was take her purse, we didn't hurt her." The attorney instructed the youth that he must not defend his action. Through a series of questions and answers the youth finally understood how to make a "pitch" that was apologetic and repentant — "It was a very bad thing to do; I don't know why I did it." With such a response on the presentence report, the attorney is then in a position to argue for a lighter sentence, and the judge is in a better position to grant it. Thus "cooperation" implies an understanding of the requirements of the other functionaries in the system, "ability" implies the capacity to fulfill those needs, and "rationality" or "reasonableness" suggests the acceptance of prevailing assumptions.

Not only does the public defender tend to follow a theory of his role similar to that of most private defense attorneys, but he is, in some respects, better equipped to carry it out. First, given the administrative concerns of the prosecutor's office, the public defender, as an *office*, ultimately enjoys a greater capacity to frustrate, precisely because he controls so many cases. To be sure, he also requires the "cooperation" of the prosecutor, but then, the prosecutor also needs the cooperation of the public defender. It is a nice question as to which actually exerts more leverage, and very difficult to measure. Nevertheless, in the course of the study, members of both offices indicated an awareness of and respect for the other's potential to impede the administrative concerns of each. Further, regardless of whether the prosecutor has more leverage over the public defender than the PD has over the DA, as a result of the cases it controls, the PD's office is in a structurally advantageous position when compared to the individual private defense attorney. Thus, contrary to the argument that the social structure necessarily imposes cooperation in DA-PD relations and, by implication, makes the private attorney a more adversarial agent in comparison, the structure of the situation would appear to give the PD relatively greater organizational leverage over the DA. . . .

## "Client Control" and Adversariness

If game theory is reviewed, we learn that models are typically based on an assumption of two sets of interests. The adversary system, as described, is clearly a "mixed-motive" game, that is, "one in which the goals of the players are partially coincident and partially in conflict" * . . . if we consider the defense attorney and the prosecutor as the players. In addition to the problem of deciding strategy vis-à-vis the prosecutor, however, the defense attorney also experiences the problem of maintaining decisional authority within the context of a normative system of *representation*. Thus the notion that an attorney "represents" a client is not altogether clear. It might mean that he accepts his client's view of the strategy of the case, and offers the client his technical knowledge of various branches of law to implement the client's strategy. In practice, however, this does not seem to be the accepted definition. On the contrary, the defense attorneys typically understand the idea of representation to suggest that the attorney is responsible both for strategy and tactics, that is, that the attorney is the "player." His task is understood as explaining to the client the legal consequences of the facts of the case, and to advise both strategy and tactics on the basis of his interpretation of the facts. His client, however, may not be disposed to accept such an interpretation of the attorney's role. When that occurs, the attorney feels that his reputation may be damaged, since it rests upon a consistent achievement of outcomes over a period of time. Thus, as between attorney and client, there is also a mixed-motive game.

* P. S. Gallo, Jr., and C. G. McClintock, Cooperative and Competitive Behavior in Mixed-Motive Games, 9 J. Conflict Resolution 68-77 (1965).

Among the attorneys studied, this game is typically referred to as "client-control." It is a problem experienced by all defense attorneys, but is exaggerated in relations between the public defender and his client. A special problem of "client control" exists for the public defender because he has not been selected by his client. For example, a private attorney might inform his client that if he insists on going to trial, against the attorney's advice, the attorney will withdraw from the case. Or he might advise his client that he will take the case to trial if the client insists, but that a trial will be costly. As between public defender and client, however, a different relationship obtains.

It is not so much that "when the defendant himself attempts to direct attention to his innocence . . . such attempts are never taken seriously by the PD but are seen as 'innocent pitches,' as 'being wise,' as 'not knowing what is good for him' ". . . . * It is rather that when the defendant declares his innocence, the public defender does not accept such declarations at face value, and in effect cross-examines his client. Such a course of action is, however, a standard practice for defense attorneys in general. There is an axiom of legal practice that the lawyer attempts to learn the truth from his client, in the interest of his client. To do otherwise would be to abrogate his responsibility to construct the strategy of the defense, since he cannot successfully construct such a strategy without being able to anticipate the strength of the prosecution's case. It is true that the private cross-examination of one's own defendant is an art, and that some members of the PD's office have not cultivated it as well as others. The art consists in separating the client's illegal behavior from his general moral character, just as a medical doctor segregates the patient's illness from his total self-conception. Thus, the discussion centers around legally related facts, inviting not a confession of immorality as much as a disclosure of reality.

The PD does not, however, "require," as Sudnow writes . . . , "that his 'clients' agree with whatever action he takes 'on their behalf.' " † Sudnow's own quotation indicates just the opposite. He quotes the public defender as stating:

> Can you imagine what might happen if we went straight to the
> DA with a deal to which the client later refused to agree? Can you

* D. Sudnow, Normal Crimes: Sociological Features of the Penal Code in a Public Defender Office, 12 Social Problems 272 (1965).
† Ibid.

see him in court screaming how the PD sold him out? As it is we get plenty of letters purporting to show why we don't do our job. Judges are swamped with letters condemning the PD. Plenty of appeals are started this way.

Thus it is not simply that the PD requires his clients to agree with his actions, but rather that the PD fears his clients or, at least, is fearful of a charge that he misled his client. He is sensitive to his vulnerability arising out of the situation of assignment rather than selection.

It is true, however, as Sudnow suggests, that when the defendant "refuses to face the facts" the PD understands he will lose when he enters the courtroom. Such a trial is referred to by Sudnow as a "routine trial," and is referred to in the system as a "slow plea of guilty" or a "second degree" trial. It is, indeed, a "fixed" trial, since the presumed antagonists merely put on a show. They have already decided what the outcome will be, on the basis of their knowledge of the facts. But two further implications drawn by Sudnow are not true. One is the suggestion that all trials conducted by the PD are "fixed." The other is that "slow pleas of guilty" are unknown to private defense attorneys.

Reliable statistics on fixed trials are, of course, impossible to obtain, and prudence prevents an observer from even speculating on the proportions of such trials. Nevertheless it is probable, in terms of the social structure of the system, that the PD goes to "routine trial" with proportionately greater frequency than does the private defense attorney, precisely because of his exceptional problems of client control. We have indicated that the PD does not command the sanctions of client control that the private defense attorney does. Furthermore, it is difficult for the PD to establish a situation of trust between himself and his client. It was not possible to interview privately more than six clients of the public defender, but of those six, three expressed the idea that since the PD is a public official, he must have a "tie-in" with the police and the DA. Several defendants also complained that they felt that nobody in the public defender's office was taking a personal interest in the case.

Clients of the public defender tend, in fact, to be treated as "files" or "cases," although in important cases they may be given considerable attention. It is fair to observe, however, that the "treatment" given to a client is usually more analogous to that given by an efficient hospital clinic than to that offered by an outstanding private physician. Whether the society can afford to give more is presently beside the point. Relevant here is the fact that the PD probably serves a more mistrustful, suspicious class of clients than private defense attorneys even if the *stated* basis of mistrust — that the PD is paid out of the same pocket as the DA while private defense attorneys are not — is mistaken. The mistrust, however, seems to lead to an incapacity to control clients, and to a measure of prophetic self-fulfillment regarding "routine trials." Since the PD cannot exert the sanctions on the client that are available to the private defense attorney, it is likely that he goes to "second degree" trials with proportionately greater frequency and less apparent adversariness than his private counterpart.

### Conclusion

The public defender represents a class of defendants who differ from those of the private defense attorney. They are more numerous. They are indigent, and are therefore more likely to exhibit such disadvantages of poverty as inarticulateness, relative inability to aid in their own defense, relative lack of knowledge of constitutional rights, and inability to make bail. They also have not selected their defense attorney by choice, and therefore tend to be more critical and hostile toward their attorney from the start of the case. Despite such differences, however, critics of the public defender have tended to underestimate the quality of defense provided by the public defender, in part because they have failed to take into account the socioeconomic differences between the public defender's clients and those of the private defense attorney, and in part because they have neglected to make distinctions among personnel in the public defender's office.

They also fail to make two important distinctions among private defense attorneys when they make implied comparisons between the PD as an institution and the class of private defense attorneys. Both Williams and Sudnow, for example, seem to have as their model of the private defense attorney someone very much like Edward Bennett Williams. That is, when they compare the public defender as an institution with the private defense attorney as an institution, the comparison is with the most able private defense attorney. Thus, when interviewed regarding their opinion of the public defender, other criminal attorneys might indicate the top men in the office, and conclude that the public defender is "just as good" as the private attorney, or they might consider a particular case that had been handled poorly by a member of the PD's staff, and conclude that the public defender was not so able.

Second, critics tend to confound ability with "hostility" when in fact the most able private defense attorneys, who operate on the local level, are no less "partners" of the district attorney than the public defender. The problem of the adversary system is maintaining the ethic of individuality and challenge in a system where the professionals will see greater advantage in cooperativeness than in conflict. That the prosecutor has his concerns for administrative efficiency and public relations creates a situation for the defense attorney — whether private or public — in which he must take account of the prosecutor's capacity to offer his client a less punitive outcome than he might receive if he were to challenge the state. Most defense attorneys strongly defend the system on pragmatic grounds. "The trial," said one cooperative defense attorney, "is a situation where reasonable minds cannot agree. Not only does it cost money to run a trial, but trials often get defendants into trouble."

Although such arguments are undeniably persuasive, their basic difficulty, in terms of the ethic of the adversary system, is that they assume the outcome. If we return to the metaphor of the *sporting event*, the pragmatic position comes down to deciding the outcome on the basis of expert estimate. It is as if sports champions were to be declared on the basis of expert predictions. Most of the time, odds-makers are correct in their estimates, but they are sometimes wrong. Just as an expert might be wrong in predicting how a fighter might fare on a particular night, or how a football team might play, so too a lawyer might be wrong in predicting how well witnesses might stand up at trial, which evidence will be admitted by the judge, the tendencies of the jury, and so forth.

The dilemma of the adversary system, however, is that the experts will so frequently be correct in their estimates. It may not be so easy to predict the outcome of a game between the Green Bay Packers and the Chicago Bears, but it does not require an expert to know that either the Bears or the Packers could defeat the Harvard eleven on any given afternoon. Many criminal cases are of this order of predictability before trial. Assuming such a situation, it might be to the advantage of Harvard to accept a recorded defeat of 21-0, when in the actual contest the Bears or the Packers could roll up 60 or 70 points. Similarly, it is frequently in the interests of the defendant to plead to a lesser charge, rather than to engage the prosecutor in an actual courtroom contest. What this situation leads to is a system where the principal combatants are continually "regressing" to a state of cooperation. This state, in turn, threatens to undermine the ethic of genuine conflict underlying the system.

Regression toward cooperation, is, however, a general propensity found in all conflict situations. As Schelling says* . . . , "Pure conflict, in which the interests of two antagonists are completely opposed, is a special case; it would arise in a war of complete extermination, otherwise not even in war. For this reason, 'winning' in a conflict does not have a strictly competitive meaning; it is not winning relative to one's adversary. It means gaining relative to one's own value system; and this may be done by bargaining, by mutual accommodation, and by the avoidance of mutually damaging behavior." It is only when the maintenance of conflict is itself a value, *as a procedural ethic*, that tendencies toward cooperation become a social control problem for the system advocating the ethic. In such a system there is always a tipping point where cooperation may shade off into collusion, thereby subverting the ethical basis of the system.

This analysis of the social control problem of the adversary system raises the further issue of the nature and scope of the adversary system. Although the paper is not specifically addressed to that question, we ought not conclude without some comment on it, since this more general issue has implications for both legal scholarship and the development of legal doctrine in the area of criminal procedure.

One way to view the adversary system is to place it squarely in the context of an adjudicatory proceeding. "The essence of an adversary system," writes Lon L. Fuller† . . . , "is that each side is accorded a participation in the decision that is reached, a participation that takes the form of presenting proofs and arguments." Fuller's view of the adversary system derives from his more general conception of adjudication, ". . . a process of decision in which the affected party — the litigant — is afforded an institutionally guaranteed participation, which consists of the opportunity to present proofs and arguments for a decision in his favor" . . . . ‡ Fuller's definition of the adversary system is used as a contrasting model to the institution of the investigating magistrate, a system familiar to Europe and to Asia. In such a system, the investigating magistrate conducts his own inquiry and forms his conclusions on the basis of the evidence thus derived. By contrast, the adversary system emphasizes procedural restraints on the judiciary. It

* T. C. Schelling, The Strategy of Conflict at 4-5 (1960).

† R. Fuller, The Adversary System, Talks on American Law (H. Berman ed. 1961).

‡ R. Fuller, Collective Bargaining and the Arbitrator, 3 Wis. L. Rev. at 19 (1963).

is not enough that the judge be informed and impartial, an expectation applying to many social roles embodying an authority relation, such as that between parents and children and teachers and pupils. "The essence of the judicial function," states Fuller, "lies not in the substance of the conclusion reached, but in the procedures by which that substance is guaranteed" . . . .**

The body of this paper, however, has indicated a number of procedural features and functional consequences that occasion variation from the preceding model of the adversary system envisioned by Fuller. If the adversary system is defined with only the trial in mind, we are blinding ourselves to the realities of a system of decision that is predominantly pretrial in character. These pretrial proceedings are played out against a background of court congestion, eliciting the prominence of administrative concerns as compared to institutionally guaranteed participation. From the point of view of those with "interests" in the proceeding, at least four parties seem to be involved in the system — the complainant, the prosecutor, the defendant, the defense attorney. From this perspective, the ideas of representation and of a "side" become problematic, since the long-term self-interest of the professionals in the system seems to influence the character of their participation in any given proceeding. Under such circumstances, adjudication does not define the adversary system, but is instead the outcome of a failure of pretrial negotiation, perhaps as frequently a failure of negotiation between attorney and client as between defense and prosecution.

It may be, however, that in stressing the centrality of adjudication in the adversary system, Fuller did not intend a *description* of the adversary system so much as a goal that the adversary system should aim toward. Such a view suggests the reordering of the conditions of decision in such a way as to maximize unity of interest between defense attorney and client, to further the ethic of challenge, and to afford to every defendant not only an attorney but also an adjudicatory proceeding — a *guaranteed* participation that takes the form of presenting proofs and arguments. In the meantime, however, we must seek to understand the realities of our present system for the administration of criminal justice, neither assuming a reality on the basis of stated ideals, nor succumbing to the inevitability of a reality that deviates from the ideal.

** Id. at 18.

# The Problem of Objectivity in Judicial Decision-Making*

## Alexander B. Smith, Abraham S. Blumberg

In no other area of judicial behavior has judicial decision-making been subjected to as much criticism and scrutiny as in the case of the sentencing power and the manner in which it is exercised by the judges of our criminal courts. The quality of "objectivity" which is so earnestly sought, is problematic at best in the social world where competing visions of truth abound. The judge as well as the social scientist can only strive to minimize the emotional, the idiosyncratic elements in his intellectual processes, but cannot eliminate them altogether. Men live in a world in which most of their knowledge and perspectives are socially constructed for them. That is to say, their stock of knowledge and motives for action are ordered within the confines of a particular biography which has been shaped in a given social context. The judge, like the scientific observer therefore, must strive to detach himself from his biographical situation, at least that is what the judicial role prescribes in ideal terms. However, in any given society, the role of a sentencing judge has been exercised in accordance with the ethos of that particular society or social order at that particular time. Over the years the judge, lawyer or anyone else connected with the enforcement of laws has performed his function in accordance with the particular demands of a given society. That has not been done in a mechanical manner, and at any one time there has been wide variation in the manner in which different judges have treated similar problems of sentencing. Consideration of these variations can in all likelihood be explained by differences in the personality of judges and the differential impact of public opinion.

There is a further problem occasioned by regional differences which make the possibilities of objectivity and uniformity in sentencing practice quite problematic. America is simply not a homogeneous nation and efforts to attain uniformity in sentencing will be frustrated by the local flavor of judicial decision-making. Attitudes toward certain crimes or types of offenders are quite different

    * From: 46 Social Forces 96-105 (1967). Reprinted by permission of the University of North Carolina Press.

from one community to another. Rape, drug selling and auto theft mean different things in terms of sentence disposition and ultimate treatment depending upon the community being examined.

When the sentences imposed within the federal and various state court systems are reviewed, a marked disparity, lack of uniformity and absence of objectivity in the severity of punishment is apparent. Within the legal framework of these court systems, the laws usually provide for minimum and maximum limits for sentences to penal institutions. Within these limits, to which are added the other possibilities for sentences: restitution, reparations, fines, suspended sentences, probation, or some combination of these forms of punishment, our judges have been given tremendous latitude in their sentencing powers.

Efforts to study sentencing and judicial decision-making generally have centered about the decisions made, rather than the judge–decision-maker. It is the purpose of this paper to present some further evidence of the structural difficulties attendant upon the possibility of "objectivity" in sentencing which flow from the judicial role-set. We will employ the bench of a major criminal court in our analysis, in order to explore some of the social and psychological problems which may inevitably be encountered, and which tend to make judicial objectivity and uniformity in sentencing illusory if not impossible. We shall for convenience call the court from which the data were drawn, "Central Sessions."

### SOCIODEMOGRAPHIC VARIABLES IN RECRUITMENT

By the time he has been elected to the bench, the mean age of a Central Sessions judge is 51 years. Retirement is mandatory at 70. In the more than 200 years of its existence, Central Sessions justices have always been males.

Of the nine justices who regularly sit in Central Sessions, only one is a graduate of one of the national law schools, the others are graduates of the part-time proprietary or "factory" type of law school. Three out of the nine justices completed their baccalaureate work before going on to law school. Insofar as their legal education was concerned, its course content did little to prepare them for their actual functions on the bench. Virtually all of the course materials in most of the law schools are of the "bread and butter" variety, directed toward the candidate passing the bar examination of the particular state. Only rarely do they concern themselves with the serious issues and questions raised in connection with law administration and virtually never do they deal with social and economic implications of law and legal decision-making. As a consequence there is no formal, systematic body of knowledge in legal education which one can point to, by way of indicating a minimal body of information one must possess as a requisite for the judicial career. Central Sessions judges are therefore, for the most part, as are most criminal court judges, poorly equipped to deal with the role challenges, dilemmas and problems with which they are to be confronted on the bench. An intricate knowledge of the criminal law is only rudimentary knowledge in the context of the onerous demands made by the criminal court bench.

Because he is ill-equipped to be a sophisticated decision-maker in a job that requires decision-making daily and routinely and at the same time requires him to be an administrator, manager, and routineer, he must lean heavily on the services of others. As a consequence, Central Sessions justices, when they are initially appointed, are "broken in" by court clerks and other civil service functionaries who will socialize them in terms of the "practical" side of all the organizational features, goals and requirements of Central Sessions. Interestingly, much of the socialization of justices in Central Sessions, being performed by minor civil service functionaries, is actually actively sought by the judges in order to make their own work lives easier, more pleasant and to assuage their personal insecurities. As a matter of organizational and personal practicality, regardless of their individual predilections, they learn to accept and internalize, for the most part, the routineering and ritualism of their socializers.

Three of the nine justices had some prior judicial experience in courts of inferior criminal jurisdiction. In addition, the only justice who had attended a national law school (who we shall hereinafter refer to as Judge A), had some prior experience in a lower civil court. All had a history of extensive political activity and close clubhouse ties, four of the group having served briefly in their careers as assistant district attorneys in the office of the prosecutor. All had engaged in private civil practice for periods ranging from six to 20 years, and also had taken on some "criminal work" as part of their law practice. None were employed by a major "Wall Street" type law firm, but were instead associates or partners in small or moderate sized firms whose major practice was in the lower-level courts. They were all moderately successful in terms of their income from practice, although two of the group possessed inherited wealth and were persons of financial means apart from their law practice. In terms of economic wealth, however, the other seven justices were never able to financially support more than an upper-middle-class life style, and that, rather precariously.

Intellectually, none were considered outstanding academically, except possibly Judge A who was, however, an average student at the Ivy League law school he attended. None possessed remarkable talents, although one of their number, Judge C liked to paint in oils. None were outstanding practitioners, or even noted political figures before their elevation to judicial office. They were, however, noted to be assiduous, loyal and reliable party workers who made considerable contributions of time, money, or both, to their respective political clubs. The first indicia of political reward for their services, was in the nature of a law clerkship to a judge, an assignment to the office of the district attorney or some minor court post. Judge A was most fortunate in not only being possessed of personal wealth, but began his judicial career as a lower civil court justice.

All the justices are sons of professional, proprietor, medium sized mercantile or managerial fathers. Except for Justice J, the only Negro on the bench in Central Sessions, they are all second or third generation individuals. Almost uniformly, they are the sons of middle- and upper-middle-class families. Political leaders have often claimed to make a tacit assumption that the bench's ethnic and religious composition, writ large, should be the same as the electorate's. The Central Sessions bench, in terms of religious affiliation, consists of four Roman Catholics, two Protestants and three Jews. For several decades, there has always been at least one Negro justice in the court, an obvious token, since the Central Sessions geographic jurisdiction includes a substantial Negro population. The Roman Catholic justices include three Irish Catholic and one Italian Catholic, which tends to indicate the still strong dominance by Irish groups in the Church, whose political influence is acknowledged by all the political professionals in Central Sessions to be considerable.

In contrast with the "grand tradition" judge, who almost invariably comes from an upper-class background possessed of family traditions and other elitist features, seven of the Central Sessions justices came from an almost prosaic middle- and upper-middle-class background. Only one justice, Judge C, is the son of a former city official, who is reputed to have garnered the family fortune in the course of his civic duties. Justice A, the other judge of considerable means derived his wealth from his father's successful mercantile venture.

The American Dream, involving as it does the belief in the triumph of achieved status, has many limitations, qualifications and exceptions in terms of the realities of the stratification system. Nevertheless, there is a continuing popular belief, that the field of politics is one area which has constituted an important exception to class rigidities and distinctions. It is for the most part assumed that politics offers greater possibilities of social mobility than any other activity. The experience of judges of Central Sessions, however, as one aspect of the political field, would appear to indicate that lower-level judges are drawn from the middle and upper-middle strata. Insofar as economic mobility is concerned, Central Sessions justices for the most part, would appear to belie any of the pervasive notions of political activity generating greater mobility than other activities. The fathers of the justices were at least as successful as their sons, although the judge's occupation is assigned higher prestige.

While minority group membership is no bar, the minority group member must have more than satisfied middle-class requisites and to have demonstrated close attachment to what are deemed the superior virtues of that social group, as well as fierce party loyalty and financial support.

### JUDICIAL DECISION-MAKING AND ANOMIE

A variety of contextual frames of reference have been employed by commentators to explain and clarify the basis for judicial decision-making, the most fundamental aspect of the judge's job. These range from exploration of the judge's personality to the employment of small group theory, game theory and Guttman scaling to measure and apprehend the nature of judicial decision-making. Indeed, the disciplined effort to identify with mathematical precision the decision process has been dubiously termed "jurimetrics."

To indicate some of the more significant variables which inhere in the decision-making dimension of judicial activity, one can begin by observing that a critical factor will be the level of the court. Upper-level judges will be more scrupulously concerned with the niceties of legalism and legal requirements, the voluminous case pressure and daily administrative stridencies and tensions of the lower courts being absent from their work situation. The relative distance of upper-level judges from the ebb and flow of the interpersonal dynamics of the persons involved, and the point of origin of the issues to be decided, affords them the structural possibilities of sagelike, rather than bureaucratic and instrumental role performance.

Of course individual aspects of a judge's social biography will be relevant in terms of his decision-making, regardless of the level of the court in which he sits. Similarly, political pressures, visible and invisible will manifest themselves. Even though there may be no pressures as to specific cases, the judge may not wish to offend those who have contributed to his past, or may control his future, when he comes up for reappointment or renomination. Only Federal judges and some higher appellate state justices are appointed for life and are thus presumably above political pressures, although even they may be interested in being promoted. Inasmuch as judgeships are often likely to be political rewards, there is likely to be an assumption of repayment by the judge for the reward, although such assumptions are apt to be tacit on both sides. Appropriate repayment may be in the form of judicial sympathy for the interests of the sponsor or former associates of the judge when litigation involving such interests comes before the judge. The judges of Central Sessions, being elected for a term of years, and not for life, must always maintain a keen sensitivity to the desires, requirements and interests of their political sponsors in their decision-making. In point of fact, the "easy" decision is the one that is politically inspired in terms of a visit to the judge's chamber by the politically visible lawyer, who represents a defendant awaiting pleading or sentence.

Socioeconomic and class variables, as these may differentially impinge upon judges in terms of attitudinal biases, are well known. Even the kind of law school he attended, or the nature of his practice before his judicial career, are elements in judicial decision-making. Thus, a judge who has been engaged in a corporate or a commercial civil practice may have an entirely different decision pattern than one who has devoted much of his prior practice to criminal law and negligence. Class factors will, of course, have been a strong influence in the sort of structural opportunities available for the kind of practice the judge will have had previously. Indeed, sometimes a judge may be reacting against his past as a criminal lawyer, and become extremely harsh and punitive when dealing with the kind of criminals he used to defend, as is the case with at least one well-known judge.

The nonrational aspect of judicial decision-making may be best summed up by a confessional statement by one of America's leading contributors to jurisprudence, Chancellor James Kent. He indicated well over a century ago, in explaining how he reached a decision, that "... I might once in a while be embarrassed by a technical rule, but I almost always found principles suited to my view of the case..." [10]

Even the much revered Oliver Wendell Holmes has indicated, "... a decision is the unconscious result of instinctive prejudices and inarticulate connections..." and "even the prejudices which judges share with their fellow men have a good deal more to do than the syllogism in determining the rules by which men should be governed." [11]

The legal literature, for the most part, deals with the problems of judicial decision-making at the appellate level. At the level of Central Sessions, the matter is much more complex because of the incredibly greater number of decisions that have to be made, the greater variety of publics that have to be served by the judge, and the greater anxiety on the part of the judge because the legal rules, in and of themselves, do not furnish adequate guidelines for his behavior. For example, were the Central Sessions judges to permit themselves to be bound by statutory provisions in connection with sentencing procedures, they would come into conflict with many groups in and out of the court, who have vested interests in mitigating sentencing requirements and other rules. The judicial ambivalence to rules is also apparent in connection with institutionalized evasions of the Canons of Judicial Ethics, especially Canon No. 14 requiring that "a judge should not be swayed by partisan demands," and No. 28 forbidding his participation in politics except in connection with his own election. These requirements are a significant aspect of "deregulation" in the daily work of a Central Sessions justice. This is so, because a key dimension in his decision-making process is responses to continuing commitments to politically visible clubhouse lawyers. They are part of a constant procession of visitors to the judge's chambers, where there is negotiation as to plea and sentence. Many of these minutiae of negotiation, and exchanges of views and information are not conducted by the judge himself, but are performed by his confidential law secretary. He, in turn, is a clubhouse emissary, sensitive to clubhouse demands, awaiting career mobility as he serves a particular Central Sessions justice in that capacity. He is also the judge's roving eyes and ears in all the other areas of court activity including

10. Jerome Frank, Law and the Modern Mind (New York: Doubleday & Co., 1963), p. 112....

11. Oliver W. Holmes, The Common Law (Boston: Little, Brown & Co., 1886), p. 35.

the office of the district attorney, probation division and the Legal-Aid group.

Central Sessions judges develop a set of rationalizations couched in "community service" and "concern with social problems" in order to obviate the more strident violations of the foregoing Canons. They are caught in a bind which by the nature of their office compels them to behave with bureaucratic concern for production, efficient administration and at the same time to be instruments of their political benefactors' particularistic designs and concerns.

Another aspect of the anomic character of judicial conduct is reflected in the negative judicial attitude in Central Sessions in connection with placing an individual on probation if he has been convicted after a jury trial. The justices, from time to time, make public affirmations to the effect that jury trial is a central element of justice and due process. But, privately, in their decision-making process they will, as a rule, deny a probation disposition to a jury-convicted offender. In point of fact, the judges, the district attorney and the probation report will upon sentence of such an individual, make explicit reference to the issue, that "the defendant has caused the state to go to the expense of a trial." In 1962, the Central Sessions probation division investigated a total of 3,643 out of the total 4,363 cases that were processed that year. Of the number investigated, 1,195 were placed on probation, or 30.88 percent of those investigated. All but three of those who had been placed on probation, had pleaded guilty *before* trial.

Lower-level judges in their decision-making and administrative conduct are much more visible than are their appellate colleagues in the middle and upper courts. In a study of 30 appellate judges, three of whom were from Federal courts and the rest of whom were members of various state superior courts, the justices were asked to define the least favorable aspects of their work. Two-thirds of the respondents identified their isolation as the least favorable aspect of being an appellate judge. "I am segregated from the political, social, and economic arenas of life in which our destinies are shaped," was a comment that tended to summarize other similar comments. Two judges simply responded with one word, "loneliness." Another judge deplored his "lack of personal contact with the litigants, witnesses and others who play a part in each case." In the case of the Central Sessions judges, the situation is reversed. Here the justices are able to diffuse the anxieties and responsibilities of the decision-making process. As in any other bureaucracy, in the lower-level court, the span and scope of decision-making is limited. Because there is perhaps even greater anxiety generated in the criminal court, due to the nature of the decisions made, the Central Sessions judges make an even more active effort to diffuse responsibility and authority than is usual in bureaucracy. They simply are reluctant to carry the entire burden, and unlike the appellate courts, there are ample intermediaries and interstitial people, and groups who can be invoked, to share in the responsibilities which are ultimately only that of the judge. Reluctant to shoulder the decision-making burden, and ambivalent toward formal rules and criteria as these may interfere with his informal relations with his political benefactors, lawyers, and other court personnel, the judge tailors each decision-making process to suit his own needs. Thus, different decisions will result in the judge involving specific kinds of personnel in the court setting, to diffuse responsibility and at the same time alleviate his own formal obligations.

In examining three fundamentally separate areas of decision-making procedures, it becomes evident that Central Sessions decision-making is anything but the traditional, Solomon-like decision role performance of the judge. While it is bureaucratic in character in terms of its rationality, the procedures also admit of the informal relations characteristic of that form of social organization. Thus for example, one of the administrative functions of Central Sessions judges is budget-making. The formal structure of the court's fiscal personnel will be involved in the mechanical aspects of drawing up the budget. But specific, politically, visible personnel, will be involved on an informal level to counsel them as to the actual distribution of the funds in a manner which will most effectively contribute to organizational discipline, morale and control. The Central Sessions judges review the final distribution, only in the most perfunctory, ministerial manner, for it represents decisions actually arrived at by others which simply awaits their signature. What on the surface appears to be an administrative delegation based on the expertise and superior knowledge of those consulted, is in reality an effort at diffusion of decision-making responsibility. It is also a subtle design for the internal distribution of patronage and rewards for continued loyalty to the judges, on the part of their subordinates.

A second area of decision-making procedure in which the judge is supposed to have a major role, but which he relinquishes in large measure, is the determination of the nature of the plea which is to be accepted when an accused pleads guilty before trial. Central Sessions judges are largely content to "pass the buck" in this decision area to the district attorney, who will ordinarily frame the nature of the lesser plea to be accepted, in connection with the original offense for which an accused has been charged. Traditional judicial formulations would require the judge to serve as an instrument of the whole community in reviewing the propriety of an accepted lesser plea. However, here too, Central Sessions judges have abdicated, and prefer to have the district attorney in negotiation with counsel, structure the dimensions of the lesser plea. While the judge may have the right to refuse a given plea, he rarely does so. Although Central Sessions procedures are highly rational, it is often surprising to observe the frequent number of spontaneous, last minute, private conferences at the judge's bench in which minor details of a lesser plea are to be ironed out.

It is, however, in the area of sentencing that judges manifest their greatest ambivalence and inconsistency, displaying wide variation in their sentence practices. While differences in sentence practice are to some extent reflections of the differential character of judicial social biography, they can in the main be accounted for in terms of pressures that are present or absent in a given sentencing situation. The harsh fact about being a criminal court judge is, that some men may glory in it, still others are entirely ambivalent about the responsibilities imposed in sentencing their fellow men to prison or death. The latter description for the most part fits the Central Sessions judges. They, therefore, have arranged for elaborate probation and psychiatric services in the form of reports which they can "lean on," in deciding the otherwise dubious case. Where there are strong political considerations or where there is a mandatory penalty, and little exercise of discretion is possible, judicial decision-making is circumscribed. However, in many instances the judge is confronted with a sentencing situation in which particularistic criteria are lacking and the universalistic criteria or rules are either attenuated, unclear or have lost their viability in regulating judicial behavior. Many criminal penalties are simply too harsh or not feasible in terms of their enforcement. It is not here suggested that Central Sessions judges completely abdicate, and permit probation and psychiatric reports or a district attorney's recommendations to supplant their judgments. On the contrary, judges deliberately involve them, not only to diffuse responsibility or to mitigate his own anxieties, but that which *appears* to be a group decision is more palatable in organizational life to client, workers and the publics concerned.

In addition, the bureaucratic admonition of "cover yourself," applies as well to judicial conduct as it does to any other individual in the organizational world. The group decision functions not only to conceal individual mediocrity, but can also be pointed to as evidence of profound efforts to individualize, and at the same time make the administration of justice more uniform and equitable.

## PATTERNS OF JUDICIAL ROLE PERFORMANCE

As in the case of any other role, there are minimal prescriptive standards which any incumbent of the judicial role must meet. Just as no two incumbents can ever fill a role in precisely identical fashion, in like manner no two judges perform their judicial role obligations in a similar manner. Minimal standards are of course met, but there is a wide range of performance which is acceptable and perhaps even desirable in terms of organizational needs. For the bench, as a source of career satisfaction and meeting ego needs, furnishes in actuality, a rich variety of possibilities of differentiated role performance. Further, organizational requirements would appear to harness and exploit individual judicial idiosyncracies for organizational ends. Distribution of the Central Sessions workload may be viewed as a source of evidence of this feature of organizational life. The judges and their retinue are loathe to ever discuss the distribution of the workload among the judges. The reason for this becomes apparent in the examination of Table 1. Each of the nine judges had been rotated among the various "parts" of the court and thus, theoretically at least, had a reasonable possibility of equal access to the court's case workload.

TABLE 1
Distribution of Central Sessions Judicial Workload in 1962

| Number of Cases Disposed of | Judge | Percent of Total Caseload |
|---|---|---|
| 1519 | A | 34.82 |
| 112 | L | 2.57 |
| 198 | M | 4.54 |
| 1326 | C | 30.40 |
| 287 | J | 6.58 |
| 132 | P | 3.03 |
| 147 | K | 3.37 |
| 229 | D | 5.25 |
| 413 | G | 9.47 |
| 4363 | | |

It will be readily apparent that two judges, A and C, were responsible for disposing of more than half the court's total caseload during 1962. Further, the differential assignment and participation in the workload responsibilities of the court organization are reflective of the individual pattern of role performance of each judge. The individual, idiosyncratic characteristics of each judge, in terms of intellectual and emotional cathexis, are structurally employed and utilized to advance organizational drives, needs and ends.

In their actual role performance, as discerned in part from their workload activity, a typology of judicial role patterns involving six major patterns of role content may be perceived.

1. Intellectual-Scholar ⎱ Workhorses of
2. Routineer-Hack ⎰ the court
3. Political Adventurer-Careerist
4. Judicial Pensioner
5. The Hatchet-Man
6. Tyrant-Showboat-Benevolent Despot

Actually, the Central Sessions court has always during the course of its modern history had on its bench at any given time, one or two justices who have performed a substantial portion of its workload. The other justices might secretly chafe under this, but they are remarkably acquiescent about a situation which relieves them of a good deal of the burden and responsibility of the court's workload. Further, as a matter of organizational practicality in advancing goals of maximum production, it is perhaps more efficient to narrow the circle of individuals whose organizational role and mission it will be to accomplish these ends.

Judges A and C who are the "workhorses" of the court, perform their respective organizational roles on entirely different levels of work performance. Judge A, a graduate of an Ivy League law school, is the bench member with intellectual and scholarly leanings, but with a great personal need to be continuously involved in the fray of practice, and of "wheeling" and "dealing." A not uncommon sight in his courtroom is the tumultuous scene of a trial in progress, interrupted for the purpose of Judge A pausing to accept 15 to 20 lesser pleas of guilty; to hear motions on various matters affecting cases before him; to sentence a number of cases previously heard; to consult with lawyers, probation officials or members of the district attorney's staff. The other justices and members of the court community refer to Judge A's courtroom as a three-ringed circus, because of the manifold activities he conducts there in simultaneous fashion. His fellow judges tend to view the fact that he frequently works on Saturday, Sunday, holidays and at odd hours of the night, with consternation and misgivings. His passion for work is regarded with suspicion. However, all in the court community admit that Judge A gets results. He is sought after by lawyers for accused persons because it is generally known that Judge A is an eminently "practical" man who is more than willing to compromise a given situation in return for a plea. He is also very sensitive to political cues and his office has a veritable procession of individuals seeking his intervention, counsel and assistance.

Possessed of personal charm, wit and intelligence, Judge A views his organizational role as that of maximizing production, even if traditional rules have to be bent. Often, he utilizes his reputation for leniency and "practicality" as a means of disposing of the welter of cases, which are for those very reasons funneled to his "part" for disposition.

Judge C is a more traditional political figure on the bench. Like Judge A, he is possessed of inherited wealth. He is the son of a former important municipal official. Basically, his career aspirations are limited, but he greatly enjoys his work, which he is really incapable of handling in other than a routine fashion. His great production is a product of his easygoing, nonpunitive attitudes, coupled with his personal desire to make his mark in the organization. Because, he is otherwise prosaic and pedestrian, he is not viewed to be as threatening an individual by other judges, as is Judge A. The judgeship, for him, is simply a comfortable slot, a means of maintaining work and other ego needs which would not be otherwise available to him.

Judges G and J, are extremely well-connected politically, and as a result, their lackluster performance in Central Sessions is of no consequence. As "Political Adventurer-Careerist" types, their incumbency there will be shortlived, the bench is simply a temporary steppingstone to other political offices they desire. They have no profound interest in law or for that matter criminal law administration. They are more concerned with building their personal as well as organization empires elsewhere, and most of their efforts will be concerned, not with cases that come before them, but in manipulating the organization for their own ends. At times, they will attempt to develop favorable newspaper and media publicity about themselves and their judicial careers, as part of their overall career plan. Of course, some of these fail and find that they have been consigned to a lower court career destiny. The resulting bitterness and querulousness can transform them into either "pensioners," "routineers" or "tyrant" types.

The "Judicial Pensioner" is simply a judge who has been rewarded rather late in his political life with a judicial sinecure. He prefers to be left undisturbed, spend as little of his time as possible in court and desires an almost anonymous existence. He takes virtually no interest in the administrative activities of the court, and it is as though he were already retired. Judges L and M and P have had long, active political careers at the clubhouse level, and their ascent to the bench is simply viewed as a way of either discharging a political obligation, or even to get them safely out of the way.

The "Hatchet-Man" role is often played by a member of the bench who has previously had a career in the office of the district attorney. He has close ties to that office, the political clubhouse and other areas of power in municipal government. It is his role and function in the court to have presented to him those cases involving special difficulty because of their "public" nature. In other words, those cases characterized by crimes of delict, malfeasance or breach of trust committed by public officials and petty civil servants which place the municipal administration on the defensive. Further, all those accused persons who have by virtue of their failure to cooperate with the prosecuting authorities or whose cases involve special features of scandal or opprobrium, and are being avidly watched by the news media, are also grist for the "Hatchet-Man's" mill. It is his function to stage-manage an impression of swift justice; impassively, clinically and uniformly administered in the case of matters which have achieved notoriety or infamy, and which tend to be viewed as a test of the administrative mettle of the court organization.

The "Tyrant"-"Showboat"-"Benevolent Despot" is quite generally all three faces of one role performance in the same incumbent, presented on alternate occasions. He is the deeply hostile, frustrated, ambition-ridden individual who has been defeated in his career aspirations. He is at a dead end, and knows it. Possessed of an unbounding contempt and scorn for others, his grandiosity is incredible. He is the terror of his courtroom. Lawyers, accused persons and probation officers fear him and loathe him. District attorneys simply abide his irascible, acidulous, querulous, surly manner. The social context of the courtroom provides an outlet for the kind of sadistic exhibitionism which is characteristic of this judicial role. Largely rejected by his colleagues, this egocentric individual exploits his judicial post as a vehicle for presenting a spectacle calculated to attract the attention of the press. He glories in the publicity he receives, even if it is of a negative kind. His harshness and intemperance are occasionally relieved by acts of charity and forbearance, which he is quick to exploit through publicity in the news media.

The most destructive aspect of his conduct, however, is in the area of meeting his professional and legal obligations in the courtroom itself. Here, he completely dominates the proceedings and manipulates them toward his own ends or what he perceives to be his version of what is the truth and reality. He has complete control over the court stenographer, virtually furnishing the material the stenographer is to include or exclude from the record in connection with his own comments and statements, which may have been improper. He manipulates juries through smiles, smirks and unrecorded off-the-cuff comments which may tend to discredit a witness or a defendant's testimony during a trial. He intimidates defendants, privately threatens lawyers. Thus, cloaked in organizational authority and while appearing to be performing important activities in furtherance of organizational goals, he is meeting the needs of personal pathology.

In large measure, however, all the judicial types, despite the differential character of their performance, contribute to the court organization as a functioning mechanism. The division of labor in the court is not as random and fortuitous as may appear at the outset. Each judicial role type that has been indicated is cultivated, for each contributes in his own way to the total institutional arrangement, performing a systemic mission in terms of his own drives, needs and personality. As long as individual aberration does not materially interfere with the attainment of organization objectives of production and efficiency, it will be permitted to proceed undisturbed.

One commentator's view of the matter, perhaps an incorrect one, is that, "The appropriation of major aspects of bureaucratic organization as means for the satisfaction of personal needs is pathological." He regards personal behavior patterns which do not advance organizational goals as defiant, or in his words, "bureaupathic behavior." However, this would be an unrealistic assessment of the matter in the criminal court and other similar organizations. For, on the contrary, the individual needs are capitalized and rendered rational in the service of the court organization, performing functions and providing for a division of labor which is most efficacious in terms of the social and organizational realities.

The problem of objectivity then, is one which is not only dependent upon individual social biographies, but also is filtered through an organizational ethos of efficiency and maximum production, which overrides concerns for the ideal of objectivity and uniformity.

# The Decision to Prosecute*

# George F. Cole

This paper is based on an exploratory study of the Office of Prosecuting Attorney, King County (Seattle), Washington. The lack of social scientific knowledge about the prosecutor dictated the choice of this approach. An open-ended interview was administered to one-third of the former deputy prosecutors who had worked in the office during the ten year period 1955-1965. In addition, interviews were conducted with court employees, members of the bench, law enforcement officials, and others having reputations for participation in legal decision-making. Over fifty respondents were contacted during this phase. A final portion of the research placed the author in the role of observer in the prosecutor's office. This experience allowed for direct observation of all phases of the decision to prosecute so that the informal processes of the office could be noted. Discussions with the prosecutor's staff, judges, defendant's attorneys, and the police were held so that the interview data could be placed within an organizational context.

The primary goal of this investigation was to examine the role of the prosecuting attorney as an officer of the legal process within the context of the local political system. The analysis is therefore based on two assumptions. First, that the legal process is best understood as a subsystem of the larger political system. Because of this choice, emphasis is placed upon the interaction and goals of the individuals involved in decision-making. Second, and closely related to the first point, it is assumed that broadly conceived political considerations explained to a large extent "who gets or does not get — in what amount — and how, the good (justice)

---

* From: 4 Law & Socy. Rev. 331-342 (1970). Reprinted by permission of The Law and Society Association, and the author.

that is hopefully produced by the legal system" . . . .[†] By focusing upon the political and social linkages between these systems, it is expected that decision-making in the prosecutor's office will be viewed as a principal ingredient in the authoritative allocation of values.

## THE PROSECUTOR'S OFFICE IN AN EXCHANGE SYSTEM

While observing the interrelated activities of the organizations in the legal process, one might ask, "Why do these agencies cooperate?" If the police refuse to transfer information to the prosecutor concerning the commission of a crime, what are the rewards or sanctions which might be brought against them? Is it possible that organizations maintain a form of "bureaucratic accounting" which, in a sense, keeps track of the resources allocated to an agency and the support returned? How are cues transmitted from one agency to another to influence decision-making? These are some of the questions which must be asked when decisions are viewed as an output of an exchange system.

The major findings of this study are placed within the context of an exchange system. . . . This serves the heuristic purpose of focusing attention upon the linkages found between actors in the decision-making process. In place of the traditional assumptions that the agency is supported solely by statutory authority, this view recognizes that an organization has many clients with which it interacts and upon whom it is dependent for certain resources. As interdependent subunits of a system, then, the organization and its clients are engaged in a set of exchanges across their boundaries. These will involve a transfer of resources between the organizations which will affect the mutual achievement of goals.

The legal system may be viewed as a set of interorganizational exchange relationships analogous to what Long . . . has called a community game.[*] The participants in the legal system (game) share a common territorial field and collaborate for different and particular ends. They interact on a continuing basis as their responsibilities demand contact with other participants in the process. Thus, the need for the cooperation of other participants can have a bearing on the decision to prosecute. A decision not to prosecute a narcotics offender may be a move to pressure the

[†] J. R. Klonski and R. I. Mendelsohn, The Allocation of Justice: A Political Analysis, 14 J. Pub. L. 323-342 (1965).
[*] N. Long, The Polity 142 (1962).

United States' Attorney's Office to cooperate on another case. It is obvious that bargaining occurs not only between the major actors in a case — the prosecutor and the defense attorney — but also between the clientele groups that are influential in structuring the actions of the prosecuting attorney.

Exchanges do not simply "sail" from one system to another, but take place in an institutionalized setting which may be compared to a market. In the market, decisions are made between individuals who occupy boundary-spanning roles, and who set the conditions under which the exchange will occur. In the legal system, this may merely mean that a representative of the parole board agrees to forward a recommendation to the prosecutor, or it could mean that there is extended bargaining between a deputy prosecutor and a defense attorney. In the study of the King County Prosecutor's Office, it was found that most decisions resulted from some type of exchange relationship. The deputies interacted almost constantly with the police and criminal lawyers, while the prosecutor was more closely linked to exchange relations with the courts, community leaders, and the county commissioners.

### THE PROSECUTOR'S CLIENTELE

In an exchange system, power is largely dependent upon the ability of an organization to create clientele relationships which will support and enhance the needs of the agency. For, although interdependence is characteristic of the legal system, competition with other public agencies for support also exists. Since organizations operate in an economy of scarcity, the organization must exist in a favorable power position in relation to its clientele. Reciprocal and unique claims are made by the organization and its clients. Thus, rather than being oriented toward only one public, an organization is beholden to several publics, some visible and others seen clearly only from the pinnacle of leadership. As Gore . . . notes, when these claims are "firmly anchored inside the organization and the lines drawn taut, the tensions between conflicting claims form a net serving as the institutional base for the organization." *

An indication of the stresses within the judicial system may be obtained by analyzing its outputs. It has been suggested that the administration of justice is a selective process in which only those cases which do not create strains in the organization will ulti-

---

* W. J. Gore, Administrative Decision Making 23 (1964).

mately reach the courtroom. . . . † As noted in Figure 1, the system operates so that only a small number of cases arrive for trial, the rest being disposed of through reduced charges, nolle pros., and guilty pleas. Not indicated are those cases removed by the police and prosecutor prior to the filing of charges. As the focal organization in an exchange system, the office of prosecuting attorney makes decisions which reflect the influence of its clientele. Because of the scarcity of resources, marketlike relationships, and the organizational needs of the system, prosecutorial decision-making emphasizes the accommodations which are made to the needs of participants in the process.

## FIGURE 1. Disposition of Felony Cases — King County, 1964

*Superior Court*
(Bound Over)    774

| | | | |
|---|---|---|---|
| Plead Guilty | 510 | | |
| Plead Innocent | 240 | Found Guilty | 216 |
| Dismissed | 24 | Found Innocent | 24 |

*Justice Court*
(Cases Filed)

| | |
|---|---|
| Felonies | 2471 |
| Gross Misdemeanors | 629 |
| Misdemeanors | 574 |
| Traffic Violations | 20 |
| Game Violations | 6 |
| | 3700 |

*Justice Court*
(Reduced to
Misdemeanor) 1697

| | | | |
|---|---|---|---|
| Plead Guilty | 1595 | | |
| Plead Innocent | 4 | Found Guilty | 3 |
| Dismissed | 98 | Found Innocent | 1 |

† W. J. Chambliss, Crime and the Legal Process 84 (1969).

*Police*

Although the prosecuting attorney has discretionary power to determine the disposition of cases, this power is limited by the fact that usually he is dependent upon the police for inputs to the system of cases and evidence. The prosecutor does not have the investigative resources necessary to exercise the kind of affirmative control over the types of cases that are brought to him. In this relationship, the prosecutor is not without countervailing power. His main check on the police is his ability to return cases to them for further investigation and to refuse to approve arrest warrants. By maintaining cordial relations with the press, a prosecutor is often able to focus attention on the police when the public becomes aroused by incidents of crime. As the King County prosecutor emphasized, "That [investigation] is the job for the sheriff and police. It's their job to bring me the charges." As noted by many respondents, the police, in turn, are dependent upon the prosecutor to accept the output of their system; rejection of too many cases can have serious repercussions affecting the morale, discipline, and workload of the force.

A request for prosecution may be rejected for a number of reasons relating to questions of evidence. Not only must the prosecutor believe that the evidence will secure a conviction, but he must also be aware of community norms relating to the type of acts that should be prosecuted. King County deputy prosecutors noted that charges were never filed when a case involved attempted suicide or fornication. In other actions, the heinous nature of the crime, together with the expected public reaction, may force both the police and prosecutor to press for conviction when evidence is less than satisfactory. As one deputy noted, "In that case [murder and molestation of a six-year-old girl] there was nothing that we could do. As you know the press was on our back and every parent was concerned. Politically, the prosecutor had to seek an information."

Factors other than those relating to evidence may require that the prosecutor refuse to accept a case from the police. First, the prosecuting attorney serves as a regulator of case loads not only for his own office, but for the rest of the legal system. Constitutional and statutory time limits prevent him and the courts from building a backlog of untried cases. In King County, when the system reached the "overload point," there was a tendency to be more selective in choosing the cases to be accepted. A second reason for rejecting prosecution requests may stem from the fact that

the prosecutor is thinking of his public exposure in the courtroom. He does not want to take forward cases which will place
him in an embarrassing position. Finally, the prosecutor may
return cases to check the quality of police work. As a former chief
criminal deputy said, "You have to keep them on their toes, otherwise they get lazy. If they aren't doing their job, send the case
back and then leak the situation to the newspapers." Rather than
spend the resources necessary to find additional evidence, the police may dispose of a case by sending it back to the prosecutor on
a lesser charge, implement the "copping out" machinery leading
to a guilty plea, drop the case, or in some instances send it to the
city prosecutor for action in municipal court.

In most instances, a deputy prosecutor and the police officer
assigned to the case occupy the boundary-spanning roles in this
exchange relationship. Prosecutors reported that after repeated
contacts they got to know the policemen whom they could trust.
As one female deputy commented, "There are some you can trust,
others you have to watch because they are trying to get rid of cases
on you." Deputies may be influenced by the police officer's attitude on a case. One officer noted to a prosecutor that he knew he
had a weak case, but mumbled, "I didn't want to bring it up here,
but that's what they [his superiors] wanted." As might be expected,
the deputy turned down prosecution.

Sometimes the police perform the ritual of "shopping around,"
seeking to find a deputy prosecutor who, on the basis of past experience, is liable to be sympathetic to their view on a case. At
one time, deputies were given complete authority to make the
crucial decisions without coordinating their activities with other
staff members. In this way the arresting officer would search the
prosecutor's office to find a deputy he thought would be sympathetic to the police attitude. As a former deputy noted, "This
meant that there were no departmental policies concerning the
treatment to be accorded various types of cases. It pretty much
depended upon the police and their luck in finding the deputy
they wanted." Prosecutors are now instructed to ascertain from
the police officer if he has seen another deputy on the case. Even
under this more centralized system, it is still possible for the police
to request a specific deputy or delay presentation of the case until
the "correct" prosecutor is available. Often a prosecutor will gain
a reputation for specializing in one type of case. This may mean
that the police will assume he will get the case anyway, so they
skirt the formal procedure and bring it to him directly.

An exchange relationship between a deputy prosecutor and a

police officer may be influenced by the type of crime committed by the defendant. The prototype of a criminal is one who violates person and property. However, a large number of cases involve "crimes without victims".... This term refers to those crimes generally involving violations of moral codes, where the general public is theoretically the complainant. In violations of laws against bookmaking, prostitution, and narcotics, neither actor in the transaction is interested in having an arrest made. Hence, vice control men must drum up their own business. Without a civilian complainant, victimless crimes give the police and prosecutor greater leeway in determining the charges to be filed.

One area of exchange involving a victimless crime is that of narcotics control. As Skolnick . . . notes, "The major organizational requirements of narcotics policing is the presence of an informational system." * Without a network of informers, it is impossible to capture addicts and peddlers with evidence that can bring about convictions. One source of informers is among those arrested for narcotics violations. Through promises to reduce charges or even to nolle pros., arrangements can be made so that the accused will return to the narcotics community and gather information for the police. Bargaining observed between the head of the narcotics squad of the Seattle Police and the deputy prosecutor who specialized in drug cases involved the question of charges, promises, and the release of an arrested narcotics pusher.

In the course of postarrest questioning by the police, a well-known drug peddler intimated that he could provide evidence against a pharmacist suspected by the police of illegally selling narcotics. Not only did the police representative want to transfer the case to the friendlier hands of this deputy, but he also wanted to arrange for a reduction of charges and bail. The police officer believed that it was important that the accused be let out in such a way that the narcotics community would not realize that he had become an informer. He also wanted to be sure that the reduced charges would be processed so that the informer could be kept on the string, thus allowing the narcotics squad to maintain control over him. The deputy prosecutor, on the other hand, said that he wanted to make sure that procedures were followed so that the action would not bring discredit on his office. He also suggested that the narcotics squad "work a little harder" on a pending case as a means of returning the favor.

* J. E. Skolnick, Justice Without Trial 120 (1966).

## Courts

The ways used by the court to dispose of cases is a vital influence in the system. The court's actions effect pressures upon the prison, the conviction rate of the prosecutor, and the work of probation agencies. The judge's decisions act as clues to other parts of the system, indicating the type of action likely to be taken in future cases. As noted by a King County judge, "When the number of prisoners gets to the 'riot point,' the warden puts pressure on us to slow down the flow. This often means that men are let out on parole and the number of people given probation and suspended sentences increases." Under such conditions, it would be expected that the prosecutor would respond to the judge's actions by reducing the inputs to the court either by not preferring charges or by increasing the pressure for guilty pleas through bargaining. The adjustments of other parts of the system could be expected to follow. For instance, the police might sense the lack of interest of the prosecutor in accepting charges, hence they will send only airtight cases to him for indictment.

The influence of the court on the decision to prosecute is very real. The sentencing history of each judge gives the prosecutor, as well as other law enforcement officials, an indication of the treatment a case may receive in the courtroom. The prosecutor's expectation as to whether the court will convict may limit his discretion over the decisions on whether to prosecute. "There is great concern as to whose court a case will be assigned. After Judge ——— threw out three cases in a row in which entrapment was involved, the police did not want us to take any cases to him." Since the prosecutor depends upon the plea-bargaining machinery to maintain the flow of cases from his office, the sentencing actions of judges must be predictable. If the defendant and his lawyer are to be influenced to accept a lesser charge or the promise of a lighter sentence in exchange for a plea of guilty, there must be some basis for belief that the judge will fulfill his part of the arrangement. Because judges are unable formally to announce their agreement with the details of the bargain, their past performance acts as a guide.

Within the limits imposed by law and the demands of the system, the prosecutor is able to regulate the flow of cases to the court. He may control the length of time between accusation and trial; hence he may hold cases until he has the evidence which will convict. Alternatively, he may seek repeated adjournment and continuances until the public's interest dies; problems such as witnesses becoming unavailable and similar difficulties make his request for dismissal of prosecution more justifiable. Further, he may determine the type of court to receive the case and the judge who will hear it. Many misdemeanors covered by state law are also violations of a city ordinance. It is a common practice for the prosecutor to send a misdemeanor case to the city prosecutor for processing in the municipal court when it is believed that a conviction may not be secured in justice court. As a deputy said, "If there is no case — send it over to the city court. Things are speedier, less formal, over there."

In the state of Washington, a person arrested on a felony charge must be given a preliminary hearing in a justice court within ten days. For the prosecutor, the preliminary hearing is an opportunity to evaluate the testimony of witnesses, assess the strength of the evidence, and try to predict the outcome of the case if it is sent to trial. On the basis of this evaluation, the prosecutor has several options: he may bind over the case for trial in Superior Court; he may reduce the charges to those of a misdemeanor for trial in Justice Court; or he may conclude that he has no case and drop the charges. The President Judge of the Justice Courts of King County estimated that about seventy percent of the felonies are reduced to misdemeanors after the preliminary hearing.

Besides having some leeway in determining the type of court in which to file a case, the prosecutor also has some flexibility in selecting the judge to receive the case. Until recently the prosecutor could file a case with a specific judge. "The trouble was that Judge —— was erratic and independent, [so] no one would file with him. The other judges objected that they were handling the entire workload, so a central filing system was devised." Under this procedure cases are assigned to the judges in rotation. However, as the chief criminal deputy noted, "the prosecutor can hold a case until the 'correct' judge came up."

### Defense Attorneys

With the increased specialization and institutionalization of the bar, it would seem that those individuals engaged in the practice of criminal law have been relegated, both by their profession and by the community, to a low status. The urban bar appears to be divided into three parts. First, there is an inner circle which handles the work of banks, utilities, and commercial concerns; second, another circle includes plaintiff's lawyers, representing interests opposed to those of the inner circle; and finally, an outer group scrapes out an existence by "haunting the courts in hope of picking up crumbs from the judicial table" . . . .* With the exception of a few highly proficient lawyers who have made a reputation by winning acquittal for their clients in difficult, highly publicized cases, most of the lawyers dealing with the King County Prosecutor's Office belong to this outer ring.

In this study, respondents were asked to identify those attorneys considered to be specialists in criminal law. Of the nearly 1,600 lawyers practicing in King County only eight can be placed in this category. Of this group, six were reported to enjoy the respect of the legal community, while the others were accused by many respondents of being involved in shady deals. A larger group of King County attorneys will accept criminal cases, but these lawyers do not consider themselves specialists. Several respondents noted that many lawyers, because of inexperience or age, were required to hang around the courthouse searching for clients. One Seattle attorney described the quality of legal talent available for criminal cases as "a few good criminal lawyers and a lot of young kids and old men. The good lawyers I can count on my fingers."

In a legal system where bargaining is a primary method of decision-making, it is not surprising that criminal lawyers find it essential to maintain close personal ties with the prosecutor and his staff. Respondents were quite open in revealing their dependence upon this close relationship to successfully pursue their careers. The nature of the criminal lawyer's work is such that his saleable product or service appears to be influence rather than technical proficiency in the law. Respondents hold the belief that clients are attracted partially on the basis of the attorney's reputation as a fixer, or as a shrewd bargainer.

There is a tendency for ex-deputy prosecutors in King County to enter the practice of criminal law. Because of his inside knowledge of the prosecutor's office and friendships made with court officials, the former deputy feels that he has an advantage over other criminal law practitioners. All of the former deputies interviewed said that they took criminal cases. Of the eight criminal law specialists, seven previously served as deputy prosecutors in King County, while the other was once prosecuting attorney in a rural county.

Because of the financial problems of the criminal lawyer's practice, it is necessary that he handle cases on an assembly-line basis, hoping to make a living from a large number of small fees. Refer-

* J. Ladinsky, The Impact of Social Backgrounds of Lawyers on Law Practice and the Law, 16 J. Legal Ed. 128 (1963).

ring to a fellow lawyer, one attorney said, "You should see ——. He goes up there to Carroll's office with a whole fist full of cases. He trades on some, bargains on others and never goes to court. It's amazing but it's the way he makes his living." There are incentives, therefore, to bargain with the prosecutor and other decision-makers. The primary aim of the attorney in such circumstances is to reach an accommodation so that the time-consuming formal proceedings need not be implemented. As a Seattle attorney noted, "I can't make any money if I spend my time in a courtroom. I make mine on the telephone or in the prosecutor's office." One of the disturbing results of this arrangement is that instances were reported in which a bargain was reached between the attorney and deputy prosecutor on a "package deal." In this situation, an attorney's clients are treated as a group; the outcome of the bargaining is often an agreement whereby reduced charges will be achieved for some, in exchange for the unspoken assent by the lawyer that the prosecutor may proceed as he desires with the other cases. One member of the King County Bar has developed this practice to such a fine art that a deputy prosecutor said, "When you saw him coming into the office, you knew that he would be pleading guilty." At one time this situation was so widespread that the "prisoners up in the jail had a rating list which graded the attorneys as either 'good guys' or 'sell outs.'"

The exchange relationship between the defense attorney and the prosecutor is based on their need for cooperation in the discharge of their responsibilities. Most criminal lawyers are interested primarily in the speedy solution of cases because of their precarious financial situation. Since they must protect their professional reputations with their colleagues, judicial personnel, and potential clientele, however, they are not completely free to bargain solely with this objective. As one attorney noted, "You can't afford to let it get out that you are selling out your cases."

The prosecutor is also interested in the speedy processing of cases. This can only be achieved if the formal processes are not implemented. Not only does the pressure of his caseload influence bargaining, but also the legal process with its potential for delay and appeal, creates a degree of uncertainty which is not present in an exchange relationship with an attorney with whom you have dealt for a number of years. As the Presiding Judge of the Seattle District Court said, "Lawyers are helpful to the system. They are able to pull things together, work out a deal, keep the system moving."

*Community Influentials*

As part of the political system, the judicial process responds to the community environment. The King County study indicated that there are differential levels of influence within the community and that some people had a greater interest in the politics of prosecution than others. First, the general public is able to have its values translated into policies followed by law enforcement officers. The public's influence is particularly acute in those gray areas of the law where full enforcement is not expected. Statutes may be enacted by legislatures defining the outer limits of criminal conduct, but they do not necessarily mean that laws are to be fully enforced to these limits. There are some laws defining behavior which the community no longer considers criminal. It can be expected that a prosecutor's charging policies will reflect this attitude. He may not prosecute violations of laws regulating some forms of gambling, certain sexual practices, or violations of Sunday Blue Laws.

Because the general public is a potential threat to the prosecutor, staff members take measures to protect him from criticism. Respondents agreed that decision-making occurs with the public in mind — "will a course of action arouse antipathy towards the prosecutor rather than the accused?" Several deputies mentioned what they called the "aggravation level" of a crime. This is a recognition that the commission of certain crimes, within a specific context, will bring about a vocal public reaction. "If a little girl, walking home from the grocery store, is pulled into the bushes and indecent liberties taken, this is more disturbing to the public's conscience than a case where the father of the girl takes indecent liberties with her at home." The office of King County Prosecuting Attorney has a policy requiring that deputies file all cases involving sexual molestation in which the police believe the girl's story is credible. The office also prefers charges in all negligent homicide cases where there is the least possibility of guilt. In such types of cases the public may respond to the emotional context of the case and demand prosecution. To cover the prosecutor from criticism, it is believed that the safest measure is to prosecute.

The bail system is also used to protect the prosecutor from criticism. Thus it is the policy to set bail at a high level with the expectation that the court will reduce the amount. "This looks good for Prosecutor Carroll. Takes the heat off of him, especially in morals cases. If the accused doesn't appear in court the prosecutor can't be blamed. The public gets upset when they know these types are out free." This is an example of exchange where one actor is shifting the responsibility and potential onus onto another. In turn, the court is under pressure from county jail officials to keep the prison population down.

A second community group having contact with the prosecutor is composed of those leaders who have a continuing or potential interest in the politics of prosecution. This group, analogous to the players in one of Long's community games, are linked to the prosecutor because his actions affect their success in playing another game. Hence community boosters want either a crackdown or a hands-off policy towards gambling, political leaders want the prosecutor to remember the interests of the party, and business leaders want policies which will not interfere with their own game.

Community leaders may receive special treatment by the prosecutor if they run afoul of the law. A policy of the King County Office requires that cases involving prominent members of the community be referred immediately to the chief criminal deputy and the prosecutor for their disposition. As one deputy noted, "These cases can be pretty touchy. It's important that the boss knows immediately about this type of case so that he is not caught 'flat footed' when asked about it by the press."

Pressure by an interest group was evidenced during a strike by drug store employees in 1964. The striking unions urged Prosecutor Carroll to invoke a state law which requires the presence of a licensed pharmacist if the drug store is open. Not only did union representatives meet with Carroll, but picket lines were set up outside the courthouse protesting his refusal to act. The prosecutor resisted the union's pressure tactics.

In recent years, the prosecutor's tolerance policy toward minor forms of gambling led to a number of conflicts with Seattle's mayor, the sheriff, and church organizations. After a decision was made to prohibit all forms of public gaming, the prosecutor was criticized by groups representing the tourist industry and such affected groups as the bartenders' union which thought the decision would have an adverse economic effect. As Prosecutor Carroll said, "I am always getting pressures from different interests — business, the Chamber of Commerce, and labor. I have to try and maintain a balance between them." In exchange for these considerations, the prosecutor may gain prestige, political support, and admission into the leadership groups of the community.

## SUMMARY

By viewing the King County Office of Prosecuting Attorney as the focal organization in an exchange system, data from this exploratory study suggests the market-like relationships which exist between actors in the system. Since prosecution operates in an environment of scarce resources and since the decisions have potential political ramifications, a variety of officials influence the allocation of justice. The decision to prosecute is not made at one point, but rather the prosecuting attorney has a number of options which he may employ during various stages of the proceedings. But the prosecutor is able to exercise his discretionary powers only within the network of exchange relationships. The police, court congestion, organizational strains, and community pressures are among the factors which influence prosecutorial behavior.

## Two Models of the Criminal Process*

## Herbert L. Packer

### INTRODUCTION

People who commit crimes appear to share the prevalent impression that punishment is an unpleasantness that is best avoided. They ordinarily take care to avoid being caught. If arrested, they ordinarily deny their guilt and otherwise try not to cooperate with the police. If brought to trial, they do whatever their resources permit to resist being convicted. And even after they have been convicted and sent to prison, their efforts to secure their freedom do not cease. It is a struggle from start to finish. This struggle is often referred to as the criminal process, a compendious term that stands for all the complexes of activity that operate to bring the substantive law of crime to bear (or to keep it from coming to bear) on persons who are suspected of having committed crimes. It can be described, but only partially and inadequately, by referring to the rules of law that govern the apprehension, screening, and trial of persons suspected of crime. It consists at least as importantly of patterns of official activity that correspond only in the roughest kind of way to the prescriptions of procedural rules. As a result of recent emphasis on empirical research into the administration of criminal justice, we are just beginning to be aware how very rough the correspondence is.

* Reprinted from: The Limits of the Criminal Sanction 149-173 by Herbert L. Packer, Stanford: Stanford University Press; London: Oxford University Press, with the permission of the publishers, © 1968 by Herbert L. Packer.

At the same time, and perhaps in part as a result of this new accretion of knowledge, some of our lawmaking institutions — particularly the Supreme Court of the United States — have begun to add measurably to the prescriptions of law that are meant to govern the operation of the criminal process. This accretion has become, in the last few years, exponential in extent and velocity. We are faced with an interesting paradox: the more we learn about the Is of the criminal process, the more we are instructed about its Ought and the greater the gulf between Is and Ought appears to become. We learn that very few people get adequate legal representation in the criminal process; we are simultaneously told that the Constitution requires people to be afforded adequate legal representation in the criminal process. We learn that coercion is often used to extract confessions from suspected criminals; we are then told that convictions based on coerced confessions may not be permitted to stand. We discover that the police often use methods in gathering evidence that violate the norms of privacy protected by the Fourth Amendment; we are told that evidence obtained in this way must be excluded from the criminal trial. But these prescriptions about how the process ought to operate do not automatically become part of the patterns of official behavior in the criminal process. Is and Ought share an increasingly uneasy coexistence. Doubts are stirred about the kind of criminal process we want to have. . . .

Two models of the criminal process will let us perceive the normative antinomy at the heart of the criminal law. These models are not labeled Is and Ought, nor are they to be taken in that sense. Rather, they represent an attempt to abstract two separate value systems that compete for priority in the operation of the criminal process. Neither is presented as either corresponding to reality or representing the ideal to the exclusion of the other. The two models merely afford a convenient way to talk about the operation of a process whose day-to-day functioning involves a constant series of minute adjustments between the competing demands of two value systems and whose normative future likewise involves a series of resolutions of the tensions between competing claims.

I call these two models the Due Process Model and the Crime Control Model. . . .

There is a risk in an enterprise of this sort that is latent in any attempt to polarize. It is, simply, that values are too various to be pinned down to yes-or-no answers. The models are distortions of reality. And, since they are normative in character, there is a danger of seeing one or the other as Good or Bad. The reader will have his preferences, as I do, but we should not be so rigid as to demand consistently polarized answers to the range of questions posed in the criminal process. The weighty questions of public policy that inhere in any attempt to discern where on the spectrum of normative choice the "right" answer lies are beyond the scope of the present inquiry. The attempt here is primarily to clarify the terms of discussion by isolating the assumptions that underlie competing policy claims and examining the conclusions that those claims, if fully accepted, would lead to.

### VALUES UNDERLYING THE MODELS

Each of the two models we are about to examine is an attempt to give operational content to a complex of values underlying the criminal law. As I have suggested earlier, it is possible to identify two competing systems of values, the tension between which accounts for the intense activity now observable in the development of the criminal process. The actors in this development — lawmakers, judges, police, prosecutors, defense lawyers — do not often pause to articulate the values that underlie the positions that they take on any given issue. Indeed, it would be a gross oversimplification to ascribe a coherent and consistent set of values to any of these actors. Each of the two competing schemes of values we will be developing in this section contains components that are demonstrably present some of the time in some of the actors' preferences regarding the criminal process. No one person has ever identified himself as holding all of the values that underlie these two models. The models are polarities, and so are the schemes of value that underlie them. A person who subscribed to all of the values underlying one model to the exclusion of all of the values underlying the other would be rightly viewed as a fanatic. The values are presented here as an aid to analysis, not as a program for action. . . .

*Crime Control Values.* The value system that underlies the Crime Control Model is based on the proposition that the repression of criminal conduct is by far the most important function to be performed by the criminal process. The failure of law enforcement to bring criminal conduct under tight control is viewed as leading to the breakdown of public order and thence to the disappearance of an important condition of human freedom. If the laws go unenforced — which is to say, if it is perceived that there is a high percentage of failure to apprehend and convict in the criminal process — a general disregard for legal controls tends to develop. The law-abiding citizen then becomes the victim of all sorts of unjustifiable invasions of his interests. His security of person and property is sharply diminished, and, therefore, so is his liberty to function as a member of society. The claim ultimately is that the criminal process is a positive guarantor of social freedom. In order to achieve this high purpose, the Crime Control Model requires that primary attention be paid to the efficiency with which the criminal process operates to screen suspects, determine guilt, and secure appropriate dispositions of persons convicted of crime.

Efficiency of operation is not, of course, a criterion that can be applied in a vacuum. By "efficiency" we mean the system's capacity to apprehend, try, convict, and dispose of a high proportion of criminal offenders whose offenses become known. In a society in which only the grossest forms of antisocial behavior were made criminal and in which the crime rate was exceedingly low, the criminal process might require the devotion of many more man-hours of police, prosecutorial, and judicial time per case than ours does, and still operate with tolerable efficiency. A society that was prepared to increase even further the resources devoted to the suppression of crime might cope with a rising crime rate without sacrifice of efficiency while continuing to maintain an elaborate and time-consuming set of criminal processes. However, neither of these possible characteristics corresponds with social reality in this country. We use the criminal sanction to cover an increasingly wide spectrum of behavior thought to be antisocial, and the amount of crime is very high indeed, although both level and trend are hard to assess. At the same time, although precise measures are not available, it does not appear that we are disposed in the public sector of the economy to increase very drastically the quantity, much less the quality, of the resources devoted to the suppression of criminal activity through the operation of the criminal process. These factors have an important bearing on the criteria of efficiency, and therefore on the nature of the Crime Control Model.

The model, in order to operate successfully, must produce a high rate of apprehension and conviction, and must do so in a context where the magnitudes being dealt with are very large and the resources for dealing with them are very limited. There must then be a premium on speed and finality. Speed, in turn, depends on informality and on uniformity; finality depends on minimizing the occasions for challenge. The process must not be cluttered up with ceremonious rituals that do not advance the progress of a case. Facts can be established more quickly through interrogation in a police station than through the formal process of examination and cross-examination in a court. It follows that extrajudicial processes should be preferred to judicial processes, informal operations to formal ones. But informality is not enough; there must also be uniformity. Routine, stereotyped procedures are essential if large numbers are being handled. The model that will operate successfully on these presuppositions must be an administrative, almost a managerial, model. The image that comes to mind is an assembly-line conveyor belt down which moves an endless stream of cases, never stopping, carrying the cases to workers who stand at fixed stations and who perform on each case as it comes by the same small but essential operation that brings it one step closer to being a finished product, or, to exchange the metaphor for the reality, a closed file. The criminal process, in this model, is seen as a screening process in which each successive stage — pre-arrest investigation, arrest, post-arrest investigation, preparation for trial, trial or entry of plea, conviction, disposition — involves a series of routinized operations whose success is gauged primarily by their tendency to pass the case along to a successful conclusion.

What is a successful conclusion? One that throws off at an early stage those cases in which it appears unlikely that the person apprehended is an offender and then secures, as expeditiously as possible, the conviction of the rest, with a minimum of occasions for challenge, let alone post-audit. By the application of administrative expertness, primarily that of the police and prosecutors, an early determination of probable innocence or guilt emerges. Those who are probably innocent are screened out. Those who are probably guilty are passed quickly through the remaining stages of the process. The key to the operation of the model regarding those who are not screened out is what I shall call a presumption of guilt. The concept requires some explanation, since it may appear startling to assert that what appears to be the precise converse of our generally accepted ideology of a presumption of innocence can be an essential element of a model that does correspond in some respects to the actual operation of the criminal process.

The presumption of guilt is what makes it possible for the system to deal efficiently with large numbers, as the Crime Control Model demands. The supposition is that the screening processes operated by police and prosecutors are reliable indicators of probable guilt. Once a man has been arrested and investigated without being found to be probably innocent, or, to put it differently, once a determination has been made that there is enough evidence of guilt to permit holding him for further action, then all subsequent activity directed toward him is based on the view that he is probably guilty. The precise point at which this occurs will vary from case to case; in many cases it will occur as soon as the suspect is arrested, or even before, if the evidence of probable guilt that has come to the attention of the authorities is sufficiently strong. But in any case the presumption of guilt will begin to operate well before the "suspect" becomes a "defendant."

The presumption of guilt is not, of course, a thing. Nor is it even a rule of law in the usual sense. It simply is the consequence of a complex of attitudes, a mood. If there is confidence in the reliability of informal administrative fact-finding activities that take place in the early stages of the criminal process, the remaining stages of the process can be relatively perfunctory without any loss in operating efficiency. The presumption of guilt, as it operates in the Crime Control Model, is the operational expression of that confidence.

It would be a mistake to think of the presumption of guilt as the opposite of the presumption of innocence that we are so used to thinking of as the polestar of the criminal process and that, as we shall see, occupies an important position in the Due Process Model. The presumption of innocence is not its opposite; it is irrelevant to the presumption of guilt; the two concepts are different rather than opposite ideas. The difference can perhaps be epitomized by an example. A murderer, for reasons best known to himself, chooses to shoot his victim in plain view of a large number of people. When the police arrive, he hands them his gun and says, "I did it and I'm glad." His account of what happened is corroborated by several eyewitnesses. He is placed under arrest and led off to jail. Under these circumstances, which may seem extreme but which in fact characterize with rough accuracy the evidentiary situation in a large proportion of criminal cases, it would be plainly absurd to maintain that more probably than not the suspect did not commit the killing. But that is not what the presumption of innocence means. It means that until there has been an adjudication of guilt by an authority legally competent to make such an adjudication, the suspect is to be treated, for reasons that have nothing whatever to do with the probable outcome of the case, as if his guilt is an open question.

The presumption of innocence is a direction to officials about how they are to proceed, not a prediction of outcome. The presumption of guilt, however, is purely and simply a prediction of outcome. The presumption of innocence is, then, a direction to the authorities to ignore the presumption of guilt in their treatment of the suspect. It tells them, in effect, to close their eyes to what will frequently seem to be factual probabilities. The reasons why it tells them this are among the animating presuppositions of the Due Process Model, and we will come to them shortly. It is enough to note at this point that the presumption of guilt is descriptive and factual; the presumption of innocence is normative and legal. The pure Crime Control Model has no truck with the presumption of innocence, although its real-life emanations are, as we shall see, brought into uneasy compromise with the dictates of this dominant ideological position. In the presumption of guilt this model finds a factual predicate for the position that the dominant goal of repressing crime can be achieved through highly summary processes without any great loss of efficiency (as previously defined), because of the probability that, in the run of cases, the preliminary screening processes operated by the police and the prosecuting officials contain adequate guarantees of reliable fact-finding. Indeed, the model takes an even stronger position. It is that subsequent processes, particularly those of a formal adjudicatory nature, are unlikely to produce as reliable fact-finding as the expert administrative process that precedes them is capable of. The criminal process thus must put special weight on the quality of administrative fact-finding. It becomes important, then, to place as few restrictions as possible on the character of the administrative fact-finding processes and to limit restrictions to such as enhance reliability, excluding those designed for other purposes. As we shall see, this view of restrictions on administrative fact-finding is a consistent theme in the development of the Crime Control Model.

In this model, as I have suggested, the center of gravity for the process lies in the early, administrative fact-finding stages. The complementary proposition is that the subsequent stages are relatively unimportant and should be truncated as much as possible. This, too, produces tensions with presently dominant ideology. The pure Crime Control Model has very little use for many conspicuous features of the adjudicative process, and in real life works out a number of ingenious compromises with them. Even in the pure model, however, there have to be devices for dealing with the suspect after the preliminary screening process has resulted in a determination of probable guilt. The focal device, as we shall see, is the plea of guilty; through its use, adjudicative fact-finding is reduced to a minimum. It might be said of the Crime Control Model that, when reduced to its barest essentials and operating at its most successful pitch, it offers two possibilities: an administrative fact-finding process leading (1) to exoneration of the suspect or (2) to the entry of a plea of guilty.

*Due Process Values.* If the Crime Control Model resembles an assembly line, the Due Process Model looks very much like an obstacle course. Each of its successive stages is designed to present formidable impediments to carrying the accused any further along in the process. Its ideology is not the converse of that underlying the Crime Control Model. It does not rest on the idea that it is not socially desirable to repress crime, although critics of its application have been known to claim so. Its ideology is composed of a complex of ideas, some of them based on judgments about the efficacy of crime control devices, others having to do with quite different considerations. The ideology of due process is far more deeply impressed on the formal structure of the law than is the ideology of crime control; yet an accurate tracing of the strands that make it up is strangely difficult. What follows is only an attempt at an approximation.

The Due Process Model encounters its rival on the Crime Control Model's own ground in respect to the reliability of fact-finding processes. The Crime Control Model, as we have suggested, places heavy reliance on the ability of investigative and prosecutorial officers, acting in an informal setting in which their distinctive skills are given full sway, to elicit and reconstruct a tolerably accurate account of what actually took place in an alleged criminal event. The Due Process Model rejects this premise and substitutes for it a view of informal, nonadjudicative fact-finding that stresses the possibility of error. People are notoriously poor observers of disturbing events — the more emotion-arousing the context, the greater the possibility that recollection will be incorrect; confessions and admissions by persons in police custody may be induced by physical or psychological coercion so that the police end up hearing what the suspect thinks they want to hear rather than the truth; witnesses may be animated by a bias or interest that no one would trouble to discover except one specially charged with protecting the interests of the accused (as the police are not). Considerations of this kind all lead to a rejection of informal fact-finding processes as definitive of factual guilt and to an insistence on formal, adjudicative, adversary fact-finding processes in which the factual case against the accused is publicly heard by an impartial tribunal and is evaluated only after the accused has had a full opportunity to discredit the case against him. Even then, the distrust of fact-finding processes that animates the Due Process Model is not dissipated. The possibilities of human error being what they are, further scrutiny is necessary, or at least must be available, in case facts have been overlooked or suppressed in the heat of battle. How far this subsequent scrutiny must be available is a hotly controverted issue today. In the pure Due Process Model the answer would be: at least as long as there is an allegation of factual error that has not received an adjudicative hearing in a fact-finding context. The demand for finality is thus very low in the Due Process Model.

This strand of due process ideology is not enough to sustain the model. If all that were at issue between the two models was a series of questions about the reliability of fact-finding processes, we would have but one model of the criminal process, the nature of whose constituent elements would pose questions of fact not of value. Even if the discussion is confined, for the moment, to the question of reliability, it is apparent that more is at stake than simply an evaluation of what kinds of fact-finding processes, alone or in combinations, are likely to produce the most nearly reliable results. The stumbling block is this: how much reliability is compatible with efficiency? Granted that informal fact-finding will make some mistakes that can be remedied if backed up by adjudicative fact-finding, the desirability of providing this backup is not affirmed or negated by factual demonstrations or predictions that the increase in reliability will be $x$ per cent or $x$ plus $n$ per cent. It still remains to ask how much weight is to be given to the competing demands of reliability (a high degree of probability in each case that factual guilt has been accurately determined) and efficiency (expeditious handling of the large numbers of cases that the process ingests). The Crime Control Model is more optimistic about the improbability of error in a significant number of cases; but it is also, though only in part therefore, more tolerant about the amount of error that it will put up with. The Due Process Model insists on the prevention and elimination of mistakes to the extent possible; the Crime Control Model accepts the probability of mistakes up to the level at which they interfere with the goal of repressing crime, either because too many guilty people are escaping or, more subtly, because general awareness of the unreliability of the process leads to a decrease in the deterrent efficacy of the criminal law. In this view, reliability and efficiency are not polar opposites but rather complementary characteristics. The system is reliable *because* efficient; reliability becomes a matter of independent concern only when it becomes so attenuated as to impair efficiency. All of this the Due Process Model rejects. If efficiency demands shortcuts around reliability, then absolute efficiency must be rejected. The aim of the process is at least as much to protect the factually innocent as it is to convict the factually guilty. It is a little like quality control in industrial technology: tolerable deviation from standard varies with the importance of conformity to standard in the destined uses of the product. The Due Process Model resembles a factory that has to devote a substantial part of its input to quality control. This necessarily cuts down on quantitative output.

All of this is only the beginning of the ideological difference between the two models. The Due Process Model could disclaim any attempt to provide enhanced reliability for the fact-finding process and still produce a set of institutions and processes that would differ sharply from those demanded by the Crime Control Model. Indeed, it may not be too great an oversimplification to assert that in point of historical development the doctrinal pressures emanating from the demands of the Due Process Model have tended to evolve from an original matrix of concern for the maximization of reliability into values quite different and more far-reaching. These values can be expressed in, although not adequately described by, the concept of the primacy of the individual and the complementary concept of limitation on official power.

The combination of stigma and loss of liberty that is embodied in the end result of the criminal process is viewed as being the heaviest deprivation that government can inflict on the individual. Furthermore, the processes that culminate in these highly afflictive sanctions are seen as in themselves coercive, restricting, and demeaning. Power is always subject to abuse — sometimes subtle, other times, as in the criminal process, open and ugly. Precisely because of its potency in subjecting the individual to the coercive power of the state, the criminal process must, in this model, be subjected to controls that prevent it from operating with maximal efficiency. According to this ideology, maximal efficiency means maximal tyranny. And, although no one would assert that minimal efficiency means minimal tyranny, the proponents of the Due Process Model would accept with considerable equanimity a substantial diminution in the efficiency with which the criminal process operates in the interest of preventing official oppression of the individual.

The most modest-seeming but potentially far-reaching mechanism by which the Due Process Model implements these anti-authoritarian values is the doctrine of legal guilt. According to this doctrine, a person is not to be held guilty of crime merely on a showing that in all probability, based upon reliable evidence,

he did factually what he is said to have done. Instead, he is to be
held guilty if and only if these factual determinations are made
in procedurally regular fashion and by authorities acting within
competences duly allocated to them. Furthermore, he is not to be
held guilty, even though the factual determination is or might be
adverse to him, if various rules designed to protect him and to
safeguard the integrity of the process are not given effect: the tribunal that convicts him must have the power to deal with his kind
of case ("jurisdiction") and must be geographically appropriate
("venue"); too long a time must not have elapsed since the offense was committed ("statute of limitations"); he must not
have been previously convicted or acquitted of the same or a substantially similar offense ("double jeopardy"); he must not fall
within a category of persons, such as children or the insane, who
are legally immune to conviction ("criminal responsibility"); and
so on. None of these requirements has anything to do with the
factual question of whether the person did or did not engage in
the conduct that is charged as the offense against him; yet favorable answers to any of them will mean that he is legally innocent.
Wherever the competence to make adequate factual determinations lies, it is apparent that only a tribunal that is aware of these
guilt-defeating doctrines and is willing to apply them can be
viewed as competent to make determinations of legal guilt. The
police and the prosecutors are ruled out by lack of competence,
in the first instance, and by lack of assurance of willingness, in
the second. Only an impartial tribunal can be trusted to make
determinations of legal as opposed to factual guilt.

In this concept of legal guilt lies the explanation for the apparently quixotic presumption of innocence of which we spoke
earlier. A man who, after police investigation, is charged with having committed a crime can hardly be said to be presumptively
innocent, if what we mean is factual innocence. But if what we
mean is that it has yet to be determined if any of the myriad legal
doctrines that serve in one way or another the end of limiting official power through the observance of certain substantive and
procedural regularities may be appropriately invoked to exculpate
the accused man, it is apparent that as a matter of prediction
it cannot be said with confidence that more probably than not
he will be found guilty.

Beyond the question of predictability this model posits a functional reason for observing the presumption of innocence: by forcing the state to prove its case against the accused in an adjudicative
context, the presumption of innocence serves to force into play

all the qualifying and disabling doctrines that limit the use of the criminal sanction against the individual, thereby enhancing his opportunity to secure a favorable outcome. In this sense, the presumption of innocence may be seen to operate as a kind of self-fulfilling prophecy. By opening up a procedural situation that permits the successful assertion of defenses having nothing to do with factual guilt, it vindicates the proposition that the factually guilty may nonetheless be legally innocent and should therefore be given a chance to qualify for that kind of treatment.

The possibility of legal innocence is expanded enormously when the criminal process is viewed as the appropriate forum for correcting its own abuses. This notion may well account for a greater amount of the distance between the two models than any other. In theory the Crime Control Model can tolerate rules that forbid illegal arrests, unreasonable searches, coercive interrogations, and the like. What it cannot tolerate is the vindication of those rules in the criminal process itself through the exclusion of evidence illegally obtained or through the reversal of convictions in cases where the criminal process has breached the rules laid down for its observance. And the Due Process Model, although it may in the first instance be addressed to the maintenance of reliable fact-finding techniques, comes eventually to incorporate prophylactic and deterrent rules that result in the release of the factually guilty even in cases in which blotting out the illegality would still leave an adjudicative fact-finder convinced of the accused person's guilt. Only by penalizing errant police and prosecutors within the criminal process itself can adequate pressure be maintained, so the argument runs, to induce conformity with the Due Process Model.

Another strand in the complex of attitudes underlying the Due Process Model is the idea — itself a shorthand statement for a complex of attitudes — of equality. This notion has only recently emerged as an explicit basis for pressing the demands of the Due Process Model, but it appears to represent, at least in its potential, a most powerful norm for influencing official conduct. Stated most starkly, the ideal of equality holds that "there can be no equal justice where the kind of trial a man gets depends on the amount of money he has." [5] The factual predicate underlying this assertion is that there are gross inequalities in the financial means of criminal defendants as a class, that in an adversary system of criminal justice an effective defense is largely a function of the resources

5. Griffin v. Illinois, 351 U.S. 12, 19 (1956).

that can be mustered on behalf of the accused, and that the very large proportion of criminal defendants who are, operationally speaking, "indigent," will thus be denied an effective defense. This factual premise has been strongly reinforced by recent studies that in turn have been both a cause and an effect of an increasing emphasis upon norms for the criminal process based on the premise.

The norms derived from the premise do not take the form of an insistence upon governmental responsibility to provide literally equal opportunities for all criminal defendants to challenge the process. Rather, they take as their point of departure the notion that the criminal process, initiated as it is by government and containing as it does the likelihood of severe deprivations at the hands of government, imposes some kind of public obligation to ensure that financial inability does not destroy the capacity of an accused to assert what may be meritorious challenges to the processes being invoked against him. At its most gross, the norm of equality would act to prevent situations in which financial inability forms an absolute barrier to the assertion of a right that is in theory generally available, as where there is a right to appeal that is, however, effectively conditional upon the filing of a trial transcript obtained at the defendant's expense. Beyond this, it may provide the basis for a claim whenever the system theoretically makes some kind of challenge available to an accused who has the means to press it. If, for example, a defendant who is adequately represented has the opportunity to prevent the case against him from coming to the trial stage by forcing the state to its proof in a preliminary hearing, the norm of equality may be invoked to assert that the same kind of opportunity must be available to others as well. In a sense the system as it functions for the small minority whose resources permit them to exploit all its defensive possibilities provides a benchmark by which its functioning in all other cases is to be tested: not, perhaps, to guarantee literal identity but rather to provide a measure of whether the process as a whole is recognizably of the same general order. The demands made by a norm of this kind are likely, by their very nature to be quite sweeping. Although the norm's imperatives may be initially limited to determining whether in a particular case the accused was injured or prejudiced by his relative inability to make an appropriate challenge, the norm of equality very quickly moves to another level on which the demand is that the process in general be adapted to minimize discriminations rather than that a mere series of post hoc determinations of discrimination be made or makeable.

It should be observed that the impact of the equality norm will vary greatly depending upon the point in time at which it is introduced into a model of the criminal process. If one were starting from scratch to decide how the process ought to work, the norm of equality would have nothing very important to say on such questions as, for example, whether an accused should have the effective assistance of counsel in deciding whether to enter a plea of guilty. One could decide, on quite independent considerations, that it is or is not a good thing to afford that facility to the generality of persons accused of crime. But the impact of the equality norm becomes far greater when it is brought to bear on a process whose contours have already been shaped. If our model of the criminal process affords defendants who are in a financial position to do so the right to consult a lawyer before entering a plea, then the equality norm exerts powerful pressure to provide such an opportunity to all defendants and to regard the failure to do so as a malfunctioning of the process of whose consequences the accused is entitled to be relieved. In a sense, this has been the role of the equality norm in affecting the real-world criminal process. It has made its appearance on the scene comparatively late, and has therefore encountered a system in which the relative financial inability of most persons accused of crime results in treatment very different from that accorded the small minority of the financially capable. For this reason, its impact has already been substantial and may be expected to be even more so in the future.

There is a final strand of thought in the Due Process Model that is often ignored but that needs to be candidly faced if thought on the subject is not to be obscured. This is a mood of skepticism about the morality and utility of the criminal sanction, taken either as a whole or in some of its applications. The subject is a large and complicated one, comprehending as it does much of the intellectual history of our times. It is properly the subject of another essay altogether. To put the matter briefly, one cannot improve upon the statement by Professor Paul Bator:

In summary we are told that the criminal law's notion of just condemnation and punishment is a cruel hypocrisy visited by a smug society on the psychologically and economically crippled; that its premise of a morally autonomous will with at least some measure of choice whether to comply with the values expressed in a penal code is unscientific and outmoded; that its reliance on punishment as an educational and deterrent agent is misplaced, particularly in the case of the very members of society most likely to engage in criminal conduct; and that its failure to provide for individualized and humane rehabilitation of offenders is inhuman and wasteful.[6]

This skepticism, which may be fairly said to be widespread among the most influential and articulate contemporary leaders of informed opinion, leads to an attitude toward the processes of the criminal law that, to quote Mr. Bator again, engenders "a peculiar receptivity toward claims of injustice which arise within the traditional structure of the system itself; fundamental disagreement and unease about the very bases of the criminal law has, inevitably, created acute pressure at least to expand and liberalize those of its processes and doctrines which serve to make more tentative its judgments or limit its power." In short, doubts about the ends for which power is being exercised create pressure to limit the discretion with which that power is exercised.

The point need not be pressed to the extreme of doubts about or rejection of the premises upon which the criminal sanction in general rests. Unease may be stirred simply by reflection on the variety of uses to which the criminal sanction is put and by a judgment that an increasingly large proportion of those uses may represent an unwise invocation of so extreme a sanction. It would be an interesting irony if doubts about the propriety of certain uses of the criminal sanction prove to contribute to a restrictive trend in the criminal process that in the end requires a choice among uses and finally an abandonment of some of the very uses that stirred the original doubts, but for a reason quite unrelated to those doubts.

There are two kinds of problems that need to be dealt with in any model of the criminal process. One is what the rules shall be. The other is how the rules shall be implemented. The second is at least as important as the first. . . . [T]he distinctive difference between the two models is not only in the rules of conduct that they lay down but also in the sanctions that are to be invoked when a claim is presented that the rules have been breached and, no less importantly, in the timing that is permitted or required for the invocation of those sanctions.

As I have already suggested, the Due Process Model locates at least some of the sanctions for breach of the operative rules in the criminal process itself. The relation between these two aspects of the process — the rules and the sanctions for their breach — is a

6. Finality in Criminal Law and Federal Habeas Corpus for State Prisoners, 76 Harv. L. Rev. 441, 442 (1963).

purely formal one unless there is some mechanism for bringing them into play with each other. The hinge between them in the Due Process Model is the availability of legal counsel. This has a double aspect. Many of the rules that the model requires are couched in terms of the availability of counsel to do various things at various stages of the process — this is the conventionally recognized aspect; beyond it, there is a pervasive assumption that counsel is necessary in order to invoke sanctions for breach of any of the rules. The more freely available these sanctions are, the more important is the role of counsel in seeing to it that the sanctions are appropriately invoked. If the process is seen as a series of occasions for checking its own operation, the role of counsel is a much more nearly central one than is the case in a process that is seen as primarily concerned with expeditious determination of factual guilt. And if equality of operation is a governing norm, the availability of counsel to some is seen as requiring it for all. Of all the controverted aspects of the criminal process, the right to counsel, including the role of government in its provision, is the most dependent on what one's model of the process looks like, and the least susceptible of resolution unless one has confronted the antinomies of the two models.

I do not mean to suggest that questions about the right to counsel disappear if one adopts a model of the process that conforms more or less closely to the Crime Control Model, but only that such questions become absolutely central if one's model moves very far down the spectrum of possibilities toward the pure Due Process Model. The reason for this centrality is to be found in the assumption underlying both models that the process is an adversary one in which the initiative in invoking relevant rules rests primarily on the parties concerned, the state, and the accused. One could construct models that placed central responsibility on adjudicative agents such as committing magistrates and trial judges. And there are, as we shall see, marginal but nonetheless important adjustments in the role of the adjudicative agents that enter into the models with which we are concerned. For present purposes it is enough to say that these adjustments are marginal, that the animating presuppositions that underlie both models in the context of the American criminal system relegate the adjudicative agents to a relatively passive role, and therefore place central importance on the role of counsel.

One last introductory note. . . . What assumptions do we make about the sources of authority to shape the real-world operations of the criminal process? Recognizing that our models are only

models, what agencies of government have the power to pick and
choose between their competing demands? Once again, the limiting features of the American context come into play. Ours is not
a system of legislative supremacy. The distinctively American institution of judicial review exercises a limiting and ultimately a
shaping influence on the criminal process. Because the Crime
Control Model is basically an affirmative model, emphasizing at
every turn the existence and exercise of official power, its validating
authority is ultimately legislative (although proximately administrative). Because the Due Process Model is basically a negative
model, asserting limits on the nature of official power and on the
modes of its exercise, its validating authority is judicial and requires an appeal to supra-legislative law, to the law of the Constitution. To the extent that tensions between the two models are resolved by deference to the Due Process Model, the authoritative
force at work is the judicial power, working in the distinctively
judicial mode of invoking the sanction of nullity. That is at once
the strength and the weakness of the Due Process Model: its
strength because in our system the appeal to the Constitution
provides the last and the overriding word; its weakness because
saying no in specific cases is an exercise in futility unless there is
a general willingness on the part of the officials who operate the
process to apply negative prescriptions across the board. It is no
accident that statements reinforcing the Due Process Model come
from the courts, while at the same time facts denying it are established by the police and prosecutors.

# PART III.
# THE POLITICS
# OF LOWER COURTS

Politics necessarily loom large in any account of lower courts. While the political functions and role of the judiciary are apparent in the policy decisions of higher courts, they are usually cloaked in the rhetoric of stare decisis and the view that judges find rather than make law. But at the lower court level such rhetoric rings hollow. Political connections jump out at every turn — the state senator who manages to win nearly all his court cases, the political contributor who becomes a judge, the radical activist whose claim of police brutality is ignored.

This section develops a political perspective on lower criminal courts by presenting materials on several facets of courts and politics. Perhaps the most blatant interface is judicial selection and the influence of local politicians over personnel and budget. Both appointive and elective selection systems suffer this ill, as the selections from Samuel Seabury's investigation of the New York magistrate system and the account of electioneering in Cleveland show. Although dating from 1920 and 1932 respectively, these excerpts were included because present procedures differ in detail only, and no studies since have been as forthright and candid in their description of the political requirements of becoming a judge. Confirmation of their relevance is found in two short newspaper accounts of Massachusetts courthouse politics. One describes how a powerful politician blocked the confirmation of a young legal services lawyer appointed to the bench in a Boston working-class neighborhood court. The second shows how court budgets and offices allow politicians to wield power and profit personally.

A less obvious political influence is the attitudes and values which judges bring to the bench. Judges usually represent one class in society — the class that holds power and defines community mores. John Hogarth's study of Canadian magistrates, who share a like jurisdiction with American lower court judges, is useful for demonstrating the social and class affiliations judges bring to the courtroom.

Martin Levin compares styles of urban politics with the kinds of sentences judges impose in criminal cases. His study of judges in Minneapolis and Pittsburgh demonstrates that both judging styles and case outcomes, far from being value-free, express political, class, and personal biases.

An obvious political function of courts is the protection of dominant values and maintenance of the status quo. The last two selections in this section illustrate two aspects of that function: The Michigan Law Review study of the Detroit Recorder's Court during the 1967 Detroit riot shows how the judges overtly became social control agents, shedding their supposedly neutral role between the individual and the state to help the police maintain order. Through high bail, denial of rights, and violations of due process, they openly assumed the role which the formal rules of the system assign to the police and executive. An important issue is to what extent the courts fulfill these functions in ordinary times.

The Stumpf-Janowitz article on the reaction of California judges to legal service programs, while not directly concerned with criminal courts, shows the policy-implementation role of lower court judges. In this case judicial ignorance or antipathy to policy goals partially frustrated a legislative program to reallocate power to poor people. It illustrates the truism so often encountered in the lower courts that not only do judges not lead social change movements, they often obstruct them when they appear. Part VI explores other aspects of this theme.

# The Root of the Problem in the Magistrates' Courts*

## Samuel Seabury

The City Magistrates' Courts, as we know them today, were created ... after an extended investigation of the inferior courts by a Commission known as the Page Commission, created by the Legislature in 1908 to conduct an inquiry into the "Courts of Inferior Criminal Jurisdiction in Cities of the First Class." The Page Commission held hearings from September, 1908 to December, 1909. The testimony adduced before the Page Commission revealed a shocking condition of affairs in the inferior courts in New York City. The record of its work, collected in five large volumes, contains a vast amount of information, which, when compared with the voluminous testimony offered before your Referee in the present investigation, has a strikingly familiar sound.

In 1910, after the Page Commission, the City Magistrates' Courts were reorganized under the Inferior Criminal Courts Act. This Act was believed at the time by many reformers to contain truly modern provisions under which justice might be administered. The atmosphere at the time was full of hope that a new era in the dispensation of justice in the inferior criminal courts had been reached. In fact, for years after the enactment of the Inferior Criminal Courts Act, reform organizations hailed it with enthusiasm and approval. The fact that the evils disclosed by the testimony taken before the Referee herein were substantially the same as those which were shown before the Page Commission is conclusive proof that the optimism with which the Inferior Criminal Courts Act was hailed was premature and ill-founded. The reason why we are no better off today under the Inferior Criminal Courts Act than we were prior to its enactment is that the Inferior Criminal Courts Act left unimpaired and free to flourish the basic vice in the Magistrates' Courts, i.e., their administration as a part of the political spoils system. It left the Magistrates to be appointed

* From: S. Seabury, In the Matter of the Investigation of the Magistrates' Courts in the First Judicial Department and the Magistrates thereof, and of Attorneys-at-Law Practicing in Said Courts, [New York] Supreme Court, Appellate Division, First Judicial Department. Final Report 25-33 (Mar. 28, 1932).

by a political agency, the Mayor, upon the recommendation of the district leaders within his political party — and these men, as we know, have regarded the places to be filled as plums to be distributed as rewards for services rendered by faithful party workers. The Courts are directed by these Magistrates in co-operation with the Court clerks, who are not Civil Service employees and who are appointed without the slightest regard to fitness or qualification, but solely through political agencies and because of political influences. The assistant clerks and attendants, though nominally taken from the Civil Service List, are still, in almost all instances, faithful party workers who, despite Civil Service provisions, have secured their places through political influence as a recompense for services performed for the Party. The insidious auspices under which the Magistrates, the clerks, the assistant clerks and the attendants are appointed are bad enough; the conditions under which they retain their appointments are infinitely worse, because they involve the subserviency in office to district leaders and other politicians. It is a by-word in the corridors of the Magistrates' Courts of the City of New York that the intervention of a friend in the district political club is much more potent in the disposition of cases than the merits of the cause or the services of the best lawyer and, unfortunately, the truth of the statement alone prevents it from being a slander upon the good name of the City.

Much, if not all, of the hideous caricature which parades as justice in these courts is avoidable; complaisancy, unconcern and corruption are alone responsible for it — and these causes, in turn, are the product of the system which permits what was intended to be a great instrument of justice to remain a part of a political system, the purpose of which is to retain and control the jobs and perquisites relating to government. As long as appointments to office in these courts are permitted to rest in the hands of a politically controlled agency, just so long must we expect the appointees to be recruited from the ranks of those whose only claim to appointment is their subservience to their political party, and as long as this remains the yardstick by which candidates for these places are to be measured and selected, there is no justification for expecting any substantial improvement in the administration of these courts.

... [T]he nauseating practices which prevail there, must leave a profound impression. These impressions in turn have a direct and potent influence upon the respect of all these persons for our institutions and upon their private as well as public conduct. ...

## MAGISTRATES.

*Appointments as Rewards for Service to Political Party.*

There is no evidence which would justify criticism of some of the Magistrates, and it is gratifying to be able to say of them that, as far as the Investigation has shown, they came by their offices under circumstances suggesting no nefarious political connections. Of the other Magistrates, however, many testified that their appointment to judicial office was the form in which their Political Party expressed its "recognition" for services previously rendered to the "organization." In practically every such case, the evidence shows the applicant for judicial office standing abjectly and, figuratively, with his hat in his hand, before the political District Leader, begging his recommendation to Tammany Hall, which was recognized to be the sine qua non. This evidence presents a situation which is a scandal and a disgrace, as well as a menace, to the City of New York.

It is true that this condition has long existed and is generally recognized — so generally recognized, indeed, that the people of this City have come to accept it as a necessary and inherent part of the Magistrates' Courts. Notwithstanding this, I propose to reproduce the testimony of some of the Magistrates on this subject because, as far as I know, the common-law proof of the condition has never before been laid before this Court for consideration by it.

*Magistrate Dreyer.*

Magistrate August Dreyer stated that when his law practice dwindled, he explained his predicament to his District Leader and demanded "recognition" for his eighteen years of work for the Party. His Leader agreed, and in due time the appointment came. The Magistrate testified:

> I was a Democrat, and I belonged to the organization about eighteen years. This theatrical practice was going downhill fast, upon the ground that the National Vaudeville Artists started, which was taking care of all differences, which were settled by arbitration by the National Vaudeville Artists. The Equity was started with Mr. Paul Turner there, and they took care of all their differences, so that really what was left in the theatrical business was nothing but to take a divorce suit, and I felt that I did not want to take any divorce suits. I simply went around to my organization at the time, which was the 25th, and I spoke to George Donnellan, who was

leader at the time, he is a General Sessions Court Judge. I said:
"Listen," — he was not a Judge at the time — I said: "Listen,
George, for eighteen years I never knew what a reference or receiver-
ship or guardianship was, never got a 5-cent piece, never held a
political office. Here is my position, my practice absolutely gone,
the National Vaudeville Artists settle their differences with the
Actors' Equity who settle their differences through Paul Turner,
what am I going to do? I think I am entitled to get a judgeship for
all I have done for eighteen years, spent my time three times a
week, never asked for anything, never bothered about references,"
I said, "I think I am entitled to some recognition." Well, he says:
"I will be honest with you, you are entitled to some recognition.
You never annoyed me or bothered me, other lawyers were after me
to see what I could get for them." I said: "I think I am entitled to
it."

When Magistrate Frothingham's place became vacant, the appointment went to a resident of his "district." Magistrate Dreyer
began to lose hope; things looked "blue," but his Leader encouraged him. "Don't give up hopes," he said, and finally Magistrate
Dreyer went to see Mayor Hylan.

... and I said: "I am a Democrat, and here you have been a
classmate of mine, and when the time came you asked me to do a
favor and I did it for you. Many an afternoon I stayed in and told
you just what happened. Now, there is an opportunity for you to
help me." Well, the result was I did not get any help. I waited and
waited, and finally one day, I went down and I said: "We will have
it over with with the organization." I wanted to know if my name
was being sent down, and what was happening, if I was being fooled
around with.

Subsequently, Mayor Hylan advised Mr. Dreyer that he was going
to appoint him a Magistrate, and he did.

# The Bench and Its Background*

## Reginald Heber Smith and Herbert B. Ehrmann

### THE UNDERLYING CAUSE FOR DISSATISFACTION

The changes in election machinery were in large part the result of the progressive wave which swept the country in the first decade of the century. They represent a revulsion against intolerable political conditions then flourishing, and it was impossible to foresee all the effects of the steps when proposed by the new leadership. Cleveland has now had ten years' experience of the wide-open method of selection, and although few would care to return to the bossed party conventions, it is safe to say there is scarcely a man in Cleveland able to weigh the qualifications for the bench who does not deplore present tendencies and fear them.

It is not altogether a question of comparing the intrinsic ability and integrity of the new judges with the old. Such a comparison might not be wholly unfavorable to some of the younger judges. Nor does the reason lie entirely in the fact that the judges are coming to the bench younger and less experienced than formerly, and that a few are markedly unsuited for judicial careers. These are symptomatic conditions only. Most serious is the present cheapening of the judicial office, so that neither the bar, the press, nor the judicial incumbents themselves any longer respect it. Young lawyers who would have viewed the bench with reverence formerly, now give voice to their disrespect, and retired and even sitting judges are openly cynical.

The situation is summed up in the universal comment that the judges are generally above the suspicion of taking direct money bribes, but find it difficult to forget the coming election. To judges who have had little or no private practice before beginning their public careers, the matter of insuring reelection is especially urgent.

Here again the trouble lies in attempting to adapt the democracy of the town meeting to a great cosmopolitan population.

---

* From: Criminal Justice in Cleveland: Reports of the Cleveland Foundation Survey of the Administration of Justice in Cleveland, Ohio 251, 259-266, 268-272 (R. Pound & F. Frankfurter, eds. 1922). Reprinted by permission of the Cleveland Foundation.

Direct nomination and non-partisan election of judges produce fairly satisfactory results in a small community, where everyone knows the nominees, and fitness for office is a matter of common appraisal. Judges from country districts are frequently sent to the Cuyahoga Common Pleas Court to help handle the crowded docket in that court, and Cleveland lawyers, on the whole, prefer these outside judges to the members of the local bench. Superior legal ability generally and greater disinterestedness are conceded to these country judges. In a community of nearly a million population, however, containing many voters who cannot even read English, it is not possible for more than a small proportion of the voters to know anything about the fitness for office of the numerous candidates for judicial office. This small group could carry the city by aggressive leadership, but so far there has been no such leadership. The result has been that a judge facing reelection has had to insure his survival through one or several of the following ways: catering to petty bosses who control votes; patronizing certain influential groups — racial, religious, or industrial; general publicity in the newspapers or otherwise. Whichever way the premium is paid, the judge and his high office are degraded. . . .

### IMPORTANCE OF THE PETTY POLITICIAN

Catering to politicians is probably the least common mode of assuring reelection for Common Pleas judges, and not the most desirable for the Municipal judges. It is not only distasteful, but dangerous. Undoubtedly, under the older methods of selection, there were forces which impelled a judge to heed the wishes of the great chieftains of the party, but it must have been less subversive of morale to deal with chiefs, who interfered rarely, than to listen continually to the unvoiced threats of petty vote controllers specializing in criminal law. When one considers that most professional or habitual criminals engage these political lawyers to defend them, the unwholesomeness of the condition is clear.

Moreover, it is often difficult to say where influence ends and "good-fellowism" begins.[1] Both judges and prosecutors have often risen through politics, and it would not be surprising to find that they have not forgotten some of their old associates. . . .

No statistics on this subject can be secured for the Municipal

---

1. Even in civil cases, where the alertness of opposing counsel minimizes the danger of favoritism, complaints are not uncommon. "Before some of the judges," remarks one lawyer, "my first worry is to wonder what 'drag' opposing counsel has with the court."

Court, but prevalent opinion is that "influence" and "good fellowism" flourish still more successfully in that court. This is to be expected where great haste and inadequate record keeping afford a screen behind which operations may be conducted.[3] It is not uncommon for lawyers to call judges on the telephone to talk about their cases. Usually publicity at the trial will thwart any tendency to favoritism by the court. In one case on a charge of rape the defendant, a politician of low order, had a reputation for slipping out of "scrapes" through influence. On the day of the preliminary hearing the court-room was filled with representatives of various women's societies, and the man was bound over. The ways of "influence" are so devious, however, that not even full publicity will avail where there is a determination to protect. "Tim" Raleigh openly and decently maintained an establishment for the placing of election, baseball, and racing bets. It was operated, as a Common Pleas judge had expressed it, "not with the connivance, but with the acquiescence, of everyone," and apparently was regarded as a public service institution. Owing to the vigorous attacks of the Cleveland *Press*, arrests were made and a trial forced. It is reasonable to suppose that no one in authority sincerely desired to convict Raleigh, who had obtained tacit, if not express, consent to the conduct of his business. The *Press* had tried Raleigh in its columns and convicted him, even to the extent of publishing names of men who had placed bets. Nevertheless Raleigh was acquitted, under such circumstances that the judge, jury, prosecutor, and police could each lay reasonable claim to have acted conscientiously and yet point the finger of suspicion at the other.

### THE INFLUENCE OF GROUPS

More important in its effect on the bench than the tendency to respond occasionally to political influence is the bid for support

3. An ex-Municipal Court judge states that when asked to defend his former office boy, he advised him to see the "boss" of his ward and not to waste time with a mere lawyer. An attorney relates that a professional criminal asked him to secure a continuance until he could get his councilman. The papers in this case were subsequently withdrawn. One of the leading firms in the city advised a client in an automobile manslaughter case to take his medicine "because the evidence against him was conclusive." The defendant retained a councilman-lawyer, however, and after several continuances was discharged.

Care should be taken not to make a blanket charge that all judges cater to politicians. Specific instances could be cited where judges have courageously stood out against politics in their court.

which many judges make to different groups and factions in the city. This is almost entirely a new influence upon the judiciary. "In order properly to play the game," observes one of the more sophisticated judges, "it is necessary for a judge to attend weddings, funerals, christenings, banquets, barbecues, dances, clambakes, holiday celebrations, dedications of buildings, receptions, opening nights, first showings of films, prize-fights, bowling matches, lodge entertainments, church festivals, and every conceivable function given by any group, national, social, or religious." Several of the judges have a reputation for "handshaking" nearly every night in the week. One judge of fine, simple nature is reported to have been inveigled into making a speech on the educational and moral value of motion pictures at the first showing of a particularly salacious film. The judge, of course, had not seen the picture. Another judge is said to have refereed a prize-fight. In the past the saloon, as the neighborhood center, has been assiduously courted.[1] Three judges of unquestioned character campaigned by visiting the saloons in the different foreign sections of the city, and were presented to long lines of foreign-speaking voters with the aid of an interpreter. No drinks were bought, not a cent was spent, only handshakes were exchanged, yet this was deemed essential campaigning. All three were reelected.

### 1. Racial and Religious Appeal

One of the most disturbing features is the intensifying of racial and religious appeals. A man is elected or appointed because he is a Pole, a Jew, an Irishman, a Mason, a Protestant, and it is sometimes difficult for a committee to reject a candidate without being charged with discrimination. On the other hand, an even more vicious tendency has begun to appear — the formation of organizations with the avowed or unavowed purpose of "knifing" every candidate who is not of a particular religion, nationality, or color. It is estimated that one such organization last fall, through the expedient of issuing thousands of marked ballots at churches and other places, succeeded in swaying 50,000 votes among the regular nominees. The marked ballot carried nothing to indicate the sectarian nature of the organization, which bore a title similar to that of the Civic League, an impartial organization, and it is not

---

1. In a campaign speech addressed to an audience containing many saloon-keepers a judge is quoted as saying the following: "I am a candidate for an office that is important, especially to men like you. You might have a little unfortunate trouble and get into the police court — when you do, you want a man on the bench who is your friend."

to be supposed that so many voters knew of the dominant motive behind the marked recommendations.

## 2. Labor Organizations

From time to time, as at present, fierce industrial controversies rage in Cleveland, and there, as elsewhere in the United States, in contrast with England, courts are drawn into the economic struggle. Naturally, therefore, each group is alert to bring its pressure — be it voting strength or dominant public sentiment — to bear upon the courts and to be concentratedly watchful of the group interests. Another manifestation, therefore, of the use of group power is the active participation of certain of the labor organizations in the election of judges. Like other groups, these organizations have often not taken a broad view of a judge's fairness and ability. "The unions have lost faith in the courts," states one of their most respected leaders; "they believe the man who has the influence gets by." So believing, they tend to act on their beliefs and fears — fears not wholly unjustified in past American experience. If a judge renders a decision, however conscientiously made, which is believed to be adverse to the interests of a labor organization, he is apt to be marked for the slaughter. Even a passing remark may be taken to stamp a judge as anti-union and be used to defeat him.[1] Naturally, the converse is also true, that unions will support those "who will give us a square deal when we get into trouble." It is not surprising that this condition produces a judge who flourishes his union card on the bench, and in a suit quantum meruit for work done, campaigns for reelection by observing that "a non-union man isn't entitled to receive the union

---

1. Judge R. M. Morgan rendered a decision in Taylor and Boggis Foundry Company v. Iron Molders' Union, limiting the extent of picketing during a strike. The union construed this decision as hostile, and fought him at the primary as "an enemy of the union." Although Morgan had been making an able judge, he was badly defeated. Even the party organization did not support him. The union claimed the credit of assisting in his defeat.

Judge F. B. Gott was opposed for reelection in 1918 because "one of our members was called before Judge Gott about a year ago and he asked this brother what he done with his money, and he told him he was a member of the —— Union. The judge in turn told him he had better drop the union, so he also must have a grudge against labor unions." The "member" referred to had failed to comply with an order of the court as to an allowance for his wife and children, giving as an excuse that part of his wages went to pay union dues. The judge told him his legal and moral obligation to his family came ahead of the union. In 1912 Judge Gott had led the ticket; in 1918 he was defeated, running fifth in a field of eight candidates.

rate of wages." A former judge relates that when he was on the bench two well-known union leaders were introduced to him by his clerk — "no particular business, just to let me know they were on the map."

This situation naturally tends to undermine the character of the judiciary.

There are some critics, notably attorneys for large employers, who would explain all of Cleveland's troubles in administering justice with the observation that "Labor is on top." Little good can come from taking such a simple partisan view. The influence of organized labor is only one of many symptoms of an unhealthy system. If organized labor disappeared completely, the system would be just as unsound and unsatisfactory. The country has had the converse experience with judges imbued wholly with the viewpoint of big business and wants no more of it. The folly of exposing a judiciary to every wind that blows, and then blaming a particular wind, is apparent.

### 3. Bar Association and the Civic League

The two organizations to which the voting public would naturally turn for leadership in the selection of judges are the Bar Association and the Civic League. The Bar Association contains the men who are best able to weigh the attainments of a judge and who have intimate personal knowledge of all the candidates. The Civic League exists largely for the purpose of furnishing the people of Cleveland with unbiased estimates of the qualifications of public officers. Its wide membership places it above suspicion of ulterior motives. Yet neither the Bar Association nor the Civic League has been wholeheartedly accepted by the people of Cleveland as a guide. That other influences have been at times more potent may be seen in the list of judges who have failed of reelection since 1912. Judges who have done well in office and become seasoned should, if possible, be returned to office, if the bench is to develop fine traditions and attract men who seek the bench as a life-work and not as a political stepping-stone. Moreover, it is an expensive work to train young and inexperienced men, and the training should not be wasted. . . .

One reason for the partial ineffectiveness of the Bar Association and the Civic League is the fact that, as a general practice, neither organization makes a fight for its recommendations, except by publishing their indorsements in the newspapers. When a real effort is made to elect its choices, as at the launching of the Municipal Court, the entire list may be elected. Few people are influenced merely by reading a list of recommendations, and many voters live beyond the city limits. Meanwhile the influence of the ward politician, the appeal to race, religion, class solidarity, and prejudice, have won the mass of the voters. Moreover, the two associations begin their efforts *after* the primary, so that often they have little or no enthusiasm for their own indorsements. These bodies have a splendid opportunity for intelligent leadership, and since the advent of woman suffrage, a new and powerful source of support.

There has been another reason for the failure of the Bar Association to lead. For a time it was like most other bar associations in the country, functioning chiefly to eulogize the dead. It has bestirred itself occasionally when vacancies occurred on the bench, and through committees has conferred with judges regarding changes in rules and practice. It has made possible such reforms, as the establishment of the Municipal Court, certainly a great improvement over the justices of the peace. It has maintained an organization for dealing with grievances against individual attorneys, which has probably functioned as well as most grievance committees. Until recently it had never set itself the definite task, however, of supplying educational advantages to its members, or of lifting the standard of admission to the bar, or of cleansing the profession of pirates and evil practices, or of improving the personnel of the bench. For these reasons the Association was not highly regarded even by its own members, or recognized as a public-spirited organization generally. . . .

### PUBLICITY

Editorially, newspaper support of candidates for the bench has in the main been wisely given. What effectiveness the recommendations of the Bar Association and the Civic League have had is due chiefly to the cooperation of the press. The gravest criticism that can be made of the increased editorial power of the newspapers in relation to the bench is that sometimes it comes perilously close to dictating important decisions, and that always the fear of it tends to weaken independence of mind.[1] In a community

1. The dilemma of the judges is clearly brought out in a story related by a court reporter of one of the local papers. A judge who had been ridiculed by this paper, in delivering an address, severely arraigned the press for attempting to influence the court and juries. The reporter walked in toward the close of the address and was discovered by the speaker. As soon as the talk was concluded, the judge rushed to the reporter and whispered, "For —— sake, don't handle me too rough tomorrow."

where the administration of justice may be interfered with by many unseen causes, however, newspaper vigilance has often been exerted in the interest of the public welfare.

## 1. Self-Advertisement

The real evil in the use of the power of the press lies not in its editorial policy, but in its news column, where the daily publication of a judge's name may lead the public to vote for a judge as naturally and unreasoningly as it asks for the most widely advertised brand of soap. Some publicity is, of course, not only justly earned by a judge, but highly desirable from the public viewpoint, as, for instance, when a judge inaugurates a reform, or hands down a decision on an important and unusual question. Such publicity means public education. However, quantity of publicity is more telling than quality. The average voter soon forgets in what connection he has read a judge's name, and knows only that some names on the ballot look familiar and some strange. Then the law of "suggestion" makes him vote for the advertised name.

This kind of voting in Cleveland has produced some curious results. At least two candidates, hitherto unknown to the public and of no marked fitness for the bench, were elected to the Municipal Court because they bore the same names as two retired Common Pleas judges who had built up good will through many years of service. In one election a blacksmith carried Cuyahoga County as candidate for Chief Justice of the Supreme Court of Ohio because his name was similar to that of the well-known judge of the Probate Court. At the next succeeding election for the Supreme Court the same man ran third in a field of seven.

The continued advertisement of a judge's name — or the name of a prosecutor who would be judge — may take place without, and even contrary to, the wish of the editor. The newspaper reporters who cover the courts naturally want copy. The judges, too, desire copy and the combination, unchecked, is bringing the bench into a disrepute which attaches alike to the conscientious judge and the guilty "juggler" on the bench. The least judicial and most immoderate judges get their actions into the papers because "it's news," while strict and competent attention to judicial duties is too commonplace for mention. Several years ago a Municipal Court judge began to sentence traffic-law violators with such a heavy hand that he furnished copy to the reporters for weeks. A society woman receiving a workhouse sentence made "a story." In the fall this judge was a candidate for the Common Pleas bench, and although opposed by the press, led the field by a big majority, partly because of the advertisement he had received. A judge now on the Municipal Court bench started the same tactics in the winter of 1921, fining the liquor law violators — for the most part foreigners making "home brew" — unprecedented sums. The newspapers promptly responded with publicity. Many of the defendants were sent to the workhouse to work out fines ranging from $500 to $3,000 at 60 cents a day. These unfortunates were immediately dubbed "lifers," and a fresh run of publicity started, with photographs and interviews. The judge then injected new life into the news by calling publicly for criticism and suggestions. Evidently the comments he received were not wholly favorably, because he soon relaxed his campaign. As a matter of fact, by means of motions in mitigation, quietly allowed, this judge was not exacting greater penalties than his more moderate colleague in the next room, but of this the public was not aware. The man who paid his huge fine without making a motion in mitigation was penalized for not having a lawyer who "knew the ropes." The judge justifies his conduct on the ground that he never intended the large fines to be paid; that they were simply warnings and had a wholesome deterrent effect.

## 2. Exploitation of the Police Court

The two judges cited are perhaps most extreme examples, but even without such campaigns the police court furnishes lime-light enough. To serve in the police court during election year is a political asset, and the schedule of the judges is apparently conveniently arranged so that all judges facing reelection are given the opportunity to serve on the criminal side during the preceding nine months. If necessary, the regular sitting of a judge not up for reelection is shifted to a colleague who is. . . .

## 4. Campaign Funds

There is one aspect of purchased publicity which ought to be stopped immediately, namely, the solicitation of campaign funds, especially among lawyers. So far the reports of such funds concern only a few judges, but unless curbed, other judges will be compelled to permit collections in their behalf. It would be difficult to conceive a more degenerating influence than the giving of campaign funds by lawyers in behalf of a judge before whom they expect to practise.

## *Gold May Judge But Not on Sonny McDonough's Turf\**

## Robert Healy

Governor's Councilor Patrick (Sonny) McDonough is a friend of Judge Jerome Troy. In fact it was because of McDonough that Troy was appointed by Gov. John Volpe to the bench in the Dorchester District Court. Mrs. Paula Gold, Gov. Sargent's nominee to be special justice of the Dorchester District Court, has directed the Fields Corner office of the Boston Legal Assistance Project and in her work there with the poor has rubbed shoulders with The People First. The People First is a group opposed to Judge Troy.

And that is why Mrs. Gold was rejected last week by the Governor's Council. It is as simple as that.

Sonny McDonough is an oldtime Boston politician whose basic rule is: Don't get mad, get even. And the process is that anyone who opposes one of his old pals has to be disposed of.

McDonough, of course, needed some help. And he received it from Councilors Edward O'Brien (D-Easthampton), George Cronin Jr., (D-West Roxbury), Thomas Lane (D-Lawrence) and Edward Bradley (D-Somerville). There is little mystery as to how he gets them to go along. McDonough is the leader of the pack. This Governor's Council is a school of diminishing returns. The only thing they have going for them now is the nomination of judges. Except for that they might just as well be out of business.

So because it is the Last Hurrah for the council, they hold on. The Dorchester District Court is Sonny McDonough's court. That is what it is known as on the streets of Dorchester. He has had a say in who is appointed as clerk of court. He has had a say as to who sits on the bench. People and lawyers who have business with the courts and with the police in Dorchester know that. A lot of trouble between police and judges can be settled at the clerk of court level. That is power in a district and McDonough is not about to give that up.

---

\* From: Boston Globe, Feb. 11, 1973, at 12, col. 1. Reprinted courtesy of the Boston Globe.

Mrs. Gold would have had no trouble getting through the council if she had been Sonny McDonough's appointment to the Dorchester District Court. That would have meant a continuation of the system. But she is not, and when she gets on the bench, if she ever does, anyone in Dorchester will know that she is not Sonny McDonough's judge and that a call to McDonough won't do any good if there is a case before her.

And that means loss of power for McDonough.

That's what the judgeship for Mrs. Gold is all about.

The Governor's Council had its sails trimmed during the long fight to abolish it in the '60s. It once was a political powerhouse. It had to OK appointments of the executive and even more important perhaps, it OK'd contracts and payments. The council's ability simply to hold up a contract or a payment was real political power. That power has been abolished. But still this archaic body, which was established to be a check against the King's governor of the colony of Massachusetts, remains to OK the judicial selections of the governor. Of course, there must be some confirmation process for judicial appointments which are made until a person reaches 70 years of age. The problem is that the Governor's Council remains as it always was, a politically isolated body. No one cares much about it until it does something outrageous. A majority of the people do not even know who serves them on the Governor's Council and that perhaps is the real cause of this political isolation.

When the reformers were after the abolition of the council, they never made a good case for a body to confirm judges and so the council remains intact but breathing hard.

Some suggested that the state Senate might be a place to confirm judicial appointments. It is a larger body but a great deal more responsive to the public than the council. . . .

## *Milford District Court**

# Gerald O'Neill

LITTLE-USED COURTHOUSE — ONE MILLION DOLLAR MONUMENT
TO DAVOREN'S POWER

The one million dollar Milford District Courthouse is a monument to patronage, nepotism and waste.

Its 100-car parking lot is usually empty, its conference rooms seldom used, its docket one of the lightest in the state.

The court is a gift self-serving local politicians gave themselves at the expense of residents.

It is a showpiece for John F. X. Davoren.

For years the district had been able to get along with the old facility in downtown Milford since the caseload from the four towns of Milford, Hopedale, Upton and Mendon has been one of the lightest in the state. But a courthouse located on the first floor of the town hall offers no prestige to a state legislator who has just become Speaker of the House of Representatives.

One of Davoren's first acts on becoming speaker in 1965 was to push a bill through the Legislature to have the courthouse built.

The original price tag on the courthouse was $600,000 but within two years, Davoren had squeezed another $400,000 out of the Legislature to build the facility.

Filing the legislation with Davoren was former Rep. Nathan Rosenfeld, a Milford Republican. A major portion of the public funds used to build the courthouse went to a company owned by Rosenfeld's brother Joseph, The Globe has learned. The Rosenfeld Concrete Co. of Milford was hired by the general contractor to supply the concrete material for the building. The Board of the Worcester County Commissioners says it paid the contractor more than $130,000 to purchase the concrete from the Rosenfeld firm.

Davoren's real estate partner, Noah DeMattia, was appointed by the Worcester County Commissioners as clerk of the works on construction of the courthouse. Local sources said DeMattia was the only person considered for the job which he was given, they

---

* From: Boston Globe, June 23, 1973, at 26, col. 1-8. Reprinted courtesy of the Boston Globe.

say, because of Davoren's backing. (DeMattia, who at the time was building inspector for the town of Milford, was constructing several cottages with Davoren in Dennis.) After the courthouse was completed, Davoren had DeMattia appointed custodian of the facility but he resigned when townspeople raised a howl over his holding two public jobs.

However, working as a town official while being employed at the courthouse is not uncommon in Milford.

William A. Murray Jr. is part-time clerk of the court as well as being chairman of the Milford Building Board of Appeals. Murray's $12,500 a year salary is the highest in the state paid to a "part-time clerk." It is fitting that he is the son of one of the most powerful women Democrats in the state, Mrs. Mary DePasquale Murray, a long-time member of the Democratic State Committee.

Arthur LeBlanc makes more than $10,000 a year as a court officer in Milford. LeBlanc is also chairman of the Milford Off-Street Parking Commission and a former member of the town planning board. At Davoren's direction, LeBlanc served on the special six-man commission which was formed to find a site for the new courthouse.

(A slice of the 5½-acre site for the structure was purchased from the then-chairman of the Milford Board of Assessors.)

A former Davoren campaign worker, LeBlanc was indicted in 1961 by a Plymouth County Grand Jury for conspiracy to overcharge the city of Brockton on a termite extermination contract. At his trial — where he was found innocent — LeBlanc was defended by Atty. Henry Sontag, who has been Davoren's closest advisor in the State House and is now his counsel as secretary of state.

The other officer at the Milford District Court is George A. Pyne, father-in-law of Massachusetts Atty. Gen. Robert H. Quinn.

The presiding judge at the court is Francis J. Larkin, a close friend and campaign contributor to Davoren. . . .

The caseload handled by Judge Larkin and the 13 other employees at the court has been one of the lightest in the state. Of the 57 full-time courts in the state, Milford ranked 50th in the number of civil cases filed and 55th in the number of criminal cases in 1971 according to the Massachusetts Supreme Judicial Court. Judge Larkin agrees it is hard to justify construction of the court. "We just don't have that much work," he said.

For much of the work week from Monday morning to Saturday afternoon the courthouse is dormant — unused by the citizens it was built to serve. For hours at a time, the only activity inside the structure is the chatter of the secretaries in the clerk's office and the sweeping of a broom by a custodian. Yet, last year the 14 employees of the courthouse cost the county and the state more than $135,000 in salaries.

While the court's case load has remained light, one man's work inside the facility has increased markedly in the last year.

Gordon A. Shaw, a full-time bank lawyer and vice president, is special justice at the court and in 1970 and 1971 he heard cases about 75 days out of the year. However, last year, with the court without a full-time judge for several months, Judge Shaw had to fill in for 179 for which he was paid more than $14,000. This year, with Judge Larkin presiding, Judge Shaw has still been able to average about two sittings a week at a cost of $82.50 a day usually for several hours work, to taxpayers.

### PART-TIME COURT CLERK, FULL-TIME LAWYER — WILLIAM MURRAY, JR.

The secretary dashed into the clerk's office of Milford District Court and shouted to her boss: "Bill, the judge is looking for you in court. They can't start without you."

William A. Murray Jr., clerk of the court, broke off the conversation he had been having with an elderly couple since arriving to work 15 minutes before. "You go back in court," Murray told the secretary. "Hold him off. I'll be in in a while."

The reason why Murray was unable to take care of his public responsibilities — for which the state pays him $12,500 a year — was that he was busy with a pair of private law clients explaining the technicalities of a relative's will.

While the court waited, Murray attended to his private law practice.

Five minutes later the secretary returned accompanied by a court officer. "Judge Larkin wants you immediately," the court officer told Murray sternly. Murray waved him away without looking up and continued speaking with his clients. Several minutes later, the conversation completed, Murray used the court phone to call his private law office in downtown Milford and direct his secretary there to draw up documents needed by his clients. He then escorted the couple out of the courthouse. His private business completed, Murray then strolled into court to begin the morning session. It was 10:45 a.m. and while Judge Francis J. Larkin claims he has forced the court to start on time, Murray was already a half hour late.

This scene — witnessed by a Globe reporter recently — is not unique for the Milford Court clerk's office. According to court employees, Murray frequently uses his court office and hours to interview private clients and when there is a conflict between the two jobs, Murray usually takes care of private business first.

Murray has held the job as clerk of the Milford Court since February 28, 1945, when he was appointed by Democratic Gov. Maurice J. Tobin. It was a strictly political appointment for Murray.

His mother, Mrs. Mary DePasquale Murray, was then, and still is, a member of the Democratic State Committee. A delegate to 13 of her party's national conventions, Mrs. Murray has long been one of the best-known and most influential Democrats in the state.

Murray's father was a well-to-do local attorney who, 10 years prior to his son's appointment, had been named special justice of Milford District Court. For more than a decade, until Judge Murray's death in 1956, the two men served together as judicial officers and attorneys in Milford.

Murray's influence was not confined to Massachusetts. His uncle, Luigi DePasquale, was a district court judge in Providence for 22 years after having been a Rhode Island state representative, senator and chairman of its Democratic State Committee.

Murray was almost removed as clerk of the court in 1960, but his political clout came to his rescue again. For three months, Murray was absent from the court while getting divorced. A bench warrant was issued for his arrest by Worcester Probate Judge Carl E. Wahlstrom after Murray reportedly fled to Florida and Mexico and failed to keep up $100 a week separate support payments to his estranged wife.

Local attorneys called for Murray to be replaced but their appeals fell on deaf ears as Democratic Gov. Foster Furcolo refused to act. Murray later returned, the arrest warrant was rescinded and the clerk's job was still his.

At present he is "actively seeking" to be appointed judge of the court to replace Judge Larkin who is retiring to become dean of Suffolk Law School.

As part-time clerk of court, Murray has been legally able to continue his law practice. He works at the courthouse only until noon and he sticks closely to his schedule. An interview with him recently had to be scheduled in the morning "because afternoons I'm on my own time."

Although Murray works only "part-time" as clerk, the court he administers employs both a full-time and a part-time judge. Only four of the 72 district courts in the state have such an anomalous arrangement. Milford is one of them. Another is Clinton District Court, but its part-time clerk, Walter E. Stukka, has found it too difficult to keep up both jobs of clerk and private attorney.

"The court is going mornings and evenings and the job requires you to be there even if you're not being paid fully. There just aren't enough hours in the day to keep up your law practice — not if you expect to do any quality work at the court," Stukka said.

Somehow, Murray has been able to fill both roles for 28 years. He says he would like to become a full-time clerk in two years "once my 30-year pension is assured." Until that time, he says, he'll continue his private practice which is one of the most lucrative in the area even though he is prohibited from handling criminal cases anywhere in the state or civil cases in his own court. His probate practice is extensive as is his tort work. "I don't have to solicit any cases from my work as clerk," he said recently. "I've got one of the best practices anywhere already. I get more cases than I can handle."

One of Murray's cases ran him afoul of state authorities in 1963 when he had to appear before then Secretary of State Kevin H. White to plead for continuance of the corporate existence of the Franklin Fair Assn. The firm, for which Murray was attorney and officer, wanted to transfer its rights to six racing days to a track 140 miles away in Hancock.

The awarding of the racing dates by the state Racing Commission resulted in an investigation by a special legislative panel. It charged that Murray's firm, the Franklin Fair Assn., was a "phantom fair," which had been revived only to get more racing dates for Berkshire Downs.

Murray argued that the fair was not a "paper organization." He admitted, however, that financial reports for nine years, which are required to be filed annually, had been backdated and filed all at once. Murray attributed the error to a part-time clerk in his law office.

Murray also admitted he signed the name of a deceased director of the fair, his uncle, Joseph DePasquale, to the necessary public documents when the fair changed hands in 1962. His explanation: "It seemed a nullity since two of the three directors signed the papers."

All this time, his court duties have apparently suffered. In the known presence of a Globe reporter recently, the three secretaries who work for Murray in the clerk's office, openly criticized him for his failure to provide them with day-to-day guidance with their jobs.

"I don't ever ask his advice anymore," one secretary said. "He tells you one thing today and the opposite tomorrow. He never knows what's going on." As the women chatted, another court worker poked his head into the clerk's office and shouted: "Everything going as usual, girls — all screwed up?" They all laughed.

Murray is currently looking to the Legislature to relieve him of most of his present tasks by providing him with a full-time assistant. The bill was filed at the State House by Murray's cousin, Rep. Emilio E. Diotalevi.

Judge Larkin, who has presided at Milford Court for more than a year, said he attempted to increase the "standard of professionalism" at the court by requiring trials to begin on time and assure all parties are treated courteously by court officials....

As one local lawyer familiar with the situation said, "Judge Larkin will shout to Murray to get into court on time and stay there but Murray never listens to him and Larkin never backs up his shouts by doing anything. The situation now is the same as it was years ago. Murray does what he damn well pleases in that court and gets away with it."

## Background Characteristics of Magistrates*

## John Hogarth

### INTRODUCTION

Over a total life span, individuals change their attitudes, values, behaviour, and self-concepts as they assume new roles and undergo new experiences. New roles and experiences vary, however, in the extent to which they affect or induce change in the individual depending on the demands of the role, the degree to which it is compatible with past roles and experiences, and the strength of the personalities concerned. Magistrates are appointed to the bench when they are well into middle age. They have had a significant background of life experience prior to appointment. One might expect that this experience will largely determine the attitudes, expectations, and frames of reference that they bring with them to the bench. On the other hand, it may be argued that the judicial role

* Reprinted from: Sentencing as a Human Process, by John Hogarth, by permission of University of Toronto Press © University of Toronto Press, 1971, pp. 50-61.

is sufficiently powerful to restrain any tendency to allow past experience to influence their behaviour once appointed. Magistrates are bound by law, their oath of office, and the traditions and values of their profession, to insulate their private biases from their public behaviour. It may also be expected that the longer magistrates are on the bench, the less important past experience will be. In any event, the role of past experience in present behaviour is a question that can, and in this study will, be tested empirically.

PREVIOUS RESEARCH

There are numerous studies which have demonstrated relationships between the social backgrounds and past experience of judges and their conduct on the bench. It has been shown that there are relationships between political affiliation, social class background, age, religion, and ethnic background, and judicial behaviour. At the same time, many criticisms have been made of attempts to *explain* judicial behaviour in terms of these characteristics.

Critics made the point that attempts to abstract a single item or variable from the background of a judge in isolation of all the other variables bearing on his behaviour, lead to an overly simplistic view of the sources and motivations of judicial behaviour. It has been pointed out that even if all relevant background characteristics are taken into consideration, research of this kind faces the problems of demonstrating how the past influences the present. Scholars have also questioned the assumption, made for the purposes of analysis, that judicial behaviour can be viewed in terms of a simple stimulus-response model. It is argued that analyses which assume that the facts of the cases (the stimulus) and the decision by the court (the response) are perceived and understood equally by all judges give a false picture of the judicial process. Finally, these studies have been criticized on methodological grounds. Nearly all of them were studies of courts consisting of several judges. Regardless of the level or type of court being studied, unanimous decisions were eliminated. This meant that the largest group of cases were excluded from analysis, and undue emphasis was placed on differences among judges.

Joel B. Grossman summarizes these criticisms particularly well:[11]

There is no doubt that preliminary attempts to isolate particular background variables have initially and necessarily overlooked the

11. Grossman, Social Backgrounds and Judicial Decision-Making, [79 Harv. L. Rev. 1551 (1966)].

essentially cumulative and often random nature of human experience, as well as slighting the impact of institutional influences on the judicial mind. That judges are (or were) republicans or catholics or corporate law professors may tell everything about some judges. More likely, it would tell only part of the story. . . . Some categorisation is inherent in all scholarship, but the demands of quantitive analysis in this regard may sometimes seem to be fulfilled at too great a cost.

Knowledge of social background characteristics of magistrates alone offers no key to understanding how they will behave on the bench. But such knowledge will, at least, shed some light on the selection method for appointment, and together with other data, may provide some insight into the judicial process. In this study, social characteristics of magistrates are presented only as a background to further analyses which are to follow. The material presented was derived from interviews with magistrates during which they related their life histories.

### THE SOCIAL CLASS BACKGROUND OF MAGISTRATES

One of the myths that many Canadians like to perpetuate is that their society has no classes. It is a comfortable myth, as it presents an image of a society that provides equal opportunity for all its members to achieve the economic and social rewards coming from success in academic, business, or professional life. This being the case, the myth holds that able people from humble origins can, primarily through education, reach the pinnacles of success and power in whatever field of activity they choose. One would expect, therefore, that the composition of the "power elite," including the judiciary, particularly at the magistrates' level, would reflect the basic structure of society.

But as John Porter demonstrated in his explosive book, *The Vertical Mosaic*, "social images are one thing and social realities another."[12] Porter destroyed effectively the myth of equality by showing that a great deal of the social, political, and economic power in Canada, particularly in eastern Canada, is represented by a surprisingly small minority of Canadian families possessing certain attributes, and that these families tend to pass on the advantages of their class position to their children, by providing advantageous educational and social environments, as well as the

12. J. Porter, The Vertical Mosaic (Toronto, 1965), 3.

goals and values that make for success in competitive society. In fact, Canada has an identifiable class-structure and this class-structure is reflected in the composition of the magistrates' bench in Ontario.

In Table 4, the occupations of magistrates' fathers are listed and ranked in order of frequency. The largest category consists of businessmen of various kinds. In actual fact, most of these owned and operated retail stores and should, therefore, be classed as small businessmen. The professional category, some twenty in all, consists of thirteen lawyers, three judges, and only four from professions not associated with the law. If one groups the three police officers with the judges and lawyers, it indicates that nearly one in three magistrates had fathers whose occupations were associated with the law in some way.

The social class backgrounds of magistrates become significant when one compares them with the distribution of occupational groups in the total labour force during 1930, when most magistrates were still living at home. As can be seen from Table 5, the skilled wage-earners category is a large one (sixteen, or twenty-three per cent). This is roughly representative of the proportion in this category in the total male labour force. What is interesting is the gross over-representation of both businessmen and professionals among the fathers of magistrates, and at the same time the gross under-representation of farmers and unskilled earners. More than half the magistrates come from business or professional families, while not many more than one in ten of the general population are drawn from these occupational groups. At the same time, more than one in three of the male labour force were in the unskilled wage-earner category, while only one magistrate had a father in this group.

These data compare with those in previous studies which have shown that a social class factor distinguished those who achieve high judicial office from the general population. It is interesting that this factor appears to hold in Canada, even at the magistrates' level.

These findings may disturb those who value an open, democratic, society which emphasizes equality of opportunity, and representation of all social groups in the agencies of governmental control. However, career choice is a complicated matter, and it must be pointed out that working-class children who reach university do not choose the legal profession as frequently as do their middle-class counterparts.

Of greater import is the possible impact of middle-class upbringing on the eventual behaviour of magistrates on the bench. As many sociologists have pointed out, social class is more than an economic category. People experience class membership in terms of beliefs and values that are associated with it. People are linked together in social groups by ideas. Social class is one such

### TABLE 4
#### Occupations of Magistrates' Fathers

| Category | Number | Per cent |
|---|---|---|
| Businessmen | 19 | 26.8 |
| Lawyers | 13 | 18.3 |
| Skilled wage-earners | 13 | 18.3 |
| Civil servants | 8 | 11.3 |
| Farmers | 4 | 5.6 |
| Other professionals | 4 | 5.6 |
| Police officers | 3 | 4.2 |
| Judges | 3 | 4.2 |
| Clergymen | 2 | 2.8 |
| Unskilled wage-earners | 1 | 1.4 |
| Total | 70 | 100.0 |

### TABLE 5
#### Per Cent Distribution of Labour Force by Occupations: Magistrates' Fathers Compared to Total Male Labour Force, 1931

| Occupational category | Magistrates' fathers | Total labour force* |
|---|---|---|
| Professional | 26.9 | 3.7 |
| Business | 26.8 | 6.9 |
| Skilled or semi-skilled wage-earner | 22.5 | 23.3 |
| Clerical | 11.3 | 10.5 |
| Farmer | 5.6 | 19.7 |
| Unskilled wage-earner | 1.4 | 35.9 |
| Total | 100.0 | 100.0 |

\* Source: H. D. Woods and Sylvia Ostry, Labour Policy and Labour Economics in Canada (Toronto, 1962), table 35.

group, and its strength depends on the degree to which its members accept its collective sentiments and values as their own. And, of course, in a pluralistic society, such as Canada's, ideas, values, and sentiments compete with one another.

By convention we are taught that the court, particularly the magistrates' court, represents the community. The standards against which behaviour is judged are supposed to be the standards of the average "reasonable man." But how is a magistrate to learn about the standards of this hypothetical "average man," when his past experience and, as we shall see, his current life activities, were and are restricted to social intercourse with a small segment of society. Is it not more likely that a magistrate will reflect the standards he learned in his pre-judicial experience, reinforced by the standards of those with whom he is currently in frequent contact, namely, middle-class standards? Whether or not this is as it should be, it is a question worth exploring....

THE PATTERN OF UPWARD MOBILITY IN MAGISTRATES' FAMILIES

It appears that magistrates come from families that are quickly ascending the social class ladder. In Table 6, the occupational distribution of brothers and brothers-in-law of magistrates is compared to that of the total male labour force in 1951. It can be seen from this table that over-representation in the professional category becomes even more pronounced in the magistrates' generation. Over one-half of the brothers and brothers-in-law of magistrates are professional people, compared to slightly more than one-twentieth of the total labour force. Together with the business category, over three-quarters of family contemporaries of magistrates are in the top fifteen per cent of the labour force. Not one of these family members is in the unskilled wage-earner category, and only fourteen per cent are in the skilled wage-earner category, compared to twenty-four per cent and thirty-four per cent in these respective categories in the general population.

The pattern of upward mobility holds for all occupational categories. If the father was a farmer or unskilled wage-earner, the sons become skilled wage-earners or businessmen; if the father was a skilled wage-earner, the sons become businessmen or professionals, and if the father was a businessman, the sons become professionals. Only in three cases did sons fail to achieve a higher class standing than their fathers. While upward mobility has been a feature of Canadian society since the war, the rate of mobility is much more accelerated among magistrates' families than in the general population.

These findings suggest that magistrates come from families that were relatively successful, at least in economic terms. This is probably a good thing, as it suggests that magistrates are likely to be capable, confident people. But it also suggests that the parents of magistrates probably encouraged ambition, hard work, delayed gratification in the expectation of long-term rewards, and held all the other values that make for success in business and professional life. Whether these values exist among magistrates, and whether the adoption of them influences the way in which magistrates deal with those who have failed in life, are questions that will be explored later.

AGE, BIRTHPLACE, RELIGION, EDUCATION, AND MARITAL STATUS

The demographic characteristics of magistrates are presented in Table 7. Comparisons are made with all adult males in Ontario, and a number of interesting facts emerge, all of which support the conclusion, among others, that magistrates represent a relatively small segment of the population.

## TABLE 6
Per Cent Distribution of Labour Force by Occupations:
Siblings of Magistrates Compared With Total Male
Labour Force, 1951

| Occupational category | Siblings of magistrates | Total labour force* |
|---|---|---|
| Professional | 54.7 | 5.5 |
| Business | 19.8 | 10.3 |
| Skilled and semi-skilled wage-earner | 13.9 | 34.4 |
| Clerical | 4.6 | 11.5 |
| Farmer | 6.9 | 13.5 |
| Unskilled wage-earner | — | 23.7 |
| Total | 100.0 | 100.0 |

* Source: Woods and Ostry, Labour Policy and Labour Economics.

## Age

Magistrates range in age from thirty-four to seventy-one, with a mean age of fifty-five. Leaving aside those persons under thirty who would normally not be considered for judicial appointment, magistrates as a group are still older than the rest of the adult population. Of males over thirty in the general population, about two-thirds (67.7 per cent) are forty or more, compared to over ninety-seven per cent of magistrates.

Despite the fact that there are no age qualifications set down in legislation with respect to the appointment of magistrates, only five magistrates in the sample were appointed before they reached forty, probably reflecting the general view that maturity and experience are essential attributes for magistrates. Comparisons with similar jurisdictions are not possible, due to the unavailability of data. The impression is that magistrates as a group are considerably younger than judges of superior, district, and county courts in Canada, and possibly somewhat younger than English magistrates. Later in this book it will be shown that the age of a magistrate is closely associated with certain attitudes and beliefs that he holds.

## Birthplace

Nearly all magistrates (sixty-five out of seventy-one) were born in Canada. Of the remainder, four were born in the United Kingdom and two in the United States. It is interesting to note that while the "other European" category comprises over twelve per cent of the Ontario male population, this group is not represented on the magistrates' bench. This probably does not reflect bias against immigrants on the part of the Attorney-General in appointing magistrates, but rather the simple fact that most foreign-born do not have the professional qualifications to become lawyers.

## Religion

John Porter has shown that the elite in each area of the Canadian social system is dominated by men of Anglo-Saxon heritage, with Anglican, United, and, to a lesser extent, Presbyterian, backgrounds. This appears to hold true in the legal setting (and as we shall see, since judicial appointments are political appointments, also in the political setting). Roman Catholics and "other protestants," are greatly under-represented among magistrates, while the Anglican, United, and Presbyterian churches are all over-represented. Roman Catholics comprise over thirty per cent of the

## TABLE 7
### Demographic Characteristics of Magistrates Compared to General Population Statistics

|  | Per cent magistrates | Per cent all males in Ontario* |
|---|---|---|
| *Age* |  |  |
| 30-39 | 2.8 | 32.3 |
| 40-49 | 25.3 | 26.6 |
| 50-59 | 39.4 | 20.0 |
| 60-69 | 28.2 | 13.4 |
| 70-79 | 4.2 | 7.7 |
| *Birthplace* |  |  |
| Canada | 91.6 | 77.9 |
| United Kingdom | 5.6 | 8.0 |
| United States | 2.8 | 1.1 |
| Other European | — | 12.6 |
| Other | — | 0.4 |
| *Religion* |  |  |
| Roman Catholic | 16.9 | 30.6 |
| Anglican | 26.8 | 17.6 |
| United Church | 29.6 | 25.9 |
| Presbyterian | 12.7 | 7.8 |
| Other protestants | 5.6 | 9.1 |
| Jewish | 2.8 | 1.8 |
| Other | 1.4 | Unknown |
| *Education* |  |  |
| None | — | 1.2 |
| Elementary | — | 46.0 |
| Secondary | 32.4 | 44.8 |
| Some university | 14.1 | 3.1 |
| Degree | 49.3 | 4.9 |
| *Marital status* |  |  |
| Single | 1.4 | 50.5 |
| Married | 96.8 | 47.00 |
| Divorced | 1.4 | 4.4 |
| Separated | Unknown | Unknown |

Source: Dominion Bureau of Statistics, Census 1961.
* These percentages were calculated only on the population of adult males aged 30-70.

general population, but only twelve per cent of magistrates are
Catholics. The majority of Catholic magistrates (nine out of
twelve) are appointed for judicial districts where the Catholic
population exceeds fifty per cent of the total.

Jewish magistrates appear to be over-represented, but the percentage figure is unreliable due to the small number (two). One
must also remember that in Ontario, Jewish men are greatly over-
represented in the legal profession from which most judicial appointments are made. Exact figures are not available, but it is estimated that about one in five lawyers in Ontario is Jewish. This
suggests that Jews are under-represented among magistrates as far
as their numbers in the profession would warrant.

These findings cannot be explained in terms of a religious bias
in appointments to the bench. Religion is closely associated with
ethnic affiliation, education and, more importantly, social class.
They do, however, show that magistrates do not represent the religious distribution in the province. Later we shall show the differences in attitudes held by magistrates of different religious affiliations.

## Education

Legal training is not a prerequisite to appointment to the magistrates' bench. However, fifty-six out of seventy-one magistrates
now on the bench, or approximately seventy per cent, are lawyers.
Of the lawyers, thirty-five (seventy per cent) took a liberal arts BA
prior to entering law school. The rest either took the required two
years at university, and then completed the three years' law school
course leading to an LL B, or, as in the case of some of the older
magistrates, entered law school direct from high school to complete the then offered five-year LL B programme.

For nearly all legally-trained magistrates (fifty out of fifty-six)
the law school of choice seems to have been Osgoode Hall, until
recently a school administered by the Law Society of Upper Canada, and not affiliated with a university. For many years, this school
had the reputation of providing a more solid practical training
than some of the newer, more academically-oriented schools in the
province.

Of the fifteen "lay" magistrates, nine were previously employed
as justices of the peace or clerks of the court, and one was a police
chief. These ten so-called "lay" magistrates probably came to the
bench with more technical knowledge of the rules of procedure and
practice in the criminal courts than many lawyers.

The policy of appointing lay magistrates has been the subject of considerable criticism from many people in and out of the profession. In general it is felt that despite the technical competence certain lay magistrates might pick up, and conceding that a number of them have admirable personal qualities, legal training is essential for a person to discharge properly the larger judicial role inherent in the resolution of both legal and social issues arising out of the cases. Moreover, it is felt that the standing of the magistrates' court among lawyers and the public at large suffers because it does not require that only professionally qualified people can be considered for appointment to the bench.

## Marital Status

Marital stability is a striking feature of magistrates as a group. All but six were married, and of the remainder, five were widowers, and only one was in each of the divorced and single categories. Single and divorced magistrates are greatly under-represented as compared with the general population.

Table 8 demonstrates that over the years there have been marked fluctuations in the proportions of legally- and non-legally-trained persons appointed. There are three discernible time periods which mark changes in the proportion of legally-trained persons appointed to the magistrates' bench. During the pre-war and war period, about four out of five new appointments were lawyers. In the immediate post-war period, only about half were legally-trained, while in the 1960s the balance again shifted in the direction of more lawyers, with about three out of four appointments coming from this group. The interesting fact is that these trends closely follow broad economic trends in the province, and more particularly, the changing size in the gap between an average lawyer's income and a magistrate's salary. To many lawyers in private practice during the thirties, and to some of the legally-trained veterans returning from overseas, the steady income of a magistrate's salary looked attractive. In the fifties, lawyer's salaries in Ontario rose sharply, while the salaries of magistrates made only modest gains. In this period, legally-trained persons did not come forward. In the 1960s, not only did magistrates' salaries make a remarkable recovery, nearly doubling in the space of five years, but also considerable effort was made to improve the office and court room facilities, working conditions, and status of the court.

*Legally-Trained Magistrates*

Of the fifty-six legally-trained magistrates, forty-nine (or eighty-seven per cent) acted primarily as defence counsel prior to appointment, while eight (thirteen per cent) were full-time crown attorneys for most of their previous legal experience. All legally-trained magistrates had at least ten years' experience at the Bar prior to appointment.

It does not appear that magistrates were selected from those lawyers whose practice was devoted largely, or even substantially, to criminal law matters. Only eight out of the forty-six magistrates with some experience as defence counsel devoted twenty per cent or more of their practice to this type of work. Like most lawyers in Ontario, these magistrates earned the greatest part of their income from the civil side of a law practice. Table 9 shows the proportions of the practices of legally-trained magistrates that were devoted to criminal court work.

Legally-trained magistrates appear to represent the Bar as a whole, rather than the minority of lawyers who can properly be called "criminal lawyers." Until recently, criminal lawyers did not enjoy much status in the profession, although there were a few outstanding exceptions. The recent introduction of legal aid has

TABLE 8

Appointment of Legally-Trained and Non-Legally-Trained
Magistrates Over a Thirty-Two Year Time Span

| Year of appointment | Lay magistrates | Legally-trained magistrates |
|---|---|---|
| 1936-40 | 6 | 19 |
| 1941-5 | 9 | 24 |
| 1946-50 | 10 | 10 |
| 1951-55 | 14 | 15 |
| 1956-60 | 3 | 9 |
| 1961-5 | 5 | 12 |
| 1966-8 | 2 | 11 |
| Total | 49 | 100 |

Source: Inspector of Legal Office, Province of Ontario, Report (Toronto, 1936-68).

made it financially possible for a young lawyer to earn a livelihood primarily from criminal court work. At the same time, renewed interest in the administration of criminal justice, on the part of both the professional Bar and the public in general, has made a career as a criminal lawyer more prestigious.

## Magistrates Without Legal Training

Of the fifteen magistrates without legal training, nine were previously justices of the peace, clerks of the court, or both; four were in private business; one was a school teacher; and one was a chief of police. In the larger urban areas, all the lay magistrates appointed had some prior court experience. Later we shall explore the similarities and differences in attitudes, beliefs, and sentencing behaviour between legally- and non-legally-trained magistrates.

## Military Service

About half the magistrates had military experience. Twenty ended their military career as commissioned officers, nine as non-commissioned officers, and five as regulars. Once again a pattern of success is evident.

## Occupational Stability

Prior to appointment, the majority of magistrates did not change jobs frequently, forty-three holding only one or two previous jobs, and only eleven holding four or more. Bearing in mind that most magistrates were at least forty when appointed, these facts assume some significance. The picture of stability in family, economic, and, as we shall see, community life is further enhanced.

### COMMUNITY TIES

## Years of Residence in Local Community

Nearly all magistrates are home town people, who have spent the greater part of their life in the local community where they now work. This fact is clearly evident from Tables 10 and 11.

For most magistrates, the only time spent away from their home community was that spent at school or in military service. The relative lack of geographic mobility of magistrates in Ontario compared with the general population is quite striking. Almost forty per cent of the total adult population was born outside the census division where they now live, compared to less than five per cent of magistrates.

*Formal Links to the Community*

Most magistrates are very active in the life of their community. Fifty-eight magistrates (nearly eighty per cent), are active members of service clubs, such as Rotary, Elks, or Kinsmen. Twenty (twenty-eight per cent) are also members of the Masonic Order. About one-third hold office in public service or charitable organizations, such as the Community Chest, and of this group, more than half are members of more than one. Two out of every three are active participants in purely social or recreational clubs, and seven out of ten are actively involved in their church.

As far as professional organizations are concerned, over half the magistrates are members of local police commissions. In rural and small town areas the figure is much higher (nearly eighty per cent), as magistrates in some of the larger cities are not normally considered for this position. One in four hold office in local Bar associations. Nearly half (forty-four per cent), sit as judges of the Family and Juvenile Court. Only fifteen magistrates (twenty-one per cent) do not have formal links to the community through club or organizational ties, but of these twelve attended church regularly.

What is the significance of all this? It appears that, on the whole, magistrates are gregarious, out-going people who are often called upon by the community to give leadership or otherwise play a part in the life of the community. In doing so, they are likely to engage in social intercourse with a highly select group of persons. For the

TABLE 9

Proportion of Practice Devoted to Criminal Court Work
Among Magistrates With Some Experience as Defence Counsel

| Proportion of practice (per cent) | Number | Per cent |
|---|---|---|
| 0 | 1 | 2.2 |
| 1-9 | 27 | 58.7 |
| 10-19 | 10 | 21.7 |
| 20-29 | 3 | 6.6 |
| 30-39 | 1 | 2.2 |
| 40-49 | 3 | 6.6 |
| 50-59 | 1 | 2.2 |
| Total | 46 | 100.0 |

most part, the organizations mentioned above are made up of professional and business people with perhaps a sprinkling of skilled wage-earners. It is these people who form the reference groups for magistrates, and the main source of information concerning the views and attitudes of the community. Because of this, one would expect that to the extent that the social and cultural milieux of a magistrate are important in the formation or change of attitudes and beliefs, middle-class values are likely to be encouraged and reinforced. . . .

### POLITICAL AFFILIATION

Appointments to the bench in Canada are "political," in the sense that most appointments are made from supporters of the

### TABLE 10
Years of Residence in Local Community

| Years | Number of magistrates | Per cent |
|-------|-----------------------|----------|
| 1-9 | 1 | 1.4 |
| 10-19 | 8 | 11.3 |
| 20-29 | 13 | 18.3 |
| 30-39 | 7 | 9.9 |
| 40-49 | 16 | 22.5 |
| 50-59 | 17 | 23.9 |
| 60-69 | 9 | 12.7 |
| Total | 71 | 100.0 |

### TABLE 11
Proportion of Adult Life in Local Community

| Proportion | Number of magistrates | Per cent |
|------------|-----------------------|----------|
| One-quarter or less | 2 | 2.8 |
| More than quarter, less than half | 7 | 9.8 |
| More than half, less than three-quarters | 9 | 12.7 |
| Three-quarters and more | 53 | 74.7 |
| Total | 71 | 100.0 |

party in power. At the magistrates' level, appointments are made by the Attorney-General for the province. While appointments to the magistrates' bench of known supporters of opposition parties are not unknown, it is unusual for such an appointment to be made unless a suitably qualified party supporter does not come forward.

This does not mean that prior to appointment most magistrates were actively engaged in politics. Out of seventy-one magistrates, six had been candidates for election, and another seventeen held executive positions in local party organizations. Of the remainder, thirty-five were known to be nominal party members, and seven had no known political affiliation. Three were known as supporters of an opposition party. On appointment, all magistrates dropped visible links to party organizations, but it was noticed in the course of this project that at least five were still active behind the scenes.

Since the Progressive Conservative Party has been in power in Ontario for more than twenty-five years, most magistrates are, or were, Conservative Party supporters. This does not mean, however, that most magistrates are overtly small "c" conservative in outlook or temperament. The Progressive Conservative Party in Ontario occupies a broad band of "right of centre" political thinking, and, if success at the polls is any guide, it enjoys support from many sections of the electorate. It is not inconsistent to be a Conservative in Ontario and at the same time support some social welfare legislation. However, it is no doubt true that most magistrates, like their fellow conservatives, would not go as far in this direction as supporters of the two main opposition parties, the Liberals and New Democrats.

### LENGTH OF EXPERIENCE AS A MAGISTRATE

One would expect judicial experience to be a powerful factor, not only in shaping a magistrate's behaviour, but also in determining his conception of himself. The judicial role is a highly specialized one, based on tradition and circumscribed by law. Norms deeply rooted in law and in the professional role of the magistrate do more than define appropriate and inappropriate judicial behaviour. They affect the nature of his relationships with other persons and determine the values and sentiments that he can properly express in dealing with them.

The judicial role is highly visible, and it is acted out in the court room with rituals and ceremonies which tend to create social distance between the magistrate and others he comes into contact with. This social distance serves the function of isolating him from influences which may alter or conflict with his concept of self as he sees it in relation to his role. The wearing of robes, the elevated position of the magistrate in the court room and all the other ceremonies of deference shown, help define and enhance his position in relation to all the other members of the court. Off the bench, the high degree of formality which characterizes relationships tends to be somewhat eased, but all the parties are likely to be aware of the pre-eminent position of the magistrate.

On appointment, the magistrate must learn quickly the specific and expected pattern of behaviour appropriate to the judicial role. Whatever his background of experience, immediately on appointment he must give the appearance of impartiality, caution, wisdom, certainty, and dignity. In other words, he must appear to be comfortable in his new role, and never show signs of conflict with it. Enormous pressure is thus placed on him to alter any dissonant attitudes, feelings, or beliefs in the direction of conformity to role expectations. Simply stated, judicial experience serves to socialize magistrates into accepting the norms of judicial office.

To the extent that a magistrate internalizes these norms they become part of his self-image. He tends to see the world from a particular point of view, and may find it difficult to behave, and in time even to think, in ways inconsistent with that viewpoint.

For all these reasons, it was felt that judicial experience is likely to be an important variable in the shaping of judicial attitudes, self-concepts and behaviour. Later in this book we will examine the relationship of length of experience to these factors. First, let us look in Table 12 at the varying lengths of experience that magistrates have.

Magistrates range in length of judicial experience from one year to thirty-six years, with a mean of approximately fourteen years. For research purposes, the wide spread in judicial experience is useful, as it allows one to examine the similarities and differences in judicial attitudes and behaviour among magistrates of varying lengths of experience.

TABLE 12
Length of Experience on the Bench

| Years | Number of magistrates | Per cent |
|---|---|---|
| 1-5 | 19 | 27.1 |
| 6-10 | 19 | 27.1 |
| 11-15 | 16 | 22.9 |
| 16 and more | 16 | 22.9 |
| Total | 70 | 100.0 |

## *Urban Politics and Judicial Behavior**

## Martin A. Levin

This paper presents an empirical analysis of the consequences of different political systems on the sentencing decisions of criminal court judges in Minneapolis and Pittsburgh. These cities represent polar models of urban political systems and judicial selection.

Some large cities have a traditional political system. This involves a formally partisan city government, with (in varying degrees) strong parties that rely on material rewards rather than issues to attract members, have a generally working-class orientation toward politics, emphasize the conferral of material benefits upon individuals, identify with local areas of the city rather than with the city as a whole, and centralize influence. Other large cities have a "good government" or reform political system. This involves a formally nonpartisan city government and weak parties that rely on nonmaterial rewards (primarily issues or personalities), have a generally middle-class orientation toward politics, emphasize the maximization of such values as efficiency, honesty, impartiality, professionalism and identification with the city "as a whole," and decentralize influence. Scholars have just begun, however, to trace the practical consequences of each system for

* From: 1 J. Legal Studies 193-221 (1972). Reprinted by permission of Journal of Legal Studies. Tables have been omitted.

urban residents. None has yet studied the consequences of the different systems for judicial behavior.

For many years attorneys, their professional associations, many judges, and reform-minded laymen have advocated taking the selection process of judges "out of politics." The proposals vary, but are typically variations of the "Missouri Plan" or "merit selection plan," in which the governor appoints the judges from a list of nominees selected by a nonpartisan nominating commission composed of lawyers and laymen (and in some instances judges). The appointees go before the voters at the next election without opposition. Another selection method, which is also designed to remove judges from politics but which reformers feel is less ideal, is the selection of judges in truly nonpartisan elections. The advocates of reform argue that judges are experts and should be selected by fellow experts in a nonpolitical manner and that expert, nonpolitical selection procedures will produce higher-quality, more efficient, more independent, and, therefore, more impartial and just judges. None of the reform advocates supports his assertions with systematic evidence indicating that taking the selection of judges "out of politics" does in fact produce such judges, or indeed that it has any consequences for judicial behavior. Opponents of taking the selection of judges "out of politics" premise their argument on democratic values, but also fail to support their assertions with evidence that a political selection procedure would help attain such values.

Pittsburgh has a formally partisan and highly centralized city government. In 1966, when this research was begun, the Democratic party organization was strong, hierarchical, disciplined and highly cohesive, and attracted workers by means of material incentives.[10] It had dominated city politics since the early 1930's and had been influential in state and national politics. Public and party offices in Pittsburgh are filled by party professionals who patiently "wait in line" because of the party's desire to maintain ethnic and religious "balance," even on a judicial ticket. The citizens tend to accept pro-union and liberal social welfare policies. There is wide acceptance of partisanship and party activity in almost every sphere of Pittsburgh local government. The public has

10. The Pittsburgh Republican organization also attracts workers with material incentives, but it is weaker and correspondingly less highly disciplined and cohesive. For a detailed discussion of the political and judicial selection systems of both cities, see Martin A. Levin, Urban Politics and the Criminal Courts (forthcoming).

displayed little enthusiasm for efforts to take the selection of judges "out of politics," and parties view positions on the courts and their related agencies as primary sources of rewards for their workers.

There are nineteen judges on the Allegheny County (Pittsburgh) common pleas court, the trial court for both criminal and civil cases, and they are elected, on a partisan basis, for ten-year terms. Party designation appears on the ballot. The political parties, especially the Democratic party, dominate both the primaries and the general elections for judicial positions in Pittsburgh; the bar association usually plays a very limited role. When a court vacancy occurs, the governor appoints a successor who must stand for reelection at the next general election. Ten of the nineteen incumbent judges in 1965 had first reached the bench in this way. These appointments have been controlled by the local parties.[11]

The Pittsburgh judges' career patterns also reflect the dominance of the parties and the limited role of the bar association in judicial selection. At the time of appointment or election almost all of the judges held a government position, such as city solicitor, assistant prosecutor, city councilman, state legislator, or congressman (all partisan offices, and all controlled by the parties), and were active members of the party organization.

Minneapolis has a formally nonpartisan and structurally fragmented city government. The democratic-Farmer-Labor (DFL) party and the Republican party play a significant role in city politics, but one that is both formally (because of nonpartisan elections) and informally (because of the wide acceptance of nonpartisanship) limited. The parties are weak, undisciplined, loosely organized, and highly democratic. They attract workers through nonmaterial incentives. The parties do not overcome the formal decentralization of authority in the city. Individuals (including "amateur" politicians) with the ability and willingness to work, but with little seniority in the party, can and do rise rapidly in

11. The only names that Democratic governors considered for a judicial appointment are those that came from the Pittsburgh organization. Some Republican governors have requested, and sometimes followed, the Pittsburgh bar association's recommendations, but its influence has been limited even during Republican state administrations (including reform-oriented administrations). Its recommendations have first been cleared (and sometimes modified) by the Pittsburgh Republican organization, and then often blocked ultimately by the Democratic organization, which has successfully opposed interim Republican judicial appointments at the next election several times since 1950.

the party and in city government. The citizens tend to be disposed toward conservative city policies. Nonpartisanship in city politics is accepted by the people (and even by many party workers and some party leaders). Indeed, the electorate has had a strong negative response to candidates or incumbents who violate, or seem to violate, the ideal of nonpartisanship. This is especially true with respect to the courts and their related agencies, and consequently party leaders and workers tend not to regard them as a source of party rewards.

There are sixteen judges on the Hennepin County (Minneapolis) district court, the trial court for both criminal and civil cases. They are elected for six-year terms on a nonpartisan basis. The political parties play almost no role in the selection of judges in Minneapolis; the local bar association plays a major role. Prior to a judicial election the Minneapolis bar association polls its members and publicizes the results. The "winner" of the poll (or the second or third highest candidate) almost always wins the ensuing election. The governor makes appointments to interim vacancies, and fourteen of the sixteen incumbent judges in 1965 had first reached the bench in this manner. When vacancies occur, the Minneapolis bar association again conducts a poll and the Minnesota governors have adhered closely to the bar's preferences. The two DFL governors who have served in the last ten years have been significant exceptions to this pattern, but they were strongly criticized for this (even by some of their own party members) and had to work carefully around the bar association. Moreover, even during the administrations of these governors, the party played almost no role in judicial selections: the appointees' relationships to these governors were personal rather than organizational.

The Minneapolis judges' career patterns also reflect the minor role of the parties and the major role of the bar association in judicial selection. Prior to coming to the bench fourteen of the eighteen Minneapolis judges in this study had been exclusively or predominantly in private legal practice (usually business-oriented, and often corporate, practices). Those who held public positions before coming to the bench did not hold elective positions (with one exception) and were generally not active in either party. . . .

To understand typical judicial behavior in each city, sentencing decisions were compared statistically for the nine most common felony offenses. To understand the judges' attitudes, decision-making processes and courtroom behavior, interviews were conducted

with all but one of the judges in both cities, and trials and courtroom proceedings were observed over a period of several months
in 1966. The judges' interview statements were cross-validated on
the basis of their actual sentencing decisions, observation of their
courtroom behavior, and interviews with more than twenty criminal court participants in each city.

There are significant differences in the sentencing decisions of
the judges in each city. Table 1 compares the percentage of probation in both cities for all nine offenses in one subset of defendants
— whites with a prior criminal record. In this subset, there is a
greater percentage of probation in Pittsburgh for all nine offenses.
This and subsequent tables . . . indicate that, on the whole, the
decisions are more lenient in Pittsburgh than in Minneapolis.
Both white and black defendants receive probation more frequently
and shorter prison terms in Pittsburgh. . . . [T]his pattern persists,
when the defendant's previous record, plea, and age are controlled,
and it is generally consistent for all of the offenses compared.
For probation, when the sentencing decisions are controlled for
type of prior record and race, there is a sufficient number of cases
to compare the nine offenses in each city for twenty-five specific
categories of offender. In 22 categories the percentage of probation
is greater in Pittsburgh; in two it is greater in Minneapolis; in one
there is no significant difference. For incarceration, we can perform the same analysis of sixteen categories, and we find that in
thirteen of these the length of incarceration is less in Pittsburgh;
in two categories it is less in Minneapolis; in one there is no significant difference between the cities.

Although both white and black defendants receive more lenient
sentences in Pittsburgh, in both cities whites receive probation
more frequently than blacks in most categories. In Minneapolis
whites also receive shorter prison terms than blacks in most categories. In Pittsburgh, however, blacks receive shorter prison terms
than whites in almost all offenses. On the whole, . . . sentencing
decisions are more favorable to blacks in Pittsburgh than in Minneapolis, both in absolute terms and relative to whites.

A comparison of sentencing decisions by type of plea . . . reveals
that the Minneapolis judges gives defendants who plead not guilty
more severe sentences more frequently than do the Pittsburgh
judges. In Pittsburgh the sentences of such defendants are, on the
whole, only slightly more severe than those of defendants who
plead guilty; in Minneapolis they are much more severe.

There is much more uniformity in the length of prison terms
in Minneapolis than in Pittsburgh. In Minneapolis, white and

black defendants with the same type of prior record receive the identical or nearly identical median term of incarceration in five of the seven offenses in which there is a sufficient number of cases for comparison. Not so in Pittsburgh. There white and black defendants with the same type of prior record receive a nearly identical median term of incarceration in only two of the nine offenses in which there are sufficient cases for meaningful comparison.

Turning to the attitudes and decision-making processes of the judges in the two cities, we find that the Minneapolis judges tend to be more oriented toward "society" and its needs and protection, and toward the goals of their professional peers, than toward the defendant. Their decision-making is also formalistic in character. The Pittsburgh judges typically are oriented toward the defendant rather than toward punishment or deterrence. Their decision-making is particularistic and pragmatic.

There are also significant differences in the judges' courtroom behavior prior to sentencing. Most nonjury trials in Pittsburgh are informal (for example, the witnesses stand at the front bar) and abbreviated. Most of the judges prefer this arrangement, and they also prefer informal procedures for obtaining information concerning defendants (the defense attorney's trial presentation, individuals intervening with the judge outside of court, the court staff's knowledge about the defendant) to the presentence investigations of the probation department. Trials in Minneapolis are formal, deliberate, and unabbreviated, and all of the judges prefer this arrangement. Presentence investigations are conducted in almost every case and most of the judges dislike utilizing any informal sources of information concerning the defendant. In both cities plea bargaining is infrequent. . . .

The Minneapolis and Pittsburgh judges' views, decision-making processes, and sentencing behavior approximate two general models of decision-making: a judicial decision-making model (Minneapolis) and an administrative decision-making model (Pittsburgh). In the judicial model, decisions are made on the basis of the evidence of record developed by the adversary system. The judge feels that he must maintain an image of detached objectivity. The judge's decisions are dichotomous (yes-no) and assign legal wrong to one of the two parties. The judge arrives at his decision by a formal line of reasoning from legal principles. He is more concerned with satisfying the requirements of "the law" conceived as an abstract ideal than producing "just" settlements of individual cases.

In the administrative model of decision-making, decisions are made on the basis of the kind of evidence on which reasonable men customarily base day-to-day decisions, evidence frequently gathered by the administrator's own investigation. The length and depth of the investigation is determined by the resources available to him. An administrator believes that he must seek intimate contact with the real world in order to be able to administer effectively, and that this is more important than maintaining an image of detached objectivity. He may adopt dichotomous (yes-no) or intermediate decisions (such as compromise decisions or delay in enforcement of a decision). He reasons to his decision, pragmatically and inductively, from the policy goals embodied in the program he administers. He has greater concern for arriving at "just" settlements based on the particular merits of individual cases than for adherence to abstract notions of justice and the law. He seeks to give individuals what he feels they "deserve," and he bases his decisions in large part on the needs of those individuals; in some instances he may perceive that one of their needs is exemption from the treatment involved in his program. He has greater concern for substantive issues than for procedure, and measures his success by the way the program he administers "fits" real-world demands and supports.[23]

The administrative model of decision-making fails to fully cap-

---

23. Herbert L. Packer has recently suggested "crime control" and "due process" models of the criminal justice process. Herbert L. Packer, The Limits of the Criminal Sanction 149-173 (1968). There are some similarities between his models and those presented here (for example his crime control model, like this study's administrative model, has assembly-line procedures, informal fact-finding and is generally "almost managerial"), but the differences in the goals and means of his models and this study's are much more significant. For example, in the crime control model the goal is the repression of crime by all possible means, and the means are routinized and uniform procedures. By contrast, in the administrative model that the Pittsburgh judges' behavior approximates, the maintenance of order is but one of several goals, which also include arriving at "just" settlements based on the particular merits of individual cases and expediting their caseload in a pragmatic fashion. These judges feel that policies of agencies such as the courts are not likely to be effective deterrents or modifiers of illegal behavior. Also, Packer's models relate to legislators, police, prosecutors, defense attorneys, and judges and emphasize the central role of counsel and the passive role of the judge. This study's models relate only to the judges; its findings indicate that in these two cities the judges dominate the counsel. Finally, unlike this study, Packer's does not analyze the behavioral consequences of the processes described in the models.

[See Part II, *supra* — ED.]

ture one major element of the Pittsburgh judges' behavior — their special emphasis on informalism and on personal and individualistic consideration. The model of Khadi justice described by Max Weber seems to capture this and other elements of their behavior. Weber describes Khadi justice as "popular justice" based on "free discretion" and appealing to "the sentiments of laymen" (especially the "underprivileged classes") because of its focus on the "concrete, ethical, or political considerations of substantive justice [rather than] formalism." Khadi justice involves eschewing written law and deciding on the basis of "practical value judgments." The source of modern Khadi justice is "the democratic ethos," and it springs from "irrational 'feelings' . . . normally instigated or guided by party leaders or the press." [24]

Let us look more closely at some of the differences in judicial attitude between the Minneapolis and Pittsburgh criminal courts. Thirteen of the seventeen Minneapolis judges appear to have little empathy for defendants, whom they often describe as "coming from low intelligence groups," "crummy people," "congenital criminals," "not learning from their mistakes," "not able to consider the consequences before they act." They tend to be resigned to the "criminality" of most defendants and often seem inclined to "give up" on them. The Minneapolis judges' tendency to penalize with more severe sentences defendants who plead not guilty seems to be an indication of their greater concern for what they consider the needs of society than for the defendant.[26]

At the same time, thirteen of the seventeen judges are also ori-

24. See Max Weber on Law in Economy and Society (Max Rheinstein, ed.; 1954), 351-352, 354, 356. [See Part I, *supra.* — Ed.]

26. Twelve of the seventeen judges feel that trials should not be used by the "guilty" to escape a conviction. Thus, if a defendant pleads not guilty and is then convicted, they are critical of him because "he has put the state through the expense of a trial." They feel that his plea indicated "a wrong attitude" or that he "wasn't repentant" and that he "deserves less consideration" in sentencing. Minneapolis defense attorneys are aware of the judges' attitudes and behavior concerning pleas of not guilty, and thus they usually encourage their clients to plead guilty. Only 14.4% of the defendants in this study's sample pleaded not guilty in Minneapolis, while in Pittsburgh, where defendants are not reluctant to do so, 71.1% of our sample pleaded not guilty. Many of the not guilty pleas in Pittsburgh are "slow pleas" — a "slower," more drawn out manner of pleading guilty. The trials that follow this type of plea are informal, abbreviated, and consist largely of the defense's presentation of statements concerning the defendant's allegedly favorable personal characteristics. These are irrelevant to his guilt or innocence; they are aimed at the judge's sentencing decision. . . .

ented toward their professional peers (such as correction authorities and law enforcement officials) and their goals. They are willing to sacrifice the exercise of some of their own discretion in order to achieve both greater consistency in their own sentencing and the goals of some of these peers (such as "professional expertise" and "better law enforcement"). In almost all instances in recent years, the effect of pursuing these goals has been more severe sentences. These judges tend to be enlightened in terms of professional doctrine rather than benevolent toward the defendant. Many Minneapolis judges explain that one reason they dislike and discourage informal sources of information about the defendant (which tend to convey personal and mitigating information) and prefer the probation department's formal presentence investigations (which tend to be professional and objective) is that they "don't want to become emotionally involved in individual cases."

Twelve of the seventeen Minneapolis judges believe in the effectiveness of institutional rehabilitation and penal deterrence, and thus are not reluctant to punish defendants by incarcerating them. Judge Rasmussen told an interviewer: "I know I am considered a tough judge here, but that doesn't bother me because punishment works. You won't sit on a hot stove if you have been burned." Few of these judges are critical of the quality of prisons, but several complain about "the failure rate of the people we put on probation." Many of the judges spoke of the therapeutic effect of the "shock" of incarceration.

These thirteen Minneapolis judges feel little "closeness" to the defendant. Rather than act as a buffer between him and the law, they act as if they *are* the law. The nature of the offense dominates these judges' considerations ("the offense itself is an indication of the man and his motives"), especially when the offense is a crime against the person. Thus, although sentences for all offenses are more severe in Minneapolis than in Pittsburgh, the differential is greater for armed robbery than for crimes against property. Still, ten of the seventeen Minneapolis judges consider most crimes against property "serious crimes."

Universalistic criteria dominate these judges' decision-making. They rarely regard individual characteristics (age, whether only property is involved in the crime, a black defendant's environment, a favorable family or employment situation, or addiction to alcohol or narcotics) as legitimate bases for making exceptions. Their consideration of individual and personal characteristics is limited to highly unusual situations. Judge Slovack described such a situation:

There are only a few situations in which I will give a fellow extra consideration. I had one in here on burglary and his attorney made a very emotional plea about the fellow's wife going blind and that he had to raise some money to help her. So I gave him probation.

Many of these Minneapolis judges seem to be aware of the non-legalistic factors they might consider, but do not think they are proper or relevant. For example, they believe that the stability of lower-income families is the proper concern of public agencies other than the criminal court.

Sixteen of the eighteen Pittsburgh judges seem to be oriented toward the defendant. Their view of most defendants is benevolent, and they describe their decision-making as "giving the benefit of the doubt" to the defendant, "taking a chance on the defendant," or "err[ing] in the direction of being too soft." They feel that "chances" are worth taking despite getting "taken in sometimes" because "some are rehabilitated." They seek to "help" defendants, especially by "emphasiz[ing] probation and parole." Moreover, they tend to feel that they have a "closeness" and "kinship with the people that come into criminal court," that they are "more human" than the judges of the past and that they have a "greater empathy and awareness of the [defendant's] problems" and "more insight into the different types of people" that come before them. Several judges explain this empathy and "closeness" as part of a general attachment to the "underdog"; others explain it as a product of experience in their previous careers in political parties and government;[33] some say it stems from their own minority ethnic and lower-income backgrounds.[34]

The Pittsburgh judges' sentencing decisions for defendants who plead not guilty, which on the whole are only slightly more severe than for defendants who plead guilty (in sharp contrast to Minneapolis), seems to be a manifestation of their greater orientation toward the defendant and his needs than toward "society." Their preference for using informal sources of information concerning

33. For example, Judge Bloom told an interviewer, "A judge should feel a kinship with the people that come into criminal court. Through my thirty years of active political work I worked with Negroes and other poor persons, and I developed a kinship with them and an awareness of their problems."

34. Judge Guggliemi explained: "I was brought up in a semi-industrial neighborhood, and my father worked in the mills. I was a solicitor for the township, so I got to know people with problems more intimately. I learned that it's really tough for some people just to get along in this world . . . ; you also see this inability to cope with life in the people in (criminal) court, particularly the minorities."

the defendant — individuals' intervention with the judge, the defense attorney's trial presentation, and the court staff — also seems to be a manifestation of this orientation. These informal sources focus almost exclusively on mitigating circumstances. By contrast, the presentence report is made by a "third party," the probation officer, whose professional ethos stresses objectivity; and it includes both mitigating and aggravating information.

The Pittsburgh judges' closeness to and empathy with the defendant cause them to stand apart from the law and act as a buffer between it and the people upon whom it is enforced. Most of them act as if they view the law primarily as a constraint within which they have to operate to achieve substantive justice for the defendant. They are critical of the law's inflexibilities and resist standardization of any of their sentencing decisions (even in offenses such as drunken driving and gambling).

The Pittsburgh judges tend to reject legalistic criteria in favor of policy considerations derived from criteria of "realism," and "practicality." Fourteen of the eighteen judges do not seem to be oriented toward institutional rehabilitation, punishment, or deterrence in their sentencing decisions because of their "realistic" attitudes concerning deterrence and the actual quality and effectiveness of prisons. They believe that prisons today are usually ineffective in achieving rehabilitation or discouraging recidivism because of their low quality ("not much is done for [defendants] in jail," "it's not helpful," the jails do "more damage" and defendants leave "worse off"), and that this consideration is relevant to their sentencing decisions.

The judges' views on the gravity of offenses also seem to be based on "realistic" criteria. Twelve of the eighteen judges tend to view criminal behavior as often a manifestation of a dispute between two private parties rather than as a conflict between an individual and society. From this perspective many acts appear less serious to the judges, especially where there is a special relationship between the defendant and the victim.[37] Similarly, thirteen of the eighteen Pittsburgh judges believe that many crimes against property that do not involve violence are "minor," involve "only money," and are "less serious than [harm to] a human being."

Thirteen of the eighteen judges indicate they should consider

37. Some of these "special" relationships include prior acquaintance and sometimes strong ties (e.g., as a relative, friend, or lover), the victim's physical or sexual provocation (e.g., in assault or rape cases), monetary provocation (e.g., in forged check or theft cases), or the "victim's" desire for revenge.

such "practical" factors as "how the defendants live," the heterogeneity of the city's population, and particularly the "mill town" character of the population, in ascertaining the standards of proper conduct. They seem often to base their sentencing decisions on frankly extra-legal standards, notably the standards of the group in which the offense occurred (youths, blacks, lower-income persons, homosexuals). For example, several of the judges believe that blacks often deserve "breaks" because of their "different code of morality." To these judges, frequent use of extra-legal standards is more realistic and equitable than the "rule of law" assumption that there is a single standard of conduct to which all individuals are expected to conform. The use of extra-legal standards tends to reduce the gravity of offenses in the judges' eyes. Similarly, most of the Pittsburgh judges justify another departure from the rule of law — their use of informal courtroom procedures that can undermine a defendant's rights to due process, such as the verdict "acquitted plus costs" — on the ground that they introduce "compromise" and "practical considerations" into law.[39]

Sixteen of the eighteen judges base their sentencing decisions on a very wide range of individual and personal characteristics as well. They feel that "everything counts"; it is the "whole system" and the "complete picture" that must be considered. They describe their decision-making as "intuitive," "impressionistic," "unscientific," and "without rules of thumb." In part they seem to base sentencing decisions on such general criteria as the defendant's offense and the "type of person" he is, but they also act as if no general norm could cover all individuals within the criteria. Thus they give weight to such diffuse and particularistic considerations as "how the defendant conducted himself" during the commission of the offense, how "cooperative" he was when arrested, and the culpability and background of the victim (for example, the degree of actual consent, provocation, and the previous "purity" of a victim, in a rape case).

39. Almost all of the judges used the verdict "acquitted plus costs" until it was declared unconstitutional in 1966 by the U.S. Supreme Court. (Giaccior v. Pennsylvania, 382 U.S. 399, a case from another Pennsylvania city.) In this verdict a defendant was acquitted but also ordered to pay the court costs and was thus, in effect, given a fine without conviction. (By contrast, almost all of the Minneapolis judges stated that they did not use a somewhat analogous procedure that had been available to them on the municipal bench.) Also, most non-jury trials in Pittsburgh are informal — witnesses often stand at the front bar — and abbreviated. The judges justify these procedures as practical necessities which do not prejudice either the judgment of guilt or the sentence.

In crimes against the person, the nature of the offense tends to become the dominant criterion in the decisions of fourteen of the eighteen judges, and thus tends to operate as a general standard. However, these judges significantly qualify the generality of this standard by making distinctions among the various types of crimes against the person (such as the degree of viciousness involved in the violence, the degree of aggressiveness, the degree of passion, whether a weapon was involved, the degree of provocation involved or whether the act caused an injury). For example, a comparison of the Pittsburgh and Minneapolis judges' sentencing decisions for armed robbery indicates that the Pittsburgh judges frequently qualify the general standard and the Minneapolis judges almost always adhere to it.

It is not surprising that sixteen of the eighteen Pittsburgh judges should describe their decision-making as exceptional and expedient. As Judge Guggliemi explained:

> If I can find a way — if the evidence ameliorates in some way I'll give [the defendant] a "break." I suppose that it's unfair, but I try to help as many as I can. . . . I'm not constrained in sentencing by viewing defendants in set categories; I'm just trying to help them out.

The bases of these exceptions are not distinctions defined by the law as being relevant; they are distinctions based on the policy considerations that the judges believe are relevant to their decision-making. For example, twelve of the eighteen Pittsburgh judges believe that it is legitimate for the court to consider the effects of its decisions on a defendant's family and employment situations. Similarly, fourteen of the eighteen judges feel that young males by nature are likely to have "escapades" and thus often deserve "breaks" — especially if they are first offenders — because their behavior is often likely to change simply with time.

The behavior of the Pittsburgh and Minneapolis judges appears to be the indirect product of the cities' political systems. These systems influence judicial selection, leading to differential patterns of socialization and recruitment that in turn influence the judges' views and decision-making processes. The pre-judicial careers of most of the Pittsburgh judges in political parties and government, and their ethnic minority and lower-income backgrounds,[44] seem to have contributed to the development of the

44. Four of the Pittsburgh judges are Jewish, two of them foreign born — in Poland and Austria. Seven of the judges are Catholic, one of them foreign

characteristic that many successful local politicians possess — the ability to understand the motives of other people by entering imaginatively into their feelings. Their political experience and — a frequent concomitant — lack of much legal experience seem to have contributed to the highly particularistic character of the judges' decision-making and their emphasis on policy. In party and policy-oriented government positions, general rules are usually subordinated to more immediate ends (such as the desires of a constituent), and personal relationships — rather than abstractions such as "the good of society as a whole" — are emphasized. A primary task of a local party worker is to view a situation in personal terms, to dispense favors, and to make exceptions rather than to apply legal rules. It is usually his job to say "yes," particularly to an individual who has a problem or who is in trouble.

The predominantly legal-practitioner pre-judicial careers of most of the Minneapolis judges, and their dominantly middle-class Northern-European-Protestant backgrounds,[46] seem to have con-

---

born — in Hungary. Three of the other Catholic judges have Irish backgrounds, two are Italian, and one is Polish. One of the judges is black, and six are white Protestants. Eleven of the judges had working-class backgrounds and seven had middle-class backgrounds. (This class categorization is based primarily on the occupation of the father of each of the judges.) The pre-judicial careers of twelve of the eighteen Pittsburgh judges were predominantly or exclusively in public positions such as congressman, state legislator, city councilman, assistant district attorney or assistant city solicitor. All of these positions are partisan, and the parties dominate the recruitment for them. Moreover, while holding these positions they were also active members of the party organization. The pre-judicial careers of five of the eighteen judges were predominantly in private legal practice, but a significant proportion of the careers of three of them involved public positions (and thus party activity) such as those just noted. Only one of the judges' pre-judicial careers was exclusively in private legal practice, and even he had had a good deal of exposure to party activities as a local and national leader of an ethnic fraternal organization.

46. Fifteen of the Minneapolis judges are Protestants, including Lutherans and also Congregationalists, Episcopalians, Methodists, and Christian Scientists. Eight of these Protestant judges have Scandinavian backgrounds (one is foreign born — Norway). Two of the Minneapolis judges are Catholic, and one is Jewish. Ten of the judges had middle-class backgrounds and seven had working-class backgrounds. The pre-judicial careers of six of the eighteen Minneapolis judges were exclusively in private legal practice. An additional eight judges were predominantly in private legal practice, but a small proportion of their careers involved public positions. (Half of these eight judges held these public positions during World War II and accordingly did not serve in the armed forces.) Most of the fourteen judges were involved in business-oriented legal practices and several were involved in corporate prac-

tributed to their development of a greater orientation toward "society." In their careers few had contact with individuals from lower-income backgrounds. Their experience in predominantly business-oriented private practice typically involved major social institutions, such as the "law," corporations, and commercial transactions.

Their pre-judicial experience (reinforced by their lack of party or policy-oriented experiences) may also explain the more formalistic character of their decision-making and their eschewal of policy and personal considerations. In their milieu, rules were generally emphasized, especially legal ones. These rules were used to maintain and protect the social institutions with which they were involved. Learning to "get around" required a skill in operating in a context of rules. Their success seems to have depended more on their objective achievements and skills than on personal relationships. Furthermore, the predominantly middle-class background of these judges may in itself have contributed directly to their emphasis on the importance of laws.

The decision-making of the few judges in both cities with cross-cutting backgrounds and experiences in effect serves as a control, and it seems to indicate that pre-judicial career experiences are a more important influence than social background. The decision-making of the few Pittsburgh judges with middle-class Protestant backgrounds who also had careers in party and government positions tends to be much like that of their ethnic-minority and lower-class-background colleagues. The decision-making of the few Minneapolis judges with middle-class Northern-European-Protestant backgrounds who had pre-judicial careers less oriented toward legal practice tends to be less oriented toward "society" and less formalistic than that of most of the other Minneapolis judges.

The covariation of the dominant socialization and recruitment patterns of the judges in each city and their decision-making processes suggests a causal linkage. This is especially suggested by the deviant socialization and recruitment patterns, which in effect serve as controls: In each city, interview and sentencing data in-

---

tices. (Only a few of them were in the less prestigious areas of law such as divorce and personal injury litigation, and none did criminal defense work.) The pre-judicial careers of four of the judges were predominantly in public positions with some experience in private legal practice. Significantly, these public positions, and those held by the eight judges who were involved in public positions for a small proportion of their pre-judicial careers, were nonpartisan and, more importantly, were in fact nonpolitical.

dicate that the decision-making of the judges whose socialization and recruitment patterns deviate from the dominant pattern also tends to deviate significantly from the decision-making of most of the city's judges. In Pittsburgh the few judges with little party or government experience tend to be less oriented toward the defendant, less particularistic, less pragmatic, and less policy-oriented than most of the other Pittsburgh judges. In Minneapolis the few judges with less legal experience and more political experience than most of their colleagues tend to be less oriented toward society and their professional peers and less formalistic than most of the other Minneapolis judges.

We have already seen how the judges' views and decision-making processes, influenced by their socialization and recruitment patterns, in turn influence the judges' sentencing decisions. The Pittsburgh judges' predominant orientation toward the defendant, their tendency to "empathize" with many of the defendants, to act as a buffer between the law and the people upon whom it is enforced, seem to make leniency "natural." Their tendency to base decisions on "realistic" policy considerations (the defendant's background, the effect of his crime, the standards of proper conduct of the group in which the offense occurred) reduces the gravity of many of the defendants' acts in the judges' minds. Their emphasis on individualistic and personal characteristics leads them to view many defendants as "exceptional" and thus deserving of a "break."

In contrast, the various elements of the Minneapolis judges' views and decision-making processes seem cumulatively to contribute to severe sentencing decisions. Their predominant orientation toward "society," which leads them to emphasize its protection, the related view of both crimes against person and crimes against property as very serious, and the tendency to be critical of defendants who plead not guilty, seem to shape their severe sentencing decisions. Their low degree of empathy for most defendants and their belief in the effectiveness of institutional rehabilitation and penal deterrence have a reinforcing effect. Mitigating exceptions are infrequent probably because the judges' formalistic decision-making rarely results in consideration of personal characteristics and because of their belief in the standards of conduct prescribed by law. The judges' orientation toward the goals of their professional peers (such as maximum indeterminate terms of incarceration and uniform severe sentencing for prostitution) contribute to severe decisions, as does their reliance on formal sources of information concerning defendants, which, unlike informal sources, provide the judge with both mitigating and aggravating information.

Some additional pieces of evidence reinforce the inference of a linkage between the cities' political and judicial selection systems, the judges' views and decision-making processes, and finally their sentencing decisions. One is the characteristics and sentencing decisions of the Pittsburgh "visiting" judges. In addition to the three Pittsburgh judges regularly assigned to the criminal bench on a rotating basis, three or four "visiting" judges from rural counties in Western Pennsylvania usually hear criminal cases in Pittsburgh. They are the same type of cases heard by the Pittsburgh judges and are tried by the same group of prosecutors and defense lawyers. Therefore the "visiting" judges' sentencing decisions in effect can serve as a limited control to test the validity of the suggested linkage between political systems and sentencing decisions.

The political systems of the rural areas from which the visiting judges are drawn are very different from Pittsburgh's. The visiting judges' social backgrounds and pre-judicial careers are also different. Conservative and business-oriented Republican party organizations dominate these areas. A high proportion of both the population and political leadership in these areas is Protestant of Northern European background. In comparison with the Pittsburgh judges, a smaller proportion of the visiting judges had pre-judicial experience in public positions, a smaller proportion were active in a political party, most were predominantly in private legal practice, and they were selected more *by* the Republican party than *from* the party. . . . the visiting judges' sentencing decisions are less lenient than those of the Pittsburgh judges. There is no direct evidence that the different political systems and different social backgrounds and career experiences are the primary factors accounting for the visiting judges' different sentencing decisions, but it is the explanation most often offered by attorneys and other participants in the Pittsburgh courts and by the Pittsburgh judges themselves. . . .

Finally, several similarities in the political systems of Pittsburgh and Minneapolis and their judges' behavior are indirectly and tentatively suggestive of the linkage between the two factors. The formal trial procedures and formal sources of information concerning the defendant which the Minneapolis judges use are generally advocated by professional and reform judicial organizations. By contrast, the informal trial procedures and informal sources of information concerning the defendant which the Pittsburgh judges use are generally criticized by professional and reform judicial organizations. Patterns somewhat similar to these forms of judicial behavior seem to exist in each city's political system. Minneapolis' political system is characterized by procedures advocated by professional and reform organizations in city government (nonpartisan elections, widespread popular participation in governmental and party decision-making, frequent referenda and grass roots party-nomination procedures, merit recruitment and appointments, and an emphasis on procedures as important ends in themselves). In contrast, Pittsburgh's political system is characterized by procedures that are generally criticized by most of these professional and reform organizations (partisan elections, hierarchical control of government and party decision-making, and party recruitment and appointments). The relationship between these patterns in each city's political and judicial systems is indirect; indeed, both may be the product of a more general factor such as a common political culture.

Alternative explanations for the linkages suggested here must be considered. Recent studies have indicated the importance of political factors in judicial decision-making. It is unlikely, however, that political influence shapes the behavior of the Pittsburgh and Minneapolis judges in criminal court. The usual felony defendant has no influence. Typically a young lower-income male, often from a minority group, he is on the bottom rung of society. In the few cases in which defendants do have political influence, the judges' decisions may be shaped by it — though this seems less likely to occur in Minneapolis. For example, organized labor is quite influential in Pittsburgh, and almost all of the judges are reluctant to preside over a case involving a union (especially strike injunction requests) because they are wary of taking the "wrong" position. But such cases are almost always civil.

Studies have also suggested that judges' social or ethnic backgrounds significantly shape their decisions. Thus it is possible that the Pittsburgh judges are lenient primarily because of their predominantly minority ethnic backgrounds and the Minneapolis judges more severe primarily because of their Northern-European-Protestant backgrounds. As already pointed out, however, our data show that while both the judges' pre-judicial career experiences and social backgrounds influence decision-making, in both cities the former seems to be the more important influence. Moreover, any relationship between the judges' background characteristics and their decision-making seems to be indirect. The crucial intervening variable is the city's political system: judges with a particular social and career background that may affect their decisions are recruited by the city's political and judicial selection systems. The ethnic composition of the bench in each city can serve as a partial test of the intervening impact of the judicial selection system on judicial decision-making. Significantly, that composition is more reflective of the influence of particular groups in the city's political system than it is of the ethnic composition of the city's population. . . .

Tension between the style of criminal court that may be preferable in an ideal context and that which may be necessary because of the actual context, and the difficulties inherent in the latter style, seem to be a product of a more general tension. According to notions of the rule of law and democratic theory, we ought to ignore class differences. But urban realities make this difficult. "Two cultures" exist in our large cities — a large lower-class as well as the dominant middle-class culture — but our theory of democracy assumes that we are able and willing to live together under a single set of rules or standards. The Minneapolis judges adhere to the rule of law, but fail to consider the two cultures. The Pittsburgh judges often tend to base their decisions on the existence of the two cultures, but usually fail to adhere to the rule of law. These shortcomings in both courts are largely a function of the two cultures, a factor external to the court systems. Any prescription for remedying these inadequacies must be directed primarily at this external factor and more basic cause.

## *Judges and the Poor: Bench Responses to Federally Financed Legal Services**

## Harry P. Stumpf and Robert J. Janowitz

In the fall of 1965 the Office of Economic Opportunity launched a major new campaign in the War on Poverty, the Legal Services Program. While legal aid to the indigent in both the civil and criminal fields had been available for decades in the United States, the many shortcomings of these old-line community agencies in serving the broader needs of the poor had been well-established and widely discussed. The OEO effort was to be a departure from

* From: 21 Stan L. Rev. 1058-1076 (1969). Copyright 1969 by the Board of Trustees of the Leland Stanford Junior University. Reprinted by permission of the editors of the Stanford Law Review, and Fred B. Rothman & Company.

traditional civil legal aid in that (1) neighborhood offices would be established within the poverty community itself, providing direct accessibility to the indigent client; (2) programs would be structured and governed to ensure their independence from local governmental agencies, other political institutions, and private groups that might have opposing interests; (3) there would be "maximum feasible participation" of the poor in policy decisions in order to increase the responsiveness of the program to the needs of the indigent community; and (4) emphasis would be placed on aggressive, creative advocacy in raising problems and pursuing issues that bear on the problems of the poor as a group. As an integral part of the War on Poverty, the Legal Services Program was to reach beyond the individualized services of traditional legal aid by using the instrumentalities of the law, broadly defined, to attack the root causes of poverty.

> We cannot be content with the creation of systems of rendering free legal assistance to all the people who need but cannot afford a lawyer's advice. This program must contribute to the success of the War on Poverty. Our responsibility is to marshal the forces of law and the strength of lawyers to combat the causes and effect of poverty. Lawyers must uncover the legal causes of poverty, remodel the systems which generate the cycle of poverty and design new social, legal and political tools and vehicles to move poor people from deprivation, depression, and despair to opportunity, hope and ambition.[4]

In the fall of 1967 the program entered its third full year of operation. Of the 299 projects then funded (at a cost of $30,457,-214), 250 were operating service programs, and 49 were research, training, demonstration, and technical-assistance grants. The typical program had a staff of seven full-time lawyers, a central office, and several neighborhood offices. The average OEO lawyer handled 500 new cases a year and was paid $8,460. Although standards for client eligibility varied widely from community to community, the average maximum income consistent with eligibility was $2,240 for a single person or $3,610 for a family of four. Cases having a fee-generating potential and criminal cases are not handled by the program.

Given the goal of fundamental social change through the legal process — to be achieved with aggressive, reform-oriented tactics

---

4. Address by E. Clinton Bamberger, Jr., to the National Conference of Bar Presidents, Feb. 19, 1966.

rare in traditional legal-aid operations — it is hardly surprising that from the start the program met with mixed reaction from the legal fraternity. After some initial reservations and misgivings, the House of Delegates of the American Bar Association endorsed the program, and since that time the ABA has proven a valuable ally in the struggle to keep the program alive. The National Legal Aid and Defender Association has in general followed suit and works closely with program officials in long-range planning. However, strong bar opposition at the local level has frequently undermined the effectiveness of community legal-services centers.

Arguments against the neighborhood-legal-services concept have been based on economic, ideological, and professional grounds. Some marginal (often solo) practitioners perceive federally funded legal services as a threat to their livelihood. Well-established lawyers often see the program as socialistic and unnecessary. Many lawyers and local bar groups believe the OEO Legal Services Program may violate several of the ABA Canons of Professional Ethics: canon 27 concerning advertising and soliciting business, canon 28 condemning barratry, and canons 35 and 47 on group practice. While national, state, and local bar reactions to the program and their influence on the program operations have been widely discussed, very little is known of the program's interaction with the judiciary — the other major component of the legal system.

## I. RESEARCH RATIONALE AND METHODOLOGY

The vast majority of problems handled by neighborhood attorneys, as by other attorneys, never reach litigation. Conferences, threats of litigation, phone calls to creditors, landlords, or local governmental agencies — these are the modi operandi of the neighborhood attorney. However, the central goal of the Legal Services Program is law reform via the adversary process, and by definition the judiciary becomes one key medium for achieving this goal. The role of appellate courts in effecting legal change is too well known to require elaboration here, but the significant role of local trial courts is much less recognized.

Whether one wishes to characterize the work of local tribunals as policy-making, norm-enforcing, or simply dispute-settling, the local judge inevitably weighs competing interests (social, political, legal, economic, and others) in arriving at decisions. That process involves the exercise of discretion, which, in incremental fashion, plays an important role in shaping community lifestyles. Because appeals from such decisions are rare and because of the low visibility of these courts, the judge's discretionary power is maximized, which results in enhancement of his political role. The most "inferior" of courts have not been reluctant to affix their stamp of approval or disapproval to many dimensions of individual and group behavior within the community. Thus, even in the less dramatic, day-to-day trial court proceedings in which the OEO attorney finds himself, the customs, attitudes, and decrees of local tribunals help to establish the framework within which the program operates.

For these reasons it was felt that the interaction of reform-oriented, federally financed legal aid with local judiciaries might prove to be an important and interesting research focus. Preliminary studies, though quite limited in both breadth and depth, supported this conclusion. For example, interviews with neighborhood legal-services attorneys in the San Francisco area revealed hostility on the part of several local judges to the aims of the program. Unusually close questioning of litigants as to their eligibility for legal services, refusal or reluctance to approve in forma pauperis proceedings, and irritation with OEO attorneys for pressing "minute" points of law were some of the judicial responses reported. Similar judicial attitudes were revealed in the findings of a recent study by the American Bar Foundation.

If research in judicial behavior over the past decade is any indication, one would expect such attitudes toward federally financed legal services to be reflected in the manner in which local judges approach and decide cases handled by the Legal Services Program. The purpose of the instant study is not to analyze decisional propensities; rather, we wish to explore in a general way the bench-program relationship and its impact on program effectiveness? Has that relationship been cooperative or conflict-ridden? How knowledgeable are local judges about the aims and operations of the program? What attitudes and administrative responses has the program evoked from local judges? . . .

From this list of 112 judges a small sample was selected in each of the counties in which target programs were established. The primary criterion of selection was the frequency with which the judge was mentioned by program attorneys. However, an effort was made to get a fairly even balance between superior- and municipal-court judges. Of the initial sample of 23, five judges declined a request for an interview, resulting in a final list of 18 respondents. Of these, 10 were superior-court judges, seven were municipal-court judges, and one was a judge in the federal district court.

Ten of the 18 judges were identified by program staff attorneys as favoring the program, four were labeled opponents, and four were named in both categories. All respondents were mentioned as judges before whom the staff attorneys frequently appear, and the names of the 18 judges appeared an average of 5.6 times each on the Staff Attorney Interview Schedules. Hence, the judicial respondents were selected primarily for their contact with (and presumed knowledge of) the Legal Services Program rather than for their representativeness as Bay Area judges.

Extended interviews were held with these judges in April 1968. The interview schedule contained 29 questions concentrating on six major facets of court-program relations: (1) the judges' awareness and knowledge of the activities of the Legal Services Program; (2) the nature of in-court and out-of-court contact with OEO lawyers; (3) the judges' past and present attitudes toward the program; (4) the program's influence on court policies and procedures; (5) the court's influence on the local program; and (6) the judges' attitudes toward the goals of the Legal Services Program. For the purposes of this Article, the data will be presented under three headings: bench attitudes toward the program in action; changes in policies and procedures; and bench attitudes toward the program's goals.

## II. BENCH ATTITUDES TOWARD THE LEGAL SERVICES PROGRAM IN ACTION

The judges' general level of awareness of the Legal Services Program was quite high. When asked "What agencies are available to provide legal assistance to the poor?" 16 of the 18 judges specifically mentioned the Legal Services Program in existence in their respective jurisdictions. When requested to describe the variety of services made available by the local program, the types of cases handled by OEO attorneys, and their disposition, the judges' replies indicated that they were generally cognizant of the emergence of OEO legal services. Most were able to describe several specific cases handled by staff attorneys in their courts, and even in relatively minor matters were often able to recall the performance of the attorneys and the outcome of the cases. Not surprisingly, divorce was the type of case most frequently mentioned by judges, and was often mentioned first. But landlord-tenant, debtor-creditor, and other matters were also mentioned as having been brought before the court by program attorneys.

However, as suggested by their answers to a number of questions, most judges seemed to be little aware of the goals of the program, apart from those it shares with traditional legal-aid programs. They were also uninformed about the structure, financing, and administration of the Legal Services Program, both nationally and locally. The judges gave simplistic replies or failed to reply to questions about their attitude toward the program when it was established, their recommendations for improving the program, their understanding of the aims of the program, and their opinions of the program's impact on the community; this suggests that the judiciary, at least as represented by these 18 respondents, has remained somewhat aloof from the program and is not at all well informed about the issues and problems with which it is concerned. Except for two who were involved in the establishment of local programs, most of the judges appeared to have little knowledge of the program beyond the confines of the courtroom.

At the introductory stage of questioning, responses from both judges and staff attorneys indicated that the programs had been well received by the bench and that relations were harmonious. When asked to characterize their current attitude toward the program, 13 of the 18 judges said it was favorable or positive. Corroborative responses were given by the staff attorneys interviewed. Nearly 80 percent of the attorney respondents said they knew of no judges who were opposed to the program when it was established. When asked how they were generally treated by members of the judiciary, 78 percent of the staff attorneys who gave specific answers indicated that the treatment had been fair, courteous, "like [that accorded] any other attorney."

Only three judges, however, supported the program without reservation. As the interviewers proceeded to more concrete dimensions of court-program relations, such as type of cases handled, attorney performance in court, and the use of specific tactics in litigation, many judges criticized the program. The most frequent complaints were directed to the performance of staff attorneys in court, especially to their lack of experience and "unprofessional" demeanor. Although the largest number indicated that OEO lawyers were "competent but inexperienced at first," and some even said that they were "highly competent," "excellent," or "highly motivated," the majority of judges were critical of program lawyers because they were either idealistic or inexperienced, or both. The flavor of these criticisms is reflected in the following three responses:

As I previously stated, they enter sloppy pleadings, [they're] not prepared, not competent; [their] appearance is weird — long hair, beards.

[I would give them a] good — all "A" for effort. They're young and have a lot to learn; [their] biggest fault [is that they are] idealistic rather than practical. Humans take umbrage at brash tactics . . . .

When [they] started [they were] green. They don't know proper conduct; they're late, don't call; [their] general conduct and demeanor [is] not good. But the judges straightened them out. [Their] legal ability is up to [that of] the average lawyer.

In comparing legal-services lawyers with private lawyers, and in commenting on the relationship between private practitioners and program lawyers, the 18 ·judges tended to comment repeatedly that though many OEO lawyers are good and are accepted, they are relatively inexperienced and sometimes are regarded as "deadbeats — financially and socially irresponsible," "social-worker types," and so forth. At the very least, these responses suggest that many staff attorneys have a hard row to hoe in their day-to-day court work.

Staff-attorney responses led to a similar conclusion: "The majority of judges are not too hot for us." "We are put down." "As soon as we're identified [as OEO attorneys] we're suspect. The Court is prone to harass us and even take the opposing attorney's position." And while many OEO lawyers felt that on the whole they were treated fairly by the majority of judges before whom they appeared, it was often reported that judges who were antagonistic toward the program visited their displeasure on the staff attorney personally. Staff attorneys frequently reported snide remarks directed from the bench in court: "You're wasting taxpayers' money," the Legal Services Program is a "gravy train," "Poverty lawyers are all the same," "You guys again," "Don't you people have anything better to do with your time?" and "This is socialized law."

While staff attorneys appear to bear the brunt of judicial antagonism — probably because they are readily available to the skeptical judge — the responses of attorneys and judges alike strongly suggest that most of the hostility is based on broader objections of an economic, ideological, and professional nature: The program was called socialistic, unnecessary, not sufficiently controlled by the local bar; it was an economic threat to the private attorney; and it engaged in unethical law practice.

The overall pattern of responses of hostile judges contained a curious twist. Those five or six judges who could be classified as hostile or strongly hostile to the program tended to develop one or two standard criticisms in the early part of the interview, which were repeated throughout the questioning, regardless of what the interviewer asked. While this may reflect a flaw in the interviewing techniques employed, it might also be seen as further evidence that judges, as a group, know little about the program beyond their immediate in-court contact and therefore tend to repeat criticisms they have heard, or which are based on preconceptions they entertained when the program was established.

Judge A, a gruff but candid respondent according to the interviewer, seemed to take a good deal of pride in the decorum of his court and was quite critical of the appearance (long hair, beards) of some of the program attorneys. He also found the OEO attorneys deficient in their preparation of cases, suspected them of handling cases "just for the social aspects," and wanted to hold seminars to train OEO lawyers in proper conduct. These themes were repeated again and again, often without regard to the question posed. He referred to the physical appearance of the attorneys in partial response to six different questions, and on five occasions he insisted that the program was "helping people involved in sit-ins," a form of representation that he strongly opposed. Yet when asked how the program should be improved or what its impact had been on the community, his responses were so brief and vague as to suggest that he knew very little about its specific aims and operations.

Judge B, also generally opposed to the program, had been involved in discussions with private attorneys regarding the role of the local bar in program management. He was quite concerned that the program be properly supervised and controlled by the bar, and he referred to this problem in responses to six questions. A third judge was unalterably opposed to the "sociological" overtones of the program and managed to squeeze in comments on this subject in each of his answers. A fourth judge became preoccupied with the program's eligibility standards, which he thought were too lenient.

### III. OEO AND BENCH INTERACTION: CHANGES IN POLICIES AND PROCEDURES

In addition to examining the attitudes judges have formed from their contacts with the program now in operation, we attempted to determine what effects, if any, the two institutions have had on each other's policies and procedures, and the role of judicial attitudes in determining those effects. Questions were directed to both judges and staff lawyers, and some of their responses are instructive. With minor exceptions, the program seems to have brought about few changes in the policies and procedures of local courts. Fourteen of the 18 judges said they had not found it necessary to alter any formal or informal policies or administrative procedures as a result of the activities of the local Legal Services Program. The remaining four judges mentioned such minor changes as the rewording of the unlawful detainer summons and requests to accept form complaints. . . .

California is one state in which the right to proceed in forma pauperis has been established by judicial decision in the absence of any statute. However, as in a good many other states, the right to the proceeding is surrounded by a host of restrictions and limitations of both a formal and a customary nature, which combine to transform the right into a privilege rarely extended. In practice, the privilege is granted at the discretion of the local judge.

In the San Francisco Superior Court the filing fee for a plaintiff complaint in domestic relations is $33; for other plaintiff actions it is $31. The fee for a defendant's response is usually $18. In municipal court all plaintiff filings cost $14. Given the extremely heavy case load of legal-services programs, filing fees, if assumed by the programs, would seriously drain already inadequate budgets. But to require indigent clients to bear these costs (the usual practice of some programs) would contradict a basic aim of OEO legal services — to encourage the poor to assert their rights through the legal process.

One way local courts could aid the OEO Legal Services Program would be to liberalize the approval of in forma pauperis proceedings. There is little evidence, however, to indicate such a practice on the part of the judges interviewed. This is not to say no such proceedings are approved; many are. And it is possible that more are being approved now than in the past, because of the programs. However, judicial responses show little movement toward liberalization, although this may be in part because judges have had few requests as a result of attorneys' hesitation to presume upon their goodwill.

Some typical responses will illustrate the point. For example, one judge said there was no provision for proceeding in forma pauperis in civil cases in California! Others have replied: "I haven't heard that term for a long time. I believe I've had one and granted it"; "I didn't have too many of these, but when I did I had a standard rule of refusing it if the client owned a car or had an income"; and "I'm not familiar with any being used here."

A more complete picture of the role of judicial attitudes in the restricted use of the "pauper's oath" emerges from the staff attorneys' extensive remarks on the subject. Attorneys in the four staffed programs plus 11 private attorneys in the Fremont Judicare Program were asked: "What have been the attitudes of judges toward the use of in forma pauperis proceedings?" Of the 58 attorneys who answered with a specific, codable response, 23 indicated that judges were quite antagonistic and hostile to the proceeding, while another 11 described the judges' attitudes as reluctant or restrictive. Two attorneys who indicated that judges were hostile to in forma pauperis proceedings said:

> [The attitude of the judges is] antagonistic. They feel the client is getting free legal service and should pay for [the] filing fee.... [Judges think it] causes a burden on the court. Private attorneys can, but usually don't have paupers as clients.

> In Muni [Municipal] Court, Judge [X] would not allow them ... wouldn't sign because he didn't believe in them. [He said] "if the client wants to bring action, he can get his own fees."

Describing a confrontation between the court and the program on the matter of in forma pauperis proceedings, two attorneys we classified as "restrictive" responded:

> Everything came to a head. [The] judges saw themselves as protectors of the public purse.... [T]he order went out ... do not allow them .... The end result was we agreed to be more careful and the judges agreed not to bitch. Now ... [we] only file in dire necessity.

> They don't like it. It is a cumulative position from clerk to judge. Snide remarks are made .... I've only filed three or four .... We've had to change our policy because judges were upset because of the number of these [requests for proceeding in forma pauperis].

... While the data strongly indicate that the emergence of federally funded legal services has had little impact on the policies and procedures of local courts, the hostility of judges, according to most staff attorneys, has had an adverse effect on local programs in a number of ways. The impact of judicial reluctance to approve in forma pauperis proceedings on program procedures has already been noted. But there are several other areas in which staff attorneys report that judicial attitudes have interfered with program activities. Many staff attorneys reported decisional manifestations of judicial hostility, such as:

> He refuses to sign petitions; he [doesn't] allow us to represent our clients. [He] tells us we shouldn't be handling these cases, especially test cases.
>
> In an unlawful detainer case he [the judge] attempted to force a settlement and indicated his bias for the landlord by declaring a verdict for the landlord. He threw a woman in jail and was going to hold me in contempt for making him realize she was on welfare and had been advised not to seek employment until her children were in school.

> In court, if you're right they will begrudgingly rule for you. If the [case is almost] 50-50, you're dead. One judge argued with [my] witness and told him to shut up.

> The only way you would get a temporary restraining order from him [another judge] is [if his] daughter were eloping with a guy. It's not that he is against the poor people so much; it is just that he is for rich people.

It was also reported that judges complained that staff attorneys quibbled over minor procedural errors, took business from private practitioners, and represented ineligible clients. When the 67 attorneys were asked what adjustments they had made, the bulk of responses (aside from "we avoid certain judges") were in the categories "we are now more careful about eligibility" and "we are more careful about avoiding minor procedural errors." The combined effect on the programs produced by judicial rigidity in in forma pauperis and other proceedings, eligibility standards, and minor procedural matters, as well as by general hostility to the program, is summarized in these comments of staff attorneys:

> We were able during the first year to get in forma pauperis in divorce cases, then this was cut off totally. So we said *all* clients now have to pay costs . . . . This coincided with our desire to cut down on our case load, [but it is] unfortunate for those who hurt the most [the poor].

> Because we find it difficult to get a TRO [temporary restraining order] we've stopped seeking them and instead are moving towards a show cause order . . . .

> Yes, we've definitely had to make adjustments in our activities. The

kind of cases we bring depends on the judges we get. I like to bring cases to Federal Court, if possible, because I know I will get good treatment.

When [Judge X] was in domestic relations court, staff attorneys were reluctant to litigate child support cases . . . [they] tried to settle out of court if possible.

When asked how their relationship with the court complicates their activities, some staff attorneys replied:

I have turned down some clients that I would have handled if I hadn't been afraid of being called on it.

It [judges' attitudes] puts the client at a disadvantage.

We now pay more attention to what should be peripheral.

We're hesitant to test cases in California state courts because judges as a whole are not interested in change on behalf of our clients . . . . Where are you going to find a sympathetic judge? [They're just] not receptive.

As these findings demonstrate, although program-bench relations may appear at first blush to be amicable, there is a considerable amount of adverse reaction from the judges, which in turn tends to affect adversely the representation of the poor by legal-services attorneys. It is true that private practitioners are frequently forced to contend with similar problems, including biased judges whom they attempt to avoid and courts that are clearly unsympathetic to certain kinds of pleadings. But it seems clear that judicial hostility to the OEO Legal Services Program has contributed to certain of the program's failures: Local judges have been reluctant to permit the introduction of new procedures in their courts, and the program has had to make some compromises in the pursuit of its goals. Moreover, this hostility has arisen in a context of limited judicial knowledge of the program. As the next section indicates, program goals less visible to the judiciary carry the potential for still greater hostility.

## IV. JUDICIAL ATTITUDES TOWARD PROGRAM GOALS

The findings regarding bench-program relations that may be of greatest interest and significance relate to judicial attitudes toward

the stated goals of the program. Following the introductory remark that "[t]he following are possible activities that the Legal
Services Program could engage in — we would like to get your
views on these activities," the goals of the program as stated in
the OEO *Evaluation Manual* [29] were presented:

1. To provide quality legal services to the greatest possible number
   consistent with the size of the staff and the other goals of this
   program.
2. To educate target area residents about their rights and responsibilities in substantive areas of concern to them.
3. To ascertain what rules of law affecting the poor should be
   changed to benefit the poor and to achieve such changes either
   through the test case and appeal, statutory reform, or changes in
   the administrative process.
4. To serve as advocate for the poor in the social decision making
   process. This can be done by representing a neighborhood association at a zoning hearing, for example, or before a city council
   at which a street improvement is being considered. It could
   mean the organization and representation of a group of tenants
   to secure a standard lease that is fair to both landlord and tenant.
   In brief, it is to provide for the poor the same type of concerned
   advocacy that others have long enjoyed.
5. To assist poor people in the formation of self-help groups such as
   cooperative purchasing organizations, merchandising ventures,
   and other business ventures.
6. To involve the poor in the decision making process of the legal
   services program, and to the extent feasible, to include target
   area residents on the staff of the program.

We added a seventh goal — "To dispose of the client's problems
in such a way as to affect the greatest number of the poor." To
each goal the judges were asked to respond: strongly agree, agree,
undecided, disagree, or strongly disagree. Because these goals, particularly goal 7, may be interpreted in different ways, each question
was followed by three probes: (1) "For what reason?" (2) "To
what extent is the Legal Services Program attempting to engage
in this activity?" (3) "With what results?"
   Most judges either explicitly or implicitly agreed that the program should pursue the first three goals: providing legal services,
educating the community on its legal rights and responsibilities,
and attempting to reform laws and administrative processes that
adversely affect the poor. Beginning with goal 4 — serving as an

29. Legal Services Program, Evaluation Manual 1-2 (1967).

advocate of the poor in the social (as distinguished from the judicial) decisionmaking process — a radical shift in judicial responses became manifest: Two judges disagreed strongly, five disagreed, five were undecided (most leaning toward disagreement), and only four supported the goal. Some responses were:

Disagree: "Lawyers should represent individuals."

Disagree: "This is not their function. This gets to the point where neighborhood associations would have funds. [This would be] interfering with private practice."

Disagree: "[OEO attorneys are] not advocates for social change. They have to have their clients' interests in mind."

Disagree: "[This would] get the programs into extremely controversial areas such as government paying people to take on a private landlord. Private attorneys would represent groups in these matters."

As the interviewers proceeded through the remaining goals, it became increasingly clear that the judges were generally unfamiliar with the broader, reform-oriented aims of the program and were appalled that such activities would be considered proper for an attorney. By the time the interviewers reached the last two activities that the Legal Services Program might engage in, judicial opposition to the new departure from traditional legal aid became quite apparent.

Of the 13 judges who responded to goal 6 — involving the poor in the program's decisionmaking process — seven disagreed outright, three expressed grave misgivings about the policy, and three were undecided. Two typical disagreeing responses were: "This gets [the program] into the political arena. This is not a true legal assistance structure," and the "poor are not equipped to be effective in the decisionmaking process. [This] requires the knowledge of the legal profession."

Only four of the 18 judges supported our hypothetical seventh goal — handling clients' problems to affect the poor as a group. Four failed to answer, and the remaining 10 judges disagreed in some measure. "This is contrary to everything an attorney is taught ...," said one judge. Another remarked: "He [a lawyer] should dispose of clients' problems to benefit the *client*; anything else is not practicing law." A third said "[i]t's shocking to suggest they would [place] the group above the individual; this is not group legal assistance, it's individual."

Three, possibly four, judges seemed to be in general sympathy with the goals of the programs, understood its social and political import, and were able to articulate reasons for a new departure in legal services to the poor. However, there was strong concern expressed by our small sample of judges when the possibility of a program extending beyond traditional legal aid was presented. The more expansive of the stated goals of the Legal Services Program, and, interestingly, those with which the judges would have least professional contact — participation of OEO lawyers in out-of-court representation of the poor, organization of self-help groups, and participation of the poor in the program — were opposed by most judges. The added hypothetical goal aroused the most severe disapproval. Clearly most judges perceive the program as a traditional legal-aid operation. Anything beyond individual, case-by-case service appears to be anathema to many members of the judiciary.

### CONCLUSIONS

When one combines these findings with the strong local bar opposition to the Legal Services Program revealed in past research, it seems clear that a significant portion of the legal fraternity is far from prepared to accept the philosophy and modi operandi of the OEO's Legal Services Program. Even the apparently firm support received at the national level from the American Bar Association may not be durable, for a recent study by the American Bar Foundation notes that the ABA-OEO agreement rests on the notion that the new program "should be consonant with the 'legal aid concept.'" Since no working definition has ever been given to this concept, the study concludes, the resolution of underlying fundamental issues has been postponed — "and this is particularly crucial in view of what the objectives of the OEO projects are."

Locally, it seems that significant elements within both bench and bar tend to remain tied to the traditions of the old legal-aid societies. Some judges emphasized case-by-case service, displayed restrictive attitudes toward in forma pauperis proceedings and eligibility standards, and disapproved strongly of systematic use of the judicial process for social reform. One can only speculate what this portends for the future of the Legal Services Program.

Some have argued that attitudes in the legal community are changing significantly, that initial opposition to the program and its philosophy is on the wane, and that in time the "new wave" in legal services will come to be accepted by the legal profession. Without the benefit of a long-term study, one can neither confirm nor refute that assertion. However, the deep-seated hostility to some of the philosophies underlying the OEO effort suggests that changes in professional attitudes and in the legal system conducive to the success of the program will be very slow in coming. In the interim, if local judges and lawyers continue to play their customary role in community affairs, the legal arm of the War on Poverty is unlikely to realize its full potential.

The use of legal reform to better the economic and social situation of the poor is the chief goal of the program. But it may be necessary first to reform the legal system itself — both private practitioners and the local judges who set the guidelines for their practice. The list of proposals for change, running the gamut from updating the ABA's canons of professional ethics to radical alterations in court structure and procedure, is already lengthy and need not be summarized here. But one area in which change would seem to be suggested is legal education.

A critical element in local lawyers' and judges' opposition to the program is their apparent inability to perceive the legal process as an instrument of social change. Most revealing were the comments of several local judges to the effect that any staff-attorney activity beyond the immediate confines of the individual case or client (such as group organization and representation of the poor, or handling clients' problems to affect the greatest number of the poor) is simply "not practicing law." Or as one judge put it, such an approach to the practice of law "is contrary to everything an attorney is taught." And so it is.

It seems likely that this phenomenon stems in part from the "splendid isolation" of American legal education from the broader academic disciplines. The stark contrast between the Legal Services Program's conception of the role of law and lawyers, on the one hand, and that of many local judges and private practitioners on the other, has a close parallel in the contrast between the functional orientation of the social and behavioral sciences and the pedagogy and epistemology of law schools. The notion of establishing a publicly financed legal-services agency for the purpose of marshaling the instrumentalities of the law for social change strikes the social scientist as logical, if not commonplace; for to him the legal process is not an end in itself, but rather a social and political instrument to achieve larger goals. While modern legal educators and the men they train may accept this truism in the abstract, they nonetheless proceed as if it were not true — as if the lawyer had no proper role beyond the immediate needs of his client.

The fact that many private practitioners and local judges not only refuse to accept, but do not even seem to understand, this essential role of law in society has become a potentially serious stumbling block for a program that offers one of the more promising alternatives to the use of violence as a means of solving social problems. The irony of it is that legal education is actually underselling the vast potential of the law and its processes as a device for peaceful social reform. To develop such a device is precisely the goal of the Legal Services Program, but given the nature and extent of opposition by local bench and bar, the program seems unlikely to succeed in that aim.

## The Administration of Justice in the Wake of the Detroit Civil Disorder of July 1967*

### Michigan Law Review

#### I. INTRODUCTION

The Supreme Court of the United States and the Court of Appeals will take care of themselves. Look after the courts of the poor, who stand most in need of justice. The security of the Republic will be found in the treatment of the poor and ignorant; in indifference to their misery and helplessness lies disaster.[1]

The belief is pervasive among ghetto residents that lower courts in our urban communities dispense "assembly-line" justice; that ... the poor and uneducated are denied equal justice with the affluent.... Too often the courts have operated to aggravate rather than relieve the tensions that ignite and fire disorders.[2]

Early Sunday morning, July 23, 1967, the Detroit Police Department raided a "blind pig" at the corner of Twelfth Street and Clairmont Street. An unexpectedly large number of patrons were present at the after-hours drinking establishment, and it took the police over an hour to remove them all from the scene. The weather was warm and humid — despite the time, many people were still on

---

* From: 66 Mich. L. Rev. 1544-1559, 1627-1630 (1968). Reprinted by permission of the editors of the Michigan Law Review.
1. Address by Charles E. Hughes, N.Y. State Bar Ass'n, 42d Annual Meeting, in 1919 Proceedings of N.Y. State Bar Ass'n 224, 240-41.
2. Report of the National Advisory Commission on Civil Disorders 183 (Government Printing Office ed. 1968).... [Hereinafter Commision Report].

the streets. A crowd of about two hundred gathered while the police were occupied with the individuals arrested in the raid. The last of the arrestees were removed shortly after 5:00 a.m. At that moment an empty bottle broke the rear window of a police car and an empty litter can was thrown through the window of a nearby store.

By 6:00 a.m., there were thousands of people on Twelfth Street. Widespread looting began as windows were broken over a wide area. Civil disorder had come to Detroit. It was to continue until Friday, July 28, 1967. In the interim, thousands of state police, Michigan National Guardsmen, and federal troops were called in to contain reported disorder activity within the city. Over seven thousand people were arrested during this six-day period.

The mass arrests imposed a tremendous burden on the legal establishment of Detroit; fair and speedy processing of the arrestees was required. The *Michigan Law Review* sent two observers into Detroit on August 1 to measure the response of the legal establishment. The observers spent countless hours in Detroit Recorder's Court. Interviewing of defense attorneys, prosecutors, judges, defendants, and others who were concerned with the proceedings continued until March of 1968. Others who studied the administration of criminal justice following the disorder volunteered pertinent information throughout the year. This Comment is the result of these efforts. . . .

## II. ARRAIGNMENT ON THE WARRANT

### A. Purpose and Normal Operation

Under normal circumstances, people arrested in Detroit are brought to one of thirteen police precincts for booking, fingerprinting, and interrogation. Each case is then assigned to a detective who investigates the charges and confers with the prosecutor to determine whether a warrant should be issued. If a warrant is authorized, the prisoner's file is sent to the warrant clerk's office in the Recorder's Court where a complaint and an affidavit are prepared. The prisoner is then brought before the court for the arraignment on the warrant.

The primary functions of the arraignment on the warrant are to inform the defendant of the charge against him, to advise him of his constitutional rights, to set bail, and to ascertain whether the defendant wishes a preliminary examination and, if so, to set a date for it. The merits of the case are not considered, and any evidence received is directed toward the setting of bail. Moreover, there are no defenses which must be asserted at this stage, no pleas are required, and, except for the arresting officer, no prosecution witnesses are present. The defendant may, if he so desires and can afford it, be represented by retained counsel at the arraignment on the warrant. The court, however, will not appoint counsel for the indigent, having adopted the view that there are no rights of the defendant which can be jeopardized or need to be protected by counsel at this stage.

With regard to the amount of bail to be set, there are statutory guidelines in Michigan which require consideration by the judge of the seriousness of the offense charged, the previous criminal record of the defendant, and the probability of his appearance at trial. Therefore, in setting bail the judges normally consult the prisoner's file, which contains his past record, the police write-up, the complaint, and any other relevant material that may have been accumulated by the police department. In addition, they will usually question the defendant with regard to such information as his employment, marital, and residence status. Bail is then set and the defendant is either remanded to custody (if he cannot post bail) or released (if he can post bail, or if he is placed on personal recognizance).

## B. Arraignment on the Warrant During the Disorder — An Overview[16]

Lining up a group of fifteen or twenty unrepresented prisoners before the bench, the judge said, "You're accused of entering without breaking, your bond is $10,000, your examination is set for August 1." Calling the next group, he continued, "You heard what I said to them, the same applies to you." This incident, witnessed by at least two observers,[17] illustrates what might be termed the

16. Information as to what transpired during the arraignments on the warrant for persons arrested on charges related to the disorder was obtained primarily from private interviews with the principals involved, including Recorder's Court judges, the prosecutor and his staff, the county sheriff, members of the Detroit Police Department, defense counsel, defendants, and interested observers present during this stage. Personal observation of court proceedings did not begin until August 1, 1967, when the arraignments on the warrant had been concluded and the preliminary examinations had begun.

17. Professor Frank Sengstock, University of Detroit Law School, who related the incident in an address given before the American Association of Law Schools at their Annual Convention on Dec. 29, 1967 (available for inspection in *Michigan Law Review* files) . . . .

salient features of the arraignment on the warrant during the disorder: high bail, absence of counsel, failure to consider individual circumstances, failure to inform defendants of their constitutional rights, and an emphasis on expediency. Although each of these things did not necessarily occur at every arraignment or in every courtroom, each was present all too often. Secondary factors contributing to and exacerbating the elements listed included a shortage of judicial manpower coupled with a desire by the court to go-it-alone, a logistics problem in keeping track of and identifying prisoners, and an atmosphere pervaded by mass confusion, fear, and panic.[18]

By far the most pervasive aspect of the arraignment on the warrant, and for that matter of all judicial proceedings in the Recorder's Court, involved in the processing of cases during the disorder was a major breakdown in the adversarial process. The court made a basic policy decision to aid the executive branch in every possible way to break the back of the disorder and restore order to the community. This decision was in some cases made explicit by public statements of the judges; in others, it was implicit, manifested by the conduct of the court.

## 1. High Bail

Although complete statistics were not immediately available, it was readily apparent that the judicial policy during the early stages of the disorder was to set extremely high bail. An unofficial sampling of court files covering the first two or three days of the disorder reveals that bonds ranged from $200,000 (for a sniper) to personal recognizance (for a curfew violating female), but the most popular figures were $10,000 and $25,000. Thus, one judge set 161 bonds out of 175 at $10,000, another set 121 at $25,000 and 42 at $10,000 out of a total of 171, and a third set 81 at $10,000 and 39 at $5,000 out of a total of 130. Interviews with 1,014 prisoners who were arrested during the disorder and incarcerated at Jackson

18. According to Professor Frank Sengstock, University of Detroit Law School, this atmosphere was not confined to the community outside the courtroom but also affected the judges and the performance of their judicial functions. In an address to the American Association of Law Schools (see note 17 *supra*) he said: "A significant number of these [Recorder's Court] judges have conceded privately that they were filled with fears and doubts about the capacity of structured society to resist the riots, as they watched, from their courtroom windows, smoke filling the sky from fires burning in the city. These fears and apprehensions affected them in the manner in which they were discharging their official responsibilities."

State Prison disclosed that at least 50 per cent of them were being held subject to bonds in excess of $10,000 and at least 70 per cent on bonds of over $5,000.

The initial decision on the bond policy seems to have been made by Wayne County Prosecutor William Cahalan some time during the first Sunday of the disorder. He publicly stated that his office would ask for bonds of $10,000 and up on all persons arrested "so that even though they had not been adjudged guilty, we would eliminate the danger of returning some of those who had caused the riot to the street during the time of stress."

Recorder's Court judges were almost unanimous in their adoption of the prosecutor's suggestion. According to Cyrus Vance, Special Assistant to the Secretary of Defense:

> [T]he judge who was on duty Sunday night and the additional judges who came on during the night followed [the prosecutor's] recommendation to the letter. . . . By Monday morning, twelve of the thirteen judges in the Recorder's Court had begun to uniformly follow the recommendation of the prosecutor and set extremely high bail on each of the prisoners arrested.

The dissenting judge was George W. Crockett, Jr. who, on Wednesday, July 26, wrote a letter to his fellow judges on the Recorder's Court informing them of his "disagreement with [the] suggested 'high bond policy' " and of his view that

> each of us has the sole responsibility of fixing bonds in cases assigned to us. I intend to exercise that responsibility as well as accept the responsibility for my action. . . . In my judgment [ten and twenty-five thousand dollar] bonds are not only excessive, they are prohibitive.[27]

On the Monday morning following the start of the disorder, executive Judge Brennan called a meeting of the bench. It was at this meeting that the bond policy was formally agreed on by the twelve judges other than Crockett. Their rationale, like Cahalan's, was that high bonds would help control the disorder by keeping

27. Although Judge Crockett admitted the amount of bond set by him was somewhat higher than under normal circumstances, an examination of court files reveals that it was considerably lower than that of his fellow judges. Out of 114 defendants whose bonds Judge Crockett set on July 25, five were placed on bonds of $5,000, the highest he set, while seven were given suspended sentences, eleven were placed on personal bond, six were released on $100 cash bonds, four bonds were set at $500, thirty-two at $1,000, twenty-seven at $2,000, and twenty-two at $3,000.

those apprehended from returning to the streets. Brennan was quoted in *The Detroit News* as saying, "We will, in matters of this kind, allocate an extraordinary bond. We must keep these people off the streets. We will keep them off." [28] In the same article, Judge Robert J. Colombo declared, "What we're trying to do here is keep them off the streets. And apparently we're being successful at that. If we let them back on, you know what would happen.... In a way we're doing what the police didn't do." [29] "Doing what the police didn't do" is not the typical analysis of the bail-setting function of an independent judiciary.

Although there was no explicit change in policy, on Wednesday, July 26, individual judges did begin to depart from the uniformly high bails, and some defendants were released.[30] By this time the

28. The Detroit News, July 26, Doc Green's Column, §A, at 12, col. 6.

29. Id. It should also be noted at this point that Justice Thomas E. Brennan of the Michigan Supreme Court, not speaking for that body, assured Recorder's Court judges that whatever the latter felt necessary to do to cope with civil disorder defendants would be upheld by the Supreme Court. (This information was volunteered independently by several trustworthy persons who asked that they not be named.) It can only be conjectured what effect this might have had on the attitude of Recorder's Court judges in adopting a high bond policy. Professor Frank Sengstock concluded (address *supra* note 17) that the prohibitively high bond set in Detroit during the disorder was in fact a dishonest way of denying bail altogether: "[A]t no time did [Recorder's Court judges] refuse to set a bond for any accused. If the object in setting a bond was to keep an individual in jail, the intellectually honest way of accomplishing this goal was to deny bond altogether and let the denial be tested with a writ of habeas corpus. The dishonest approach, which was in fact adopted by the court, to a basic constitutional right can only produce extreme skepticism about the value of constitutional liberties for those detained by this procedural subterfuge."

30. ... At some point during the early part of the week of the disorder, Wayne County Sheriff Peter Buback was ordered by Judge Vincent J. Brennan, Executive Judge of the Recorder's Court, to report back to the court before releasing a prisoner who had met bond. According to Judge Brennan, this was done so that a check on the prisoner's record could be made to see whether he had been involved in disorders elsewhere around the country, especially Newark, or had a "wanted" or "parole" status. If the man's record was clear, his bond was reduced and he was released; if not, the bond was not to be honored by the sheriff until further notice. According to Sheriff Buback and some Detroit attorneys who attempted to obtain release for clients, a notice was posted on the door of the sheriff's office on Tuesday and Wednesday of the week of the disorders saying that no bonds would be honored until further notice. Thus, although bonds were beginning to be set at lower amounts, within the financial reach of some defendants, there was a great deal of difficulty in obtaining release even if the bond could be met.

This practice of refusing release until records were checked met with con-

community had begun to return to normal, and the jails in the city and throughout the state were filled beyond capacity. Therefore, "at the urging of a number of persons including federal officials, [the prosecutor's office] began to think in terms of releasing prisoners on personal bond or on reasonable bond."

It is significant that once again it was the prosecutor's office that initiated a judicial policy. According to Cahalan, his office engineered the major part of the release program by undertaking an examination of all the prisoners' files in regard to prior criminal records. If the defendant had no prior convictions, he was recommended for personal recognizance; otherwise, no further investigation was made and the original bond was maintained. Since the court invariably approved the prosecutor's recommendations, this program resulted in the release of 3,000 prisoners on personal recognizance in a period of a few days. An additional 650 were also released on personal bond after a review of their files by the judges themselves. The arraignments on the warrant were completed by August 1, at which time the preliminary examinations began. At this later stage those people still in custody who had not been charged with serious offenses such as sniping or arson were either released on personal bond or their bonds were lowered to what they probably would have been under normal circumstances.

It was noted earlier that a Recorder's Court judge ordinarily has the prisoner's file before him when he sets bond. Because of a clerical log jam, those files were unavailable during the disorder. Although the Clerk's Office of the Recorder's Court operated around the clock, the attempt to process within one week the equivalent of one half of the entire caseload for all of 1966 proved understandably impossible for an office unprepared for such an emergency. In addition, the Records Bureau of the Detroit Police Department bogged down and was unable to supply necessary records at the pace they were demanded. Finally, the task was complicated even further by the fact that many prisoners gave incorrect names or had the same name as other prisoners.

---

siderable resistance from some Recorder's Court judges, notably Judges Crockett and Schemanske. Judge Crockett in fact told Sheriff Buback that if the bonds he had set were not honored, he would cite the sheriff for contempt of court. The notice was soon thereafter removed from the sheriff's door and what few prisoners could meet bond were released.

Charles Goldfarb, one of the principal professional bondsmen in Detroit, reported that he wrote about 700 bonds, 80% of which were for less than $2,000, and only two or three of which were for $10,000. Although he did three months business in one week, most of this was done during the latter part of the week when the bonds were considerably lower.

Many of the judges, including Judge Brennan, asserted that this absence of records was an additional factor necessitating the high bonds. They took the position that since they were unable to tell which of those appearing before them required custody to insure their appearance at trial, prohibitively high bails had to be set until a judgment could be made on the basis of prior record. Whether this approach was consistent with the presumption of innocence will be examined later. At this point it is enough to note that Judge Crockett was unimpressed with the argument that the serious clerical problem necessitated high bonds, and that in light of the announced policy of "trying to . . . keep them off the streets." [43] it is questionable whether the absence of records actually did account for the high bails.

## 2. Representation by Counsel

Since Recorder's Court does not consider it necessary to appoint counsel at the arraignment on the warrant, the existence of the disorder did not alter the situation in regard to the representation of indigent defendants at this stage. As usual, there was no representation. The disorder did, however, have an effect on the representation of those who had retained counsel. In most instances the efforts of those retained attorneys who were present at this stage were greatly impaired by the mass confusion in the community, the courtroom, and the jails. As one attorney put it:

> There was no real effort to comply with the elementary right of a defendant to see his lawyer. You couldn't find your client at all except by blind luck. When I did find somebody, I couldn't get to him as there was no procedure by which a lawyer could interfere with the administrative procedures of the police. It was futile to try anything.[44]

Also, the organized bar, which later responded so well to the need for counsel at the preliminary examinations, made no effort to intervene during the arraignments on the warrant. According to Judge John Emery, a municipal judge of Birmingham, Michigan, the bar was wholly inactive during the disorder period, which is when the arraignments were being conducted. Similarly, Professor

43. See text accompanying note 29 *supra*.
44. Interview with Detroit Attorney Ernest Goodman in Detroit, Feb. 5, 1968. Mr. Goodman also related that during the first few days of the disorder, "[g]oing into the court building was a devastating experience. It was surrounded by armed guards with machine guns. The building was practically a tomb and prisoners were being processed by some method I couldn't fathom."

Frank Sengstock of the University of Detroit Law School observed that "the legal profession in Detroit did not check the court of justice throughout most of the week in which the riot occurred. In fact, the profession was paralyzed."

Although the organized bar as such did not come forward to assist defendants during the early stages of the disorder, several individuals did. On Monday of the week of the disorder Emery suggested to the judges that they consider providing representation for indigents, and volunteered his own services, and those of a few other attorneys, for this purpose. Most of the judges, however, were opposed to the idea. They thought that providing counsel at the arraignments was unnecessary and would only impair the process of appointing counsel at later stages in the proceedings; initially, only three judges permitted attorneys to be present in their courtrooms to "assist" those who requested it, and even they did not formally assign counsel to any one case.[48]

When the volunteer attorneys were present, they attempted to induce over-all reductions in the amounts of bail and to increase judicial sensitivity to individual circumstances and hardship cases. In some cases involving pregnant women, although not in all, this resulted in a release on personal bond. But their efforts on the whole were described by Emery as "perfunctory and ineffectual." "We were running around, frustrated, helpless, not able to accomplish much of anything."

### 3. Failure to Consider Cases Individually[50]

Apparently it was commonplace during the disorder for a group of suspects to be "rounded up" and arrested at the same place (often a store which had already been broken into or burned), charged with the same offense (typically, entering without break-

48. Interview with John Emery, municipal judge of Birmingham, Michigan, in Detroit, Aug. 2, 1967. It has become customary in the practice of Recorder's Court judges to appoint counsel for trial of indigent defendants primarily from a group of Detroit attorneys known pejoratively as the "Clinton Street Gang" (so named because of the site of the courthouse on Clinton Street in Detroit....), who devote the bulk of their practice to court appointments and are paid by the state.

50. According to mimeographed Recorder's Court statistics, there was a total of 3,166 felony defendants on 1,390 separate files, or an average of slightly over two and one quarter defendants per file. A sampling of the files by the writers revealed that files of six to eight defendants were not uncommon. Further analysis of the information included in the files suggests a pattern of group treatment from the arrest through, in some instances, the arraignment on the information....

ing but with intent to commit larceny),[51] brought to a police station for booking, and taken to the court to be arraigned — still as a group — before one judge. Moreover, most of the judges continued the pattern of group treatment by addressing the defendants collectively, rather than as individuals, and by setting identical bails for all. Obviously the adoption of these procedures precluded any consideration of individual circumstances or of the probability that any particular defendant would return for trial on the appointed day. Bail was set for offenses, not for people.

Again, the notable exception was Judge Crockett, who attempted to individualize the bail procedure and adhere to the statutory guidelines. He took advantage of the offers of help from attorneys and members of the Neighborhood Legal Service (NLS) Bail Bond Project, using them to aid in the gathering of the information necessary to set an appropriate amount of bail. According to Dennis James, head of the Bail Bond Project, defendants were interviewed privately, the information was presented to the judge, the advice of the interviewer was requested, and bond was then set. And, a stern and clear warning was given on the consequences of lying to the court.

The chief reasons given by the other judges for not employing Judge Crockett's procedure were the lack of time, the conviction that the defendants could not be believed, and the fear that dangerous individuals would be freed to engage in further destruction. However, Judge Crockett's experience indicates that in fact it took very little extra time to arraign defendants his way, and that in the long run it actually saved his court a great deal of time by eliminating the necessity of reviewing every bond at a later date. Moreover,

51. "Entering without breaking but with intent to commit larceny" was the legal translation of "looting" settled upon by the prosecutor. Cahalan, . . . [The Detroit Riot, 3 The Prosecutor 431 (1967)], Prosecutor Cahalan, in an interview in Detroit, Sept. 7, 1967, emphasized the importance of settling upon this charge, a felony (maximum, five years) to the implementation of a high bond policy and thus keeping people off the streets. He felt that had the looting charges been designated as misdemeanors it would have been far more difficult to justify high bonds.

As might have been expected in a disorder, by far the greatest number of arrests were for looting. Thus, Recorder's Court statistics show 2,694 arrests for entering without breaking, followed distantly by 1,337 for violation of the Governor's Emergency Proclamation (curfew violation, the greatest single misdemeanor charge), 623 for breaking and entering a business place, 337 for larceny over $50, and 288 for receiving stolen property. A number of other offenses with considerably fewer offenders follow these in order of frequency.

he felt there was very little misrepresentation by defendants, and that questionable bail risks and dangerous persons could be weeded out by the volunteers or the court. In addition to the warning to the defendant about lying, telephones were available to the volunteers to aid in verifying information when that was possible and necessary. Finally, Crockett did not think that the absence of any official report of the defendant's prior record precluded individualizing the bond procedure, or that setting bonds at an amount within the financial reach of the defendant jeopardized the safety of the community.

It should be noted that there were a few judges, besides Crockett, who made some attempt to individualize the bond procedure. According to James, Judge Davenport followed Crockett's lead on the second day of arraignments and began to utilize the services of NLS, and to provide a phone for verification purposes; but he also continued to set bonds which were higher than those of Judge Crockett. Two other judges had defendants interviewed and received advice from volunteers in the courtroom — only, apparently, to ignore completely the information and continue to set $10,000 and $25,000 bails across the board.

### 4. Failure to Inform Defendants of Their Constitutional Rights

Many of the people who witnessed the arraignments on the warrant during the early part of the disorder have expressed the view that Recorder's Court judges failed to explain adequately to defendants the offenses with which they were charged and to inform them of their constitutional rights. According to Professor Sengstock,

> The right to counsel was not adequately explained to the accused. His right to have an attorney appointed, if he could not retain one, was not explored. He was not advised what a preliminary examination was. . . . The nature of his offense was not explained to the accused and often he was not informed of his right to a jury trial. The assembly line technique adopted by the court left those uneducated in the process as bewildered after their arraignments as before.

Similarly, Judge Emery has maintained that "[p]eople just were not advised of their constitutional rights at the arraignment on the warrant — they were shuffled through the line."

Recorder's Court judges reject these assertions. Judges Brennan and Gillis, for example, claim that in their courtrooms each defendant was advised of the charges against him, his right to counsel, and his right to remain silent.

The discrepancy between these two accounts is probably due to a difference of opinion in regard to what constitutes an "adequate" explanation of a defendant's rights. Those who criticize the court's performance may feel that it performs unsatisfactorily even under normal circumstances, since ordinarily the accused is not informed that he has a right to have counsel "appointed," or that he can exercise this right "immediately." On the other hand, if less than the usual amount of time was devoted to this aspect of the arraignment as a result of the pressure on the court to process suspects quickly, the disorder may also have exacerbated any deficiencies which normally inhere in the court's warning procedure.

## 5. Expediency

Many of the previously mentioned features of the arraignment on the warrant can also be explained by the Recorder's Court's preoccupation with expediency. Indeed, expediency seemed to be the prevailing philosophy during this stage of the proceedings. Thus, the high bail policy was a means of removing those allegedly engaged in the disorder from the streets with a minimum of legal complications, and the failure to provide counsel or to accept the offers of assistance from various volunteers reflected a desire to dispense with interruptions on behalf of defendants which would slow the work of the court. The group arraignments, too, indicated a predisposition to proceed as quickly as possible. And even the alleged failure to provide adequate warnings of constitutional rights may be attributed in part to an attempt to dispose of cases rapidly.

The reasons for this judicial commitment to expediency are readily apparent. According to Recorder's Court statistics a total of 7,231 persons were arrested on charges related to the disorder. This means that nearly one half of the *entire* caseload for 1966 was thrust upon the court within one week in 1967. By the night of July 23, the first day of the disorder, 255 people had already been arrested; that number climbed to 3,740 by July 27, when the worst of the disturbance ended and the rate of arrests per day began to decline. To cope with this onslaught of prisoners the court remained open around the clock. The judges divided the day into four six-hour shifts, each of which had one judge handling misdemeanors and the rest handling felony arraignments.[60] This

60. The situation confronting the Recorder's Court is forcefully demonstrated by the fact that within a period of six days there were as many felony arrests as normally occur in a six-month period. Thus, while in 1966 the total number of felony warrants issued was 7,360 and in 1965 the number was

left only three judges at any given time to handle felony arraignments, and forced each to arraign approximately eighty prisoners per shift, or an average of one prisoner every four and one-half minutes, in order to keep up with the pace of arrests.

Despite these enormous burdens, it is questionable whether the expedient measures employed by the court were in fact necessary.[61] During the week of the disorder, the Circuit Court of Wayne County had suspended its operations, leaving twenty-six judges with no official duties. On July 25 the services of these judges, and the facilities of the Circuit Court, were offered to the Recorder's Court to aid in the arraignments. Moreover, a number of municipal judges from nearby communities also offered their services.[62] Although accepting these offers would have resulted in at least tripling the judicial manpower available to process the disorder defendants, they were rejected by the Recorder's Court. The reasons given were that the Circuit Court judges would be unfamiliar with the procedures of the Recorder's Court, which has jurisdiction over all criminal cases within the corporate limits of Detroit, that in any event the problem was not judicial manpower but a clerical impasse, and that an attempt was made to use clerks from the Circuit Court but they could not be taught the necessary clerical procedures in time to be of any assistance.[64]

---

6,307, there were 3,164 felony warrants issued during the period of the disorder alone. In addition, there were 1,014 misdemeanor arrests prosecuted. Recorder's Court Statistics on Civil Disturbance Cases (unpublished mimeos).

61. Despite the generally hectic atmosphere, it was asserted by Dennis James, head of the Bail Bond Project, that conditions in the courtrooms were much better than under normal circumstances because all other business had been suspended and unauthorized persons were excluded from the courtroom. According to Mr. James these conditions contrast markedly with the normal "squeezing in" of arraignments among other business of the court, and extensive commotion caused by officers, bondsmen, attorneys, spectators, and others. He added that in his opinion the judges had ample time to arraign individually and according to statutory guidelines. Interview with Dennis James in Detroit, Aug. 8, 1967.

62. According to Judge Horace Gilmore, Wayne County Circuit Judge, some thirty-five municipal judges from Wayne County and nine judges from Common Pleas Court would have been available in addition to the twenty-six circuit court judges. Interview with Judge Gilmore in Detroit, Aug. 17, 1967.

64. Cyrus Vance reports that on Tuesday morning of the disorder the prosecutor estimated that arraignments were about eight hours behind arrests, that by Wednesday morning a police survey indicated that 2,200 prisoners were waiting in various precincts to be recorded and that by Thursday morn-

These reasons are self-defeating. If there was in fact no problem with judicial manpower (there are reports that some judges were often waiting for people to arraign), then whatever justification did exist for employing the "assembly-line techniques" disappears. If, on the other hand, the concern was that a more deliberate approach would put the court behind schedule, even though it was at the time caught up, then the extra manpower should have been welcome, especially since the claim that it would have been difficult to inform judges from another court how to perform what in essence is a simple procedure lacks conviction. Finally, if it is urged that the lack of records was the key factor compelling the procedures used and that expediency was merely a by-product, the experience of Judge Crockett would be evidence to the contrary.

The explanation one is left with is that the expedient procedures were actually the result of a policy decision by a majority of the court to forgo their judicial function and act instead as an arm of the executive and administrative branches in an effort to help quell the disorder. Given this judicial attitude, it is doubtful that the presence of records would have resulted in any significant differences in the court's approach. Their absence merely provided a convenient explanation for the procedures used, albeit a weak one — considering the experiences of one or two judges and the candid remarks of some members of the court. It remains to be considered whether the court's approach to restoring order did in fact contribute to the immediate, or ultimate, good of the community, and whether it was constitutional. . . .

---

ing there were still 1,500 prisoners in precinct stations. . . . [C. Vance, Special Assistant to the Secretary of Defense, Final Report Concerning the Detroit Riots 47 (1967).] Some have suggested that a major contributing factor to the refusal of the court to accept help is the present controversy in Detroit over whether to continue the existing court structure or to abolish the Recorder's Court and merge its functions with those of the Circuit Court. The proffer of judicial assistance might have been regarded as an implicit criticism suggesting the Recorder's Court was incapable of performing its function in times of stress. See 47 Mich. St. B.J. 31 (1968), which quotes a post-disorder "resolution of policy" by the Michigan supreme court on the orderly treatment of persons accused of crime during a civil disturbance. Adopted pursuant to Mich. Const. art. VI, §4, which vests the Michigan supreme court with superintending control over all courts, the resolution states that, in the event of a judicial emergency, the Chief Justice or his designate "shall direct and coordinate the work of all affected courts, court employees, court officers and judicial personnel for the duration of the emergency."

V. A FINAL REFLECTION: THE EFFECT OF THE LEGAL PROCEEDINGS
ON THE ACCUSED AND THE GHETTO COMMUNITY

Perhaps the most important factor for consideration in any attempt to evaluate the administration of criminal justice after the Detroit civil disorder is the effect which the legal procedures that were utilized had on the individual defendants and the community in which they live. Because of the confusion which existed, some observers of the legal proceedings in the wake of the disorder might assert that this Comment presents a distorted view of the facts. Judges may argue that they did strictly observe the rights of all defendants; prosecutors may feel the same way; and, some volunteer attorneys might insist that the proceedings were actually worse than those described. Each individual judge, prosecutor, and attorney has his own viewpoint and his own interest to protect. But, in the final analysis, it is the effect on the individuals which is important; this must provide the framework for all considered evaluation of the legal process. Whether lawyers are able to argue that "due process" was followed is irrelevant to an individual arrestee; what matters to him is what he saw and how he reacted to the legal process.

Sociologists have stated that ghetto dwellers have a suspicious view of the outside system, and this "system" clearly includes the courts. This view is sometimes distorted — a product of their own socioeconomic position.[409] If those who appeared before the Recorder's Court did have a distorted and suspicious view of society as a whole, it seems that one of the court's objectives in processing the defendants should have been to insure that this attitude was not reinforced. The problem, as the President's Task Force on the Administration of Justice stated it, is that

409. See Commission Report 183 (GPO ed.), 337 (paper ed.): "Some of our courts, moreover, have lost the confidence of the poor. This judgment is underwritten by the members and staff of this Commission, who have gone into the courthouses and ghettos of the cities torn by the riots of 1967. The belief is pervasive among ghetto residents that lower courts in our urban communities dispense "assembly-line" justice; that from arrest to sentencing, the poor and uneducated are denied equal justice with the affluent, that procedures such as bail and fines have been perverted to perpetuate loss inequities. We have found that the apparatus of justice in some areas has itself become a focus for distrust and hostility. Too often the courts have operated to aggravate rather than relieve the tensions that ignite and fire disorders."

[t]he many persons who encounter . . . [the lower] courts each year can hardly fail to interpret that experience as an expression of indifference to their situation and the ideals of fairness, equality, and rehabilitation professed in theory, yet frequently denied in practice. The result may be a hardening of antisocial attitudes in many defendants and the creation of obstacles to the successful adjustment of others.[410]

The reinforcement of antisocial attitudes in some and the creation of antisocial attitudes in others appears to have been one result of the administration of criminal justice in the wake of the Detroit civil disorder.[411]

410. [The President's Commission on Law Enforcement and Administration of Justice, Task Force Report: The Courts 29 (1967)].

411. The effects of the post-disorder legal proceeding on the individual are best gleaned from statements made by various released accused who were interviewed by Dr. Nathan Caplan, a sociologist associated with the University of Michigan Institute for Social Research. Dr. Caplan went into Detroit and interviewed a substantial number of persons who had been involved in the disorder; some of these had been arrested and others had not.

One man, who was released at the examination because of lack of probable cause, stated his attitude about what he would do if another civil disorder occurred. He said:

"I will not stay here and watch. . . . Why? You get the same treatment as the rest of them. I might just as well be out rioting with the rest of them. I get the same treatment. . . .

"They might kill me but they won't arrest me. You can believe that. I don't intend to go through the same thing again. . . ."

Another man related his feelings after his case was dismissed because there was no evidence against him. He said: "When I remember it I get angry. I get mean as hell, you know. That's an ugly thing that you do to people. Then you expect them to be nice. You know, that you pat them on the back and say, be nice little niggers and say conform to our laws. Hell no! No we can't conform to your laws because you didn't give us the due process of your laws. That's what."

Another portion of Dr. Caplan's interview with this particular individual is as follows:

Dr. Caplan: Did he ever look up at you?

W: No, he didn't look at you. He just looked down at this thing and ripped you on off.

Dr. Caplan: How did you feel when he said $3,000 and then didn't look up at you?

W: I wanted to kill him. Cuz' I wanted to have a chance to explain. I wanted to tell him that I just got a job this summer and I was trying to go back to school, you know. And it was the first break I'd had in a long time. And I didn't get a chance to say it. And because of it I lost my job, locked up in that joint, you know. And there I was again, like I was last summer, trying to hustle getting back in school. Some thing. You know each year you

Generally, the released arrestees displayed an extremely negative, hostile attitude toward the Recorder's Court and the system which supports it. This reaction resulted not only from the in-court procedures but also from the effect which the in-court procedures had on the arrestees' personal lives. Hurried mass arraignments with little or no opportunity for defendants to justify their activities at time of arrest, the imposition of high, unreasonable bails, and the subsequent delay in the preliminary examination, meant that each

---

got to work a little harder and a little harder, and these people don't care. You tell them and they say, sorry, regulations. Man, damn your regulations! You gotta give somebody a chance to live. We can't meet up to your regulations and your rules. Because we haven't got the tools. You don't give us anything to work with. That was the thing that really got me when I didn't have a chance to say, "Look, I got a job." I'll come back man, I ain't going no place. Look, I'll face it. If I did something, I'm gonna be right back here you know, but let me go out and hold onto my job. This means a living, and do what I want to do and, you know, have money to do it and live like somebody. And he said . . . he didn't say nothing, he just said $3,000.

W:   Then my court date came up. It was August 8, that was the day August the 8th.

Dr. Caplan:   That was two weeks after you were arrested.

W:   Yeah.

Dr. Caplan:   Two weeks?

W:   It seemed like a hundred weeks to me. Well, I went to court and I walked into the courtroom and the man, Judge Columbo, he just looked at me and he say, I suspended your case, you know. That's all he said — he said, cause we ain't got nothing on you. He told me to go on home. I turned around to that man — I was like a beast let loose to the wilderness. That's just what I was, I was an animal.

On outside I was yelling and screaming — I jumped down the street. I was just like a hyena, I was an animal. I looked like one too. And I felt like one. Every white face I passed I wanted to smash it. That's just what I wanted to do.

Dr. Caplan:   How do you feel today?

W:   I could knock some man's head off. I feel like this now: if one of you should dare touch me again, try to dehumanize me again, I'd kill you.

Dr. Caplan:   Are there many people who feel like you because they were arrested?

W:   We all do. We all do.

Dr. Caplan:   How does being arrested and having all this happen to you affect you?

W:   Affect me? Before I was quite passive. You know, I couldn't hurt a fly. I was really a passive person — hard working — trying to reach this goal, trying to get that degree. That's what I wanted. And I wasn't messing with nobody. I didn't break no laws or nothing. I got too much resentment inside me, or bitterness now, to let it happen again — to let somebody say to me, you have to do this.

arrestee spent a considerable amount of time in a crowded, unsanitary detention center. Time in detention facilities was spent under the control of often hostile police officials; little, if any, contact with family and friends was permitted. A rushed preliminary examination meant the possibility of more time in jail and an increased likelihood that present employment would be lost. The pressures to plead guilty at the arraignment-on-the-information stage meant that many individuals emerged from the legal process with a sometimes undeserved but always detrimental criminal record. To many defendants, all of this appeared to be happening without reasonable justification. Because of the way the disorder criminal proceedings affected their lives, both the innocent and the guilty may well be more willing to respond to an agitator in the future.

It can be argued that the court did the best it could under the circumstances. As has been done in the past, it is possible to say that during periods of strife the Constitution and its safeguards must be pushed to the side in the interest of order. Some might argue that it is impossible to accord the strict constitutional guarantees to all arrestees during an "insurrection." However valid this argument might be in other factual contexts, its cogency is surely subject to question in the context of the Detroit disorder and perhaps in every similar disorder. This Comment has demonstrated that there was no justifiable reason (except perhaps lack of planning, which is in itself unjustifiable) for the inadequate procedures utilized in Detroit. Absent a sound and compelling reason for abandoning constitutional protections they must and should be rigidly adhered to by all. The Constitution and its guarantees are applicable to all citizens at all times. Panic, disorganization, and lack of preparation should never excuse granting a defendant less than his full measure of constitutional rights.

# PART IV.
# THE PERFORMANCE OF
# LOWER CRIMINAL COURTS

The materials in this section, describing the actual performance of lower criminal courts, were selected to achieve two objectives. One was to describe the atmosphere, decorum and "feel" of a lower criminal court — the swiftness and impersonality of disposition, the tsar-like power of the judge, and the relative unimportance of rules and legal procedure. The courts described here are not essentially different from the 1921 account of the Cleveland Municipal Court in Part I. The time, however, is thirty to fifty years later. Samuel Dash's observations of the Chicago Municipal Court in 1951 underscore this point. They point backward in time to the 1928 Chicago Crime Survey, and forward to the 1967 Crime Commission study and the Bing and Rosenfeld account of judicial power and defendant denigration in Boston in 1969. Throughout one is struck by the powers of the lower court judge, epitomized by the judge who says the Supreme Court doesn't count in his court, or who, not knowing whom to believe, believes the police.

The second objective of these selections was to present statistical data on the actual outcomes defendants experience in lower courts. By now, no one should be surprised to find that poor, nonwhite defendants fare worse than wealthy white persons; that lawyerless defendants fare worse than those with lawyers; and that a public defender in some cases may be worse than no lawyer at all. Indeed, such facts account for the judgment of the Kerner Commission that the performance of the lower criminal courts contributes to the oppressive conditions leading to civil disorder. The Bing and Rosenfeld study and Donald Warren's research on the Detroit Recorder's Court are paradigmatic examples of what occurs in most lower courts. Surprisingly, these are pioneering studies. The municipal court reformers of the early twentieth century prided themselves on the statistics which the new courts generated. Today court bureaucracies churn out reams of statistics, but with few exceptions these numbers are too crude or unrefined to serve evaluative purposes, and often do not even indicate gross changes occurring within one jurisdiction. In Massachusetts, for example, official court statistics do not distinguish type of offense or sentence imposed. Studies relating social background, wealth, race, and dress with defendant outcomes are rare. Statistical studies, for example, of Baltimore and Detroit completed for the President's 1967 Crime Commission grossly tabulated cases and dispositions by offenses, but neglected the ties to social characteristics. Unfortunately the two statistical studies included here were not able to control for all relevant variables — previous record and offense charged may have biased some of the conclusions. And we are not always told whether the findings are statistically significant. The findings, however, fit with most lower court observations, and are a firm basis for evaluating the quality of lower court justice.

Rounding out this section are accounts of Los Angeles and Cincinnati lower courts. Judge Nutter's discussion of the Los Angeles Municipal Court emphasizes the effect of mass-production procedures on the deterrent power of the law and the benefits which hardened criminals derive from lower court procedures. The Cincinnati study shows the reaction of a lower court to a change in arraignment procedures designed to alleviate an injustice to defendants. Its account of why that reform, minor as it was, failed tells much about lower court performance.

# Cracks in the Foundation of Criminal Justice*

## Samuel Dash

...One of the most discouraging findings of a study made of the Municipal Court of Chicago is the similarity between most of the poor conditions existing today in the Municipal Court with those reported in the Illinois Crime Survey of 1928. After so intensive a study as the one made then by the Illinois Association of Criminal Justice and after 23 years of opportunity to improve, that there should be no improvement is indeed shocking. One of these unchanged conditions is the non-judicial atmosphere of the criminal proceedings and of the court itself, which is an important element in impressing spectators and defendants alike with a sense of unfairness and corruption. In 1928 the Illinois Crime Survey reported on the atmosphere of the then Harrison Street Court:

When the court is in session in the morning, the room is crowded almost to suffocation. The noise is very great. On one side of the room is a runway fenced in by wire which, in a very inadequate way, separates the prisoners coming from their cells from the people in the room. There is no reason why communication cannot be carried on between prisoners and visitors and articles passed through from the latter to the former. The section before the bench is jammed with policemen, lawyers, bondsmen, reporters, visitors, curiously and genuinely interested — men, women, and children, young and old, rich and poor, vicious and innocent. The bailiffs during the entire session of the court go through ineffective motions of seeking a better order. They are constantly rapping for order and pleading with the mob to move back from the bench and open the way to the bull pen. Benches are provided for those who have legitimate business in the court but usually no one is sitting on them. For self protection and in order to see and hear better, people prefer to stand. The smoke is always thick. There is much laughing, loud talking, whispering and expectorating. At times the noise rises to almost deafening proportions, due to the shuffling about and the loud shouts of the bailiff and the pounding of the gavel and the remarks of the bystanders and the efforts of the judge to elicit infor-

* From: 46 Ill. L. Rev. 385, 386-406 (1951). Reprinted by special permission of the Illinois Law Review. Copyright © 1951 by Illinois Law Review Corporation, Vol. 46, No. 3.

mation from reluctant witnesses. It is probable that many cases are dismissed for want of prosecution because the complaining witness fails to hear the case called.[2]

The Felony Branch of the Municipal Court was established in 1930 as an improvement on such courts as the Harrison Street Court. Yet the atmosphere of the new court is identical with that described above. It resembles that of a bustling railroad station, filled with both smoke and movement as well as with loitering attorneys and noise.[3]

The activities of defense attorneys have also remained unchanged. In 1928, the Illinois Crime Survey reported:

> Many of the branches of the Chicago Municipal Court seem to tolerate a condition in connection with attorneys for the defense which is more serious even than the lack of prosecution which has already been described. It seems to be customary for certain lawyers to assume a proprietary attitude toward defense cases. These privileged characters come to the court daily, deposit their coats and hats immediately upon arrival and participate in the activities exactly as if they were paid attendants. They solicit business very largely through the assistance of clerks, bailiffs, assistant prosecutors, and occasionally through the judges themselves. They also mingle freely among the unfortunates who are hauled before the court and get business first hand. The continuous presence of such a permanent defense lawyer in the courtroom means that pleasant and sometimes profitable relationships are established between them and court attachés. Such lawyers have been known to divide the profits from their activities with the kindly officers who throw business to them. In fact, it is stated on good authority that occasionally such a privileged position in a given branch court is paid for by the lawyer, either on a percentage basis or as an initial fee, for the advantage of preying upon the victims of that particular neighborhood.[4]

The same observations may be made on the activities of defense attorneys today. A new face among this group of attorneys is rarely seen. Direct solicitation of business is common, and collab-

2. Illinois Crime Survey 404 (1929).
3. Dash, Report to the Chicago Crime Commission on the Administration of Criminal Justice in the Municipal Court of Chicago 6 (Unpublished report in the files of the Chicago Crime Commission 1951).
4. Illinois Crime Survey 408-409 (1929).

oration between the attorneys and the other "officers" of the court is notorious.[5]

Other striking similarities are apparent between conditions existing today in the Municipal Court and those that existed in 1928. Some important changes were made after the Illinois Crime Survey, but strangely enough, not through the recommendations of the survey, but on the advice of a special judicial advisory committee set up by the chief justice in 1929. In 1930 a separate branch, the felony branch, was established in the Municipal Court to conduct the preliminary hearings of felony cases. Before that time preliminary hearings were conducted in each of the 16 branches of the Municipal Court. In 1931 the public defender system was set up to aid the indigent defendant at the trial of a felony. In that same year a new criminal court building was opened. But many equally if not more important abuses disclosed and emphasized in the Illinois Crime Survey were never considered or remedied, and exist today in an even more aggravated state.

## SPEED AND LACK OF DECORUM

Speed and the resulting careless handling of facts remain important evils. One is impressed immediately by an air of hurry when he enters any branch of the Municipal Court. Along with the hurried atmosphere is the confusion which dominates most of the

---

5. Report, note 3 *supra* at 5-6: "It is not often that a new face is seen among this group of attorneys. They appear day after day representing persons accused of crime. How they obtain their clients is an interesting story. I believe some of the clients are obtained through direct solicitation by the attorney. In one case I had the opportunity to observe such solicitation. While a defendant was before the court, an attorney rushed past him, and I heard him whisper to the defendant, 'Get a continuance.' He was overheard by the judge who asked him if he was representing the defendant. The attorney replied that he didn't know yet and had not received a fee. The court made him make a choice then and there. The attorney spoke a few hurried words to the defendant, then pleaded him guilty, and that was that. It is easy to see that many of the clients are obtained for the attorneys by way of the bailiffs. I have seen these officials approached often by the family of a defendant and then have observed the official lead these persons over to one of the attorneys. The source of clients lies in the hands of policemen, jailors and bailiffs. I am sure they engage in the profitable marketing of this commodity to criminal attorneys who 'belong.' Collaboration between this group of criminal attorneys and police officers is apparent. I have often observed a lawyer in long huddled conversation with a police officer who later turned

stages of the proceedings. The bailiffs set up systems to insure the rapid presentation of defendants before the court. A defendant is held "on deck" while one is before the bench and is shifted into place before the judge as soon as the prior defendant is snatched away. A minute's delay caused by the judge's request for additional information from the witnesses or the defendant antagonizes the bailiffs and makes them work with redoubled effort to make up for the lost time.[8] In any event they must be out of the court by noon, and they let very little stand in their way to reach this objective.

Often the continuing of a case before the defendant has arrived before the bench results in a new case being called with the defendant in the prior case being presented to the court. After the police testify as to the facts of the case, this misplaced defendant is asked what he has to say for himself. He denies the story which is absurd and strange to him. He receives a strong rebuke from the judge for lying to the court and he is about to be threatened by the prosecutor when the police officer discovers that he is not the man he arrested. It is then that the bailiff realizes that this man is the defendant whose case was continued on the prior call and that the defendant for the present call is waiting in the bull pen. The mistaken and confused defendant is grabbed and pushed back to the bull pen, with as little explanation as possible, and the proper defendant is rushed out to the court and placed in position, arriving too late to hear the case against him, and facing a judge already impatient with a case that has taken up too much of his time.

The speed with which cases are tried often results in the failure of crucial facts to be brought before the court. The movement is so swift that facts and testimony are ignored or unheard. An example of this situation was the case of a man sentenced to the

---

out to be the arresting officer in the case and whose testimony freed the defendant. I have observed a lawyer and a police officer leave together and go into the corridor, where I have seen the lawyer slip a bunched up something to the police officer. The attorney who doesn't make use of the services offered by the bailiffs and the police officer may find his going tougher, if not impossible."

8. A judge's popularity among the bailiffs in the Felony Branch of the Municipal Court depends almost entirely on his speed of action. It is not unusual for the most conscientious judges who attempt to get all the facts of the case disclosed before the court to be extremely unpopular with the bailiffs and the targets of many a curse throughout the morning.

county jail in spite of the testimony of the complaining witness that the defendant was not the man who had robbed him.[9] In the confusion and noise around the bench the judge had not heard this testimony.

In the outer branches of the Municipal Court, judicial swiftness is even more pronounced. The judge arrives usually between 9:45 and 10:00 A.M. He leaves at 10:30, sometimes at 10:45 A.M., after having disposed of about thirty to forty cases. On one day I clocked the speed at which cases were handled and came out with an average of seven cases every ten minutes, less than two minutes a case. The fastest judge I observed would arrive at 9:45 A.M. and be out at 10:00 A.M., having disposed of twenty cases.

In the great rush of prosecution little attention is paid to ceremony or courtroom decorum. Oath-taking in the Municipal Court is little more than a mockery. In every case I observed, regardless of its gravity, there was in fact no oath-taking. The defendant was hurried before the court and the clerk barked at all witnesses to raise their right hand. Some did, some did not. The clerk then rattled off in the manner of a tobacco auctioneer a jumble of words which were completely incomprehensible. When he was through the witnesses were supposed to say "I do." Most of them said nothing. A few moved their lips a little. But nobody had waited for them anyway, since the police officer had already begun to give his testimony. Certainly none of the witnesses were impressed with the fact that they were under oath or influenced in any exceptional way to tell the truth.

In cases where the court is trying the defendant on a misdemeanor charge, the defendant must be asked whether he wants to be tried by the court or by a jury. Again this question is asked in a mumbled manner, without any intention being paid to the defendant's reaction or answer. At times the question is asked in a clear enough manner so that the defendant understands what is being asked him. But if he is unrepresented by an attorney, which is the usual case, he does not know how to answer. If he delays,

9. In this case the complaining witness looked over at the defendant and said, "He doesn't look like the man who stole my wallet." The judge failed to hear this statement because of the noise and confusion around the bench, and mechanically sentenced the defendant. This case also serves as a shocking lesson of what can happen to a defendant who is not represented by counsel, since had counsel been present he would have quickly brought the witness' statement to the attention of the judge.

however, the clerk barks at him and tells him that he wants to be tried by the court, and the case is commenced. Jury trials in these cases are almost unheard of.

## CORRUPTION

There seems to be common agreement among all people who have studied the courts that there is often corruption present in criminal proceedings. Because of the inherent nature of corrupt practice, its workings are secret and only rarely can concrete evidence be collected. Sometimes the boldness with which illegal influence is accepted in the courts of Chicago convinces one that the perpetrators of this activity think themselves firmly entrenched. On one occasion, a judge in the Municipal Court in open court, in my presence, told a defendant, "You're in Joe . . . .'s precinct, aren't you? Well, he called me up today. Somebody must have told him you were in trouble. Well, you can go, and tell Joe that we got his message."

Political pressure is common in the outer branches of the Municipal Court and I have witnessed this kind of activity actually determine the disposition of cases. Because court officials such as bailiffs and deputy sheriffs are recipients of political favors for their work during political campaigns and in their very jobs are participants in the spoils system, it is little wonder that these officials look to the political boss as their master rather than to the city or state which they are under oath to faithfully represent.

A shocking example of the failure of law enforcement because of corruption is an activity which is a common occurrence in one of the branches of the Municipal Court. In this court 70% of the gambling cases are dismissed on a motion to suppress the evidence because of an illegal search and seizure. Day after day the same police squad testifies as to the nature of the raids and the same small clique of lawyers make[s] the motions to suppress. The routine has become so common that there is now very little attention paid to the facts and the motions are made and sustained as a matter of course. . . .

## THE LESSER PLEA

The most important contributor to injustice in the Municipal Court today is the process by which a great number of felony cases in the Felony Branch are eliminated through pleas of guilty to a lesser offense. The percentage of these eliminations amounts to

36% of the felony cases presented before the court.[16] Such felonies as robbery, burglary and rape are cut down to petty larceny, assault and battery, and contributing to delinquency of a minor. Crimes which carry penalties such as twenty years or life in the penitentiary are punished with as little as 30 days in the county jail. This compromise, if not nullification, of the criminal law is a daily process in the Felony Branch, and goes on completely unsupervised. There is no requirement that the prosecutor give a reason for the reduction of the offense. There is no attempt to curb the efforts of the prosecutor to bargain in open court for such a plea to a lesser offense. In fact, the judge, himself, often enters the bargaining process and attempts to sell the defendant on the advantages of the misdemeanor plea.

This practice is all the more insidious when it is worked on unrepresented defendants. Many such defendants appear in the Felony Branch since the public defender system does not extend its protection until after an indictment is returned. The methods used by the prosecutor and the judge to obtain a plea of guilty to a lesser charge from an unrepresented defendant often amount to downright coercion performed in open court. I have heard one prosecutor tell a defendant, "Don't be a fool — if you buck us you will wait six months in jail for your trial. Now if you take a plea, you'll get six months and at the end of that time you will be a free man." Another prosecutor told an unrepresented defendant, "You had better plead guilty to petty larceny or we'll make sure

16. The following table comprises the breakdown of the disposition of cases in the Felony Branch of the Municipal Court of Chicago for the past three years. . . .

|  | 1948 | 1949 | 1950 |
|---|---|---|---|
| Total Cases Beginning as Felonies | 8,146 | 8,519 | 7,897 |
| Cases Disposed of as Felonies |  |  |  |
| Discharged | 1,163 | 769 | 874 |
| Nolle Prossed | 2,527 | 2,959 | 2,494 |
| DWPa | 592 | 604 | 443 |
| Grand Jury | 1,271 | 1,254 | 1,226 |
| % Discharged | 14.2 | 9.2 | 11.5 |
| % Nolled | 31.2 | 34.8 | 31.6 |
| % DWP | 7.2 | 7.3 | 5.6 |
| % Grand Jury | 14.3 | 14.8 | 15.6 |
| Cases Reduced at Preliminary Hearing |  |  |  |
| from a Felony to a Misdemeanor | 2,593 | 2,833 | 2,860 |
| % Reductions | 31.8 | 34.4 | 36.2 |

a—Dismissed for want of prosecution.

you are sent up for ten years in the penitentiary. With the record you have nobody will believe your story, and it's a sure thing we'll get you found guilty of robbery at the trial." The defendants in both these cases pleaded guilty and were sentenced for a misdemeanor. Unquestionably there are innocent men who have pleaded guilty to a misdemeanor from fear of being "railroaded" to the penitentiary for a long period of years. While few of these men would be considered desirable citizens since most have long records of prior convictions for crimes of which they were actually guilty, the fact remains that they are innocent of the crime to which they have pleaded guilty. A system of justice which permits this type of conviction is in reality a system of injustice. Moreover the convicted person finds in this practice confirmation of his belief in the futility of reform.

In many of the cases observed, suspicions arose that an innocent man was being forced to plead guilty to a misdemeanor. Two cases present absolute proof of this shameful practice. In both the prosecutor failed to force a plea of guilty and the trial of the felony vindicated the defendants. These cases present an unusual opportunity to observe the real nature of the coerced plea, since luckily they went to the stage of trial where the absolute failure of the State's evidence proved that the prosecutor had no basis whatsoever to threaten the defendant with a conviction.

The defendant in the first of these two cases had been warned by the prosecutor in open court that if he would not cooperate with the state in pleading guilty to a misdemeanor, he would be "put away" for twenty years in the penitentiary. After being subjected to this kind of threatening for a period of time, the defendant begged the court to accept his plea of guilty, while insisting that he was innocent. It happened that the judge sitting on this case was one of the most competent and conscientious judges in the court, and he refused to accept the plea of guilty in the face of a claim of innocence. The defendant was bound over to the Grand Jury and at the trial was acquitted when the State failed to produce any evidence that could link him to the crime charged.

In the second of these cases, the defendant fought both prosecutor and judge in his battle to resist pleading guilty to a misdemeanor. After the prosecutor had threatened the defendant with a long prison term if he refused to take a plea, the judge advised the defendant not to throw away the "gift" that was being offered to him. When the defendant continued to claim he was innocent, the judge attempted to persuade him to plead guilty by promising him a term of only four months in the county jail instead of the six months originally offered him for a plea. At the point of tears the defendant demanded his right to a trial and was bound over to the Grand Jury. He was acquitted at the trial, when again the State failed to produce evidence supporting its charges against the defendant. It is safe to say that few persons would have withstood the pressure that this defendant did in refusing to make a plea of guilty.

The problem of the unrepresented defendant is not the only one produced by the practice of the reduced plea. With respect to represented defendants, this evil sullies the entire legal profession. Criminal attorneys who are in the Felony Branch every day know well this practice of the prosecutor to accept a plea to a lesser charge. When they receive a case involving a felony charge, they often approach the defendant and impress upon him the seriousness of the charge and the danger he faces of a long term in the penitentiary. This technique works especially well with young first offenders. The attorneys inform the defendant that they know the judge and the prosecutor and with a little money can buy them off and get them to accept a plea of guilty to a misdemeanor. The frightened defendant doesn't care how he is saved, so long as he is saved. Somehow he raises the money his lawyer demands. The lawyer pays no money to the judge or prosecutor, but pockets the money. Surely enough at the preliminary hearing the prosecutor asks the defendant if he will plead to a lesser charge. The judge accepts the defendant's plea and gives him a light sentence or places him on probation. The defendant informs his friends that his lawyer is a "sharp operator" and that the judges and prosecutors can be bought off. This belief that the courts are open for this type of bribery spreads and clings to all courts and lawyers.

A third and equally as important a result of the practice of the lesser plea is its effect in undermining the deterrent theory of punishment. A principal purpose for long sentences in felony cases is to deter persons from committing felonies. But when the seasoned criminal knows that he will be permitted to plead to a lesser charge and get a few months in the county jail, he may well conclude that it is worth his while to commit the crime in face of such light punishment. The prosecutor accepts the lesser plea regardless of the prior record of the defendant. In his own discretion, without any supervision, the prosecutor makes the law for the State even though such a practice is directly contrary to the legislative provisions. The Illinois Crime Survey reported in 1928 that, "The criminal who knew his way about had no fear of prosecution." [23] The same is true today....

23. Illinois Crime Survey 17 (1929).

What is the motivation behind the prosecutor's willingness to accept a plea of guilty to a lesser charge? Various reasons have been given by the crime surveys and experts who have written on the subject, and on some of these reasons there is mutual agreement. It is agreed, for instance, that neither the courts nor the prosecutors' staffs are able to care for the increased volume of crimes. Some writers found that prosecuting officials have regarded certain laws as too severe, which is reminiscent of the attempt of prosecutors in the seventeenth century to evade a felony charge that would bring the death penalty. Professor Jerome Hall believes that three important factors leading a prosecutor to compromise cases are the desire not to try on a felony charge a person with a good reputation in the community; the weakness of the State's case making it probable that the trial would result in an acquittal; and the fervent desire of the prosecutors to establish a record of numerous convictions the quickest and easiest way. Other reasons put forward are political corruption and influence and the reluctance of persons to admit criminal liability because of the stigma of moral delinquency resulting in a strong opposition to serious charges.

My observation of this practice has led me to believe that the major reasons which lie behind this abuse are the desire of the prosecutor for a record of numerous convictions by the quickest and easiest method and the weakness of the State's case resulting from poor police work and inadequate trial preparation. The job of prosecution becomes easy indeed when most cases can be disposed of on a plea of guilty. Of course, a factor which continues to generate this activity is the prosecutor's past success in chalking up quick convictions. Where innocent men are before the prosecutor, and especially those who are unrepresented, he applies the kind of pressure described earlier to get a plea of guilty. That the man might be innocent appears not to worry him for he seems to have the attitude that regardless of whether the defendant is guilty of the crime charged, because of his record, he must have committed some undetected crime and deserves any sentence he gets. That this practice is handled carelessly and on a wholesale basis is proved by the request for a plea of guilty made by the prosecutor to almost every defendant that comes up before the bench. The prosecutors in the Felony Branch of the Municipal Court have made one exception. They usually will not accept a plea to a lesser offense in the case of robbery with a gun. But in all other cases regardless of the record of the defendant, or the facts of the case, the prosecutor stands ready to reduce the charge — in fact more than ready, since he usually makes the initial offer himself. Many complaining witnesses who have been victims of serious crimes committed by the defendant are shocked to see the man who has committed a crime which calls for a long prison term trot off merrily on a short tour in the county jail. . . .

Basically, the solution is getting better prosecutors and not eliminating the discretion of the prosecutor. Professor Hall recognized this when he wrote, "It follows that the task for legal reform lies not in the direction of eliminating discretion, but rather in the direction of securing a wiser use of it by intelligent delegation of authority, a more competent, honorable personnel, and careful checks." [60] The problem, however, is fraught with so much danger of abuse, and the experience of "checks" has been so completely unsatisfactory in the New York courts, that there is need for a step even more drastic to rid the courts of this market street bargaining and coercion.

A necessary step is the divorcement of the sentencing power from the court. While there are many other reasons why this change in procedure is necessary for the betterment of the administration of criminal justice, it is in any event a change that will directly wipe out the dangers of the reduced plea. With the court no longer in a position to offer lesser sentences, there will be no advantage to the defendant in pleading guilty to a misdemeanor. As Professors Weintraub and Tough pointed out, "The average defendant will not plead guilty unless he feels that he is getting the better of what under any circumstances must be for him a bad bargain." [62] The trial under such a system will serve its only proper function, the determination of the guilt or innocence of the defendant. Most judges today admit that they are incompetent to sentence. As a result of their insecurity and lack of knowledge in this field, they seize on any pretext to shift the burden, and have welcomed the chance to give light sentences on a plea of guilty to a lesser offense. The sentencing power could be given to a treatment board made up of experts in the fields of psychology, psychiatry, and sociology. Its approach would be on an individual basis and hinged on the problems and needs of the particular defendant. Prediction tables such as have been developed by the Gluecks would be valuable in the determination of a convicted person's chances for reform and his ability to live a socially desirable and acceptable life. Finally, the removal of the prosecutor's bargaining power will force him to prepare better for trial and it will give confidence both to the police and the victim of the crime

---

60. Hall, Theft, Law and Society 121 (1935).
62. Hall, op. cit. supra note 60, at 529.

that the accused will, if found guilty, be found guilty of the crime for which he was arrested.

## CONCLUSION

If the activities of the lower criminal court discussed in this article were recounted in a Dickens' novel, they would indeed be the subject matter of many a hearty laugh. But reality in this respect is no laughing matter. These activities take place not only in the courts of Chicago, but in the courts of every large city in this country. The most tragic thing about it all is that most lawyers generally are unconcerned, and those who care have convinced themselves that there is nothing that can be done about it. And so we are left with the most important area of the law being abandoned to the weeds and the vermin. Young men with ideals graduating from law schools today shun the criminal law as if it were the black death. Perhaps they show good judgment in their decision, since there is little room for young men with ideals in the practice of the criminal law today. Syndicates of criminal lawyers maintain a strangle hold on the practice of criminal law and they have control of the avenues leading to clients. Even were a young man fortunate enough to get a client, this client would be spirited away from him before the case came up for trial. In short, there is no money in the honest practice of criminal law.

It is inevitable that a study of the lower criminal courts leads to the desire to change procedure. But the study of these courts also makes it clear that there can be a decent administration of criminal justice without changing any of the procedures now in practice. It perhaps seems obvious that the real change that is needed is in the personnel administering the procedures. Though this may be true in all fields of the law, it is particularly true in the criminal law. All of the prior surveys on crime named this the principal solution to the abuse of criminal justice and they warned that no procedural changes could withstand corrupt and inefficient administrators.

The first and main responsibility for getting decent and honest lawyers in the field of the administration of criminal justice lies with the Bar. Until the Bar recognizes its neglect and sets up methods by which it can clean its house, little can be expected of the public in the way of a desire to do anything. How many more studies must be made before the Bar is convinced? How much longer will the Bar put up with its reputation being soiled by the activities in the no-man's land on the other side of the tracks?

There have been sufficient studies and adequate proof. It seems that the need for action has long been apparent, and that we are now very late.

# The Quality of Justice in the Lower Criminal Courts of Metropolitan Boston*

## Stephen R. Bing and S. Stephen Rosenfeld

PART II. THE OFFICIALS IN THE DISTRICT COURT PROCESS

*Introduction*
Ultimately, the judge controls the lower court. The role played by other personnel depends in large part upon how important the judge considers him to the criminal process. Prosecutors, clerks, probation officers and defense counsel, practically speaking, all serve at the will of the presiding judge. For example, in most cases tried in the district courts, a police officer acts as prosecutor. Often, the judge takes an active role in the prosecution of the case, filling crucial gaps left by a police prosecutor unfamiliar with the requirements of proving guilt.

The importance of the probation officer in the court process depends exclusively upon how much reliance the judge places upon pre-sentence reports. Often, as is his prerogative, the judge ignores the pre-sentence process entirely and imposes sentence guided solely by the defendant's prior record and the nature of the crime. In such cases the responsibilities of the probation officer are greatly diminished, beginning only after the process of judging is completed and the correctional process has begun.

We have also observed the influence enjoyed by clerks of courts. Many judges delegate much of their own authority, or acquiesce in the clerk's exercise of powers shared by both clerk and judge. Thus in many courts the decision to issue a complaint, while by statute within the province of both judge and clerk, is made almost exclusively by the clerk of court.

Finally, the ability of a defense counsel to represent his client adequately certainly depends upon the thoroughness of his preparation and his commitment to his client. However, the willingness

* From: Pp. 23-34, 51-58, 79-94 (1970). Reprinted by permission of the Committee on Law Enforcement and Administration of Criminal Justice, Commonwealth of Massachusetts.

of the judge to allow counsel the time in court to develop defenses and establish reasonable doubt of the defendant's guilt plays a significant role in the final outcome in the district court. We have observed judges who view attempts to develop thorough defenses as obstructing the court. A comment made by one judge characterizes this attitude: "The case is open and shut, why are you taking up the court's time." In such instances, the role of the defense counsel is reduced to a technical compliance with the requirement of legal representation. . . .

### The Judge — Power Derived from Absence of Review

All district court judges are appointed for life by the Governor subject to approval by the Governor's Council. Their substantive powers include issuing search warrants and arrest warrants, conducting pre-trial commitment proceedings, issuing complaints for criminal offenses within the jurisdiction of the district court, setting bail both at arraignment and after defendant's application for trial de novo, holding trials, deciding guilt or innocence, and imposing sentence upon defendants found guilty.

In most court systems which function without juries, the judge occupies, unchallenged, the most powerful position in the process. In the district courts of greater Boston the absence of prosecuting attorneys heightens the judge's power. In Washington, D.C. a strong prosecutor's office engages in pre-trial bargaining and often decides to drop cases for want of evidence. In many cases, the judge merely rubberstamps decisions already made by others. In Boston, one institution — the police department — makes the arrest and prosecutes the case. There is less opportunity either for bargaining between prosecutor and defense counsel or for an independent appraisal, prior to court appearance, of the strength of the government's case. Consequently, here in Boston, the judge controls virtually all post-arrest decision making.

The absence of a traditional system of judicial review further enhances the district court judge's power over proceedings in his own courtroom. Throughout the report we shall stress this feature of the trial de novo system. Trial de novo provides the individual with a new trial. Given the alternative, virtually every defendant dissatisfied with the result in district court will, as is his right, choose a complete new trial in another court rather than settle for the one other opportunity to contest the district court decision open to him — a narrow claim by writ of error to the Supreme Judicial Court that the district court acted contrary to law. . . .

The absence of a stenographic record in the district courts

places a practical and severe limitation upon the usefulness of the writ of error in contesting the district court proceeding. Currently much error which might be laid bare by a full stenographic record falls below the Supreme Judicial Court's level of visibility, since the record in the district court consists only of the formal court papers. Were the stenographic transcript included as part of this record, and were stenographers freely available in the district courts, the potential for effective judicial scrutiny of district court proceedings might be enhanced.

The infrequent use of the writ of error is perhaps best underlined by our interviews with many defense lawyers active in the district courts. Most lawyers confessed ignorance about the specific procedures to be followed in pursuing the writ of error. They emphasized that the exclusive remedy used by almost all defense lawyers contesting district court decisions was trial de novo.

The exoneration of the defendant after a new trial establishes his innocence but involves no scrutiny of the process in the district court that reached the improper result in the first trial. No opportunity exists for higher courts to discover or rectify whatever errors exist, e.g., in (a) court procedure, (b) taking of evidence, (c) the lower court's view of defendant's constitutional rights, or (d) the court's interpretation of the criminal statutes. Each district court judge continues in his own court as the unchecked arbiter of the law.

The injury inflicted by placing the district court beyond effective review does not end with errors of law. The absence of a reviewing court promotes patterns and practices that may not rise to the level of illegality, but nonetheless take a serious toll. No direction is provided district court judges in the uniform application and observance of court procedures. There results a marked disparity in the procedures followed in different district courts. The absence of court rules further encourages the disparity in procedures. For example, in the setting of bail, the taking of pleas, the assignment of counsel to indigent defendants, and the granting of continuances, the practice of the courts varies from court to court, and within one district court, may vary from judge to judge. This lack of uniformity stemming from the absence of rules and the absence of judicial review places a premium upon the defense counsel's familiarity with the peculiarities of each court and each judge. He is thus forced to respond to the man rather than to the law.

Finally, the absence of traditional judicial review actually discourages the establishment of affirmative standards and a system of court rules. Such rules are usually discussed and developed by panels of judges and distinguished legal scholars. Such men have no day to day involvement in the business of the district criminal courts. They must derive their knowledge, their understanding, their sense of need for change, by some other means. Absence of traditional review closes off one crucially important source: the appellate cases that, taken together, may indicate a persistent problem requiring the imposition of rules. Official transcripts of court proceedings would also provide information to guide the development of court rules. Similarly, the absence of review that shields problems from the rulemakers' attention will subsequently shield from the scrutiny of appellate courts any abuse and disregard of drafted rules, once instituted.

In other jurisdictions where judicial review is available, these same problems exist and often flourish. An unfortunate characteristic of virtually every lower criminal court system is the insulation of the courtroom from scrutiny, with or without a system of judicial review. That insulation persists with the help of many factors: (a) the defense bar is apathetic in pursuing appellate cases; (b) neither defendant nor victim has appreciable political and economic power; (c) the influential segments of the established bar are uninterested in practicing here regularly. That insulation frustrates lasting improvement in the quality of justice. Decisions can be ignored with little fear of admonition. If intelligent recommendations for improving the courts are to have a telling impact, insulation must be stripped away, layer by layer, by addressing each of the problems that causes such insulation. In Massachusetts, the absence of traditional judicial review is one cause of this insulation. Absence of rules, and of court stenographers are others. While providing appellate review will not by itself bring widespread uniformity and fidelity to rules of law into all district courts, this step would be helpful to the ultimate achievement of these objectives. In an imperfect system, we as pragmatists have asked not how we can make matters perfect, but rather how we can minimize the imperfections.

### Court Clerks

The Governor appoints court clerks to a life tenure. They have been given defined substantive authority concurrent with the district court judge. They do not, however, receive any special training to fulfill these responsibilities. While many clerks have had a legal education, the Governor need not appoint persons trained in the law.

Clerks may, after taking evidence, issue complaints, warrants for arrest, and search warrants. The clerk must, in considering the request before him, follow the recognized standard of probable cause. It is, in fact, the normal practice for all warrants to be issued by the court clerk. One police officer told us that a clerk once refused his request to issue an arrest warrant. The officer, in what he considered a highly unusual occurrence, had to secure the warrant from the judge.

The clerks have power, concurrent with judges, to set bail, and to issue summonses to witnesses in criminal trials. In cases involving misdemeanor offenses, the clerks may hold hearings, with both complainant and accused present, to determine whether a complaint should be granted. This clerk's hearing serves as an informal adjustment mechanism, and is regular practice for certain offenses, principally domestic relations matters.

The clerk's administrative duties include keeping records of the court's business, receiving fines and fees owing to the court, calling in other judges in the event of death or disability of the presiding judge, and adjourning the court if no judge is present or available. The court clerk may appoint one or more assistant clerks to carry out these tasks.

### Police Prosecutors

In our six courts, as in virtually every district court, police officers act as prosecutors. The prosecutor is either the arresting officer or a police officer assigned to the courts as a full time prosecutor. No statute or judicial decision has been uncovered which authorizes the police prosecutor system. This practice dates back to the late nineteenth century and has become firmly established throughout the state as an acceptable, if imperfect, method for representing the interests of the government in the criminal process.

There is no established policy for designating cases to be tried by the arresting officer and cases tried by the regular police prosecutor. We have occasionally observed the regular police prosecutor handling only drunkenness charges, while simultaneously in another courtroom, an arresting officer represents the state in a complex probable cause hearing.

Police officers receive little formal training in the law, much less in prosecution of cases. Those officers who prosecute infrequently rely primarily on their native ability to improvise, past observation of court cases, and frequent prompting from the presiding judge. The regular police prosecutor develops a practical working knowledge of courtroom procedure over a period of years.

He transmits a sense of confidence in his prosecutorial ability, through a combination of offhand courtroom manner and an actual understanding of many legal requirements involved in presenting the government's case. Experienced police prosecutors believe that they possess sufficient skill to prosecute cases successfully. And they realize that the judge can be relied upon to step in and pull the threads of the prosecution's case together in a difficult matter.

The state accepts an obvious handicap in all criminal cases by having police officers assume the tasks fulfilled in most jurisdictions by professional, trained prosecutors. Lack of skill and training results in cases being lost when convictions are justified.

Moreover, this system demeans the criminal process. The necessity of the judge injecting himself into the prosecution — often presenting the state's case if the police prosecutor stumbles — casts doubts upon his impartiality. Also, the prosecuting attorney, if he is the arresting officer, is the state's chief witness. This ambiguity of roles makes the uniform application of rules of evidence practically impossible, and reduces the trial process to an informal argument.

### Defense Counsel

Two out of three defendants charged with "real crime" are represented by a lawyer in the district courts. Thirty-nine percent have private retained counsel. The other 28 percent after being found indigent and therefore unable to pay for defense services, have a lawyer assigned by the court. The private lawyers in the district courts are individuals whose practice for the most part consists of criminal cases. The lawyers and law firms with the greatest influence in the private bar and in established bar associations seldom find themselves appearing in a district criminal court. Rather, their time is spent in civil courts, where the practice of law brings greater financial gain. If they represent criminal defendants, the cases usually involve white collar crime, high fees, and a higher court.

It is no coincidence that courts where such influential lawyers practice have better trained personnel than the lower criminal courts and well developed rules or practice which are closely followed for the client's benefit. Judges are likely to be drawn from this same influential segment of the legal profession. With substantial amounts of money in controversy and high fees involved, these lawyers would abide nothing less. It is also no coincidence that when the established law firms and bar associations are absent, as in the Massachusetts district courts, there exists serious inadequacies in the system of defense counsel provided indigent defendants.

The weight of criminal defense for the poor falls almost exclusively upon the overworked Massachusetts Defenders Committee. The MDC is a statewide, state financed organization staffed presently with sixty lawyers. Each lawyer carries an average of 360 cases a year in the district courts alone. In addition, the MDC is responsible for the defense of persons being charged in the Superior Court. In each of the courts we studied except the BMC [Boston Municipal Court] we observed but one MDC lawyer available to take cases assigned by the judge. In the BMC two or three lawyers are always present. In all of Suffolk County in 1968, nine public defenders took responsibility for assigned cases. These nine lawyers made a total of 7,836 court appearances, about three per man per day. This small staff finds itself further burdened by insufficient support personnel. In 1968 there were only ten investigators to assist all MDC lawyers with preparation of district court cases. Not surprisingly, MDC lawyers tell us that they have less than adequate time to prepare a full defense.

And as a consequence of the lack of resources and the large caseload, defendants are depersonalized. They became cases, charges, numbers, instead of clients.

The pressure of their caseload also forces the Massachusetts Defenders to make some very practical decisions in representing their clients. These decisions are partially reflected in the way the Massachusetts Defenders Committee compiles its annual statistics, evaluating its defense work during the year. According to these statistics any disposition in the district court short of a jail term is viewed as a "favorable result." The MDC definition of a "favorable result" thus includes findings of guilt and pleas of guilty as well as dismissals and findings of not guilty. This grouping accurately suggests that the MDC uses plea bargaining freely, to obtain the defendant's freedom while avoiding the time necessary to provide a full dress defense at trial. The MDC considers the results of that bargaining as satisfactory. Plea bargaining is used by all attorneys to obtain freedom for a client when the defense appears weak. For the Massachusetts Defenders Committee, plea bargaining becomes a necessary technique to deal with an overwhelming caseload.

The statute articulating the responsibility of the Massachusetts Defenders Committee directs them to represent those persons "legally entitled" to counsel. The MDC has interpreted this standard as requiring that a judge find the defendant entitled to counsel. Thus the MDC only accepts cases assigned by the court.

The judge makes the decision to assign counsel at arraignment when the defendant first appears in court. The public defender will in most cases meet with his client only after arraignment; after the judge has set bail and taken the defendant's plea.

In later sections we shall discuss in greater detail the problems of assigned counsel. And as Table D . . . indicates, defendants with assigned counsel — i.e., poor people — receive fewer continuances — especially in the Boston Municipal Court — have higher bail set, and are found guilty more often than defendants with private counsel. What is more startling, defendants with assigned lawyers fare little differently, sometimes worse, than defendants who have no lawyer at any time during the district court process. See Table D. . . .

### The Probation Department

The formal duties of probation officers fall into two separate categories, (a) assisting the judicial process and (b) supervising the corrections process for probationers. In assisting the process, the probation officer provides information about the defendant to the judge to guide him in setting bail and imposing sentence. As a corrections officer, he serves both as monitor, insuring that all conditions of probation are met, and as counselor, assisting the probationer to resolve personal difficulties during the period of probation.

The actual role of the probation officer in the judicial process varies widely. In some courts the officer is in fact a respected advisor to whom the judge turns for guidance and detailed information. Other judges use the probation officer merely to provide the court with records of previous arrests and convictions.

In most courts, the officer's responsibilities outside the courtroom — therefore outside direct control by the judge — are quite similar. In domestic relations matters, the probation officer serves as a collection agency recording the husband's regular payments. Also, probation officers in Boston decide whether persons charged with drunkenness should be released prior to court appearance. In Boston in 1967, some 11,178 drunk arrests — 62.7 percent of the total — were finally resolved through release by a probation officer at the police stationhouse. . . .

### Assignment of Counsel

When a defendant appears at arraignment unrepresented by counsel, the judge asks if he wants a lawyer to represent him. Most

**TABLE D**
Effect of Defense Counsel on Court Process

| | Continuances (% of defendants pleading not guilty) | | | Bail (% of those for whom bail is set) | | Adjudication (% of defendants pleading not guilty) | | |
|---|---|---|---|---|---|---|---|---|
| | None | At least one | Unknown | Pretrial Release (on P.R. or money bail) | Committed for failure to make bail | Found Guilty | Found not Guilty | Other* |
| Defendants with no Attorney | 43 | 53 | 4 | 75 | 25 | 48 | 37 | 15 |
| Defendants with Attorney | 29 | 68 | 3 | 73 | 27 | 56 | 27 | 17 |
| —Private Attorney | 21 | 75 | 4 | 82 | 18 | 49 | 35 | 16 |
| —Assigned Attorney | 40 | 58 | 2 | 58 | 42 | 65 | 17 | 18 |

\* Probable cause
Jurisdiction declined
Unknown

defendants who appear without a lawyer do so because they cannot afford the fee. Rule 3:10 promulgated by the Supreme Judicial Court guarantees the right to counsel. However, the procedures used to implement the rule vary greatly from court to court. Few judges make an effort to explain that a lawyer will be assigned free of charge if the defendant is indigent.

In the suburban courts, we observed a generally explicit process for telling defendants about their right to counsel. In the urban courts, however, the judges we observed made little effort to explain that a lawyer would be assigned free of charge if the defendant was indigent. Consequently, for many defendants, especially those in court for the first time, the lawyer assignment process was confusing and appeared arbitrary. For example, one observer interviewed a defendant who had gone to trial without an attorney. The defendant said that he had not requested legal assistance because, although he was unemployed, he did have ten dollars in his pocket. The judge initiated the assignment process by asking the defendant, "Do you have any money?" When the defendant answered "yes," the judge went no further.

In another court, the judge asked a Spanish-speaking defendant who understood English with difficulty, "How much money do you have in your pocket?" The defendant answered, "Forty cents." The judge then told the defendant that since he had forty cents in his pocket, he should hire a forty cent lawyer. Unable to understand the twist of intended humor — or ridicule — involved, the defendant proceeded to trial without a lawyer and was found guilty.

There are no standard procedures or criteria guiding or directing court judges in establishing the defendant's indigency. One judge, for example, has a rule of thumb that defendants who can afford to make bail are not indigent. This of course ignores that (a) the bail premium may devour the defendant's resources, and (b) a great disparity exists between the amounts of bail premium and lawyers' fees. Another judge has advised defendants to sell property they own to pay a lawyer's fee.

To some degree then, whether a defendant is assigned a lawyer depends not on a realistic assessment of his ability to pay, but upon the court where he is tried.

Confusion also exists within each court. In one case the judge criticized the Massachusetts Defenders, declaring that a defendant who earned one hundred and thirty-five dollars a week should not have assigned counsel. The Massachusetts Defender then told him that the agency had been appointed in that case by another judge in the same district court. In another court a judge asked how the

Massachusetts Defenders got into a case, since the defendant apparently earned enough money to pay his own attorney. The reply by the Defender was: "We were wondering that ourselves, your honor."

Since no formal criteria or standards exist for the determination of indigency, the courts are able to use assignment of counsel for purposes unrelated to the defendant's financial need. In one case, a defendant vigorously protesting his innocence at arraignment was told to behave himself or the court would find that he could afford his own lawyer. In another court the assignment process reflects the judge's attitude toward certain crimes. The court categorically refuses to assign counsel for minor motor vehicle offenses and charges of drunkenness, thus enabling it to expedite the handling of these cases. While we have suggested elsewhere that administrative handling of this type of case might be appropriate, such a procedure should be adopted by rule and statute, not by the use of the assignment process.

Most importantly, the absence of controlling standards and criteria allows easy use of the assignment process as a tool for in-court bargaining. We observed several incidents where judges implied that a lenient sentence was available if the defendant would waive his right to counsel. In one court the judge assured the defendant that his rights would be protected if he would proceed without a lawyer. The defendant was told that the matter could be "worked out." In another court a young narcotics defendant was told that he would be "satisfied" with the results of the trial if he would proceed without a lawyer.

Our statistics suggest that defendants who proceed without attorneys do indeed receive more lenient treatment than those who insist on the assignment of counsel. Table G ... compares the sentences for defendants represented by assigned counsel and those with no lawyer at all. Those without lawyers receive a fine as the only sentence more often, and jail sentences less often than those represented by an assigned attorney. Moreover, if we look specifically at findings of not guilty or no probable cause, the people with no counsel are substantially better off than those with assigned lawyers. As Table H ... illustrates, 37 percent of those without lawyers are found not guilty. Only 17 percent of those represented by assigned counsel are found not guilty. Further, Table I ... compares the relation between not guilty findings and lawyers, court by court. Finally, Table J ... indicates that this result — favoring defendants with no lawyer — remains virtually unchanged regardless of the crime charged.

## TABLE G
Comparison of Sentences for Defendants With Assigned Lawyer
and Defendants With No Lawyer
(Percentages of those found guilty and pleading guilty)

| Attorney | Jail Sentence | Suspended Sentence | Probation | Filed | Fine only or Restitution |
|---|---|---|---|---|---|
| No Attorney | 12 | 38 | 13 | 11 | 26 |
| Assigned Attorney | 35 | 41 | 6 | 8 | 10 |

## TABLE H
Comparison of Adjudication for Defendants With
Assigned Lawyer and Defendants With No Lawyer
(Percentages of defendants pleading not guilty)

| Attorney | Found Guilty | Found not Guilty | Probable* Cause | No Probable Cause | Other** |
|---|---|---|---|---|---|
| Assigned Attorney | 65 | 17 | 11 | 5 | 2 |
| No Attorney | 48 | 37 | 8 | 3 | 4 |

* Includes high felony plus decline of jurisdiction for crimes within district court's jurisdiction.
** Includes continued without a finding and unknown.

Later we shall discuss other forms of plea bargaining in the district courts. The failure to develop and impose proper indigency standards is reflected in the persistence of a bargaining process designed to encourage defendants to waive their right to counsel.

The absence of a uniform and reliable procedure for determining indigency takes a severe toll on defendants in the district courts. Between one-half to two-thirds of these defendants are semi-skilled or unskilled workers. At least 40 percent are unemployed at the time of arrest. The median income of these defendants is between $50 and $75 per week. Many are married and have children. See Table K. ... Despite this stark poverty, most district courts make no inquiry into the defendant's financial status,

## TABLE I
Comparison of Not Guilty Findings — Court by Court —
Assigned Lawyer vs. No Lawyer
(Percent of defendants pleading not guilty
who are found not guilty)

|  | Assigned Attorney | No Attorney |
|---|---|---|
| All Courts | 17 | 37 |
| Urban | | |
| Court 1 | 9 | 14 |
| Court 2 | 35 | 32 |
| Court 3 | 26 | 61 |
| Suburban | | |
| Court 4 | 18 | 74 |
| Court 5 | 0 | 50 |
| Court 6 | 18 | 20 |

## TABLE J
Comparison of Not Guilty Findings* in Major Offense Categories
No Attorney vs. Assigned Attorney
(Percent found not guilty of defendants pleading not guilty)

| Danger to Person | Assault | Robbery** | Theft and Property | Narcotics | Public Regulation | Non-Support |
|---|---|---|---|---|---|---|
| Defendants with no attorney | | | | | | |
| 7 | 63 | 0 | 35 | 19 | 47 | 32 |
| Defendants with Assigned Attorney | | | | | | |
| 9 | 29 | 10 | 16 | 18 | 26 | 16 |

* Includes only cases where full trial was held — excludes probable cause hearings.
** Small sample — most cases involved probable cause hearings.

employment, number of dependents, or related information which, easily obtained, gives a generally accurate picture of the defendant's ability to afford counsel.

Should the defendant choose to proceed immediately to trial without a lawyer, he must sign a waiver of counsel form, required by the Supreme Judicial Court. The form states simply that the defendant has been informed of his right to counsel but nevertheless chooses to proceed alone. The district court judge must sign a parallel form indicating that he has informed the defendant of his right to counsel.

Our study indicates that, in fact, only 21 percent of those defendants who plead not guilty proceed without counsel. Of those with counsel approximately 6 out of 10 have private counsel.

Once the district court judge does find a defendant eligible for assigned counsel, he appoints (a) a member of the Massachusetts Defenders Committee, (b) a member of a private group offering free legal service, or (c) a lawyer willing to serve without a fee.[86] As mentioned earlier, the bar associations and other institutions representative of the legal profession have shown little concern with representation of indigent defendants in the district courts.

In most cases, the public defender assigned a defendant does not actually confer with his client until after arraignment is completed. The court thus hears the plea and sets bail before the defendant is able to avail himself of his lawyers' advice. Also, the lawyer is unable to argue for low bail or present facts that would dictate release on personal recognizance.

Our statistics make clear the results of delayed consultation. Eighteen percent of all defendants with private lawyers — i.e. a lawyer available to argue on bail — are committed for failure to raise bail. For defendants with no one to argue bail, the commitment rate is 38 percent. If the defendant is unable to raise bail, he will be committed until trial or until his lawyer petitions the Superior Court under the Bail Reform Act for a reduction in bail. . . .

### Trial in the District Court

Trials do not consume as much of the district court's time as (a) the high rate of not guilty pleas and (b) the length of time assumed necessary for a trial together might indicate.

(a) Not every defendant who pleads not guilty has a full trial. Ten percent of defendants pleading not guilty have been charged with high felonies and appear in district court only for a probable cause hearing. In addition, the court declines jurisdiction of 3 percent of all defendants pleading not guilty.

86. On April 10, 1969, the Supreme Judicial Court amended Rule 3:10. . . . The effect of this amendment was to require the appointment of MDC attorneys except in special circumstances. However, the Dorchester District Court and the BMC continue to assign and compensate private attorneys out of court funds.

## TABLE K
Profile of Defendants Family Status, Occupation, Income
(Figures are percentages of all defendants charged
for whom personal background information was available)

|  | All courts | Urban courts | Suburban courts |
|---|---|---|---|
| *Family status* |  |  |  |
| Unmarried* | 58 | 58 | 59 |
| Married | 42 | 42 | 41 |
| No children | 60 | 59 | 62 |
| One or more children | 40 | 41 | 38 |
| *Income* |  |  |  |
| Unemployed | 41 | 53 | 30 |
| $1-75/wk. | 14 | 11 | 16 |
| $76-$100/wk. | 23 | 21 | 25 |
| Over $100/wk. | 22 | 15 | 29 |
| *Occupation* |  |  |  |
| Prof., Sales, Clerical, Craftsman | 17 | 17 | 16 |
| Unskilled, Semi-skilled | 66 | 66 | 66 |
| Student | 8 | 8 | 8 |
| In Service | 2 | 2 | 1 |
| None | 7 | 6 | 8 |

\* Includes single, divorced, separated, widowed.

(b) The total court time spent in the average full trial in the district court is small, markedly less than criminal trials in the Superior Court. The district courts we studied sit for an average of four hours each day, excluding recesses and luncheon breaks. During this period the courts conduct (1) arraignments, (2) probable cause hearings, (3) acceptance of guilty pleas in drunkenness cases, (4) traffic offenses (in those courts with no separate traffic session), and trials on "real" crime.

The courts processing the highest number of trials were Courts 1 (BMC), 2 (Dorchester), and 3 (Roxbury). The fewest trials each day occur in Courts 5 (Malden) and 6 (Waltham). It is also in these two suburban courts that greatest care is taken in holding trials. Judges in these two courts, despite their lighter caseload, sit as many hours as judges in the three urban courts.

Many factors influence the speed with which trials are held and disposed. There is no need for empanelling jurors. And the judge need not interrupt trials to inform the jury about rules of procedure or inform them of the applicable substantive law.

Few motions are made by defense counsel in district court trials, further shortening the time for trial. Defense counsel in the urban courts do not take pains to develop questions of law that might take up much of the court's time. They recognize that the judge may become irritated by this departure from custom.

The few motions presented are usually motions to suppress illegally obtained evidence and motions to dismiss to charge. In the 2,000 cases we studied in detail, however, only ten motions were noted on the record. Five of ten motions were successful.

Quite apart from the dim view some judges take of motions, the process itself discourages their use regardless of how great the justification. First, if a lawyer fails to file motions in the lower court trial, he may nonetheless bring these motions in the new trial in the Superior Court. Conversely, when a motion is brought and improperly denied, the Supreme Judicial Court has said that this error is wiped away by a trial de novo in the Superior Court. Also, in the courts with the heaviest caseloads, unless the question of law presents itself with unchallengeable clarity, the judge may view the defendant's case less favorably if time consuming legal arguments are introduced. The defendant consequently has much to lose and very little to gain by injecting motions, however cogent the argument.

During the course of trial, defense counsel sometimes make motions to dismiss informally. One important use of informal motions is to implement a plea bargain. As the court hears evidence, gains a rough familiarity with the case, opportunities to bargain arise. In cases with multiple charges, a guilty plea on one charge may be traded for dismissal of another by oral, in-court motion.

Motions to suppress illegally obtained evidence are made in writing, but briefs are seldom prepared. District court judges frequently reserve decisions on motions to suppress until the entire case has been heard. Then if he thinks the defendant committed the offense charged, influenced in part by the questionably obtained evidence, the judge is in the position to balance the legal merits of the motion against the seriousness of the crime. One judge stated, after taking this approach, and finding the defendant guilty: "the day I throw out a (search) warrant that uncovers 100 decks of heroin is the day they'll throw a net over my head."

The ennui caused by the trial de novo system influences private and assigned lawyers alike. Both are generally reluctant to employ the legal tools developed to protect the defendant in the adversary process — the filing of motions, vigorous cross-examination, arguments in summation after the case has been presented on both sides, and a carefully prepared presentation on the defendant's behalf at sentencing. In one case, we observed defendant's private attorney request a continuance to prepare a brief. The court ordered that the motion be argued orally, denied the motion immediately after oral argument, found the defendant guilty and sentenced him immediately to six months in the house of correction. The defendant's lawyer then claimed a new trial on his client's behalf. Sufficient repetition of this process, which takes no more than ten minutes, impresses even the most aggressive defense counsel with its futility, and the practical advisability of saving his energies for the Superior Court.

Arguments on motions, when they are brought, pit judge and defense counsel as adversaries. The police prosecutor participates only to comment upon the facts in the case. Regardless of how lengthy his experience, he has little more than a capsule knowledge of controlling court decisions. The burden falls upon the judge first to develop the arguments in opposition to the motion, then decide who has made the better argument.

Our daily observations convince us that discouraging careful defense preparation is but one dangerous result of improper judicial practices. All court personnel, defendants, and eventually the community — which because of the nature of the court's jurisdiction means the poor people within that community — come to recognize that the judge's personal power and personal prejudices overshadow established rules of law in the district courts.

The trials themselves are brief. If the judge estimates that a trial will take up some time, he will transfer the case to another session in the courthouse to avoid slowing the process of clearing the docket. If a trial gets underway and becomes unavoidably complicated, the court will continue the case until another day. One judge's impatience with zealous legal defenses was illustrated when he remarked to a defense counsel, "We don't follow those Supreme Court decisions here."

Use of police prosecutors further shortens the time for trial. Unfamiliar with the methods for marshaling his evidence in a logical, persuasive fashion, or for using cross-examination effectively, the police prosecutor presents a perfunctory case, relying on the judge to fill the obvious holes. Since the judge is expected to understand implicitly the complexities of the government's case, the police prosecutor virtually never makes a closing argument that a sufficient case has been presented for a guilty finding.

Finally, defense counsel who are interested only in getting to the Superior Court use the district court proceedings exclusively for discovery. They do not object to evidence presented, hoping to learn about all the evidence the government possesses. In such cases, the defendant will not testify and, at the close of trial, will merely note his "appeal" to the Superior Court.

*Adjudication*

When the trial is over, and the prosecutor and defense counsel (or defendant) have finished presenting their sides of the case, the judge almost immediately delivers his decision. He may find the defendant not guilty of the one or more crimes charged against him. Thirty-five percent of the defendants who go to trial are found not guilty of *all* charges. The judge may find the defendant guilty of one or more of the crimes charged. This occurs in 62 percent of the cases that go to trial. See Table W. . . . In a very few cases the judge makes a third kind of disposition, "continued without a finding." Under this arrangement, the court places the defendant on informal probation. If within a time period set by the court the defendant remains out of trouble, the charge itself will be dismissed. If during the period of this extended continuance the defendant is charged and found guilty of another crime, the judge will record a guilty finding in the first case and impose sentence for both crimes. In our study only 0.3 percent of the defendants charged were "continued without a finding." [105] Table W . . . compares adjudication, court by court.

The formal requirement for a guilty finding is proof beyond a reasonable doubt. In trials before a judge in the district court, there are strong indications that the government's burden is reduced to showing that the preponderance of the evidence points to the defendant's guilt. The most graphic admission by a district court judge that the burden of proof is reduced came in a closely contested case. The defense presented a number of witnesses to counter the sole prosecution evidence, the testimony of the arresting officer. The judge resolved the case by declaring: "Well, I don't

---

105. But given the one year lapse between the time the cases were in court and our data collection, some cases that were first continued may have finally appeared in the record as not guilty findings.

## TABLE W
### Adjudications in District Court
(Percentages are of all defendants
pleading not guilty and tried in district court)

| Court | Found Guilty | Found Not Guilty | Continued Without finding | Unknown |
|---|---|---|---|---|
| All courts | 62 | 35 | 0.3 | 2.7 |
| Urban | | | | |
| 1 | 75 | 23 | 0 | 2 |
| 2 | 48 | 40 | 2 | 10 |
| 3 | 50 | 45 | 1 | 4 |
| Suburban | | | | |
| 4 | 47 | 51 | 0 | 2 |
| 5 | 53 | 44 | 0 | 3 |
| 6 | 50 | 50 | 0 | 0 |

know who to believe. Just to be safe I'll find you guilty." The defendant, given a suspended sentence and a short period of probation, did not assert his right to a new trial.

Boston courts are by no means unique in reducing the burden for proof of guilty. Other studies have made clear that when cases are presented in an erratic, perfunctory manner, when few rules are imposed to guide development of the case, and more is implied than proven, rigid application of the burden of proof required by law would bring few convictions. The judge thus feels he must judge what is "really" the case rather than what formal rules of court would require him to decide.

Perhaps the primary evidence that district courts require less than proof beyond a reasonable doubt is the greater inherent credibility given the testimony of police officers. This claim is made most often and most predictably, by defendants and their lawyers. But probation officers have also suggested that certain judges favor police testimony.

Moreover, we have observed trials where the testimony of the police officer alone convicted the defendant. In one case the defendant was charged with assault and battery on a police officer. The defendant claimed that the police had beaten him while arresting him on a domestic relations complaint. The defendant's arm had been broken and his wife testified that the police had beaten him. The court responded by saying:

I don't believe a word she said. Here is a domestic argument that she brought the police into and now she wants to implicate them. I have seen this policeman before me for a number of years and have no doubt as to his integrity. Guilty.

This illustration suggests an attitude we observed in the three urban courts studied. Guilt was not determined by a process where the defendants were protected and presumed to be innocent, but rather by a process which, if it determined the defendant to be guilty, overlooked violations of guaranteed rights and rules of evidence. At the heart of this attitude, as defense lawyers, police, and judges themselves admit, is the belief that a defendant can always protect himself with a new trial at the Superior Court level. The district court need not run the risk of exonerating a defendant who may have committed a crime. The new trial removes responsibility from the judge. And the consequence is a practical softening of the presumption of innocence and the burden of proof.

One cannot be certain that a true system of judicial review would remedy these shortcomings in the district court. Determining the standard of proof applied by the judge is difficult for any reviewing court. However, true judicial review would at least establish that the standards of proof applied would be scrutinized. At least in the clearest of cases this scrutiny would result in a reversal of the conviction. This would serve as a signal to the lower courts that the application of proper standards of proof will be required.

### Sentencing

The judge, in sentencing, may impose a jail sentence or fine the defendant, and in some cases he may do both. Further, he may impose a sentence but suspend its execution, choosing to place the defendant on probation. Under this alternative, the judge may execute the sentence at a later date if he finds that the defendant has violated his conditions of probation. This later process is called revocation of probation. Although the defendant has the right to seek trial de novo from a sentence when it is originally imposed after trial, he has no right to trial de novo if and when it is executed at a later date.

The judge may decide to impose no sentence at all but nonetheless place the defendant on probation for whatever time he considers appropriate. Should the defendant subsequently violate this "straight probation" — the phrase used to distinguish probation without sentence from probation coupled with a suspended sentence — the judge may call the defendant into court and reconsider the sentence. This procedure has reportedly never been used. In fact, no defense attorney or court official interviewed were certain what would happen to a defendant placed on straight probation who later violated his probation.

Judges, with the consent of the defendant, sometimes place a case "on file," after finding the defendant guilty. No formal sentence is imposed. Nor is the defendant subjected to probation, with formal conditions dictated by statute. The judge by filing a case puts the defendant on notice that the case may be called forward at any future time for sentencing. And the possibility of a later sentence acts as a continuing incentive to avoid further involvement with the criminal court. If a jail sentence is later imposed, the defendant may at that point assert his right to a new trial.

The suspended sentence is the sentence most often imposed. As Table X . . . indicates, its frequency varies from court to court. When one adds together suspended sentence, straight probation and defendants whose cases are placed on file — i.e., sentences where the judge stops short of imprisonment — the total percentage amounts to 54 percent of those found guilty. By comparison, 23 percent are sent to jail. And the remaining 23 percent receive a fine as their only punishment.

## TABLE X
### Sentencing in the District Court
(Percent of defendants found guilty or
pleading guilty)

| Court | Jail Sentence | Suspended Sentence | Straight Probation | Filed | Fine only* |
|-------|-----------|-----------|-----------|-------|-----------|
| All courts | 23 | 35 | 8 | 11 | 23 |
| Urban | | | | | |
| 1 | 28 | 34 | 5 | 12 | 21 |
| 2 | 8 | 51 | 5 | 6 | 30 |
| 3 | 21 | 32 | 21 | 11 | 15 |
| Suburban | | | | | |
| 4 | 26.5 | 26.5 | 6 | 3 | 38 |
| 5 | 14 | 46 | 0 | 7 | 33 |
| 6 | 15 | 19 | 15 | 23 | 27 |

* Includes restitution.

PART IV DECIDING ON TRIAL DE NOVO

*Influence of the Sentence on Trial de Novo*

The sentence is related closely to the defendant's decision on trial de novo. Certainly the relative leniency or severity of the sentence will have some influence on the defendant's determination whether or not to pursue a new trial. Judge and defendant may, by tacit understanding or by straightforward discussion, strike a bargain in open court. The defendant is looking for the lightest sentence practically possible. The judge looks for the defendant to accept his lot in district court, sacrificing his right to a new trial.

The defendant's sentence and his decision to seek trial de novo are related in another way. First, it is true that every defendant convicted in the district court after pleading not guilty or admitting to a finding may have a new trial in Superior Court. But judges have over the years come to accept the notion that there can be no *"appeal"* — i.e., no trial de novo — *from a suspended sentence.* Thus, even when the judge has no blatant discouragement of trial de novo in mind, he feels obligated, once the defendant chooses trial de novo, to "execute" a sentence he has just suspended.

This rule has a marked effect in discouraging trial de novo, often without the specific intent of the judge. We have observed defendants in some cases change their minds and decide against "appeal," once the judge shifts from sentence suspended to sentence imposed. Characteristically, this practice is related to the defendant as follows: "The court sentences you to six months in the House of Correction. The sentence is suspended. If you appeal, the sentence will be imposed." Another version is: "The court sentences you to six months in the House of Correction. You have the right to appeal. Not appealing, the sentence will be suspended."

District court judges have arrived at the notion that they must impose a jail sentence to qualify a case for trial de novo through a questionable reading of several appellate court cases.[110] The judges

110. None of these cases has treated these questions squarely, because the trial de novo system prevents a direct presentation of the issues. Once the defendant has accepted the jail sentence in order to get to Superior Court, the issue is perforce wiped away by the substitution of the second trial for all phases of the first. There is thus no opportunity to challenge the injustice to other defendants who may have been dissuaded from seeking trial de novo by the specter of a jail sentence — since a suspended sentence is assured. Thus, imposing a jail sentence has the practical effect of discouraging new trials.

believe these cases to hold that there must be a final judgment in the district court before the defendant can exercise his right to "appeal." They believe further that only an imposed jail sentence or a fine can satisfy the requirement of a final judgment. The cases cited suggest that suspended sentences have the effect of holding a case open, i.e., the word "suspended" is defined literally.

In court trials the need for final judgment before "appeal" is a well-established principle. It assures that all issues will be raised once and only once in appellate court. We believe, however, that suspended sentences have all the relevant features of final judgment as do imposed jail sentences. If the suspended sentence is executed at a later date, the judge may only impose the original term. No re-examination of the length of the original sentence is permitted.

Some make the argument that, because at a subsequent time, the court may be asked to consider whether probation has been violated and whether the suspended sentence should then be executed, the consequence is to keep the case open, preventing "appeal." However, this possible later consideration has no relationship whatsoever to the original charge and the trial that determined guilt. The sole question at this later probation revocation hearing will be whether the conditions of probation have in fact been violated by some activity or conduct occurring *after* the probation period has begun. The proceedings in the district court that determined guilt are in no way affected.

Significantly, suspended sentences are considered final for certain other purposes under Massachusetts law. For example, a finding of guilt in the district court coupled with a suspended sentence is sufficient "final judgment" for use in impeaching the credibility of that convicted individual should he testify in a later court action.

## Influence of Final Judgment Rules on Right to Jury Trial

When conditions such as final judgment are attached to trial de novo, they may help choke off defendant's free exercise of his right to jury trial. Finality may be desirable and necessary for traditional judicial review. However, the exclusive rationale of trial de novo — the "preservation" of jury trial — demands separate consideration.

Quite simply, if the defendant's free exercise of trial by jury is of paramount importance, it makes little sense to hinge jury trial upon the type of sentence handed down. Recent cases suggest that *any* precondition to the exercise of one's right to jury trial — per-

haps even the trial de novo process itself — may be improper and
unconstitutional. Elaborating on an earlier decision in Duncan v.
Louisiana,* the Supreme Court held in Baldwin v. New York†
that the Constitution requires that the defendant be afforded a
jury trial whenever he faces imprisonment of six months or more.
Since the Baldwin v. New York opinion sought to define the point
at which the right to a jury trial accrued, it naturally focused on
the practice in the various jurisdictions. Thus Duncan v. Louisiana
continues to express the Court's views on the extent of the Sixth
Amendment's protection.

The Supreme Court in Duncan relied heavily upon an older
federal case Callan v. Wilson.‡ Callan, in a section not cited in
Duncan, rejected expressly the process of trial de novo, as it currently exists in the Massachusetts courts, as an interference with
the right to jury trial in *federal* courts. The Supreme Court has
not yet chosen to apply this same evaluation of trial do novo to
state court proceedings. Importantly, Duncan indicates that the
Supreme Court will step in if they see a state *denying* trials by jury.
Were they to take the next step and reject *interferences* with jury
trial, relying upon the same case Callan v. Wilson, trial de novo in
state courts would be held unconstitutional.

Given the shaky status of the trial de novo system itself, a rule
such as "final judgment" that limits jury trial even further, whether
born of judicial custom or state law, should be examined with the
gravest suspicion. Nothing other than vague and inapplicable notions of finality have been offered in support. The limitation
should be eliminated.

### How the District Court Actively Discourages Trial de Novo

The harm caused by discouraging trial de novo transcends the
right to jury trial. Only trial de novo effectively frees a defendant
from whatever errors may have occurred in his first trial. And as
long as there exists no judicial review in the district courts, free
exercise of trial de novo must be aggressively encouraged. Otherwise, not only do errors persist, but the system closes off the only
recourse available to escape those errors.

Unfortunately, the district courts pay little heed to maintaining
free access to trial de novo. Through the years, certain courts and

---

* 391 U.S. 145 (1968).
† 399 U.S. 66 (1970).
‡ 127 U.S., 540, 549 (1888).

judges have developed pernicious practices specifically designed to discourage defendants from asserting their right to a new trial. The two practices regularly employed are:

(1) Offering probation or a suspended sentence if the defendant foregoes his new trial. Here the judge makes an express bargain with the defendant.

(2) Setting a new bail requirement, often at a higher amount than was originally set at arraignment, forcing the defendant to pay a new premium to remain out of jail pending his new trial in Superior Court.

These two limitations, in series, impress upon the defendant that loss of immediate freedom may be the price he pays for persisting in his defense. If the judge imposes a jail sentence and if the bail is too high, the defendant goes immediately to jail.

(1) *Using the Sentence to Discourage Trial de Novo.* Our observations of the district courts made clear that some judges consistently use the sentencing power to discourage requests for trial de novo. The judge here goes far beyond the "final judgment" rationale. We have observed judges lengthen the jail term as a penalty for asserting a new trial. For example, one judge imposes sentence as follows:

J: "You (defense attorney) ask him (defendant) if he wants to pay the money back. If not I'll sentence him to six months on the Island (Deer Island).* If he wants to appeal, I'll make it a year."

(2) *Using Bail to Discourage Trial de Novo.* The district court judge must reconsider the conditions of bail once a defendant decides upon trial de novo. In approximately one-half of the new trial cases, the district court judge decides to increase the amount of bail beyond that set at the time of arraignment. See Table Y. . . . Moreover, even if the bail is set at the same or lower amount than at arraignment, the district court routinely requires that the defendant pay a new premium to the bail bondsman. The urban courts increase bail substantially more often than do the suburban courts. For example, in Court 2 (Dorchester) bail is increased in 71 percent of the new trial requests.

At this stage the district court continues to have jurisdiction over the case. Consequently, the provisions of the Bail Reform Act — requiring a presumption in favor of personal recognizance

---

* Deer Island is the location of the Suffolk County House of Correction.

— still apply. But after conviction in the district court, personal recognizance is a rarity. This process illustrates the irony of requiring the judge to presume a defendant innocent, for bail-setting purposes, a moment after he has heard evidence and found the defendant guilty. As one judge stated in open court, while imposing a higher bail:

"Before this trial he was presumed innocent. Now he is guilty."

In one case we observed, a defendant, charged with larceny, appeared in court under personal recognizance. He was found guilty and noted his intent to have a new trial. The court thereupon reset bail at $300. Defendant changed his mind and accepted his sentence.

In another court, a woman appeared on her own recognizance charged with prostitution. Found guilty, she withdrew her request for trial de novo after the court set new bail at $500.

Resetting bail for trial de novo not only deters defendants from asserting a new trial but also works considerable hardship upon defendants who have the will to proceed. In our study 37 percent of the defendants who sought trial de novo were committed for failure to make bail. What is more disturbing is that our statistics

TABLE Y
District Court Bail Practice for Defendants
Requesting Trial De Novo
(Percent of defendants requesting trial de novo)

| Court | Bail Decreased | Bail Same | Bail Increased | Committed Pending Trial de novo |
|---|---|---|---|---|
| All courts | 23 | 24 | 50 | 37 |
| Urban | | | | |
| 1 | 21 | 17 | 62 | 50 |
| 2 | 14 | 14 | 71 | 71 |
| 3 | 35 | 39 | 22 | 39 |
| Suburban | | | | |
| 4 | 33 | 19 | 43 | 10 |
| 5 | 13 | 50 | 25 | 25 |
| 6 | 0 | 20 | 80 | 10 |

indicate that increases in bail for trial de novo are preserved for those defendants who have the least ability to pay. For professional or skilled workers, bail is more frequently set at the original or lower amount at this stage than for semi- or unskilled workers. Higher bail is most often preserved for those most vulnerable to economic pressure.

Finally, a disparity exists between the pre–trial-de-novo commitment rate of black and white defendants. Fifty-two percent of all black defendants seeking a new trial are committed for failure to make bail. The figure for whites is 29 percent.

Our statistics for trial de novo indicate only how many defendants *did not* change their minds. Unfortunately, we cannot determine how many might have gone ahead had there been no new bail, no higher bail, no threat to impose a harsher sentence.

## SUMMARY

A combination of influences and circumstances discourages routine assertion of trials de novo by defendants. Only the defendants who have actively contested the charges against them even get to the point of considering trial de novo. As is true throughout, most defendants at this stage are poor.[121] The trial de novo will require more lawyers' fees of the defendant who has retained a private lawyer. In most cases, the offer of a suspended sentence beckons the defendant to let the new trial pass, especially when he is told by the judge that his appeal will "force" the execution of the jail sentence he might escape by foregoing his trial de novo. Finally, if the defendant does seek trial de novo, a new bail premium will be set, often at a higher amount. If the defendant is poor, if he is unable to raise the money for bail, he will be sent to jail. It matters little to him that the sentence levied by the district court is now vacated because of the new trial. What is important to him is the knowledge that if he persists, he will be taken to jail to await his new trial. For many, this can be a period of weeks, often months. Had he not been so aggressive, had he accepted his suspended sentence, he would now be free. And this simple choice between immediate freedom and immediate incarceration forms at least part of the weighing process that besets a defendant at the time of his decision on trial de novo. . . .

121. See Table 1 [omitted] which shows that 55% of all defendants earn less than $75 per week. [See also Table K, *supra* — Ed.]

# The Municipal Court Misdemeanor Arraignment Procedure of Hamilton County, Ohio: An Empirical Study*

## Cincinnati Law Review

### I. INTRODUCTION

The arraignment procedure for the Hamilton County Municipal Court prior to January 2, 1970 was as follows:

Cases shall be tried in their order, at the convenience of the Court, preference however being given to cases under the following circumstances and in this order:

FIRST: Cases wherein demands for trial by jury are filed.

SECOND: Cases wherein applications for continuances shall be made.

THIRD: Cases wherein counsel or witnesses must be present at other court rooms.

FOURTH: Cases wherein officers on night duty are summoned as witnesses.[1]

In practical effect, this rule meant that an accused person would be arraigned the morning following his arrest. At his arraignment, the complainant or the arresting officer and other witnesses were present, and unless the defendant requested a continuance, his case would be heard immediately, regardless of whether he entered a plea of guilty, not guilty or no contest.

Pursuant to a resolution adopted by the judges of the Hamilton

* From: 42 U. Cinc. L. Rev. 206-240 (1973). Reprinted by permission of the editors of the Cincinnati Law Review.

1. Rules of Practice, Hamilton County Municipal Court (1952) at 8.

The Hamilton County Municipal Court, Criminal Division, is a court of limited jurisdiction. The court has jurisdiction to take dispositive action in misdemeanor cases and can hold preliminary hearings in felony cases to determine whether or not there was probable cause to arrest the accused. The court also has jurisdiction to hear probation violation cases if the probation violator was originally paroled by a judge of the Municipal Court.

County Municipal Court in joint session, this rule was abolished, effective on January 2, 1970. The new procedure alters the old method by providing for an immediate disposition of an accused's case only when the defendant enters a plea of guilty or no contest. The following excerpt from the instructions that are read by the judge when each session of court convenes outlines the current procedure:

> ... If you enter a plea of "guilty" or "no contest" the prosecutor will read a statement of facts involved in your case, and it will be disposed of immediately.

> If you enter a plea of "not guilty," your case will be set at a later date for trial.

> Some of you have already had your cases continued one or more times. You should be ready to enter a plea now.

> For those of you who have already entered a plea of "not guilty," the trial of your case will take place today.

Under the new arraignment system, if the defendant enters a plea of not guilty the witnesses need not appear until the date that has been set for trial. Theoretically the trial will then be held on that date and the witness will have to appear only one time. If the defendant enters a plea of guilty or no contest the witnesses need not appear at all; the affidavit is read and the defendant is sentenced.

There were two reasons for this change. The first was that under the old arraignment system witnesses were greatly inconvenienced by the requirement that they be in court each time the defendant appeared. Their first appearance would be wasted if the defendant requested and received a continuance. Second, the old system resulted in large, wasted payroll expenditures for police officers' courtroom time. Defendants were frequently granted continuances after the police officers had spent much time in the courtroom waiting to testify.

Another problem with the arraignment system, sought to be corrected by the Hamilton County Municipal Court judges, was lack of courtroom space. The courtroom in City Hall was grossly inadequate in size and seating facilities because, in addition to daily arraignments, all trials were held there except those in which a jury demand had been filed. Thus, over 300 people were present at each session of criminal court. To correct this situation and thereby create an atmosphere more conducive to judicial reflection, two additional courtrooms were provided in the Hamilton County Courthouse solely for the purpose of hearing cases in which defendants had entered a plea of not guilty. These cases were broken down into two groups: (1) those that could be disposed of in a relatively short time; and (2) those, which, due to factors such as the number of witnesses to be called, were expected to take a longer time. It was thought by the judges that if these more complex cases were segregated from those which were more routine, the less frenzied atmosphere would be more conducive to judicial reflection; in short, that "justice" would be improved. . . .

This project was designed to study the comparative merits of the two arraignment procedures. Specifically, its purpose was to ascertain whether the new arraignment procedure is achieving the goals outlined above, and whether the new system has induced misdemeanants to enter a plea of guilty or no contest, by requiring a second appearance if they do not. . . .

### III. THE ATTORNEYS

Twenty-two lawyers, whose clients comprise substantially all of the defendants in the Municipal Court who are represented by private attorneys, were interviewed. All 22 appear in the Criminal Court at least once a week, and all but one have practiced law in Hamilton County under both the former and the present arraignment procedures.

### A. Advantages and Disadvantages of the Old System

In comparing the major advantages and disadvantages of the two systems, five attorneys stated that the old procedure was ideal for the defendant who wanted an immediate trial because he was spared the inconvenience of having to return for trial at a later date. They also stated that the old procedure was ideal for the individual who could not make bond because he would not have to await trial in jail for more than the 24 hour maximum period between the time of his arrest and his first appearance before the magistrate.

However the disadvantages of the old system were manifest to most of the lawyers interviewed. They agreed that the former requirement of an immediate trial, regardless of the plea, created substantial risks for the defendant. If he entered his plea on the morning after his arrest, he gambled that his attorney, assuming he was able to retain one, had not had time to become fully apprised of the facts of the case. Far worse, according to the lawyers, were the difficulties encountered by the defendant who entered his plea without having first discussed his case with an attorney. If a defendant entered his plea oblivious to the fact that the affidavit was defective, the judge would not permit an attorney subsequently retained to file a motion to challenge it. Consequently, the accused would be required to proceed to trial on a charge which should have been dismissed. The defendant without counsel who entered a plea of not guilty to a crime in which physical force was an element was often compelled to argue his case in the presence of a prosecuting witness or victim whose openly-displayed emotions (and wounds) had not been soothed in the short interval between arrest and trial. In the same case, a defendant represented by an attorney would have requested a continuance. Furthermore, defendants who argued their own cases felt pressured to clear the docket because the judges became impatient with them in the presence of great crowds of persons whose cases were yet to be heard.

Another problem with the old system, candidly expressed by one attorney, was the facility with which the client could be denied an attorney's full services. Since the defendant's trial could be held the morning after his arrest, his attorney could be tempted to proceed with the trial with very little preparation, and collect his fee quickly, using the established court procedure as a justification.

## B. Advantages and Disadvantages of the New System

The attorneys almost unanimously (18 of 22) agreed that the new procedure has advantageously eliminated many of the time-consuming and unnecessary court appearances that were formerly required of police officers and witnesses. A second frequently mentioned advantage afforded by the new arraignment procedure is, in the phrase of four attorneys, that "better justice is accomplished," since the additional courtrooms theoretically allow the judges more time to spend on each case, in less hectic surroundings, more conducive to careful cogitation.

A benefit to defendants, noted by several attorneys, is that defendants now enjoy in a limited way the opportunity to choose which judge will hear their cases. The procedure works as follows. A defendant is charged with possession of marijuana and is scheduled to be arraigned before Judge A the following morning. Prior to arraignment, the defendant's attorney examines the Municipal Courtroom assignment card. The card, which is published annually and is ubiquitously displayed in elevators, hallways and courtrooms

in both the Alms & Doepke Building and the Main Courthouse,
lists the individual Municipal Court judges and the courtrooms in
which they will sit for each of the next twelve months. The defendant's attorney determines from the assignment card that Judge
B will be sitting in the courtroom to which Judge A will probably
send the defendant for trial. (Most cases reassigned from Criminal
Court are transferred to room E for trial.) Knowing that Judge B
has a reputation for being particularly harsh on drug offenders,
the attorney will request a jury trial in a different courtroom in
which Judge C, who is reputedly lenient in drug cases, is sitting.
Prior to the trial, the defendant's attorney will waive the jury demand. The defendant is then tried without a jury before Judge C.
Although only five of the attorneys interviewed conceded that they
engaged in such practices, all admitted that they knew attorneys in
Municipal Court who did.[9]

There were two other advantages to the new system in the attorneys' eyes. Several welcomed the new system because it enabled
them to collect a bigger fee per case, since a not guilty plea now
requires at least two paid court appearances — arraignment and trial
— rather than the single appearance which could have disposed of
the case under the old system. Secondly, as noted by two attorneys,
Municipal Court judges now have more free time.[10]

Most of the attorneys cited a wide-ranging number of new problems created by the new system. Some attorneys complained that
the prosecutors were able to judge-shop. Others claimed that there
were too many dismissals for want of prosecution, attributing the
dismissals to what they considered to be a ramshackle method of
notifying prosecuting witnesses and police officers of their court
appearances. One attorney blamed the increase in the total number
of arrests for the problems that still remained after the institution
of the new procedure. Another criticized the supposed advantages

9. One attorney was interviewed immediately after an unsuccessful attempt
to maneuver his client before a judge whom the attorney considered to be
sympathetic to the defendant. Prior to the trial, the attorney had succeeded
in continuing his case four times for reasons which he characterized as "pre-
texts," including the jury demand waiver method. He finally received the desired judge, but discovered on the trial date that the judge was ill and had
been replaced by the one judge the attorney had tried so hard to avoid. Crest-
fallen because his client had received an unusually harsh fine and jail sentence, the attorney remarked that the practice of judge-shopping "probably
should not be allowed, but as long as it is available, an attorney owes it to his
client to make use of it."

10. While it is true that most of the court sessions are adjourned by noon
each day, all judges denied that they sometimes "take the afternoon off."

of preparation time for attorneys and stated that the prosecutor's office was correspondingly disadvantaged by an increased preparation burden.

The bulk of the comments from the attorneys interviewed, however, was directed toward the various ways in which the new arraignment procedure adversely affected defendants. Five of the attorneys declared that the procedure was "dreadful" for the defendant who could not afford bail money and who was not released on his own recognizance (O.R.). One attorney emphasized that the skeletal staff maintained for purposes of determining which defendants were eligible to be released O.R. was so overworked with felony cases alone that it rarely had time to consider misdemeanants. And even when the staff members were able to interview a defendant charged with a misdemeanor, he would automatically be disqualified if he had a record of prior conviction, or, one attorney believed, he belonged to a militant minority group.

In addition, the attorneys felt that the arraignment system had induced many defendants who did not want to return for trial at a later date or be incarcerated during the period between arraignment and trial to plead no contest or guilty.

Finally, two attorneys observed that the fact that the prosecuting witnesses are not present when the defendant pleads guilty or no contest disadvantages both the judge and the defendant, since the judge is denied the opportunity to observe the demeanor of the prosecuting witness for purposes of determining their credibility, and the defendant is sentenced on the basis of an unsworn, hearsay statement written by a person who is not in court. . . .

The attorneys' list of reasons that continuances were requested was the most instructive. A very frequent reason for the request was the failure of the client to pay the attorney. The euphemism employed to convey this fact to the judge was "continuance requested for reason number one, your honor." Its use appears to have diminished; many attorneys reported that judges no longer consider it to be a good enough reason to delay criminal proceedings. However, the current arraignment system allows for a technique which accomplishes the same purpose. The attorney who has not received his fee now instructs his client to request a continuance and to explain that the attorney is "unavoidably detained" in another courtroom.

As discussed above, the continuance device is commonly used by defense attorneys who desire that their cases be heard by a particular judge. In addition, the continuance may be used in cases involving physical contact between the defendant and the prosecuting witness to gain time to "cool off" the prosecuting witness before testifying. Such continuances are commonly asked and are notably effective in "family squabble" cases, where the charge is often dismissed for want of prosecution after one or more continuances. But several attorneys complained that continuances are becoming increasingly difficult to obtain and that they are more readily granted to the state than to the defense attorney. . . .

## IV. THE PROSECUTOR'S STAFF

### A. *The Assistant Prosecutors*

Two Hamilton County Municipal Court assistant prosecutors were interviewed during this study. They were asked the same questions as the defense attorneys and, like the attorneys, both assistant prosecutors noted that the former procedure allowed the defendants to be tried on the morning after their arrests, regardless of their pleas. Unlike some of the attorneys, however, the assistant prosecutors emphasized that this procedure was harmful to defendants, explaining that some attorneys would plead their clients guilty so that their time would not be consumed by the long wait before the case was called. And both assistant prosecutors agreed that witnesses and police officers are spared many of the frustrations of the past that arose from repeated, unnecessary appearances. Although they maintained that the arraignment procedure "makes things work more smoothly," they noted that there has been a "tremendous increase in the length of the docket in the last few years, so the system itself is becoming increasingly burdened." Problems intrinsic to the system were also cited by the assistant prosecutors. For example, where a plea of guilty or no contest is entered, municipal court judges no longer possess the thorough knowledge of a case that was formerly possible. The present procedure is simply to read a statement of facts prepared at an earlier time by an arresting officer or complainant whose presence at the arraignment is no longer required. The assistant prosecutors also concurred in the view of the attorneys that no contest pleas have increased considerably, estimating an increase of as much as 50%. In the assistant prosecutors' opinion, this increase is dangerous because many defendants do not know what the no contest plea means. . . .

### B. *The Chief Prosecutor*

The Hamilton County Municipal Court Prosecutor, well-informed by virtue of the fact that he formulated the proposal for the new arraignment procedure, stressed that although the arraignment system is quite simple and should theoretically operate without difficulty, many problems have arisen due to a lack of cooperation by the different groups affected by the change. He felt that the lack of an assignment commissioner to schedule and co-ordinate cases, courtrooms, and judges resulted in an inefficient use of facilities, and created a situation in which one court may be in session until 3:00 p.m., while another may be adjourned by 11:00 a.m.

The Prosecutor also complained that the Municipal Court judges frequently alter the court procedure, and fail to consult the prosecutors. And once the procedure is altered, the judges do not apply it consistently. For example, the variations in time are allowed for continuances granted when attorneys have not been paid by their clients (some judges feel a week is sufficient; others will grant a four-week delay), and often the judges refuse to enforce the rule that requires a timely filing of a demand for a jury. In addition the judges retain cases which have the potential for making headlines rather than assigning them to other rooms where they could be handled without clogging the Criminal Court docket. According to the Prosecutor, this practice will continue "as long as judges are elected in popularity contests."

The other difficulties which have blocked the effective functioning of the arraignment procedure, the Prosecutor felt, are caused by a lack of co-ordination between his office and the Police Department, rather than a defect in the new system itself. For example, the reoccurring problem of dismissals for want of prosecution due to the arresting officer's failure to appear at the trial, is due to a breakdown in the police notification system rather than a lackadaisical attitude about court appearances among individual officers. An officer's failure to appear wastes the time of the court and witnesses, and also of the police officers who must then re-arrest the defendant on a new affidavit and await the setting of a new trial date if the defendant again pleads not guilty.

Police frustration with the court's current method of operation was recently brought to light when a check was made to determine whether officers were giving false information about their work shifts in hopes of getting an early call. A Prosecutor's spot check revealed that in a single day no less than 16 officers had lied to get an early call. Even after reprimands were issued, it was the Prosecutor's estimate that approximately four instances of this type occur each day, again, causing needless delay.

Significant as they are, however, the problems discussed by the Prosecutor thus far pale when they are compared with two others.

Section 2935.10 of the Ohio Revised Code allows an attorney to file a motion to dismiss at any time prior to a finding in the case. The Prosecutor was of the opinion that the statute encourages defense attorneys to file as many motions to dismiss as they possibly can in order to delay the progress of a case, hoping thereby that the witnesses for the prosecution will find the delays frustrating and unproductive, will lose interest, and will simply go home.

The biggest single problem viewed by the Prosecutor is the issuance of affidavits by the clerks in situations when "there is absolutely no basis for the charge." Hamilton County allows its clerks to issue misdemeanor affidavits with virtually no control on their discretion to dispense them. The Prosecutor has found that the clerks, who are not highly educated and receive little or no training for their jobs, will issue affidavits for arrest on the strength of an unchallenged statement offered "by anyone who walks in the door — drunks, illiterates, people who want a shoulder to cry on, etc." This practice produces a wave of dismissals, with a consequent waste of court time.

## V. THE JUDGES

All eight of the judges who were on the bench during the year preceding the change, as well as during the year subsequent thereto, were interviewed for purposes of this study. The major part of these interviews was unstructured.

In a local bar association publication, one of the Municipal Court judges wrote that "the primary purpose of the new procedure is to expedite the orderly disposition of cases and to minimize the inconvenience to witnesses." Five of the eight judges, in personal interviews, agreed that this purpose was being accomplished. Although the inconvenience formerly caused to witnesses was declared to be the primary motivating factor for the change, four of the judges also indicated that the true beneficiary has been the defendant because fewer police officers appear in court each day. There is no longer the bank of officers flanking the bench, the familiar "police chorus" which one judge accused of exerting a "chilling effect" on defendants who were not accustomed to such an array. . . .

In addition, three judges recognized that under the former procedure a defendant would often proceed with his trial on a not guilty plea without adequate preparation. This pitfall was sought to be avoided by the mandatory delay requirement of the present procedure when a not guilty plea is entered. The better preparation made possible thereby allows more "real justice" to be dispensed. Although delays in going to trial under the old system were anything but unknown, the defendant under the new arraignment procedure is tried sooner than he would have been formerly — attributable to a general insistence by judges that the defendant go to trial on a set date and an awareness by attorneys that additional continuances will be parsimoniously awarded. . . .

Most of the judges agreed that the defendant benefits significantly when the plea is no contest or guilty because of the absence of the officer or complaining witness. The affidavits which are read in court upon a plea of guilty or no contest are often written so sketchily by the complainant that defendants are given penalties smaller than deserved.

One judge witnessed the assault and battery of a woman on a public street. The arrested defendant was brought into Criminal Court before this judge, charged with disorderly conduct, and entered a no contest plea. It was not until the defendant was about to be sentenced on the disorderly conduct charge that he realized that the defendant was the man he had observed perpetrating the assault and battery. The affidavit recited merely that the defendant had "acted in a disorderly manner" at a certain time and place.[23]

The judges disagreed with the attorneys that the new procedure induces pleas of guilty and no contest, saying that this inducement is simply "not a problem." One judge acknowledged the pressure on a defendant to dispose of the matter in one appearance by means of a guilty plea, but felt that there has been "too much concern for the rights of the defendant," and not enough concern for the rights of society. And while conceding that inducement is definitely a by-product of the arraignment procedure, another judge felt that a person who is not guilty, but lacks sufficient "respect for the system to demand that the state prove its case or demand a trial by his peers," is "not worthy of concern." As for the importance of the factors of loss of wages and inconvenience to the average Municipal Court defendant, a judge declared:

I don't consider lost wages at all. Guilty or innocent, the system is there.

23. The incident has ramifications which apparently were not appreciated by the witnessing judge. After he realized that the defendant should have been charged with assault and battery, he questioned the defendant about the facts of the incident, and then sentenced him to a jail term. Perhaps the judge should have disqualified himself on the grounds of personal knowledge of all the facts in the case.

You risk every day getting involved in some fashion in a criminal action.

I'm not about to run someone through [the arraignment and trial process] just to avoid having him lose a day's pay. It's the price you pay, and it's a small price.

While the judges generally agreed that the new arraignment procedure constitutes an improvement over the former system, they all mentioned several further significant problems.

1. The lack of a Public Defender's staff capable of handling the great numbers of indigent defendants in the Municipal Court. The indigent defendant is especially handicapped if he takes it upon himself to vindicate his innocence with a not guilty plea. Once his case has been assigned to be heard in a room other than the Criminal Courtroom, he must abandon all hopes of professional assistance, since there is no Public Defender in these other rooms.

2. The large number of continuances currently being granted. The judges placed the blame for these delays on defense attorneys who have not been compensated for their services by the time of the trial. . . .

3. The loss of wages to defendants. "Loss of wages to the average man is a critical loss. Under this system, we make people come down to court three times to prove their innocence. It is not fair to the defendant to require so many appearances."

4. The slowness of the new system, which creates a "windfall for the bail bondsman," and causes "defendants without money to spend more time in jail. There are two systems of justice in the same courtroom: one for the rich and one for the poor."

5. Failure to return police officers to their primary job of patroling the streets. The compensatory time off program is a false economy. Although the police are not receiving additional pay for their court appearances, the community is being deprived of the benefit of having the policeman back on his beat. One judge said that the police "are milking the system." It was his opinion that the police desire court appearances despite their almost universal protestations to the contrary; "they're afraid they'll get shot in the streets, and they feel safe in the courtroom."

6. The failure of the police notification system. One judge termed this failure a police tactic.

It's not that the officers aren't notified, but that they ignore the notification. They show up only when they want to. Two days to notify the police is too long, basically, but it's justified only because the police are sometimes off duty. If the police department can get off-duty police officers to the scene of a riot in minutes, why can't they get one into the courtroom in less than two days?

7. Docket backlogs in not guilty plea cases. Responding to a suggestion made in the local press, all eight judges disapproved of the idea that Municipal Court judges remain in the courtroom from 9:00 a.m. to 5:00 p.m. in order to clear up docket backlogs in not guilty plea cases. They felt that five continuous hours in the courtroom was the maximum time for effective functioning. They also cited the demands of massive paperwork upon their time, work which could not be finished if the entire day was spent in the courtroom.

### VI. THE POLICE

In order to elicit spontaneous responses, 45 police officers were interviewed at the Hamilton County Courthouses while they waited for their cases to be called. Of the 45, many were unaware of even the fundamental mechanics of the two systems. They disagreed on such basics as which defendants were tried immediately and which were eligible for continuances under the old and new systems, and whether there are more or less continuances granted under the new than the old. Despite their lack of knowledge, the police did voice strong preferences for one or the other system. . . .

### B. Criticism of the Present System

Almost all of the officers had criticisms of the effects on the police of the arraignment system or court system in general:

1. *The Need for Better Scheduling.* Since the police are not in court when the trial date is set at the first or second appearance of the defendant, not infrequently a day is chosen which is inconvenient for the police — either a day off or a day on which they have been assigned the third relief shift.

The physical structure of the Hamilton County Municipal Court, consisting of the two courthouses with four courtrooms between which cases are bounced back and forth is believed to slow up court schedules; cases and witnesses get lost in the shuffle. This physical structure also results in officers being scheduled to testify in two or three cases on the same day, each of which is held in a different courthouse or courtroom. Hence, cases are often called and then dismissed for want of prosecution when officers do not appear.

Attorneys also may have trials scheduled on the same day in more than one courtroom. If, when one case is called, the attorney is busy in another courtroom, the police who are to testify in the case called must await the second call of the case, which may not occur until all the other cases are disposed of.

Several police felt that an assignment commissioner, responsible for scheduling all of the trials, would be of tremendous value in coordinating the schedules of the police and attorneys. It was also suggested that if trials were scheduled for a particular time block such as 9:00-10:30, or 10:30-12:00, police could spend less time in court waiting for a case to be called since it would be less likely, with scheduling by the assignment commissioner, that two cases would be called simultaneously....

4. *The Problem of Notification.* Nine officers commented on the fact that there is a notification problem between the prosecutor's office and the police department. The police are often told to appear in court on a certain date, but they are not told in which case they will be required to testify. They may not know what the case is about even five minutes before the trial begins. Even when notification of the proper case is given to the officers, it is only given one or two days before the trial. With such short notice, it is often difficult for the police to locate and notify witnesses of the impending trial, especially when much time has elapsed between the arrest and the trial date. Occasionally, a total absence of notification causes dismissal of the case. And since there is no communication between the police and prosecutor prior to trial, the prosecutor often must try the case with very sketchy facts.

The police are not the only ones who suffer when there has been no notification; the defendant and other witnesses suffer as well since when the police fail to appear, the prosecutor is often able to obtain a continuance. Thus, the defendant and all the witnesses have come to court needlessly and are forced to return again. This breakdown in communication is disastrous for a defendant who is not able to post bail and is forced to spend additional time in jail....

## VII. THE DEFENDANTS UNDER THE NEW SYSTEM

Defendants under the new system were observed by the authors during their arraignment or trial (when possible), and approached afterward in the hallway outside the courtroom for an interview....

7. *No Knowledge of the Automatic Continuance.* Nineteen of the 63 defendants who pled guilty did not know at the time of

the plea that they would have to return to court at a later date — a striking 30% of the group. Although the defendants are told at the beginning of each court day that if they plead not guilty their trials will be scheduled for a later date, it is obvious that this statement is insufficient to properly appraise the defendants of the procedure. A better method should be devised by the courts. However, fourteen of these nineteen defendants who did not know they would have to return to court said they would not have been influenced in their plea had they known of the automatic continuance, and one had no opinion. But the remaining five of these defendants, eight percent of the total number who pled not guilty, did assert that knowledge of the automatic continuance would have influenced them. One of these would have been reassured in his not guilty plea because he needed time to obtain a witness. Three of the five would not have wanted to lose additional wages due to missing work. One of these five, thinking she could have her trial immediately, was shocked to have to spend four days in jail and to pay a babysitter $40 to watch her children. Another defendant tried to change her plea to guilty after the judge told her she would have to come back, but she was not permitted to do so. It seems incontrovertible that the automatic continuance following a not guilty plea under the present arraignment system does indeed induce some pleas of guilty. . . .

9. *Whether The Continuance Was Helpful.* Twenty-seven of the 63 defendants who pled not guilty stated the delay following arraignment was not helpful (43%), 22 said it was helpful (35%), three had ambiguous feelings, nine had no opinion and two gave no response.

The 22 defendants who considered the delay between their plea and their trial as helpful gave a total of 27 reasons for their response. Four said it gave their attorneys time to prepare their cases, three used the time to contact or hire an attorney, six were able to obtain a needed witness, four utilized the time to work out their differences with the prosecuting witness, one said he had wanted to talk to his witnesses before the trial, among other reasons.

The 27 defendants who did not consider the delay helpful gave a total of 36 reasons for their opinions. Prominent among these were lost wages, adequate preparation for trial at the first court appearance, time spent in jail between arraignment and trial, inconvenience of returning to court and failure of defense witnesses to appear following the delay. . . .

It should be noted that the single most frequent complaint was the loss of wages that resulted from multiple court appearances. This refutes the judges' general feeling that the chilling effect the continuance has on a defendant is minimal, although it may be true in individual cases. In fact most defendants, especially those who are paid hourly and who thus lose wages if they enter a plea of not guilty pay a price for asserting their innocence. One defendant, not able to post bail, was incarcerated for six days. "I've probably been fired by now," he stated. This is a heavy price to pay for a finding of not guilty for petit larceny. Thus not all the defendants agreed with an interviewee who stated that while lost wages were "important," not having a record was "more important." Defendants should not be forced to pay a double penalty for a crime — loss of wages and the former sentence. Nor should defendants ultimately found innocent have to suffer loss of wages as a penalty for maintaining their innocence. A system which demands this much operates on faulty premises. . . .

Of those 71 defendants who pled as they did for reasons other than that they lacked a desire to return for trial, 26 (20 guilty plea defendants and 6 no contest plea defendants) stated the prosecutor's case was of only "slight" or "moderate" strength. Thus, even though these 26 defendants declared their reason for pleading as they did to be that they were guilty or knew that their penalties would be small, they still maintained that the case against them was not strong.

When asked to characterize their chances for acquittal had they pled not guilty, 40 of the 103 defendants (27 guilty plea and 13 no contest plea) stated that their chances were "moderately strong" or "very strong." Of these 40, 21 defendants gave reasons for pleading guilty or no contest other than lack of desire to return for trial.

These figures indicate that the 21 defendants who characterized their chances for acquittal as "moderately strong" or "very strong" and the 26 defendants who characterized the prosecutor's case as "slight" or "moderate," and did not merely express a disdain for returning for trial, may actually have been motivated to make their pleas by that reason alone. It is reasonable to suppose that a man who pleads guilty, believing that the case against him is not strong or that he had a chance for acquittal, must have entered his guilty plea for reasons extraneous to the question of guilt. When these defendants are added to the 32 who initially admitted that they pled guilty because they did not want to return for trial, the total number of defendants who pled guilty or no contest for reasons other than the fact of their guilt exceeds 50% of the total defendants interviewed.

A high percentage of defendants are arrested (81%) rather than being merely cited into court (19%). This fact plus the statistics that slightly more than 50% of the interviewed, arrested defendants utilized bailbondsmen, substantiate the statement of one of the Municipal Court judges that the new arraignment procedure is a windfall for bail bondsmen. . . .

Thus, approximately 85% of the defendants were prepared to knowledgeably answer whether the mechanics of the arraignment system affected their plea decision. Although 60 defendants (46 guilty plea and 14 no contest plea) replied in the negative, 43 defendants answered that they had weighed this factor in making their pleas. These 43 defendants include 18 defendants (11 guilty plea and 7 no contest plea) who had not originally stated in response to question three that the arraignment system was a reason for pleading as they did.

In order to gauge the degree to which the arraignment system was a factor influencing the defendant's plea, the defendants who had entered a guilty plea were asked whether they would still have pled guilty or no contest had they been able to have their trials immediately. Almost one-third of the 103 defendants interviewed (a total of 30, including 20 guilty plea and 10 no contest plea defendants) responded that they would have pled not guilty under the hypothetical circumstances. . . .

## VIII. CONCLUSIONS AND RECOMMENDATIONS

### A. *Conclusions*

The new system was adopted for three reasons: to alleviate witness inconvenience, to decrease police payroll expenditures, and to improve courtroom conditions in order to achieve more just results.

The new system has failed to completely alleviate witness inconvenience. The complainant who files an affidavit is often in court when the accused is arraigned. Thus, either the information that he need not be present at the accused's arraignment has not been communicated to him or he does not consider it an inconvenience to be present at the arraignment. If the former possibility is correct, the new system is not being properly implemented; if the latter conclusion is correct, institution of the part of the system intended to alleviate witness inconvenience was unnecessary. Not only is complainant and witness inconvenience not being alleviated at the present time but the complainant's presence at the accused's arraignment produces congestion in the courtroom because the facilities in the Alms and Doepke Building are still not adequate to accommodate the people present at each session of criminal court.

Yet, courtroom congestion was a primary reason for the adoption of the new system. Immediately prior to the new system's adoption, the court was moved to the more spacious, yet still inadequate, facilities in the Alms and Doepke Building and two additional courtrooms were established in the county courthouse to hear cases transferred from criminal court in the Alms and Doepke Building. But courtroom congestion remains; fewer and fewer cases are actually being transferred to the additional courtrooms and presently the number of transferred cases has leveled off at 16 percent. . . .

The new arraignment system was also designed to provide better justice for the accused. The additional courtrooms were meant to allow the presiding judge greater time in a less hurried atmosphere to consider all factors in a case before making a finding. However, a comparison of the ultimate results under the old and new systems demonstrates that the new system is not yielding ultimate results that differ significantly from those attained before the changes were instituted. Longer workhouse terms are however being imposed upon defendants under the new system.

It cannot be ascertained whether tax savings have accrued since the presence of the arresting officer at the accused's arraignment was dropped as a requirement, since, at the same time that the new arraignment system went into effect, the police department abolished overtime pay for court appearances.

The only other characteristic that sharply distinguishes the new system from the old is the difference in the number of cases that are disposed of at the accused's first appearance. Under the old system, 72.5% of all cases were heard to conclusion immediately after the accused was arraigned. Under the new system, the immediate conclusion of a case occurs in only 48.2% of the cases. This delay is caused by the automatic continuances required after a not guilty plea is entered. In effect, the new system punishes the accused who enters a plea of not guilty by occasioning a loss of wages or a stay in jail. A system that imposes such a burden on the accused for entering a not guilty plea is inherently unjust. This conclusion refutes the statements of several municipal court judges and lawyers who did not recognize the "chilling effect" that the system has on the defendants passing through it. . . .

Thus, there are no easy solutions to the real problems that are inherent in the new system as it now operates. Although the new system has fulfilled some goals of its originators, such as bringing

great savings in witness time, it has created new problems unantici-
pated by its founders. The most serious of these is the influence it
wields over defendants in their choice of a plea. The large number
of complaints made during this study by people involved in all
phases of the criminal process demonstrates that it is imperative
that action be taken soon to remedy the system's defects and enable
it to realize its full potential for effective and efficient criminal
law administration.

# The Quality of Justice in Misdemeanor Arraignment Courts*

# Ralph H. Nutter

The massive increase of population in Los Angeles has had a
peculiarly harmful effect on the conditions of our municipal arraignment courts. The increasing volume of cases now scheduled
for hearing in Los Angeles arraignment courts has raised many
serious problems concerning the quality of law enforcement and
the quality of justice meted out in these courts.

Recently, community leaders and the newspapers have been
clamoring for stiffer penalties and greater individual attention on
the part of judges in cases involving vice, narcotics, drunk driving,
traffic safety, and delinquent parents. In excess of 1,000 cases involving these problems are brought before municipal arraignment
courts every day. During March, 1961, there were 27,442 arraignments in the Los Angeles Judicial District. Arraignment courts
must assume a major share of the responsibility in these fields
because in excess of 80 per cent of the defendants plead guilty at
the time of arraignment.

The tremendous volume of cases which must pass through these
arraignment courts in a given period of time necessarily limits the
opportunity of the judge, city attorney, and the defendant or his
attorney to give more than perfunctory attention to any individual
case. Frequently, it is physically impossible for the deputy city
attorney to know anything about the details of the charge, the
background of the defendant, or his record. As a result, both the
quality of law enforcement and the rights of the defendants are

* From: 53 J. Crim. L. Crim. & P.S. 215-219 (1962). Reprinted by permission of the Journal of Criminal Law and Criminology, and the author.

made to suffer. Police officers and complaining witnesses often feel that their case has not received proper attention. In many cases, defendants enter a plea without any conception or understanding of the law. Often, the defendant pleads guilty "to get it over with." Under such conditions, remedial or beneficial results to the community or the defendant are only incidental.

### TRAFFIC CASES

In the main traffic arraignment court, Division 50, there are more than 400 arraignments a day. This means that with a court day from 9:00 to 12:00 a.m. and from 1:30 to 4:30 p.m., with two ten-minute recesses, there are only 220 minutes to handle these cases, *or an average of 51 seconds per case.* Of course, many traffic citations involve routine matters, and in such cases a minimum of time is required to arraign the defendant, receive the plea, and impose sentence. But it should be remembered that the Los Angeles Municipal Court does not require a defendant to make a personal appearance in traffic court until he has received citations for three moving violations within a 12 month period, or has been cited for an extremely high rate of speed, or some other more flagrant type of alleged violation. By the time a defendant is obliged to make a personal appearance in a traffic court, he has developed a pattern of unsafe driving habits quite unlike the average driver. (According to a survey of the National Safety Council, the average driver receives an average of three traffic citations in ten years.)

The appearance of a citizen in traffic court should be a meaningful experience. Defendants should not get the impression that the purpose of the appearance is to shepherd them in lines to the cashier's window. Each case should receive individual attention from the judge, the deputy city attorney, and the defendant or his counsel. Under the present physical conditions this is impossible.

In a study of "California Traffic Law Administration," the authors state:

> It is clear that the average traffic court is ill equipped to handle the pressure traffic violations place upon it. . . . This pressure, as well as the factual simplicity and general minor character of the offense, has motivated the use of a simplified procedure. But considering the important part played by procedure in our system of justice such a simplification could constitute the denial of fair trial. This danger is intensified by the fact that appeals from traffic convictions are so rare that in effect the *traffic* court is a court of last resort.

...the traffic court ... does not adequately promote traffic safety because it fails to deal effectively with the convicted violator.... Adequate treatment directly affects traffic safety through deterrence of future violations.[1] (Emphasis supplied.)

In commenting upon the traffic courts, Associate Justice Tom Clark, of the United States Supreme Court, has stated:

> Those who are charged, or who go into our traffic courts not being charged but just as visitors, see in action perhaps the only court they know anything about. The condition of that courtroom, the manner in which its procedures are carried out, the demeanor of the judge and the attachés of the court, the method in which the court is carried on, and the time, perhaps, one has to wait in order to have his case called, all these things are impressed indelibly upon those people who come and sit in that courtroom .... There can be no more important court in this whole land than the traffic courts .... Here is where respect or disrespect for law, for order, for the courts, and for government is fostered.

### PHYSICAL CONDITIONS IN ARRAIGNMENT COURTS

The physical conditions in Los Angeles Municipal arraignment courts are not conducive to either justice or individual attention. In Divisions 50, 58, and 59, defendants are informed of their constitutional rights in crowds ranging in size from 100 to 300 defendants. In Divisions 58 and 59, there are no seats available for the defendants, and they are crowded into a small space between the counsel table and the courtroom seats, in conditions similar to those of New Yorkers crowded into a subway during the rush hour.

After defendants are informed of their constitutional rights, to facilitate the arraignment process, bailiffs are obliged to line up the defendants in long lines, blocking up the aisles of the courtroom. As the names of individual defendants are called off, each defendant moves up in the line, shepherded ahead by the bailiffs. Under such physical conditions, the deputy city attorney and the defendant are primarily concerned with a quick disposition of the case. By the time the defendant appears before the judge, frequently his only objective is to get out of the courtroom as fast as possible. Like assembly line workers in a factory, all parties operate under a climate which makes it appear that nothing may be per-

1. California Traffic Law Administration, 12 Stan. L. Rev. 388, 388-89 (1960).

mitted to interfere with the smooth operation of the line. Under such conditions, it is possible that defendants plead guilty without adequate knowledge of the charges against them, or sufficient information concerning the specific counts in a complaint, or even the number of counts in the complaint.

A plea of guilty under such circumstances does not create respect for the law enforcement process. It certainly does not create a climate for the education of the defendants.

### THE IMPORTANCE OF LAW ENFORCEMENT IN MUNICIPAL COURTS

In the field of general criminal law, a larger number of defendants with felony records appear in Division 59 than in any other court in Los Angeles County. "The minor offense is often a prelude to a major crime. While usually only the more violent or vicious crimes make the headlines, the so-called 'petty' offenders or misdemeanants are also a serious problem and worthy of public concern. The minor offense of today may very well be the prelude to a major offense." [2]

Frequently, crimes of violence or crimes involving the use of concealed and deadly weapons, are reduced from felonies. In many of these cases, defendants who have been involved in an attempted robbery, rape, or stabbing are more than happy to plead guilty to a misdemeanor.

Although narcotic addiction cases are treated as misdemeanors, the confirmed narcotic addict usually has a long felony record to support his habit. The illegal use of dangerous drugs is frequently the beginning of a habit which will lead to heroin and other narcotic use and addiction, and later felony appearances for other crimes committed for the support of the habit.

Delinquent fathers who fail to support their families and neglectful parents are prosecuted for conduct which endangers the welfare of children or permits child delinquency. Husbands are prosecuted for wife beating under misdemeanor battery charges. The disposition of cases involving the family relationship is important to the continuance of the marriage and the well-being of the home and the children. In many cases, the conduct which is the subject of the complaint is the predecessor of future superior court proceedings in the domestic relations courts.

All forms of minor fraud are prosecuted in the municipal courts:

2. J. Edgar Hoover, The Minor Offense — Prelude to a Major Crime? 1 Munic. Ct. Rev. 6 (1961).

petty theft, checks issued with insufficient funds, petty "bunco" schemes, and unemployment insurance fraud. Also included are violations of the Labor Code, the Revenue and Taxation Code, the Business and Professions Code, and even misdemeanor manslaughter cases. In such a wide area, affecting the entire scope of social relations, the community has a right to expect more than perfunctory attention in the disposition of cases. They should not be disposed of by a court in times averaging one minute or less.

### SENTENCING IN ARRAIGNMENT COURTS

Justice Henry Alfred McCardie once said: "Trying a man is easy, as easy as falling off a log, compared with deciding what to do with him when he has been found guilty."

But in the municipal arraignment courts, where formal probationary procedures are used in only a minority of cases, it is difficult for a judge, under the physical conditions described above, to devote a sufficient amount of time to the sentencing of defendants. In a book published since his death, Judge Charles Fricke stated:

> The imposition of a sentence or the granting of probation and the conditions attached thereto cannot, if justice is to be done, be based on a schedule or rule of thumb fixing a more or less standard penalty for each particular crime. Each case is a problem by itself depending partly upon the crime committed, partly on the manner in which it was committed and partly, and this is most important, upon the particular defendant before the court, his past education and environment, intelligence, predispositions and tendencies, his employment record, health and accident record, his past home life, the attitude of his parents and their treatment of him, his married life, if any, and his dependents, mental defects or disease, his habits and excesses, if any and, in fact, everything that can be learned about him and his past, even including his favorite manner of spending his leisure hours.[3]

I am aware of the argument that added attention to the record and background of each defendant will not change the habits or conduct of certain "repeater" defendants. But if this be true, conversely, the practices and system of the arraignment courts should not give advantage to the chronic law violator.

The sentencing of repeater defendants in vice and gambling cases is a continual problem. The "professionals" in these fields

3. Fricke, Sentence and Probation 4 (1960).

are continually shopping for sentences which may be considered no more than a tax or business expense for continued operation.

The "repeaters" or their advisers are well versed in the calendar problems of the arraignment courts and are often able, because of the pressure of physical conditions, to induce the deputy city attorney to accept a reduced plea.

There seems to be a presumption among "repeaters" that in return for a plea of guilty in the arraignment or master calendar court, the sentence will be within a certain range, and lighter than in the trial court. This expectation is founded upon the understanding of a simple fact. An increase in not guilty pleas of only 5 per cent in the arraignment and master calendar courts would result in a flooding of the trial courts and a breakdown of the entire system. Cases which could not be sent to trial within the statutory 30-day period would be dismissed.

Of course, "judicial shopping" has always been a serious problem in any busy metropolitan court which utilizes a master calendar and arraignment system, separate from the trial courts. Nor is reference to this fact to be construed as a criticism of the statutory right of a defendant to exercise his challenge of an individual judge. Judicial "shopping" is largely confined to defendants who make regular appearances in municipal arraignment courts. This practice, when used in conjunction with and under the physical conditions of the present overcrowded arraignment courts, has redounded in favor of the professional criminal or "repeater" as opposed to the first offender.

In many occasions, the "repeater's" knowledge of the arraignment system enables him to obtain a sentence of less severity than the first offender, who, in many cases, can neither afford the price of bail nor obtain counsel.

### POSSIBLE DENIAL OF RIGHTS TO DEFENDANTS

Recently, Attorney General Robert Kennedy stated: "I have a strong feeling that the law, especially in criminal cases, favors the rich man over the poor in such matters as bail, the cost of defense counsel, the cost of appeals and so on." This statement is pertinent to our municipal arraignment courts.

The present Los Angeles system of having separate courts for arraignment and for trial may make the choice of plea a difficult one even for a defendant who believes himself to be innocent. A defendant who pleads guilty in arraignment court will be sentenced at once; one who pleads not guilty will be forced to wait several weeks because of the separation of arraignment and trial courts. The delay will usually involve additional detention if the defendant cannot afford the cost of a bail bond, and the trial will necessitate a higher lawyer's fee.[6]

The great majority of our defendants who have any financial resources or earn their living are not represented by attorneys in misdemeanor arraignment courts. Court attaches estimate that less than ten per cent of all defendants are represented by counsel.

The indigent defendant is entitled to representation by the public defender, and, of course, has the benefit of the public defender's experience in the arraignment courts. But the average citizen, without benefit of counsel, is completely unfamiliar with the processes of the criminal law. If he has enough money to make bail, it is extremely unlikely that he will have sufficient funds to pay the cash required by most attorneys before they will make an appearance. In addition, those defendants who are not paid on a weekly salary basis are faced with loss of a day's wages for every day they make an appearance (usually a minimum of three days if they plan to litigate the case). Under such circumstances, in a case involving a first offense, the average citizen without benefit of counsel will plead guilty.

The law enforcement process will not be materially benefited if a guilty plea is entered under such conditions. A plea of guilty must be meaningful to the defendant. If the defendant has not received competent legal advice, he can always rationalize a guilty plea on the ground that he was forced to do so by conditions, or he had no other choice because of financial reasons. In such a case, the sentence may have some deterrent effect, but it is extremely unlikely that it will have any rehabilitative effect. The defendant will not feel that the sentence is based on his needs, because he will feel that he never should have pleaded guilty in the first place.

### CONCLUSION

Each defendant is an individual and must be treated as such. This concept is fundamental to our American system of democracy. It requires that punishment shall not only fit the crime, but that it shall also fit the character of each individual defendant in so far

6. [Note, Metropolitan Criminal Courts of First Instance, 70 Harv. L. Rev. 320, 337 (1956).]

as this may be achieved within the framework of the law in question. Our aim should not only be to prevent future crime by the individual defendant and others who learn of this punishment, but also in some way assure that the defendant who has admitted his guilt in the arraignment court will, in the future, be more of an asset than a liability to the community.

The problem of maintaining justice in a mass society, with a population exploding in geometric ratios, may be one of the greatest challenges of our democracy. Justice cannot be mass produced. We must be ever alert that our traditional concepts of justice are not eroded by the sheer volume of cases which are now flooding our courts. Under the present physical conditions in our arraignment courts, it is increasingly more difficult to give even the appearance of justice.

Obviously, there are no quick remedies for these problems. As tentative solutions, I would suggest the following:

(1) The alarming increase in crime makes it imperative that lawyers and judges must devote more time to the problems of law enforcement and misdemeanor courts. There has been a tendency to minimize misdemeanors as matters of small importance. In many cases the distinction between misdemeanors and felonies is artificial. This is particularly true in crimes involving violence to the person and cases involving drugs and narcotics.

(2) It has been necessary for municipal courts to use summary probation procedures more frequently than formal probation. Summary probation must be made a meaningful experience. At the time sentence is imposed defendants should be given a written copy of the terms. Violation of the terms should not be ignored. Procedures must be instituted to insure that violations of terms are brought to the attention of the court. This is a joint responsibility of the court and the city attorney's office.

(3) Lawyers who have little or no contact with municipal courts and have no occasion even to advise a defendant in a criminal proceeding must be made aware that criminal proceedings which are conducted with the great majority of all defendants unrepresented is an indictment of their profession. It is true, even in an arraignment court, that the right to be heard is, in many cases, of little avail, if it does not comprehend the right to be heard by counsel. A better system for lawyer references in criminal cases must be developed.

(4) An increase in the number of judges will assist in solving some of the problems related above. But serious consideration must be given to changing the present master calendar and ar-

raignment system. The Los Angeles Bar Association should appoint a committee to visit the arraignment and master calendar courts. This committee should consult with the judiciary, the City Attorney, law enforcement officials, and experienced criminal attorneys. It should seek to advise the courts on methods to cut down the number of court appearances required in traffic cases, and if possible increase the number of arraignment courts. A study should be made of the new Metropolitan Court in Dade County, Florida, with particular attention devoted to the traffic court reforms there instituted. New arraignment courts might be combined with trial courts to function as part-time trial courts, as is now the case in Divisions 51 and 59.

(5) The arraignment courts must be considered as an important part of our judicial system. The arraignment court must not be considered the "stepchild" of our criminal courts. For a great many citizens, arraignment courts are courts of last resort. They are the courts where the greatest number of defendants receive sentences and penalties imposed by law, and where many of our citizens learn about our judicial system and the law enforcement process.

## The Urban Courts*

## The President's Commission on Law Enforcement and Administration of Justice

*Practices and Procedures of the Lower Courts*
Every day in the courthouses of metropolitan areas the inadequacies of the lower criminal courts may be observed. There is little in the process which is likely to instill respect for the system of criminal justice in defendants, witnesses, or observers. Some representative observations are set forth below.

*Initial Presentment.* Following arrest, the defendant is initially presented in court, often after many hours and sometimes several days of detention. In theory the judge's duty is to advise the defendant of the charges against him and of his rights to remain silent, to be admitted to bail, to retain counsel or to have counsel

* From: President's Commission on Law Enforcement and Administration of Justice. Task Force Report: The Courts 30-36 (1967).

appointed, and to have a preliminary hearing. But in some cities the defendant may not be advised of his right to remain silent or to have counsel assigned. In others he may be one of a large group herded before the bench as a judge or clerk rushes through a ritualistic recitation of phrases, making little or no effort to ascertain whether the defendants understand their rights or the nature of the proceedings. In many jurisdictions counsel are not assigned in misdemeanor cases; even where lawyers are appointed it may not be made clear to the defendant that if he is without funds he may have free representation. One Commission staff report notes:

> In the cases observed no defendant was told that he had a right to remain silent or that the court would appoint a lawyer to represent him if he were indigent, notwithstanding the court rule that counsel will be assigned whenever a defendant may be sentenced to more than six months or fined more than $500. We were told that at least one judge takes great care to advise defendants fully, but the three judges we observed did not.[5]

The judges have little time to give detailed consideration to the question of bail. Little is known about the defendant other than the charge and his prior criminal record. The result is that bail is based on the charge instead of on the circumstances of each case; high money bonds are almost invariably set by established patterns, and large numbers of defendants are detained.

*Disposition.* The initial appearance is also the final appearance for most defendants charged with misdemeanors or petty offenses. While those who can afford to retain counsel are released on bond to prepare for trial at a later date or to negotiate a disposition, a majority of defendants pleads guilty immediately, many without advice of counsel. Pleas are entered so rapidly that they cannot be well considered. The defendant is often made aware that if he seeks more time, his case will be adjourned for a week or two and he will be returned to jail.

> Most of the defendants . . . pleaded guilty and were sentenced immediately, without any opportunity for allocution. When they tried to say something in their own behalf, they were silenced by the judge and led off by the bailiff. . . .[6]

5. Staff Study, Administration of Justice in the Municipal Court of Baltimore . . . [Task Force Report: The Courts at 121].

6. Staff Study, Administration of Justice in the Recorder's Court of Detroit . . . [id. at 129].

*Trial.* An observer in the lower criminal courts ordinarily sees a trial bearing little resemblance to those carried out under traditional notions of due process. There is usually no court reporter unless the defendant can afford to pay one. One result is an informality in the proceedings which would not be tolerated in a felony trial. Rules of evidence are largely ignored. Speed is the watchword. Trials in misdemeanor cases may be over in a matter of 5, 10 or 15 minutes; they rarely last an hour even in relatively complicated cases. Traditional safeguards honored in felony cases lose their meaning in such proceedings; yet there is still the possibility of lengthy imprisonment or heavy fine.

In some cities trials are conducted without counsel for either side; the case is prosecuted by a police officer and defended by the accused himself. Staff observations in one city were summed up as follows:

> A few defendants went to trial, but the great majority of them did so without counsel. In these cases the judge made no effort to explain the proceedings to the defendants or to tell them of their right to cross-examine the prosecution's witnesses or of their right to remain silent. After the policeman delivered his testimony, the judge did not appear to make any evaluation of the sufficiency of the evidence but turned immediately to the defendant and asked, "What do you have to say for yourself?" Where counsel appeared at a trial, the procedure was slightly more formal, but the judge conducted most of the questioning himself.[7]

*Sentence.* Most defendants convicted in the lower criminal courts are sentenced promptly. Usually there are no probation services or presentence investigations. Unless the defendant has an attorney who has taken time to inquire into his background, little will be known about him. Sentence may be based on the charge, the defendant's appearance, and the defendant's response to such questions as the judge may put to him in the few moments allotted to sentencing. In the lower courts of one State

> the availability of violator's records is the exception rather than the rule. Even in the larger cities when the judge wishes to see the record of individual defendants he must send for the record and then delay the trial until it arrives. Delay and inconvenience so caused often lead to a situation where the judge merely asks the defendant what his record is and relies upon his word for its accuracy. . . .[8]

7. Ibid.
8. Sheridan, [Urban Justice 41 (1964)].

Short jail sentences of one, two, or three months are commonly imposed on an assembly line basis. A defendant's situation can hardly be considered individually. When a defendant is fined but is unable to pay, he may be required to work the penalty off at the rate of $1 to $5 for each day spent in jail.

*Petty Offenses.* The conditions described above are found in more aggravated form in lower courts which handle petty offenses. Each day in large cities hundreds of persons arrested for drunkenness or disorderly conduct, for vagrancy or petty gambling, or for prostitution are led before a judge. Among the defendants are slum dwellers who drink in public and young men who "loiter" on street corners or "fail to move on" when ordered to do so. Typically, they have no private place to go, no money to spend, and no family or lawyer to lend them support.

Judges sometimes seem annoyed at being required to preside in these courts. Defendants are treated with contempt, berated, laughed at, embarrassed, and sentenced to serve their time or work off their fines. Observers have sometimes reported difficulty in determining what offense is being tried in a given case, and instances have come to light in which the disposition bears little relationship to the original charge. A trial of a defendant charged by police with drunkenness consisted of this exchange:

MAGISTRATE: "Where do you live?"
DEFENDANT: "Norfolk."
MAGISTRATE: "What are you doing in Philadelphia?"
DEFENDANT: "Well, I didn't have any work down there, so I came up here to see if I could find . . . ."
MAGISTRATE (who had been shaking his head): "That story's not good enough for me. I'm going to have you investigated. You're a vagrant. Three months in the House of Correction." [12]

The offender subjected to this process emerges punished but unchanged. He returns to the streets, and it is likely that the cycle soon will be repeated in all its futility.

*Causes of the Problems of the Lower Courts*
*The Volume of Cases.* More than in any other courts in the system the problems of the lower courts center around the volume of cases. It is estimated that in 1962 over 4 million misdemeanor cases were brought to the lower courts of the United States. The

12. Foote, [Vagrancy-Type Law and Its Administration, 104 U. Pa. L. Rev. 603, 610-611 (1956)].

crux of the problem is that there is a great disparity between the number of cases and the number of judges.

Data from various cities illustrate this disparity. For example, until legislation last year increased the number of judges, the District of Columbia Court of General Sessions had four judges to process the preliminary stages of more than 1,500 felony cases, and to hear and determine 7,500 serious misdemeanor cases, 38,000 petty offenses and an equal number of traffic offenses per year. In Detroit over 20,000 misdemeanor and nontraffic petty offense cases must be handled by the single judge sitting in the Early Sess'ons Division. In Atlanta in 1964 three judges of the Municipal Court disposed of more than 70,000 cases.

It is not only judges who are in short supply. There are not enough prosecutors, defense counsel, and probation officers even in those courts where some of them are available. The deluge of cases is reflected in every aspect of the courts' work, from overcrowded corridors and courtrooms to the long calendars that do not allow more than cursory consideration of individual cases.

There are other less visible consequences of volume problems. In the lower courts the agencies administering criminal justice sometimes become preoccupied simply with moving the cases. Clearing the dockets becomes a primary objective of all concerned, and cases are dismissed, guilty pleas are entered, and bargains are struck with that end as the dominant consideration. Inadequate attention tends to be given to the individual defendant, whether in protecting his rights, in carefully sifting the facts at trial, or in determining the social risk he presents and how he should be dealt with after conviction. A former municipal court judge summed up his experiences in these words:

> The tremendous volume of cases which must pass through these arraignment courts in a given period of time necessarily limits the opportunity of the judge, city attorney, and the defendant or his attorney to give more than perfunctory attention to any individual case. Frequently, it is physically impossible for the deputy city attorney to know anything about the details of the charge, the background of the defendant, or his record. As a result, both the quality of law enforcement and the rights of the defendants are made to suffer. Police officers and complaining witnesses often feel that their case has not received proper attention.... Under such conditions, remedial or beneficial results to the community or the defendant are only incidental.[16]

16. Nutter, The Quality of Justice in Misdemeanor Arraignment Courts, 53 J. Crim. L., C. & P.S. 215 (1962). [See *supra.* — ED.]

The heavier the volume, the greater delay between arrest and disposition for many defendants. This delay weakens the deterrent effect of the criminal process. It can cause the collapse of the prosecutor's case as witnesses tire and fail to appear and as memories fade. In addition, continuing cases time and again needlessly expends witnesses' time, including that of a large number of police witnesses. From the point of view of the defendant delay increases the length of pretrial detention for those who cannot afford to post bail.

*The Quality of Personnel.* It is clear that the lower courts are generally manned by less competent personnel than the courts of general jurisdiction. There are judges, attorneys, and other officers in the lower courts who are as capable in every respect as their counterparts in more prestigious courts, but the lower courts regularly do not attract such persons.

In almost every city judges in courts of general jurisdiction are better paid, are more prominent members of the community, and are better qualified than their lower court counterparts. In some cities lower court judges are not required to be lawyers. The conduct of some judges reveals inaptitude and a lack of familiarity with rules of evidence or developments in case law.

In jurisdictions in which the State is represented by a district attorney, the most inexperienced members of the staff are usually assigned to the lower courts. As they gain experience, the more able assistants are moved to the felony courts to handle more "important" cases, a move commonly regarded as a substantial career advance. For example, in the District of Columbia, five members of the U.S. Attorney's office were transferred from the lower court to the felony court in a four-month period in 1965. In some cities prosecutors are part time and police officers serve as prosecutors.

As has been noted, in many lower courts defense counsel are not provided for defendants without funds. In those places where counsel are assigned, frequently he is not compensated and often his performance is poor. A community gets the kind of legal service it pays for, and typically it pays little or nothing for defense counsel in its lower courts.

Attorneys operating regularly in these courts rarely appear in other courts. Often they seem to be more concerned with extracting a fee from their clients than with defending them. They operate on a mass production basis, relying on the plea of guilty to dispose of cases quickly. Frequently these lawyers are unprepared, make little contact with their clients, fail to investigate their backgrounds, and make little effort aside from the plea bargaining session to protect their interests or to secure a favorable disposition. For all the shortcomings of these attorneys who regularly operate in the lower courts, however, probably most defendants are better off with them than without any lawyer at all.

Probation services in the lower courts frequently are not available. More than one-third of the sample counties in the Commission's national survey of corrections had no probation services for misdemeanants. In jurisdictions where probation departments are attached to the lower courts, the probation services are markedly inferior, with few exceptions, to those available in the felony courts. Salary schedules for misdemeanant probation offcers are generally too low to attract competent personnel, and in some counties the position of probation officer is filled by persons of limited qualifications who must rely on a part-time job to supplement their inadequate salary.

However, the greatest obstacle to effective probation services in the lower courts is the insufficient number of probation officers. The corrections survey estimated a national average of 114 misdemeanant cases per probation officer, an average which is far in excess of the minimum standards recommended in chapter 6 of the Commission's General Report. Under such heavy caseloads probation is at best a checking rather than a counseling or assisting function. The result is that lower court judges are unable to make the fullest appropriate use of probation, and presentence reports, when possible at all, are likely to lack sufficient information for effective sentencing.

*Administrative Problems.* The lower courts usually have separate personnel, facilities, and budgets from courts of general jurisdiction, but they generally manifest the same administrative deficiencies. The problems of lack of coordination among judges of a single court and of burdening judges with administrative chores which are found in many court systems are discussed in chapter 7 [omitted]. However, it should be noted that the effects of these problems are greater in the lower courts because of the greater volume of business which must be processed. Moreover, such attention as is directed to problems of court administration tends to be focused on the higher courts, in which more prominent judges and more experienced prosecutors are far more likely to take the initiative than their counterparts in the lower courts. The absence of defense counsel in many lower courts, apart from the "regulars" in the courthouse who often have vested interests in the status quo, also eliminates a source of initiative for reform.

Commission staff research revealed a pervasive lack of statistical data necessary for any attempt to improve the operations of the lower courts. In the District of Columbia Court of General Sessions, for example,

> there is nothing which approaches a comprehensive profile of the offender, . . . [but] the problems are far more basic. There is no agreement among the agencies even as to the volume of business of the court . . . . There are no statistics on the rate or length of pretrial detention. The incidence of indigency at the court is unknown. There is no comprehensive analysis of the manner in which cases are charged, broken down, or disposed of by the prosecutor. There is no description of sentencing patterns or of the workloads of individual judges. And there are no reliable statistics on recidivism.[18]

In most cities cases are listed in terms of charges rather than defendants, and there is no way to determine how many persons entered the system. Quite often inconsistencies appear between statistics kept by the police and those kept by the court. In the District of Columbia, for example, some 5,000 defendants shown on police records to have reached court do not appear on court records at all. The lack of data makes it difficult to pinpoint critical areas of need, renders comprehensive assessment of the performance of the court impossible, and restricts sound management control over court business.

## Unification of the Criminal Courts

Division of the criminal courts has produced lower standards of judicial, prosecutorial, and defense performance in the misdemeanor and petty offense courts. Procedural regularity has been a prime casualty. The function performed by these courts, ultimate disposition of misdemeanors and petty offenses only, has meant that community attention is directed to the higher courts where felony cases are processed.

When community resources are committed to criminal justice, the lower courts, largely lacking in articulate spokesmen, are commonly ignored. The result has been the development of two separate court systems of strikingly disparate quality. The distinction between felonies on the one hand and misdemeanors and petty offenses on the other may be useful in fixing the range of punishment and the collateral effects of conviction, but it certainly does not justify the present dual court system. In many respects the distinction between felonies and misdemeanors is an artificial one.

18. Subin, [Criminal Justice in a Metropolitan Court 155 (1966)].

Misdemeanants are sometimes liable to lengthy imprisonment, and a large percentage of these offenders were initially charged with felonies which were reduced to misdemeanors as a result of plea bargaining; they may represent the same danger to society and the same need for rehabilitative measures as those processed through the felony courts.

It is hard to see why a defendant charged with a felony should be accorded so many more of the elements of due process than his counterpart charged with a less serious offense in a misdemeanor court: better representation, more care in disposition, and better facilities for rehabilitation.

The community and the offender both suffer when the offender is processed through the lower courts, for he often receives a lighter sentence than is appropriate, and he is denied access to the rehabilitative facilities of the higher courts. The hardened offender does not develop overnight; generally he has a history of repeated misdemeanor and petty offense violations. At the initial stage of a criminal career there should be reason to hope for successful rehabilitative efforts. Yet at just that crucial phase the community's resources fail to be effective. The disturbing rate of recidivism among offenders processed through the lower courts alone is reason enough to try another approach.

The problems of the lower courts can best be met by unification of the criminal courts and abolition of the lower courts as presently constituted. The National Commission on Law Observance and Enforcement reached this conclusion over 30 years ago. Conditions in the lower courts today have not improved, and increases in caseloads have multiplied the problems. The experience of this century suggests that the lower courts will remain a neglected segment of our criminal justice system unless sweeping reforms are instituted.

All criminal prosecutions should be conducted in a single court manned by judges who are authorized to try all offenses. All judges should be of equal status. Unification of the courts will not change the grading of offenses, the punishment, or the rights to indictment by grand jury and trial by jury. But all criminal cases should be processed under generally comparable procedures, with stress on procedural regularity and careful consideration of dispositions.

Complete unification of the criminal courts would entail central administration which may take a number of forms. The logistics may be handled by a court's chief judge, by a small administrative committee of judges, or by an administrative judge, an office established in the New York Criminal Court and in other cities. The services of professional court administrators to assist the judges charged with administrative duties will be needed for the larger courts, and the use of business management techniques, including the use of data processing equipment, should be developed. It is in the lower court, with a higher volume of routine cases than the felony court, that mechanical and electronic equipment would have the greatest impact.

In addition to unification of the courts, centralization of the prosecutive function in a single office responsible for all criminal prosecutions and operating on a county level or on a citywide basis in major cities would result in more efficient use of manpower and a higher level of prosecution. The often found systems of special prosecutors, city prosecutors, part-time employees, and police prosecutors should be eliminated.

Two improvements may be anticipated in a unified court system. Such facilities as probation services and presentence investigations, currently of limited availability in most jurisdictions, would be available for all criminal cases, and all defendants would be entitled to assigned counsel to the extent suggested in chapter 5 [omitted]. High-volume courts present the opportunity for experimentation with ways of providing counsel to the poor, including variations of the familiar assigned counsel and defender approaches.

The precise form unification should take in each jurisdiction will have to be considered in light of local conditions. An initial question is whether the civil courts should be included in the unified court structure or whether separate civil and criminal courts should be maintained. The merits and demerits of specialization by judges, and the effects of the several approaches on the administration of the courts and the quality of court personnel must be weighed. Procedural and administrative differences in the processing of petty offenses may lead some jurisdictions to follow the pattern set by Detroit, where an integrated court handles all phases of criminal cases but a special branch of that court deals with petty offenses. At first there will be problems of housekeeping and of the use of the courthouse and other facilities of the merged courts, but the recent accomplishments of court integration efforts in a number of States have demonstrated that these problems can be met.

Unification of the criminal courts may place additional burdens on judges, prosecutors, and lawyers, and additional personnel may be required. More time and attention must be devoted to misdemeanor and petty offense cases by all participants in the administration of criminal justice. But the efficiency which will follow use of modern court administration and management techniques should help to meet some of these burdens. And implementation of proposals to reduce the volume of cases entering the criminal justice system by eliminating drunkenness and other offenses from the criminal law should also result in significant relief.

Inauguration of procedures to screen cases, for early diversion from the criminal process, and for referral to the appropriate social, medical, and psychiatric community services would free substantial resources now processing such cases through the criminal justice system. Other proposals of the Commission concerning court procedures should facilitate the processing of cases within a unified court system. Early assignment of counsel holds the promise of quantitative improvement in the disposition of offenders of the lower court: greater deliberation, more attention to procedural regularity, and careful sifting of evidence and of sentencing information.

Plea negotiations at as early a stage as possible in the proceedings and adoption of procedures for precharge conferences would focus the parties' attention on dispositional decisions at an early stage. Court business would be facilitated by scheduling more than one session each day for the initial appearance of defendants. This reform would enable the prompt arraignment of defendants, would permit the court's business to be spread over a longer period of the day with more time for each case, and would substantially reduce time lost for police witnesses. In most medium- and large-size cities the caseloads justify at least three sessions each day for initial appearances, one of which should be at night.

Communities may wish to experiment with the use of laymen to facilitate the initial processing of cases. Many arrested persons need information and advice on a variety of subjects — how to obtain a lawyer, what the charges are, and what the next steps in the proceeding are. These functions could be performed by a defendants' aide, a layman trained to provide basic information and advice and assigned to each precinct or a central detention point. This same person could be given the broader functions of conducting bail and indigency investigations. He might be an employee of a legal aid or public defender's office, or of a community social service agency or bail project. The services of a defendant's aide could help to speed the flow of cases through the courts by reducing the time required to process requests for assignment of counsel and to set the conditions of pretrial release.

## JUSTICE OF THE PEACE COURTS

Justice of the peace courts are the rural counterparts of the urban lower criminal courts. These courts developed in an era of slow transportation and communication to provide isolated small communities with a quick means of hearing minor criminal cases and exercising committing authority locally. But the conditions which gave rise to the development of justices' courts largely disappeared with the advent of modern means of travel and almost instantaneous communication. As a result, the lay-manned, fee-paid court is an anachronism.

Legal authorities, reform groups, and laymen long have drawn attention to deficiencies in justice of the peace courts. While some improvements have been made, there is pervasive evidence that substantial problems still must be solved in the operation of these courts and in the quality of justice they dispense.

As of 1965, in 32 of the 35 States in which the justice of the peace heard criminal cases or exercised committing authority, he was remunerated for his services by a fee or assessment against the parties depending upon the outcome or volume of litigation. In three States the justice still receives payment only when he convicts and collects his fee from the defendant, despite a Supreme Court decision 40 years ago holding such a practice unconstitutional.

Use of the fee system in justice courts has been condemned for years. Most authorities have agreed that it distorts the administration of justice. One writes:

> The primary evil . . . is the pressure it exerts on each justice who operates under it to get more business in order to enlarge his income . . . .
>
> . . . Most criminal complaints are made by officers exercising police powers. These officers naturally seek convictions, and would be expected to patronize justices who aid them in their efforts rather than those who insist too rigidly upon protecting the rights of the defendants. A sympathetic attitude toward the views of the police is therefore quite likely to result in more business and an increase in the justice's income.
>
> It is very common in all states where justices . . . compete for business, to find instances where the sheriff's office, or the state police, or any other agency engaged in enforcing the criminal law, take most or all of their cases to certain justices notwithstanding the

fact that other justices may be more conveniently accessible. In such cases it is difficult not to conclude that the favored justice renders service acceptable to the officers who bring in the business . . . .[24]

Reports from States in which justices are paid on an annual basis by the county or State for cases resulting in acquittal indicate that justices tend to convict to avoid having to wait for the county to pay. No matter what form of fee system is used, the public is unlikely to go beyond the fact that fees are collected and can draw only adverse conclusions from the fact.

Other widespread criticisms of the justice of the peace are that he lacks legal training and is ignorant of proper judicial procedure. Recent research indicates that the justice is not required to be a lawyer in all or some part of 34 States. In addition, there are indications that justices occasionally fail to carry out the requirements of due process and keep abreast of current developments in the law and that they sometimes have disregarded or failed to understand jurisdictional limitations.

Other defects in the justice-of-the-peace courts arise from the lack of supervision and control of their activities. Questionable practices may often go unchecked. One Maryland judge recently criticized local justices of the peace in these terms:

[They have] "treated some good, decent citizens like common criminals.

"The justice of the peace system is completely outmoded . . . If things keep going like they've been going, some of these people are going to get us into serious trouble. . . .

"[M]any of the JP's are just plain nasty to people.

"There have been all sorts of instances where they've been rude to people and when the person complains they tell him to 'go to see your congressman.'

"These people aren't controlled by us. They deny they have any connection with the police department. They tell the police to jump — and they tell us the same thing.

"It's time these people were put under us — or the Circuit Court — or somebody." [28]

The chaotic and disorganized nature of the system also makes difficult its improvement:

24. Sunderland, [A Study of the Justices of the Peace and Other Minor Courts, 21 Conn. B.J. 300, 331-34 (1947)]. . . .
28. Sentinel (Montgomery County, Md.), Feb. 17, 1966, § A, P. 3, col. 3.

[F]or the most part the individual justice works below the threshold of judicial visibility. His acts are very often discretionary in nature and are seldom subject to judicial review . . . . Moreover, the failure to maintain adequate records for all justices . . . means that the entire system is likewise obscure in its outline and workings.

[J]ustices who earn over 2500 dollars per annum are required to disclose their entire source of income from the discharge of their duties . . . . Those who earn less than 2500 dollars per annum must file a statement to that effect . . . . One official . . . estimates that less than 50% of the justices comply with this requirement. . . .

. . . No one knows exactly how many justices there are, how much aggregate income they receive, how many are active or inactive, or any of a host of other facts necessary for an intelligent appraisal of the system. . . .[29]

Because most of these courts are independent entities dependent on local financial resources, they are often unable to afford courtrooms, office facilities, or clerical assistance necessary for effective operation. In Montana one justice reportedly tried a case while repairing an automobile; another justice disposed of a case while sitting on a tractor during a pause from plowing his field. Where courtrooms are available, undignified and inconvenient physical conditions are the rule rather than the exception.

The unhealthy tendency to view these courts as local revenue-producing devices as well as the justice's political responsibility to a small area colors the quality of justice dispensed in these courts. It has often been noted that local offenders may have cases, usually traffic offenses, fixed in advance, while out-of-State defendants must pay the full fine or penalty.

### Remedying Deficiencies

The defects of justice of the peace courts are in large part inseparable from problems involving the rest of the lower courts. What is needed is a basic revision of the judicial system. Careful consideration should be given to replacing local justice of the peace courts with a small number of State district or county courts of limited jurisdiction, having a wide territorial basis, and manned by salaried, law-trained judges. All fees and fines should go to the State.

An outstanding example of progress is found in Illinois. The

29. [Virginia Comm. of Judicial Conference of Courts of Record to Study Problems of Justices of the Peace, Report to Judicial Council of Comm. of Circuit Judges, 30-31, 35-36 (1965).]

legislature abolished some 4,000 fee system courts and replaced them with circuit courts. Salaried magistrates, appointed by circuit judges, are limited in number to 207 (no more than 1 for each 35,000 of population). Ordinarily, magistrates must be legally trained and must serve full time.

Other States also have eliminated justice of the peace courts. Connecticut abolished JP courts and created a system of circuit courts which began operating in 1961. Circuit court judges are appointed by the Governor, must be admitted to the bar, and must serve full time. Maine replaced its justices with a State district court system in 1961.

While elimination of the traditional justice of the peace system is preferable, until that is accomplished, there are other steps that should be taken to improve the high quality justice where these courts are retained.

First, fee systems of compensation, no matter how remotely related to litigation, must be replaced. Many jurisdictions have already done so. During 1965 Delaware revised its laws to provide for payment of salaries instead of fees; some counties in Florida have abolished the fee system; in North Carolina all judicial officers performing the functions of justices of the peace will be salaried as of 1970.

Changing to a salary system is complicated by the large number of justices. Many justices hear too few cases to justify a reasonable salary. The fact that several States have managed to replace justices of the peace with a smaller number of full-time judges indicates that the number of justices can be decreased substantially. Unnecessary concentrations of justices of the peace should be eliminated.

Second, all persons exercising judicial functions should either be lawyers or be required to complete rigorous judicial training prior to assuming office. Several States have instituted such requirements. All New Jersey judicial officers attaining office after 1947 must be trained to practice law; Washington's legislature has provided that all judicial officeholders in the State's three largest counties must be attorneys. New York, Mississippi, and Iowa justices have been required to complete training courses of various types. While such courses may prove beneficial, to ensure a better quality of training and higher interest in the work performed, it is far preferable that judicial officers be lawyers.

Third, the justice of the peace courts should be administratively accountable to and under the supervision of the court system of the State. They should be required to keep records, and they should be provided with administrative help, with an administrative officer for a set of courts.

## Justice in Recorder's Court: An Analysis of Misdemeanor Cases in Detroit*

## Donald I. Warren

### I. THE COURT WATCHING SURVEY

The impetus for this study of the Recorder's Court in Detroit was the civil emergency during July of 1967 when thousands of arrested persons crowded the courts and created what was widely recognized as a crisis in due process of defendants. In the Annual Report of the Recorder's Court for 1967, it was stated:

> From Sunday July 23 to the following Sunday the court was virtually inundated with humanity.... There was considerable difficulty in keeping up with the heavy flow of requests for police records. The courts were arraigning defendants without benefit of knowledge of previous police records, therefore not knowing who or how bad an individual might be when we were arraigning. We instituted high bonds.... Members of the President's Civil Rights Commission ... arrived Monday night and virtually lived with us the entire two weeks.... They continually and constantly praised the Recorder's Court for the manner in which it was handling prisoners and cases [Annual Report, p. 4].

This report is dated January 15, 1968. The Report of the National Advisory Commission on Civil Disorders (the Kerner Report) came out on March 15, 1968. Here is what it had to say about Recorder's Court:

> In Detroit defendants where herded to arraignment in groups.... One thousand defendants were arraigned in a single day in the Detroit Recorder's Court (250 per six hour shift). There was little chance to screen out those cases that could best be handled out of court or which could not survive trial. Defense counsel were not

* From: Unpublished report prepared for the Equal Justice Council of Detroit (1971). Reprinted by permission of the author.

allowed to represent defendants at this stage in Detroit. Some judges failed to advise the defendants of their legal rights. After one group arraignment, a Detroit Judge told the next group of defendants, "You heard what I said to them. The same thing applies to you."

Trial and sentencing proved equally vulnerable to the tyranny of numbers. Sentences meted out during the riots tended to be harsher than in those cases disposed of later. Some judges in the early days of the riots openly stated that they would impose maximum penalties across the board as deterrents.... Circumstances of the arrest, past record, age, family responsibilities or other mitigating factors were not considered. The burden of this policy fell on the poorest defendants — those unable to raise bail — who agreed to immediate trials.... Once the riots were over, defendants were frequently sentenced to time already spent in detention, if they consented to plead guilty [Kerner Report, pp. 341, 343].

In the wake of what can only be termed a community disaster, the Interfaith Action Council and its subsidiary arm, the Justice Office — now the Equal Justice Council — were formed. This latter group was initially given the responsibility to start a program to place volunteer Court Watchers in Recorder's Court. Out of this effort has evolved a systematic survey of misdemeanor cases handled by that court. The central thrust of the current analysis grew out of emergency conditions. However, irrespective of the inequities attendant upon such circumstances as civil disorders, *the purpose of the present study is to look at the typical, normal, daily meting out of justice in Recorder's Court.*

To accomplish the goal of a sound and thorough analysis of the treatment of minority-group and low-income defendants in a court of justice, a program was initiated during the summer of 1969 to provide the data necessary to examine cases processed in Recorder's Court. The two-step process of court watching involves (a) training, and (b) systematic observing. During the months of July and August of 1969 a special questionnaire for Court Watchers was developed and tested which embodied the principle of objective reporting of court proceedings. A plan for the team or "buddy" approach to court watching was instituted. Here two volunteers work together, one person gathering information on the defendant and the other following details of the court proceedings. Without such a plan, the rapidity with which misdemeanor cases are handled and the fact that information about defendants is scant or unavailable would make any study of cases difficult if not impossible. In practically all respects this approach is totally unique. While court-watching programs exist in several cities around the country, all of them rely on the writing up of highly subjective reports by relatively untrained lay persons whose information cannot be correlated or summarized.

In September of 1969, our program of standardized coverage of individual cases began to operate. By the end of the year the program had fully evolved and continues at the present time. This paper reviews the findings of the period from September 1969 to August 1970. During this period, the Court Watcher teams — composed of up to 50 white and black volunteers — participated in the effort. A total of 3624 cases were sufficiently complete to be processed for analysis. Another 107 forms were insufficiently complete or contained major errors in their completion.

## II. RACE DIFFERENCES IN MISDEMEANOR CASES

Apart from describing the general setting within which cases are processed, the key job of the court watching project is the systematic recording of how each case was handled and with what result. One major dimension of this task involves race of the defendant as a determining factor. Table 1 illustrates that the type of charge brought against a defendant differed in several instances according to the race of the individual. We find, for example, that black defendants were more likely to be charged with simple larceny (value under $100) while white defendants were more likely to be charged with drunk and disorderly conduct. Firearms violations were more frequent for black defendants, assault and battery for white defendants. All told, one out of two cases observed dealt with simple larceny or drunk and disorderly conduct.

The reason for these differences cannot be addressed in this paper. Nor should any implication be made that the incidence of one type of alleged law violation is more prevalent for one racial group than another. Instead, we can say that over an eight-month period the cases observed by court watchers show the differences noted above. The cases heard in Recorder's Court may be very unrepresentative of crime in the community, but our sample is probably representative of the offenses for which different racial groups are likely to be brought to trial. We have a good cross section of cases handled by the court. As we shall see, the processing of these cases produced several important effects related to the race of the defendant.

Of the 3624 cases observed, 2570 involved black defendants and 985 involved white defendants. Another 69 cases where the race of the defendant was not clearly established have been omitted from our subsequent analysis.

*Sentencing: The Crucial Test*

Aside from the procedural protections that each defendant is entitled to, the most significant aspect of the judicial process is focused in the determination of punishment. Even if injustice might be tolerated in the preliminary steps of the legal system, the most basic measure of justice lies in the final disposition of each case. Let us now examine that issue. Table 2 [omitted] presents data on the sentencing patterns observed for black and white defendants. Three of the possible outcomes — a jail only sentence, a jail-fine combination sentence, or a probation sentence — involve either the actual or imminent taking away of the individual's freedom. Keeping this in mind, we find that for black defendants such a deprivation occurred in 86.0 percent of the sentences while for whites the comparable figure was 73.3 percent. In Chart 1 we can clearly observe the race differences in sentences where no loss of freedom was implicated in the outcome of the case. Whites were more than twice as likely to receive a suspended sentence as were blacks. They were one and one-half times as likely to receive

## TABLE 1
Type of Charge Brought Against Defendant

|  | Total % | % Black | % White |
|---|---|---|---|
| Simple larceny | 30.1 | 33.1 | 21.7 |
| Drunk and disorderly | 18.2 | 13.2 | 29.9 |
| Assault and battery | 9.9 | 9.3 | 11.7 |
| Firearms violations | 8.9 | 10.0 | 5.9 |
| Nonsupport | 8.3 | 10.1 | 3.8 |
| Accosting and soliciting | 7.4 | 7.3 | 7.8 |
| Engaged in an illegal occupation | 3.5 | 4.2 | 1.7 |
| Malicious destruction of property | 2.2 | 2.1 | 2.4 |
| Vagrancy | 2.2 | 1.2 | 4.5 |
| [Other] ... | [7.2] | [9.5] | [10.6] |
| Total | 99.9 | 100.0 | 100.0 |
|  | (N = 3624) | (N = 2570) | (N = 985) |

a psychiatric care sentence. The same ratio held in regard to a fine only sentence.

Let us now examine the size of fines and the length of jail terms as they relate to the race of the defendant. Table 3 shows the pattern for jail sentences — 57.9 percent of black defendants compared to 46.9 percent of white defendants received a sentence of 100 days or longer. In Chart 2 we observe the pattern for the dollar value of fines and length of jail sentence. In both instances the differences of 5.5 percent and 10.0 percent respectively are statistically significant, that is, not due to chance factors of the sample of defendants.

Turning now to the matter of setting bail, we find that where the trial had been adjourned 39.4 percent of the white defendants but only 24.8 percent of the black defendants had bond set at under $1000. . . .

### III. ROLE OF DEFENSE COUNSEL

One of the issues most focused upon in dealing with the problem of adequate justice in lower courts is the presence and quality of defense counsel. In the cases analyzed, we find that an attorney was present 22.2 percent of the time. No difference by race of the defendant occurred in this pattern. These findings clearly suggest the problem of having defendants represented either in preliminary hearings or at their trial.

With regard to the important issue of how a defendant pleads, we find that the role of the attorney is a major one. Thus, where

### TABLE 3
#### Length of Jail Sentence in Relation to Race of Defendant

|  | % Black | % White | Total % |
|---|---|---|---|
| 1-29 days | 13.7 | 16.7 | 14.5 |
| 30-59 days | 17.3 | 21.3 | 17.9 |
| 60-99 days | 11.1 | 15.1 | 12.0 |
| 100-399 days | 45.7 | 38.8 | 44.3 |
| 400 days or more | 12.2 | 8.1 | 11.3 |
| Total | 100.0 | 100.0 | 100.0 |
|  | (N = 1615) | (N = 519) | (N = 2134) |

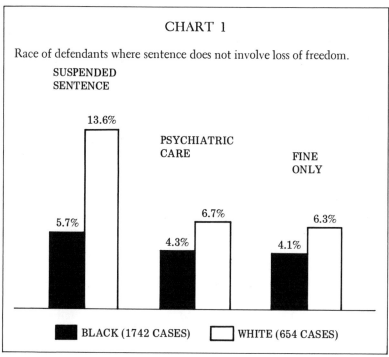

**CHART 1**

Race of defendants where sentence does not involve loss of freedom.

SUSPENDED
SENTENCE

13.6%

PSYCHIATRIC
CARE

FINE
ONLY

5.7%

6.7%

6.3%

4.3%

4.1%

■ BLACK (1742 CASES) □ WHITE (654 CASES)

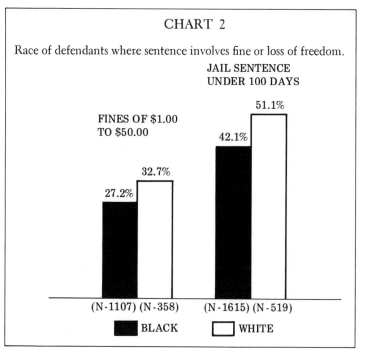

**CHART 2**

Race of defendants where sentence involves fine or loss of freedom.

JAIL SENTENCE
UNDER 100 DAYS

51.1%

FINES OF $1.00
TO $50.00

42.1%

32.7%

27.2%

(N-1107) (N-358)   (N-1615) (N-519)

■ BLACK   □ WHITE

a black defendant lacked counsel a plea of guilty occurred 59.8 percent of the time compared to 25.2 percent where counsel was present. For whites the figures were 71.1 percent and 23.5 percent respectively. For a white defendant a "not guilty" plea was twice as often entered where an attorney was present.

A defendant may enter an automatic "not guilty" plea by standing mute (and thereby not be required to have his own remarks entered as required testimony). Both black and white defendants did so several times more often where there was an attorney in the case. . . .

What about the verdict in each case? What differences occur with an attorney representing the defendant? Table 5 contains the relevant information. For blacks, a "not guilty" verdict occurred three times as often if defense was present. For whites the ratio was 5 to 1. Dismissal of cases was twice as frequent for whites when an attorney was present. The difference for black defendants was even more pronounced: 6.2 percent with an attorney, only 2.4 percent without an attorney. Quite clearly, then, having an attorney changes both the original plea as well as the final verdict rendered by the judge.

Now let us examine the sentencing patterns where defense counsel was present or absent. Table 6 shows the pattern of race differences when no attorney was available — the fact in nearly four out of five misdemeanor cases. Whites received a suspended sentence twice as often as blacks, psychiatric care one and one-half times as often. At the same time whites received a jail only sen-

TABLE 5
Verdict in Relation to Race of Defendant
and Presence of Defense Counsel

|  | % Black | | % White | |
|---|---|---|---|---|
|  | Attorney | No Attorney | Attorney | No Attorney |
| Guilty as charged | 59.3 | 73.1 | 59.2 | 74.6 |
| Guilty of lesser offense | 1.3 | 2.1 | 1.0 | 1.2 |
| Not guilty | 11.4 | 3.7 | 12.2 | 2.7 |
| Case dismissed | 6.2 | 2.4 | 4.6 | 2.7 |
| Not stated | 21.8 | 18.7 | 23.0 | 18.7 |
|  | (N = 546) | (N = 1735) | (N = 196) | (N = 657) |

tence more often than blacks. Taking the three sentences involving loss of freedom for a defendant, the proportions were 85.1 percent for blacks without an attorney and only 72.6 percent for whites.

Now let us see the pattern where an attorney was present.

In Table 7 we find that loss of freedom occurred 87.1 percent of the time for blacks, 76.3 percent for whites. Examination of the jail only sentence shows that *even with an attorney* blacks were more than twice as likely to receive such a sentence but half as likely to be given a psychiatric care determination. The fine only sentence was given to 13.6 percent of the white defendants with an attorney compared to only 8.5 percent of the blacks with counsel.

The patterns we have noted indicate that the presence of counsel does not affect race differences, although it does alter the severity of sentencing in general. In Chart 4 the fine only sentence is depicted and shows that for both racial groups having an attorney increased the chances of receiving this type of sentence.

Chart 5 [omitted] shows what occurred in the absence of counsel in terms of the amount of fines and length of jail sentences. Nearly twice as many white defendants received a fine of $25 or less compared to black defendants. A smaller but similar difference occurred with jail sentences of less than sixty days.

IV. THE DUAL HANDICAPS: RACE AND CLASS

We have already indicated the important role which the race of defendant plays in the procedures and outcome of misdemeanor cases in Recorder's Court. In addition, the indicator of social posi-

TABLE 6
Type of Sentence in Relation to Race of Defendant
Where Counsel Is Not Present

|  | % Black Defendant Without a Lawyer | % White Defendant Without a Lawyer |
|---|---|---|
| Probation | 50.5 | 35.5 |
| Jail only | 18.6 | 24.7 |
| Fine or jail | 16.0 | 12.4 |
| Fine | 3.1 ⎫ | 4.4 ⎫ |
| Suspended sentence | 7.1 ⎬14.8 | 16.3 ⎬27.3 |
| Psychiatric care | 4.6 ⎭ | 6.6 ⎭ |
|  | (N = 1304) | (N = 498) |

tion based on type of attire in court has been shown to be a source of discrimination. Is it possible to conclude that racial bias is only economic bias in disguise?

In Detroit, misdemeanor cases cannot be analyzed using a direct measure of a defendant's economic or occupational status, the approach of comparing the effects of social class. Records are scant and access by court watchers would require a research effort not now in existence. The only way to assess economic bias is through the appearance of the defendant in court. In many respects this is the only information the court itself employs. To obtain relatively objective evidence of economic discrimination, the questionnaire form employed by observers stipulated a set of categories of male and female dress. *Only one out of seven cases involved a defendant appearing in middle-class attire — coat and tie.* Over one third of all defendants appeared in clothing fitting the definition of "work clothes." The remainder were classified as wearing "sport clothes."

Since most blacks who come to court are in a low-income category, are they merely — along with poor whites — the victims of social class inequities? To examine this question we have analyzed cases of male defendants separated according to *both* their race and type of dress in court. In Chart 6 we have presented such an analysis for male defendants in terms of sentencing involving no loss of freedom. *Low-status clothing meant a greater chance of a jail sentence for both blacks and whites compared to sport clothes or a coat and tie. However, the greatest probability of*

TABLE 7

Type of Sentence in Relation to Race of Defendant
Where Counsel Is Present

|  | % Black Defendant With a Lawyer | % White Defendant With a Lawyer |
|---|---|---|
| Probation | 50.5 | 49.2 |
| Jail only | 13.3 | 5.9 |
| Fine or jail | 23.3 | 21.2 |
| Fine | 8.5 ⎤ | 13.6 ⎤ |
| Suspended sentence | 1.2 ⎬13.0 | 1.7 ⎬22.8 |
| Psychiatric care | 3.3 ⎦ | 8.5 ⎦ |
|  | (N = 331) | (N = 118) |

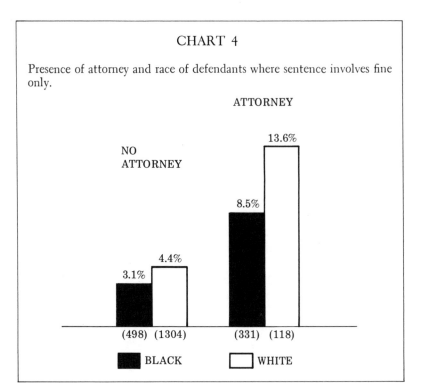

# CHART 4

Presence of attorney and race of defendants where sentence involves fine only.

ATTORNEY

NO
ATTORNEY

13.6%

8.5%

4.4%

3.1%

(498) (1304)     (331) (118)

■ BLACK     ☐ WHITE

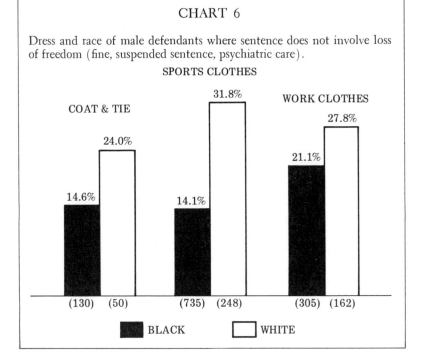

# CHART 6

Dress and race of male defendants where sentence does not involve loss of freedom (fine, suspended sentence, psychiatric care).

SPORTS CLOTHES

COAT & TIE

WORK CLOTHES

31.8%

27.8%

24.0%

21.1%

14.6%     14.1%

(130) (50)     (735) (248)     (305) (162)

■ BLACK     ☐ WHITE

*receiving the sentence of jail was for the low-status black defendant: in one out of two instances he received a jail or jail-fine sentence. The best situation was the white defendant wearing sport clothes — he was given a comparable sentence only one out of five times.*

*We find that even where the black individual was wearing middle-class attire — coat and tie — he was three times less likely to get a fine only sentence than his white counterpart. In the case of sport clothes, black defendants were half as likely to get a fine only sentence compared to similarly dressed whites. And finally, in the case of work clothes whites were three times more likely than blacks to get a fine only sentence.* Note that both whites and blacks suffer a form of class discrimination. But for blacks this is not merely something which reflects economic position, but it is added to what is purely racial discrimination in sentencing. In other words, the black male defendant is a victim of a double dosage of injustice.

Whites dressed in coat and tie were nearly twice as likely to receive a sentence involving a fine, suspended sentence, or psychiatric care as blacks with the same attire. In the case of defendants in sport clothes the race difference was even larger. Only in the instance of persons appearing in court in work clothes did the race difference narrow. Quite clearly, then, the handicap of class is not the reason that blacks receive different sentences.

Chart 7 [omitted] shows the same analysis for female defendants as we have described for male defendants. Once again, we find that a race factor was present and separate from the dress factor. In fact, what both the male and female sentence analyses show is that the role of race is greater than that of dress.

### V. PATTERNS OF SENTENCING BY RACE AND CLASS FOR SPECIFIC TYPES OF CHARGES AGAINST DEFENDANTS

While much of our discussion has shown patterns for the total number of cases observed in our analysis, it is possible to raise the objection that no race or class differences are present once we are focusing on a specific type of criminal offense. We know from Table 1 that black defendants were more often brought before Recorder's Court on simple larceny charges than were whites. Likewise, whites were much more frequently charged with drunk and disorderly conduct. Can it be valid to compare whites and blacks unless we are examining their treatment on the same charge?

In this section of the report, we shall analyze the most frequently brought charges in order to determine if the class and race differences we have previously noted are present when the type of offense is identical.

Let us begin our review with the most frequently noted charge against defendants in the 3624 cases, that of simple larceny. Taking the sentencing of whites versus blacks, we find in Chart 8 [omitted] a striking confirmation of race differentials discussed earlier. Blacks were more than twice as likely as whites to be given a jail only sentence for simple larceny. By contrast whites were more than twice as likely to receive a fine only sentence. In terms of a suspended sentence, none of the 365 blacks were given this disposition while 3.5 percent of the whites received such a sentence.

If we introduce the factor of defendant dress, we can again determine for a specific type of charge whether differential treatment was occurring. Chart 9 reflects the dual role of race and class when the sentencing in a case is a jail only alternative. We find that black defendants for each type of attire grouping were substantially more likely to receive such a sentence than whites. Moreover, the lower the status of the clothing worn by a black defendant, the more likely was a sentence of jail only to be given. A similar trend occurred for white defendants in regard to the coat and tie versus sport clothes comparison.

Turning to the second most frequent charge — drunk and disorderly conduct — we find racial and dress differences in sentencing are somewhat attenuated. Taking those alternatives in punishment where no loss of freedom is implied, the following pattern occurs: 64.5 percent of the white defendants in coat and tie and 55.5 percent of the similarly attired black defendants received such sentences; with sports clothes, 58.4 percent of the whites and 47.6 percent of the blacks were given this type of sentence; but for persons in work clothes, 35.4 percent of the whites and 42.5 percent of the blacks received such sentences. As in the case of simple larceny, both dress and race differences occurred — whites and higher-status-appearing defendants generally were given more desirable types of punishment. Table 8 contains the full sentencing pattern.

When assault and battery cases are analyzed, we see from Table 9 that the role of race and dress follows the trends of simple larceny and drunk and disorderly conduct. Taking, for instance, defendants appearing in sport clothes, we find that 25.3 percent of the black defendants compared to only 3.8 percent of the white defendants received a jail only sentence. Table 9 also shows whites

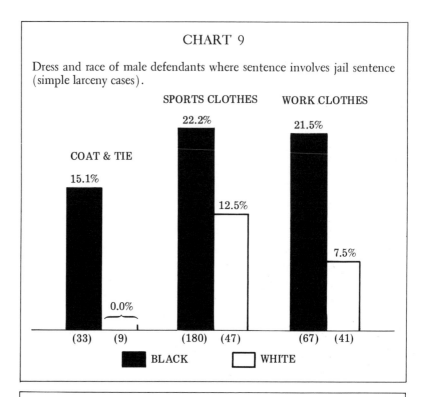

**CHART 9**

Dress and race of male defendants where sentence involves jail sentence (simple larceny cases).

SPORTS CLOTHES    WORK CLOTHES

22.2%    21.5%

COAT & TIE

15.1%

12.5%

7.5%

0.0%

(33)  (9)    (180)  (47)    (67)  (41)

■ BLACK    □ WHITE

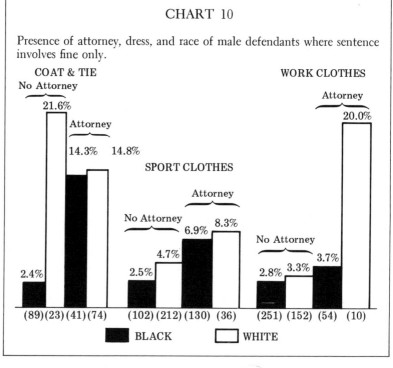

**CHART 10**

Presence of attorney, dress, and race of male defendants where sentence involves fine only.

COAT & TIE    WORK CLOTHES
No Attorney                                    Attorney

21.6%                                          20.0%

Attorney

14.3%  14.8%
                SPORT CLOTHES

                        Attorney

            No Attorney    6.9%  8.3%

                    4.7%                    No Attorney    3.7%
2.4%        2.5%                    2.8%  3.3%

(89)(23)(41)(74)    (102)(212)(130)(36)    (251)(152)(54)(10)

■ BLACK    □ WHITE

## TABLE 8
### Sentencing Pattern for Drunk and Disorderly Conduct by Race and Dress of Male Defendant

|  | % Coat and Tie | | % Sport Clothes | | % Work Clothes | |
| --- | --- | --- | --- | --- | --- | --- |
|  | Black | White | Black | White | Black | White |
| Fine only | 0.0 | 44.4 | 3.0 | 2.2 | 1.0 | 2.9 |
| Jail only | 0.0 | 9.1 | 19.8 | 22.5 | 22.0 | 41.7 |
| Fine or jail | 22.2 | 26.4 | 17.8 | 12.4 | 23.2 | 13.3 |
| Probation | 22.2 | 0.0 | 14.9 | 6.7 | 12.1 | 9.6 |
| Psychiatric care | 11.1 | 0.0 | 3.0 | 7.9 | 6.1 | 2.9 |
| Suspended sentence | 44.1 | 26.4 | 41.6 | 48.3 | 35.4 | 29.6 |
|  | (N = 17) | (N = 11) | (N = 147) | (N = 126) | (N = 151) | (N = 145) |

## TABLE 9
### Sentencing Pattern for Assault and Battery
### by Race and Dress of Male Defendant

| | % Coat and Tie | | % Sport Clothes | | % Work Clothes | |
|---|---|---|---|---|---|---|
| | Black | White | Black | White | Black | White |
| Fine only | 0.0 | —* | 3.8 | 11.5 | 0.0 | 5.0 |
| Jail only | 0.0 | — | 25.3 | 3.8 | 11.5 | 5.0 |
| Fine or jail | 21.7 | — | 5.1 | 3.8 | 11.5 | 0.0 |
| Probation | 78.3 | — | 57.0 | 69.2 | 57.7 | 65.0 |
| Psychiatric care | 0.0 | — | 8.9 | 11.5 | 15.4 | 15.0 |
| Suspended sentence | 0.0 | — | 0.0 | 0.0 | 3.8 | 10.0 |
| | (N = 14) | (N = 6) | (N = 121) | (N = 49) | (N = 39) | (N = 33) |

* Less than 10 cases.

regardless of clothing type more often received a fine only sentence or a suspended sentence.

Table 10 contains an analysis of dress and race in regard to firearm violations. Whites in sport clothes received a fine only sentence 13.0 percent of the time compared to 2.5 percent for black defendants similarly dressed. While 13.4 percent of the white defendants in work clothes received a sentence not involving loss of freedom, blacks in the same attire received a similar sentence only 7.2 percent of the time.

In each of the five specific charges we have analyzed, the patterns of both social class and race differences in sentencing have appeared. The higher status of attire, the less severe the sentence. A black defendant in general receives a more punitive sentence than his similarly dressed white counterpart.

One additional question that might be raised to explain the role of defendant dress and race is to argue that both factors result in different sentencing because better-dressed defendants are likely to have an attorney. Granted this bias, it might still be argued that having defense counsel eradicates class or race bias. In Chart 10 we can assess this argument. Taking persons with high-status attire — coat and tie — we find that receiving a fine only sentence increases sharply if the defendant is black and has an attorney. If the defendant is white, the role of the attorney is to reduce the probability of such a sentence. In cases of defendants in sport clothes and work clothes, a fine only sentence was least likely when the defendant was black and lacked an attorney, but it was greatest when the defendant was white and had defense counsel.

### VI. SUMMARY OF FINDINGS

The following patterns emerged from the case sample analyzed.

1. In sentencing, black defendants were found to be half as likely to receive a sentence of fine only, suspended sentence, or pyschiatric care compared to white defendants.

2. In the dollar amount of fines and the length of jail sentences, black defendants were significantly more likely than white defendants to receive a longer jail term and a higher dollar fine.

3. In the case of adjourned cases, black defendants were nearly twice as likely as white defendants to be released on a bond of $1000 or more.

## TABLE 10
### Sentencing Pattern for Firearms Violations
### by Race and Dress of Male Defendant

| | % Coat and Tie | | % Sport Clothes | | % Work Clothes | |
|---|---|---|---|---|---|---|
| | Black | White | Black | White | Black | White |
| Fine only | 3.7 | 12.5 | 2.5 | 13.0 | 3.6 | 6.7 |
| Jail only | 7.4 | 0.0 | 7.6 | 13.0 | 7.1 | 6.7 |
| Fine or jail | 25.9 | 25.0 | 41.8 | 56.5 | 42.9 | 33.3 |
| Probation | 63.0 | 50.0 | 45.6 | 13.0 | 42.9 | 46.6 |
| Psychiatric care | 0.0 | 12.5 | 2.5 | 4.3 | 3.6 | 6.7 |
| Suspended sentence | 0.0 | 0.0 | 0.0 | 0.0 | 0.0 | 0.0 |
| | (N = 28) | (N = 7) | (N = 81) | (N = 20) | (N = 28) | (N = 16) |

4. Defendants were represented by counsel in somewhat more than one of five cases analyzed.

5. Misdemeanor cases where there was defense counsel were more likely to be of longer duration — five or six times more frequently lasting ten minutes or longer.

6. For both black and white defendants, the absence of defense counsel meant a two and one-half times greater probability of entering a plea of "guilty." A plea of automatic "not guilty" by standing mute occurred overwhelmingly where a defense counsel was present.

7. For both black and white defendants, the presence of counsel reduced the probability that a sentence would involve actual or potential loss of freedom either in terms of jail or probation punishments.

8. Where an attorney was present, blacks had twice the probability of receiving a jail only sentence and half the probability of a psychiatric care sentence compared to whites. A fine only sentence occurred one and one-half times more often for the white defendant with an attorney than for a black defendant with counsel.

9. In the absence of counsel, nearly twice as many white defendants received a fine sentence for an amount of $25 or less than did black defendants. A smaller differential occurred regarding the length of jail sentences.

10. In the instances of the adjournment of a case, defendants — both black and white — who had defense counsel were less likely to be given a surety bail.

11. A black defendant without a lawyer received a jail only sentence three times as often as a white defendant with a lawyer. At the same time, the fine only sentence was given four times as often to a white defendant with a lawyer than to a black defendant without defense counsel.

12. For the specific charge of simple larceny, black male defendants and persons dressed in low-status attire received sub-

stantially more frequent sentences of loss of freedom, including jail only determinations.

13. For the charges of drunk and disorderly conduct, assault and battery, and firearms violations, male defendants who were black and who appeared in low-status attire received more severe sentences than other defendants.

## VII. BASIC CONCLUSIONS

The analysis of 3624 cases of misdemeanor charges reveals that the problems facing Recorder's Court are of two types: (1) biases of a class and race nature which can be attributed to the individual prejudices of judges or other judicial officials; and (2) institutional racism — the effects of particular rules, legal philosophies, or principles which tend to produce race or class discrimination without the direct influence of individual attitudes.

In the first category, it would seem that the significant differences between individual judges noted in our preliminary report can be seen as individual racism. This is not necessarily associated with the race of the judge himself. Therefore, attitudes may be held by a white or black judge which accept certain stereotypes of a race or class variety. To a very great extent, our report suggests that the problem is still a major one in the courtroom and must be viewed at the individual level. Certainly the differences linked to the attire of the defendant fall into this category.

Equally as important, and perhaps even more difficult to confront and deal with, is the institutional racism which is reflected in sentencing, bonding, and availability of quality defense counsel to defendants charged with crimes. Our analysis shows a persistent and pervasive pattern of differential sentencing based on the available penalties in the law and the response of the judicial system to individual problems of alcoholism, mental illness, and marital problems which constitute a major part of the misdemeanor case load in Recorder's Court.

# PART V.
# ALTERNATIVE MODELS:
# THE PARENTAL FUNCTION
# AND DISPUTE RESOLUTION

The formal model of the criminal justice process holds that the system disposes of cases through an adversarial confrontation between state and accused, presided over by a neutral judge. The reality, as we have seen in preceding sections, is extensive elements of exchange, bargaining, and cooperation in a conflict-oriented setting. Where the adversary model prevails, the balance is heavily weighted against the poor, non-white defendant. The lower court judge, in short, often does not adjudicate, but rather compromises, teaches, or reconciles the parties before him. Or, he ratifies the compromise reached by prosecutor and defendant.

Relinquishing the strict adversary posture may in certain cases enhance the fairness of outcomes, and optimize the impact of proceedings for all parties. In other instances, deviation from a formal adversarial role is the central vice of the lower court. Other cultures, however, are less committed to formalistic procedures; their wide experience with informal modes of conflict resolution suggests the important benefits for human values of explicitly cooperative arrangements. The American juvenile court movement is the most noteworthy example of a similar effort within our own system. This section explores the significance of nonadversarial models of adjudication for lower courts, a theme partially continued in Part VI.

John Griffiths' critique of the adversary or "battle" model, to use his term, shows the conceptual and practical limitations that flow from a narrow conception of the criminal process. Viewed and operated as a reconciling or communitarian enterprise, a court may deal more successfully with crime and succeed in integrating the offender into the social system. Griffiths argues that individual rights will still be protected in such a "family model." As an exercise in demystification, his article is essential to an understanding of the criminal process.

The same issue is then explored in Joel Handler's account of proposals to judicialize the juvenile court, a forum which deliberately avoided the adversary approach to focus on total welfare of the child and to work toward his best interests. The experiment failed and the revisionists are now in command. Since Handler's article, the Supreme Court has judicialized extensively the juvenile court.* But the switch to an adversary approach, as Handler argues, produces trade-offs. Technical and administrative factors may prevent judicialization in practice, as several studies of the impact of In re Gault have shown. When successful, sterile formalism may conflict with individual welfare.

Lon Fuller's classic discussion of role moralities — the morality of arbitration (or adjudication) and the morality of mediation — shows the demands imposed by the primary roles fulfilled by the lower court judge. While mediation or conciliation has distinct advantages in restoring harmony, pitfalls await the judge who switches roles in the same case, or who eschews too quickly the ordained role of adjudicator.

The final two pieces present a comparative perspective on the resolution of disputes through greater community participation. In Jesse Berman's account of lower Cuban courts under socialism, and in James Gibbs, Jr.'s analysis of Kpelle moots, the relation of the court to the community becomes all-important. In Cuba the court is a neighborhood affair. Highly decentralized, staffed by lay people, and attended faithfully by neighbors who often offer evidence spontaneously, the court reinforces community norms and disciplines while reintegrating or maintaining the parties in the social fabric. Similarly, in Liberia the Kpelle have devised a way of resolving disputes which depends on strong family and community bonds to reconcile the parties to a conflict. From these solutions the relevance of conciliatory, nonadversarial techniques operating more openly than the cooperative features of lower courts is made clear, though their workability in a less communal society is open to question.

---

* In re Gault, 378 U.S. 1 (1967), held that juveniles are entitled to the fundamental fairness required by due process of law, including the right to notice of charges, the right to be represented by counsel, the right against self-incrimination, and the right to confront and cross-examine witnesses. Proof beyond a reasonable doubt was also required. In re Winship, 397 U.S. 358 (1970). However, the Court has recently held that juveniles are not constitutionally entitled to jury trials. McKiever v. Pennsylvania, 403 U.S. 528 (1971).

# Ideology in Criminal Procedure, or
# A Third "Model" of the Criminal Process*

## John Griffiths

American thought about criminal procedure is confined within a prevailing ideology. By describing an alternative, I shall seek to illustrate that our present assumptions are not the inevitable truths they often seem to be. The alternative presented is not especially novel, nor is it one to which I necessarily subscribe. My purpose is merely to explore the problem of ideology in criminal procedure, and to that end the self-conscious posing of an alternative is justified by its heuristic value.

### I. HERBERT PACKER'S "TWO MODELS OF THE CRIMINAL PROCESS"

As the title of this article will have suggested to those familiar with Herbert Packer's "Two Models of the Criminal Process," † it is my point of departure. Packer's article nicely represents the fundamental underlying ideology of American thought. It is largely by way of contrast with Packer's implicit ideological assumptions that I will formulate an alternative ideology. . . .

### B. The Contents of Packer's Theory

The poles are the "two separate value systems that compete for priority in the operation of the criminal process." Packer calls them "models" — the "Crime Control Model" and the "Due Process Model." They are the "extremes" of the spectrum of possible choice in criminal procedure, and one is led to anticipate that they will reflect assumptions about "the uses of power" which differ as widely as the imaginations of human beings have been fertile, and their convictions deep, on the place and use of power in society. *The Crime Control Model* "is based on the proposition that the repression of criminal conduct is by far the most important function to be performed by the criminal process." "Criminal conduct" must be kept under "tight control" in order to preserve "public

---

\* From: 79 Yale L.J. 359-369, 371-376, 380-386, 410-417 (1971). Reprinted by permission of the Yale Law Journal Company, Fred B. Rothman & Company, and the author.

† See Part II *supra*.

order." The primary concern is efficiency. The process "must produce a high rate of apprehension and conviction," and must therefore place "a premium on speed and finality." It should "throw ... off at an early stage those cases in which it appears unlikely that the person apprehended is an offender and then secure, as expeditiously as possible, the conviction of the rest ...." To this end, a quick, accurate, and efficient administrative fact-finding role carried out by police and prosecutors should predominate over slow, inefficient, and less accurate judicial trials; and interference with this administrative process should be kept to an absolute minimum so as not to compromise "the dominant goal of repressing crime."

*The Due Process Model* seems radically different. Its system of values revolves around "the concept of the primacy of the individual and the complementary concept of limitation on official power." Because of its potency in subjecting the individual to the coercive power of the state, "the criminal process must ... be subjected to controls that prevent it from operating at maximal efficiency." "Power is always subject to abuse," and the Due Process Model "implements ... anti-authoritarian values" by limiting state power over an accused in the criminal process. This central thrust is complemented by a skepticism about the reliability of uncontrolled administrative fact-finding and a general intolerance of any significant margin of error — again, denying to efficiency in "repressing crime" a predominating position among relevant considerations. The main incidents of a central concern for limiting power and protecting against its abuses are: the concept of legal guilt and the corollary presumption of innocence; the conception of the criminal process as an appropriate forum for the correction of its own abuses; and the insistence upon the state's duty to ensure that an accused is not deprived by poverty of the capacity effectively to invoke the protections which the process must afford.

Given the scope of Packer's claims, one might expect that the two Models would be developed with considerable depth and rigor, but the brief summary I have given in fact encompasses virtually all that Packer has to say about them. The reason for this is critical to an understanding of his theory. For Packer, the Models seem to be defined primarily by their relationship to each other. Their contents are determined by the nature of that relationship, rather than the other way around. It is the essential fact of tension between two diametrically opposed reactions that the relationship of the state to the individual can elicit which sets the problem of criminal procedure, and thereby defines the Models. For the Crime Control Model, the problem is effective protection of society as a whole from the threat of a breakdown of law and order posed by unrepressed criminal activities. The concern of the Due Process Model is with the need to protect individuals caught up in the criminal process from the coercive, easily abused power of society. Each Model, in its polar form, subordinates other considerations to its central, animating conception of the problem. Criminal procedure as it is, and also as it might be, is determined by a selection from among the possibilities for compromise located on the spectrum between the two polar Models.

The "functional approach" is by now so ingrained that at least a genuflection toward "substance" is mandatory in any discussion of "procedure." Thus one instinctively wonders what relationship there might be between the two Models and the range of possible substantive functions of the criminal law. At the outset of his article, Packer describes its "major premise": "that the shape of the criminal process has an important bearing on questions about the wise substantive use of the criminal sanction." He wants to limit the ends of the process so that the means will be able to be subservient — so that the process will not be overburdened or put to tasks for which it is unsuited. But one will search his essay in vain for the suggestion that substantive functions should have any role whatsoever in the making of procedural choices or that the substantive functions of the process include anything more than enforcement of prohibitions. One would suppose, nevertheless, that procedure has no independent, intrinsic value, and that the more fundamental relationship runs from substantive functions to procedural techniques; it is wise to suggest that we build the sort of houses for which the available materials are suitable, but it is surely even wiser to insist that we look for materials suited to the kinds of houses we wish to build.

I think there are three explanations for Packer's strange lack of interest in what the process, after all, is all about. First, his attention is so dominated by his "major premise" — the need to put fewer and more narrowly defined demands on the process — that he is simply not concerned about the more fundamental reverse relationship of means to ends. Second, he takes the *general* substantive functions of the criminal law (i.e. those common to all crimes) as pretty well fixed; elsewhere he argues that "[t]he function of the criminal sanction is to help prevent or reduce socially undesirable conduct through the detection, apprehension, prosecution, and punishment of offenders. This is the only function that its rationale permits . . . ." If the general substantive function can be treated as given, I suppose it follows that an analytic structure for dealing with choice about process need not make room for other kinds of possible functions. Both of these explanations are perfectly reasonable so long as the limitations they imply are kept clearly in mind.

The third explanation is especially interesting. Packer's sentence, begun above, continues: "[The detection, apprehension, prosecution and punishment of offenders] is the only function that its rationale permits *and this is the only function with which its processes are adequately equipped to deal.*" Here we can clearly see the ideological limits within which his conception of two Models is confined: despite his intention to lay bare the entire spectrum of procedural possibility, the two Models in fact give us only that which is relevant to a particular and limited conception of the substantive function of criminal law — prevention and retribution. Packer does this not only because he thinks that function is substantively fixed, but also because he has made an initial judgment that the criminal process is intrinsically unsuited to any other. Starting with narrow assumptions about both procedural and substantive possibilities, Packer is easily led to a unidimensional conception of the total range of procedural choice.

The prejudicial impact of Packer's initial assumptions appears, to give a single instance, in his off-hand characterization of the Due Process Model's protections as impairing the "efficiency" of the process. These protections can only be deemed simply "inefficient" if the values they serve are not included among the substantive goals of the criminal process. It might be, for example, that the privilege against self-incrimination serves rehabilitative ends; if one of our substantive goals were rehabilitation, the privilege could hardly then be described, without qualification, as making for an "inefficient" process. If we believe the substantive criminal law should be designed to minimize social interference in the lives of citizens, many of the protections of the Due Process Model, far from being compromises with the interest in "efficiency," may be essential to it.

## II. A THIRD "MODEL" OF THE CRIMINAL PROCESS

### A. *Packer Has Given Us Only One "Model" — the Battle Model*

A single unifying conception underlies Packer's two Models, despite the fact that he presents them as diametrically opposed. He derives the two Models from the alternative responses he conceives to the problem of the relationship of the state to the individual in the criminal process; and the unarticulated major premise of his article is that the essential nature of that problem is such as to permit only two, polar responses.

The basic object of the criminal process is "to put a suspected criminal in jail," as he puts it at one point. In the service of this fundamental dogma, Packer consistently portrays the criminal process as a struggle — a stylized war — between two contending forces whose interests are implacably hostile: the Individual (particularly, the *accused* individual) and the State. His two Models are nothing more than alternative derivations from that conception of profound and irreconcilable disharmony of interest. Since the metaphor of battle roughly suits this silent premise about the nature of the relationship of state and individual reflected in the criminal process, I shall use it to characterize Packer's position: the Battle Model of the criminal process.

Since one or the other party to a process for settling disputes between irreconcilables must win in every case, the crucial question for criminal procedure so conceived is what bias to build into the rules. This is where Packer's Models differ. The Crime Control Model reflects a primary concern with the threat which individuals pose to the general social order and welfare; accordingly, it is designed to protect society by favoring it as much as possible through the rules of battle. The Due Process Model represents the alternative reaction to the assumed state of irreconcilability — an inclination to offset state power in the battle by providing rules as favorable as possible to an accused. Packer characterizes the processes required by his two Models as resembling, respectively, an "assembly line" and an "obstacle course" in their approach to the common goal of putting a suspected criminal in jail. Given his unarticulated, unifying assumption of unyielding disharmony, the process can vary fundamentally only from the pole at which one party is most favored to the pole at which the other party is most favored. What he gives us is a single Battle Model with two possibilities of bias.

The achievement of Packer's article, then, is neatly and methodically to have laid out the differences which animate current debate over the criminal process within the context of an implicitly agreed-upon ideological premise which unites it. While it does not seem feasible to *demonstrate* that the ideological underpinnings of Packer's position are generally shared, it will be helpful at least to illustrate the point briefly.

First, rhetoric is revealing. There are many trite turns of phrase which give away a writer's underlying ideology. One has found an instance of the Battle Model when he comes across the process

conceived as a "battle" or "fight" or "duel," with any of the associated military terms: the defense counsel is a "champion of
the accused" (or a "hired gun"); the defendant is the "target" of
the criminal process; to confess is to "surrender"; the initial police
warning before a suspect makes incriminating statements serves
as a "declaration of war"; the defense must not be precluded, by
procedural rules which give "tactical advantages" to the prosecution, from a fair opportunity to "muster" its forces or "marshal"
its proofs; the judge's role is "to see that the battle is fought according to law." . . .

### B. An Altogether Different Conception of the Criminal Process — the Family Model

If Packer's article rests not upon two but upon a single, albeit
unarticulated, basic conception of the nature of criminal process
— that it is a battleground of fundamentally hostile forces, where
the only relevant variable is the "balance of advantage" — we can
expand the conceptual (and perhaps the practical) possibilities
available to us if we create another fundamental conception to
substitute for it. It may well be that there are many possibilities,
but we can do a great deal even while confining ourselves to the
simple opposite of Packer's ideological starting point. He assumes
disharmony, fundamentally irreconcilable interests, a state of war.
We can start from an assumption of reconcilable — even mutually
supportive — interests, a state of love.

Of course, it is easy to react reflexively that such an ideological
premise is utopian, or confused, or absurd. Like Packer, I make no
claim of direct applicability for my alternative "model." I should
nevertheless induce the doubter to suspend disbelief, at least temporarily, by making the proposed alternative ideology as plausible
as possible. So I propose to gather some respectability by using
an allusive name for it: a name, that is, that invokes a "real world"
institution which occasionally inflicts punishments on offenders
for their offenses but which is nonetheless built upon a fundamental assumption of harmony of interest and love — and as to
which no one finds it odd, or even particularly noteworthy, that
this is the case. I will, then (following Packer in using the word
"model" only for convenience' sake, and preferring to think of it
as an ideological metaphor), offer a "Family Model" of the criminal
process. I wish to emphasize, however, that this allusive reference
is to our family *ideology* as I take it to be, not to the facts of all
or particular families.

In what follows, it should be emphasized that I am talking about "punishment" in the strict sense which requires that it be exacted from an offender for his offense — not about things done for the good of the person concerned, nor about things done prophylactically for the good of society, and certainly not about things called "punishment" metaphorically because they share the element of unpleasantness. That "punishment" in this strict sense goes on in a family is plain. I spank my child for tearing my books, not because to tear them is bad for him, nor because he "needs to learn" about books, but because I and the rest of the members of the family don't want our books destroyed and want to accomplish that objective by appealing to our children's capacity for self-control rather than by taking preventive measures.

"Punishing" thus does go on in a family. One could impose a conceptual "process" of adjudication and exaction upon the facts of family life if it seemed worthwhile. Although punishments are expected to and do come out of the family's adjudication process, it is not a bitter "struggle from start to finish." A parent and child have far more to do with each other than obedience, deterrence, and punishment, and *any* process between them will reflect the full range of their relationship and the concerns growing out of it. Everyone expects and believes that whatever is done, it will be consistent with what the parent recognizes as the basic well-being of his child.

What, then, would be the general thrust of a Family Model?

*The Changed Conception of Crime and of the Criminal.* A thoroughgoing Family Model of the criminal process would be accompanied by a basic change of attitude toward "anti-social" behavior; the very vocabulary with which the subject is discussed would necessarily be affected. People operating within a process built upon the assumption of an ultimate reconcilability of interest between the state and the accused (and the convicted as well, of course), could not lose sight, while concerned with the criminal process, of the range and variety of relationships between the state and its citizens. Seeing "criminal" conduct in its essential variousness and its inseparability from other social events, they would reflect this perception through their attitudes and behavior in the criminal process. They would be unlikely, that is, to think about or try to deal with "crime" or "criminals" in the isolated way which is characteristic of our criminal process because they would regard these categories as of very limited and specialized usefulness.

Under a Family Model, the entire concept of a "crime" would also be quite different. One could be expected to recognize quite explicitly the role of society in perceiving an occurrence as criminal deviance, and reacting to it accordingly, as of joint importance with the actual uncharacterized conduct of the "criminal" in producing "a crime." This approach now prevails only among sociologists, who impose detachment on themselves by special discipline. For the rest of us, it is very hard to adopt so balanced an attitude toward an enemy in a battle. What now derives from sociological discipline could equally well, it seems to me, derive from a genuine acceptance of the idea that criminals are just people who are deemed to have offended — that we are all of us both actual and potential criminals — that "criminals" are not a special kind and class of people with a unique relation to the state. So adherents to the Family Model would not talk (or think) about "offenders," or "criminals," or "people who commit crimes," as if these words referred to people in any other aspect than their exposure to the criminal process.

It is important not to press this point too far. I do not think that there would be no place at all for a distinct concept of "crime" in a Family Model. There are good moral and prudential reasons for public non-interference in the lives of individuals. One might expect the reduction in artificial categories of thought to produce greater sensitivity than we now can muster to the insidious kinds of communal nosiness which we now tolerate only because they are not "penal." Thus, we might expect more appreciation under a Family Model that one great advantage of the criminal law is the way it minimizes social intervention by limiting such intervention to situations in which an individual has failed to exercise the required self-control. The same respect for the value of punishment as a method of control is characteristic of its use in the family. There, punishment in the strict sense is also part of an effort to secure the minimum conditions of social life by appealing to the capacity for self-control. The size and intimacy of a family permits this special function to succeed even in ambiguous situations. Punishment as a response to a failure to exercise the capacity for self-control can effect its purpose without being clearly denominated punishment and without being kept clearly distinct from the other things a parent does to or for a child. One may doubt whether this ambiguity is possible within a larger society. My hunch is that even a society which did not see criminal behavior as a discrete phenomenon, and which had little use for the notion that the word "criminal" describes a particular sort of person or the word "crime" an a priori category of behavior, would nevertheless find it essential to maintain some integrity in the idea of a "crime" and its "punishment" — enough to keep the concept of self-control and its culpable failures clearly in focus.[70] Thus I want to distinguish between the role of a concept of "crime" as a failure of expected self-control, consistent with the Family Model (in fact, a necessary condition of *any* system which imposes "punishment"), on the one hand, and the traditional concepts of "crimes" or "criminal behavior," and "criminals," as categories of events and persons, on the other. It is only these latter which, under a Family Model, should be expected to wither away.

In short, much of the special vocabulary and underlying assumptions which Packer (reflecting all of us rather well, I think) uses in discussing the criminal process, would undoubtedly seem cramped or distorted, or simply irrelevant to a person thinking about it from the perspective of a Family Model. Caught as we are in our present ideology and in our modes of speech which reflect it, it is difficult even to imagine thinking and talking as they would be if we accepted the assumptions of the Family Model. We can get glimpses, as I have suggested, by looking at our own behavior in family life itself. Offenses, in a family, are normal, expected occurrences. Punishment is not something a child receives in isolation from the rest of his relationship to the family; nor is it something which presupposes or carries with it a change of status from "child" to "criminal child." When a parent punishes his child, both parent and child know that afterward they will go on living together as before. The child gets his punishment, as a matter of course, within a continuum of love, after his dinner and during his toilet training and before his bed-time story and in the middle of general family play, and he is punished in his own unchanged

---

70. It is my belief, which I cannot try to develop here, that much of the General Part of the criminal law is a latent effort (which should be made manifest, coherent, and rational) to address the concept of the capacity for self-control and to distinguish situations of lack of capacity from situations of failure to exercise capacity. If this is true, a Family Model would need to maintain the concept of a "crime" — including all of the excusing conditions — in order to maintain a system premised upon appeals to the capacity for self-control; and things done as "punishment" would have to be kept plainly and intelligibly separate from things done for reasons other than a failure of self-control.

It seems that the special reasons for maintaining the concept of "crime" would necessarily be manifest to people thinking within a Family Model and that there would therefore be an inherent disinclination to use the criminal law for the delivery of social services — a practice eloquently deplored by F. Allen, The Borderland of the Criminal Law: Problems of "Socializing" Criminal Justice, in The Borderland of Criminal Justice 1 (1964). Contrast Powell v. Texas, 392 U.S. 514, 526-28 (1968).

capacity as a child with failings (like all other children) rather
than as some kind of distinct and dangerous outsider. The ideology
of family-life on the place of punishment is contained in the
straightforward and simple reply a parent gives to a child who is
anxious about the fundamental relationship because of his guilt
at an offense or his reaction to its punishment: "Of course I *love*
you, but just now I don't *like* you." A family is what it is, and
punishment within a family seems to us as it does, because the
ideology of the family permits such a reply. . . .

*Changed Attitudes Toward the Participants in the Process.* What
other implications would follow from a Family Model? For one
thing, that ideology would necessarily be accompanied by a basic
faith in public officials; everyone would assume, as a general matter,
that if a public official has a particular role or duty, he can be expected to carry it out in good faith and using his best judgment.
The Family Model could not exist without such confidence. Absent
the notion of absolute irreconcilability of interest between the
state and the individual, no a priori obstacle would preclude it.

Basic faith in public officials would revolutionize American criminal procedure. We are all used to the proposition that legal procedures — indeed, the organization of government in general —
must be designed with the bad man, or the man who will unwittingly misuse his powers, primarily in mind. In a sense, we have
begged the central ideological question when we define the problem we see as having to do with *power*, and thereby almost necessarily with its potential abuse.[81] Our assumption that the state and
the individual are in battle compels us to believe that any "discretion" — any active responsibility going beyond the umpiring role
of a judge — will necessarily be exercised either on behalf of the
individual's interest or on behalf of the state's. We see only Packer's
two poles as the possible outcomes of discretion.

Inevitably our starting assumption defines the object of our investigation and thereby affects the facts which we uncover. We
conclude that we are right to suspect any man who wields power.
But anyone who has discussed the question with a lawyer from a
country which traditionally trusts its public servants more than

81. . . . I say it begs the question, not because the matter of power is unimportant, but because putting it at the center of concern, . . . necessarily
fixes the whole ideological tone of a conception of criminal procedure. We
would not, I think, be inclined to start out that way with respect to the family, because our family ideology does not conceive of the question of power
and its abuses as the first and dominating question to be asked (although it
does not rule it out of consideration).

we do, will have found himself shaken in his American cynicism by the direct and almost incomprehending answer he receives to his suggestion that we must always expect abuse of power — willful or mindless or misguided — by the man who is charged with wielding it: "Yes, but why *should* he?" Differences in this most fundamental kind of reaction separate systems of criminal procedure so radically that useful communication across the gulf between them is nearly impossible; and an endless stream of misunderstandings has resulted. In every system, ideological assumptions work as self-fulfilling prophesies. Thus officials of the criminal law system seem to do their jobs competently and fairly on the whole in countries which manifest confidence in them, whereas in the United States each new glimpse behind the veil of "legality" reveals unspeakable horrors and abuses.

Just as a change in assumptions concerning the relation of the individual to the state would be accompanied with new attitudes toward officials who act in the name of the state, so also would it require new attitudes toward the agents of the individual, that is, toward defense counsel. So long as the state's interest is solely "to put a suspected criminal in jail," the suspected criminal's corresponding interest, amost necessarily, is simply to stay out of jail. The roles of prosecutor and defense counsel are thereby defined. The competing concerns of efficiency and abuse of power affect the size of the role defense counsel is allowed to play but not the nature of that role. Defense counsel should do for the accused what the accused could do for himself if he had legal training. He is not expected to concern himself with whether the accused is in fact guilty, nor with any interest of the accused beyond that defined by the process — to win his case, to avoid exile.

I doubt that a Family Model outlook on the process would involve less reliance on counsel, since there are good reasons for an adversary process which have nothing to do with irreconcilability of interest. Certainly though, a process which is not primarily a "struggle from start to finish" will require a defense counsel role which is cooperative, constructive, conciliatory. Together with the representative of the state, defense counsel would direct his energies toward assisting the tribunal to come to that decision which best incorporates and reconciles the interests of all concerned. He could hardly be unconcerned with whether his defendant was actually guilty and with enabling the tribunal to reach an appropriate judgment on that question since the defendant's own interest depends upon this, among other factors.

An analogous change in our attitude toward criminal defendants

would bring with it a thoroughgoing respect for their rights and
their dignity and their individuality, going far beyond the purely
formal respect which now attaches to the defendant in his role as
party to a tournament. This different attitude would be part of the
Family Model ideology not only because an offender would be
perceived first and fundamentally as a *person*, rather than as a
member of the special category of "criminals," and because treating *people* with respect would be among the substantive goals a
Family Model process would seek to promote — not an extrinsic
value for which sacrifices of "efficiency" are made. Respect and
concern would be a fact in the process, not something stimulated
artificially for the promotion of some other end — such as the risk
that an accused might turn out to be innocent. Our own criminal
process operates on quite a different basis. For example, in the
Armstead case, the trial judge insisted that the prosecutor address
the defendant by his first name alone, rather than as "Mr. Armstead." The Court of Appeals for the District of Columbia held
that this was improper. Why? Because the man was not yet convicted, so must be "presumed" (i.e. "treated as if") innocent, or
in other words, respectfully. Only Judge Edgerton, concurring,
observed that the "presumption of innocence" should be irrelevant,
because all men, accused, innocent, or convicted, are entitled to
be treated with respect. The Canons of Professional Ethics afford
another illustration of our purely instrumental attitude toward a
defendant's rights under the Battle Model ideology. Canon Five
derives the lawyer's right to defend any accused person, no matter
how unsavory, from the concern that "otherwise *innocent* persons
. . . might be denied a proper defense." Again, among the standard
arguments for the exclusionary rules attached to the Fourth and
Fifth Amendments is the necessity to find effective means of
protecting *the innocent* — one sometimes wonders how much remains of the idea that guilty defendants, too, are entitled to have
the integrity of their persons and homes protected. Concern for
the guilty — for the vast bulk of those exposed to the criminal
process — does not have a comfortable place in our ideology.

It is not difficult to see the main outlines of the patterns of
attitude and behavior toward defendants which differentiate criminal law and procedure according to the Battle Model from the
analogous institutions within a good family. Even though we all
know in an abstract way that offenses happen regularly and for all
kinds of understandable and forgivable reasons, and even though
most "offenders" are not caught, and even though all of us are
ourselves "offenders," frequently for rather serious offenses, we

nevertheless persist in thinking of a convicted person as a special sort of individual, one cut off in some mysterious way from the common bonds that unite the rest of us. To this rather arbitrarily selected group, we purposefully attach "stigma." The more perceptive and candid of us go so far as to recognize that the criminal process is a form of "status degradation ceremony." We know, the accused knows, the other parties to the process know, and all onlookers know that if the accused loses, he becomes another sort of person. Hence, I think, the special air of desperateness so characteristic of Battle Model trials. The accused and his champion are fighting for his right to remain a member of the common society — not to be treated as an outcast. That is what is at stake. In short, we could sum up the difference in attitude toward the accused which separates the Battle from the Family Model in terms of their respective contemplation and noncontemplation that, if convicted, he will suffer a fundamental breach in the ties of love, respect and concern that normally bind members of a society to one another. . . .

### IV. CONCLUSIONS

The intellectual apparatus Packer presented with such revealingly extravagant claims is in fact a clear, if unself-conscious, articulation of the ideology which is responsible for the characteristic limitations of most contemporary thinking about the criminal process. What Packer does is to make distinct the competing directions in which that ideology leads, and the resulting strains and compromises in our criminal process. But his Two Models will not help us come to real terms with the basic problems of the process; they will not permit a real understanding of guilty pleas and plea bargaining, of the juvenile court, of legal ethics, or of any of the other topics that could equally well have been chosen. Confined by the assumptions which unite his Models, we can imagine no significantly different ways of doing and understanding things from those we already know.

All of us who have had our formative experiences in an atmosphere so dominated by the Battle Model that it has seemed to exhaust the universe of possibility find it difficult to suspend disbelief in favor of a radically competing ideology, even if only temporarily and for speculative purposes. The initial and seemingly insuperable obstacle in approaching the Family Model is its basic premise of reconcilability of interest. One's instinct is to put the issue bluntly: Isn't this notion completely phony? Won't it necessarily be hypocritical, or question-begging, or brute rationalization, whenever invoked in a concrete case? We ought to be aware of such reactions, not because they may not be true, but because they are so easy. They are exactly the reactions that the ideology of the Battle Model demands. We should try not to mistake our ideological limitations for necessary truths.

Reconcilability plainly cannot mean *harmony* of interest; except in a completely mystical and analytically useless sense complete harmony can never exist in a punishment situation. Reconcilability, if it exists at all, must be consistent with some conflict, or at least difference, of interest. As Allen has shown, Judge Waite's famous observation that unlike an ordinary court, which would "do something *to* a child because of what he *has done*," a juvenile court is concerned only with "doing something for a child because of what he *is* and *needs*," is not and cannot be true. The inescapable fact is that the juvenile court often has "purposes to serve that involve more than the interests and welfare of the particular children coming before it." Nor would Waite's notion be true in a family. My child is punished for what he *has done* — torn my books — and so long as punishing is what I am doing, past misconduct is a definitional and ethical prerequisite.

The problem of the plausibility of the Family Model cannot be solved by Waite's attempt to obliterate the essential and unavoidable distinction between a punitive and a best-interests proceeding. We have to discover, before deciding what sense can be made of the Family Model, whether reconcilability of interest can exist in a punitive proceeding. Allen is right that conflict is inevitable in punitive proceedings, but the question is whether we can come to terms with this conflict within an overall relationship which is not based upon hostility. It seems to me that we can, and that a sense can be given to the idea of reconcilability of interest which does not depend upon the fiction of harmony or identity of interest. Even when we are concerned with doing something *to* a person for some end other than to benefit him, we can nevertheless sensibly describe some kinds of systems — to be distinguished from others — as resting upon a fundamental assumption of reconcilability.

Reconciliation takes place in the Family Model particularly in the energetic pursuit by society of the convict's interest in every way consistent with the social need that he be punished. His sacrifice for the general good is kept to a minimum. The experience is made as painless and as beneficial for him as possible. In concrete ways we can make plain that while he has transgressed, we do not therefore cut him off from us; our concern and dedication to his well-being continue. We have punished him and drawn him back in among us; we have not cast him out to fend for himself against our systematic enmity.

I do not think that this sort of fundamental approach is a priori impossible, although I certainly do not want to be taken as arguing that we can await its timely appearance. I am by no means sure that it is consistent with mass social life, although (unlike Pound) I am also not sure that it is inconsistent. In applying such an ideological metaphor to the real world, it is, of course, foolish to imagine that a Family Model in a "pure" form would be a conceivable state of human affairs — but surely we can place plausible criminal law systems on some kind of spectrum leading in that direction. In any case, what is perfectly clear is that any significant movement toward the assumptions of the Family Model would inevitably produce a criminal process which would be altogether different in the most fundamental ways.

Basic procedural questions can never be significantly understood without attention to their implications for and relation to issues of political philosophy. The difference between the Family Model and the Battle Model lies precisely in their opposed approaches to the central problem of political speculation: the possible and proper relationship of individual man to the state. This is an obvious point, and yet it is usually ignored by those who treat criminal procedure on a theoretical level as if it raised nothing but the technical problems of efficiency and accuracy. Even those who do recognize the relationship of political philosophy to criminal procedure have generally begged the essential question by assuming the inevitability of a state of irreconcilable hostility between the individual and the state. Packer, for example, begins his book with the observation that criminal law presents the problem of the use of and limitations upon state power, but he does not develop the procedural implications of this idea beyond the confines of his Two Models because he takes fundamental hostility for granted. The Battle Model ideology has foreclosed interesting speculation about the relationship between political philosophy and criminal procedure because it has brought with it an incapacity to think about the sort of genuinely radical political changes which would have fundamental procedural consequences. That is to say, the Battle Model is a part of a consistent political philosophy, and so long as it dominates the mind as an unself-conscious ideology no contrary speculation is possible.

If there is a direct relationship between political philosophy and ideology, and criminal procedure, there is also a complicated relationship between social fact and ideology. No one whose humanity is intact and vulnerable can have failed to recoil from exposure to the way in which criminal justice is "administered" upon the persons of its objects. In 1970, as in 1905, it is "a disgrace to our civilization." The Battle Model ideology accepts the situation as, in its most essential aspects, inevitable; it purports to explain, to rationalize, even to justify the system we have and the ways we apply it to individuals. It does this in terms of supposed laws of human nature (selfish and anti-social individualism) and official behavior (power corrupts), and the consequent necessities of social organization (the coerciveness of social power and the corollary need for limitations upon its exercise). The Battle Model, in short, derives directly from the conception of the war of all against all associated with Hobbes, whose candid views have always been most piously deplored by those whose ideology is based upon them.

It is worth wondering whether something akin to "counter-revolutionary subordination" may not be entering into the "scholarship" which continually seems to confirm the inevitability of the war of all against all and its ideological derivation in criminal procedure, the Battle Model. Asked in a slightly different way, "If it is plausible that ideology will in general serve as a mask for self-interest," then we should perhaps feel some duty to think about the kinds of self-interest which might underlie the Battle Model. One ought to be troubled that the criminal-law-that-is, and the ideology which seems symbiotic with it, can readily be interpreted as serving mainly the class benefit of the comfortable middle classes.

If one were to analyze the criminal process itself, and the "benefits" it has to offer to those who are exposed to it, it seems to me possible that one might conclude that the Battle Model ideology rationalizes and justifies a system whose "balance of advantage" rules give considerable advantage to middle-class defendants, but offer precious little protection to the great bulk of those who are processed by it and whose offenses are perceived, realistically or not, as directly threatening the social position of the middle class. For the ordinary offender, the filigree of procedural rules which consumes, the attention of the Supreme Court, academic lawyers like Packer, and the public generally, is of doubtful significance. These rules seem to reflect little more than the concerns of the middle class in connection with the rare occasions on which it has to fear prosecution. The Battle Model's lack of concern for what follows conviction — its reliance on social exile — perhaps responds to an accurate perception of what is, for the middle classes, unimportant. The Due Process Model in particular — the Model, as Packer says, of the "schools," of liberal intellectuals and enlightened judges and lawyers — sometimes seems mostly a reflection of a vaguely left-wing concern about political prosecutions, rather than a response to the actual experiences of the sorts of people on whom the system ordinarily operates. Surely the Fourth and Fifth Amendments, and all of their refinements, are fairly marginal in the actual administration of criminal justice; what is *not* marginal is the way ordinary defendants are treated during the process, and what happens to them afterwards. It is this reality which is so grim, which affects mainly the poor, and which the ideology of the Battle Model serves conveniently to explain, to excuse, and to justify. It seems to me, in short, that we ought to feel queasy about the sources and the functions of the Battle Model.

This brings me to my ultimate conclusion, which is that speculation about fundamental change in criminal procedure must begin with the development of ideological self-consciousness and speculation about the possibilities of ideological change. This is not a conclusion which is very favorable to the prospects of significant reform, but at least it might help us avoid moral and practical disasters like the juvenile court movement. The canons of American "scholarship" tend to make it difficult to approach ideological issues, which are, among other things, not very amenable to the manipulative techniques and "scientific" jargon on which the social sciences pride themselves. It is difficult to be fashionably "hard" about them; and I rather doubt the effort would be rewarding. Nevertheless, it seems to me that very little substantial progress is to be made in thinking about criminal procedure until we address ourselves to the ideological underpinnings of our thought. The first step in doing that is simply to set our minds free to wonder.

## What Problems Can Be Solved by Some Form of Adjudication?*

## Lon L. Fuller

### III.

Let me now turn to the other major controversy surrounding labor arbitration, that of the proper role of the arbitrator himself. Is his office essentially judicial, with all the restraints that term implies? Or shall we assign to him a freer role, something like that suggested by the term "labor-relations physician"?

Here we encounter the difficulty of defining the restraints of the judicial role in the case of one who does not hold public office in the ordinary sense of the word. Even the most ardent advocate of the view that the arbitrator's function is essentially judicial would hardly argue that his procedures should be patterned precisely after those applicable to courts of law. The problem then becomes that of defining in some more general sense what it means to act like a judge.

At this point one is tempted to discern the essence of the judicial function in a requirement that the decision reached be *informed* and *impartial*. This will not do, however. The expectation that judgments should be informed and impartial applies to many social roles: that of supervisors toward those under their direction, of teachers toward pupils, of parents toward children, and so forth. The essence of the judicial function lies not in the substance of the conclusion reached, but in the procedures by which that substance is guaranteed. One does not become a judge by acting intelligently and fairly, but by accepting procedural restraints designed to insure — so far as human nature permits — an impartial and informed outcome of the process of decision.

I believe there is open to us a relatively simple way of defining the procedural restraints to which the judicial role is subject. We can do this by looking at adjudication, not through the eyes of the judge, but through the eyes of the affected litigant. Adjudica-

* From: Collective Bargaining and the Arbitrator, 1963 Wis. L. Rev. 3, 18-30. © Wisconsin Law Review. Reprinted by permission of the Wisconsin Law Review.

tion we may define as a social process of decision which assures to the affected party a particular form of participation, that of presenting proofs and arguments for a decision in his favor.

Viewed in this light, adjudication is only one form of social decision in which the affected party is afforded an institutionally guaranteed participation. Elections grant to the affected party participation through voting; contracts grant to him participation through negotiation, either in person or through representatives. No procedure of decision guarantees any particular outcome and least of all an outcome favorable to any particular participant. But the essence of the rule of law lies in the fact that men affected by the decisions which emerge from social processes should have some formally guaranteed opportunity to affect those decisions.

Within this framework of thought we may say, then, that adjudication is a process of decision in which the affected party — "the litigant" — is afforded an institutionally guaranteed participation, which consists of the opportunity to present proofs and arguments for a decision in his favor. Whatever protects and enhances the effectiveness of that participation, advances the integrity of adjudication itself. Whatever impairs that participation detracts from its integrity. When that participation becomes a matter of grace, rather than of right, the process of decision ceases to deserve the name of adjudication.

From the analysis just presented can be derived, I believe, all of the restraints usually associated with an adjudicative role. Thus, interest or bias on the part of the adjudicator constitutes an obvious impairment of the interested party's participation through presenting proofs and arguments. So does the holding of private conferences, for the party not included in such a conference cannot know toward what he should be directing the presentation of his case. Matters are not squared when both parties are separately consulted, for then both are dependent on the candor and intelligence of the adjudicator in learning what the other side is saying, not to mention the more usual objections, such as the lack of an opportunity to cross-examine.

The test here suggested by no means coincides with popular prejudice concerning the judicial role. In this country there is a strong inclination to identify judicial behavior with passiveness, the judge being viewed as an umpire over a game in which he takes no active part until called upon by one of the parties to do so. The test here proposed renders a quite different judgment. If the arbiter of a dispute judges prematurely without hearing what both sides have to say, he obviously impairs the effectiveness of the parties' participation in the decision by proofs and arguments. On the other hand, that participation may be equally impaired if the parties are given no inkling at any time as to what is happening in the arbiter's mind. One cannot direct an effective argument into a vacuum. Accordingly it is the part of the wise arbitrator at some time, usually toward the end of the hearing, to convey to the parties some notion of the difficulties he finds in supporting or in answering certain of the arguments that have been addressed to him. He may find it useful also to summarize the arguments on each side, asking the parties to make corrections or additions so that he may be sure he fully grasps what each is contending for. Such discussions, initiated by the arbitrator himself, take him out of a purely passive role. It is plain, however, that they enhance meaningful participation by the parties in the decision and thus enhance the integrity of adjudication itself.

Perhaps the crassest infringement of adjudicative integrity consists in what has been called the "rigged award." In its most extreme form this means that although the affected parties think their case is being submitted to arbitrational decision, in fact their representatives have already agreed on the outcome to be incorporated in the award. It might seem that this procedure involves not so much an abuse of arbitration as a fraud by representatives on their constituents. But it should not be forgotten that the object of the whole manipulation is to secure the moral force of adjudication for what is in fact not adjudicated at all. The apparent participation of the affected party — through proofs and arguments presented on his behalf — is an empty sham. This problem of the "rigged," or more politely, the "informed" award deserves some analysis. Such an analysis will reveal that, while in some cases to clothe an agreement with the trappings of an award will constitute a plain abuse of adjudicative power, in other instances the appraisal is less obvious.

Let me take two extreme cases, beginning with an instance where the practice is presented in its most innocent form. Six grievances are scheduled for hearing over a three-day period. These grievances are all closely related, involving, let us say, a series of work-load or machine-assignment problems. Late on the third day the sixth case has still not been heard. If it is to be heard at all, a new hearing will have to be scheduled and this will be difficult. Though the arbitrator has as yet rendered no formal award in any of the cases heard, the drift of his mind has become apparent during the hearing of the first five cases, and the disposition of the sixth is not hard to predict. The parties' representatives agree on a solution of it and ask the arbitrator to incorporate their settlement in an award. If the first five cases were reported to the membership as settled by arbitration, while the sixth was reported as settled by agreement, quite unjustified suspicions and doubts would be aroused. Hence the arbitrator is willing to put the agreed settlement "in series," as it were, with its five companions. It would take a purist indeed to discern any real wickedness in this action.

At the other extreme is the case where an arbitrator is paid handsomely to hold extended hearings, where a parade of witnesses is heard, where lawyers plead with heart-stirring eloquence, when all the while the whole thing has been rigged and fixed from the beginning and the whole hearing is a farce from start to finish. I agree with Willard Wirtz that even if awards rendered in cases like this always produced a short-run advantage judged from the standpoint of public welfare, the long-run cost would be too high to pay. Such an arbitrational practice is essentially parasitic. It takes advantage of the fact that most awards are honest, for if all awards were known to be fixed there would be no point in masquerading an agreement as the decision of an arbitrator. One recalls here the remark of Schopenhauer, that the prostitute owes her bargaining power to the restraint of virtuous women.

It should be observed that in cases like that just suggested, the "fixed" award may involve a by-passing of procedural guarantees surrounding the negotiation of the collective bargaining agreement itself. Those representing the union in an arbitration would seldom possess the power acting by themselves to negotiate a contract binding on the union. Thus, in the typical case where the arbitration involves the wages to be paid under a new contract, the arbitrator becomes an accomplice in circumventing limitations on the agency of the union's representatives.

At the extremes, passing judgment on the "agreed" award is relatively easy. In the middle area of gray, arriving at a valid appraisal requires a greater exercise of individual responsibility. One thing seems to me clear, however. In deciding what he should do the arbitrator is not entitled to take the easy way out by saying, "After all, the purpose of arbitration is to promote good labor relations. If I can head off an unjustified and futile strike by issuing as an arbitrator's decision what is really an agreed settlement, then my conscience is clear." Before taking this escape the arbitrator should reflect that he is trustee for the integrity of the processes of decision entrusted to his care. He should ask himself whether the argument for bending his powers for good is not like that of the man who, in order to give to a worthy charity, embezzles funds entrusted to his care for an undeserving nephew. In practice the temptation to take short cuts in order to do good is a much greater threat to the integrity of arbitration than the temptation to use its forms for evil purposes.

Before leaving this question of the "informed" award — so that none of its nuances may be left unnoticed — it should be remarked that the problem can arise within the framework of an arbitration wholly conducted within the strictest judicial restraints. Effective advocacy sometimes suggests that the advocate give some intimation in his argument of the most acceptable form of an adverse decision in the event such a decision should be rendered. It needs hardly to be said that such intimations, though conveyed "in open court" and in the presence of all affected, are not always perceived by an inattentive audience. This tincturing of the argument with intimations of settlement, instead of employing more direct and reliable channels of communication, may seem to some the essence of hypocrisy. To others it will represent that deference for symbolism without which social living is impossible.

There remains the difficult problem of mediation by the arbitrator, who instead of issuing an award, undertakes to persuade the parties to reach a settlement, perhaps reinforcing his persuasiveness with "the gentle threat" of a decision. Again, there is waiting a too-easy answer: "Judges do it." Of course, judges sometimes mediate, or at least bring pressure on the parties for a voluntary settlement. Sometimes this is done usefully and sometimes in ways that involve an abuse of office. In any event the judiciary has evolved no uniform code with respect to this problem that the arbitrator can take over ready-made. Judicial practice varies over a wide range. If the arbitrator were to pattern his conduct after the worst practices of the bench, arbitration would be in a sad way.

Analysis of the problem as it confronts the arbitrator should begin with a recognition that mediation (or conciliation, the terms being largely interchangeable) has an important role to play in the settlement of labor disputes. There is much to justify a system whereby it is a prerequisite to arbitration that an attempt first be made by a skilled mediator to bring about a voluntary settlement. This requirement has at times been imposed in a variety of contexts. Under such systems the mediator is, I believe, invariably someone other than the arbitrator. This is as it should be.

Mediation and arbitration have distinct purposes and hence distinct moralities. The morality of mediation lies in optimum settlement, a settlement in which each party gives up what he values less, in return for what he values more.[19] The morality of arbitration lies in a decision according to the law of the contract. The procedures appropriate for mediation are those most likely to uncover that pattern of adjustment which will most nearly meet the interests of both parties. The procedures appropriate for arbitration are those which most securely guarantee each of the parties a meaningful chance to present arguments and proofs for a decision in his favor. Thus, private consultations with the parties, generally wholly improper on the part of an arbitrator, are an indispensable tool of mediation.

Not only are the appropriate procedures different in the two cases, but the facts sought by those procedures are different. There is no way to define "the essential facts" of a situation except by reference to some objective. Since the objective of reaching an optimum settlement is different from that of rendering an award according to the contract, the facts relevant in the two cases are different, or, when they seem the same, are viewed in different

---

19. In exchange ". . . the rule must be that you give, so far as possible, what is less valuable to you but more valuable to the receiver; and you receive what is more valuable to you and less valuable to the giver. This is common sense, good business sense, good social sense, good technology, and is the enduring basis of amicable and constructive relations of any kind. This does *not* mean that you give as little as you can from the *receiver's* point of view. . . . What conceals this simple fact of experience so often is that subsequent evaluations may change, though this is then beside the point. I may pay a man $10 today with pleasure, and find tomorrow that I need $10 very badly, but cannot use the service I paid for. I am then perhaps disposed to think I made a bad exchange. I read the past into the present. This leads to the false view that what exchange *should* be is as little as possible of what the *receiver* wants, regardless of its value to me. This philosophy of giving as little as possible and getting as much as possible in the *other man's values* is the root of bad customers relations, bad labor relations, bad credit relations, bad supply relations, bad technology. The possible margins of cooperative success are too limited to survive the destruction of incentives which this philosophy implies." Barnard, The Functions of the Executives 254-55 (1950).

Barnard may simplify the matter somewhat in this passage. If in making a deal today I look forward to possible future deals with the same party tomorrow, then it may sometimes be wise to hold back something he wants badly, even if it would cost me little to give it. By doing so I improve my bargaining position tomorrow. But without doubt this consideration is in practice grossly overemphasized. Barnard is certainly right in pointing up the social destructiveness of the conception that you have won an important victory just because you have deprived the other party of something he wanted badly. One of the most important tasks of the mediator is to keep the discussions within the frame recommended by Barnard, so that this conception will have no chance to work its havoc.

aspects. If a person who has mediated unsuccessfully attempts to assume the role of arbitrator, he must endeavor to view the facts of the case in a completely new light, as if he had previously known nothing about them. This is a difficult thing to do. It will be hard for him to listen to proofs and arguments with an open mind. If he fails in this attempt, the integrity of adjudication is impaired.

These are the considerations that seem to me to apply where the arbitrator attempts to mediate before hearing the case at all. This practice is quite uncommon, and would largely be confined to situations where a huge backlog of grievances seemed to demand drastic measures toward an Augean clean-up. I want now to pass to consideration of the case where the arbitrator postpones his mediative efforts until after the proofs are in and the arguments have been heard. In doing so I pass over the situation where the arbitrator interrupts the hearing midway in order to seek a voluntary settlement. The standards properly applicable to this intermediate situation may be derived from those governing the two cases that lie on either side of it.

One might ask of mediation first undertaken after the hearing is over, what is the point of it? If the parties do not like the award, they are at liberty to change it. If there is some settlement that will effect a more apt adjustment of their interests, their power to contract for that settlement is the same after, as it is before, the award is rendered. One answer would be to say that if the arbitrator undertakes mediation after the hearing but before the award, he can use "the gentle threat" of a decision to induce settlement, keeping it uncertain as to just what the decision will be. Indeed, if he has a sufficiently Machiavellian instinct, he may darkly hint that the decision will contain unpleasant surprises for both parties. Conduct of this sort would, however, be most unusual. Unless the role thus assumed were played with consummate skill, the procedure would be likely to explode in the arbitrator's face.

There is, however, a more convincing argument for mediative efforts after the hearing and before the award. This lies in the peculiar fact — itself a striking tribute to the moral force of the whole institution of adjudication — that an award tends to resist change by agreement. Once rendered it seems to have a kind of moral inertia that puts a heavy onus on the party who proposes any modification by mutual consent. Hence if there exists the possibility of a voluntary settlement that will suit both parties better than the award, the last chance to obtain it may occur after the hearing and before the award is rendered. This may in fact be an especially propitious moment for a settlement. Before the hearing it is quite usual for each of the parties to underestimate grossly the strength of his adversary's case. The hearing not uncommonly "softens up" both parties for settlement.

What, then, are the objections to an arbitrator's undertaking mediative efforts after the hearing and before rendering the award, this being often so advantageous a time for settlement? Again, the objection lies essentially in the confusion of role that results. In seeking a settlement the arbitrator turned mediator quite properly learns things that should have no bearing on his decision as an arbitrator. For example, suppose a discharge case in which the arbitrator is virtually certain that he will decide for reinstatement though he is striving to keep his mind open until he has a chance to reflect on the case in the quiet of his study. In the course of exploring the possibilities of a settlement he learns that, contrary to the position taken by the union at the hearing, respectable elements in the union would like to see the discharge upheld. Though they concede that the employee was probably innocent of the charges made by the company, they regard him as an ambitious trouble maker the union would be well rid of. If the arbitrator fails to mediate a settlement, can he block this information out when he comes to render his award?

It is important that an arbitrator not only respect the limits of his office in fact, but that he also *appear* to respect them. The parties to an arbitration expect the arbitrator to decide the dispute, not according to what pleases the parties, but by what accords with the contract. Yet as a mediator he must explore the parties' interests and seek to find out what would please them. He cannot be a good mediator unless he does. But if he has then to surrender his role as mediator to resume that of adjudicator, can his award ever be fully free from the suspicion that it was influenced by a desire to please one or both of the parties?

Finally, in practice, the settlement mediated after the hearing will seldom be free from some taint of being "rigged." Indeed, when an agreement is reached under the express or implied threat of an award, the distinction between agreement and award is lost; the "rigged award" blends into the coerced settlement, and it may at a given time be uncertain which will emerge from the discussions. During these discussions it is most unusual for all affected to know at all times just what is going on.

These, then, are the arguments against the arbitrator's undertaking the task of mediation. They can all be summed up in the phrase, "confusion of role." Why, then, should any arbitrator be

tempted to depart from his proper role as adjudicator? In what
follows I shall try to analyze the considerations that sometimes
press him toward a departure from a purely judicial role. I shall
also offer suggestions as to how these considerations can be met
without that departure — by methods that keep the arbitrator within
the proper limits of his role.

IV.

The most obvious case where an arbitrator is tempted to mediate
is where the decision dictated by the terms of the contract is plainly
less advantageous to the parties than one that lies within their
powers of agreement. Suppose, for example, the following situation. Certain employees called out in an emergency, occurring
outside their regular shifts and on a holiday, claim triple pay for
the work done. Though the arbitrator has no personal fondness
for pyramided overtime, it seems clear to him that under the relevant provisions of the contract the grievants are entitled to triple
pay. The company advances as one of its arguments that if triple
pay is allowed, the employees may connive to make available in
emergencies only those whose shift schedules are such as to qualify
them for triple pay. The union offers during the hearing to work
out an agreement by which any such practice would be forestalled.
    In such a case the arbitrator will be strongly tempted to propose
private consultations, during which he could explain to the company that if the case goes to an award, he will have to grant triple
pay and that he will have no way of qualifying his award so as to
avoid the abuse about which the company is concerned. I think,
however, that there is no need for the arbitrator thus to step down
from the bench. He may, for example, explain toward the end of
the hearing that he finds it useful to request each party to state
how he would write an opinion in his own favor. He then asks
the company representative to give in outline form an opinion
that would justify a refusal of triple pay. He may thus bring home
to the company the plight he has in writing his award. He may
further at this point ask the union to clarify its proposal for avoiding abuses. Thus without abandoning his role as judge of the dispute he may open the way for a voluntary settlement. At least in
one case like that just related the arbitrator received a letter two
days after the hearing that the case had been settled by agreement.
It may be objected that this procedure is an hypocrisy and constitutes mediation from the bench. In a sense this is true. But the

procedure suggested avoids what is always undesirable and suspicion-arousing: private consultants with the parties. The procedure in no way impairs the integrity of adjudication, for each party has his full chance to present his proofs and arguments in open court and each knows every consideration that the other is advancing for a decision in his favor.

A second situation where an arbitrator may be moved to undertake mediation is presented by a case where there is really no intelligible standard of decision — where decision by a roll of the dice would be about as rational as one reached by an artificial and unconvincing manipulation of contractual phrases. In international law the concept of justiciability is largely associated with the presence or absence of available standards of decision. A judge is one who applies some principle to the decision of the case; if there are no principles, then the decider cannot be a judge — the case is not justiciable. In terms of the analysis proposed in this paper, the participation of the litigant by presenting proofs and arguments becomes meaningless if there is no rational standard that can control the decision. One cannot join issue in an intellectual void. Unless there is some standard by which the relevance of proofs can be judged and the cogency of arguments measured, the litigant's participation in the process of decision becomes an empty form.

In actual practice I don't think the arbitrator tempted to mediate can find much justification in considerations like those just outlined. Justiciability in the sense in which the term is commonly used in international law is not a serious problem in labor arbitration. In arbitrations arising under a contract, the source of the standards that should govern the decision is clear: it lies in the contract itself. In comparison with contracts generally, labor agreements are tolerably well drafted. The fact that crucial provisions are sometimes drafted at 4 a.m. by tired and angry men does not make them as different from other contracts as labor negotiators are likely to suppose. The difficult problems of interpretation are those common to contracts generally: overlooked situations, apparent or real inconsistencies, carelessness of thought and language, passages drafted by one party in his own terms and never closely examined by the other, provisions knowingly left vague or ambiguous either for later resolution through arbitration or simply through an inability to find an apt verbal solution for the problem addressed. These problems are not, I would say, as difficult as they are in many other branches of contract law. The factual foundation of reciprocal dependence on which a labor agreement rests supplies guide lines for interpretation that may be lacking when business contractors part permanently in a bitter litigational feud. In labor contracts a high specificity of standards often impedes justiciability instead of advancing it. I think most arbitrators would rather decide discharge cases under a simple provision requiring "just cause" than under an elaborate table of detailed offenses. Such a table, because of the limitations of human foresight, usually does more harm than good. (An explicit rule against storing liquor in your locker seems simple enough until the offending employee testifies it was on doctor's orders that he bought a bottle for his ailing grandmother at lunch time so that he could rush it home after work.)

The procedural limitations that surround the adjudicative function are designed to insure as rational a decision as possible. The essential open-endedness of all human arrangements makes it impossible to guarantee that every dispute that arises will find waiting for it a rule conclusively dictating its decision. Every system of rules yields occasional cases that could be decided either way with equal persuasiveness. This is as true of labor arbitrations as it is of other adjudicative processes, but no more so. The important thing is that in arbitrations arising under a collective bargaining agreement both parties know where to go to get the standard of decision. It lies in the contract itself. This is the standard by which they must judge, as best they can, what proofs to offer and what arguments to advance.

The problem of finding appropriate standards of decision may seem somewhat more difficult in the case of arbitrations to set the terms of a new contract — almost invariably, of course, wage terms. Here the problem is not so much a lack of standards as a multiplicity of standards — all, curiously, of a conservative nature, being directed toward the restoration of a disturbed balance of some sort. George W. Taylor has suggested a procedure by which the arbitrator may in such cases secure a firmer basis for decision. This consists in requesting the parties to include in their agreement of submission a stipulation of the criteria by which judgment should be rendered. Even in the absence of such an agreement, however, the arbitrator will generally find himself compelled to do the best he can. Arbitration being usually a last resort in such cases, the chances of agreement have usually been sufficiently explored to make mediation pointless. If there is any hope that mediation could result in a settlement, it ought to be conducted by someone other than the arbitrator. . . .

# The Juvenile Court and the Adversary System: Problems of Function and Form*

## Joel F. Handler

... The establishment of the Juvenile Court of Cook County at the turn of the century was the first success of reform movements directed towards removing adolescents from the criminal law process and improving programs for dependent and neglected children. The revolutionary experiment apparently reflected widely shared attitudes. By 1917 juvenile court legislation had been passed in all but three states. By 1932 there were over 600 independent juvenile courts and over 2,000 juvenile sessions of regular courts in the United States alone, all providing for the separate disposition of adolescents who transgressed or were considered to be about to transgress accepted standards of behavior.

The bold, exciting experiment is now more than 60 years old. With the passage of time the experiment has been exposed to increasing scrutiny and criticism; indeed, it may now be said that practically every significant aspect of the juvenile legal process is under heavy attack. In several states there have been official investigations and statutory revisions of the basic legislation.

The serious critics of the juvenile court experiment do not question the initial decision that adolescents ought to be handled in a legal process separate from adults. The battle is over the treatment of adolescents within the separate process. It is charged that the standards by which they are adjudicated delinquent, dependent, or neglected — the three most common routes to formal, official intervention — are so loosely defined as to be meaningless. Coupled with looseness in standards is looseness in procedures. In pre-adjudication stages, police or probation officers take it upon themselves to regulate significant aspects of the conduct and relationships of adolescents and their families. At the adjudication stage important elements of procedural due process are given lip service or, in some jurisdictions, not provided for at all. The original reformers, in their zeal to extricate the adolescent from the cruelty and harshness of the criminal law courts, left behind, it is

* From: 1965 Wis. L. Rev. 7-19, 24-39. © Wisconsin Law Review. Reprinted by permission of Wisconsin Law Review.

charged, basic concepts of responsibility and standards of due process. The great humanitarian reform movement has led to un-
bridled official discretion often resulting in capricious decisions.
What is needed, the argument runs, is a return to clearer standards
and orderly procedures which will facilitate the rendering of sound
decisions and at the same time safeguard the rights of adolescents
and their parents.

This article is concerned with only one aspect of the current
battle over the juvenile court movement: the formal procedures
for deciding statutory status and disposition. The original reformers
rejected the adversary system of adjudication. The current critics
and reformers (hereinafter referred to as the "revisionists") charge
that this decision was a fatal error and they call for a reintroduc-
tion, in varying degrees, of adversary procedures. The inquiry here
is concerned with this basic problem: What role, if any, does the
adversary system have in deciding the issues of statutory status
and disposition for juveniles? If it is to play a role, what forms
should it take to best perform that role? . . .

### THE ORIGINS AND CURRENT STATUS OF THE
### JUVENILE COURT MOVEMENT

*The Original Understanding: Substantive and Procedural*

The critical philosophical position of the reform movement was
that no formal, legal distinctions should be made between the delinquent and the dependent or neglected. The adolescent who
broke the law should not be viewed and treated as an adult offender. He should be viewed and treated in the same manner as
a wise and understanding parent would view and treat a wayward
child. He should not be considered an enemy of society but
society's child who needs understanding, guidance and protection.
The goals of the program are rehabilitation and protection from
the social conditions that lead to crime.

This foundational concept of parens patriae is the theoretical
underpinning for the rejection of the criminal law adversary procedures. The adult offender is the enemy of society. He stands
accused and is to be tried. He is given the opportunity to defend
himself as best he can, but if he is adjudged guilty, he will be
punished according to the gravity of the offense. The delinquent,
on the other hand, is not the enemy of society. He is society's
child, and therefore the interests of the state and the child do not
conflict but coincide. Since the interests coincide there is no need
for the criminal adversary adjudicatory procedure. The adolescent

offender is not brought before the court to be accused and given the opportunity to defend himself. The juvenile court, as a parent, is only concerned with trying to find out what can be done on the adolescent's behalf. The issues are not criminal responsibility, guilt and punishment, but understanding, guidance and protection.

If objectives such as understanding, guidance and protection are to be realized, then juvenile court justice must be "personalized," "socialized" and "humanized" — again, as a parent would treat individually his own child. The traumatic effects and stigma of exposure to the regular criminal law courts must be avoided.

The single criminal act is no longer important; it is only a symptom or end product of drives over which the adolescent has little or no control. It is more scientifically appropriate to view the total personality in order to decide what best can be done for the adolescent to save him from a downward career in crime.

The first statute, the Illinois Act of 1899, remarkably reflected the original understanding. With the exception of provision for a right to trial by a jury of six (perhaps to meet constitutional objections), the act eliminated the contentious adversary aspects of formal criminal procedures. Among other things, it provided for petition instead of complaint, special court rooms, specially selected judges, informal hearings instead of formal trials, separate juvenile records, probation officers to investigate and act in the best interests of the adolescent and to supervise the adolescent either in the home or in some "suitable" family home or institution, and the segregation of adolescents sentenced to adult institutions. . . .

## METHODS OR PROCEDURES

The failure to impose effective statutory limits on the jurisdiction of the courts and their powers of disposition is compounded, it is charged, by the methods or procedures for deciding the issues of status and disposition. Under the guise of seeking to find out not necessarily what the adolescent did but how he can be helped, the court, through its arm, the probation department, conducts a social investigation allegedly in the best interests of the adolescent. The results of this investigation, in the vast majority of cases, constitute the basic findings of fact. The so-called nonadversary, nonpunitive, solicitous judicial procedure operates to prevent any effective challenge to these findings. Depending on the jurisdiction, the alleged offender may be denied a specific charge, appointment of counsel or advice that he has a right to counsel, the privilege against self-incrimination or the right to be advised of the privilege, confrontation, trial by jury, the defense of double jeopardy, the right to make a complete record, and appeal. In other jurisdictions, the alleged offender may have these rights but he will be effectively discouraged from exercising them by the police, the probation officers or even the judges.

Summarizing the charge, we find very broad statutes, an extremely informal procedure where there is no defense counsel to challenge the findings of the social investigation or to insist on other procedural safeguards, and the possibility of very serious consequences. Whatever protection the adolescent might receive from the hazards of the arbitrary, the vicious, the incompetent or even the tired, rests solely with the judge. He alone must take it upon himself to challenge the facts and to insist on competent and relevant evidence.

Lodging such unfettered power even in the best of men should give one pause; yet, in the opinion of the critics, the quality, interest and training of the juvenile court judges leave much to be desired. The original understanding called for dedicated, highly-trained specialists of prestigious status. What has generally happened, however, is that the juvenile court is considered to be the lowest rung on the judicial ladder. Rarely does the court attract men of maturity and ability. The work is not regarded as desirable or appropriate for higher judgeships. In courts of mixed jurisdiction, judges seek to avoid assignment to the juvenile division and rotation must be employed.

Given this state of affairs, plus the extreme press of business (at least in the large urban courts), effective decision making tends to shift from the court to the probation staff or the police. The court hearings are usually very perfunctory. The judges, in effect, rubber stamp the findings and recommendations of the reports either because the judges are uninterested or overworked, or because the investigators have learned to tailor the findings and recommendations to the judges' proclivities. But whatever the reason, the judicial hearing does not serve the purpose of detached, independent, and conscientious fact-finding before the application of official sanctions.

Needless to say, the critics of this type of administration do not find much solace in judicial reliance on the probation staff or the police. The thoroughness, quality, and soundness of the findings and decisions will depend on the ability, training and incentives of the officers. In too many jurisdictions, it is charged, probation officers are political appointees who lack the requisite training and motivation. But the system is doubtful even where the probation officers are trained and properly motivated. It is said that these officers are even less interested than the judges in proving specific conduct; their attitude is to avoid "legal technicalities" which may slow or prevent the application of what they think is needed therapy. The position of the adolescents and their families rests on the officers' notions of what is best for them.

The same type of objections apply, but more forcefully, to the regulatory practices of station adjustment or unofficial delinquency. There is no legal authority for this practice and there are no controls unless the adolescents or their parents have the temerity to challenge the officer. In view of the type of persons brought before the police, the power relationships, and even the threats to send adolescents to court if they do not comply, such challenges would be exceedingly unlikely.

According to the critics, then, the present administration of juvenile justice represents, for all practical purposes, unfettered official discretion. The critics would add the further charge that the officials who are exercising this discretion are ill-suited for the task. But their point would still be valid even if the best of men were administering the system and even if, in individual cases, adolescents and their families were helped by the results. The fact remains that the system allows intervention by the government into the affairs of people without their consent and without standards and controls. Experience has taught us that this is objectionable even if it may be characterized as "disinterested benevolence. . . ."

### The Revisionist Program: "Judicializing" the Juvenile Court

The revisionists start with the very realistic premise that no matter what the label — "treatment" instead of "punishment"; "we want to help you, not convict you"; "we're on your side" — the basic fact is that the juvenile process represents significant governmental interference in individual affairs without consent. The community is exercising the power to take an adolescent from his home and place him under governmental restraint. This force should only be exercised pursuant to rules and standards meaningfully set forth in advance and after a scrupulous determination of the facts. An adolescent as well as an adult is entitled to protection from arbitrary or well-meaning but mistaken government. In the minds of the revisionists, this means that the legal process for juveniles must be "judicialized" as distinguished from what is characterized as the present pattern of administrative disposition.

It is proposed that the more serious charge of delinquency be separated from neglect, dependency, waywardness and the like and that only specific instances of serious antisocial conduct should justify a finding of delinquency. The others would include anti-social behavior but behavior falling short of violation of criminal laws or willful neglect by parents. In either case, the emphasis should be on specific acts but the difference in status should make clear that there should be a difference in treatment. An adolescent should not be allowed to suffer harsh consequences merely because a government official wants to help him.

The emphasis on fault or personal transgression does not mean abandonment of the concept of the total personality. But it does mean the separation of issues in the decision-making process. Jurisdictional status must be decided first. What did the adolescent do? Or what have the parents done? After that is decided, the next question is disposition. In view of the total situation, what should be done?

The separation of issues facilitates the introduction of the procedural safeguards commonly found in the adversary system — a clear and definite charge, the separation of functions between the prosecutor and judge, a meaningful right to counsel, the right of confrontation, proof by competent and relevant evidence, a relatively high degree of burden of proof and the right of appeal.

Remedial proposals vary from critic to critic, but there constantly reappear two main points. On the basis of past experience, and in view of the structure, personnel, and community resources, it is neither safe nor sound to decide important issues in the lives of families on the basis of social and psychological data. "The nature of . . . [the] illegal act, together with . . . prior history of violations and the circumstances surrounding . . . [the] offense, are the best evidence of the present and future threat that . . . [the adolescent] poses to the community. An agency that is interested only in its client's welfare and adjustment is not oriented to the nuclear problem of lawlessness." [73] Combined with a feeling of unreliability of welfare notions and practices is an extreme revulsion at the informal investigatory procedure of the juvenile courts. Even the best of judges, it is urged, will make unsound decisions if all the facts are not properly brought before him. Experience has shown that despite its faults, the adversary system of adjudication is better designed to insure the proper presentation of the

73. Tappan, Judicial and Administrative Approaches to Children with Problems, in Justice for the Child 154-55 (Rosenheim ed. 1962).

facts. The essential conceptual error in the juvenile court reform movement has proved to be the departure from the adversary system; this departure has generated most of the due process problems.

## Evaluation of the Present Views on the Applicability of the Adversary System

The procedural side of the current controversy over the future direction of the juvenile court reform can be analyzed in terms of a search for an appropriate method of fact-finding. The original reformers had many reasons for rejecting the adversary system of adjudication; but two of the important reasons were that that procedure was not suited for the development and presentation of the relevant scientific behavioral data and that the trauma of a trial-by-battle adversary system would destroy rehabilitative goals. The revisionists, on the other hand, are equally convinced that in both theory and practice the nonadversary, solicitous approach hinders the determination of the facts and may produce fear and cynicism on the part of the adolescents and their families; and that rehabilitative goals cannot be accomplished under either circumstance.

### A PRELIMINARY ARGUMENT

Before evaluating the two positions, a preliminary but important argument must be disposed of. It is to be noted that both positions are concerned with the scrupulous determination of the facts. Nonconsensual governmental intervention of this order should not be based on surmise or conjecture. This is true whether the basic facts are the commission of specific acts, as the revisionists would have it, or aspects of the total personality as the original understanding and current practice stress. It would be unnecessary to emphasize this point but for the fact that the argument is often raised that the task of devising a procedure for the scrupulous determination of the facts is unimportant because in the overwhelming majority of cases the basic facts are not in dispute; the adolescents and the parents rarely if ever challenge the findings.

This argument must be rejected for a number of reasons. First, on occasion adolescents will contest and there has to be a procedure available for handling this type of case. If adolescents experience a sense of injustice when they try to contest, then rehabilitative goals will be set back.... Second, it is very doubtful whether the confession cases mean that adolescents agree with the allegations in the petition. The crucial question is why there is such a high rate of confessions? Is the adolescent confessing because he agrees with the allegations in the petition or is he confessing because rightly or wrongly he fears a contest? Is he confessing because he has been led to believe (which may be true) that disposition will be lighter if he tearfully and remorsefully promises to behave? Have threats of court referral with potentially harsh consequences induced the confession? In short, does the adolescent think that he will be better off if he plays ball? Answers to these questions have relevance to the accomplishment of rehabilitative goals.

In addition, the confession argument serves to defeat the community's interest in having official power exercised only in proper cases. It is curious that those who adopt this argument seem to have borrowed unwittingly a concept from the adult world that is even questionable there. In the world of adults it is assumed that if two antagonists agree on a solution, the state generally has no further interest in the dispute. In commercial litigation, for example, it is usually open to the litigants to settle the matter before or even after judgment. The same idea applies in criminal proceedings. With comparatively few exceptions, if the accused agrees to the charge, society's quest for the truth and the just disposition will be considered satisfied. Grown-ups, it is assumed, can look after their own interests and public policy will be satisfied by the result. In the world of commerce this assumption can be defended, at least where bargaining positions are relatively equal; with private law-making, the immediate parties are probably more capable of tailoring a satisfactory solution than the state. In the world of crime, the assumption is to say the least, very questionable. We already have evidence that many adult confessions are badly bargained for by psychiatrically disturbed persons who really do not understand what it is they are admitting or the likely consequences. Accordingly, there is increasing concern that the trial judge not rely on the face value of confessions by adults. Viewed in this light, the confession argument in the world of juvenile delinquency is, literally, incredible. Those who adopt this argument as a substitute for a scrupulous determination of the facts are satisfied that the public interest in accurate fact-finding may depend on the wishes of the adolescent and his parents even though agreement with the allegations may be induced through confusion, fear, or manipulation. The interest of the community in finding out who is within the statutory standards is far broader than what a particular adolescent or parent thinks is best for them. The public interest is in having official intervention and control only when the facts warrant such action. This means that the public must have a method of finding out what the facts are.

### THE UNSOUNDNESS OF THE NONADVERSARY APPROACH

It is argued here that the procedural approach of the original reformers, and as presently practiced, will more likely than not hinder the accurate determination of the facts. This is because the nonadversary, solicitous procedure seriously underestimates the extraordinary task placed on the fact-finder adjudicator. More often than not in juvenile delinquency cases the existence of facts rests in perceptions laden with tensions, hostilities and personal animosities. Finding out what happened, or what the environment is, in such a context, is not easy. To do the job well, the fact-finder must first rid himself of his own biases and preconceptions. He must investigate the facts to the best of his ability and consider all the inferences from the point of view of one side. What is the position of the police or complaining witness? What are they charging and is it credible? Then, he must completely extricate himself from that mental position and perform the same mental processes from the other point of view. What does the adolescent have to say? (The fact of confession does not satisfy this obligation.) Assuming that he can survive this ordeal, he must then reassume his completely neutral position and decide where the truth lies.

Even the relatively simple charge requires this type of investigation. Suppose that a twelve year old boy is charged with burglarizing a residence and the evidence is that he was seen leaving the residence, through a window, on the night in question. One need not trace through the investigative steps that competent prosecution and defense counsel would take if the accused were an adult. Can we expect the same type of investigation on the part of a single fact-finder? Is it realistic to expect the fact-finder, after investigating the prosecution side, to then approach the accused's side with the frame of mind, the tenacity, doggedness and imagination of defense counsel? Note that the case might very well involve more than testing the credibility of the prosecution witnesses in court. If the boy did not do the act, it might be necessary to establish his presence elsewhere at the time in question. Even if the boy did commit the act, there may have been unusual circumstances such as coercion by a gang or by members of his family. The proper ascertainment of the facts requires more than the negative check, a healthy suspicion of one side of the story (a difficult

enough task for a single fact-finder). It also requires the development of affirmative facts on the other side. And then, the detached, objective, cool look at where the truth lies. This is what is
called for when statutory status depends on a single act of misconduct. How much more severe are the demands on the single
fact-finder in . . . [the] example where the relevant facts are elusive
and complex and perceptions are shot through with vindictiveness and spite.

What is needed, then, for the accurate determination of delinquent behavior is a clear separation of fact-finding roles. A clear
separation is needed because as a realistic matter the drive of the
single fact-finder would be to try to label the case, to try to fit it
into a familiar pattern in an effort to order the mass of facts
around a tentative theory. "It is a mistake to suppose that this
premature cataloguing must necessarily result from impatience,
prejudice or mental sloth . . . But what starts as a preliminary
diagnosis designed to direct inquiry tends, quickly and impercep-
tibly, to become a fixed conclusion, as all that confirms the diagnosis makes a strong imprint on the mind, while all that runs
counter to it is received with diverted attention." [82] The existence
and force of this drive — the drive to fit the case into the familiar
pattern — tends to cast the facts as the single fact-finder would
have it, which could differ from what the facts are. This is the
difficulty with the nonadversary, solicitous procedure. It fails to
take sufficient account of this drive. Merging the roles means that
the only counter to the biases and preconceptions of the single
fact-finder will be what he himself can generate. The accurate
determination of the facts will be hindered to the extent that the
single fact-finder is unable to perform this feat.

If this analysis is correct, then a number of conclusions follow.
First, the unsoundness of the nonadversary procedure will not be
cured by a tighter definition of statutory status. Where status depends on very broad definitions of delinquency ("so deports himself as wilfully to injure or endanger the morals or health of himself
or others"), the dangers of professional biases, proclivities and preconceptions are clear. But, as the burglary example demonstrates,
procedural reform is still needed even if the meaning of juvenile
delinquency is narrowed to a specific act. Second, it makes little
difference whether effective decision-making has shifted from the
judge to the probation staff or the police. The judge, of course,

82. A.B.A. Joint Conference on Professional Responsibility, Report, 44
A.B.A.J. 1159, 1160–61 (958). . . .

has less opportunity to perform the required fact-finding function, but the inherent vice of the nonadversary system does not lie in the lack of opportunity. It lies in the fact that psychologically the single person attempting three roles will be less inclined to take the opportunity. Third, so far the argument has been in terms of the trained, capable and dedicated official. It need hardly be mentioned that the task of finding the facts under this procedure is intensified if the fact-finders are poorly trained, underpaid, overworked or temperamentally unsuited for this type of work.

The nonadversary, solicitous procedure tends to destroy rehabilitative goals in two respects. It will destroy goals to the extent that it is ill-suited for the accurate determination of what the adolescent did or what he is like. This would be clearly true if the boy is declared guilty of a burglary he did not do or the father of [a] girl [is] lying. Suppose, however, that the boy or girl needed some sort of official control anyway. This fact, of course, is fortuitous and should not be used to cover up a slipshod method of finding the facts; a proper procedure can also be used for the exercise of official control when needed. But even more important, if [the] analysis is correct, despite the fact that the adolescent does need official control, rehabilitative goals will still have been set back by this procedure. Whether or not the girl needed treatment, or even whether or not her father was telling the truth, as far as the girl is concerned — and this is the critical point — her father is still lying, no one is seriously interested in hearing her side of the story, the procedure is completely stacked, and this is one more telling example of the hypocrisy and treachery of the adult world.

The point of the matter is that despite what the original reformers may have thought, "hearing both sides of the story" is not a lawyer's invention to free the guilty by throwing sand in the eyes of the adversary; it is a procedure which through the ages seems to reflect basic notions of what is the proper way to find out what happened before important decisions are made.

### SOME QUESTIONS ABOUT "JUDICIALIZING" THE JUVENILE COURT PROCEDURE

In efforts to get away from the defects of the nonadversary procedure, the emphasis in current programs for reform has been on the granting of "rights" — the right to counsel, the right of confrontation, the privilege against self-incrimination and the right to be advised of the privilege, the benefits granted by stricter rules of evidence and the right of appeal; that is, the more important rights of the criminal adversary system. A number of questions may be raised, however, as to whether the granting of these rights in the juvenile courts will accomplish the claimed objectives.

A program of rights, to be effective, requires affirmative exercise or intelligent waiver, which, in turn, assumes notice, understanding, and motivation. The accomplishment of notice, understanding and motivation in the juvenile process presents great problems. For a long time the New York Court of Appeals has said that many of the rights now called for must be observed in juvenile court proceedings. Nevertheless, it was found that for all practical purposes there was no representation, no objections were taken despite flagrant violations of the rules of evidence, and there were no appeals. Why the discrepancy between what the high court wanted and what it got?

The reason could lie in the hostility of juvenile court judges, probation officers and the police to the exercise of these rights. Such hostility would result in failure to comply with formal standards declared by the court or legislature or even active discouragement of the exercise of these declared rights by these officials.[86]

86. ... The California Governor's Special Study Commission on Juvenile Justice [Report (1960), hereinafter cited as California Report,] documented several instances of official hostility to the exercise of rights:

"3. Many parents are not informed of this right to be represented by counsel ... and in other instances, this information is not transmitted until the child is actually at the hearing itself and the court is ready to proceed.

"4. Many judges discourage the presence of counsel in their courts in an effort to reduce the time devoted to the juvenile court assignment.

"5. Some courts believe that attorneys have no place in the juvenile court and use coercive means to discourage their presence.

"6. Probation officers will frequently counsel the parents against hiring attorneys as a needless expense, assuring them there will be no difference in the case's outcome.

. . . .

"8. Some judges are concerned that more frequent appearance of counsel will invite more appeals, and thereby upset traditional, local juvenile court procedures.

"The commission knows of several counties where representation by counsel is actively discouraged by threatening parents that if they insist on counsel a more severe disposition will be imposed or the case will be transferred to the criminal courts. In addition, information concerning right to counsel is sometimes transmitted to the parents in a manner which discourages employment of counsel. Such advisory statements as 'you are entitled to counsel, but he won't be able to do you any good,' are not likely to augment the number of persons hiring counsel." California Report, pt. II, ... at 13.

On the privilege against self-incrimination, the report stated that the overwhelming majority of judges do not advise adolescents that they have a right

Anyone who has witnessed the proceedings in lower criminal courts knows that the routine of giving of notice (i.e., the formal compliance with appellate court or legislative commands) is not enough.

In addition, the reason could lie in a connection between the extraordinarily high number of respondents pro se and the extraordinarily high number of "tearful" confessions. Leaving aside the problem of the confused, the frightened, and feeble minded, why should even the intelligent and understanding insist on his rights? Does the shrewd adolescent have more or less to gain by rejecting unofficial delinquency or the informal inquisitorial hearing and insisting on his rights? Given the present state of affairs, one might well have serious doubts as to whether or not the adolescent would think that he will be better off by insisting on his rights. The police or probation officer may be acting illegally and in some cases, no doubt arbitrarily, incompetently and oppressively. But in the eyes of the adolescent compliance may seem far safer than the unknown but potentially harsh consequences of a litigated contest. Before rights will be exercised, the possessor of the rights must know what advantages, real practical advantages, he can tangibly expect by insisting on his rights.

In other words, in the total context of the present administration of juvenile justice, if the program of rights is to be effective, it must deal with the problem of waiver — waiver by those who do

---

not to testify. In addition, *"some courts unfortunately take coercive action when a child refuses to testify.* This is evidenced by the following excerpt from the transcript of a recent juvenile court hearing:

'Counsel: "I'm instructing my client not to testify."

'The Court: "Then, in that case, we will find that this matter is an unfit case for this particular court and certify him to the adult court for trial. He will be ordered confined here until the time of the trial."

'Clerk: "Your Honor, is that a dismissal of the petition in regard to the youth?"

'The Court: "That's right."

'Counsel: "Your Honor, is that a dismissal of the petition in regard to the youth?"

'The Court: "That's right."

'Counsel: "Your Honor, in that respect, I withdraw the objection."

'The Court: "Now, James, what do you have to say about this?" ' " California Report, pt. II, . . . at 11.

As to the extreme infrequency of appeals, the Report noted that since few attorneys appear in the juvenile court proceedings, judicial error is often not detected, parents are either unaware of the right to appeal or do not know how to make an appeal, and in only a minority of courts is there a stenographic record. California Report, pt. II, . . . at 11, 13, 18.

not understand and waiver by those who, rightly or wrongly, think, or have been coerced into thinking that they have more to gain by playing ball or by manipulation. Waiver under either circumstance should not be allowed. As already discussed, the community's interest here is greater than that which the adolescent or the parent thinks his best interests are. Furthermore, if these rights are to serve the important function of testing and questioning the juvenile process, allowing waiver should increase coercive tactics by the officials who are going to be questioned. Paradoxically, then, for "rights" to be effective, they must be made mandatory. If the community is seriously interested in these rights, it must be prepared to require the adolescents and parents to exercise them; otherwise, as in New York (at least under the previous regime) the program will remain largely vacuous.

The most serious conclusion implicit in the foregoing is that granting the right to counsel on request will not do. For many jurisdictions recognizing the right to counsel and affording counsel to the indigent will be a step forward. But laudable as such programs are, they will not meet the problem of waiver. If the respondent is either unwilling or unable to retain counsel, counsel must be assigned.

In addition, it is questionable whether assigning counsel at the hearing will be enough. No doubt counsel at the hearing can perform many important functions — insisting on competent and relevant evidence, questioning witnesses, and speaking on behalf of his client. But, as the discussion of the burglary example indicates, if the adolescent is to be represented effectively, he will need investigative services as well as trial services. The need is no less acute if the hearing is bifurcated. Criminal lawyers traditionally emphasize the adjudicatory hearing but at least in juvenile delinquency, the dispositional hearing may be the really crucial one. And it is at this hearing — on the question of what is to be done with the adolescent — that the probation officer's social report will have its most significant impact. At the same time, this is the area where the truth is most elusive and the report's conclusions and recommendations are most subject to the hazards of bias, overwork or incompetence. How effective will the defense lawyer be if he only performs at the hearing? Does he not also have a responsibility to offer an alternative plan? Properly functioning defense lawyers would not restrict their roles to the negative check at the hearing and the revisionists should expect no less for counsel representing juveniles.

Assuming that lawyers in sufficient quantity are available to man such a program (and assuming that the community is willing to bear this burden), a further question may be raised as to whether lawyers are properly equipped to handle the assignment. The emphasis in this paper is in terms of a sound procedure, a procedure that will further the community interest in finding the facts before official power is exercised. This is what the community is entitled to. This is also what the adolescent and the parents are entitled to; they are entitled to freedom in their future relationships unless it is found that past conduct warrants official control. It is on this basis, the search for a sound method of finding the facts, that the procedure of the original understanding and the current administration is rejected, and that an adversary system is urged. So the question then becomes: Will the lawyers staffing the program envisaged by the revisionists but trained in the adversary system of criminal and civil justice carry with them this approach? Can these lawyers provide the kind of representation that the adolescent and the family need for the sensible resolution of the case? Is it clear that the tactical advice given to an adult in investigative and adjudicative proceedings would be appropriate for an adolescent in juvenile proceedings?

The New York experience under the recent Family Court Act is already proving instructive. The Act provides for a system of "law guardians" to represent adolescents in delinquency, and persons-in-need-of-supervision proceedings if the adolescents are unable to obtain independent legal representation. Also, the court may appoint a law guardian on its own motion. Although the statute is silent as to the time of his appointment it seems to be contemplated that the guardian will be appointed at the time of the initial hearing.

What is the role envisaged for the law guardian? Although the Act does not define the role, in several sections it speaks in terms of partisan representation. On the other hand, the Joint Legislative Committee report and another section of the Act seem to view the law guardian more in terms of an aid to the court. The ambiguity of positions was not helped by an assembly bill which would have permitted the appointment of an attorney as a Family Court representative. An able commentator said of the bill that if it had become operative, "the complete return to an adversary system of proceeding would have been all but inevitable." Yet the Governor vetoed the bill on the ground that it duplicated the responsibilities of the law guardians.

Thus far the literature on the role of the law guardian has been sparse. Jacob L. Isaacs, a member of the Family Court Committee of the Judicial Conference of the State of New York, and a former chairman of the Committee on the Domestic Relations Court and Family Law of the Association of the Bar of the City of New York, described that role as follows: As advocate, the law guardian "should bring to this task the usual tools of the advocate — familiarity with the applicable law, the ability to make a thorough investigation and logical presentation of the relevant facts and the faculty for forceful and persuasive exposition of his client's position." [98] On the other hand, "conscientious counsel will have to exercise intelligent discrimination in the use of tactics learned in other courts since wholesale importation of techniques developed in the handling of criminal or civil cases before other tribunals may not only threaten the objectives of the court but will rarely serve the interest of the minor child." [99] As guardian, the lawyer must be concerned with not only "legal rights" but "the general welfare of the minor." [100] As officer of the court, in addition to other duties, the lawyer must disclose to the court "all facts in his possession which bear upon a proper disposition of the matter," subject to the attorney-client privilege.[101] Isaacs significantly points out that the attitudes of the lawyer will have important consequences for the rehabilitative goals of the program. "If counsel condones the 'beat the rap' approach and substitutes deception for honest but firm concern for the protection of his client's rights, he will not only be doing the court and his profession a disservice, but he will be rendering an even greater disservice to his client." [102]

The role envisaged by Isaacs does not seem to differ from the role envisaged by the American Bar Association for trial counsel in general. It is seriously questionable, however, whether these positions represent the attitudes of lawyers themselves as to the advocate's role and his strategy and tactics. In civil litigation, authoritative commentators, including no less a paragon than the late Samuel Williston, take a position on the trial lawyer's role which is quite different from Isaacs. Williston states flatly: "If ... [unfavorable] evidence was unknown to ... [the lawyer] when he took the case, he may sometimes withdraw from it, but while he is engaged as counsel he is not only not obliged to disclose unfavorable evidence, but it is a violation of his duty to his client if he

98. Isaacs, [The Role of the Lawyer in Representing Minors in the New Family Court, 12 Buffalo L. Rev. 501, 506 (1963)].
99. Ibid.
100. Id. at 507.
101. Ibid. . . .
102. [Ibid.]

does so." [104] The lawyer's duty is to do everything for his client that the law permits. He violates this duty if he sacrifices the client's legal rights for what he, the lawyer, thinks is the most just result. In criminal litigation, the push toward duty to client is intensified by the policies of the privilege against self-incrimination, the attorney-client privilege, and the strict burden of proof on the state.

This is not the place to comment on what role the lawyer should play either in court or in pre-trial bargaining. If, however, lawyers are to be used successfully in the juvenile process, one must reckon with the attitudes of the profession. As long as one assumes that the representation of juveniles calls for standards of behavior different from those practiced in adult proceedings, then, the critical problem of whether lawyers are willing or capable of changing their patterns of behavior must be faced. Furthermore, the change in behavior will probably have to be self-imposed. The experience of the criminal trial and appellate courts in attempting to control the excesses of advocacy has not been a happy one. In the juvenile process, where standards are much more vague, effective court control seems unlikely.

These then are some of the important problems of "judicializing" the legal process for juveniles. If the benefits of an adversary system are to be realized, representation cannot depend on the wishes of those caught in the system. The effectiveness of the representation depends on whether it is supplied at levels preceding formal hearing and whether the profession is equipped to handle the job. A program of this type will require an extensive commitment of the legal talent in the community (assuming that such talent is available). Unless these problems are resolved satisfactorily, the program of "rights" in the administration of juvenile justice might very well not be much more effective than such programs have been in the past.

104. Williston, Life and Law 271 (1940)....

# The Kpelle Moot: A Therapeutic Model for the Informal Settlement of Disputes*

## James L. Gibbs, Jr.

Africa as a major culture area has been characterized by many writers as being marked by a high development of law and legal procedures. In the past few years research on African law has produced a series of highly competent monographs such as those on law among the Tiv, the Barotse, and the Nuer. These and related shorter studies have focused primarily on formal processes for the settlement of disputes, such as those which take place in a courtroom, or those which are, in some other way, set apart from simpler measures of social control. However, many African societies have informal, quasi-legal, dispute-settlement procedures, supplemental to formal ones, which have not been as well studied, or — in most cases — adequately analysed.

In this paper I present a description and analysis of one such institution for the informal settlement of disputes, as it is found among the Kpelle of Liberia; it is the moot, the *bɛrɛi mu mɛni saa* or 'house palaver.' Hearings in the Kpelle moot contrast with those in a court in that they differ in tone and effectiveness. The genius of the moot lies in the fact that it is based on a covert application of the principles of psychoanalytic theory which underlie psychotherapy.

The Kpelle are a Mande-speaking, patrilineal group of some 175,000 rice cultivators who live in Central Liberia and the adjoining regions of Guinea. This paper is based on data gathered in a field study which I carried out in 1957 and 1958 among the Liberian Kpelle of Panta Chiefdom in north-east Central Province.

Strong corporate patrilineages are absent among the Kpelle. The most important kinship group is the virilocal polygynous family which sometimes becomes an extended family, almost always of the patrilineal variety. Several of these families form the core of a residential group, known as a village quarter, more technically, a clan-barrio. This is headed by a quarter elder who is related to most of the household heads by real or putative patrilineal ties.

* From: 33 Africa 1-10 (1963). Reprinted by permission of the International African Institute, and the author.

Kpelle political organization is centralized although there is no single king or paramount chief, but a series of chiefs of the same level of authority, each of whom is superordinate over district chiefs and town chiefs. Some political functions are also vested in the tribal fraternity, the Poro, which still functions vigorously. The form of political organization found in the area can thus best be termed the polycephalous associational state.

The structure of the Kpelle court system parallels that of the political organization. In Liberia the highest court of a tribal authority and the highest tribal court chartered by the Government is that of a paramount chief. A district chief's court is also an official court. Disputes may be settled in these official courts or in unofficial courts, such as those of town chiefs or quarter elders. In addition to this, grievances are settled informally in moots, and sometimes by associational groupings such as church councils or cooperative work groups.

In my field research I studied both the formal and informal methods of dispute settlement. The method used was to collect case material in as complete a form as possible. Accordingly, immediately after a hearing, my interpreter and I would prepare verbatim transcripts of each case that we heard. These transcripts were supplemented with accounts — obtained from respondents — of past cases or cases which I did not hear litigated. Transcripts from each type of hearing were analysed phrase by phrase in terms of a frame of reference derived from jurisprudence and ethno-law. The results of the analysis indicate two things: first, that courtroom hearings and moots are quite different in their procedures and tone, and secondly, why they show this contrast.

Kpelle courtroom hearings are basically coercive and arbitrary in tone. In another paper I have shown that this is partly the result of the intrusion of the authoritarian values of the Poro into the courtroom. As a result, the court is limited in the manner in which it can handle some types of disputes. The court is particularly effective in settling cases such as assault, possession of illegal charms, or theft where the litigants are not linked in a relationship which must continue after the trial. However, most of the cases brought before a Kpelle court are cases involving disputed rights over women, including matrimonial matters which are usually cast in the form of suits for divorce. The court is particularly inept at settling these numerous matrimonial disputes because its harsh tone tends to drive spouses farther apart rather than to reconcile them. The moot, in contrast, is more effective in handling such cases. The following analysis indicates the reasons for this.[1]

The Kpelle *berei mu meni saa*, or 'house palaver,' is an informal airing of a dispute which takes place before an assembled group which includes kinsmen of the litigants and neighbours from the quarter where the case is being heard. It is a completely ad hoc group, varying greatly in composition from case to case. The matter to be settled is usually a domestic problem: alleged mistreatment or neglect by a spouse, an attempt to collect money paid to a kinsman for a job which was not completed, or a quarrel among brothers over the inheritance of their father's wives.

In the procedural description which follows I shall use illustrative data from the Case of the Ousted Wife:

> Wama Nya, the complainant, had one wife, Yua. His older brother died and he inherited the widow, Yokpo, who moved into his house. The two women were classificatory sisters. After Yokpo moved in, there was strife in the household. The husband accused her of staying out late at night, of harvesting rice without his knowledge, and of denying him food. He also accused Yokpo of having lovers and admitted having had a physical struggle with her, after which he took a basin of water and 'washed his hands of her'.
>
> Yokpo countered by denying the allegations about having lovers, saying that she was accused falsely, although she had in the past confessed the name of one lover. She further complained that Wama Nya had assaulted her and, in the act, had committed the indignity of removing her headtie, and had expelled her from the house after the ritual hand-washing. Finally, she alleged that she had been thus cast out of the house at the instigation of the other wife who, she asserted, had great influence over their husband.
>
> Kolo Waa, the Town Chief and quarter elder, and the brother of Yokpo, was the mediator of the moot, which decided that the husband was mainly at fault, although Yua and Yokpo's children were also in the wrong. Those at fault had to apologize to Yokpo and bring gifts of apology as well as local rum[2] for the disputants and participants in the moot.

1. What follows is based on a detailed case study of moots in Panta Chiefdom and their contrast with courtroom hearings before the paramount chief of that chiefdom. Moots, being private, are less susceptible to the surveillance of the anthropologist than courtroom hearings, and we have fewer transcripts of moots than of court trials. The analysis presented here is valid for Panta Chiefdom and also valid, I feel, for most of the Liberian Kpelle area, particularly the north-east where people are, by and large, traditional.

2. This simple distilled rum, bottled in Monrovia and retailing for twenty-five cents a bottle in 1958, is known in the Liberian Hinterland as 'cane juice' and should not be confused with the imported varieties.

The moot is most often held on a Sunday — a day of rest for Christians and non-Christians alike — at the home of the complainant, the person who calls the moot. The mediator will have been selected by the complainant. He is a kinsman who also holds an office such as town chief or quarter elder, and therefore has some skill in dispute settlement. It is said that he is chosen to preside by virtue of his kin tie, rather than because of his office.

The proceedings begin with the pronouncing of blessings by one of the oldest men of the group. In the Case of the Ousted Wife, Gbenai Zua, the elder who pronounced the blessings, took a rice-stirrer in his hand and, striding back and forth, said:

> This man has called us to fix the matter between him and his wife. May *yala* [the supreme, creator deity] change his heart and let his household be in a good condition. May *yala* bless the family and make them fruitful. May He bless them so they can have food this year. May He bless the children and the rest of the family so they may always be healthy. May He bless them to have good luck. When Wama Nya takes a gun and goes in the bush, may he kill big animals. May *yala* bless us to enjoy the meat. May He bless us to enjoy life and always have luck. May yala bless all those who come to discuss this matter.

The man who pronounces the blessings always carries a stick or a whisk (*kpung*) which he waves for effect as he paces up and down chanting his injunctions. Participation of spectators is demanded, for the blessings are chanted by the elder (*kpung namu* or '*kpung owner*') as a series of imperatives, some of which he repeats. Each phrase is responded to by the spectators who answer in unison with a formal response, either **ɛ** *ka ti* (so be it), or a low, drawn-out **ɛɛɛɛ**. The *kpung namu* delivers his blessings faster and faster, building up a rhythmic interaction pattern with the other participants. The effect is to unite those attending in common action before the hearing begins. The blessing focuses attention on the concern with maintaining harmony and the well-being of the group as a whole.

Everyone attending the moot wears their next-to-best clothes or, if it is not Sunday, everyday clothes. Elders, litigants, and spectators sit in mixed fashion, pressed closely upon each other, often overflowing on to a veranda. This is in contrast to the vertical spatial separation between litigants and adjudicators in the courtroom. The mediator, even though he is a chief, does not wear his robes. He and the oldest men will be given chairs as they would on any other occasion.

The complainant speaks first and may be interrupted by the mediator or anyone else present. After he has been thoroughly quizzed, the accused will answer and will also be questioned by those present. The two parties will question each other directly and question others in the room also. Both the testimony and the questioning are lively and uninhibited. Where there are witnesses to some of the actions described by the parties, they may also speak and be questioned. Although the proceedings are spirited, they remain orderly. The mediator may fine anyone who speaks out of turn by requiring them to bring some rum for the group to drink.

The mediator and the others present will point out the various faults committed by both the parties. After everyone has been heard, the mediator expresses the consensus of the group. For example, in the Case of the Ousted Wife, he said to Yua: 'The words you used towards your sister were not good, so come and beg her pardon.'

The person held to be mainly at fault will then formally apologize to the other person. This apology takes the form of the giving of token gifts to the wronged person by the guilty party. These may be an item of clothing, a few coins, clean hulled rice, or a combination of all three. It is also customary for the winning party in accepting the gifts of apology to give, in return, a smaller token such as a twenty-five cent piece to show his 'white heart' or good will. The losing party is also lightly 'fined'; he must present rum or beer to the mediator and the others who heard the case. This is consumed by all in attendance. The old man then pronounces blessings again and offers thanks for the restoration of harmony within the group, and asks that all continue to act with good grace and unity.

An initial analysis of the procedural steps of the moot isolated the descriptive attributes of the moot and shows that they contrast with those of the courtroom hearing. While the airing of grievances is incomplete in courtroom hearings, it is more complete in the moot. This fuller airing of the issues results, in many marital cases, in a more harmonious solution. Several specific features of the house palaver facilitate this wider airing of grievances. First, the hearing takes place soon after a breach has occurred, before the grievances have hardened. There is no delay until the complainant has time to go to the paramount chief's or district chief's headquarters to institute suit. Secondly, the hearing takes place in the familiar surroundings of a home. The robes, writs, messengers, and other symbols of power which subtly intimidate and inhibit the parties in the courtroom, by reminding them of the physical force which underlies the procedures, are absent. Thirdly, in the courtroom the conduct of the hearing is firmly in the hands of the judge, but in the moot the investigatory initiative rests much more with the parties themselves. Jurisprudence suggests that, in such a case, more of the grievances lodged between the parties are likely to be aired and adjusted. Finally, the range of relevance applied to matters which are brought out is extremely broad. Hardly anything mentioned is held to be irrelevant. This too leads to a more thorough ventilation of the issues.

There is a second surface difference between court and moot. In a courtroom hearing, the solution is, by and large, one which is imposed by the adjudicator. In the moot the solution is more consensual. It is, therefore, more likely to be accepted by both parties and hence more durable. Several features of the moot contribute to the consensual solution: first, there is no unilateral ascription of blame, but an attribution of fault to both parties. Secondly, the mediator, unlike the chief in the courtroom, is not backed by political authority and the physical force which underlies it. He cannot jail parties, nor can he levy a heavy fine. Thirdly, the sanctions which are imposed are not so burdensome as to cause hardship to the losing party or to give him or her grounds for a new grudge against the other party. The gifts for the winning party and the potables for the spectators are not as expensive as the fines and the court costs in a paramount chief's court. Lastly, the ritualized apology of the moot symbolizes very concretely the consensual nature of the solution. The public offering and acceptance of the tokens of apology indicate that each party has no further grievances and that the settlement is satisfactory and mutually acceptable. The parties and spectators drink together to symbolize the restored solidarity of the group and the rehabilitation of the offending party.

This type of analysis describes the courtroom hearing and the moot, using a frame of reference derived from jurisprudence and ethno-law which is explicitly comparative and evaluative. Only by using this type of comparative approach can the researcher select features of the hearings which are not only unique to each of them, but theoretically significant in that their contribution to the social-control functions of the proceedings can be hypothesized. At the same time, it enables the researcher to pin-point in procedures the cause for what he feels intuitively: that the two hearings contrast in tone, even though they are similar in some ways.

However, one can approach the transcripts of the trouble cases with a second analytical framework and emerge with a deeper understanding of the implications of the contrasting descriptive attributes of the court and the house palaver. Remember that the coercive tone of the courtroom hearing limits the court's effectiveness in dealing with matrimonial disputes, especially in effecting reconciliations. The moot, on the other hand, is particularly effective in bringing about reconciliations between spouses. This is because the moot is not only conciliatory, but *therapeutic*. Moot procedures are therapeutic in that, like psychotherapy, they re-educate the parties through a type of social learning brought about in a specially structured interpersonal setting.

Talcott Parsons has written that therapy involves four elements: support, permissiveness, denial of reciprocity, and manipulation of rewards. Writers such as Frank, Klapman, and Opler have pointed out that the same elements characterize not only individual psychotherapy, but group psychotherapy as well. All four elements are writ large in the Kpelle moot.

The patient in therapy will not continue treatment very long if he does not feel support from the therapist or from the group. In the moot the parties are encouraged in the expression of their complaints and feelings because they sense group support. The very presence of one's kinsmen and neighbours demonstrates their concern. It indicates to the parties that they have a real problem and that the others are willing to help them to help themselves in solving it. In a parallel vein, Frank, speaking of group psychotherapy, notes that: 'Even anger may be supportive if it implies to a patient that others take him seriously enough to get angry at him, especially if the object of the anger feels it to be directed toward his neurotic behaviour rather than himself as a person.' In the moot the feeling of support also grows out of the pronouncement of the blessings which stress the unity of the group and its harmonious goal, and it is also undoubtedly increased by the absence of the publicity and expressive symbols of political power which are found in the courtroom.

Permissiveness is the second element in therapy. It indicates to the patient that every-day restrictions on making anti-social statements or acting out anti-social impulses are lessened. Thus, in the Case of the Ousted Wife, Yua felt free enough to turn to her ousted co-wife (who had been married leviratically) and say:

You don't respect me. You don't rely on me any more. When your husband was living, and I was with my husband, we slept on the farm. Did I ever refuse to send you what you asked me for when you sent a message? Didn't I always send you some of the meat my husband killed? Did I refuse to send you anything you wanted? When your husband died and we became co-wives, did I disrespect you? Why do you always make me ashamed? The things you have done to me make me sad.

Permissiveness in the therapeutic setting (and in the moot) results in catharsis, in a high degree of stimulation of feelings in the participants and an equally high tendency to verbalize these feelings. Frank notes that: 'Neurotic responses must be expressed in the therapeutic situation if they are to be changed by it.' In the same way, if the solution to a dispute reached in a house palaver is to be stable, it is important that there should be nothing left to embitter and undermine the decision. In a familiar setting, with familiar people, the parties to the moot feel at ease and free to say *all* that is on their minds. Yokpo, judged to be the wronged party in the Case of the Ousted Wife, in accepting an apology, gave expression to this when she said:

I agree to everything that my people said, and I accept the things they have given me — I don't have *anything else* about them on my mind. (*My italics.*)

As we shall note below, this thorough airing of complaints also facilitates the gaining of insight into and the unlearning of idiosyncratic behaviour which is socially disruptive. Permissiveness is rooted in the lack of publicity and the lack of symbols of power. But it stems, too, from the immediacy of the hearing, the locus of investigatory initiative with the parties, and the wide range of relevance.

Permissiveness in therapy is impossible without the denial of reciprocity. This refers to the fact that the therapist will not respond in kind when the patient acts in a hostile manner or with inappropriate affection. It is a type of privileged indulgence which comes with being a patient. In the moot, the parties are treated in the same way and are allowed to hurl recriminations that, in the courtroom, might bring a few hours in jail as punishment for the equivalent of contempt of court. Even though inappropriate views are not responded to in kind, neither are they simply ignored. There is denial of *congruent* response, not denial of *any* response whatsoever. In the *bɛrɛi mu mɛni saa*, as in group psychotherapy, 'private ideation and conceptualization are brought out into the open and all their facets or many of their facets exposed. The individual gets a "reading" from different bearings on the compass, so to speak, and perceptual patterns . . . are joggled out of their fixed positions. . . .'

Thus, Yua's outburst against Yokpo quoted above was not responded to with matching hostility, but its inappropriateness was clearly pointed out to her by the group. Some of them called her aside in a huddle and said to her:

> You are not right. If you don't like the woman, or she doesn't like you, don't be the first to say anything. Let her start and then say what you have to say. By speaking, if she heeds some of your words, the wives will scatter, and the blame will be on you. Then your husband will cry for your name that you have scattered his property.

In effect, Yua was being told that, in view of the previous testimony, her jealousy of her co-wife was not justified. In reality testing, she discovered that her view of the situation was not shared by the others and, hence, was inappropriate. Noting how the others responded, she could see why her treatment of her co-wife had caused so much dissension. Her interpretation of her new co-wife's actions and resulting premisses were not shared by the co-wife, nor by the others hearing a description of what had happened. Like psychotherapy, the moot is gently corrective of behaviour rooted in such misunderstandings.

Similarly, Wama Nya, the husband, learned that others did not view as reasonable his accusing his wife of having a lover and urging her to go off and drink with the suspected paramour when he passed their house and wished them all a good evening. Reality testing for him taught him that the group did not view this type of mildly paranoid sarcasm as conducive to stable marital relationships.

The reaction of the moot to Yua's outburst indicates that permissiveness in this case was certainly not complete, but only relative, being much greater than that in the courtroom. But without this moderated immunity the airing of grievances would be limited, and the chance for social relearning lessened. Permissiveness in the moot is incomplete because, even there, prudence is not thrown to the winds. Note that Yua was not told not to express her feelings at all, but to express them only after the co-wife had spoken so that, if the moot failed, she would not be in an untenable position. In court there would be objection to her blunt speaking out. In the moot the objection was, in effect, to her speaking *out of turn*. In other cases the moot sometimes fails, foundering on this very point, because the parties are *too* prudent, all waiting for the others to make the first move in admitting fault.

The manipulation of rewards is the last dimension of therapy treated by Parsons. In this final phase of therapy the patient is coaxed to conformity by the granting of rewards. In the moot one of the most important rewards is the group approval which goes to the wronged person who accepts an apology and to the person who is magnanimous enough to make one.

In the Case of the Ousted Wife, Kolo Waa, the mediator, and the others attending decided that the husband and the co-wife, Yua, had wronged Yopko. Kolo Waa said to the husband:

> From now on, we don't want to hear of your fighting. You should live in peace with these women. If your wife accepts the things which the people have brought you should pay four chickens and ten bottles of rum as your contribution.

The husband's brother and sister also brought gifts of apology, although the moot did not explicitly hold them at fault.

By giving these prestations, the wrong-doer is restored to good grace and is once again acting like an 'upright Kpelle, (although, if he wishes, he may refuse to accept the decision of the moot). He is eased into this position by being grouped with others to whom blame is also allocated, for, typically, he is not singled out and isolated in being labelled deviant. Thus, in the Case of the Ousted Wife the children of Yokpo were held to be at fault in 'being mean' to their step-father, so that blame was not only shared by one 'side,' but ascribed to the other also.

Moreover, the prestations which the losing party is asked to hand over are not expensive. They are significant enough to touch the pocketbook a little; for the Kpelle say that if an apology does not cost something other than words, the wrong-doer is more likely to repeat the offending action. At the same time, as we noted above, the tokens are not so costly as to give the loser additional reason for anger directed at the other party which can undermine the decision.

All in all, the rewards for conformity to group expectations and for following out a new behaviour pattern are kept within the deviant's sight. These rewards are positive, in contrast to the negative sanctions of the courtroom. Besides the institutionalized apology, praise and acts of concern and affection replace fines and jail sentences. The mediator, speaking to Yokpo as the wronged party, said:

> You have found the best of the dispute. Your husband has wronged you. All the people have wronged you. You are the only one who can take care of them because you are the oldest. Accept the things they have given to you.

The moot in its procedural features and procedural sequences is, then, strongly analogous to psychotherapy. It is analogous to therapy in the structuring of the role of the mediator also. Parsons has indicated that, to do his job well, the therapist must be a member of two social systems: one containing himself and his patient; and the other, society at large. He must not be seduced into thinking that he belongs only to the therapeutic dyad, but must gradually pull the deviant back into a relationship with the wider group. It is significant, then, that the mediator of a moot is a kinsman who is also a chief of some sort. He thus represents both the group involved in the dispute and the wider community. His task is to utilize his position as kinsman as a lever to manipulate the parties into living up to the normative requirements of the wider society, which, as chief, he upholds. His major orientation must be to the wider collectivity, not to the particular goals of his kinsmen.

When successful, the moot stops the process of alienation which drives two spouses so far apart that they are immune to ordinary social-control measures such as a smile, a frown, or a pointed aside. A moot is not always successful, however. Both parties must have a genuine willingness to co-operate and a real concern about their discord. Each party must be willing to list his grievances, to admit his guilt, and make an open apology. The moot, like psychotherapy, is impotent without well-motivated clients.

The therapeutic elements found in the Kpelle moot are undoubtedly found in informal procedures for settling disputes in other African societies also; some of these are reported in the literature and others are not. One such procedure which seems strikingly parallel to the Kpelle *berei mu meni saa* has been described by J. H. M. Beattie. This is the court of neighbours or *rukurato rw'enzarwa* found in the Banyoro kingdom of Uganda. The group also meets as an ad hoc assembly of neighbours to hear disputes involving kinsmen or neighbours.

The intention of the Nyoro moot is to 'reintegrate the delinquent into the community and, if possible, to achieve reconciliation without causing bitterness and resentment; in the words of an informant, the institution exists "to finish off people's quarrels and to abolish bad feeling." ' This therapeutic goal is manifested in the manner in which the dispute is resolved. After a decision is reached the penalty imposed is always the same. The party held to be in the wrong is asked to bring beer (four pots, modified downwards according to the circumstances) and meat, which is shared with the other party and all those attending the *rukurato*. The losing party is also expected to 'humble himself, not only to the man he has injured but to the whole assembly.'

Beattie correctly points out that, because the council of neighbours has no power to enforce its decision, the shared feast is *not* to be viewed primarily as a penalty, for the wrong-doer acts as host and also shares in the food and drink. 'And it is a praiseworthy thing; from a dishonourable status he is promoted to an honourable one . . .' and reintegrated into the community.

Although Beattie does not use a psychoanalytic frame of reference in approaching his material, it is clear that the communal feast involves the manipulation of rewards as the last step in a social-control measure which breaks the progressive alienation of the deviance cycle. The description of procedures in the rukurato indicates that it is highly informal in nature, convening in a room in a house with everyone 'sitting around.' However, Beattie does not provide enough detail to enable one to determine whether or not the beginning and intermediate steps in the Nyoro moot show the permissiveness, support, and denial of reciprocity which characterize the Kpelle moot. Given the structure and outcome of most Nyoro councils, one would surmise that a close examination of their proceedings would reveal the implicit operation of therapeutic principles.

The fact that the Kpelle court is basically coercive and the moot therapeutic does not imply that one is dysfunctional while the other is eufunctional. Like Beattie, I conclude that the court and informal dispute-settlement procedures have separate but complementary functions. In marital disputes the moot is oriented to a couple as a dyadic social system and serves to reconcile them wherever possible. This is eufunctional from the point of view of the couple, to whom divorce would be dysfunctional. Kpelle courts customarily treat matrimonial matters by granting a divorce. While this may be dysfunctional from the point of view of the couple, because it ends their marriage, it may be eufunctional from the point of view of society. Some marriages, if forced to continue, would result in adultery or physical violence at best, and improper socialization of children at worst. It is clear that the Kpelle moot is to the Kpelle court as the domestic and family relations courts (or commercial and labour arbitration boards) are to ordinary courts in our own society. The essential point is that both formal and informal dispute-settlement procedures serve significant functions in Kpelle society and neither can be fully understood if studied alone.

## The Cuban Popular Tribunals*

# Jesse Berman

### INTRODUCTION

Cuba's Popular Tribunals, which have been in operation since 1964, are the embodiment of a theoretical approach to the role of a legal system in a communist society, one which, in a relatively short period of time, has undergone much profound economic, political, and social change. Dissatisfaction with conventional Western courts in Cuba was voiced early in the revolution by its leadership. In 1953, Fidel Castro, a lawyer by training, while defending himself for his abortive raid on the Moncada barracks in that same year, argued that courts should "judge people, and not crimes," and that individuals must be judged in the context of their environment:

> When you judge a defendant for robbery, your honors, do you ask him how long he has been unemployed? Do you ask him how many children he has, which days of the week he ate and which he didn't, do you concern yourselves with his environment at all? You send him to jail without further thought.[1]

The Popular Tribunals have developed, within their sphere of competence, as an attempt to provide an alternative to the system which Castro condemned as unresponsive. This article, based in large part on personal observations and interviews made and con-

---

* From: 69 Colum. L. Rev. 1317-1354 (1969). Reprinted by permission of the Columbia Law Review and the author.
   1. F. Castro, History Will Absolve Me (1967).

ducted in Cuba, will discuss the present day operation of the Tribunals, and evaluate their progress in light of their professed goals.

## I. PURPOSES AND FUNCTIONS

The first Cuban Popular Tribunals were organized, in the rural areas of the provinces, on an experimental basis. By November 3, 1966, the number of experimental Tribunals already functioning was thirty-one, and these were made permanent on that date. Forty-five new permanent Tribunals were to be established in November and December of 1966, and the first two sections of a Judges' Manual were published that November. Popular Tribunals were set up in Habana del Este (a newly-built suburb of the capital) in late 1966 and early 1967, and Tribunals were formally established in Havana proper beginning in January 1968.

The avowed, theoretical purposes of the Popular Tribunals have been outlined by Blas Roca, a member of the Central Committee of the Communist Party of Cuba (*Partido Comunista de Cuba*) and chairman (*presidente*) of the Commission for Constitutional Studies of the P.C.C.:

> [with the creation of] the Popular Tribunals, the revolutionary and socialist content of our justice is made more complete and profound, and the form, structure and organization of the courts is made more in accord with this content.
>
> The fact that the masses, in a profoundly democratic manner, choose and elect those who can be popular judges, is a decisive blow against the idea, prevalent among the people, that justice is something official, something which comes down from above, something alien to them.
>
> ... people's justice, applied to the people, through tribunals elected by that same people.
>
> The fact that the Popular Tribunals are organized and function in the neighborhood, so that neighbors and acquaintances of those being judged can attend the trials and can make these trials truly public, and that the judges sitting in these trials come from the same community in which they live and work, reinforces the idea that the justice they administer is that of the working people, the expression of the power of the working people in the socialist state.
>
> ... to edify and consolidate the new society of socialism and communism, to educate the new man, to secure and to perfect the rules of the socialist community.[6]

6. [Manual de los Tribunales Populares de Base vi (1966), hereinafter cited as Manual].

More practically speaking, the purpose of the Popular Tribunals is to encourage acceptance of the laws of a new society by making the courts, which enforce these new laws, not institutions of coercion, but familiar, popularly accepted institutions. If the people can identify with the courts, they can identify with the law they learn in those courts, and can learn to avoid voluntarily what these courts term "anti-social conduct." As Parsons has noted, "Defining an act as a crime, so long as that definition is accepted in the community, is an effective way of discouraging other people from following that example." [7] Voluntary acceptance of new definitions, fostered by presenting these new definitions in a palatable, identifiable context, greatly lessens the need to resort to coercion for enforcement. Thus one practical function of the Popular Tribunals is to encourage voluntary compliance with the severe rationing now in force in Cuba. Illustrative of this is the fact that almost every evening's docket in a Popular Tribunal contains at least one petty black market case.

Another function of the Popular Tribunals is to introduce a revolutionary mentality into the solution of personal quarrels. The most common cases in the Havana Popular Tribunals are those involving "public disorder," often resulting from the acute housing shortage in Havana (new housing is no longer being constructed in Havana, in order to encourage migration to the rural areas, so that more labor will become available for work in agriculture). According to Rogelio Buznego, director of the Popular Tribunals for the province of Havana, this urban overcrowding results in children fighting in the streets, and in their mothers defending them, creating large numbers of disputes which require peaceful settlement. This incidentally results in the fact that most litigants before the Popular Tribunals are women.

An increase in the frequency of divorces has also compounded the housing shortage, and some divorced couples are forced to remain together for months while they await separate housing. Quite naturally, numerous quarrels ensue during the interim. According to Buznego, the Popular Tribunals are often dealing with "social problems, not penal problems," because of these various environmental factors.

It must be stressed that although the Popular Tribunals do impose sanctions on litigants and on criminal defendants, these are of a relatively mild, rehabilitative nature. The essential function of

7. Parsons, Personality and Social Structure, in Personality and Political Crisis 74 (A. Stanton & S. Percy eds. 1951).

the Popular Tribunals is not to settle quarrels and not to sanction, but to involve and educate the community in the day-to-day laws of their society, especially in the new laws promulgated by the revolution. This is perhaps best illustrated at this point with a summary of a sample case I observed in Havana:

Woman A and her daughter accused woman B of stealing woman A's pants. B's defense was that she bought the pants in a government clothing outlet in the neighborhood. She offered, as evidence, her ration booklet, showing that she had purchased a pair of pants of the type in question in May, 1968. One of the three judges (*jueces*) of the Tribunal interrupted to say that his daytime work was in the distribution of clothing, and that he personally knew that the particular type of pants in question were not available in that neighborhood in Havana in May of 1968 and that, therefore, B must be lying and the ration booklet entry must have been falsified. This sudden revelation determined the outcome of the case, and the audience was clearly impressed with the Solomon-like wisdom of this *coup de théâtre*. B never admitted her guilt, but at this point she ceased her protestations of innocence. B was given a public admonition (*amonestación pública*) and was sentenced to 60 days confinement (*confinamiento*) to her house and her work in agriculture. The head judge (*presidente*) then lectured *both parties* on the necessity for friendship between workers. The Tribunal also noted that the *daughter* of the complainant (*acusadora*) had lied about her educational level (inquiries around the neighborhood by the judges had revealed this), and she was ordered to go to school at night until attainment of the minimum, sixth-grade literacy level (*superación educacional*). The pants were then publicly returned to A.

The quarrel was effectively settled and appropriate sanctions ordered. But clearly the function of the Popular Tribunal was, in this instance, to educate the audience of community people. The Tribunals' opportunities to fulfill these various functions is, of course, directly related to the statutory powers vested in them. Section II will briefly survey these powers.

## II. THE POWERS OF THE POPULAR TRIBUNALS

### A. Jurisdiction

. . . Each Popular Tribunal has jurisdiction over certain civil and criminal wrongs—*conductas antisociales* — committed in its particular zone or committed elsewhere by inhabitants of its particu-

lar zone. This jurisdictional scope allows the Tribunal to adjudge
most petty crimes and torts of the inhabitants of its zone, a relatively small area averaging less than thirty square blocks and containing an average population of only four thousand people.

... The types of delicts which the Tribunals are empowered to
deal with, in addition to the manner in which cases are commonly
disposed of, illustrate vividly the important role which the Tribunals perform in the day-to-day life of their respective communities. The following discussion, therefore, will center on selected
delicts within the competence of the Popular Tribunals, for which
observed trials can be offered as examples.[24]

One such offense is a delict against individual rights, limited to
the two categories of threats (*amenazas*) and coercions (*coacci-
ones*). With regard to threats, no distinction is made between
civil and criminal assaults. A coercion is the forcing of someone
to do something by utilizing a threat. A specific illustration can
be seen in a case actually observed in Havana:

The *acusadora* claimed that the *acusado*, her neighbor (a soldier), who shared a common water main with her, kept his faucet
on too long every day — water is available in their neighborhood
only twelve hours a day and must be stored daily in a tank in
each apartment — thus preventing her from filling her tank. She
further claimed that when she criticized him, he talked to her
abusively, threatened her, and forced her to abandon the faucet.
He denied this and claimed instead that she had monopolized the
water. He also claimed that he was a good soldier, a member of
the *Fuerzas Armadas Revolucionarias* (regular army), and that
she was a counterrevolutionary. She answered that she was a good
citizen and charged that he was a counterrevolutionary. There
were two "spontaneous" witnesses who tended to corroborate the
*acusadora's* testimony. The court admonished both litigants, lectured them on the high value which socialism places on cooperation, and set up a schedule for the use of the water main.

It may be inferred that the Popular Tribunal in the above case

24. In all, the Tribunals possess competence over thirteen different types
of delicts. Although a detailed discussion of each is not necessary or helpful
to an understanding of the functioning of the Tribunals, a list of these delicts
follows: (a) delicts against individual rights, (b) against public order, (c)
against the administration of justice, (d) against the public faith, (e) delicts
committed by public employees in the exercise of their powers, (f) against
the integrity of the body, (g) against health, (h) against collective security,
(i) against "good customs," (j) against the order of the family, (k) against
honor. Manual at 34-74.

felt that the threats and the name calling were less important than the immediate problem of devising a method for sharing the water. Although there probably actually were threats and perhaps even coercion, the Popular Tribunal here declined to make any factual findings and limited its sanctions to an admonition. This case is typical of what Buznego termed a social, rather than a penal problem.

Delicts against the integrity of the body primarily consist of *lesiones,* defined as intentional physical aggression causing bodily injury short of death. Various personal, rehabilitative sanctions may be imposed on the *acusado,* depending upon the severity of the injury, the weapon or other means employed, the *acusado's* conduct before and after the act, his personal circumstances (previous record, family situation, etc.), and his motive. In addition to the rehabilitative sanctions, the *acusado* may be required to indemnify his victim. An observed *lesión* case follows:

A wife had claimed that her husband had hit her, while she was pregnant, breaking her nose. A medical certificate (which I personally examined before the trial) was introduced as evidence, and showed extreme damage to the wife's nose, obviously the result of a beating rather than a fall or other accident. On the night of the trial, the wife said that she wanted to withdraw the charges, explaining that at the time when she made the complaint she feared that her baby would be born abnormal as a result of the beating, but since the baby had been born normal, she no longer wished any ill toward her husband. The Tribunal ruled that she could not unilaterally drop the charges, because the people had an interest in discouraging wife beatings, even if this particular wife no longer cared. The trial proceeded. The husband's defense was that it had been an accident, based on a claim that his wife fell as he was helping her get into bed. The Tribunal viewed this story as being inconsistent with the medical report and less credible than the wife's written complaint. The wife then offered to testify that she had hit her husband first. Neither the Tribunal nor the onlookers seemed to believe this. The husband was found guilty, but in view of the circumstances was sanctioned with only a public admonition.

By contrast, when a husband was tried in Camagüey for knifing his wife, the Tribunal, after noting that the *acusado* had thirty-six prior convictions, and had fathered children by three different women, sentenced him to one hundred eighty days deprivation of liberty, the maximum Popular Tribunal sanction. . . .

Another illustrative case, actually observed, follows: A wife accused her husband of *injuria*, namely that he had told people in the community that she was having affairs with other men (adultery is not a crime, so husband's statements would not be a *calumnia*). The husband denied the charge, and claimed that his wife was often drunk and did not feed their child, and that he believed that she was crazy. In the opinion of most observers at the trial, the woman was clearly disturbed. The judges stopped the trial and ordered the wife to report to a hospital for a psychiatric examination later that week.

Some of the delicts within the competence of the Popular Tribunals are based on laws promulgated since the Revolution, and thus, are more substantively related to societal concepts. One such offense is the delict against the popular economy, subdivided into seven categories.

(1) Altering prices. The Judges' Manual refers to an "owner or administrator" who alters prices. Since the *Ofensiva Revolucionaria*, there are virtually no private owners.
(2) Hoarding.
(3) Selling disproportionate amounts of scarce commodities to oneself or to friends.
(4) Exporting illicit goods.
(5) Infringement, in any manner, of the rationing regulations.

The last is a very common offense and is taken very seriously. Rice, beans, meat, lard, butter and milk are rationed, and sugar and cigars were added to the list in January 1969. Also rationed are clothing and gasoline (a Chevrolet, for example, is alloted twenty gallons per month). Until recently bread was not rationed, but one was limited to a certain number of loaves for each long wait on line, so that the effect was that of rationing. A typical rationing violation case which I witnessed occurred as follows:

On trial were five adults (over the age of sixteen): the father, mother and three oldest daughters in a poor family of fourteen. The oldest daughter held her illegitimate baby on her lap throughout the trial, paying attention to the child, rather than to the proceedings. There was no *acusador* present. All five were charged with having alterations on their respective clothing pages in the family ration booklet. All five denied that there were any alterations, and denied having made the alterations, if there were found to be any. They were also charged with having resold the excess clothing. The Tribunal ruled that anyone over age sixteen was responsible for alterations found on his pages of a family ration booklet, even if he himself was not the person who made the alterations. The evidence that the family had resold the extra clothes was not offered at the trial. Presumably such evidence was in a written deposition taken by the investigating judge from a policeman or militiaman (*miliciano*) who caught them. Since the private sale of one's own clothing is not a crime, the whole issue was neither the fact of sale of clothing nor the identity of the alterer, but rather, whether or not there were alterations on each *acusado's* page. The only evidence on this point was the fact that the entry "1½" in a box on one page was in smaller print than the entry "1" on another page. Since both entries were supposed to have been made by the same government official, yet were of different sized figures, the Tribunal reasoned that there had been some forgery, and sentenced all five *acusados* to no new clothes for six months and gave them a public admonition. The *Presidente* of the Tribunal was especially vehement in his admonition and indeed during the entire trial. (During its private deliberations before arriving at a verdict, the Tribunal members asked me for my opinion of the evidence. I noted that a "1½" had to be written smaller than a "1" in order to fit into the same size space and that, therefore, both entries might have been made by the same official and that there was not necessarily any alteration. The Tribunal was not convinced by my argument.)

Another actual case of ration booklet alteration was observed in the "pants" case, discussed earlier.

(6) False weights or measures.
(7) Clandestine businesses. Here, too, an actual case can be described:

A retired baker sold bread clandestinely at forty centavos a loaf. The government price is fifteen centavos per loaf. Because of the enormous length of bread lines, people were willing to pay this high premium to a private source. The *acusado* had been caught in the act by local *milicianos*, who were not present at the trial, but whose testimony had previously been taken by the investigating judge. The *acusado* was sentenced to one hundred eighty days confinement to his house.

## 2. Contraventions.

As previously discussed, contraventions are *conductas antisociales*, of commission or of omission, which are less severe than delicts and which do not affect the fundamental interests of society.

Nevertheless, the manner in which the Tribunals dispose of these cases is also highly illustrative of the functions they perform within their communities.

An example of this is the contravention against good customs and public decorum. This consists of a widely diversified array of conduct, including indecent exposure, obscene language in public, selling pornography, nude swimming, and peeping Toms. I witnessed one fascinating peeping Tom case in Havana:

A man, aged twenty-four, was accused of peeping through a window at the wife of his good friend while she was undressing. The *acusadora* was a middle-aged, severe, prudish, Madame Defarge type and chairman of the women's division of the local Committee for the Defense of the Revolution. (The victim of the alleged peeping did not appear at the trial.) The *acusado* admitted having seen her undressing, twice, from an alley. He claimed, however, in requesting a lighter sanction, that he was drunk at the time, was returning from work, went into the alley to urinate, and accidentally happened to see her undressing. He also argued that when the C.D.R. woman (the *acusadora*) caught him, he went along peacefully and did not resist. The *acusadora*, however, claimed that the *acusado* had not been drunk and had been standing on a chair while peeping, implying that the act was premeditated. The *Presidente* of the Tribunal mockingly asked the *acusado* why he had to stand on a chair to urinate and why had this so-called coincidence happened twice. The *acusado* could provide no answers; he only bowed his head remorsefully and wiggled his legs continuously. A second C.D.R. witness, this one a good looking young girl, added that the C.D.R. had followed the *acusado* for fifteen days in order to catch him in the act. A third C.D.R. member, who rose from the audience as a "spontaneous" witness, testified that he had been on *miliciano* duty that night, that the incident occurred at 1:40 a.m., and that even before the *acusado* was caught, all the neighborhood knew of his peeping activities. A final witness, another girl, testified that she had awakened at 4 a.m. on the morning in question (to go to her job in a hospital), that she heard noises, and that she saw the *acusado* peeping.

The *acusado* was found guilty on the basis of his confession taken together with the testimony of the four witnesses. The *Presidente* of the Tribunal noted that a confession alone could not sustain a guilty verdict in this type of case. The *acusado* was sentenced to one hundred eighty days deprivation of liberty (*privación de libertad*), the most severe sanction possible, and to a public admonition. For the one hundred eighty days he would have to work on a farm (and would be paid for this work at the same rate as all agricultural laborers). In the admonition, the *acusado* was told that his crime was all the more severe because the woman he peeped at was the wife of his friend and neighbor. The *Presidente* was very vindictive in this case. (In private discussion of the case with the members of the Tribunal, they stressed to me the fact that the *acusado* was twenty-four and was unmarried, implying that this meant something unhealthy.)

## C. The Sanctions Available to the Popular Tribunals

The seven principal and two secondary sanctions which the Popular Tribunals are empowered to impose are viewed as rehabilitative in nature. Capital punishment and imprisonment are outside of the scope of the Tribunals' power to impose, and fines, which are included in the 1966 Judges' Manual as a permissible sanction, were abolished in 1968 because they were considered to be essentially punitive in nature.

The public admonition (*amonestación pública*) is the least severe and the most common of all the Popular Tribunal sanctions. It consists of a lecture or warning given to the *acusado* (and sometimes to the *acusador*) by the *Presidente* of the Tribunal. It may be given either in the courtroom at the close of the trial, or later, in the *acusado's* place of work. It is given in almost all cases and is usually accompanied by other, more severe sanctions. By definition, it involves an audience; and, as virtually all Popular Tribunal trials are public and are well attended, the public admonition also serves as a useful means for educating the community. Its use has been described earlier in the "pants" case, the "water main quarrel" case, the "wife-beating" case, the "altered ration booklet" case, and the "peeping Tom" case.

The sanction of educational improvement (*superación educacional*) is generally used to bring the person being sanctioned up to a sixth-grade school level, which is considered the literacy level in Cuba. This is achieved by the Popular Tribunal's ordering the person to attend a local educational center, to participate in a study group, or to undertake specific tasks which embody a direct educational purpose. The Tribunal often certifies the sentence to the director of a school, who must send the Tribunal periodic progress reports on the person being sanctioned. An example of this sanction is offered in the Judges' Manual:

A young man, twenty years of age, employed as a mechanic in a shop, and having achieved a fourth grade level of education, is brought before the Tribunal for the second time, and it again finds him responsible for a minor public disorder, this time in the town movie house. The Popular Tribunal, knowing that the young man has all of his evenings free, and that he does not devote them to anything useful — laziness being one of the causes of his anti-social conduct — decides to compel him to use those evenings for educational improvement, imposing upon him, as a sanction, obligatory enrollment and attendance in a night course of labor and agricultural education, until completion of the sixth grade....[49]

This is a typical case of public disorder, but the real cause was perhaps not so much the young man's "laziness" as the lack of sufficient recreational facilities in Cuba. Another instance of the educational sanction was observed in the "pants" case, where it was the *acusadora's* daughter who was given this sanction.

The deprivation-of-rights sanction (*privación de derechos*) is a punishment specifically designed to correspond to the offense. The person sanctioned is deprived of the same "social right" which the Tribunal found his *conducta antisocial* had abused. Thus, one who gets drunk may be deprived of the right to drink alcohol for a period of up to two years. This sanction does not have the one hundred eighty day maximum to which some of the other sanctions are limited.

The Tribunal might have utilized this sanction in the case of the young man who created the disorder in the movie theatre; instead of, or in addition to, the educational improvement sanction he could have been deprived of the right to go to the movies. For an actual illustration, note the "altered ration booklet" case, where extra clothes had been procured illegally and the Popular Tribunal decided that the defendants could have no new clothing for six months.

The sanction of banishment from a specific place (*alejamiento*) also illustrates a close relationship between the punishment and the offense committed, differing only in its emphasis on geography, rather than a particular activity. The person sanctioned is prohibited from going in or near the place where he is prone to indulge in the type of *conducta antisocial* for which he has just been tried. Thus one who habitually gets drunk may be barred from the saloons in his town; a gambler may be banned from places where

49. Manual at 13.

cock fights are likely to be held; one might be banned from his mother-in-law's house if he had previously committed *conductas antisociales* there. The police (D.O.P.) and "especially" the Committees for the Defense of the Revolution are specifically charged with enforcing this sanction by informing the Popular Tribunals if the sanction is violated.

Confinement to a specific place (*confinamiento*) is a relatively severe sanction and is reserved for those who would otherwise be totally deprived of their liberty (sent to a work farm) but for the fact that they are mothers with children at home, elderly, or for some similar reason. The person thus sanctioned is not allowed to leave his home, except to go to work, for a period of up to six months. Once again, the D.O.P. and the C.D.R. are charged with enforcing this sanction.

In the highly illustrative "pants" case, the *acusada* (woman B) was sentenced to three months confinement to her home and job, because she had young children. In the "clandestine bread business" case, the old baker was sentenced to six months confinement to his house. He then, however, appealed to the Tribunal to let him visit a health spa (he was sixty-seven years old). The court said it would modify the sanction and allow him to be confined to the spa instead, if a doctor would verify that the old man needed the care available at the spa.

When sanctioned with relocation (*reubicación*), the guilty party and his family are relocated permanently in a different neighborhood, with the assistance of *Reforma Urbana*, the agency in charge of housing and urban development. Our legally-trained guide said that this sanction was very rare, and I never witnessed an instance of its being imposed. Its rarity is probably due at least in part to lack of housing, especially in Havana. This is the only sanction where the whole family suffers directly for the actions of one member.

The sanction of deprivation of liberty (*privación de libertad*) is composed of two classes: with internment and without. In the latter case, the person sanctioned is required to do specific tasks, without remuneration, in his spare time, but he is otherwise at liberty. The example offered is that of a man who has ridden his horse through his neighbor's garden, destroying the flowers. This sanction might require him to work without compensation in his neighbor's garden for a certain number of Sundays, perhaps until the flowers have been restored. In cases where the sanction is imposed with internment, the person sanctioned is forced to live and work elsewhere (usually in agriculture) for up to one hundred eighty days. Examples of this sanction were observed in the "peeping Tom" case, and in the Camagüey "wife-knifing" case.

Two other sanctions which the Tribunals may impose are considered secondary in nature. The Tribunals may order confiscation (*decomismo*) of the fruits or instrumentalities of the offense. Thus, they may confiscate black-marketed items in excess of the legally allowable limit, playing cards, dominos, money used in gambling, and weapons. The sanction of indemnification (*indemnización*) is used primarily to indemnify a victim for physical injuries. The guilty party may indemnify his victim by paying money damages, by surrendering to the victim goods equal in value to the amount of damage done, or, in cases of property damage, by performing certain tasks aimed at correcting the damage.

From time to time a Popular Tribunal will hold a mass trial purely for educational purposes, imposing no sanctions, but informing the large group of *acusados* that they are all habitually guilty of the same offense (usually a contravention) and that there will be sanctions for future violations. Especially common in the provinces are mass educational trials of parents who are truant in not sending their children to school or of villagers who let pigs roam loose in the streets.

In addition, in cases cited earlier and in other cases which I observed, several remedies not listed in the Judges' Manual were employed. Among these were medical and psychiatric referrals, referral to *Reforma Urbana,* partition of disputed property, referral to a spa for recuperation (as in the case of the old baker), and the setting up of various equitable compromises (such as the schedule for use of the common water main). Thus, the Tribunals would seem to possess considerable flexibility in choosing proper sanctions for cases before them. . . .

### III. THE POPULAR TRIBUNALS IN ACTION

## A. *Personnel*

When one attends a Popular Tribunal trial, his attention is likely to focus first on the judges. Indeed this reaction is virtually guaranteed by the sudden shout of a uniformed *miliciano*. "A pie!" (On your feet!), which announces the judges' entrance into the courtroom. The judges then seat themselves behind a simple table at the front of the room, and there are no stenographers or bailiffs to impede one's view of the proceedings. Soon other actors appear on the scene. Seated off to one side, near the front of the room, there is usually an *Asesor*, and he can be seen leaving and returning with the judges each time they retire for deliberations.

The parties themselves sit among the other members of the audience, unnoticed until their respective cases are called. Members of the local Committee for the Defense of the Revolution are present, but they cannot be distinguished by an outside observer, unless they are called as witnesses and elect to identify themselves in terms of their Committee affiliation. The *miliciano* who gives the cry is always obvious, and there occasionally are regular policemen present, if they are needed as witnesses. Also among the unobtrusive actors are the "spontaneous" witnesses, some of them more camouflaged than spontaneous. These, and the regular witnesses, sit among the audience until called, either by spontaneity or by the court, to come forward.

Finally, the observer cannot ignore the audience, the residents of the *zona*, who habitually pack the courtroom. In a theoretical sense, at least, the whole show is for them, and the show is not devoid of audience participation.

### 1. *The Judges.*

a. *Selection and Training.* The Popular Tribunal judges are laymen. Aside from a three-week training course, their only legal experience is that which they gain while serving as Popular Tribunal judges. They are laymen, not because of any lack of professionally trained judges in Cuba (although such a shortage may exist), but because laymen are actually preferred for this position. As Blas Roca observed, the fact "that the judges sitting in these trials come from the same community in which they live and work, reinforces the idea that the justice they administer is that of the working people." Perhaps it is not unfair to say that it is deemed more important that the people know the judges, than that the judges know the law.

The judges do indeed come from the community; they are among the four or five thousand residents of the *zona* over which their Tribunal has jurisdiction. They are workers, employed in various full-time jobs during the day, and they serve in the Popular Tribunals, which meet at night, without pay. Their working class background is genuine. In the Luyanó section, in Havana, for example, the judges also do all the plumbing and cleaning in the courtroom. In Havana's San Miguel del Padrón section, while I was observing a night's trials in one *zona*, a judge from a *zona* whose Tribunal was not in session that night busied himself filling a water pitcher for the judges who were sitting. While Cuba cannot yet be termed a classless society, the Popular Tribunal judges of any given *zona* appear to be relatively indistinguishable from the *acusados*, from the audience, or from the people of that *zona* in general.

How, then, are these judges selected? There is no official, written description of the whole procedure, but it appears to begin with a given number of men and, occasionally, women, being nominated by the local Party officials and by the neighborhood Committee for the Defense of the Revolution. For example, if a new Tribunal is being set up and six judges are needed (a *zona's* complement of judges may be more than three, but only three sit at one time), the names of perhaps ten residents will be suggested by the Party and the C.D.R. These ten candidates are then trained by an *Asesor* for about three weeks. The *asesor* also makes inquiries as to their reputations in the community and verifies the fact that each is over twenty-one years old and has at least a sixth-grade education.

At the close of the training session, the candidates are given an examination by the *Asesor* and he determines which six men are best qualified, based upon the exam and the inquiries made into their reputations. These six names are then submitted to the people of the *zona* for ratification, by secret ballot, evidently by majority vote. Those selected serve for an indefinite term, theoretically as long as they continue to satisfy their constituents. Since the Popular Tribunals are, at present, only four or five years old at most, it is impossible to estimate the average duration of judicial tenure. The average age for a Popular Tribunal judge in Havana seems to be in the late thirties; judges in the provinces are somewhat younger.

b. *The Judges' Manual.* Once ratified, the Popular Tribunal judges are to a very great degree on their own. Although the *Asesor* who trained them will advise them closely during their first few months in office, he will then take an increasingly less active role, and after a while he may not even attend the trials at all on some nights. These newly-trained laymen must therefore depend, to a large extent, on the Judges' Manual for guidance. This manual, published in November 1966, will ultimately have six sections:

I. Fundamentals

II. Structure and Function of the Popular Tribunals

III. *Conductas Antisociales* within the Popular Tribunals' Competence

IV. Penal Procedure in the Popular Tribunals

V. General Regulations

VI. Model Forms for Use in the Popular Tribunals

Only sections III and VI had been published as of September 1968, and the judges were often observed referring to these two sections. But the lack of any code of procedure forces the judges to interpolate rules of procedure from the anecdotal examples found in Section III and from their own notions of what procedure is or used to be like. As for substantive law, Section III provides the judges not with a code, but rather with names of crimes and with illustrative examples of some of these entitled offenses. The methodology, then, is one in which each judge, or at least each tribunal, is free to analogize from the hypotheticals in the Manual to the behavior of the residents in his *zona*, with only the *Asesor*, if anyone, to check if that which one Popular Tribunal deems *conducta antisocial* conforms at all to the types of behavior which the revolutionary government had sought to render sanctionable.

2. *The Asesores.*

. . . In addition to being the legislators for the Popular Tribunals, the *Asesores* also participate in the selection and training of the Popular Judges. It has also already been noted that at least during the first few months of a Tribunal's operation, the *Asesor* is present at all trials to advise the judges and to correct serious errors. Since the Popular Tribunals each meet one weekday night a week, often more than one Tribunal in a given *Asesor's* section will be meeting on the same night. Thus, once an *Asesor* has all the Tribunals in his section functioning regularly, it is not unusual for him to be absent from some of the trials. During the judges' deliberations, the *Asesor* may be present with them, but theoretically is not allowed to speak unless the judges ask him a question. In practice, some *Asesores*, although present at the trials, do not enter the deliberation room with the judges at all. More direct intervention or observation on the part of the *Asesores* appears to be limited to *zonas* with newly trained judges.

With the Revolution strongly wary of "bureaucracy," the administrative work of the Popular Tribunals is handled entirely by the *Asesores*, who spend four days each month in Havana, at the Ministry of Justice, reporting on the functioning of their respective sections and receiving the latest directives. . . .

Another role of the *Asesores* in the Popular Tribunals is that of appellate judge. When a verdict is appealed (rather than an appeal of severity of sanction), it is decided by the *Asesor* of that *zona*, in conjunction with two other judges from the same *zona* who were not on the panel that originally heard the case. This type of appeal may be initiated by the *Asesor* himself, in the name of justice, as well as by the party found guilty. Such appeals, however, are very rare (as opposed to appeals of severity of sanction), and I never observed one. In the "woman's honor" case discussed earlier, the *acusadora* was clearly mentally disturbed. During the trial I mentioned this fact to the *Asesora*, who replied that she had already passed a message to the judges to stop the trial and to order a psychiatric examination for the *acusadora*. It was perhaps another ten minutes before the judges stopped the trial, and during this interval the *Asesora* had assured me that if the tribunal were to ignore her message and were to find the husband guilty, she would bring an appeal "in his name." I do not believe that this concern on her part for the rights of the husband was due to the presence of foreign observers, but this was the closest I came to seeing an actual appeal. . . .

5. *The Spectators.*

Two basic concepts inherent in the Popular Tribunals are that they "function in the neighborhood, so that neighbors and acquaintances of those being judged can attend the trials and can make these trials truly public," and that the public trials "educate the new man . . . secure the socialist laws" and "correct those who still keep the customs of the old oppressor society." These ideas may be capsulized as popular involvement and popular education. Thus, audience participation is encouraged and the residents of each *zona* show up each week in overflow crowds. When asked why they come, their answer is often simply "to see the trials." These spectators generally pay close attention to the proceedings, reacting with "oohs" and "ahs" at appropriate intervals. One is at first tempted to conclude that the trials are seen by the people as merely entertainment, but it is perhaps more accurate to state that people come because they are interested, and overflow crowds can be observed even in *zonas* where the Popular Tribunal has been in operation for more than a year.

The ultimate in audience participation is the emergence of "spontaneous" witnesses from the audience. While in instances like the "peeping Tom" case, these witnesses appear to be less than spontaneous, especially when they identify themselves as C.D.R. members, often the witnesses are truly spontaneous, as in the "water main quarrel" case. With the audience coming almost entirely from the same neighborhood, there is nothing unusual in expecting that some of its members were, in fact, witnesses to neighborhood occurrences.

## B. The Setting and Atmosphere in the Courtroom

In cities and villages the Popular Tribunals meet in storefronts, either those belonging to the local Committee for the Defense of the Revolution or in storefronts which have been assigned exclusively to the Tribunal. The rooms are relatively small and bare, with virtually none of the trappings found in a traditional courtroom. A photograph of Che Guevara and a Cuban flag are often on the wall behind the judges, and in one *zona* the judges had a small bell which they rang at the close of each case. In another *zona* the judges personally passed out pages from old magazines during the trials, so that the spectators could fan themselves on that hot summer night.

The spectators usually sit on plain wooden benches, demonstrating great interest and involvement in the trials. Often there are not enough seats and the crowd overflows out into the street. In Camagüey, one Popular Tribunal had a small fluorescent sign outside over the doorway saying "Popular Tribunal," but that was the fanciest element of Popular Tribunal decor I ever observed. Trials of "exceptional interest" are held out of doors so that all may come and observe, as in the "wife-knifing" case, which had an audience of five thousand persons in the town of Nuevitas. Occasionally the setting differs, as when there is a mass trial, such as the educational, simultaneous, "warning" trials of several dozen habitual violators of the same minor contravention.

## C. Procedure . . .

### 1. Chronology of a Case.

A case begins when a complaint is made to the Tribunal by an *acusador*, the combination plaintiff and complainant. There is no prosecutor and both the *acusador* and the *acusado* are virtually never represented by counsel. Consistent with revolutionary legal training in Cuba, the Popular Tribunals are not adversary proceedings; one judge conducts an investigation prior to the trial, taking depositions from all parties, witnesses, experts, and whomever else he deems appropriate. At the trial, all questioning is done by members of the court.

An offender is supposedly "brought to justice" within seven to ten days. What this probably means is that within seven to ten days after a complaint is made, one of the judges begins an investigation. When this investigation is completed, if a trial is merited it is scheduled for the next night the Tribunal is due to meet. At the trial the parties are advised of their rights, they and the witnesses are questioned once again, and, after the judges recess to deliberate, a verdict including sanctions is announced. From the date of the alleged offense through complaint, investigation and trial, an average of perhaps two months have gone by. An exception is the case of delicts against the popular economy, where a trial must be held within seven days of the alleged offense.

Appeals are usually made right after the verdict and sanctions are announced. . . .

### IV. COMPARISON AND EVALUATION

#### A. *Other Systems of Popular Justice*

The discussion which follows is limited to a comparison with those Soviet and Chinese institutions which utilize, through several methods and with varying degrees of intensity, popular involvement in the administration of justice. This limitation is not meant to suggest that "popular justice" is restricted to these two models and to the Cuban Popular Tribunals, nor does it imply any conclusion that these institutions necessarily embody "popular justice" in any absolute sense. The Soviet and Chinese cases were chosen because they are prototypal in this area, and because enough has been written about them to permit some intelligent basis for comparison with the Popular Tribunals.

#### 1. *The Soviet Union.*

There are a number of parallels between the Cuban Popular Tribunals and the two Russian institutions charged with administering "popular justice," the People's Courts and the Comradely Courts.

a. *The People's Courts.* On the surface, the Soviet People's Courts seem to be similar to the Cuban Popular Tribunals. These

Russian courts have a "homespun" atmosphere, and although a professional judge presides, he sits with two lay people's assessors. Also somewhat similar to the Popular Tribunals is the fact that the most frequent charges in the People's Courts are of disorderly conduct, and that half of the cases in the People's Courts are "dwelling area" disputes.

But the differences between the Popular Tribunals and the People's Courts far outweigh these few similarities. The latter are run almost exclusively by the professional judges, with the lay assessors saying and doing virtually nothing. Investigations are carried out by specific bureaucrats charged with this function. In the Popular Tribunals, on the other hand, all the functions of investigation and adjudication are performed by the lay judges, who are unpaid volunteers from the neighborhood. The Soviet People's Courts are not neighborhood tribunals — there are only seventeen of them for all of Moscow, for example, while there is, at least theoretically, a Popular Tribunal for each zona of four or five thousand residents in Cuba. The People's Courts meet during the day; Popular Tribunal trials are held in the evening, in order to encourage popular attendance and participation. Finally, the sanctions administered by the People's Courts are essentially punitive, and, at times, severely so. In a majority of cases the sanction is "deprivation of freedom," meaning six months to fifteen years in a labor colony. In the Popular Tribunals, on the other hand, the maximum sanction is six months deprivation of freedom. The People's Courts' other sanctions are also punitive: fines and corrective labor (present employment is continued, but up to twenty per cent of salary is deducted). The Popular Tribunals impose no fines, and the emphasis is on rehabilitative sanctions, such as educational improvement. In general, in comparison with the Soviet People's Courts, the Cuban Popular Tribunals have a more popular and localized administration, greater popular attendance and involvement, and more strongly emphasize social education and rehabilitation.

b. *The Comradely Courts.* The Soviet Comradely Courts, whose functions have increased considerably since 1959, are the Soviet courts which most closely parallel the Popular Tribunals. These courts are primarily intended as organs of persuasion rather than coercion, and their emphasis on popular involvement is very similar to that found in the Cuban Tribunals. The judges are non-professionals, the trials are during non-working hours, and audience participation is encouraged. There are Comradely Courts for residential areas, as well as in enterprises, collective farms and universities, and 197,000 Comradely Courts were reported to exist in the Soviet Union in 1963. One Comradely Court, for example, serves a Moscow apartment-house group that has 16,000 residents. Popular participation in the Comradely Courts is encouraged through the cooperation of the People's Patrol and the street, block and house committees, analogous to the participation of the Cuban *milicianos* and Committees for the Defense of the Revolution, described earlier, in the Popular Tribunals.

In addition to similarities in their emphasis on popular involvement, both courts operate within similar spheres of competence, the major difference being the criminal area. While the Popular Tribunals have considerable competence over criminal offenses, handling all violations of approximately a misdemeanor level, the Comradely Courts usually can hear only those criminal cases delegated to it by the People's Courts.

In areas of sanctions, the Comradely Courts are limited to warnings, censures and reprimands, or to relatively minor financial sanctions, such as fines of no more than ten rubles, transfer to a lower-paying job, or awards of compensatory damages of no more than fifty rubles. The Comradely Courts have no sanction of a rehabilitative nature, such as educational improvement or banishment from a part of town where one is prone to trouble, which the Popular Tribunals can impose. Nor do the Comradely Courts possess any sanctions as forceful as deprivation of freedom, even for a period as brief as a few weeks.

The Comradely Courts are also less formal than the Popular Tribunals. The audience is not made to stand when the judges enter, and legal terminology is intentionally avoided to the point of not calling anyone the "accused." The Comradely Courts do not meet regularly and there is no set procedure. Perhaps this lesser degree of formality might be seen as more revolutionary and might be thought to render the Comradely Courts more popular, but one observer indicates that the Comradely Courts are not taken seriously and that the whole proceeding is farcical. Others report that "[t]he sessions of Comrades' Courts sometimes degenerate into a kind of hurly-burly, disrupted by the presence of drunks and by the irrelevant remarks of busybodies." The Cuban Popular Tribunals, as far as I could observe, are decorous and are respected by the people; indeed, the Popular Tribunals seem to have increased popular involvement by retaining some of the traditional formalities of a court.

## 2. The People's Republic of China.

Here again the Cuban Popular Tribunals find two possible analogues, the People's Courts and the People's Mediation Committees.

a. *The People's Courts.* The Chinese People's Courts were most widely used during the period which began in 1953 and ended in 1957 with the commencement of the "anti-rightist" movement. These courts were similar to the Soviet People's Courts in that both served districts having several hundred thousand inhabitants and both were tribunals composed of a professional judge and two lay assessors. But the Chinese People's Court judges were "professional" only in that they worked full time as judges. Any citizen who was at least twenty-three years old and who had never been deprived of political rights was eligible for selection as a people's judge. The selection of laymen to serve as judges more closely resembles the Cuban Popular Tribunals than the Russian People's Court.

With the beginning of the "anti-rightist" movement, however, the role of the courts, in any formal sense, was drastically diminished. "Work groups," consisting of police officers, a procurator and a judge, were organized to rush to the scene of a crime and to administer the "three on-the-spots" (investigate on-the-spot, mediate on-the-spot, try and sentence on-the-spot). Eighty per cent of all cases in one province were reportedly tried "on-the-spot." Regular trials in the People's Courts are reserved for only the most serious criminal offenses, and trials in the People's Courts are no longer public, except for cases which the Security Bureau chief deems especially serious. Judges have been required to perform physical labor, such as collecting manure. The courts are used almost exclusively for "problems between the 'people' and the 'enemy,' " and the only remedy in such cases is punishment. Indeed, Mao Tse-tung has discussed punishment as a means for satisfying society's sense of just retribution. Thus, the Chinese People's Courts today do not seem to stress either the popular involvement or the education and rehabilitation which are among the essential functions of the Cuban Popular Tribunals.

b. *The People's Mediation Committees.* Most civil disputes in the People's Republic of China are settled extra-judicially, by mediation. Mediation committees, the street-level counterpart of the judiciary in China, were established nationally in 1954. There are three to eleven members to a committee, and they are all unpaid "activists." One writer estimates that there were more than 200,000 such committees in 1966 and observes that the Soviet Union has "no institutional counterpart to the 'people's mediation committees....'" [130] The theory of this system of mediation, although it has Confucian antecedents, is essentially Mao's principle that "disputes among the people" (as opposed to those "between the people and the enemy," which are handled by the People's Courts) should be resolved by "democratic methods, methods of discussion, of criticism, of persuasion and education, not by coercive, oppressive methods."

Although the Chinese mediation procedures are infinitely less formal than the procedures followed in the Cuban Popular Tribunals, and while concepts such as "self-criticism" and "thought reform" have no true equivalents in Cuba, the Chinese system of Mediation Committees and the Cuban Popular Tribunals are similar in their emphasis on popular involvement, on the administration of justice in the neighborhood, and on legality as a means of social re-education.

## B. An Evaluation of the Popular Tribunals

### 1. Effectiveness.

The essence of any evaluation of the Cuban Popular Tribunals must be an inquiry into how successful the Tribunals have been in effecting the ends for which they were created. The degree of achievement in the direction of six goals will be discussed: (a) popular involvement, (b) popular education, (c) settling private disputes, (d) discouraging anti-social conduct, (e) administering justice, and (f) efficiency.

a. *Popular Involvement.* As far as popular involvement is concerned, the Popular Tribunals have met with success both in theory and in practice. There is or soon will be a Popular Tribunal for every *zona* of four or five thousand persons, within walking distance of every home in the *zona*. The Tribunals meet in the evenings, when all can attend the trials, which are virtually all public. The judges are laymen from the neighborhood, and the cases deal with essentially local problems, such as housing shortages or disputes over use of a water main. Attendance is high, with the crowds actually overflowing the small courtrooms. The local resi-

130. Cohen, [Chinese Mediation on the Eve of Modernization, 54 Calif. L. Rev. 1201, 1203 (1966)].

dents view the Popular Tribunals as something of their own, not as a mechanism imposed on them from outside. At least some of the "spontaneous" witnesses are truly spontaneous — neighbors with personal knowledge of the case who want to offer their cooperation. The judges elicit questions and comments from the audience and explain the proceedings carefully. Most cases come to the Popular Tribunals on the complaints of local residents; the *acusadores* are policemen in only a small minority of the trials. Finally, enforcement is delegated to unpaid local people — the C.D.R. members who live in the *zona*. All of these factors, which have previously been discussed, illustrate the increased level of popular involvement, which is most apparent when compared with the traditional *Audiencia*. And despite the popular participation, there seems to be a general respect for the Tribunals among the people.

b. *Popular Education*. A major goal of the Popular Tribunals is to teach the population the laws in general and the new laws in particular, as well as to instill in the people a revolutionary consciousness and a socialist mentality. This idea of education is one of the prime reasons for all of the stress on popular involvement. It is no doubt too soon to expect the Popular Tribunals, which have been in existence only a few years, to have achieved total success in this endeavor. Nevertheless, there is already some question as to whether all this popular involvement may not be taken by the people more as entertainment than as education. Rogelio Buznego, director of the Popular Tribunals for the province of Havana, for example, has observed that women are attracted to the Popular Tribunals because they view the trials as a substitute for the other ceremonies which have declined since the Revolution.

The "entertainment" reaction is perhaps best illustrated by the reactions from the audience when the *acusadora* was ordered to go for a psychiatric examination in the "woman's-honor" case. Similarly, the outdoor trial of the "wife-knifer," before an audience of five thousand, is a bit reminiscent of a public execution, although perhaps that particular public stigmatization in Nuevitas was an exception and was chosen because it was felt that the educational, deterrent value outweighed the entertainment interest. By way of contrast, there are some trials which are purely educational, with no sanctions being imposed, and these are well attended even though they have no entertainment value. To support the argument that the Popular Tribunals are indeed educational, one might point to the absence of strictly punitive sanctions, such as prison terms or fines, and to the emphasis placed on rehabilitative sanctions, such as banishment from an area of potential trouble, and educational improvement.

Finally, one must appreciate the positive educational effect of the trials themselves as almost classic demonstrations of points of law. The visual effect of returning the pants from the *acusada* to the *acusadora* in the "pants" case or the lecture on the virtue of cooperation in the "water-main quarrel" case are perfect illustrations of the Popular Tribunals fulfilling their educational function.

c. *Settling Private Disputes.* What is more significant for dispute settlement is that all citizens, no matter how poor or uneducated, are now able to bring their disputes to a court for resolution. Such a remedy was unavailable in the days when the only court one could turn to was the grandiose *Audiencia.* Another measure of effectiveness in settling private disputes might be the extremely small number of appeals, although this could be attributed to other factors. Similarly, I never witnessed a single "comeback" case, which might suggest that cases are settled satisfactorily the first time they come to the Popular Tribunals. I cannot say, however, that I witnessed a statistically significant number of cases to make this particular conclusion.

d. *Discouraging Anti-Social Conduct.* It is probably too early in the history of the Popular Tribunals to measure their effectiveness in discouraging anti-social conduct. One possible indication of the deterrent effect of the Tribunals might be Premier Castro's address of March 13, 1969. Based on a fragmentary newspaper account of the speech, it appears that Castro believes that Cuba has "fallen behind" in dealing with crime. He discussed juvenile delinquency and truancy, and disclosed that a study of Cuba's penal system was under way. The thrust of these remarks, however, seemed to be directed at "incorrigible" prisoners "who cannot be rehabilitated" and who commit killings in prison. If so, the speech was not a criticism aimed at the Popular Tribunals, except perhaps the part concerning juvenile delinquency and truancy.

e. *Administering Justice.* The prime consideration in administering justice is that the results be correct — that the facts be determined accurately enough to lead to a verdict consistent with the equities of the case and to insure that the sanctions imposed or the remedies granted by appropriate. The Popular Tribunals appear to be quite successful in reaching correct, fair results. This is due to a large extent to the fact that in most Popular Tribunal cases the facts are relatively simple and are often well known around the *zona* even before the trial. Thus, in the "pants" case, for example, all observers left the courtroom convinced that the pants were returned to their rightful owner. Similarly, in criminal cases, there is rarely any real doubt that the person convicted was guilty — there was no doubt that the old man had sold the bread on the black market in the "clandestine bread sale" case, or that the "peeping Tom" was really peeping. Occasionally the sanction seems to be a bit severe, but severity of sentence is appealed more often than is the verdict itself, and the Popular Tribunals are more likely to make modifications in the sanction, as in the case of the old man who sold the bread. It should also be remembered that an *Asesor* is usually present to correct serious errors.

Another element of justice is procedural fairness, affording to a litigant or to an accused an opportunity to be heard and guaranteeing some degree of predictability in the proceedings. Cuba has essentially a civil law system, and comparisons with common-law procedural safeguards are no more appropriate in the case of the Popular Tribunals than in those of any French or Italian court. Once it is understood that the Popular Tribunal trials are not intended to resemble American adversary proceedings, the rights of the *acusados*, as described earlier, are quite substantial. As to the question of predictability, the absence of a code of procedure is somewhat remedied by the careful attention which the judges pay to the Judges' Manual. Procedure, although improvised at times, does not vary greatly from one Popular Tribunal in Havana to the next. The only unpredictable element is the question of which sanction will be imposed, and broad discretion in sentencing is a phenomenon not limited to the Cuban Popular Tribunals.

f. *Efficiency*. One measure of efficiency is speed. Accusations brought before the Popular Tribunals are adjudicated within an average of perhaps two months, while defendants to be tried by the *Audiencia* may spend a year in prison before they are brought to trial.

Another measure of the efficiency of the Popular Tribunals is the fact that they have no bureaucracy, since all administrative work is done by the *Asesores*.

## 2. Possible Faults.

a. *Excessive Party Intervention*. The problem of Party intervention does not seem to occur in the Popular Tribunals. The only direct Party involvement is in the nomination of the Popular Judges. There is, however, indirect Party influence, through the Judges' Manual, the local C.D.R. members, and the *Asesor*. Despite this, the general impression of this observer is that once a Popular Tribunal is in operation it is fairly independent of outside influence. Furthermore, as noted, the role of the *Asesor* in a given Tribunal often lessens with the passing of time. The situation in the Popular Tribunals appears to differ drastically from that in China, where there is "explicitly articulated, persistently avowed espousal of local Party control over judicial decisions. . . ." [150]

b. *Invasion of Privacy.* Invasion of privacy may indeed be a problem, but one which relates more to the Committees for the Defense of the Revolution than to the Popular Tribunals, as was seen in the "peeping Tom" case.

Private trials are guaranteed for "personal issues," such as a woman's honor, juvenile delinquency or homosexuality. The one juvenile case I observed in Havana was handled privately, but the "woman's-honor" case discussed earlier, which should have been private, was conducted as a public trial.

c. *Puritanical Attitudes.*

> [R]evolutions have at their crises a quality unmistakably puritanical or ascetic. . . . There is a serious attempt by those in authority to eradicate the minor vices, as well as what some might feel inclined to call the major pleasures. . . . [I]n '93 and '94 there was an earnest attempt to clean up Paris, to shut up brothels, gaming houses, to eliminate actual drunkenness. Virtue was the order of the day. You couldn't even be lazy. Some Jacobin would be sure to report you to the club, with the suggestion that the best place to cure you of unrepublican laziness was the army. The puritanism of the Bolsheviks may seem even more paradoxical, but it most certainly existed. . . . [154]

Sexual offenses are among the most typical cases before the Popular Tribunals, both in Havana and in the provinces. The Tribunals are not only interested in such cases, but often handle them quite vindictively, as in the "peeping Tom" case. Yet this attitude on the part of the Popular Judges is not a true reflection on the inherent nature of the Popular Tribunals, but seems rather to be part of a view currently held by the revolutionary government in general, and which seems to have filtered down to most persons in

150. Cohen, [The Criminal Process in the People's Republic of China: An Introduction, 79 Harv. L. Rev. 469, 485 (1966)].

154. C. Brinton, An Anatomy of Revolution 180-81 (Vintage rev. & exp. ed. 1965).

positions of authority, a phenomenon which is perhaps described, if not explained, by the paragraph quoted just above.

### CONCLUSION

The Cuban Popular Tribunals are a considerable step forward in popular involvement in the administration of justice, at least when compared with the situation in Cuba before their inception. Although the Popular Tribunals are a revolutionary advancement when compared with the traditional Cuban *Audiencia*, they cannot be termed especially original within the realm of the socialist legal systems. However, they do appear to be considerably effective in achieving popular involvement and respect, and their decisions are for the most part just, as are their procedures, although perhaps to a lesser degree. Thus, while they have only recently come into existence, and to some extent are still in a developmental stage, the Cuban Popular Tribunals are close to being institutions which truly administer "popular justice."

# PART VI.
# REFORMING THE
# LOWER COURTS

The lower criminal courts, as several of the preceding sections show, lack neither proposals for reform nor obstacles to achieving them. This section deals directly with ideas for reform and the system dynamics which are likely to frustrate or facilitate those goals.

The first selection deals with reform of a lower court problem that has not been discussed extensively in the preceding pages. The traffic jurisdiction of lower courts comprises the bulk of their caseload — in numbers if not in time. Due process problems are, if anything, accentuated because of the apparent triviality of most traffic offenses, their great numbers, and the exposure of otherwise law-abiding citizens to lower court justice. No reform of lower courts will be complete until the traffic offense problem is solved. This selection presents a comprehensive reform proposal which would achieve that end.

Argersinger v. Hamlin, the recent decision of the Supreme Court extending the right of counsel to indigents in misdemeanor cases in which a sentence of imprisonment is imposed, represents the due process segment of the traditional approach to lower court reform. Its antidote for rough justice is further judicializing — here by provision of an attorney, the actor most necessary to assure fairness. Justice Powell's concurring opinion highlights the administrative problems posed by such a reform. An important issue, however, is whether appointed counsel will assert defendant rights vigorously enough to move lower courts to more careful and orderly disposition of cases.

Lewis Katz's proposal for community courts, which echoes Berman's description of Cuban popular tribunals, would solve the lower court problem through the reestablishment of the community basis of the court. Katz takes seriously the anthropologist's dictum:

"No community, no court." His proposal is interesting and well conceived. While experimentation along these lines has occurred in the New York small claims court, community courts are unlikely to overcome the entrenched power of existing systems, though further experiments would be welcome. The community versus anomie issue is here starkly raised.

The next three selections illuminate the obstacles to reform efforts. The Massachusetts materials show the responses of two chief justices when faced with a well-documented attack on lower court procedures. Any reform effort from outside the system will initially meet such resistance — outright hostility or delay to study the problem. This, then, is the system response. Ironically, in Massachusetts a shift toward reform did in fact occur. Chief Justice Adlow never relented, but in November 1972 he was retired and replaced by a more progressive judge. Chief Justice Flaschner, developing his own timetable and strategy, became an effective and farsighted leader for court reform, eventually implementing rules, included here, similar to those proposed in the petition. The typicality of the initial response was followed by the untypicality of the final outcome.

Beverly Cook's study of judicial politics in Kansas shows both the slowness of judicial change and the configuration of forces likely to confront reformers. The political nature of the problem — the effect of change on the status, power, and interests of incumbent lawyers and judges — thus calls for political solutions. Adept planning on this level can make or break reform.

Finally, Warren Lehman's reflections on the pervasive inability of men to change their institutions and behavior, contribute more than tough-minded skepticism, and highlight the true nature of the reform problem. The subjection of men's conduct to rules is never finalized — it is an enterprise that succeeds partially, if at all, and requires constant vigilance. In the final analysis the lower courts reflect, more than they direct, social forces. The true community and brotherhood lacking elsewhere in the social order will not be achieved in the lower courts. Although reforms and changes will occur, and conditions incrementally improve at different times and places, the enterprise of realizing justice in the criminal courts is never finished.

# Traffic Court Reform*

## Columbia Journal of Law and Social Problems

At the lowest level of the American judicial system are the "minor courts" such as the justice of the peace courts, the small claims courts, and the traffic courts. It has been said that, "[T]he minor courts are seriously misnamed. In many ways they are far more important than state supreme courts. For [sic] in the lower courts the people of America actually come into contact with our system of justice. It is here that they form concepts about law and order." [1] This statement is particularly true of the traffic courts. "It is in the traffic court that most of us learn how the American system of justice works. What we experience there influences our attitudes toward all courts and our system of justice as a whole." [2]

The present system of traffic courts has been widely criticized. Former U.S. Supreme Court Justice Charles A. Whittaker has voiced a common complaint of the traffic tribunals:

> [W]ith notable but all too rare exceptions [they] are so poorly housed, staffed and equipped, the proceedings in them are so lacking in deference, dignity and decorum and their judgments are so stereotyped and perfunctory, that they not only miserably fail to create respect, but in the defendants brought before them — a greater number than appear in all other courts combined — they actually create disrespect, if not, indeed, contempt, not just for the traffic laws and traffic courts, but for all laws and courts.[3]

This article will discuss the reasons why the traffic courts fail to command public respect and evaluate the various proposals which have been made to reform the system.

### I. THE NEED FOR REFORM

#### A. Procedural Abuses

The main factor contributing to the tarnished image of the traffic courts has been the flaws and abuses in their procedure. Traffic

\* From: 4 Colum. J. Law & Soc. Problems 255-266 (1968). Reprinted by permission of the Columbia Journal of Law and Social Problems.
1. H. James, Crisis in the Courts 56-57 (1968).
2. Id. at 51-52.
3. Whittaker, Lawyers, Laymen and Traffic Courts: Concerted Effort Needed for Improvement, 49 A.B.A.J. 333, 334-35 (1963).

courts are most often burdened by a large volume of cases. Frequently this is due to understaffing, both at the clerical and judicial levels. The New York City traffic court illustrates the problem. Defendants often have to wait several hours before their case is called. Once called, the procedure is extremely rapid, even summary. One group of defendants is lined up at the side of the courtroom. The bridgeman, a combination bailiff-clerk, calls each defendant and rapidly recites the charges. The actual exchange between the judge and the defendant is generally quite brief. Defendants who are in court only because an appearance is required often have no explanation to make and want only to get on their way. The judges, faced with a seemingly endless line of defendants, are more than willing to let them do so. The appearance before the judge has been described as consisting of "one word by the defendant, and two by the judge" (presumably "Guilty" and "X dollars".[6] The defendant then lines up in front of a window on the other side of the courtroom to pay his fine to a clerk.

A further problem is created by the use of the rules of criminal procedure in traffic proceedings. Since most defendants are not represented by counsel, they are not aware of the content and intricacies of this procedure. Thus, the defendant who wishes to contest the charges against him may find himself frustrated by his inability to present his case fully.

It is also felt by some that the use of judges in traffic courts, where the problems are routine and few real questions of law arise, is a waste of judicial talent. This is particularly true in New York City, where all judges of the Criminal Court spend a certain amount of time presiding over the traffic court. They continue to do so despite the fact that the backlog of other criminal cases is so great and the shortage of judges so acute that in Bronx County civil trials were recently suspended for a month so that other judges might be free to help reduce the backlog.

It is clear that the traffic laws are inefficiently administered. As a result, the proceedings may leave the traffic court defendant with a cynical view of the administration of justice.

## B. A Traffic Offense Is Not a Crime

The current treatment of the traffic offense as a crime and the offender as a criminal should be changed. There are two reasons why the traffic offense should not be treated as a crime. First, the

6. Public Hearings, State of New York Joint Legis. Comm. on Court Reorganization, Supreme Court Building, Brooklyn, N.Y., Feb. 10, 1966. . . .

state of mind of the offender is irrelevant to a conviction for a traffic violation, and second, such an offense is too commonplace for the imposition of a criminal sanction.

1. *Strict Liability: The Offender's State of Mind Is Irrelevant.* Over a century and a half ago, Blackstone said that "[T]o constitute a crime against human laws, there must be, first, a vicious will; and, secondly, an unlawful act consequent upon such vicious will." [12] The essential element of a crime according to this traditional definition is the state of the actor's mind. Over the years, however, exceptions developed to this rule, and today there are offenses punishable as crimes without any reference to the actor's intent. Most of them are called public welfare offenses. Although the theoretical boundaries of this class of offenses have never been clear, Professor Sayre was able to point out eight types of offenses for which a person could be convicted without proof of mens rea; traffic offenses were among those listed.[15] Courts have consistently recognized that no proof of intent is required for conviction for a traffic offense.

A strong case can be made for the attachment of strict liability to public welfare offenses. Such liability serves as a "prod to stimulate increased care and efficiency." Moreover, strict liability in such cases is often a practical necessity:

> The slightness of the penalty prevents individual interests from being seriously jeopardized; and it would be practically impossible for courts to investigate individual states of mind where adequate enforcement depends upon prosecution by the thousand. If violation threatens serious and widespread public injury, courts have no other course open to them. The orthodox fundamental principles of criminality must be sacrificed in such cases in the interest of enforcement.[18]

Acceptance of the necessity for strict liability does not compel the conclusion that a penalty so imposed should be criminal in nature. The overwhelming weight of opinion is that the public welfare offense should not be treated as a crime. Criminal conduct, by definition, is that which merits moral condemnation; there can be no such condemnation without an inquiry into the actor's mental state. Treatment of these offenses as noncriminal would

12. 4 Blackstone Commentaries at 21 (9th ed. 1783).
15. Sayre, [Public Welfare Offenses, 33 Colum. L. Rev. 55, 84-87 (1933)].
18. Sayre, *supra* note [15], at 78-79.

not be impractical. There can be effective regulation by means of strict liability without the additional onus of criminality.

This view has been endorsed by the draftsmen of the Model Penal Code. The Code classifies any offense for which absolute liability is imposed with respect to any material elements as a "violation." A "violation" is noncriminal, and the only penalties which can be imposed are fines and/or forfeitures.

2. *Incidence of Traffic Infractions Too Widespread.* It is highly probable that every adult American has either received at least one traffic ticket himself, or knows several friends who have. Indeed, the recipients of the estimated 30 million tickets dispensed annually represent a significant percentage of the adult population of this country. It is inconceivable that the community at large considers all of these traffic violators to be criminals, worthy of moral condemnation. By continuing to treat these offenses as crimes, the present system weakens the impact of the criminal law. As Professor Sayre has said, "[O]nce it becomes respectable to be convicted, the vitality of the criminal law has been sapped." [26]

## II. APPROACHES TO REFORM

### A. *The American Bar Association Traffic Court Program*

The most vocal advocate of traffic court reform has been the American Bar Association Traffic Court Program, which was established in 1943. The Program conducts an active series of regional and national conferences for judges, prosecutors, and court personnel. The conferences offer technical information for improving standards of traffic law enforcement and court administration, as well as a forum for mutual exchange of practical problems solutions. It performs studies of local traffic courts at the requests of judges, city officials, and other local agencies, and gives annual awards to communities which have notably improved their traffic court procedures. Through its newsletter, *Traffic Court Justice*, the Program keeps the legal profession informed of its activities as well as legal developments bearing on traffic problems.

These activities of the A.B.A. Program are based on what have become known as the National Standards for Improving the Administration of Justice in Traffic Courts, often called the National Standards. These Standards are the compilation of the recommendations made by several studies conducted over the past

26. Sayre, *supra* note [15], at 80.

three decades. The most important reforms proposed by the National Standards can be summarized as follows:

1. *Upgrading the Status of the Traffic Courts.* The National Standards would elevate the traffic courts to the level of other courts of first instance. They should be courts of record, integral parts of the state judicial system. Traffic court judges should be highly qualified and specially trained. The judge should be a full-time, non-political official. He should be fairly compensated, and the fee system, whereby the judge receives a percentage of the fines he levies, should be abolished where it still exists. Courtroom facilities should be improved, and the proceedings made more dignified.

2. *Emphasis on the Seriousness of the Traffic Offense.* According to the National Standards, all moving violations should require an appearance in court. Use of any type of violations bureau, i.e., clerical levying and collection of fines, should be kept to a minimum. It is apparently felt that forcing the defendant to appear in court will impress upon him the seriousness of a traffic offense and thus have a stronger rehabilitative effect.

3. *Administrative Tightening.* Ticket-fixing should be reduced to a minimum by giving the judge the sole authority to reduce fines and by use of the multiple-copy ticket. More stringent systems of internal accounting and financial control should be introduced.

The National Standards have served a useful function by bringing to light many of the procedural shortcomings of the present system of traffic courts. Their failure, however, lies in the fact that they do not recognize that a traffic offense is essentially noncriminal. In fact, their emphasis on the seriousness of the offense together with their approach of upgrading the existing system of traffic courts, which are essentially criminal courts, would seem to have exactly the opposite effect.

## B. *The Present New York Approach*

New York's approach has been to define traffic infractions as non-criminal, but to maintain criminal procedure in their prosecution. Section 155 of the Vehicle and Traffic Law defines a traffic infraction as follows:

[A traffic infraction is] [t]he violation of any provision of this chapter or of any law, ordinance, rule, or regulation regulating traffic which is not declared by this chapter or other law of this state to be a misdemeanor or a felony. A traffic infraction is not a crime and the punishment imposed therefor shall not be deemed for any purpose a penal or criminal punishment and shall not affect or impair the credibility as a witness or otherwise of any person convicted thereof. . . . Outside of cities having a population in excess of one million, courts and judicial officers heretofore having jurisdiction over such violations shall continue to do so and for such purposes such violations shall be deemed misdemeanors and all provisions of law relating to misdemeanors . . . shall apply. . . . In cities having a population in excess of one million, the criminal court of the city shall have exclusive jurisdiction to hear and determine any complaint alleging a violation constituting a traffic infraction. . . .[35]

It would seem that the intent of the legislature was that the stigma of criminality should be removed from most traffic violations. There is some indication that it was thought a mere denominatory change would be sufficient to accomplish this objective, and that no change from criminal procedure was necessary.

Such an approach to traffic court reform is little better than no change at all. Merely changing the statutory classification of a traffic infraction does not cure procedural abuses. Moreover, it does not succeed in its limited objective of removing the stigma of criminality from the traffic offense. It is unlikely that many violators are even aware of the statutory definition of the infraction as noncriminal; all are aware, however, that infractions are processed through the criminal courts. There is evidence that the public resents being forced to appear in criminal court. It would seem that only a complete shift from the use of the criminal process will be effective to place the traffic infraction in its proper context.

### C. Civil Court

Another possible alternative would be to remove jurisdiction over traffic offenses from the criminal courts, and transfer it to a civil court. This would remove any stigma of criminality, and the problem would then become one of effecting the necessary procedural reforms within the structure of a civil court. While it may be possible to bring about reform in this manner, it is submitted that use of a civil court is not a desirable solution to the problem. The nature of efficient traffic law enforcement is such that nonjudicial treatment would be more appropriate.

35. N.Y. Vehicle & Traffic Law §155 (McKinney Supp. 1967). There are several traffic violations which are misdemeanors or felonies and are thus crimes. See, e.g., N.Y. Vehicle & Traffic Law §1190 (McKinney 1960) (reckless driving). . . .

In New York City the great majority of summonses which are answered are processed clerically, either through the mail or in person at the Traffic Summons Control Bureau. The recent crackdown on those who ignore summonses has been conducted by means of computers and an expansion of the towaway program to cover habitual scofflaws. The overwhelming majority of traffic infractions, therefore, are dealt with outside the courts. It would seem that the vesting of authority over all aspects of traffic offenses in a single administrative agency would be the most effective and efficient way to deal with the administration of traffic laws.

## D. Administrative Agency

There have been several proposals in recent years to transfer jurisdiction over traffic offenses to an administrative agency; the most recent is legislation currently pending before the New York Legislature. The New York proposal would remove the jurisdiction of the New York City Criminal Court over some traffic infractions and vest it in a Traffic Infractions Board.

1. *Advantages of an Administrative Agency.* An administrative agency would have several advantages over any of the previously discussed approaches to traffic court reform. It is the only approach which deals with both the problems of procedure and criminal status of the offense. Any basic reform which could be made by upgrading the existing system of courts could also be made through an administrative agency. In fact, it probably could be done more effectively. Inaugurating an entirely new system would undoubtedly bring about more sweeping reform than would piecemeal changes in the present system. Moreover, taking jurisdiction away from the courts and placing it in an administrative agency would be the most affirmative way to recognize the fact that a traffic offense is noncriminal.

If it is recognized that driving is an activity that must be regulated in the public interest, the appropriateness of vesting authority in an administrative agency becomes apparent. The administrative agency has become a most common and effective method of government regulation. The State of New York has, in fact, provided for a large degree of administrative authority to regulate drivers. The Department of Motor Vehicles issues and renews licenses, and it has the power to revoke or suspend them for good reason. There would seem to be no reason why authority over individual "infractions" as well could not be delegated to an administrative agency.

2. *Criticism of the Administrative Agency Approach.* The

American Bar Association Traffic Court Program has been the most outspoken critic of the use of an administrative agency as the solution to the problems of traffic law enforcement. Spokesmen for the Program are of the opinion that dealing with traffic infractions through an administrative agency would minimize the seriousness of the offense. Apparently the ABA feels that any shift from the present system of enforcing traffic laws through the criminal courts would remove the main deterrent to irresponsible driving. Nothing in the literature published by the Program, however, has demonstrated that it is the criminal process that is the compelling force behind effective traffic law enforcement. It would seem that such sanctions as fines and revocation or suspension of licenses are the effective means of enforcement, and these can just as well be applied by an agency as by a court.

The ABA Program is also of the opinion that the abolition of criminal procedure in favor of an administrative agency would be a violation of due process. The administration of civil sanctions by an administrative agency is not a violation of due process if the respondent is afforded hearing and judicial review. As will be seen, the only sanctions proposed are civil.

## PROCEDURE FOR PROPOSED ADMINISTRATIVE AGENCY

The remainder of this article will suggest structure and procedure for an administrative agency with authority over traffic infractions.

The defendant should be allowed to file pleas by mail in most cases. If a hearing is required, it would be before a hearing officer appointed by the administrative agency. At such hearing, the rules of evidence would not be strictly applied. The hearing officer would determine whether the charge has been proven. The sanctions which the hearing officer may impose would include fines and license suspension or revocation, but not imprisonment. Appeal to a court of general jurisdiction would be available.

### A. Response to Summons

1. *Not Guilty Plea.* There would seem to be no valid reason why a defendant who wishes to plead "not guilty" to an offense should not be allowed to enter his plea by mail. Formerly in New York City, the defendant had to appear once to make his plea and be assigned a trial date, and again for the trial itself. Since there were usually lines at both stages, the process was quite time consuming and especially oppressive to those who worked during

the day. There seemed to be little reason for the extra visit, and it is believed that the change is beneficial.

2. *Guilty Pleas.* It is suggested that most guilty pleas should be allowed by mail. Supporters of the National Standards have argued that payment of fines by mail without a personal appearance demeans the traffic offense. They feel that "The more defendants know that they will not be required to appear in court in person, the more they have a right to assume that a 'violate for a price' policy exists." This argument, however, overstates the case.

The defendant who is in court only because an appearance is required often has no explanation to make and wants only to be on his way. It is doubtful that his mere presence in court is of much corrective value; on the contrary, it is likely that he regards it as an unnecessary nuisance. Further, although it is not denied that a dignified procedure promotes respect for the processes of justice, it has yet to be convincingly demonstrated that even an ideal hearing procedure will have a significant effect on the defendant's driving habits. Perhaps as more communities across the nation upgrade their traffic tribunals, more data will be available as to whether these improvements actually help lower the accident rates. At the present time, however, there seems little reason for taking the strict view that personal appearance is always necessary.

Required appearances for defendants pleading guilty should be limited to "repeaters" and to those whose summonses are the result of traffic accidents. This would ensure that the most serious offenders are personally warned of the consequences, both legal and practical, of their behavior. On the other hand, it would give violators the benefit of the belief that their infractions were only momentary slips. It would also significantly decrease the appearance load.

3. *Scofflaws.* One of the most serious problems faced by a traffic tribunal, whether it be a court or an administrative agency, is ensuring that those who have received summonses answer them. In 1965, approximately 20 per cent of the summonses issued for moving violations in New York City were never answered. Another 20 per cent were answered only after letters and/or citations were issued by the Department of Motor Vehicles or by the traffic court. Fifty per cent of all parking tickets were ignored.

There are several possible means to compel violators to respond to a summons. One would be to continue the present New York procedure whereby a citation is sent to the nonresponding violator's address. If this is ignored, a warrant is issued for the defendant's arrest. The warrant is executed personally by the police;

the defendant, if he has been found, is brought into court. The disadvantages of this technique are obvious. The defendant who has ignored the summons will frequently ignore the citation as well. This is especially true in the case of habitual scofflaws. Further, the police manpower required could be better utilized for other purposes.

A more effective approach would treat nonappearance as a ground for automatic license suspension. The logic of this approach is clear: contempt of the legal process used to regulate the driving privilege is punished by suspension of the privilege itself. This plan could be implemented in several ways.

One novel method would be for the traffic officer, when issuing a summons, to take the violator's permanent license and give him a temporary one in its place. This temporary license would expire on the date set for appearance, or, alternatively, after a period sufficient to allow the violator to set a hearing date. If the driver did not appear, he would not thereafter have a valid license, and would be subject to penalties for driving without a license. Driving without a license is a misdemeanor in New York State. This plan has considerable merit in theory, but is impractical. The permanent license of every accused violator would have to be confiscated until the hearing. This would impose a huge burden on the agency.

A more reasonable solution would be to notify the defendant, upon his nonappearance, that his license was to be suspended. The suspension would not become effective until the license was surrendered. Failure to turn in the license within a specified period would be a misdemeanor. Moreover, the longer the defendant delayed such presentation, the longer would be the suspension. After a certain period of delay, revocation of the license would result. Even if respondent never surrendered his license, the penalty would be automatically effective when his license came up for renewal and he found such renewal blocked. This plan lacks the immediate effect of the one previously discussed, but involves much less paperwork, and limits such paperwork to cases where the sanction will actually be applied.

## B. Hearings

1. *Cases Requiring a Hearing.* Hearings would be held in three classes of cases:

(1) Cases in which the respondent has entered a not-guilty plea;

(2) Cases in which respondent pleads guilty but appearance is required by statute; e.g., those respondents who are "repeaters" or

recipients of summonses because of involvement in a traffic accident;

(3) Cases in which respondent pleads guilty but requests a hearing.

2. *Hearing Officers.* There should be a permanent staff of referees to preside over all hearings. Such an arrangement would promote consistent treatment of traffic infractions.

Dean Daniel Gutman of the New York Law School has suggested that the hearing officers could be taken from a panel of volunteer lawyers, similar to the system currently used in the New York City Small Claims Court. Such a proposal, however, would hinder the establishment of uniform treatment of traffic violators. In addition, practicing lawyers could not as easily keep abreast of the growing body of knowledge concerning effective traffic-law enforcement. Such disadvantages more than outweigh the economic savings of a volunteer system.

3. *Hearing Procedure.* Proposed New York legislation sets forth a hearing procedure suitable for general adoption. In many respects it is similar to current criminal trial procedure. Under this bill, the respondent could appear with or without counsel, and could testify, call witnesses, and submit legal arguments in support of his position. The hearing officer would have the power to subpoena and compel production of documents. This power would be enforceable by the supreme court.

The bill proposes two changes in the rules of evidence. First, proof beyond a reasonable doubt would no longer be required. The suggested standard is that the evidence be "clear and convincing." This seems appropriate in view of the traditional use of the reasonable-doubt standard only for crimes. Such lesser standard is used in the Administrative Procedure Act, and its adoption here seems wise.

The second change is that the exclusionary rules, except for statutory rules relating to privileged communications, will not apply to traffic hearings. This is in accord with the rules for hearings before other administrative agencies in New York and the federal government. The exclusionary rules have been applied with full force only in jury cases. In judge-tried and administrative actions, there has been a more lenient attitude toward the admission of evidence. Abolition of the exclusionary rules in the proposed traffic agency would greatly simplify the disposition of cases, without any violation of the driver's rights.

4. *Appeals.* The proposed New York legislation provides for appeal on both questions of law and fact to the supreme court.

There is no appeal as of right from the decision of the supreme court to the appellate division, but such an appeal may be taken if special permission is granted. The process is simpler than that normally provided for appeals from the decisions of administrative agencies in New York. This recognizes that the cases themselves are relatively uncomplicated and that the vast majority of parties will not be represented by counsel.

## C. Sanctions

The three most common sanctions for traffic offenses are fine, imprisonment and license control. The sanctions available to the proposed traffic agency would be limited to fine and license control. The elimination of the sanction of imprisonment is proper. Imprisonment by an administrative agency is unconstitutional. In addition, commentators have heavily criticized the practice of allowing jail sentences for strict liability offenses.

1. *Fines.* An administrative agency with jurisdiction over traffic violations should have the power to levy fines on those who plead guilty or are found guilty at a hearing. The proposed New York legislation gives such power to the Traffic Infractions Board. Some courts, including the United States Supreme Court, have questioned the power of an administrative agency to use a fine as a penalty. Since the more drastic power of an agency to suspend or revoke a license is allowed, it would seem that a fine would also be appropriate. The question is actually whether the fine is criminal or civil in nature. Provisions making clear the civil purpose of the fine and setting forth civil means for its enforcement would seem to eliminate the constitutional objection.

2. *Suspension and Revocation.* Perhaps the most effective method of traffic-law enforcement is by the suspension or revocation of licenses. As early as 1935, a survey showed that traffic violators considered license control a much more effective means of regulation than fines. Writers dealing generally with the subject of public welfare offenses have also concluded that license suspension or revocation is more suitable for these offenses than the traditional criminal penalties.

Existing New York law gives the Department of Motor Vehicles, an administrative agency, the power to suspend or revoke licenses. The exercise of this power has been upheld. Thus there should be no doubt that the proposed agency could exercise a similar power. The proposed New York legislation would give the Traffic Infractions Board the power to suspend or revoke, but the Department of Motor Vehicles would still maintain concurrent power. A more efficient and effective system would be to grant the Traffic Infractions Board the exclusive power to suspend or revoke for infractions, thus eliminating the need for a second hearing before the Department of Motor Vehicles. Such a unified procedure would result in a saving of both time and money to the State and motorist alike.

## IV. CONCLUSION

Current methods of processing traffic violations are unsatisfactory. The procedure leaves the defendant with a poor impression of the administration of justice. Present law classifies the traffic offense as a crime while the offense itself may involve no culpability.

Various reforms have been proposed for the handling of traffic cases. The American Bar Association Traffic Court Program has recommended an increased emphasis on the criminal aspects of the traffic offense in order to deter offenders. The present New York statute makes the traffic offense an "infraction" rather than a crime, but requires hearings in the criminal court. The use of the civil court would remove the traffic offense from the criminal court completely, but would still require the case to be handled by a court.

It is submitted that the proposed traffic enforcement agency is the best solution to the processing of traffic cases. The agency would remove most traffic cases from the criminal law and the courts. Many of these cases would be quickly processed by mail. The others would be handled by hearing officers. Sanctions would be fines and license control, but not imprisonment. There would be an opportunity of appeal to the courts from agency decisions.

Such a system would make quick and effective enforcement of the traffic laws possible, and would help relieve the overcrowded dockets of our nation's courts.

# The Formation of Community Councils*

# Lewis R. Katz

### V. A PROPOSAL FOR REFORM

The following proposal is two-fold: (1) remove most original criminal jurisdiction except for traffic offenses from the municipal courts in communities over 75,000, and (2) vest the remainder of that jurisdiction in a system of lay courts known as Community Councils which would have jurisdiction over a population of 5000 and whose members would be chosen by that population.

A. *Limiting the Jurisdiction of the Urban Municipal Criminal Court*

The urban municipal court should have its criminal jurisdiction curtailed for many reasons, certainly not the least of which is "the municipal court mentality." That state of mind is quite common among judges and one can turn to a former judge for a description of the syndrome.

Prolonged service on the criminal side of the municipal court, the judge said, produces in each judge a sense of frustration from repeatedly hearing the same minor claims and offenses and realizing that any action taken in the courtroom will probably have negligible, if any, effect on the lives of the participants. He said that this point is driven home by the fact that judges, even in the largest metropolitan courts, see many of the same people back before them time after time. This, he contends, hardens the attitudes of the judges, breeds contempt for the defendants, and encourages a lack of concern for why these defendants are before the court and what will happen to them in court. After years of people with the same old problems, judges "tune out" and "turn on" to the numerous people who have no business to transact in court but who come to the court each day to watch it in action. At this point the judges begin to concentrate on "entertaining" this audience of spectators, even when the jibes and asides are at the expense of

* From: Municipal Courts — Another Urban Ill, 20 Case W. Res. L. Rev. 87, 119-139 (1968). Reprinted by permission of the Case Western Reserve Law Review.

defendants and witnesses. He theorized that judges do this not only to break the tension and boredom within themselves, which results from hearing the same problems continuously, but also as a political gesture and a method of campaigning. The judges make themselves personalities to the spectators, personalities who will be remembered in the voting booths.

Compounding the atmosphere and the attitudes of the court is the lack of social service agencies connected with the municipal court. The lack of adequate social services in the municipal courts is attributable to the absence of any meaningful community commitment for funds to inquire into the social causes of crime. Instead, the middle-class community and its representatives, the judges, tend to believe that crime is the intrinsic problem, instead of crime being a manifestation of deeper problems within the community. Operating under this delusion, the courts should not be surprised to see the same people before them repeatedly.

To expect concrete positive results from present judicial attitudes is, at best, naive. Especially tragic is the alcoholic who appears repeatedly before these judges and has often appeared in other municipal courts throughout the state. Transient alcoholics are treated in a way that is reminiscent of American frontier justice: they are simply ordered to leave town. Repeaters are made sport of in the courtroom and often instructed by a judge or prosecutor to choose the number of days themselves that they will be sentenced to the county farm. While apropos of an O'Henry short story, these practices should be offensive to a 20th century society that unjustifiably prides itself on protecting the dignity of its citizens through the court system. These practices are likely to continue because of a recent Supreme Court decision which reversed a trend growing in lower courts and held that conviction and imprisonment of chronic alcoholics for public drunkenness does not violate the eighth amendment's prohibition against cruel and unusual punishments.[68] Finally, the judges themselves — who they are, whom they represent, their attitudes and concerns — make the development of the municipal court mentality inevitable.

Municipal court judges in most urban centers are chosen neither because they have demonstrated great legal talent nor for their compassion. On the contrary, they are chosen by partisan political machines for their faithfulness to the party and their past work on behalf of the party. From the overall lack of quality judges, one might surmise that the bar association recommendations carry

68. Powell v. Texas, 392 U.S. 514 (1968)....

little weight with the voters. Many of the lawyers willing to accept
these posts have not been too successful in the private practice and
find a judge's salary — though certainly not high — both attractive
and secure. Whatever their career backgrounds, the municipal court
judges soon become callous toward the people who come before
them. Rarely is a judge concerned with mitigating circumstances,
and often he refuses to hear them at all. Too often these judges
seem to forget that they are dealing with human beings whose
problems have brought them before the court. The one consuming
concern is to run the docket and dispose of the cases. Congestion,
however, should not serve as an excuse for the municipal court
mentality, because it does not explain the blatant racism exhibited
by some of the judges.[70]

The white municipal court judge is representative of the white,
middle-class community, and he is too often responsive only to
that community. Consequently, he reflects the white community's
uneasiness with the black community's restiveness, and he is more
concerned with charges that the court is coddling criminals than
he is with charges that the courts treat blacks unfairly. Finally, the
municipal court judge deals constantly with the police and is concerned with maintaining a good working relationship with them.
Unfortunately, the police departments that acknowledge good
working relationships with the municipal court judges are generally
those that have pretty free reign in those courts. As a result of all
of this, many municipal court judges do not even make a pretense
of impartiality when hearing a case. The police officer's word is
rarely doubted unless an attorney is representing the defendant and
in six out of 10 cases involving lawyers, the case will not get far
enough to have the policeman's assessment of the situation chal-
lenged. The prosecutors, who do not get the physical and mental
relief that the judges do from alternating between the civil and
criminal sides of the court, become the epitome of the municipal
court mentality. In the great majority of cases they become masters of ceremony hurrying the various performers on and off the
stage.

More than 100,000 criminal cases, not including minor traffic
offenses, flow through the Cleveland Municipal Court every year.
When one compares this with the more than 5 million arrests
yearly in the United States, most of which are at least processed

70. The condescending way in which one judge and a prosecutor in Cincinnati called all black men by their first names and repeatedly made jokes at
their expense, set the tone of that courtroom.

through, if not terminated in some form by a municipal or police court, the burdens on these courts and their personnel become clearer. When it is fully realized that the number of arrests and charges signifies that one out of every 40 Americans passes through the criminal process yearly — the figure is much higher if traffic arrests are included — it should be obvious that a deliberate and considered method of disposing of these matters is impossible. The burdens imposed by such a caseload make the docket the ultimate concern. Under these circumstances, it is also easy to understand why fairness, fact finding, and problem solving become much lesser concerns.

Survival of the municipal criminal courts is predicated upon maintaining conditions as they presently exist — conditions consisting of uninformed poor people appearing before the courts, confessing to their misdeeds by a plea of guilty and receiving inequitable punishment. Those who know better, or who can afford to retain someone whose business is to know better, fare better. Putting the state to its proof, its obligation under our system of law, and forcing the state to present its case within the bounds provided by the rules of evidence, creates chaos and the system falls apart. Only 27 of the more than 1000 cases tabulated in the Cleveland Municipal Court involved requests for jury trials. Only five guilty verdicts resulted from these jury trials, while there were seven not guilty verdicts returned by the juries, and in 15 of these cases the state threw in the towel and the charges were nolled or dismissed.

At the heart of the American legal system is the concept of due process of law. Implicit in the meaning of this term is its underlying notion: *fairness*. Fairness dictates that, above all, the government deals evenly with its citizens, does not attempt to victimize the citizenry even at the expense of disrupting the machinery, and, finally, insures that the citizens are apprised of both rights and obligations so that the functioning of the government or any of its component parts is not dependent upon the citizenry remaining uninformed. To the extent that maintenance of the municipal court system is dependent upon continuing unequal administration of justice, victimizing a substantial part of the community and perpetuating an ignorance of how the system actually functions, it is repugnant to the concept of due process.

Drastic reforms are needed to convert the municipal courts into an integral part of a democratic system of government. One approach would be to apply those specific provisions of the Bill of Rights, currently applicable to persons charged with serious of-

fenses, to all persons charged with any crime. Principally, this
would mean the appointment of an attorney for every person
charged who claims that he is financially unable to obtain counsel.
Since it would be administratively impossible to verify the claims,
the appointment would be automatic. The administrative task of
notifying private attorneys to represent all indigents would likewise be impossible, not to mention the prohibitive cost of such a
system. It would require the establishment of enormous public
defender staffs in every urban center just to handle the traffic in
the municipal courts. It is questionable whether there are even
enough laywers to handle this task. A minimum of 10 laywers
per 100 cases would be required in each courtroom per day, and
this would be sufficient only to handle the initial counseling and
entering of pleas. Vast additional legal talent would be required
for actual trial work. Law students provide an untapped resource
which could be mobilized for much of this work, and there is no
reason why law students should not be incorporated into the practice of law in intern programs comparable to those for medical
students. Law students are for the most part interested in public
service, dedicated to the improvement of this country's legal institutions, and are presently questioning the relevance of much of
their legal training. Pilot programs involving law students have
demonstrated their maturity, ability, and the high quality of their
work.

The problem of providing massive legal assistance will be acute
in localities where there are no law schools or where they are insufficient numbers of advanced law students to participate in this
work. In any event, the introduction of legal assistance for all
defendants would in all likelihood sound the death knoll for the
present system the very existence of which is dependent upon its
ability to dispose summarily of its massive docket. When defendants are apprised of their rights, it is doubtful that the great numbers of guilty pleas will continue, a situation which will then
require trials or dismissals. Once this occurs, and the municipal
courts are unable to summarily dispose of hundreds of cases a day,
the system will come to a complete halt. Any attempt to substitute
a single representative to counsel all those who desire it will be of
no value because of the number who need counseling, as evidenced
by Cincinnati where the presence of the Legal Aid Defender has
had no visible effect as far as misdemeanants are concerned. Implicit in any plan to permanently station lawyers in the municipal
courts to assist any defendant who desires their help is the danger
that repeated exposure to that court may develop in the lawyers the

same callousness that presently signifies the municipal court mentality. Finally, it is doubtful that the presence of public defenders would guarantee a greater equality in sentencing than presently exists because the reasons many attribute, perhaps erroneously, to the discrimination in sentencing between defendants with attorneys and those without — a realization that the defendant must pay a substantial legal fee to the attorney — would not abate. The discrimination could conceivably become greater if the municipal court lawyers, who jealously guard their prerogatives, and their allies felt the presence of competition.

The former judge of an urban municipal court who discussed the municipal court mentality indicated that one cure-all for the most recurring abuses would be to require a verbatim transcript of all municipal court sessions. . . .

Finally, the basic deficiency of the existing municipal courts in urban centers is that they are white men's institutions handling black men's problems. Just as the number of black defendants in the municipal courts is disproportionately higher than that group's percentage of the total population, the number of black officers of the court — whether police, attorneys, prosecutors, and especially judges — is disproportionately lower than the percentage of blacks in the community. There are numerous reasons for both facts. The reasons for the greater percentage of black defendants has often been explained and belabored. The reasons for the disproportionately low number of black police, black attorneys, black prosecutors, and black judges are equally self-revealing. Destructive discrimination in job and educational opportunities, although lifted in these areas in the past decade, has taken its toll in frustration and a rechanneling of both goals and values. Second-class education in de facto segregated schools continues to disqualify great numbers from advancement, and, as 7 years of college and graduate school grow more costly each year, it becomes more out of reach for impoverished families. Moreover, there was even less financial assistance available in the past when most of the lawyers practicing today were educated.

The lack of communication between the white and black communities which is being magnified across this country reaches tragic proportions in the urban municipal criminal courts where the black man appears most often as the accused. Certainly, under these conditions, meaningful dialogue is precluded. Mutual distrust exists between the black defendant and the white establishment, foreclosing any meaningful attempt to reach the core of the individual's problem which results in anti-social conduct. Few, if any, whites can empathize with the black Americans of the second-half of the 20th century, and surprisingly, few of those entrusted with the task of the administration of criminal justice actually sympathize with the black man's problems or the black community's aspirations. When a judge sitting in a court of law cannot recognize the most basic demand, that of being addressed like a human being, any more ambitious expectations, such as fairness, are utopian.

There are solutions to many of the personal problems, but they are not to be found for black defendants in white municipal courts. The people who can understand the defendant's problem, secure his confidence, and possibly assist him towards finding a solution are those in his own community, sharing many of his own experiences. The power must be transferred to the source of the solution and the creation of Community Councils represents the first step.

### B. The Formation of Community Councils

At least 30 percent of the 1034 Cleveland Municipal Court cases studied during this project could be assigned to Community Councils, neighborhood courts staffed by laymen,[84] to settle issues

---

84. The proposed Community Council should not be confused with or analogized to the outdated counterpart of the urban municipal court — the justice of the peace court. These lay-manned, fee-paid courts have fallen into as much or more abuse in the rural areas as have the urban courts. The justice of the peace courts were organized long ago because travel and communication were troublesome. They placed arbitrary decision-making power in one individual with little or no judicial or administrative review, and were based on a fee system which often meant that the justice did not receive remuneration unless a conviction and fine were imposed. See [The President's Commission on Law Enforcement and Administration of Justice,] Task Force Report: The Courts, . . . at 34-35. The Community Councils, although manned by a board of laymen, contain none of these aspects for potential abuse. Instead, these Councils are predicated upon a look backward to the old common law lay jury system where neighbors applied the law to their neighbors in the context of a fact situation that occurred within their neighborhood.

Lay participation in the decision-making process is not uncommon in civil law countries. In Germany, for example, criminal jurisdiction over minor crimes is vested in the *antsgericht*, a court composed of a single professional judge and two laymen, called *Schoeffen*. Unlike the contemporary Anglo-American lay jury, the *Schoeffen* are not confined to determining issues of fact alone, but are responsible to hear and examine witnesses, weigh the evidence, and decide legal issues. At the conclusion of a trial the laymen and the judge deliberate and vote on issues of guilt and penalty, with a two-thirds vote of the joint tribunal required. Sweigert, The Legal System of the Federal Republic of Germany, 11 Hastings L.J. 7, 12 (1959).

and disputes of a local nature. Of the 1034 cases studied, 619 involved charges of simple assault and battery — by far the most common offense. In an effort to determine how many of these assault cases arose between members of a single family, the cases where the surname of the prosecuting witness was the same as the defendant's were separately classified. By this process of selection 214 cases were classified as arising in a domestic situation. In addition, it is probable that many of the cases involving charges of disturbing the peace, harassment, malicious destruction of property, pointing firearms, trespass, and throwing stones also arose in the home neighborhood. The remainder of the serious misdemeanors could be tried in the municipal courts. Since one of the chief problems of the urban municipal court is its overcrowded docket, the elimination of at least 30 percent of its criminal caseload would have a positive effect on the administration of justice. The municipal court should, however, retain its jurisdiction over civil matters and traffic offenses and serve as the appellate court for the Community Councils.

But why form Community Councils? Basically, the answer is that so many misdemeanors are in essence neighborhood dilemmas and if solutions to the *causes* of these crimes are to be found, they will probably best be determined within the neighborhood. Additionally, the present method of "supermarket justice" as dispensed in the municipal courts has simply not worked, and an alternate means for providing justice must be devised.

For purposes of forming Community Councils, every city with a population greater than 75,000 should be divided into communities of 5000. It is obvious, however, that artificial community lines would not provide the structure envisioned for Community Councils because the people within each subdivision must have a natural mutuality of interests, concerns, and, when possible, similar backgrounds. The Councils would function best, then, in those neighborhoods that existed — and still exist in many cities — where people with similar national origins naturally group together. But the concept of Community Councils extends also to suburbia or the non-ethnic, integrated, middle class areas, for while perhaps not sharing similar backgrounds, the people of these areas today share what may be even more essential — common aspirations for the future and common difficulties with the present. Uniting these people today in a "natural" neighborhood are the problems of deteriorating neighborhoods, zoning interests, fear in the streets, school issues, and many other common concerns.

In the inner city, the neighborhood concept of government

would have the effect of bringing some power into the community and organizing it. In the ghetto, the Community Council will have the additional benefit of providing elected leaders from small population centers who can serve as the voice of that community. More important than one-man-one-vote at this level of government is the concept of natural neighborhood divisions. In that respect, then, deviations of 2500 from the 5000-person community figure should be permitted if necessary to define a natural community. Unnatural gerrymandering, to exclude a racial or ethnic group for instance, would be fairly evident and should not be permitted.

Resorting to ethnic, racial, and economic divisions to create these communities might be viewed derogatorily as a kind of racism. That brand of thinking, however, is not consonant with existing conditions in American cities. If America is a melting pot, as far as the residents of the inner cities are concerned, it stopped melting when it came to them. Nor is social and economic mobility as fluid as it once may have been, as is evidenced by the families now in their third generation on welfare subsistence. One of the few genuine points of understanding in this decade has been that people cannot lift themselves up unless they have the power to do so. The Councils provide a vehicle through which the necessary power can be restored to the community. Moreover, power placed within the community will be in the hands of people who share common problems and not in the hands of distant theoreticians who are unfamiliar with the real needs and concerns of the people. The creation of Councils in the suburbs may activate the melting operation because it will bring people together through a working organization which can stimulate communication and understanding. While there are differences among people in the suburbs, they are generally not caused by racial or religious differences.

The Community Council should be composed of three members, whose sole qualifications are that they be of voting age and residents of the voting district. The absence of other qualifications would encourage the political novice into the field and also encourage a great number of women and younger people. All of this would be beneficial because women are most intimately concerned with the daily problems of their neighborhood and involved young people act as catalysts for change and are vociferous exponents for reform. Councilmen should be selected in a nonpartisan election held at a time different from the general election and party primaries. Separate elections would help to elevate purely local issues and distinguish them from other state and city-wide problems.

The election process must be carefully policed and a strictly enforced limit should be placed on the amount of money that each candidate is permitted to spend or that may be spent on his behalf. Any time a candidate and his supporters exceed that limitation, he should be disqualified as a candidate. Similarly, each candidate must run individually, and not as a part of a ticket. Violation of this requirement should also result in disqualification. The reasons for the monetary limitation and the prohibition against tickets are threefold. First, it is essential to make the Councils function as truly representative so that the councilman campaigns on his own personality and personal record and that three candidates not be permitted to piece together achievements that would be popular to one-third of the electorate. Prohibiting tickets would prevent the organization of local party movements which might also de-emphasize the personal nature of the job and the election. Second, by limiting the amount of money that can be spent on any candidate — perhaps equivalent to the cost of one general mailing to the constituency — those without great financial means, who may be more representative of the community as a whole, will not be discouraged from entering the race. This would make soliciting of contributions unnecessary and prevent a candidate from being obligated to any interest within the community. Finally, the spending restriction would encourage a personal, door-to-door campaign which works in the interest of the Community Council concept. Candidates would have to meet nearly everyone in the community this way, would become familiar with the problems of the voters, and the voter would feel more secure in approaching the Council when a problem develops. This is the essence of any good judicial system and should distinguish the Community Council from the present municipal courts. Operating on a wise-man principle, the people should have confidence in the judgment of the councilmen and feel that the Council is their own court.

Terms of office should be 12 months and no Councilman should be permitted to serve more than four consecutive terms in office. While the wise-man principle might dictate that a popular Councilman be permitted to serve as long as the voters continue to indicate their approval of his judgment and conduct, there are competing values involved in this determination. It is essential to prevent the development of a municipal court mentality on the part of the councilmen, an attitude which could occur if year after year councilmen are faced with the same problems and people. The object is to have an interested tribunal rather than one whose members have a chance to become insensitive to the problems of the people appearing before it. The 4-year limitation would have the additional advantage of bringing other citizens into the public arena, acquainting them with the problems and needs of their neighbors and society, and generally getting them involved.

There is no need to establish a bureaucratic structure around the Community Councils, nor is it necessary to attach great salaries to the jobs. Council duties will not be so great that the position cannot be part-time and the remuneration modest. The most feasible time for the Council to hold sessions would be in the evenings and on weekends, thereby permitting people to appear with the least amount of dislocation. Valuable time would not be lost from jobs. Interested citizens could observe with the least amount of inconvenience. One full-time employee, a clerk of the Council, should be retained who should be responsible for assisting citizens coming forward so that their problem is in presentable form. The clerk would also issue subpoenas, prepare the agenda for the Council, and prepare the reports that the Council will be required to submit to a supervising authority. The office of clerk should be a civil service position and persons holding the position should be fully trained by the city. Again it becomes important to insure that the clerk does not become entrenched so that he wields too much power in the community and influences the Council. To meet that need, the clerks should not serve in any community for more than one year, but should be transferred to a different Council at the end of each term.

One of the long hard-fought battles in the annals of Anglo-American jurisprudence was to secure to an individual the right to be represented in a court appearance by an attorney. As for persons able to retain an attorney, that battle is over. For those who do not have funds, the battle continues. But the criminal side of the municipal courts has evolved into a place of privilege for the attorney class. Lawyers do not serve as officers of those courts, cognizant of their responsibility to the process. On the contrary, they have become manipulators of the process. If this is permitted to happen in the Community Council, it will no longer be a people's tribunal and will not serve its proposed purposes. Since the Council is envisioned primarily as a conciliatory agency without the power to incarcerate citizens, it is submitted that attorneys should not be permitted to appear before the Council in any capacity other than as a party to a dispute. Obviously, there is no way to prevent people from consulting with lawyers prior to their appearance before the Council, nor is there any way, or need, to bar attorneys from attending the proceedings, but the need exists to permit citizens freedom from the rules of evidence in order to explain their positions to lay judges and to permit those judges to reach an equitable solution. To some this may appear as a reactionary attempt to dilute the constitutional protections of citizens, but before that conclusion is reached the following question should be asked: Is this notion truly repugnant to American constitutional precepts or is it simply questionable because we as a people are not conditioned to doing it this way? The entire concept of conflict resolution by lay judges deciding these matters purely on the basis of common sense is radical to 20th century notions about justice.[93] The breakdown of the present system of administering justice, however, demands radical innovations. There will be safeguards provided to prevent a "Star Chamber" atmosphere from arising, more so than under the present municipal court structure, and there is nothing in the basic ingredients of lay justice that would make the Council system repugnant to concepts of due process. Certainly, criticism from the practicing bar will be suspect, for they have a vested interest in maintaining the present structure and are responsible for many of its crippling abuses. The American public is extremely disenchanted with the present deficiencies of the judicial system, and it is doubtful that it is indissolubly wed to the present institutions.

There is no reason why the arresting officer of the complainant cannot appear before the Council, present his side of the controversy, and request that subpoenas be issued to bring in witnesses who can contribute to the Council's understanding of the problem. The same holds true for the party against whom the complaint is made. Certainly, the defending party may remain mute if he chooses, in which case the Council could render its decision on

---

93. There is nothing inherent in the concept of lay justice that makes it unfair and consequently a violation of due process. Countless courts of inferior jurisdiction throughout the country remain staffed by judges or justices of the peace who do not have legal training. In its most recent attempt to delineate how far down the judicial ladder the specific guarantees of the Bill of Rights incorporated into the 14th amendment extend, the Supreme Court once again used the "serious" as opposed to "petty" offense distinction. Duncan v. Louisiana, 391 U.S. 145 (1968). In Duncan, the Court said, "we hold no constitutional doubts about . . . prosecuting petty crimes without extending a right to jury trial." Id. at 158. Furthermore, the Court seemed to ratify the federal standard which requires jury trial for offenses punishable by more than 6 months in prison and carrying more than a $500 fine. The Community Councils, which will not have the authority to order incarceration and will serve as a conciliatory agency, would not run afoul of these requirements.

the basis of only one side of the controversy.[95] Observation of the municipal courts, however, indicates that defendants often have something to say in their defense, but when unaccompanied by an attorney they rarely have the opportunity. Councils should be granted the power to subpoena witnesses. These subpoenas should be issued in the name of the supervisory court, and that court should have the power to enforce them.

Resolving disputes will be the principal function of the Community Councils, not punishing law breakers. To this end, the Councils will be expected to ascertain the facts of each dispute in detail and attempt to reach an agreement with the parties which would resolve the conflict. Operating within a small community, they should not experience the same difficulties that courts with a much larger jurisdiction seem to encounter. Similarly, with constituencies of 5000 people, the Councils will not be overwhelmed with so many cases that they are unable to devote a sufficient amount of time to any one dispute. The fewer cases the less prone the judges are to become callous and handle the matters by rote. Finally, within a small, somewhat homogeneous community of which the lay judges are an integral part, it will be easier for them to dig out facts, find witnesses, and generally get to the crux of a controversy. Functioning this way, the Councils will be able to learn the reasons for antisocial behavior and should have the full means of the city at their disposal to alleviate oppressive conditions.[97] Councilmen should be continuously trained in the social and welfare services that are available in the city, and they should have direct access to city employment agencies, welfare agencies, guidance centers, and domestic counselors. Individualized treatment of problems is the only way to solve the revolving door com-

95. The presumption of innocence in the Anglo-American system of jurisprudence which dictates that the burden of proof rests upon the state is virtually non-existent in the urban municipal courts. Along with the presumption has been lost the privilege against self-incrimination. No explanation is given to the uncounseled defendant as to what the procedure is in determining guilt or innocence and it is not at all uncommon for a judge to address a defendant and ask him what he has to say for himself. Often the response from the uninformed defendant is the only evidence against him and results in his conviction. The Council system's ability to take time to discover the facts of the controversy is one of its greatest advantages over the present system.

97. This would mean full community support in providing the Councils with the traditional probation and parole services, as well as the development of other special community programs such as guided group interaction programs and prerelease guidance centers, to mention a few.

plexion of our present criminal courts and jails. A few days, weeks, or months in jail do not solve the problems that lead individuals to commit the acts for which society punishes. The alarmingly high rate of recidivism among people who commit petty crimes indicates that a more individualized approach is required, one which would be the function of the Community Councils.

In the area of neighborhood squabbles, the Council's job would be to assist the participants in reaching an agreement to restore peace to the neighborhood. Most people would be amazed how many petty disagreements among neighbors over noise, children, dogs, and the general maintenance of property are escalated until they result in municipal court charges of malicious destruction of property, petty larceny, or assault.[99] . . .

[Usually] . . . there is no opportunity to find out the facts and generally the participants become objects of levity in the courtroom and are sent home disgruntled. Rather than using the traditional criminal process to resolve these disputes, the Community Councils would be in an excellent position to ascertain the true facts and serve as conciliators.

As incarceration has not proved to be the answer as far as petty crimes are concerned, there is no reason to vest the Councils with this power. Their primary power should be to work out equitable arrangements with which the parties could live, and which would be binding upon the parties. The Councils should have the authority to order restitution for property damaged by wrongdoers, to

99. Under the present system a large proportion of urban marital arguments and neighborhood quarrels are not settled at home or in the backyard or in church, but are litigated before a municipal criminal court of first instance. A typical example is the assault-and-battery charge with the wife as complainant. This type of case and others like it now consume much of a municipal court's time and patience, but ironically these courts can do little in this area for the charges basically are not criminal in nature. These people seek the aid of an arbitrator who has the time to come to a reasonable disposition or compromise for their present difficulty; they rarely get either time or a reasonable disposition from a heavily docketed municipal court. A good example of the municipal courts' inadequacies in this area can be seen in the typical assault-and-battery complainant described above, who is almost always shocked by a magistrate's suggestion that her spouse be sent to jail. These problems do not belong in an urban municipal court, unless of course they are permitted to continue and create tension which may result in true criminal conduct, but could effectively be handled by the Community Councils. Early dispositions of these private disputes, plus the possible use of the peace bond, a deposit guaranteeing future good conduct, would do much to obviate future misconduct of a more serious nature. . . .

order a party to pay the bills occasioned by his wrongdoing, or to work for a certain period of time to undo the damage which he did. Probably, many disputes would be considered by the Councils long before there is serious escalation, so that the rulings would be on minor matters such as directing a party not to play a phonograph after a certain hour, to leash a pet, to clean out the garbage from a yard, or to make sure that children are home at a certain hour. These are the disputes that fester until a criminal act is committed. The present judicial structure has neither the authority nor the time to handle the disputes at an incipient stage, but the Community Councils would. They would also be in a position to continue supervising the arrangement and, if it is unsuccessful, to modify their determination. Knowing the participant becomes all important at this stage. The Councils will be in an advantageous position because of their ability to judge credibility and operate with the continuing support of the neighborhood.

The closeness of the Community Council to the people of the neighborhood, and the pressure of the general community's support for the Council in most instances will insure compliance by the parties with its orders. Arrangements must be made, however, for those parties who are either dissatisfied with the Council's determination and order, or who simply fail to comply with the order. Thus, an appellate procedure must also be created to cope with these cases, but the system devised for appeals should be tailored to the Community Council system. Appeals should be heard in the next highest court which should also maintain some supervisory powers over the Councils. If the municipal courts are retained for civil and traffic cases, and criminal cases too serious for the Councils to handle, the appeals should be handled there. If the municipal court does not retain this jurisdiction, the general trial court should be assigned the appellate responsibility.[102] The

102. ... The President's Commission on Law Enforcement and Administration of Justice believes the best way the problems of the lower courts can be met is unification of the criminal courts and abolition of the lower courts as presently constituted. The commission points out that, "procedural and administrative differences in the processing of petty offenses may lead some jurisdictions to follow the pattern set by Detroit, where an integrated court handles all phases of criminal cases but a special branch of that court deals with petty offenses." [The President's Commission on Law Enforcement and Administration of Justice,] Task Force Report: The Courts, ... at 34. Implementing the commission's sensible suggestions, especially with respect to the abolition of the lower courts, would not at all conflict with the Community Council concept, for the Councils would merely assimilate the function of the special branch of the Detroit court that handles the neighborhood-type

deemphasis on law that exists in this proposed structure for the Councils should also carry over into the appellate procedure. Instead of an appeal as that term is generally used in the law, the proceeding in the "appellate" court should be handled as a trial de novo where all of the factual issues are presented and the court makes its own findings of fact. If the findings are the same as those of the Community Council, then that body's judgment should be entered as the judgment of the appellate court, assuming the Council's order is equitable. The Council's order should take precedence, because the Council is closer to the problem and better able to determine what corrective measures are suitable.

The failure of a party to a dispute to comply with an order of the Community Council presents a more difficult question than the appeal. The Council should be responsible for determining whether there has been satisfactory compliance, and in the event compliance is not forthcoming a report should be made to the city prosecutor who could issue a complaint in the municipal court based upon the failure to comply. Even though the person charged in the municipal court failed to appeal the Council's order, the facts in issue in the case should include the original facts in dispute. If the municipal court determines that the Council's findings of fact are substantially correct, the Council's order should be reinstated. It would be wise at this point to empower the reviewing court to add a penalty, including a jail sentence, as punishment for the failure to comply. Similarly, if a Council has repeated trouble from one member of the community, it should have the power to waive its jurisdiction and have the person charged and tried in the municipal court.

Although procedures are recommended to provide for appeals and those cases where individuals fail to abide by the decisions of the Community Councils, the Council's authority to settle disputes actually stems from its closeness to its constituency. It should, therefore, benefit from the natural support of the community. There will emerge pressures from within — family, neighbors, and associates — to abide by the decisions of the Council. It is submitted that this natural support, coupled with the mechanism to resolve conflicts at an early stage, will insure that the failure to comply is not an extensive problem.

No doubt there are those who would argue that a lay council

---

petty offense. Of course, since the lower courts would no longer exist under such a system, appeal from Council would be taken to the unified criminal court of first instance.

could easily become an instrument through which a small, but highly vocal, segment of the community would seize control and manipulate the system to serve the minority's own purposes. The net effect of such a minority takeover would simply be the substitution of an internal tyranny for the externally imposed tyranny that presently exists. Inherent in the Community Council concept, however, are certain structural controls which will insure that the Councils do not become a vehicle for minority control. Review by a duly constituted court is provided, and the mechanism by which councilmen are elected each year provides the means whereby the citizens of the community can protect themselves from a new tyranny. In any event, the argument that an articulate, militant minority will control the Councils is characteristic of the conservative and paternalistic attitude of the existing power structure, an attitude largely responsible for the municipal courts' present inability to help black people solve their problems. In light of this failure, is it unreasonable to suggest that the citizens of the inner city communities be given an opportunity to solve their own problems?

Restoring power to the people is not the panacea for all this society's ills. In the area of maintaining order and preventing petty crime, however, it is a solution that has been too long neglected. If the Council concept proves pragmatic at this level, there is no reason why it cannot be considered in landlord-tenant disputes and other litigation-producing relationships. It is not inconceivable that it may even be found that the best way to maintain order in a modern community is by borrowing from the past and having local constables, drawn from the community and backed up — but not directed — by modern police departments.

In any event, perhaps the sickness in our cities calls for a home, or neighborhood, remedy.

### ARGERSINGER V. HAMLIN
### 407 U.S. 25(1972)

Mr. Justice Douglas delivered the opinion of the Court.

Petitioner, an indigent, was charged in Florida with carrying a concealed weapon, an offense punishable by imprisonment up to six months, a $1,000 fine, or both. The trial was to a judge, and petitioner was unrepresented by counsel. He was sentenced to serve 90 days in jail, and brought this habeas corpus action in the Florida Supreme Court, alleging that, being deprived of his right to counsel, he was unable as an indigent layman properly to raise and present to the trial court good and sufficient defenses to the charges for which he stands convicted. The Florida Supreme Court by a four-to-three decision, in ruling on the right to counsel, followed the line we marked out in Duncan v. Louisiana, 391 U.S. 145, 159, as respects the right to trial by jury and held that the right to court-appointed counsel extends only to trials "for non-petty offenses punishable by more than six months imprisonment." 236 So. 2d 442, 443.

The case is here on a petition for certiorari, which we granted. 401 U.S. 908. We reverse.

The Sixth Amendment, which in enumerated situations has been made applicable to the States by reason of the Fourteenth Amendment (see Duncan v. Louisiana, *supra*; Washington v. Texas, 388 U.S. 14; Klopfer v. North Carolina, 386 U.S. 213; Pointer v. Texas, 380 U.S. 400; Gideon v. Wainwright, 372 U.S. 335; and In re Oliver, 333 U.S. 257), provides specified standards for "all criminal prosecutions."

One is the requirement of a "public trial." In re Oliver, *supra*, held that the right to a "public trial" was applicable to a state proceeding even though only a 60-day sentence was involved. 333 U.S., at 272.

Another guarantee is the right to be informed of the nature and cause of the accusation. Still another, the right of confrontation, Pointer v. Texas, *supra*. And another, compulsory process for obtaining witnesses in one's favor. Washington v. Texas, *supra*. We have never limited these rights to felonies or to lesser but serious offenses.

In Washington v. Texas, *supra*, we said, "We have held that due process requires that the accused have the assistance of counsel for his defense, that he be confronted with the witnesses against him, and that he have the right to a speedy and public trial." 388 U.S., at 18. Respecting the right to a speedy and public trial, the right to be informed of the nature and cause of the accusation, the right to confront and cross-examine witnesses, the right to compulsory process for obtaining witnesses, it was recently stated, "It is simply not arguable, nor has any court ever held, that the trial of a petty offense may be held in secret, or without notice to the accused of the charges, or that in such cases the defendant has no right to confront his accusers or to compel the attendance of witnesses in his own behalf." Junker, The Right to Counsel in Misdemeanor Cases, 43 Wash. L. Rev. 685, 705 (1968).

District of Columbia v. Clawans, 300 U.S. 617, illustrates the point. There, the offense was engaging without a license in the business of dealing in second-hand property, an offense punishable by a fine of $300 or imprisonment for not more than 90 days. The Court held that the offense was a "petty" one and could be tried without a jury. But the conviction was reversed and a new trial ordered, because the trial court had prejudicially restricted the right of cross-examination, a right guaranteed by the Sixth Amendment.

The right to trial by jury, also guaranteed by the Sixth Amendment by reason of the Fourteenth, was limited by Duncan v. Louisiana, *supra*, to trials where the potential punishment was imprisonment of six months or more. But, as the various opinions in Baldwin v. New York, 399 U.S. 66, make plain, the right to trial by jury has a different genealogy and is brigaded with a system of trial to a judge alone. . . .

While there is historical support for limiting the "deep commitment" to trial by jury to "serious criminal cases," there is no such support for a similar limitation on the right to assistance of counsel:

> Originally, in England, a person charged with treason or felony was denied the aid of counsel, except in respect of legal questions which the accused himself might suggest. At the same time parties in civil cases and persons accused of misdemeanors were entitled to the full assistance of counsel. . . .
> [It] appears that in at least twelve of the thirteen colonies the rule of the English common law, in the respect now under consideration, had been definitely rejected and the right to counsel fully recognized in all criminal prosecutions, save that in one or two instances the right was limited to capital offenses or to the more serious crimes. . . . (Powell v. Alabama, 287 U.S. 45, 60, 64-65.)

The Sixth Amendment thus extended the right to counsel beyond its common-law dimensions. But there is nothing in the language of the Amendment, its history, or in the decisions of this Court, to indicate that it was intended to embody a retraction of the right in petty offenses wherein the common law previously did require that counsel by provided. See James v. Headley, 410 F.2d 325, 331-332, n. 9.

We reject, therefore, the premise that since prosecutions for crimes punishable by imprisonment for less than six months may be tried without a jury, they may also be tried without a lawyer.

The assistance of counsel is often a requisite to the very existence of a fair trial. The Court in Powell v. Alabama, *supra*, at 68-69 — a capital case — said:

The right to be heard would be, in many cases, of little avail if it did not comprehend the right to be heard by counsel. Even the intelligent and educated layman has small and sometimes no skill in the science of law. If charged with crime, he is incapable, generally, of determining for himself whether the indictment is good or bad. He is unfamiliar with the rules of evidence. Left without the aid of counsel he may be put on trial without a proper charge, and convicted upon incompetent evidence, or evidence irrelevant to the issue or otherwise inadmissible. He lacks both the skill and knowledge adequately to prepare his defense, even though he have a perfect one. He requires the guiding hand of counsel at every step in the proceedings against him. Without it, though he be not guilty, he faces the danger of conviction because he does not know how to establish his innocence. If that be true of men of intelligence, how much more true is it of the ignorant and illiterate, or those of feeble intellect.

In Gideon v. Wainwright, *supra* (overhauling Betts v. Brady, 316 U.S. 455), we dealt with a felony trial. But we did not so limit the need of the accused for a lawyer. We said:

[I]n our adversary system of criminal justice, any person haled into court, who is too poor to hire a lawyer, cannot be assured a fair trial unless counsel is provided for him. This seems to us to be an obvious truth. Governments, both state and federal, quite properly spend vast sums of money to establish machinery to try defendants accused of crime. Lawyers to prosecute are everywhere deemed essential to protect the public's interest in an orderly society. Similarly, there are few defendants charged with crime, few indeed, who fail to hire the best lawyers they can get to prepare and present their defenses. That government hires lawyers to prosecute and defendants who have the money hire lawyers to defend are the strongest indications of the widespread belief that lawyers in criminal courts are necessities, not luxuries. The right of one charged with crime to counsel may not be deemed fundamental and essential to fair trials in some countries, but it is in ours. From the very beginning, our state and national constitutions and laws have laid great emphasis on procedural and substantive safeguards designed to assure fair trials before impartial tribunals in which every defendant stands equal before the law. This noble ideal cannot be realized if the poor man charged with crime has to face his accusers without a lawyer to assist him. (372 U.S., at 344.)

Both Powell and Gideon involved felonies. But their rationale has relevance to any criminal trial, where an accused is deprived of his liberty. Powell and Gideon suggest that there are certain fundamental rights applicable to all such criminal prosecutions, even those, such as In re Oliver, *supra*, where the penalty is 60 days' imprisonment:

> A person's right to reasonable notice of a charge against him, and an opportunity to be heard in his defense — a right to his day in court — are basic in our system of jurisprudence; and these rights include, as a minimum, a right to examine the witnesses against him, to offer testimony, *and to be represented by counsel*. (333 U.S., at 273 (emphasis supplied).)

The requirement of counsel may well be necessary for a fair trial even in a petty-offense prosecution. We are by no means convinced that legal and constitutional questions involved in a case that actually leads to imprisonment even for a brief period are any less complex than when a person can be sent off for six months or more. See, e.g., Powell v. Texas, 392 U.S. 514; Thompson v. Louisville, 362 U.S. 199; Shuttlesworth v. Birmingham, 382 U.S. 87.

The trial of vagrancy cases is illustrative. While only brief sentences of imprisonment may be imposed, the cases often bristle with thorny constitutional questions. See Papachristou v. Jacksonville, 405 U.S. 156.

In re Gault, 387 U.S. 1, dealt with juvenile delinquency and an offense which if committed by an adult, would have carried a fine of $5 to $50 or imprisonment in jail for not more than two months (id., at 29), but which when committed by a juvenile might lead to his detention in a state institution until he reached the age of 21. Id., at 36-37. We said (id., at 36) that "[t]he juvenile needs the assistance of counsel to cope with problems of law to make skilled inquiry into the facts, to insist upon regularity of the proceedings, and to ascertain whether he has a defense and to prepare and submit it. The child 'requires the guiding hand of counsel at every step in the proceedings against him,'" citing Powell v. Alabama, 287 U.S., at 69. The premise of Gault is that even in prosecutions for offenses less serious than felonies, a fair trial may require the presence of a lawyer.

Beyond the problem of trials and appeals is that of the guilty plea, a problem which looms large in misdemeanor as well as in felony cases. Counsel is needed so that the accused may know precisely what he is doing, so that he is fully aware of the prospect of going to jail or prison, and so that he is treated fairly by the prosecution.

In addition, the volume of misdemeanor cases, far greater in number than felony prosecutions, may create an obsession for speedy dispositions, regardless of the fairness of the result. . . .

That picture is seen in almost every report. "The misdemeanor trial is characterized by insufficient and frequently irresponsible preparation on the part of the defense, the prosecution, and the court. Everything is rush, rush." Hellerstein, The Importance of the Misdemeanor Case on Trial and Appeal, 28 The Legal Aid Brief Case 151, 152 (1970).

There is evidence of the prejudice which results to misdemeanor defendants from this "assembly-line justice." One study concluded that "[m]isdemeanants represented by attorneys are five times as likely to emerge from police court with all charges dismissed as are defendants who face similar charges without counsel." American Civil Liberties Union, Legal Counsel for Misdemeanants, Preliminary Report 1 (1970).

We must conclude, therefore, that the problems associated with misdemeanor and petty offenses often require the presence of counsel to insure the accused a fair trial. Mr. Justice Powell suggests that these problems are raised even in situations where there is no prospect of imprisonment. Post. . . . We need not consider the requirements of the Sixth Amendment as regards the right to counsel where loss of liberty is not involved, however, for here petitioner was in fact sentenced to jail. And, as we said in Baldwin v. New York, 399 U.S., at 73, "the prospect of imprisonment for however short a time will seldom be viewed by the accused as a trivial or 'petty' matter and may well result in quite serious repercussions affecting his career and his reputation."

We hold, therefore, that absent a knowing and intelligent waiver, no person may be imprisoned for any offense, whether classified as petty, misdemeanor, or felony, unless he was represented by counsel at his trial.[7] . . .

7. We do not share Mr. Justice Powell's doubt that the Nation's legal resources are insufficient to implement the rule we announce today. It has been estimated that between 1,575 and 2,300 full-time counsel would be required to represent *all* indigent misdemeanants, excluding traffic offenders. Note, Dollars and Sense of an Expanded Right to Counsel, 55 Iowa L. Rev. 1249, 1260-1261 (1970). These figures are relatively insignificant when compared to the estimated 355,200 attorneys in the United States (Statistical Abstract of the United States 153 (1971)), a number which is projected to double by the year 1985. See Ruud, That Burgeoning Law School Enrollment, 58 A.B.A.J. 146, 147. Indeed, there are 18,000 new admissions to the bar each year — 3,500 more lawyers than are required to fill the "estimated 14,500 average annual openings." Id., at 148.

We do not sit as an ombudsman to direct state courts how to manage their affairs but only to make clear the federal constitutional requirement. How crimes should be classified is largely a state matter.[9] The fact that traffic charges technically fall within the category of "criminal prosecutions" does not necessarily mean that many of them will be brought into the class[10] where imprisonment actually occurs.

Under the rule we announce today, every judge will know when the trial of a misdemeanor starts that no imprisonment may be imposed, even though local law permits it, unless the accused is represented by counsel. He will have a measure of the seriousness and gravity of the offense and therefore know when to name a lawyer to represent the accused before the trial starts.

The run of misdemeanors will not be affected by today's ruling. But in those that end up in the actual deprivation of a person's

---

9. One partial solution to the problem of minor offenses may well be to remove them from the court system. The American Bar Association Special Committee on Crime Prevention and Control recently recommended, inter alia, that:

"Regulation of various types of conduct which harm no one other than those involved (e.g., public drunkenness, narcotics addiction, vagrancy, and deviant sexual behavior) should be taken out of the courts. The handling of these matters should be transferred to non-judicial entities, such as detoxification centers, narcotics treatment centers and social service agencies. The handling of other non-serious offenses, such as housing code and traffic violations, should be transferred to specialized administrative bodies." ABA Report, New Perspectives on Urban Crime iv (1972). Such a solution, of course, is peculiarly within the province of state and local legislatures.

10. "Forty thousand traffic charges (arising out of 150,000 non-parking traffic citations) were disposed of by court action in Seattle during 1964. The study showed, however, that in only about 4,500 cases was there any possibility of imprisonment as the result of a traffic conviction. In only three kinds of cases was the accused exposed to any danger of imprisonment: (1) where the offense charged was hit-and-run, reckless or drunken driving; or (2) where any additional traffic violation was charged against an individual subject to a suspended sentence for a previous violation; or (3) where, whatever the offense charged, the convicted individual was unable to pay the fine imposed." Junker, The Right to Counsel in Misdemeanor Cases, 43 Wash. L. Rev. 685, 711 (1968).

Of the 1,288,975 people convicted by the City of New York in 1970 for traffic infractions such as jaywalking and speeding, only 24 were fined and imprisoned, given suspended sentences, or jailed. Criminal Court of the City of New York Annual Report 11 (1970). Of the 19,187 convicted of more serious traffic offenses, such as driving under the influence, reckless driving, and leaving the scene of an accident, 404 (2.1%) were subject to some form of imprisonment. Ibid.

liberty, the accused will receive the benefit of "the guiding hand of counsel" so necessary when one's liberty is in jeopardy.

Reversed.

Mr. Justice Powell, with whom Mr. Justice Rehnquist joins, concurring in the result.

Gideon v. Wainwright, 372 U.S. 335 (1963), held that the States were required by the Due Process Clause of the Fourteenth Amendment to furnish counsel to all indigent defendants charged with felonies. The question before us today is whether an indigent defendant convicted of an offense carrying a maximum punishment of six months' imprisonment, a fine of $1,000, or both, and sentenced to 90 days in jail, is entitled as a matter of constitutional right to the assistance of appointed counsel. The broader question is whether the Due Process Clause requires that an indigent charged with a state petty offense be afforded the right to appointed counsel. . . .

I am unable to agree with the Supreme Court of Florida that an indigent defendant, charged with a petty offense, may in every case be afforded a fair trial without the assistance of counsel. Nor can I agree with the new rule of due process, today enunciated by the Court, that "absent a knowing and intelligent waiver, no person may be imprisoned . . . unless he was represented by counsel at his trial." *Ante*, at 25. It seems to me that the line should not be drawn with such rigidity.

There is a middle course, between the extremes of Florida's six-month rule and the Court's rule, which comports with the requirements of the Fourteenth Amendment. I would adhere to the principle of due process that requires fundamental fairness in criminal trials, a principle which I believe encompasses the right to counsel in petty cases wherever the assistance of counsel is necessary to assure a fair trial.

I

I am in accord with the Court that an indigent accused's need for the assistance of counsel does not mysteriously evaporate when he is charged with an offense punishable by six months or less. In Powell v. Alabama [*supra*] and Gideon, both of which involved felony prosecutions, this Court noted that few laymen can present adequately their own cases, much less identify and argue relevant legal questions. Many petty offenses will also present complex legal and factual issues that may not be fairly tried if the defendant is not assisted by counsel. Even in relatively simple cases, some defendants, because of ignorance or some other handicap, will be incapable of defending themselves. The consequences of a misdemeanor conviction, whether they be a brief period served under the sometimes deplorable conditions found in local jails or the effect of a criminal record on employability, are frequently of sufficient magnitude not to be casually dismissed by the label "petty."

Serious consequences also may result from convictions not punishable by imprisonment. Stigma may attach to a drunken-driving conviction or a hit-and-run escapade. Losing one's driver's license is more serious for some individuals than a brief stay in jail. . . . When the deprivation of property rights and interests is of sufficient consequence, denying the assistance of counsel to indigents who are incapable of defending themselves is a denial of due process.

This is not to say that due process requires the appointment of counsel in all petty cases, or that assessment of the possible consequences of conviction is the sole test for the need for assistance of counsel. The flat six-month rule of the Florida court and the equally inflexible rule of the majority opinion apply to *all* cases within their defined areas regardless of circumstances. It is precisely because of this mechanistic application that I find these alternatives unsatisfactory. Due process, perhaps the most fundamental concept in our law, embodies principles of fairness rather than immutable line drawing as to every aspect of a criminal trial. While counsel is often essential to a fair trial, this is by no means a universal fact. Some petty offense cases are complex; others are exceedingly simple. As a justification for furnishing counsel to indigents accused of felonies, this Court noted: "That government hires lawyers to prosecute and defendants who have the money hire lawyers to defend are the strongest indications of the widespread belief that lawyers in criminal courts are necessities, not luxuries." Yet government often does not hire lawyers to prosecute petty offenses; instead the arresting police officer presents the case. Nor does every defendant who can afford to do so hire lawyers to defend petty charges. Where the possibility of a jail sentence is remote and the probable fine seems small, or where the evidence of guilt is overwhelming, the costs of assistance of counsel may exceed the benefits. It is anomalous that the Court's opinion today will extend the right of appointed counsel to indigent defendants in cases where the right to counsel would rarely be exercised by nonindigent defendants.

Indeed, one of the effects of this ruling will be to favor defendants classified as indigents over those not so classified, yet who are in low-income groups where engaging counsel in a minor petty-offense case would be a luxury the family could not afford. The line between indigency and assumed capacity to pay for counsel is necessarily somewhat arbitrary, drawn differently from State to State and often resulting in serious inequities to accused persons. The Court's new rule will accent the disadvantage of being barely self-sufficient economically.

A survey of state courts in which misdemeanors are tried showed that procedures were often informal, presided over by lay judges. Jury trials were rare, and the prosecution was not vigorous. It is as inaccurate to say that no defendant can obtain a fair trial without the assistance of counsel in such courts as it is to say that no defendant needs the assistance of counsel if the offense charged is only a petty one.

Despite its overbreadth, the easiest solution would be a prophylactic rule that would require the appointment of counsel to indigents in all criminal cases. The simplicity of such a rule is appealing because it could be applied automatically in every case, but the price of pursuing this easy course could be high indeed in terms of its adverse impact on the administration of the criminal justice systems of 50 States. This is apparent when one reflects on the wide variety of petty or misdemeanor offenses, the varying definitions thereof, and the diversity of penalties prescribed. The potential impact on state court systems is also apparent in view of the variations in types of courts and their jurisdictions, ranging from justices of the peace and part-time judges in the small communities to the elaborately staffed police courts which operate 24 hours a day in the great metropolitan centers.

The rule adopted today does not go all the way. It is limited to petty offense cases in which the sentence is some imprisonment. The thrust of the Court's position indicates, however, that when the decision must be made, the rule will be extended to all petty offense cases except perhaps the most minor traffic violations. If the Court rejects on constitutional grounds, as it has today, the exercise of any judicial discretion as to need for counsel if a jail sentence is imposed, one must assume a similar rejection of discretion in other offense cases. It would be illogical — and without discernible support in the Constitution — to hold that no discretion may ever be exercised where a nominal jail sentence is contemplated and at the same time endorse the legitimacy of discretion in "nonjail" petty offense cases which may result in far more serious consequences than a few hours or days of incarceration.

The Fifth and Fourteenth Amendments guarantee that property, as well as life and liberty, may not be taken from a person without affording him due process of law. The majority opinion suggests no constitutional basis for distinguishing between deprivations of liberty and property. In fact, the majority suggests no reason at all for drawing this distinction. The logic it advances for extending the right to counsel to all cases in which the penalty of any imprisonment is imposed applies equally well to cases in which other penalties may be imposed. Nor does the majority deny that some "non-jail" penalties are more serious than brief jail sentences.

Thus, although the new rule is extended today only to the imprisonment category of cases, the Court's opinion foreshadows the adoption of a broad prophylactic rule applicable to all petty offenses. No one can foresee the consequences of such a drastic enlargement of the constitutional right to free counsel. But even today's decision could have a seriously adverse impact upon the day-to-day functioning of the criminal justice system. We should be slow to fashion a new constitutional rule with consequences of such unknown dimensions, especially since it is supported neither by history nor precedent.

II

The majority opinion concludes that, absent a valid waiver, a person may not be imprisoned even for lesser offenses unless he was represented by counsel at the trial. In simplest terms this means that under no circumstances, in any court in the land, may anyone be imprisoned — however briefly — unless he was represented by or waived his right to counsel. The opinion is disquietingly barren of details as to how this rule will be implemented.

There are thousands of statutes and ordinances which authorize imprisonment for six months or less, usually as an alternative to a fine. These offenses include some of the most trivial of misdemeanors, ranging from spitting on the sidewalk to certain traffic offenses. They also include a variety of more serious misdemeanors. This broad spectrum of petty offense cases daily floods the lower criminal courts. The rule laid down today will confront the judges of each of these courts with an awkward dilemma. If counsel is not appointed or knowingly waived, no sentence of imprisonment for any duration may be imposed. The judge will therefore be forced to decide in advance of trial — and without hearing the evidence — whether he will forgo entirely his judicial discretion to impose some sentence of imprisonment and abandon his responsibility to consider the full range of punishments established by the legislature. His alternatives, assuming the availability of counsel, will be to appoint counsel and retain the discretion vested in him by law, or to abandon this discretion in advance and proceed without counsel.

If the latter course is followed, the first victim of the new rule is likely to be the concept that justice requires a personalized decision both as to guilt and the sentence. The notion that sentencing should be tailored to fit the crime and the individual would have to be abandoned in many categories of offenses. In resolving the dilemma as to how to administer the new rule, judges will be tempted arbitrarily to divide petty offenses into two categories — those for which sentences of imprisonment may be imposed and those in which no such sentence will be given regardless of the statutory authorization. In creating categories of offenses which by law are imprisonable but for which he would not impose jail sentences, a judge will be overruling de facto the legislative determination as to the appropriate range of punishment for the particular offense. It is true, as the majority notes, that there are some classes of imprisonable offenses for which imprisonment is rarely imposed. But even in these, the occasional imposition of such a sentence may serve a valuable deterrent purpose. At least the legislatures, and until today the courts, have viewed the threat of imprisonment — even when rarely carried out — as serving a legitimate social function. . . .

To avoid these equal protection problems and to preserve a range of sentencing options as prescribed by law, most judges are likely to appoint counsel for indigents in all but the most minor offenses where jail sentences are extremely rare. It is doubtful that the States possess the necessary resources to meet this sudden expansion of the right to counsel. The Solicitor General, who suggested on behalf of the United States the rule the Court today adopts, recognized that the consequences could be far reaching. In addition to the expense of compensating counsel, he noted that the mandatory requirement of defense counsel will "require more pre-trial time of prosecutors, more courtroom time, and this will lead to bigger backlogs with present personnel. Court reporters will be needed as well as counsel, and they are one of our worst bottlenecks." [18]

After emphasizing that the new constitutional rule should not

18. Tr. of Oral Arg. 34-35.

be made retroactive, the Solicitor General commented on the "chaos" which could result from any mandatory requirement of counsel in misdemeanor cases:

> [I]f . . . this Court's decision should become fully applicable on the day it is announced, there could be a massive pileup in the state courts which do not now meet this standard. This would involve delays and frustrations which would not be a real contribution to the administration of justice.[19]

. . . The majority's treatment of the consequences of the new rule which so concerned the Solicitor General is not reassuring. In a footnote, it is said that there are presently 355,200 attorneys and that the number will increase rapidly, doubling by 1985. This is asserted to be sufficient to provide the number of full-time counsel, estimated by one source at between 1,575 and 2,300, to represent all indigent misdemeanants, excluding traffic offenders. It is totally unrealistic to imply that 355,200 lawyers are potentially available. Thousands of these are not in practice, and many of those who do practice work for governments, corporate legal departments, or the Armed Services and are unavailable for criminal representation. Of those in general practice, we have no indication how many are qualified to defend criminal cases or willing to accept assignments which may prove less than lucrative for most.

It is similarly unrealistic to suggest that implementation of the Court's new rule will require no more than 1,575 to 2,300 "full-time" lawyers. In few communities are there full-time public defenders available for or private lawyers specializing in petty cases. Thus, if it were possible at all, it would be necessary to coordinate the schedules of those lawyers who are willing to take an occasional misdemeanor appointment with the crowded calendars of lower courts in which cases are not scheduled weeks in advance but instead are frequently tried the day after arrest. Finally, the majority's focus on aggregate figures ignores the heart of the problem, which is the distribution and availability of lawyers, especially in the hundreds of small localities across the country.

Perhaps the most serious potential impact of today's holding will be on our already overburdened local courts. The primary cause of "assembly line" justice is a volume of cases far in excess of the capacity of the system to handle efficiently and fairly. The Court's rule may well exacerbate delay and congestion in these

19. Id., at 36-37.

courts. We are familiar with the common tactic of counsel of exhausting every possible legal avenue, often without due regard to its probable payoff. In some cases this may be the lawyer's duty; in other cases it will be done for purposes of delay. The absence of direct economic impact on the client, plus the omnipresent ineffective-assistance-of-counsel claim, frequently produces a decision to litigate every issue. It is likely that young lawyers, fresh out of law school, will receive most of the appointments in petty offense cases. The admirable zeal of these lawyers; their eagerness to make a reputation; the time their not yet crowded schedules permit them to devote to relatively minor legal problems; their desire for courtroom exposure; the availability in some cases of hourly fees, lucrative to the novice; and the recent constitutional explosion in procedural rights for the accused — all these factors are likely to result in the stretching out of the process with consequent increased costs to the public and added delay and congestion in the courts.

There is an additional problem. The ability of various States and localities to furnish counsel varies widely. Even if there were adequate resources on a national basis, the uneven distribution of these resources — of lawyers, of facilities, and available funding — presents the most acute problem. A number of state courts have considered the question before the Court in this case, and have been compelled to confront these realities. Many have concluded that the indigent's right to appointed counsel does not extend to all misdemeanor cases. In reaching this conclusion, the state courts have drawn the right-to-counsel line in different places, and most have acknowledged that they were moved to do so, at least in part, by the impracticality of going further. In other States, legislatures and courts through the enactment of laws or rules have drawn the line short of that adopted by the majority. These cases and statutes reflect the judgment of the courts and legislatures of many States, which understand the problems of local judicial systems better than this Court, that the rule announced by the Court today may seriously overtax capabilities.

The papers filed in a recent petition to this Court for a writ of certiorari serve as an example of what today's ruling will mean in some localities. In November 1971 the petition in Wright v. Town of Wood, No. 71-5722, was filed with this Court. The case, arising out of a South Dakota police magistrate court conviction for the municipal offense of public intoxication, raises the same issues before us in this case. The Court requested that the town of Wood file a response. On March 8, 1972, a lawyer occasionally employed by the town filed with the clerk an affidavit explaining why the town had not responded. He explained that Wood, South Dakota, has a population of 132, that it has no sewer or water system and is quite poor, that the office of the nearest lawyer is in a town 40 miles away, and that the town had decided that contesting this case would be an unwise allocation of its limited resources.

Though undoubtedly smaller than most, Wood is not dissimilar to hundreds of communities in the United States with no or very few lawyers, with meager financial resources, but with the need to have some sort of local court system to deal with minor offenses. It is quite common for the more numerous petty offenses in such towns to be tried by local courts or magistrates while the more serious offenses are tried in a countywide court located in the county seat. It is undoubtedly true that some injustices result from the informal procedures of these local courts when counsel is not furnished; certainly counsel should be furnished to some indigents in some cases. But to require that counsel be furnished virtually every indigent charged with an imprisonable offense would be a practical impossibility for many small town courts. The community could simply not enforce its own laws.

Perhaps it will be said that I give undue weight both to the likelihood of short-term "chaos" and to the possibility of long-term adverse effects on the system. The answer may be given that if the Constitution requires the rule announced by the majority, the consequences are immaterial. If I were satisfied that the guarantee of due process required the assistance of counsel in every case in which a jail sentence is imposed or that the only workable method of insuring justice is to adopt the majority's rule, I would not hesitate to join the Court's opinion despite my misgivings as to its effect upon the administration of justice. But in addition to the resulting problems of availability of counsel, of costs, and especially of intolerable delay in an already overburdened system, the majority's drawing of a new inflexible rule may raise more Fourteenth Amendment problems than it resolves. Although the Court's opinion does not deal explicitly with any sentence other than deprivation of liberty however brief, the according of special constitutional status to cases where such a sentence is imposed may derogate from the need for counsel in other types of cases, unless the Court embraces an even broader prophylactic rule. Due process requires a fair trial in all cases. Neither the six-month rule approved below nor the rule today enumerated by the Court is likely to achieve this result.

## III

I would hold that the right to counsel in petty offense cases is not absolute but is one to be determined by the trial courts exercising a judicial discretion on a case-by-case basis. The determination should be made before the accused formally pleads; many petty cases are resolved by guilty pleas in which the assistance of counsel may be required. If the trial court should conclude that the assistance of counsel is not required in any case, it should state its reasons so that the issue could be preserved for review. The trial court would then become obligated to scrutinize carefully the subsequent proceedings for the protection of the defendant. If an unrepresented defendant sought to enter a plea of guilty, the Court should examine the case against him to insure that there is admissible evidence tending to support the elements of the offense. If a case went to trial without defense counsel, the court should intervene, when necessary, to insure that the defendant adequately brings out the facts in his favor and to prevent legal issues from being overlooked. Formal trial rules should not be applied strictly against unrepresented defendants. Finally, appellate courts should carefully scrutinize all decisions not to appoint counsel and the proceedings which follow. . . .

In concluding, I emphasize my long-held conviction that the adversary system functions best and most fairly only when all parties are represented by competent counsel. Before becoming a member of this Court, I participated in efforts to enlarge and extend the availability of counsel. The correct disposition of this case, therefore, has been a matter of considerable concern to me — as it has to the other members of the Court. We are all strongly drawn to the ideal of extending the right to counsel, but I differ as to two fundamentals: (i) what the Constitution *requires*, and (ii) the effect upon the criminal justice system, especially in the smaller cities and the thousands of police, municipal, and justice of the peace courts across the country.

The view I have expressed in this opinion would accord considerable discretion to the courts, and would allow the flexibility and opportunity for adjustment which seems so necessary when we are imposing new doctrine on the lowest level of courts of 50 states. Although this view would not precipitate the "chaos" predicted by the Solicitor General as the probable result of the Court's absolutist rule, there would still remain serious practical problems resulting from the expansion of indigents' rights to counsel in petty-offense cases. But the according of reviewable discretion to the courts in determining when counsel is necessary for a fair trial, rather than mandating a completely inflexible rule, would facilitate an orderly transition to a far wider availability and use of defense counsel.

In this process, the courts of first instance which decide these cases would have to recognize a duty to consider the need for counsel in every case where the defendant faces a significant penalty. The factors mentioned above, and such standards or guidelines to assure fairness as might be prescribed in each jurisdiction by legislation or rule of court, should be considered where relevant. The goal should be, in accord with the essence of the adversary system, to expand as rapidly as practicable the availability of counsel so that no person accused of crime must stand alone if counsel is needed.

As the proceedings in the courts below were not in accord with the views expressed above, I concur in the result of the decision in this case.

## Memorandum in Support of the Petition of the Massachusetts Law Reform Institute for the Adoption and Enforcement of Rules Governing Practice in Criminal Cases in the District Courts*

\* In May 1970, the Massachusetts Law Reform Institute (officially known as Voluntary Defenders Committee, Inc.), an OEO-funded legal services program in Boston, petitioned the Supreme Judicial Court of Massachusetts to promulgate rules of criminal procedures for that state's 73 district courts. Law No. 71303. The petition cited the court's inherent and statutory authority to regulate the administration of justice in inferior courts. Mass. Gen. Laws. Ann. ch. 211, §3; ch. 213, §3 (1972 Supp.). It supported the petition with affidavits from lawyer and law student observers concerning the conduct of four district court judges. The memorandum of law in support of this petition was prepared by Diane Lund, Allan G. Rodgers, and Melvyn Zarr, and was filed on October 21, 1970.

In November 1970, the Supreme Judicial Court without public hearing or argument transferred the petition and affidavits for investigation and appropriate action to the two chief justices with authority over the courts involved — Elijah Adlow of the Boston Municipal Court, and Franklin N. Flaschner of the District Courts of Massachusetts. Their initial responses are reprinted here. Chief Justice Adlow was one of the judges complained of in the institute's petition.

The Initial Rules of Criminal Procedure reprinted *infra* took effect on August 1, 1971. They were the product of the efforts of Chief Justice Flaschner and a committee of district court judges to remedy the problems identified in the petition.

Petitioner's request that this Court adopt and enforce rules specifying certain procedures to be followed in criminal proceedings in district courts of the Commonwealth is made for three reasons. First, at the present time individual rights are being disregarded in some of the district courts. The procedural safeguards which give substance to the concept of due process are seldom observed in these courts; as a result defendants appearing there frequently are treated in a manner which fails to satisfy the standards set for criminal proceedings by this Court and the United States Supreme Court. Circumstances such as these theoretically are susceptible to correction on a case-by-case basis through the mechanism of appellate review. In practice, however, this technique is not available to the appellate courts as a means of supervising and guiding the activities of the district courts of the Commonwealth. The record of the district court trial is subject to review only when a defendant found guilty in those proceedings chooses to bring a writ of error instead of claiming his right to a trial de novo in the superior court. Due to the understandably infrequent use of a writ of error, many district court practices of doubtful validity have developed and continue unchallenged. The rules proposed by petitioner, if adopted, will eliminate many of the existing procedures which infringe upon individual rights and will guard against the emergence of others.

Second, more regularity and formality in district court proceedings in criminal cases is needed to increase respect for these courts and their decisions. The emphasis upon the efficient and expeditious processing of criminal cases has led to the adoption of shortcut procedures in some of the district courts. Unfortunately, using shortcuts tends to suggest that the matters being dealt with are not important enough to merit careful consideration. This impression is confirmed whenever the courtroom is noisy, the judge is inattentive or the assigned lawyer makes only a token effort. All these things happen far too often. They combine to produce an atmosphere which both reflects and reinforces lack of respect for the courts. On the part of the community, the decline in respect for some district courts is a direct response to the failure of those courts to preserve the dignity and solemnity traditionally associated with judicial proceedings. This regrettable trend can be checked by prompt action to reestablish procedural formalities in the district courts. The proposed rules are a beginning.

Finally, enacting specific rules to identify these particular judicial responsibilities will remind the courts and inform the public of the importance of the district court judge as a protector of individual liberties. Our existing system tends to burden a district court judge with many of the functions customarily performed by a prosecuting attorney. In this context his role as an enforcer of constitutional safeguards is often obscured. Establishing procedures which demonstrate his responsibilities in this area, as the rules which have been submitted propose to do, will clarify the role which the judiciary and the community expect him to perform.

Most of the rules which have been proposed to the Court embody existing obligations of district court judges, as mandated by decisions of this Court and the United States Supreme Court interpreting the Constitution of this Commonwealth and that of the United States.... Those which do not have a constitutional basis represent efforts to make proceedings in the district courts more dignified, more predictable and more comprehensible.

Petitioner specifically requests this Court to exercise its rule making powers with respect to the subject matter of the petition. Although the proposed rules themselves can be jointly adopted by the chief justices of the courts concerned, this will accomplish only part of what is needed. The efficacy of rules without sanctions is uncertain. Only this Court has the authority to prescribe the sanctions which might be imposed in the event of a failure to observe the rules. Moreover, only this Court is capable of developing and implementing a supervisory arrangement which will ensure that violations of the rules do not pass unnoticed. In short, effective systemic reform in this area of individual rights must be initiated by and carried forward by this Court for the practical reason that it alone possesses the range of powers needed to accomplish the task. The ultimate responsibility for the judicial system of the Commonwealth lies with this Court. When the problem to be dealt with is of the magnitude of the one now under consideration, the initial responsibility should also be with this Court.

The supplementary procedures needed to ensure compliance with rules such as those proposed will have to include a method of monitoring district court sessions, a disciplinary procedure for use when the rules are violated and a means of educating lawyers, judges and the public about the existence, purpose and operation of this procedure.

There are two principal ways for this Court to acquaint itself with what transpires during criminal proceedings in the district courts of the Commonwealth. One is to provide for recording those sessions in which criminal cases are heard, either by using a stenographer or by using a mechanical device. The other is to establish an observer committee which would report to the Court at regular intervals.

Petitioner recognizes that the expense of recording presents difficulty. The present base salary of a stenotypist trained for court employment is $12,500. To this must be added the cost of transcribing the material (currently $1.25 per page). The alternative is to use mechanical devices. These should be less expensive than stenographers on a long-term basis, but the initial outlay would be high. One choice investigated is a videotape system. This would provide the most complete record of proceedings. Microphones, a tape recorder and a camera would be set up in each courtroom and a monitor used for subsequent viewing. At the present time an estimate of approximately $5,000 per courtroom for the cost of purchasing and installing this equipment (including a monitor) has been obtained. This amount may decrease if a large number of courtrooms are equipped under a single contract. The cost of slow-motion videotapes (72 hours of recording) is between $40.00 and $50.00 per tape. The equipment can be operated by anyone; no special training is needed. The alternative of video-taping court proceedings is being considered elsewhere; a full discussion of the experiments undertaken in Illinois can be found in the Interim Report to the Supreme Court of Illinois on Experimental Video-Taping of Courtroom Proceedings, issued by the administrative office of the Illinois Courts in November, 1968. Petitioner has proposed to the Justice of the District Court of Newton that a videotape experiment be conducted in that court. Arrangements are in the process of being made to install the equipment there in the near future and to record criminal sessions over a one-week period. The results of this experiment should demonstrate whether videotape could be used satisfactorily to record courtroom proceedings.

Less costly, although perhaps less satisfactory, are simple tape recordings of trials. In Alaska, tape recording is standard procedure, but the courtrooms were constructed for this purpose, with the advice of acoustical engineers. Tape recorders are being used successfully in Israel's courts. Gershoni, The Development of Tape-Recorded Court Proceedings in Israel, 53 Judicature 330 (1970). Particularly pertinent to the present inquiry is the system now being put into effect in New Jersey. The use of tape recorders in municipal courts serving towns and villages with a population of 100,000 or more was ordered by the Administrative Director of the Courts in New Jersey to begin last January 1st. Municipal courts serving towns and villages with a population of 200,000 or more will have to comply with this order on January 1, 1971. Although there is an ongoing dispute about which governmental entity must bear the costs of this new system, it has proved very satisfactory in practice. The New Jersey municipal courts try misdemeanors carrying a penalty of no more than a $500 fine. The system assumes that no jury trial is required for these offenses. Before the tape recording system was initiated, a defendant who appealed from the verdict of a municipal court judge was given a trial de novo in the Law Division of the County Court. This avenue of appeal continues to exist when the municipal court proceeding is recorded, but the appeal is now "on the record"; the county judge considers the record of the court below and hears oral argument. He may in his discretion permit either side to enlarge the record.

It should be noted in this connection that there is authority supporting the proposition that the judiciary has the power to incur expenses necessary to the administration of justice and to order their payment from the public treasury. See, e.g., People ex rel. Conn v. Randolph, 5 Ill. 2d 24 (1966); Dunn v. State ex rel. Corydon, 204 Ind. 390 (1933); Leahey v. Farrell, 362 Pa. 52 (1949) (qualified statement of the principle).

The second alternative — that of an observer committee — would result in a program of intermittent inspections. The method has a number of practical drawbacks. The accuracy of the observations is bound to be questioned. In some district courts it is almost impossible to ascertain what is being said and done, and an observer might well be wasting his time in these courtrooms. The deterrent effect of the program might become sporadic to the extent the presence or absence of an observer became known. One virtue (which hardly seems sufficient to balance these disadvantages) is that an observer program is likely to require assistance and cooperation from the organized bar and perhaps the local law schools as well. The increased interest in the operation and problems of the district courts which this might stimulate would be beneficial.

The knowledge that the proceedings are being recorded or that they might be observed is likely to result in the adoption of higher standards of judicial conduct. Nevertheless it must be clear — both to the judiciary and to the public — that a district court judge who fails to comply with prescribed procedural rules will be disciplined. In developing the necessary disciplinary procedure the Court will have to decide (1) what will constitute a violation of the rules;

(2) the sources from which information about alleged violations will be received; (3) who will be responsible for making a preliminary evaluation of the information; (4) the procedures to be followed in determining whether a violation warranting disciplinary action has occurred; and (5) the kinds of disciplinary action which might be taken when a violation occurs.

The adoption of rules should be accompanied by a public announcement of the sanctions which this Court might impose when a violation warranting disciplinary action is proven. Knowledge that definite sanctions are contemplated will have a deterrent effect upon judges who otherwise might be careless about compliance. Equally important, awareness of the sanctions will reassure those in our society who are beginning to doubt both the ability of our judicial system to correct itself and its desire to do so.

The ongoing value of such a prescribed system of sanctions — as a deterrent and as a method of preserving public confidence in the courts — depends to a great extent upon making the imposition of any sanction a matter of public record. The judicial conduct which is being corrected will have occurred in open court. In a public forum, the judge will have demonstrated his negligent indifference to or purposeful disregard of rules designed to protect individual rights. A system which values these rights clearly will not hesitate to publicly reprimand that judge out of any concern for his personal reputation but it might pause to consider the effect of such a reprimand upon the reputation of the judiciary as whole. Petitioner respectfully submits that concern for the reputation of the judicial branch is a cogent reason in favor of making public any sanction imposed because of the in-court behavior of a judge. When a pattern of misconduct exists, the community knows of it; anyone can observe it by the simple expedient of spending some time in the courtroom. Unless the community is equally well informed when corrective action is taken, the popular belief is likely to be that nothing is being done. The resultant cynicism and low level of expectation is far more damaging to the judiciary in the long run than any consequences of a public sanction possibly could be. An honest and forthright program to correct and improve in-court judicial conduct appears to us to be a necessary part of any effort to engender and preserve respect for the legal process among people who are acquainted with the realities of some of our courts. The public's interest in such a program should be acknowledged by making the program's results a matter of public record.

A two-stage system of sanctions appears to be the most desirable. The first stage would be the sanction of reproval, or public reprimand. This is used in New York. See In re Sobel and In re Leibowitz, 8 N.Y.S.2d (Ct. on the Judiciary 1960). A public rebuke has been used as a disciplinary method in other jurisdictions as well. See, e.g., Podlasky v. Price, 87 Cal. App. 2d 151 (1948); In re Eugene L. McGarry, 380 Ill. 347 (1942); In re Burton, 67 Utah 118 (1926). Of particular interest is the case In re Judges of Municipal Court of Cedar Rapids, 256 Iowa 1135, 1136 (1964). In this case the court found that its power to exercise "supervisory and administrative control over all inferior Judicial tribunals" obliged it to publicly correct judicial abuses such as "a pattern of practice which shows a consistent disregard for the rights of litigants, or an arbitrary and capricious course of conduct in the handling of cases, or an oppressive and improper use of the power of the court...."

It seems improbable that a second-stage sanction ever will be required. If such a circumstance should arise, however, it will be necessary for this Court to act to protect the public interest. The judge in question would be purposefully continuing to disregard rules enacted to assure that every defendant receives the benefit of all the safeguards and protections afforded him by the laws of the nation and the Commonwealth. The public could not be expected to accept and abide by decisions rendered by such a judge. Immediate curtailment of his judicial functions, or their complete cessation, would be imperative.

The extent of the Court's power to act in a situation such as this is a matter which it must determine for itself, of course. Petitioner recognizes the limitations imposed by c. 3, article 1, of the Constitution of the Commonwealth, as interpreted by this court in Opinion of the Justices, 271 Mass. 575 (1930). However, the distinction between actions which are clearly temporary expedients and those which result in lasting consequences in and of themselves should not be overlooked. Interim measures which might be considered include excusing the judge from the performance of all duties for a specified period of time or imposing restrictions, again for a specified time period, as to the types of cases to be heard by him. It is assumed that efforts would be made during this period to resolve the matter by negotiated agreement and that if this could not be done, more formal means would be pursued. It is always open to the Court, when all else fails, to recommend to the legislature that it address the governor requesting removal of the judge.

The question of the action which the judicial branch of the government can take with respect to an erring judge has not been frequently considered by courts. In the recent decision of Chandler v. Judicial Council, 398 U.S. 1003 (1970), the narrow issue of the power of the U.S. Judicial Council for the Tenth Circuit to reassign cases as a means of enforcing administrative rules was touched upon and some of the broader issues of judicial power were raised, but no conclusions were drawn which could serve as precedents here. In Connecticut, a legislative attempt to give a court administrator broader disciplinary powers over judges was rejected by their highest court as being inconsistent with that state's constitutional provisions. Adams v. Rubinow, 157 Conn. 150 (1968). The court, however, noted the difference between a temporary suspension intended to protect the public during an interim period and the measures proposed in the legislation being considered, and indicated that such a temporary suspension would, in its view, present no constitutional difficulties. The use of this alternative of temporary suspension was permitted in the course of the Chandler proceedings as an interlocutory action which would not be examined on the merits. Chandler v. Judicial Council, 382 U.S. 1003 (1966). Many states have made it unnecessary for their courts to confront this problem by revising their constitutions or laws to permit the creation of judicial commissions or special courts to deal with problems involving individual judges. For those states which have not — a group which includes Massachusetts — the issue must be dealt with by the courts themselves. Although this situation requires a court to face difficult questions, it also presents an unparalleled opportunity for a court to demonstrate its awareness of and concern for the problems faced by citizens in their dealings with the courts.

A corollary to the development of a flexible system of sanctions is the development of a definite complaint procedure and a method of informing the public about it. The present Rule 3:17 does not deal with the subject in any comprehensive fashion. Moreover, knowledge of its existence is not widespread outside the legal profession. While there may be administrative advantages to having complaints emanate from lawyers or undergo a preliminary screening by a bar association committee, and good reasons for handling some complaints privately, a large segment of the public views such arrangements as self-serving and deliberately unresponsive to the community's interest in visibility and accountability. A more favorable climate of public opinion is much more likely to result if standards of in-court conduct are clearly prescribed for judges, a method of complaining about failures to observe these standards is developed and precisely described and the functioning of the mechanism is made visible. The remarks of Judge Jerome Frank, quoted in the American Judicature Society's series on prominent individuals, 41 J. Am. Jud. Soc'y 32 (1957), are pertinent here:

> [J]ohn Q. Citizen should be told the flaws in the workings of the court and should be taught how to become well qualified to consider them — differentiating between inherent ineradicable difficulties in the administration of justice and those which are eradicable.... For, in a democracy, the courts belong not to the judges and lawyers but to the citizens.

Petitioner's concern with establishing prescribed procedures in the lower criminal courts and for ensuring that there will be compliance with them stems from the belief that individual justice is more likely to be achieved in a regularized proceeding. In this, petitioner is in good company. Chief Justice Warren, dissenting in Spencer v. Texas, 385 U.S. 554 at 570 (1970), pointed out that "this Court has long recognized the central importance of courtroom procedures in maintaining our constitutional liberties. As Mr. Justice Frankfurter often reminded us, the history of individual liberty is largely coincident with the history of observance of procedural safeguards...." Petitioner urges this Court to indicate its agreement with this concept by taking positive action on the petition for rules presently before it.

### Response of Chief Justice Elijah Adlow to the Petition

October 26, 1970

Hon. G. Joseph Tauro, Chief Justice
Supreme Judicial Court of Massachusetts,
New Court House
Boston, Massachusetts 02108

Dear Chief Justice Tauro:

I appreciate the privilege you have granted of submitting a reply to the grievance claimed by the New England Law Reform Institute [sic].

The impressive name carried by this organization belies its true character. It is part and parcel of the Voluntary Defenders Committee, Inc., a publicly supported project designed to assist indigent defendants. Its members are novices at the Bar with slight, if any, court experience. The only time that I have seen them about my court is on occasions when rioters and demonstrators have been brought to trial. They are intense partisans in the class struggle now being waged and in large measure share the sentiments and opinions of the clients for whom they appear at the expense of the taxpayers. Naturally they have a loathing and contempt for the police and for the courts. I am emphasizing this fact at the very outset for the reason that it is important in considering this petition to recognize the animus which inspired its presentation.

At my request, Mr. Richard Gerould, Executive Secretary of the Supreme Judicial Court has permitted me to examine the affidavits which the petitioners filed with your court. I have examined these affidavits and desire to discuss one in detail. I am satisfied that a discussion of one will suffice for them all.

I shall take the first affidavit which comes to hand. It is numbered "Exhibit 1A," and I propose to annex a copy of it to this communication. This affidavit of Warren Bruce Baum, a student at Boston University Law School consists of 6 paragraphs which I shall consider in order.

Paragraph 1 states in effect that six defendants, Gillis, Carpenter, Ewalt, Hobperry, McKenney and another were charged with drunkenness; that none of the defendants had a lawyer; none was asked if he wanted a lawyer prior to the time he was asked to plead. He complains further that all six pleaded guilty, and none was asked by the court whether his plea was voluntarily made.

In reply to this complaint, let me state that there was no defendant named Ewalt. Nor was there a defendant named Hobperry. There was a defendant named Halfpenny and I assume that this was the man to whom the affiant referred.

In the first place, our files reveal that every one of these men was asked if he wanted a lawyer, declined the offer, and signed a waiver. All of those waivers are in the files of my court. As for the defendants whose rights were so ruthlessly disregarded, let me give you the disposition of the cases of these alcoholics. (1) Gillis was released without arraignment, he having no previous record; (2) the cases of Carpenter and McKenney were filed on a plea of guilty; (3) and Halfpenny, who had a long record as an alcoholic, was surrendered on a Bridgewater State Farm suspended sentence which sentence was confirmed.

Paragraph 2. In this paragraph the affiant alleged that although the defendant was asked whether he wanted a lawyer, he was not told that the court would appoint one if he could not afford one. The fact is that there are two Mass. Defenders Committee representatives in our court at every session, and they speedily make themselves available for whoever indicates an inability to provide for counsel. If the records of our court for this day are consulted it will appear that the Mass. Defenders were in court and handled business for indigent defendants on that day.

Paragraph 3. The affiant complains that where a defendant named Croyer stated that he did not want a lawyer, the court did not advise the defendant that he did not have to testify, and further that the defendant did testify.

In reply to Paragraph 3, let me state that the name of the defendant was not Croyer but Proia. This defendant was asked if he wanted counsel, declined the offer and signed a waiver. He then pleaded guilty. Having pleaded guilty he rested on the statement of the store operator who had arrested the defendant for a larceny in Jordan Marsh's store. The defendant did not testify. According to the probation department records this defendant had been convicted of 54 larcenies in his lifetime, and in 1964 he was adjudicated a common and notorious thief. He received a one-year sentence from me and was remanded to the jail for 24 hours to decide whether he would appeal. The next day he appeared in court and declined to exercise his right of appeal. In my opinion this defendant knew more about his rights than all the members of the Voluntary Defenders Committee combined. What is astounding about this paragraph is the disparity between what the observer from the New England Law Reform Institute actually reported and what actually happened.

Paragraph 4. The affiant protests that in the cases of DeOriole, Croyer, Moore, Buckly, Kennebrew, Best and Baldwin, the Chief Justice asked the probation officer for the defendants' prior records before he announced his verdict. With respect to these allegations the fact is that Proia (Croyer) pleaded guilty and waived his right to counsel as was explained in reply to paragraph 3.

As for DeOriole, he was represented by Attorney Martin Leppo of 40 Court St., Boston. Attorney Leppo is no stranger to the criminal court, and his client's constitutional rights were amply protected.

Kennebrew, Best and Baldwin were all represented by counsel. Of course I asked the probation officer for their records before I rendered a finding, because the case was not tried on that day, but was put over for a hearing on December 4. The request made to the probation officer was in connection with setting bail, a normal and proper procedure.

As for the defendant Moore, he was charged with trespass and disturbing the peace. Asked if he wanted a lawyer, he assented, and I assigned Robert Fandel of the Mass. Defenders Committee to represent him.

All the above facts can be confirmed by the records in the office of the Clerk.

Paragraph 5 states that "Three defendants, Kennebrew, Best and Baldwin, who did not have lawyers present, were held in $10,000 bail. None of the defendants was asked any questions by Chief Justice Adlow about his ties to the community or his employment record, and none was advised of his right to petition for a bail reduction."

This particular paragraph deserves examination. The only thing the affiant has correctly recorded is the amount of the bail. These three defendants were charged with kidnapping, rape, and assault and battery. Each one was represented by counsel.

Kennesbrew was represented by Charles Nayor and Howard Newell of 89 State Street.

Best (true name Rowe) was represented by Attorney Ed. Shapiro of 126 State St., Boston.

Of course I did not inquire about their roots in the community. When I am interested in these matters I rely on my probation department to investigate. Nor did I advise them of their right to bail reduction. They had lawyers, and it was none of my business.

As for paragraph 6, I do not propose to waste time on it. I seriously doubt whether the remark attributed to me was uttered. Whether it was or not it is hardly pertinent to this petition.

In view of the variety of blunders revealed in this single affidavit I am satisfied that it would be foolhardy to follow through the remaining affidavits. The student employed by the Law Reform Institute has revealed a complete lack of experience in matters concerning the administration of justice. It is amazing that so many things could happen in a courtroom without a young man realizing what was going on. His report of the events of November 21 are so muddled and untrue that we must attribute its fictional character either to stupidity or to deliberate distortion. Whatever it is it is a most vicious libel on me and on the court over which I preside.

Frankly, it is rather stultifying and demeaning for one who presides over a court to be called upon to answer the petty but annoying charges embraced in this petition. I trust that your court will treat it with the contempt which it deserves.

Sincerely yours,

Elijah Adlow
Chief Justice
Boston Municipal Court

## Response of Chief Justice Franklin N. Flaschner to the Petition

November 24, 1970

Richard D. Gerould, Esq.
Executive Secretary
Supreme Judicial Court
New Court House
Boston, Massachusetts

Dear Mr. Gerould:

At a time when respect for duly constituted and responsibly exercised authority needs shoring up from every civic resource in our community the District Courts of Massachusetts have been broadly attacked by two study groups. The resultant petition of the Voluntary Defenders Committee, Inc. d/b/a Massachusetts Law Reform Institute and Report of the Lawyers Committee for Civil Rights Under Law* have engendered considerable attendant publicity. This is unfortunate for a number of reasons.

Firstly, the critical focus of both of these studies has been narrowly drawn to only a few Courts where the investigators knew before they started they would find meal for their grist. The criticisms are then framed as if they were warranted throughout the

---

* [In October 1970, this group issued an empirical study of six district courts in the Boston area which supported the institute's petition. An excerpt from that report is reprinted *supra* Part IV — Ed.]

system. I believe the contrary is true, that the system is substantially free of the abuses alleged. If I am correct, the responsible way to proceed is to acknowledge that the 72 Courts and the 160 Judges in the system are substantially adhering to the challenges of providing defendants with all of their constitutional safeguards, while at the same time attending to the constantly increasing volume of criminal cases and adjudging the same on an individual basis with compassion, fairness and firmness. If the allegations are to be taken up in a proper perspective they should be examined within their actual context, not used to criticize the whole system.

Secondly, the investigators have proceeded to promulgate their work products without any prior reference of the same to the Judges whose conduct is criticized nor without any prior reference to the Chief Justice of the District Courts. An opportunity for explanation, and if explanation is deemed unsatisfactory, a provision for the simultaneous publication of explanation — these are principles of fair play which ought to be afforded to any officials whose conduct is criticized, not excluding Judges. Why have the investigators proceeded as if in an adversary proceeding? Why do they assume that the Judges they criticize and/or the Chief Justice would not meet them around a table to discuss, indeed to argue, but in good faith to try to resolve the problems they pose? If they represent the public, as they would presume since they are paid by public and foundation grants, why would they assume the Judges have any less of an obligation to the public than they do?

Thirdly, when all of the allegations are examined closely it turns out that they fall into different categories, some of the most serious of which do not at all reflect upon the conduct of the Judges. Two examples: Much is made of the failure in so many cases for indigent defendants to have the benefit of effective legal assistance. The primary cause for this is acknowledged to be the gross under-staffing for lack of funds of the Massachusetts Defenders Committee whose lawyers strive valiantly to represent their assigned clients while suffering under staggering and dehumanizing case loads. The recent MDC letter to Chief Justice Tauro detailing this crisis and notifying the judiciary of the intended discontinuance by MDC to represent defendants in juvenile and misdemeanor cases actually dwarfs all other considerations of public responsibility to provide constitutional safeguards to defendants in criminal cases.

The second example of a broad criticism which unfairly rubs off on the District Court Judges is the discussion of police station bail practices. These take place outside of the Courts and will depend for their reform mostly on further acts of bail legislation.

Other allegations against the system have purportedly been corrected by legislation, thereby making these points moot. For example, the bail reform law of 1970 and the new statutory requirements for probation officers to provide Judges with written reports to assist in determining indigency on the question of appointment of counsel at public expense.

As to the allegations reflecting on the conduct of the Judges, some relate to procedures the Judges are legally bound to follow, such as not permitting an appeal from a suspended sentence and probation. Any change here is going to require legislation or a decision by a higher court, and the subject does not admit of an easy answer. The same may be said of a number of other criticisms made relative to the so-called appeal from a district court finding of guilty and the sentence imposed to a de novo trial in the Superior Court. It may be time to review this system against suggestions for basic changes, but this does not warrant criticism of judicial conduct.

Admittedly there are some allegations of judicial conduct which do deserve prompt attention. I should be the last person to want to avoid them, but I will not deal with them as if the District Courts of Massachusetts were on trial. Instead, I would like an opportunity to convene rationally, factually and deliberately on these allegations with some of my colleagues, especially the more experienced, including the Administrative Committee. I believe we can establish some common ground between ourselves as representative district court Judges and representatives of these study groups, if the latter will bring reason and maturity to their meetings with us. Out of this process I would hope to develop some guidelines I could use in mitigating some of the problems which have been called to my attention, not alone by these studies.

Therefore, on behalf of the District Courts of Massachusetts I would strongly urge that any matters presently pending before the Supreme Judicial Court be disposed of in such a manner as to avoid any adversary confrontation, with the understanding that I shall use my office to corral the complaints and allegations of abuse, to sift them through an examination by my colleagues and myself, and to do what we can to resolve any legitimate problems which are thereby identified and defined. As the Supreme Judicial Court might wish, I would be happy to report further on this process.

One caveat: We are only a band of Judges who are hard at work full time on our jobs. We have no adjunctive staff. I will not be stampeded by eager staff personnel on these study groups who must justify their grants. Would that some of them were working for me. However, this takes us into the whole subject of the underlying deficiencies in judicial administration which I believe are so crucially related to the quality of justice but which I shall not delve into at this time. For now, I merely suggest respectfully that, while the process I have outlined above may not fit into certain timetables the investigators have devised for their own convenience, such an approach is intended to be in the best interests of the Commonwealth.

Respectfully yours,

Franklin N. Flaschner
Chief Justice
District Courts of Massachusetts

## *Initial Rules of Criminal Procedure for the District Courts of Massachusetts**

### GENERAL COMMENTS

These rules do not purport to be a comprehensive set of rules of criminal procedure. These initial rules stretch from arraignment to appeal and concentrate on procedures in open court in which the judge and the session clerk participate.

These rules necessarily build upon existing Rule 3:10 of the General Rules of the Supreme Judicial Court entitled "Assignment of Counsel in Noncapital Cases." The rules are framed to protect certain fundamental rights of the defendant. They are also intended to afford opportunity to the public to observe and understand what is going on in the courtroom. The primary function of the judicial process is to do justice by the parties and to the cause before the bench. Nevertheless, justice should be done in a manner which will result in public understanding and confidence.

* From: Memorandum to the Justices, Special Justices, Clerks and Probation Officers from Chief Justice Franklin N. Flaschner, Re: Initial Rules of Criminal Procedure and Other Matters, July 9, 1971.

Finally, it should be understood that most of these rules represent no innovations in what have been regarded as good District Court criminal procedures. They are all drawn from approved practices, which are now generally observed. The practices, as stated in the rules, are hereby affirmed.

It is intended that the District Courts shall adopt a comprehensive set of rules of criminal procedure. However, a number of subjects must first be studied to determine whether additional rules are desirable before a complete set of rules may be promulgated. Among these subjects are aspects of criminal procedures which cost money, such as interpreters, summoning witnesses for the defendant, appointing expert witnesses for the defendant, and providing for some method of recording proceedings. The comprehensive rules also should deal with receiving complaints, issuing search warrants, pre-trial motions, probation and sentencing practices, and methods of keeping dockets and papers. Other areas of necessary study doubtless exist. The office of the Chief Justice and the appropriate committees will continue to work on all of these problems. It is expected that new rules will be promulgated from time to time as particular studies are completed.

*Rule 1.*

At arraignment each complaint, or the material portions thereof, shall be read aloud to the defendants by the session clerk or the judge. In the event co-defendants are arraigned at the same time charged with the same offense, the complaint need be read only once with the stated identification of each defendant so complained against. Waiving of the reading shall not be permitted unless the defendant is represented at arraignment by counsel who shall make the waiver in open court, the same to be recorded by the session clerk.

> *Comment:* The number of items to be recorded by the session clerk is increasing beyond the capacity of the present form of the complaint backer. The use of a separate sheet stapled to the complaint for the purpose of recording items is suggested until the form of the complaint backer is revised and adequate provision uniformly made for this purpose.

*Rule 2.*

On any complaint setting forth a charge for which a sentence of imprisonment may be imposed, unless the defendant has waived his right to counsel pursuant to Rule 3:10 of the General Rules of the Supreme Judicial Court, no plea other than "not guilty" shall be taken or entered and recorded unless his counsel is present. Any examination of the defendant on the application of Rule 3:10, other than the examination conducted by the probation officer pursuant to G.L. ch. 221, sec. 34D, shall be conducted in open court by the judge.

> *Comment:* An arraignment, including the defendant's plea, in some cases may turn out to be a multiple step process, in which the case is continued pursuant to this rule without taking or entering a plea until counsel is present. In the absence of counsel a defendant may plead "not guilty" or the court may enter for the defendant a plea of "not guilty." On the second sentence of the rule see Mulcahy v. Commonwealth, 352 Mass. 613 (1967).

*Rule 3.*

If an appointment of counsel is made pursuant to Rule 3:10 (including a senior law school student pursuant to Rule 3:11) and the appointee is available during the same day within such time as the judge in his discretion shall permit, no determination of bail other than release on personal recognizance shall be made without a reasonable opportunity being given to the appointee to confer with the defendant and to be heard on the question of bail. Notice of the right to a speedy review of any bail determination by a judge shall be given to the defendant by the judge at the time the determination is made, and a record of the giving of this notice shall be recorded by the session clerk.

> *Comment:* It is not contemplated by this rule (1) that arresting officers and government witnesses shall be forced to remain in court for undue periods of time pending the completion of arraignment; (2) that judges and other court personnel shall be forced to disturb an orderly process of handling all of the court's necessary daily business; nor (3) that a representative of the Massachusetts Defenders Committee or any comparable agency present in court shall be subject to serve in the capacity of counsel to a defendant upon arraignment on the question of bail unless assigned by his or her agency for that purpose either in the particular case or generally within a particular court. It is contemplated by this rule that a defendant shall be represented by counsel at the hearing on determination of bail whenever it is feasible in the relevant circumstances. For this reason counsel should be appointed, if required, as promptly as possible.

*Rule 4.*

No plea of guilty or, with the consent of the court, nolo contendere, to any complaint to which Rule 3:10 is applicable, whether or not an appointment pursuant thereto has been made, shall be accepted without the judge addressing the defendant personally and being satisfied that: —

(a) the plea is made voluntarily;
(b) the defendant understands the nature of the offense described in the complaint;
(c) the defendant understands such a plea, unless later withdrawn by leave of court, will preclude his right to a trial by jury on the question of guilt; and
(d) the defendant has notice of the minimum and maximum sentence provided by law therefor.

This rule shall not be applicable to a defendant who has pleaded not guilty and at the trial admits to a finding of facts sufficient to warrant a finding of guilty.

> *Comment:* Rule 11 of the Federal Rules of Criminal Procedure is adapted in this rule to the criminal procedure in the District Courts. This rule only applies, however, to a complaint setting forth a charge for which a sentence of imprisonment may be imposed [Supreme Judicial Court Rule 3:10]. It requires the judge to be satisfied that the defendant understands the consequences of a plea of guilty or nolo contendere to the extent stated in the rule and particularly that the judge notify the defendant of the range of penalties for the offense (with which he is charged) provided by law. It may be appropriate in connection with this rule for the judge to remind a defendant of his right to counsel if he has none. No prescription of particular language is set forth for compliance with this rule. Each judge may accomplish the objective in his own words and in his own manner so long as he reasonably complies with the substance of the rule. The emphasis should be on substance and not on form.

*Rule 5.*

If the defendant refuses to plead or if the court refuses to accept a plea of guilty for any reason set forth in Rule 4, the court shall enter a plea of not guilty. The court shall not enter a judgment upon a plea of guilty nor make a finding of guilty upon the defendant admitting to a finding of facts sufficient to warrant the same, unless it is satisfied that there is a factual basis for such plea or finding.

> *Comment:* It is contemplated, particularly in the case of a defendant admitting facts sufficient to warrant a finding of guilty, that at least one prosecution witness will be sworn and testify to the factual basis of the finding, even if the testimony includes hearsay not objected to on account of the admission.

*Rule 6.*

An unrepresented defendant who has pleaded not guilty to any complaint shall be advised by the judge at the time of his hearing or trial that on any material matter pertaining to the offense charged he has the following rights: —

(a) to cross examine any witness offered by the prosecution; and
(b) subject to cross examination to offer testimony by himself or any other witness.

The judge shall also then advise him of his rights not to testify and not to be prejudiced if he remains silent. If the prosecution offers an exhibit the judge shall allow the defendant to examine it.

> *Comment:* The judge need not become an unrepresented defendant's attorney although he should endeavor to give reasonable guidance to a defendant who insists on conducting his own defense. Therefore, not all of the defendant's rights and defenses as to which he might be advised by counsel need be explained to him. The basic rights set forth in this rule, however, should be explained by the judge in some simple and effective manner.

*Rule 7.*

Except when in the discretion of the judge he shall deem it to be necessary or desirable in the interest of the defendant or the public,

(a) no room shall be used for a hearing or trial other than a room where a court session is customarily held; and
(b) no evidence shall be taken at bench conferences during a hearing or trial, including the hearing of the factual basis referred to in Rule 5, until the time of the judge's consideration of matters bearing on disposition.

*Comment:* This rule establishes a policy discouraging hearings and trials by conference and encouraging maximum use of open court proceedings. It is not intended, however, to preclude protecting the interests or sensibilities of the public or a defendant in proper cases. Bench conferences on matters bearing on disposition are not covered by the rule. Trying a case at a bench conference or its equivalent should be avoided.

## Rule 8.

During the trial on any complaint wherein the District Court has and does not decline final jurisdiction, no consideration of any probation department records or reports shall take place until the termination of the trial. If the judge then finds the defendant not guilty, the session clerk shall so announce and notify the defendant that he is discharged of the offense set forth in that complaint. If the judge indicates a finding of guilty or facts sufficient to warrant such a finding, he shall only thereafter consider any probation department records or reports and instruct the session clerk to announce his decisions on adjudication, disposition or continuance, as the case may be.

*Comment:* This rule attempts to draw a distinct line in conducting a criminal case, between adjudication and disposition. Procedures having to do with adjudication of guilt or innocence should be insulated from, and should be generally concluded before, any aspect of the duty of fixing a penalty is commenced. Once a judge has made up his mind at the end of the trial that the case has been proved against the defendant, he should so state. Only thereafter should he receive any probation department records or reports.

## Rule 9.

In all cases where the defendant has a right to appeal to the Superior Court or to a jury of six sitting in a District Court he shall be so notified by the session clerk or the judge and shall be granted a reasonable time to make a decision after conferring with his counsel, or, if unrepresented, to make reasonable inquiry of the judge as to the procedures afforded him for this purpose.

*Comment:* The notice given must include the alternative of the appeal to a jury of six where applicable. This notice, as well as all others included in these rules, should be given directly to the defendant and in an audible and understandable manner.

EFFECTIVE DATE

These rules shall take effect on August 2, 1971.


Franklin N. Flaschner
Chief Justice
District Courts of Massachusetts


# The Politics of Piecemeal Reform of Kansas Courts*

## Beverly Blair Cook


The progress of judicial reform in Kansas appears to be related to the security of the judges and secondarily to the interests of the lawyers, the political parties, and the legislators. A judge is not likely to take any leadership in a reform campaign for structural or personnel changes unless his position is safeguarded and his autonomy and authority increased rather than decreased. Judges and lawyers are intimately and immediately affected, the "formal parties" to reform, while local and state public and party officers are the "necessary parties" to reform, who make the prior decisions of the indispensable parties into legitimate policy.

For a reform to be put into law, and then realized in practice, the judges affected must be in agreement with the proposal and committed to its purposes. If the old system has kept him in office, no judge will be likely to join in a campaign for a change with unpredictable consequences. He has a personal political interest in the mode of selection, retention, discipline, and removal of the position which has given him power and prestige. Although judges are interested in benefits, such as larger salaries, retirement provisions, vacations, professional allowances, and staffing, attitudes toward such improvements will depend upon a calculation of interest.

The basis for the private organization of judges is likely to be practical and to relate to conditions of work or to salary. Kansas district judges had a loose organization with partial membership and with poorly attended annual meetings for many years. Since

* From: 53 Judicature 274-281 (1969-1970). Reprinted by permission of Judicature, the Journal of the American Judicature Society.

1966 the Kansas District Judges' Association has had the paid membership of all district judges and semi-annual meetings with almost full attendance. The group supports an occasional lobbyist, usually a retired judge, with its dues money of $15 per head and with the $50 assessment levied in 1966 for political action.

### BAR DISINTERESTED

Although judges, with their daily contact with serious court problems, are concerned enough to act as a political interest group in Kansas, the bar, composed only 10 percent of trial lawyers, is harder to involve in organized reform activities. Trial lawyers have a vested interest in the status quo, in institutions with which they are familiar, in routines which they can trace blindly, in people they know in official positions. Such lawyers are often satisfied with their control over elected judges and fear the independence of an appointed and tenured judge; they prefer the status quo to selection reforms which would produce more responsible and decisive authorities on the bench.

Officials of the other two branches tend to develop permissive attitudes toward judicial reform. Except on the rare occasions when the change would affect a core interest, such as reducing their own authority or costing too much money, these decision-makers look to the bar and bench for clues. Since they are not involved enough or indiscreet enough to reform another branch's bailiwick unless enthusiastically pressed, the burden of responsibility for winning or losing reform measures rests with the judges and the lawyers.

The reforms of the judicial branch urged by various associations, institutes, and special committees since the turn of the century cover four overlapping areas: court structure, judicial personnel, administration, and procedure. Kansas has accomplished three major reforms in structure and administration and four partial reforms in structure and personnel. The various detailed revisions of procedure are not included in this study.

An examination of the Kansas reforms indicates that two political variables, the maintenance of the status quo and the location of decision-making, have a relationship to their political acceptance. The status quo variable has six dimensions, involving 1) the legal existence of the judicial position, 2) the autonomy of the judicial office, 3) the protection of the incumbent in office, 4) the distribution of judicial offices among the political parties, 5) the expectations of stability of the trial bar, and 6) the expense of the plan to the public coffers. The greater the degree of change that a reform threatens to any level of the court system or judicial process, the less likely the reform is to pass.

## DECISION-MAKING VARIABLE

The decision-making variable is defined by the level of the decision-maker, whether the judicial branch, the legislature, or the public. If the proximate policy-maker of the reform is the Supreme Court making a rule, the likelihood of success is greater than if the proximate policy-maker is the legislature and the governor passing a statute or the legislature with the voters ratifying a constitutional amendment. A rough scheme for quantification will assign 1 to a decision by the Supreme Court, 2 to the legislature, and 3 to the people. For the status quo variable, 1 is assigned to an impact on appellate judges only, 2 to an impact on trial judges of general jurisdiction courts, and 3 to an impact on the 1,000 inferior court judges.

If in fact there is pressure to maintain the status quo and to avoid reform decisions, then we would expect that the Kansas reforms accomplished earliest and most completely would involve the least change in the judicial world and the fewest participants in the choice, while the reforms most recently attained, partially or never achieved would be more complex and disturbing to more individuals. Table 1 shows seven reform measures which have passed and three which have been considered but not accepted to date. To show how the quantification scheme operates, the notation of 2 in column two of the status quo variable indicates that the autonomy of the trial court judges was threatened by the reform. A notation of 3 under column four indicates that the control by a political party of judicial offices on the inferior court level was threatened. A notation of 1 in column six indicates that the legislature was requested to appropriate money for the appellate court level. A notation of 3 under the Location of Decision column indicates that the reform was presented as a constitutional amendment to the people. If these political variables are significantly related to the adoption of reforms, then the total of the weights should increase for each accomplished reform listed from first to seventh. The ranking of the last three proposals signifies the relative difficulty of their accomplishment and predicts the order of their eventual passage.

1. Judicial Council. In 1927 the Kansas legislature created the Judicial Council to provide advice, channel attitudes, and offer support to the courts. The Kansas council requires a modest annual

appropriation, but the inclusion on the council of two legislators, the chairmen of the two committees on the judiciary, compensates for the expense. The bar as well as the bench is satisfied with its representation: of the nine members, one is a Supreme Court Justice, two are district judges, and four are lawyers, appointed by the chief justice. The facts that the members have other occupations and receive no salary and that its functions are not bureaucratic but advisory reduce the fear that such a group would try to build its own power center. However, the council has two vital resources for political ends: the accumulation of information and the leadership of intelligent professionals. The council served as a channel for proposing the comprehensive redistricting of 1969 and continues to urge the adoption of a unified court structure. Translating the above data into the quantitative measure gives this first reform a weight of 3 units.

2. Missouri Plan for Supreme Court justices. The next major reform did not take place for 30 years. Then, in 1958 the voters approved a constitutional amendment introducing the Missouri Plan for the selection of Supreme Court justices; efforts to include the district court judges in the amendment failed. The impact on the political world was minimal; the position and powers of the justices were not changed and the elimination of the embarrassment and risk of competitive campaigns almost guaranteed life tenure. Over the long run, the governor of Kansas could be expected to be Republican, so that the new selection process would be unlikely to change the political makeup of the court. The nominating commission gave representation to both the state and local bars, with a majority over the laymen, so that lawyers were not disappointed by the innovation. The weighting of this reform is 4 units.

3. Court administrator. The Kansas Judicial Department Reform Act of 1965 created the position of judicial administrator, appointed by the Supreme Court justices to serve at their convenience. The statutory duty of the administrator is to analyze reports of district courts on pending cases and to determine the need for the assignment of additional judges to particular courts. The Supreme Court delineated his duties to include the management of fiscal affairs, cooperation with the Judicial Council, supervision and examination of administrative methods employed by district courts, and drafting of legislative proposals and Supreme Court rules. He takes responsibility for the official judicial conferences and processes the complaints which are directed to him about the lower courts.

TABLE I

Ranking of Kansas Judicial Reforms, 1927-1969

| | Maintenance of the Status Quo | | | | | | | Total |
|---|---|---|---|---|---|---|---|---|
| | Position Existence | Judicial Autonomy | Incumbent Protection | Party Protection | Trial Bar Security | Public Expense | Location of Decision | |
| 1. Judicial Council (1927) | 0 | 0 | 0 | 0 | 0 | 1 | 2 | 3 |
| 2. Missouri Plan for Supreme Court (1958) | 0 | 0 | 0 | 1 | 0 | 0 | 3 | 4 |
| 3. Court Administrator (1965) | 0 | 2 | 0 | 0 | 0 | 1 | 2 | 5 |
| 4. Unified Court-partial (1965) | 0 | 2 | 0 | 0 | 2 | 0 | 2 | 6 |
| 5. Salary and Retirement-partial (1969) | 2 | 0 | 0 | 0 | 0 | 2 | 2 | 6 |
| 6. District Reapportionment (1969) | 0 | 2 | 2 | 0 | 2 | 0 | 2 | 8 |
| 7. Inherent Judicial Power-partial (1969) | 0 | 2 | 0 | 0 | 2 | 2 | 2 | 8 |
| 8. Missouri Plan for Trial Courts    a. | 0 | 0 | 2 | 2 | 2 | 0 | 3 | 9 |
| b. | 0 | 0 | 3 | 3 | 3 | 0 | 3 | 12 |
| 9. Removal and Discipline of Judges    a. | 0 | 2 | 2 | 2 | 2 | 0 | 3 | 11 |
| b. | 0 | 3 | 3 | 3 | 3 | 0 | 3 | 15 |
| 10. Unification and Rationalization of Court System | 3 | 3 | 3 | 3 | 3 | 3 | 3 | 21 |

Key:   Maintenance of Status Quo:
1. Supreme Court
2. District Court
3. Inferior Courts

Location of Decision:
1. Judicial Branch
2. Legislature
3. Public

Plans for Election, Discipline, Removal
a. District Court
b. Inferior Courts

A full-time professional administrator, in contrast to the part-time judicial council, provides the Supreme Court with a tool for more aggressive planning for the efficiency of the entire court system. He symbolizes a unified court system, for although the change was on the state level of government, it has implications for the rest of the hierarchy. In quantitative terms the impact of this reform measures 5 units.

4. Unified court. With the passage of the departmental justice bill in 1965 the Kansas court system moved a step closer to unification by providing for a new relationship between the associate justices and the trial judges. The law directed the Supreme Court to divide the state into six judicial departments (geographical areas) and to assign one justice to each department as supervisor. His task was to survey the condition of the dockets in his area and to assign or request assistance of district judges inside or outside of his department to help to distribute the caseload.

The 1965 act also formalized the use of the judicial department conference, as an adjunct to the annual conference which the chief justice first called in 1963. These conferences are held for several days overlapping the State Bar Association and the Kansas District Judges' Association meetings, and the judges slip back and forth from their public roles as conference members to their private roles as members of pressure groups. At the conference the judges discuss the condition of the dockets, the impact of recent Supreme Court decisions, and pending legislation affecting the courts.

The conferences perform both a solidary and an educational function. Since judicial education for new judges is not provided by the state, a number of Kansas district judges and a few juvenile court judges have "gone to college." Eight senior Kansas trial judges served as instructors and 17 of the new judges attended the National College of State Trial Judges between 1964 and 1968. The Kansas judge gives up his vacation and unless he receives a scholarship pays his own way.

## UNIFIED COURT SYSTEM

A unified court system in Kansas would provide responsibility, flexibility, and the conservation of judicial power at the price of disturbing the security of lower court judges and threatening the purse of the state legislature. Local financing, with its attendant problems of poor facilities, unconstitutional use of fees, and erratic interference in judicial affairs by local units of government, would be replaced by state support and concomitant state control. Such a complete unification of the Kansas courts has been proposed by the Judicial Council, by the president of the Kansas District Judges' Association, by the Citizens' Conference of 1964, and most recently by the Citizens' Committee on Constitutional Revision in 1969. But the fears of the lower court judges have been evidenced by the texts of proposed constitutional amendments. The 1969 proposal named the Supreme Court and the district courts as parts of the "one court of justice," but provided that no lower courts would be abolished without specific implementing legislation. A totally unified court of justice would involve an impact measured at 21 points, but the 1965 reforms measured only 6 points.

### JUDICIAL COMPENSATION

5. Salaries and retirement benefits. Effective in 1969 the legislature raised the salaries of the Supreme Court and district court judges. The legislature had been increasing the salaries very slowly due to their continuous concern with the state budget, the tax burden, and their own re-election. The Supreme Court justices moved gradually from $6,000 in 1944 to $16,500 20 years later, and in 1969 to $21,500. The district judges improved their income from $5,000 in 1947 to $14,000 in 1967 and to $17,500 in 1969. Urban district judges receive an additional $2,500, ostensibly for service on the Parole Board.

The situation of the lower court judges is often neglected, although probate and juvenile court judges have their own pressure groups. In Kansas probate salaries are fixed by statute and vary according to county population from $4,000 to $12,000. In 93 counties the same judge acts as county court judge and receives an additional salary. All probate judges act as juvenile court judges and in the larger counties receive additional recompense of $2,500 to $3,500. City judges earn from $3,000 to $12,000, and justices of the peace are paid from court fees. Police court judges receive salaries in some cities and are paid by court costs in others.

Since 1953 Kansas has had a judicial retirement program which covers only Supreme Court and district judges. A judge contributes 6 percent of his salary to the fund and is limited to a pension of 65 percent of his last salary. Retired judges are considered senior judges, available by invitation to serve without compensation except for expenses. Kansas has no hospital or medical plan for judges to join. The financial benefits provided up to 1969 have only upset the political system by 6 points. A major escalation of salaries for all judges in a unified state system would cause a larger disruption.

6. District reapportionment. The redistricting reform of 1969 was the first modern measure with an important impact in counties throughout the state. The revision of the district boundaries and the reduction in the number of districts from 38 to 29 touched the 60 trial judges and the local bar associations. Only nine districts retained their former boundaries and a total of 24 revisions were made in the county composition of the districts. The number of multi-judge districts was increased from 10 to 13 and the number of single-judge districts reduced from 28 to 15, thus requiring more judges to give up judicial autonomy in favor of joint administration. The change in the population which elected the judge shattered his stable relations with the voters and for several districts necessitated campaigning over larger areas. The success of the plan was due primarily to the care taken to protect the positions of incumbent judges by relating the elimination of judgeships to retirement dates.

The change also caused some discomfort for lawyers who had to relate to different personnel and institutional arrangements. Minor adjustments were made in the plan to suit the convenience of a potential judicial candidate and a local bar association. Party considerations were also taken into account since the district bench contained representatives of both political parties and neither party favored a change which would reduce its share of such influential posts. In 1968 41 judges were Republican and 19 Democratic for a distribution of 68 percent to 32 percent. Projecting the reapportionment to its final stage in 1977 with 56 judges, on the basis of the current voting propensities by county, the division of seats would by 37 Republican and 18 Democratic, or 67 percent to 33 percent. The difference of 1 percent met the test of party acceptability.

The impact of this reform upon the political system weighs 8. Since no judge was directly deprived of his position, the first column is given a zero, but column three on protection of incumbency is loaded because of the uncertainties inherent in new constituencies.

### INHERENT JUDICIAL POWER

7. Inherent judicial power. The most recent recognition of inherent power in Kansas was the 1969 delegation of power to the Supreme Court to increase the number of judges in four urban districts at its discretion. The statute provides that in 1970 and every

two years thereafter the Supreme Court may certify the need of a new division in order to expedite the business of the district court.

There are two varieties of inherent power: 1) control over court procedures and 2) control over structure and personnel. In Kansas the Supreme Court has power to adopt rules "consistent with statutory provisions for regulation of procedure in the supreme court and inferior courts," and since 1965 power to adopt rules to carry out the department reform act. As a matter of policy, the legislature does not revise or veto the rules. In regard to structure and personnel, the court submits its own budget directly to the legislature, increases its own staff, sets their salaries, and names the administrative judges for the urban courts.

The steps taken in the direction of full recognition of inherent judicial power can be measured at 8 units.

8. Missouri Plan for trial courts. Selection reform in Kansas has not touched the judges below the peak of the judicial pyramid. District court judges are chosen every four years and judges of the probate court and justices of the peace every two years on ballots with party designation. Judges of the 14 city courts are elected on a partisan ballot for two-year terms, except in Kansas City, Wichita, and Olathe where the term is four years. Police court judges are appointed in the 13 first-class cities in a variety of ways: appointment by the mayor and city council, by the city manager, by the city commissions, or by the district judge, and in the second- and third-class cities, where the position has been created, by election.

Any selection procedure involves some kind of politics, but the degree and the source of judicial vulnerability to pressure will be affected by the particular mode of selection. Switching from partisan to nonpartisan election would subject judges to the politics of the bar association more directly, but since political parties have failed in the past to share much of their budget with judicial candidates, dependence upon local lawyers would be no novelty for Kansas nominees. Any competitive election requires the collection of funds for campaign expenses; an urban judge in 1964 spent twice his annual salary to protect his position against a well-organized group of lawyers in opposition. Another urban judge gave up his invitation to the National College of Judges in 1966 for fear that his absence would give his opponent an advantage. The most serious complaint of judges in competitive districts is that they spend two months of the election year on campaigning instead of on the bench.

Attempts since 1958 to extend the Missouri Plan to lower court judges have failed. Many district judges prefer the "Illinois Plan" in which the initial election is partisan but subsequent elections of incumbents are on merit. The absence of unanimous judicial support for the Missouri Plan may be explained by the resistance of Democrats who fear that in a Republican state Democratic lawyers would be cut off from the trial bench by the initial appointment. The failure of the Missouri Plan to be adopted can be understood by noting that it would have an impact of 9 if applied to district courts and 12 if applied to all lower courts. However, since the next two reforms to be discussed are even more upsetting, selection reform is predicted to be the next major reform.

### REMOVAL AND DISCIPLINE

9. Removal and discipline. Kansas has adopted no new technique to discipline and remove judges. In the case of discipline, the pride, reputation, and autonomy of the judge are at stake, and in the case of removal, his incumbency in the position is at issue. In a state with a partisan system of election, innovations which could be misused for partisan purposes are looked upon with suspicion. Under present law the Supreme Court and district judges in Kansas may be removed by impeachment or address, the probate judges and justices of the peace by impeachment, and other judges under the ouster statutes. All judges may be removed by recall. In practice the traditional techniques are not utilized since they are cumbersome, politically embarrassing, and restricted to serious offenses. There is no provision for complaint by the public or for disciplinary measures to correct less serious misdeeds.

The 1969 Citizens' Committee on Constitutional Revision suggested the addition of a section to the judicial article providing for retirement of Supreme Court justices by the governor upon recommendation of the nominating commission after appropriate hearing, and for the discipline, suspension, or removal of trial judges for cause by the Supreme Court after hearing. The prognosis for this reform is very poor, unless the groundwork is laid by related changes in unification and selection. Judges are unlikely to accept surveillance and insecurity of office without the benefits of tenure and the esprit de corps of a single unified court.

10. Unification and elimination of lower courts. The most difficult reform to achieve is the legal destruction of a court. The goal of a simple judicial hierarchy requires the rationalization and elimination of overlapping local courts and the raising of the standards on the remaining courts. Opposition to such a reform springs

from incumbents who would lose their official positions, particularly if they are not eligible for other judicial offices. The numerous city, county, and township judges in Kansas have close political connections with their city, county, and state representatives and so are able to veto reforms unless the change takes into account their needs and interests. The local bar, law enforcement officers, and local businessmen also have a stake in changes in the lower courts. Traffic officers want a convenient court for weekend offenders; businessmen want a court of limited jurisdiction for collection cases; lawyers want inferior courts where costs are not out of line with the value of the case.

Although the justice of the peace in Kansas remains a constitutional officer and the total number of positions authorized is 3,320, for all practical purposes the officer has been stripped of judicial functions and left with the power of performing marriages. In 1929 the legislature lowered the jurisdiction of justices of the peace to cases involving $1 or less where a city court operated, and in 1963 where a county court was established. The last vestiges of jurisdiction were removed in 1967 when the legislature *required* the establishment of a county court where no city or county court already existed. The lack of opposition to the decimation of the justice court can probably be explained by the unpopularity of the position to the incumbents. Many elected justices did not bother to qualify and others ran only under pressure as a community service. A majority handled only one case per month and the remuneration from fees was therefore insignificant. The only drawback to this reform was financial for the counties required to provide a county court. The rating for this partial reform is 5, 3 for the public expense and 2 for the location of the decision.

Unlike justices of the peace, probate and juvenile court judges are organized in an association which holds annual conferences, promotes a professional attitude, and protects the interests of members. The urban magistrates are well paid and have political ties in the communities, and the police judges perform a local service. The achievement of a complete rationalization and unification would cause distress measured at 21 points and is predicted to be the last reform, unless it is accomplished piecemeal and with careful attention to the needs of all interested parties.

The thesis of this examination of the Kansas experience with reform is simple and graphically reflected in Table 1. The practical reformer needs to take into account the impact of his proposals upon the status quo, particularly of the incumbent judges, and to consider the arena of policy-making involved. The analysis would suggest that reformers invest their resources on the least distressing changes first and on piecemeal rather than comprehensive plans.

## The Method of Reform*

### Warren Lehman

The criminal justice system as a social institution has only recently become the subject of widespread attention. And only very recently has that attention begun to mature, here and there, into completed studies. As a result, knowledge of the social institution through which the law is administered is minuscule compared to knowledge of the substantive law. Reformist capital, however, promises rapid growth in this intellectually underdeveloped territory; the new interest is the by-product of dissatisfaction with the way criminal justice is administered and of the resulting desire for change.

Reform as a motive for research is likely to encourage two related biases — an overemphasis upon the most easily manipulable parts of a system and a corresponding willingness to view the faults of a system as accidents. In a judicial system, the most easily manipulable part is the body of rules describing court organization and procedure. (For convenience, we will refer to these rules as the constitution of a criminal justice system — a notion less disconcerting if one thinks of the constitution and by-laws of a private club, rather than of the United States Constitution.) The court system's constitution is designed to produce an ideal legal procedure in which values such as due process are maximized. In fact, the way a criminal justice system operates corresponds only roughly to this ideal. Each research project intended to guide reform seems to reinforce the claim that reform is needed because each demonstrates "how very rough the correspondence is." The kinds of behavior that fail to correspond to the ideal are likely to be viewed as aggravating accidents and the means of treating those aggravating accidents to be sought in manipulation of the constitution.

* From: D. Oaks and W. Lehman, A Criminal Justice System and the Indigent 178-196 (1964). Copyright 1968 by the University of Chicago. Reprinted by permission of the University of Chicago Press and the authors. The author wishes to thank Dallin Oaks for his generous assistance in the preparation of this chapter in a book that was otherwise fully a joint venture.

Although attractive and accessible as the focus of reform, the constitution of a criminal justice system is far less responsible for the way the system operates than one — especially one trained in the law — would be tempted to believe.[390] The first purpose of this concluding chapter is to place the constitution of a criminal justice system in perspective as but a relatively insignificant force in a very complex social institution. In the course of doing so it should become evident that the disjuncture between the ideal and the reality is not an accident, but a result — healthy or unhealthy — of the interaction among the myriad forces, including the constitution, that contribute to the creation of the system. We will conclude this chapter by examining the effects upon a criminal justice system of reforms achieved through manipulation of the system's constitution, for the ultimate goal of this study, too, is to guide reform.

## THE SYSTEM: AN INPUT-OUTPUT MODEL

We have described the criminal justice system as a device for selecting those whom society wants to treat specially because they have violated the law. The first point to be noted about this definition is that a criminal justice system is a system, capable of being

---

390. The error of overemphasizing the significance of rule-making has been noted more often in the context of substantive than of procedural rules. However, since both substantive and procedural rules are rules — attempts to direct behavior — they are subject to essentially the same kinds of resistance to their universal enforcement. Twenty-five years ago Underhill Moore described the underlying intellectual error as the belief "that a proposition of law, or its administration, is the single and only cause of its effect; that is to say, that the behaviour which follows enactment of a law or its enforcement is a dependent variable, the value of which depends alone upon the law or its enforcement and upon no other variable." Moore and Callahan, Law and Learning Theory: A Study in Legal Control, 53 Yale L.J. 1, 2 (1943). The article goes on to demonstrate the degree to which the behavior of drivers is influenced by traffic laws. A similar problem in a different context is discussed in Lehman, Thinking Small About Urban Renewal, 1965 Wash. U.L.Q. 396, 418-19.

The limited impact of both procedural and substantive law is perhaps most dramatically demonstrated in those situations in which a culture is subjected to an alien legal system. See Gray, Nature and Sources of the Law 320-25 (2nd ed. 1921), where Gray discussed the reception of the Roman Law in Germany (following Stobbe, Geschichte der Deutschen Rechtsquellen). "By degrees only was the foreign law assimilated to the domestic, and not even today have many legal principles, taken over from foreign law, become popular, that is, corresponding to a general legal feeling." Id., at 332.

analyzed in systematic terms. It has an input, a mechanism, and an output.

If we look exclusively at the judicial subsystem, the input consists of those persons delivered by the police to the courts. The output is those same persons as they leave the system to serve time in jail or to reenter society either on probation or as free men. For the moment, we will deal with the mechanism simply as a sealed box in which the input is shuffled to produce the output. The heuristic device of ignoring the content of the box will make it possible to isolate some of those forces that affect the system regardless of its constitution.

*The Impact of Input.* Our definition states that the purpose of the criminal justice system is to sort. Without looking at the mechanism we may infer, from the fact of its relatively fixed size and its purpose to sort, that the way it operates will be influenced by its input. This can be illustrated by several observable effects. One of the simplest is the relatively direct effect by which the crimes charged against the defendants entering the system determine the distribution of penalties among defendants when they leave the system, and hence, necessarily, the frequency with which various decisions are made inside it. . . . Penalties differ for different crimes, and so does the likelihood that a defendant will be found guilty. Therefore, a change in the input mix would tend to have an automatic effect on the output, achieved through changes within the mechanism in the guilty plea rate, the conviction rate, and sentencing behavior.

The crime charged is a feature of the input to which the mechanism is supposed to respond. The machinery inside the sealed box is consciously calibrated to react to such things as the crime charged, factual guilt, mitigating circumstances, and so on. It is not supposed to respond to the color of a defendant's hair. Nonetheless, the machinery can be influenced by defendants' characteristics that have little or nothing to do with the criteria by which it is supposed, ideally, to do its sorting. The sensitivity of the system to ideally irrelevant characteristics of input is, of course, not intentionally programmed into its machinery.

Any number of causes irrelevant to the sorting activity of the mechanism may result in clogging: an absolute increase in the numbers of the input; an increase of a certain type of defendants (juveniles, for instance) that overburdens a portion of the system; or a decision of the police to be either more or less careful in selecting the input. Clogging will slow down the system and affect the accuracy of decision-making, the morale of personnel, and the satisfaction of parties with both process and result. A system is likely to respond to these undesirable effects of clogging by reducing the care and even the fairness with which it processes persons charged with "crimes" considered less important. The pressure of volume may even encourage the notion that petty or less dangerous crimes are non-crimes and that they should be removed from the jurisdiction of the judicial system and placed within that of other agencies. The possibility of such a chain of reaction to input is not intentionally designed into the judicial system. The implicit decision of the relative importance of dangerous crime may or may not be a good one. The response is, however, a healthy one in the sense of the system's self-preservation. That the system can make such responses, although it was not designed to, is a good thing, not a bad.

An increase in a particular type of crime has an effect different from an overall increase in criminal business. The participants may become inured to what had been considered an evil or be impressed with an evil previously not thought significant. The increase in automobile theft by juveniles has resulted in an apparently serious crime being treated as a petty one; a narcotics scare, on the other hand, can result in a rash of stiff penalties. A general increase in criminal business may therefore affect the perception and treatment of those crimes considered by preexisting standards the least serious; a change in the mix of crimes can change the judgment of seriousness itself.

A variety of personal characteristics irrelevant to the sorting function can affect the system's responses. The racial biases of the society can be felt in the criminal system. Defendants of lower income or status are likely to be less well treated; the system responds to effective demand, and the vocal, the educated, and the affluent can exercise effective demand by their ability to attract public attention. Because the system is an adversary one, the treatment accorded by the system is bound to reflect the resources — financial, psychological, and intellectual — a defendant brings into the system. These differences affect the way the system operates in respect to any given person; by changing the proportion in the input of poor or minority group members, the whole texture of the system can change. Exactly such a change is set in motion by providing the poor some of the resources previously available only to the rich. Although this does not reduce the numbers of the poor, it achieves a comparable effect by helping to eliminate the impact of their poverty on the criminal justice system.

Responses such as these to variations in input are not intentionally provided for in the system's constitution. It is, however, more than fortuitous that a judicial system should grow more complex than its designers intended, and become sensitized to features of the input considered by the designers as irrelevant. The designers were concerned primarily with programming the system to decide whether a person should be convicted. At least in the past they were likely to pay little heed to how the system ought to react if the volume of its business exceeded its capacity. No doubt the ability of a system to respond to "irrelevant" facts permits it to deviate from democratic ideals by responding to such things as a defendant's race. But despite such unfortunate effects, the ability of a system to do more than it is designed to do may be essential to its survival.

*Inside the Sealed Box.* The mechanism inside the sealed box can vary, as it does among American and other common-law systems and more radically between common-law and code systems. The exact effect of a given change in input depends upon the peculiarities of a given system. How seriously and in what ways a system is disrupted by an increase in juvenile defendants depends on the efficiency and on other characteristics of the machinery for handling juveniles. The effects of changing patterns of input are the result of a clash between the input and the mechanism of the specific system.

The machinery in the sealed box includes the constitution (procedure and organization) to which so much attention is usually directed. But the constitution is hardly an adequate description of the sorting mechanism. Many other things play their part in defining the way the mechanism operates, including the way it responds to variations in input. The quality and quantity of personnel and their distribution within the mechanism, the adequacy of physical facilities and communication and recording systems, and the existence of subsidiary services for investigative or social welfare work would all affect the way the mechanism would respond to such a change as an increase in the volume of juvenile business.

*Feedback.* What we have so far described is really little more than a simplified court-organization flow chart, which makes it appear that the system is isolated from the outside world except for its input and that cause and effect within the system always move in straight lines from left to right. Such a flow chart is misleading, no matter what detail is added. To make a diagram that better corresponds with reality, we must add lines indicating feedback — causal sequences going in the direction opposite that assumed by the normal system diagram.

We know the machinery reacts to what is fed into it; the persons responsible for selecting the input also react to the machinery's reaction. The machinery may disapprove of the method by which the input is chosen. Disapproval in the form of appellate criticism, as by directing the police to operate in different ways, is an intentionally programmed feedback avowedly designed to influence future police conduct. There can also be informal, unintended feedback when police or prosecutors respond, without specific command, to what they learn of the mechanism's behavior. The police may learn that it is bootless to bring certain types of complaints, and they adapt their behavior to this information. We have, then, causal forces running from the mechanism to the input, as well as the reverse. The same is true from the output to the mechanism. Judges in sentencing may respond to available penal or treatment facilities and to recidivism. Information or impressions about the recidivism rate of persons convicted of specific types of crimes or of persons with varying social and economic backgrounds can affect sentencing judgments. That an individual defendant is a recidivist is likely to affect a judge differently than general knowledge about recidivism, and the path of causation is also different. In this case, the cause goes from the output all the way back to the input. The output, most of which is ultimately returned to the pool from which the input is drawn, changes the character of the input, as by creating sophistication among defendants in the way they attempt to deal with the mechanism. And judges are likely to respond differently to a two- or three-time loser than to a first offender.

*The Boundaries of a Judicial System.* The model of the system so far described still leaves the impression that the system is self-contained. This is not so. The boundaries that separate a legal system from the world are hazy indeed. The criminal justice system, as our definition runs, is a device for selecting those *whom society wants* to treat specially. It is because of the interpenetration of society and the judicial system that society can communicate to the system its view of who should be penalized or treated and in what way. Public opinion, knowledge, and emotion playing upon a criminal justice system have as essential a part in defining how the system operates as the constitution by which its machinery is organized. It is the reasonable responsiveness of the criminal justice system to society's expectation and sense of justice that makes the system legitimate in the eyes of the society it serves. Without that interplay between society and the system, the system can only endure so long as the sovereign has power to impose its will. When there are ways, programmed or not, by which the criminal justice system and the society can interact, can we say where the legal system begins and where it ends?

The routes are many and varied by which the criminal justice system interacts with the society it serves. Many external conditions affect the criminal justice system only because they accidentally intersect it. The dyspepsia of the judge, if its cause is personal rather than professional, is such an accidental intersection. In the same class are the efforts of politicians either to use the system for political purposes or to evade their responsibilities to it. Unresponsive as the court system is to innovation, changes in technology can and will inevitably influence the system's operation. So, too, will advancing knowledge of social organization and of the nature of the psyche. All these forces are at large in society and, without design, inevitably run into the judicial system, then go their way beyond it.

Other forces more directly related to the system may be conceived as beginning and ending with it. A rash of violent crimes committed by persons released from prison may arouse public indignation which, expressed in the press, has an impact on the behavior of judicial personnel. There is also a formal system of criticism through the medium of the academic community, which in simplest form consists of a short loop emanating from the judges and returning to them.

But, undoubtedly the most powerful external influence is the public attitude toward crime, toward particular crimes, toward punishment, and toward culpability. The personnel of the judicial system, because they live in the world, impact these judgments willy-nilly into the system. But such an accidental influence is apparently inadequate, for a means, the jury, is provided to funnel into the system the judgments and knowledge of the community. And . . . it is just this institution — the criminal jury — that operates to set standards for the whole trial-court system. The system is designed to get, because it needs, the guidance of the outside world regarding the way in which the world would judge the events that the system must judge. This information must be fed in so that the system can earn and keep the confidence of the community it serves.

### THE SYSTEM: A BIOLOGICAL ANALOGY

Once the constitution of a criminal justice system is put in its place as but one relatively minor nexus of forces within that system, the whole begins to resemble more a natural construct than an artificial one. It looks like a system that, without much conscious guidance, just grew, and that in growing developed means of responding to and compromising the forces that play upon it. Man is, after all, at least an animal; there is no reason why a system developed by man to control his aggression may not usefully be viewed as a natural system, much like the carbon cycle or the social organization of the baboon. If the criminal justice system is a natural system, we may further our understanding of its operation by studying other natural systems.

A brief excursion into cell biology, to illustrate a biologist's notion of a natural system, will point up features common to legal systems and to those a biologist studies. Biologists are currently at issue on whether life is a characteristic of the whole cell or is to be found in its molecular constituents, particularly in DNA (deoxyribonucleic acid), a protein molecule that appears able to reproduce itself by dictating, through another protein molecule (ribonucleic acid or RNA), the synthesis of more DNA molecules resembling the original. Professor Barry Commoner, speaking for the classical approach to biology, argues that DNA is exactly reproducible only in the context of the whole cell. He states that in the test-tube experiments so far conducted, second-generation DNA cannot be made to resemble exactly first-generation DNA; moreover, particular differences between first- and second-generation DNA molecules appear to depend upon the presence or absence of the kind of environmental influences that may be found within the cell of which the DNA molecule is normally a constituent. The reproductive process (which is by definition the characteristic of life) therefore would appear still to be a phenomenon of the whole cell system rather than of a part. On that basis, Professor Commoner argues that the whole is greater than its parts. "[C]omplex systems," he says, "may, for perfectly natural reasons, exhibit distinctive properties which are not at all discernible in the behavior of their isolated parts." [408]

The legal system shares with the cell at least two characteristics: the whole is, like a compound, different from its parts or their sum; and the distinctive properties of the whole (undiscoverable in a study of the parts) are created in the complex interaction of the parts. If legal and biological systems share these characteristics, the experience of intervention in biological systems may be relevant to those interested in intervention in a legal system. Two

408. [Commoner, Science and Survival 41 (1966).]

effects of intervention in a biological system are particularly important — amplification and dampening. Amplification makes intervention dangerous; dampening may make it a waste of time.

If, like any other natural system, a legal system is bound together and defined by the ties of interacting forces, "it is not surprising ... that the introduction of any [new factor] ... into the environment is bound to cause a change somewhere in the tangled web of relationships." [409] Those changes, often the unexpected and unwanted consequences of well-intended intervention, cannot be conceived as accidents. They are inevitable in the nature of the system. The system is a web of forces (or of routes along which forces can travel) that spreads the impact of intervention. Under certain circumstances the effect of intervention can become more intense as it spreads through the system. This can be true when poisons are introduced in the biosphere; it may also be true when a change in the constitution of a legal system seriously affects the morale of its participants or the confidence of the public.

On the other hand, the complexity of the natural system is a source of stability. "[T]his complexity is the source of their remarkable staying power.... [A]nything which reduces the complexity of a natural biological system renders it less stable and more subject to fatal fluctuations." [411] The variety of routes through a system makes it possible for the system to weather interventions by achieving much the same results in new ways. In a complex system there is often more than one way to skin a cat.

The argument so far has been intended to support the philosophy that guided our entire study. An existing system has a claim to validity and to our respect simply because it is a working system that manages, apparently reasonably satisfactorily, to absorb and balance the forces that are playing upon it. Intervention in a complex system that works, imperfect though we may consider it, is to be undertaken only with the greatest of caution and on an experimental scale, until it is clear that the overall effects will not be undesirable.

### THE EFFECTS OF INTERVENTION

We have not demonstrated that the improvement of a system is impossible, even improvement through conscious intervention.

409. Id. at 27.
411. Id. at 26.

The point is, rather, that improvement is often a difficult and chancy activity. Recognition of the complexity of the criminal justice system may be the beginning from which we can learn to predict whether an essay at intervention can succeed.

*Intervention by Rule Enforcement or Penalty.* When considering possible efforts to change an undesirable behavior pattern by means of penalty, we should ask two questions. The first is whether the practice can be eliminated or only contained. The second is whether elimination or containment of that practice will produce a net improvement in the system.

The criminal justice system is peculiarly likely to encourage misleading impressions about the effectiveness of rule-making and modification. With respect to many rules of a criminal justice system, almost every violation can be detected and either punished or counteracted. This situation is unusual because few regulatory laws do more than inhibit the objectionable behavior. The judicial system's self-policing of its public activities makes it likely that the violation rate of a rule such as that prohibiting the use in court of non-free-will confessions would be nearly zero. (Of course, the non-use in court of such confessions does not mean that no confessions are illegally obtained, only that they are not directly used.) The relative ease of enforcement of some rules tempts the observer to believe that the system is in all respects easily modifiable by adjustment in the constitution or by the introduction of penalties for violation of its rules. It is well to recognize that most rule-making will have only limited success, for this avoids the trap of judging as a failure a rule that restricts but does not completely eliminate an undesirable practice. The costs of increasing the effectiveness of a prohibition may be too high.

An objectionable pattern of individual behavior can be controlled in three ways (other than by physically preventing the individual from acting):

1. by eliminating the circumstances (other than the individual's system of values) that give rise to the behavior;
2. by persuading the individual who has been engaging in the objectionable behavior of the rightness of obeying the rule prohibiting it, either by inducing him to internalize the value underlying the rule or by convincing him of the propriety of obeying all rules of properly constituted authorities;

or

3. by enforcing the rule with (a) a certainty of detection and

(b) a severity of penalty sufficient to overcome the pressure of
circumstances giving rise to the behavior.

Since all these approaches admit of degrees of success, an effort
to eliminate a particular behavior pattern may include programs of
all three types. Usually, however, only the second and third are
employed. (The very act of rule-making creates a pressure encouraging internalization, so the second and third methods are almost
inevitably conjoined.) Social action usually does not attempt to
eliminate the structural causes of undesirable behavior.

Punishment and internalization can produce complete conformity with a rule in only two circumstances. The first is when the
forces conducing to the behavior are so weak that they are neu-
tralized by the individual's internalization of the new value. Cases
of this sort are rare because it is unusual for a weak force to create
a problem that is sufficiently egregious to be dealt with by rule-
making rather than by counseling. The second is when the behavior can be so effectively subjected to punishment or to having
its effects nullified that it is pointless to attempt to engage in it.
The possibility of such complete control rarely occurs. In any
other circumstances, containment is the best that can be expected
from any effort directed at effects.

*The Impact of Intervention on the System.* If it is questionable
whether intervention can eliminate or only contain an objectionable behavior pattern, it is even more questionable whether containment or elimination of that behavior will result in a net improvement in the system. The answer to this, our second question,
depends on the impact upon the system as a whole of containing
or eliminating a pattern of behavior that had previously existed
within it. An intervention that succeeds in reducing the incidence
of objectionable behavior is likely also to produce one or more of
three characteristic patterns of response within the system:

1. The forces creating the original behavior will be expressed in
   a new way.
2. Where, as is often the case, policy goals are incompatible and
   can only be dealt with by balancing, the advancement of the
   policy goal that led to the intervention in the system may
   unintentionally be at the expense of other goals.
3. Because the prohibition is itself a force interjected into the
   system, it may, while prohibiting the action directly, encourage it indirectly.

Any of these effects might be viewed as so undesirable that if the possibility of their occurring had been recognized in advance, the intervention would not have been undertaken. It is by that test that net improvement is measured. We will illustrate each of these patterns of response with examples related to law.

*The New Expression of Existing Forces.* The response most likely to result from any intervention is for the forces that gave rise to the objectionable behavior to find new channels through which to express themselves. If the forces are alive, they will continue to work themselves out. If every channel for their overt expression is closed, they will express themselves internally — in the psyches of the persons upon whom the forces impinge. Although difficult to detect and measure, results of that sort can be as damaging to a system, by way of demoralizing its personnel, as the continuation of undesirable behavior. But the judicial system is so complex that there is slight chance of successfully preventing a force from being overtly expressed somewhere (likely in areas less subject to regular policing than those in which it was first expressed, so that detection and suppression become more difficult). As containment approximates elimination, or as more doors are closed against alternative expressions, the discomfort of persons subject to the rules increases, magnifying the urge to evasion.

If the force producing an undesirable behavior pattern is scarcity of resources, suppressing one effect of scarcity will produce a redistribution of the system's resources so that the scarcity will be felt somewhere else. The redistribution may be judged a net improvement, but that is unlikely. First, those interested in intervention as a means of improvement almost certainly judge the legal system by an ideal to which the system nowhere completely conforms. Any new expression of scarcity will appear to be a retreat from that which had been, at best, barely acceptable. Second, redistribution caused by an order prohibiting the effect of scarcity is achieved by placing more resources at one point without considering where they are to come from; the redistribution is, from the rulemaker's view, simply a matter of chance. A redistribution that takes into consideration where resources are to come from — the only way the result is likely to be viewed as a net improvement — requires an attitude of mind prepared for concessions.

There are ways to counteract scarcity other than the corset technique, which merely relocates the difficulty. Where the original design of the system was bad or when technology offers cost savings, existing resources may be used more efficiently. This approach

presents no problem of the generic type under consideration since
it deals with the cause of the difficulty — by reducing scarcity
within the system.[423]

423. Since it would appear at first glance that scarcity can be solved by
money we can test the generality of our theory by examining whether financial intervention may be effective in solving problems of scarcity in the criminal justice system. This inquiry assumes that state and local governments will
support a redistribution of society's resources by allocating more money to the
judiciary. Infusion of more money may be an effective way of dealing with
forms of scarcity that can be eliminated by money, but not all scarcity is of
that sort. (A want of understanding of a problem, for example, is a scarcity
that cannot be compensated for by money.) An additional question is what
the money will buy. Some things indeed can be readily obtained. Whether a
given commodity is available depends on the flexibility of supply over a reasonable time span. Furniture can be obtained quickly; as long as the building
industry has surplus capacity new structures can be obtained in a few years.

Getting additional skilled and intelligent people is another matter. Both
the total supply of people and more particularly the supply with attractive
levels of skill and ability are limited; any increase in response to demand is
likely to be quite slow. Since we cannot order more and better people into
the judicial system by law, as we can money, to get more people the judicial
system must compete on the personnel market with everyone else. To the
extent that the judicial system is successful in attracting able people, the rest
of society will react by devoting more resources to wages and recruiting.
While this does not mean that money will not help, the cost to the judicial
system of any significant gain by this method must be measured by the cost
of positions added at the higher wage levels established as a result of increased
competition, plus the increment in the wages that must be paid present employes to retain them when the new wage level is reached. The cost of this
method, is, therefore, much greater than appears at first glance. And because
the cost of each person added to the total in the judicial system is greater
than the cost of the previous one, the cost of additions increases geometrically
while the number of additional personnel increases arithmetically.

Another tack would be to raise skill levels among those people who, because of lack of skill, are in oversupply. This moves the judicial system's problem over into another system. To raise skill levels would require devoting
more resources to education, both money and skilled manpower. This effort,
although worthwhile, is in conflict with immediate improvement of the judicial system. Moreover, the success of an educational program has as a natural
limit the skills of its pupils. The only other approach, it seems, would be the
even slower one of increasing the total number of people, but that is a
chimera because the burdens on the judicial system and hence its need for
yet more personnel will increase at least as rapidly as the population.

The most obvious difficulties of financial intervention in the judicial system arise in the relation between the judicial and other systems, rather than
within the judicial system. More properly, we may say that the problems arise
in the larger system of which the judicial system is a part. The difficulties of
shifting resources in that larger system are much the same as those encountered in reallocating resources within the judicial system.

A less tangible, but nonetheless important, force is that created by the expectations of society and by the system's participants concerning the success of the system in convicting the factually guilty. When rules are created that make conviction more difficult, the participants will make efforts to approximate the expected result while complying with the specific restriction. Other channels, inside and outside the system, will be sought to achieve that expectation. There is reason to believe that even defendants lose respect for a system that, because of inefficiency, poverty, or the stringency of its own procedural rules, cannot convict them with at least reasonable frequency.

*Conflict Among Goals.* The three patterns of a system's response to intervention are not mutually exclusive. A single intervention can simultaneously result in the causal force seeking a new expression and in making it more difficult to achieve an apparently unrelated policy goal. The example of intervention designed to control police behavior exemplifies the problem of incompatible purposes when it makes conviction more difficult. Much of the recent concern with procedural regularity is but a concern to make the law legitimate in the eyes of those sophisticated enough to detect a moral void behind the traditions that support some of the law's substantive rules. If one is not sure that the substantive rules have any ultimate validity, at least procedure can be purified. The purification is consoling in itself and reduces the number of persons who must suffer under the questioned rules. But the cost of purifying procedure and enhancing legitimacy in the eyes of the sophisticated may be to reduce the system's legitimacy in the eyes of the majority in society, who do not question the substantive rules and who are concerned only that the system effectively enforce them. Whether or not we analyze its causes correctly, there is certainly a grave tension today between those primarily interested in enlarging civil liberties and those primarily concerned with safety on the street.

A less speculative illustration of the problem of conflict in goals can be found in the recommendations of the President's Commission on Law Enforcement and the Administration of Justice. On the one hand, the Commission expresses concern with disparate sentencing, recommending that ways be devised to pressure judges to adopt uniform sentencing practices. On the other hand, recognizing that the negotiated guilty plea is essential to the viability of the court system, the Commission recommends that the system face up to the need for plea bargaining, admit the existence of the practice, and bring it under judicial control in open court. But plea bargaining is unlikely to be successful without disparate sentences that will benefit those who save the system the trouble of a trial. The individual judge's solution for this required disparity has been to pretend that plea bargaining does not exist. This pretense, although perhaps intellectually culpable, may be the only reasonable psychological retreat for persons who, as most, would prefer to act in a consistent manner. The proposals of the Commission will tend to increase the general pressure for sentencing uniformity while simultaneously resulting in public exposure and judicial review of plea bargaining situations in which sentencing cannot be uniform. We have no accepted locution or legal fiction by which this conflict can be avoided or resolved.

*Contradictory Effects (Neutralizing Intervention)*. We have considered two typical patterns — that in which a force continues to attempt to work itself out after repression of a symptom and that in which the achievement of one purpose is in conflict with the achievement of another. There remains yet one more to consider — that in which a force introduced into the system simultaneously discourages and encourages the same result. An obvious example is in the treatment of vice crimes such as prostitution, gambling, and narcotics addiction. Repressing vice makes it more economically attractive for suppliers to provide what is desired. Restricting sources of supply does not affect demand. Consumers appear willing to pay whatever price is necessary to induce suppliers to take whatever risks the enforcement mechanism imposes. Because of the high prices that can be charged, the laws repressing dope peddling make it attractive to attempt to expand the market by increasing the number of addicts. To the extent that the law is successful by controlling supply or use, in reducing the number of users, it may reduce the number of persons who commit crimes to support their habits; on the other hand, by increasing the cost of the habit for the remainder, the number of crimes these persons must commit goes up. A similar phenomenon appears to have occurred in the judicial system, where the number of criminal defendants whose cases are terminated adversely without trial appears to have increased as a result either of the right of a cost-free appeal or of the general impact of the due process revolution.

If these three patterns of response to intervention are typical rather than unusual, one may appropriately ask if anything can usefully be done with a system that seems unsatisfactory. We are not entirely facetious in suggesting that some failings must be lived with, for a shorter or longer time. The surest way to solve systemic problems is the slowest: to advocate ideals rather than to institute them. Ideals that are absorbed by the participants in, and by the clients of, a system are likely to find expression in the system, and to find expression in ways that do not disrupt the system. The general pressure of ideals is unlikely to be disruptive because the demands of those ideals will be put into effect by people who are subjected to all the pressures of the system. People so placed will probably act only when they can act without sacrificing conflicting goals. The participants in a system are in much the same position as a judge considering a case or controversy. One of the most important reasons why judges are generally limited to the disposition of cases and controversies is that only in a real case is the judge likely to have presented to him the real pressures that must be resolved before action is taken. The participant in the system, subjected willy-nilly to the forces within it, is likely to respond with cautious steps, constantly testing the response they evoke, in much the same way the judiciary approaches a new problem. Patience, however, is not a virtue of our time. There is only one substitute for patience — knowledge.

Although our conclusion may seem a damper to the reformer, it is not intended to be. Idealism has its own and noble place among the forces that have made the system what it is and that are in process of making it what it will be. But the idealist cannot safely be too near the seat of power. So situated both the idealist and the sovereign are likely to fall victim to the notion that fiat and money can make the society what the idealist would have it become. That is a delusion.

# INDEX

## DATE DUE

| DATE DUE | | | |
|---|---|---|---|
| FEB 2 6 1982 | | | |
| DEC 0 6 1987 | | | |
| FEB 2 3 1990 | | | |
| APR 2 2 1991 | | | |
| | | | |
| | | | |
| | | | |
| | | | |
| | | | |
| | | | |
| | | | |
| | | | |
| | | | |
| | | | |
| | | | |
| | | | |
| GAYLORD | | | PRINTED IN U.S.A. |